CASEY ANTHONY MURDER TRIAL
A MODERN AMERICAN TRAGEDY

Abacus Books, Inc.
P.O. Box 55302
St. Petersburg, Florida 33732-5302, U.S.A.
www.abacusbooks.com

Library of Congress Cataloging in Publication Data
Walker, Claudette & Filia, Matrix

THE CASEY ANTHONY MURDER TRIAL
I.   Title

ISBN# 0-9716292-7-7
EAN# 978-0-9716292-7-1

Release eBook 2011
©Copyright Abacus Books, Inc. 2011

Printed in the United States of America
Set in New Courier

This work is the personal opinions and interpretations of the authors and contributors of a public murder trial, the legal cases involved and cited, and the persons and actions involved in and surrounding the trial. It is not a verbatim transcript of any proceedings, comments, or testimony. This work should not be taken as exact regarding the statements, actions, or proceedings concerned or regarding any persons, public figures, involuntary public figures, or limited public figures mentioned in this work. This work is the real time trial documentation effort, research, document review, and personal opinions of the authors and contributors.

"The Casey Anthony Murder Trial"

A Modern American Tragedy

Written by

Claudette Walker
&
Matrix Filia

This book is an opportunity to look inside the American criminal legal system, in action. The Casey Anthony Murder Trial is the most complete account known of this high-profile murder trial of a mother, charged with killing her child. The trial occurred in Orlando, Florida in 2011.

Comment from the authors:

"The history of the death of this lovely child and the murder trial of her mother that followed cannot be rewritten or deleted. It has been preserved."

Dedication

"Caylee, the wind whispers your name."

FOREWORD
By David E. Siar, Esquire

How many times in my career have I hopefully asked for a
judge's reconsideration of a ruling? I have no idea, but
I question whether I could count that high. In my nearly
thirty years as a lawyer, with many of those spent as an
assistant public defender handling only criminal cases, I
have represented clients in hundreds of cases, including
murder and serial murder cases. I have spent hundreds,
even thousands, of hours preparing for trials with
conferences, depositions, pre-trial motions, hearings,
and just plain hard work. Those trials may last for eight
hours or for weeks, or result in a plea just before or
even during the trial. I have been kept in court by a
judge until after one in the morning, worked innumerable
nights and weekends. I have been lied to by my clients,
witnesses, and opposing counsel. I have represented
clients who insist on trial, despite all odds, and those
who insist that they will not risk a trial, even though
their chances of victory are high. The lawyer may be
influential in the client's decision whether to proceed
to trial, but it is ultimately the client's right, and
therefore the client's choice. I have felt the thrill of
victory and the agony of defeat. I have been exposed to
questionable and unethical conduct from (thankfully, a
precious few) opposing counsel. I have received rulings
both favorable and unfavorable, and seen my share of
cantankerous judges and outstanding jurists.

There have been times when I have been required to
advance a defense based on facts or theories I question,
but no ethical lawyer will put on evidence that the
lawyer knows is false. The Florida Bar, in its Rules of
Professional Conduct, Rule 4-3.3(a)(4), sets out the
procedure to be used. "A lawyer shall not… offer evidence
that the lawyer knows to be false. A lawyer may not offer
testimony that the lawyer knows to be false in the form
of a narrative unless so ordered by the tribunal. If a
lawyer, the lawyer's client, or a witness called by the
lawyer has offered material evidence and the lawyer comes
to know of its falsity, the lawyer shall take reasonable
remedial measures including, if necessary, disclosure to
the tribunal. A lawyer may refuse to offer evidence that
the lawyer reasonably believes is false." The defendant
in a criminal trial is a special case, because he or she
has the absolute constitutional right to testify or to
refuse to testify. If a defendant cannot be dissuaded

i

from testifying falsely, the law provides a procedure for the lawyer to allow that testimony without participating in it.

Capital murder trials are like no other for a defense lawyer. No other criminal case has stakes so high. Literally, the defense lawyer holds his client's life in his hands. Despite the acts that the client may or may not have committed to reach the courtroom, a failure of the lawyer can result in the client's demise. Once a person is executed, there is no turning back the clock, no possible compensation for a life lost. That is not to say that the lawyers do not also feel for the victims; we do. There is no way for us to restore them to life, and the goal at trial is often to prevent the legal system from taking another. The responsibility is awesome, and the stress can be enormous. If you ask any attorney who tries criminal cases, you will hear the same story.

For those of you who think that being a criminal defense attorney is all glamour, think again. For those who wonder why anyone would subject himself or herself to this life of torture, the reason is that there can be no greater satisfaction than the search for justice. William Blackstone, a famous English jurist said, "It is better that ten guilty persons escape than that one innocent suffer", in his Commentaries on the Laws of England, published in the 1760s. He echoed the views of those who went before him. That is the rationale for our law's presumption of innocence. Those of us on both sides of the aisle who labor in the courtroom trenches seek justice. Justice is not always done; sometimes the guilty do go free and the innocent are incarcerated, but the rule of law exists for us all.

I was asked to assist with some legal definitions and explanations in the book you are about to read. I am the "house lawyer" you will see mentioned. Since I am married to one of the authors, how could I refuse such an invitation? This book is a glimpse of the trials and tribulations experienced by all who are involved in the judicial process, from defendants to bailiffs, court reporters and clerks of court. The intense, often overwhelming work that happens outside the confines of the courtroom by the judge and the attorneys can be gleaned from the words of the participants. The lawyers, the judge, and the witnesses are the ones who, with the exception of the defendant, people seem to love or dislike most. In reading this book, you will likely understand the editorial commentary of the authors, even if you do not agree with their views. Trials engender strong emotions in us all, at least if we are paying attention to the details and are not simply listening to sound bites. Even if you have been a juror in the past, you will be able to get some idea of why you may have been bounced in and out of the courtroom, and what happens while you are gone. What may surprise you is that the work does not stop when jurors are in recess.

Very few of us have ever actually witnessed an entire murder trial. I believe you will get a representative look at what really occurs in and outside the courtroom by reading this book. Speaking as one who has been there, this book gives a real feel for the action both inside and outside the courtroom in the trial of a high-profile capital murder case.

THE CASEY ANTHONY MURDER TRIAL
A MODERN AMERICAN TRAGEDY

The estimated cost of this trial will be in the millions of dollars, paid from Floridians' and Orange County residents' tax dollars.

"To lose a child is out of the natural order of things; I have lost a son. Any failure to participate in the police discovery of information pertaining to a missing child leads to overshadow my objectivity in this case."

That was a statement during jury selection by an honest prospective juror who was excused for cause, and who is **not** on the final jury panel for the trial of Casey Anthony.

This book contains the opinions of the two co-authors regarding this public case, the trial's participants, the legal system, and the media.

PART ONE

Chapter 1

WHY?

No other single word is less relevant or more relevant in the death of Caylee Anthony. A lovely child, she was allowed only 34 months to dance on this earth.

Caylee Anthony, not quite three years old, had been missing for 31 days before a police report was filed. That, we believe, is what brought worldwide media attention to this case. Since that day, the media has brought every detail they could find to the attention of the public, including the arrest of the child's mother, who will be tried for first-degree murder over the next month.

The media has provided us with everything from pictures of the beautiful child to pictures of the mother out dancing during the 31 days she did not report her child missing. We have heard the 911 calls and seen thousands of pages of discovery documents filed in the court by the prosecution and defense for the upcoming criminal case. All which are available online in a click, from the media. TV coverage from the Discovery Channel, 48 Hours, Geraldo Rivera, True TV, and Nancy Grace has played week after week during the three years the criminal charges have been pending. Some of that coverage has been because of the peculiarities of the case, some of it because the defendant is a pretty young white woman, and some of it because of Florida's position among the top five states in both death row population and the imposition of executions.

The mother, Casey Anthony, has been tried in the media and presumed guilty by most who have heard the massive media coverage. Now the questions are what of this information will be admissible and what other evidence yet unknown will make the courtroom? Who will judge her on that evidence and what will the result be under the judicial system of the United States of America?

Lawyers have debated this case on national TV. The defense team's lawyers have granted interviews for pretrial publicity. To us, that is simply stunning – their job is not to aggrandize themselves but to defend their client, and most of the media interviews seem to be the former and not the latter. Casey has a legal dream team that has been paid in part by her parents, in part by her sale of photos of her child, in part by taxpayers, and in part pro bono (without pay) except for the massive media advertising the lawyers are receiving for free. And the people of the State of Florida are paying for all other costs: investigators, costs of prosecution, discovery documents, hearings, judges, bailiffs, and so forth. The list is unending, and the dollars spent are said to be in the millions.

Chapter 2

THE BACKGROUND

The background of this case based on media coverage – At around 1PM on June 16th, 2008, 22-year-old Casey Anthony left her parents home with her nearly three-year-old daughter Caylee Anthony. It was the home where Casey Anthony had been living since before Caylee was born. Despite their repeated requests over the next weeks, Casey told her parents that she was too busy for them to see or talk to their granddaughter.

In mid-July, the grandparents discovered that Casey's car had been towed. Upon picking up the car from the towing facility, the grandfather told the towing yard employee who took him to the car that the smell made him afraid his daughter and granddaughter could be dead in the trunk. They checked, and found only a bag of trash.

Casey was found by her mother to be living with a boyfriend; she was bought back to the mother's home, but her three-year-old child was missing. Later that day at the home of her parents, Casey stated that Caylee was with a babysitter, but that Casey did not want to disturb them. She later stated to the grandmother that Caylee had been taken and had been missing for 31 days. The grandmother called 911 and reported Caylee missing.

Casey told investigators that Caylee was with a babysitter. No one had ever seen the babysitter she spoke of, although police eventually located a woman by that name. Detectives began an immediate investigation into Caylee, now missing 31 days, and found many discrepancies in Casey's statements. Searches for Caylee ensued. Casey was arrested and charges with Neglect of a Child, False Official Statements, and Obstruction of an Investigation. She was jailed, but the child Caylee was still missing.

Caylee's bodily remains were located in a wooded area on December 11th, 2008. Her body was found approximately a mile from the home Caylee had always known. Hers was a life unlived, given to the world and then taken by someone. Who took Caylee's life is the question. We are seeking the answer to that question through the police investigation, in the media, and finally in the American judicial system.

It is our intention to enter this story like most of us, with preconceived notions about the guilt of Casey Anthony in the death of her daughter Caylee. Our bias, like that of most, is based on the massive media coverage of this case.

However, at the moment we enter the courtroom trial, we will attempt to leave all of our preconceived notions outside the courtroom and judge this case, not based on the media coverage, but only by the evidence as it is presented in the trial. We are able to do this because it is being broadcasted live from courtroom audio and video feeds.

The decision of many higher courts to allow media in the courtroom has created this nonstop trial coverage live. It has also created huge problems for the courts in high-profile cases. In this case, the judge, lawyers, the defendant, and courtroom personnel traveled two hours from Orange County to Pinellas County, Florida to attempt to pick an unbiased jury that was less tainted by media coverage. All of the people who came to Pinellas County, our home, stayed in hotels at the expense of the taxpayers for the duration for jury selection. The sole exception was Casey Anthony, who was transported from the Orange County Jail to the Pinellas County Jail, also at taxpayer expense. After two weeks of jury selection, a jury was sworn, and then the Pinellas jury was taken to Orange County for the two months the trial is expected to last. It is the jurors who are **sequestered** (isolated and locked away without contact from the media, news or other people not in the jury) to minimize the potential for outside influences. They now live in hotels, as they will for the duration of the trial.

We do not have more than general knowledge of the legal system. Although we do have one criminal defense lawyer in this family, we are not lawyers. It is our intention to guide you through this trial with a layman's explanation of what really happens in this case, and therefore a standard criminal law case if there is any such thing. Does the justice system really work or not? Who are the characters of the courtroom drama? We will freely express our own opinions of the actions and the inactions of the lawyers, the judge, and the witnesses. Still, we will base our verdict only on the evidence we see and hear in the courtroom. The media has fought very hard to place cameras inside the courtroom. Whether that is for good or bad, it does allow us to view the proceedings.

Since in our lives, we have seen the best and the worse of the judicial system's judges and lawyers, we find this an interesting experience with a purpose. We do not know what the result will be. On this journey over the next months, together we will discover many things about ourselves, other people, the effect of the media, and the judicial system.

As of this moment, it is our belief based on media coverage only, that Casey Anthony is guilty of second-degree murder and the numerous obstruction charges in the indictment. From the media reports, we believe that Casey Anthony was sedating her daughter in the trunk of the car with chloroform so she could have her freedom, live with her boyfriends, and party. We believe Caylee died from an overdose in the trunk of the car. We do not believe that Casey Anthony had the fully formed intent to kill Caylee, which is among the requirements for first-degree murder, with which Casey is charged. However, we cannot comprehend such malicious, reckless, and self-serving behavior. Thoughts of the needless death of a young child at the hands of another person horrify us, no matter what the circumstances.

We believe Casey Anthony has lied to everyone to cover her daughter's death, and that she will take anyone down with her to prevent a long jail or death sentence. Her

4

"clever" maneuvering now has her in trial for her life on first-degree murder. Will the evidence hold up? We will also tell you that if we had to judge her guilt or innocence on what we know now from the media coverage, she would walk out free of any charges, for she is innocent until proven guilty. We shall see how or if our opinion changes by the end of our story. Along the way, you will discover who Matrix Filia is and why we chose to write this book.

Chapter 3

THE SETUP

An impartial juror and pretrial publicity – Every newspaper, TV, radio and social network has followed this case to a greater or lesser degree. Most news sources have and continue to give excruciating coverage of the story. The court is not looking for someone who has not seen the minute-by-minute coverage of the death of this beautiful child, the arrest of her mother for murder and more – that would be unrealistic, for nearly everyone has heard something about the circumstances of the case. The lawyers and the judge want to know what prospective jurors saw or heard. They want to know the sources of information and how often the jurors heard about the case: daily, weekly, more? The real purpose for questioning jurors about pretrial publicity is to look below the surface to see if each juror selected can put any prior information aside and look only at the evidence presented in the courtroom, then render a fair verdict based on only that evidence introduced in the trial. The judge conducts the first round of questioning, and then the lawyers for each side get a chance, if the prospective juror is not excused before that.

Our answers to the judge's questions, strangely enough, would be yes, we have heard extensively about the death of Caylee Anthony and the case. We are certain that we would not be selected as jurors for three reasons. A criminal defense lawyer lives in the house, *strike one*. This would be a mistake, because we could and would do what is required without bringing our prejudices based upon the occupation of a household member. We are both writers – *strike two*. There is one huge problem for the prosecution… we cannot be death qualified, and Florida law requires that each individual juror seated on a death penalty case be able to recommend a death sentence, if the circumstances warrant it. If Casey Anthony were to be found guilty, we would lock her up and toss away the key for the killing of this child, but we do not believe in the death penalty. Ours should not be a vengeful society, although we admit that when Usama bin Laden died in the raid on his compound, we were not sad. Our unwillingness to recommend death means – *strike three!* Florida law prohibits us from serving as jurors in cases like this where death is a possible sentence, because we cannot recommend that a death sentence be imposed in any case.

Now we begin with the questions of the potential jurors by the judge, the prosecution, and the defense in this case. Based on the prospective jurors' answers the attorneys will compromise on the fairest jury possible to decide the fate of Casey Marie Anthony. This is the **voir dire** (two French verbs meaning to see and to speak) of the jurors. Each juror is being questioned individually outside the presence of other jurors, to avoid the answers of one prospective juror from tainting a whole group.

The jury selection has just begun in the courtroom and the defense seems to have presented its theory of the case, while debating with the judge and the prosecution over the questions that can be asked of the potential jurors, before the questioning begins. Based on the questions the defense wants to ask, it appears that they are heading for a defense of mitigating circumstances to the charges. It seems that they may argue that she did it but there were reasons why she did it, such as her mental state and the like.

Because of the way she is charged, if Casey Anthony is found guilty of first-degree murder, some of the other charges (assuming she is found guilty of those charges) could become statutory **aggravating circumstances**. (Florida has a list of factors the jury can consider, and no other reasons are supposed to be considered by the jurors as justification for a recommendation of death.) Even one aggravator might be enough to result in a death sentence.

We think this is where their questions appear to be headed in terms of mitigating factors: Casey's mom and dad abused her and therefore she killed her child. My family all saw this one coming… which parent will they throw under the bus? We think the answer is Dad.

Is any or all of this abuse true? Are the parents aware of this defense, which may be a last ditch effort to save the child who killed their only grandchild? We will hear the evidence soon. Then if it is true, it could become a **mitigating circumstance** in the penalty phase of the trial, if Casey is convicted of first-degree murder. Such things as the defendant's age, a history of abuse of defendant, a defendant's mental state at the time of the crime, and any other factor that tends to lessen the defendant's culpability are considered mitigating circumstances that can be shown by the defense's evidence in penalty phase. Could it be that the defense expects to use such a factor as some sort of defense in the first phase of the trial?

This case involves the report of a child who had been missing for 31 days before any report was made to the police. If the evidence supports this, it raises the largest question in our minds. Could anything stop you from reporting your child missing immediately? Yet, according to the 911 call on July 16th, 2008, the grandmother Cindy Anthony appeared to have just found out and immediately called 911. Then, Casey got on the 911 call and stated, "My daughter has been missing for 31 days." Will this call make the evidence in the courtroom? I think so, but justice is strange and we will have to wait and see. We need to know the why. What could have caused that failure to report? There are possibilities. Was Casey protecting someone? No, that would not do it for us.

This is our view for the millions of dollars that we as tax payers will pay for the trial of Casey Anthony, investigators, experts, testing, housing, food, and the multiple lawyers at the defense and prosecution tables.

We are the shadow jurors of the trial by media, the judge, the lawyers, the evidence and how our system really works or does not. It is up to you to decide. We will not lay aside our prejudices, guided by the media, about the guilt of this woman *until* the trial begins. Then, we will attempt to put aside all we have heard in the media and base our shadow verdict only on the evidence. The jurors will tell us their verdict. Will our verdict agree with theirs?

We would like to introduce you to our favorite character of this trial so far. The mitigation expert for the defense team is a woman by the name of Rosalie Bolin, who was a court reporter and then an investigator in the Public Defender's Office in Hillsborough County, Florida. She divorced her lawyer husband and married Oscar Ray Bolin after meeting him through her work. He was already in jail when they met, and was already charged with multiple murders. He is a serial killer of at least three women, and he now sits on death row. Oscar Ray Bolin is a man our house lawyer had the "pleasure" of representing during his days as a public defender, as one of his many

7

lawyers in numerous hearings, and in one of Mr. Bolin's trials. Our lawyer will not discuss the specifics of the case, so we cannot provide you with details.

Chapter 4

TEARS OF FEAR

The Prosecution:

1. Linda Drane Burdick (Lead Counsel);
2. Jeff Ashton;
3. Frank George.

The Defense:

1. Jose Baez (Lead Counsel);
2. Cheney Mason (the old dog with forty years experience trying murder cases);
3. Ann Finnell (the penalty phase expert);
4. Dorothy Clay Simms;
5. William Slabaugh (a lawyer who works in Baez's firm);
6. Lisabeth Fryer (a dark-haired lady lawyer who does complicated case law arguments).

Bevin Perry Jr., is the judge for the Casey Anthony trial. He is the Chief Judge of the Ninth Judicial Circuit of Florida, serving Orange and Osceola counties. He has come to Pinellas at the request of the defense for a **change of venue** (change of the location of trial, or in this case, jury selection) to pick a jury. Typically, when venue is changed the case is tried in the county where jury selection is held. In this case, Pinellas County, Florida is being used only for jury selection. Once a jury is chosen, the entire case and the jurors will go to Orlando for trial. The judge and the attorneys are looking for a jury of people who have less exposure to the pretrial publicity than people in Orlando. Judge Perry has over twenty years on the bench, and has vast experience to bring to bear as the judge for this trial. This could be a very good thing or he could be simply a man jaded from all the years of hearing about people at their worst and the worst things people can do. We will judge this as well.

Sometimes, on the high end of the scale, experience as a trial judge will bring a seasoned professional and legal scholar to the courtroom. On the low end of the scale it can bring an angry, empty person, who never was or never will be a legal scholar, with an agenda other than justice. We will wait to see what kind of Judge Bevin Perry is…

In the three years Casey Anthony has been awaiting trial, her hair has grown from a well-manicured short cut to a long pony tail. Her hair is something only a woman would notice, mostly for the precision with which she keeps part of her pony tail over her shoulder. She walks with a side sweep into the courtroom which would make even Cleopatra blush. She is continuously cleaning up the table and napkins under the glasses of everyone, so far she has cried only when the charges against her were read. We suppose that is understandable, since it is her life which hangs in limbo.

Now we notice that Casey is rubbing her hands, and also holding her female attorney's hands. It is clear that she is cold. We find ourselves thinking (remember, we are not in trial yet, so our opinions will flow freely) how cold was the grave of Caylee, whether Casey is guilty or not. This thought crosses our minds. She has shed no tears since the charges were read against her today.

Those charges are contained in the **indictment**, the charging document based on a grand jury that heard and reviewed evidence based only on the prosecution's case. No defense attorney was present or was heard. The indictment is a finding of probable cause, and is required if the prosecution intends to seek the death penalty. A grand jury is made of citizens of the area in which the crime was committed. Once an indictment is rendered by a grand jury, the case will be tried with a defense team and prosecution team before a judge and **petit jury**. Although its name means "small" in French, the job of a petit jury is anything but small – it is the jury that hears the evidence at trial, and it cannot include members of the grand jury that heard evidence presented for the indictment. In only a few types of trials, including first degree murder, are there 12 jurors. The "State" (the prosecution) must prove every **element** (part) of each of the charges to convict the mother, Casey Anthony of that charge. That means that the mother of Caylee Anthony must be proven by evidence to be criminally responsible for the child's death in only one of the charges below, while other charges require proof of separate, although possibly related crimes.

Phase one of the trial relates solely to Casey Anthony's guilt or innocence. The question before the jury is whether she committed the crime, as to each of the charged offenses. In phase one, the guilt phase, it takes a unanimous jury to reach a decision. That means 12 votes for guilty of the crime charged, 12 votes for a less serious, included offense, or 12 votes for **not guilty**, as to each charge in the indictment. A verdict of not guilty does not necessarily indicate innocence; it can also mean that despite the jurors' suspicions, the evidence did not prove guilt to the standard required by law. Without all likeminded votes there would be a hung jury or mistrial. **Phase two of the trial** relates to the punishment if she is found guilty of first degree murder in phase one. There are only two possible sentences after conviction of first degree murder in Florida; they are death by lethal injection and life imprisonment without any possibility of parole or release. A sentence of death requires a guilty verdict of first degree murder and proof of at least one aggravating factor. In the penalty phase, there are still 12 jurors voting, but the vote need not be unanimous. A vote of 7-5, with at least seven jurors voting for death is a recommendation for a death sentence to be imposed. If the vote is 6 jurors or less voting for a death sentence, the jury's recommendation is one of life in prison without the possibility of parole.

To paraphrase the judge, a **reasonable doubt** is not a possible doubt, a speculative, imaginary, or forced doubt. On the other hand, if after carefully considering and weighing all the evidence, there is not an abiding conviction of guilt, or if, having a conviction, it is one which wavers and vacillates, then the charge is not proved beyond a reasonable doubt. A reasonable doubt can arise from the evidence, the lack of evidence, or conflict in the evidence. If the juror has a reasonable doubt, he or she should vote not guilty, but if there is no reasonable doubt, the jury should find the defendant guilty.

The jurors must weigh the evidence, the accuracy of the witness's memory, and whether witnesses are honest and straightforward in answering questions. The weight given to the testimony of an expert witness such as a scientist is based on the credit the jurors give to the expert. As with any witness, factors to be considered include whether the witness has anything to gain from the testimony, (whether it is monetary, notoriety, or the obvious considerations such as a mother protecting a child). The jurors should also consider whether at some other time any witness made a statement inconsistent with their trial testimony. Based upon reason and common sense, after careful and impartial consideration of all the evidence or lack of evidence in a case, a verdict is rendered. Proof beyond a reasonable doubt, therefore, is proof of such a convincing character that the jurors would be willing to rely and act upon it without hesitation in the most important of their own affairs. However, it does not mean an absolute certainty.

The indictment filed in the Casey Anthony case charges a total of seven crimes. They are:

1. First Degree Murder;
2. Aggravated Child Abuse;
3. Aggravated Manslaughter of a Child;
4. Providing False Information to a Law Enforcement Officer;
5. Providing False information to a Law Enforcement Officer;
6. Providing False information to a Law Enforcement Officer;
7. Providing False information to a Law Enforcement Officer.

It is important for us to understand that even though the charge is first degree murder in the first count of the indictment, the jury will be advised by the judge that they can find her guilty of a lesser charge including second degree depraved mind murder and manslaughter, if the main charge has not been proven beyond a reasonable doubt. Other lesser included offenses, such as third degree felony murder may also be read, depending on the evidence presented at trial. Conviction for any of those offenses carry a lesser penalty than first degree murder's potential for a death sentence, and most of the offenses do not include a life sentence as a possibility. Similarly, the second and third crimes charged also have lesser included offenses.

PART TWO

Chapter 5

JURY SELECTION

On the first day of jury selection, Casey is presenting herself in her best possible light to the media and the prospective jurors, paying attention to her dress and her hair. She is making a first impression today. That devolves fairly quickly as the day progresses. She begins fidgeting, wiping water rings from the defense counsel table, sorting and rearranging papers. Defense attorney Baez chastised her loud enough for the courtroom microphones to pick up. He told her she was acting like a two-year-old, and told her to stop. We think his choice of words was ill-advised.

This is the first ever televised jury selection. We find that this causes us issues. Should those who are obligated by law to sit on a jury be required to reveal their personal information on TV, YouTube and more? The information that comes out about the prospective jurors in the jury selection process can make it seem as though the jurors are on trial. As we go on, you will see just how much personal information is released. This is very unnerving to us. Judge Perry is moving this case along to his goal of starting the trial in four days in Orlando. Once they have 12 jurors going forward, at that time the lawyers must use **their peremptory challenges** (remove a juror for any reason, except discrimination of a protected class such as race, disability and the like) or he will seat the 12 and then need five to eight alternate jurors. This procedure is long for everyone involved.

There are two kinds of challenges to a prospective juror. The first is a **challenge for cause**. Challenges for cause are unlimited in number, and are based upon undue hardship to the prospective juror or responses by the juror that show that the prospective juror has a bias that could prevent the juror from fairly judging the facts of the case. For instance, a juror who insists that he must hear the defendant testify or that weighing the evidence requires hearing from defense witnesses despite being told that the defendant has the absolute right to remain silent and has no obligation to present any evidence, would not be able to sit as a juror, since the jury cannot hold the defendant's silence or failure to present an affirmative defense against her. The other type of challenge is the peremptory challenge. The significant difference between the two types is that the number of peremptory challenges is limited, based on the nature of the charge(s). Each side has the same number of peremptory challenges. Obviously, both sides want to try to get prospective jurors removed with cause strikes, so they can preserve their peremptory challenges for those prospects who answer questions in a way that makes one side or the other think that the juror would be less favorable to that side than other prospective jurors. The lawyer in the family says lawyers don't really pick juries; they just get to pick who to knock off!

The prospective jurors are not shown on television, but their voices are not electronically altered. It will not be hard for many who know them to recognize their voices or recognize their most personal stories and discover who these people really are, even with each juror being called by a number. However, if after the trial they do not accept the media's invitations to talk about the case or write a book, it may be reasonably easy for them to resume their lives.

Judge Perry uses a somewhat unusual procedure for questioning jurors for this case. Each juror is brought to the courtroom several times to individually face rounds of questions. This individual questioning is known as **sequestered voir dire**, and it is used to make sure that the answers of one prospective juror do not affect the responses of others. The questions involve hardship to the juror, pretrial publicity, whether they are willing (or too willing) to impose death, and then general voir dire about the specific case. What we describe in a few pages takes ten days to accomplish, and requires calling for additional prospective jurors several times. As a result, the questioning has to start all over again for new potential jurors.

As each juror passes to the next round of questioning, Judge Perry tells them to call a telephone number to find out when (or what day) they will next be needed in court. He also tells them not to talk to anyone about the case, not to read or listen to any news or social media about the case, but only to prepare to make arrangements as necessary to be away from Pinellas County for a while. Each time a prospective juror returns to the courtroom, he or she is asked if they have observed the judge's orders regarding outside influences.

The judge begins by selecting 110 jurors to begin a process of questions. First, would they face true hardship if they were sequestered for eight weeks, the estimated length of this trial, without access to telephones, the internet, without being able to discuss of the case, in Orlando Florida, for thirty dollars a day plus food and lodging? Seems harsh don't you think? But it is necessary to insure that the jury is not tainted by the media and more – even friends and families. Each juror is individually questioned by the judge and sometimes the attorneys about whether being in Orlando for six to eight weeks would cause them an undue hardship, such as loss of a job, falling into (or deeper into) debt, whether they will be paid by their employer for the duration of jury service, whether they care for others who would be unable to obtain or afford care, and so forth. That results in quite a number of jurors being excused.

Next, as jurors are cleared to go forth in the selection process, they will be faced with rounds of questions on the pre-trial exposure to this case, ability to set aside any feelings they may have about the case and base a verdict only on the evidence and the law.

The prospective jurors are asked questions to determine if they are **death qualified.** Can they render a verdict resulting in the death penalty if the defendant is found guilty? Will the potential for a death sentence affect their voting in the guilt phase of the trial? Are they too willing to vote for death, or can they carefully consider and weigh both life and death as alternative punishments? The law does not mandate that anyone vote for death in the penalty phase, but all jurors must consider it when deciding a sentence if Casey Anthony is found guilty of first-degree murder. Remember, a vote of 7-5 for death is all they need in the penalty phase. So, sitting on this jury and voting for a life sentence in the penalty phase could still mean that you sit on a jury that gives a death sentence.

The prosecution and the defense attorneys ask questions of potential jurors such as: Have you ever been in the position of smelling something terrible? Have you ever trained a dog other than just your personal dog? Would you like to be a juror on this case? How many people have approached you wanting to talk, since you have become a prospective juror?

As the prospective jurors are asked more questions, keep in this in mind. The questions may seem insignificant, but each does pertain to something surrounding the life and death of Caylee or relates to the juror's background. If a juror has something in their life which could taint them, the judge and the lawyers needs to know. Here are some of the questions asked of potential jurors:

Have you ever heard of this case?

You said that being on this jury is like solving a mystery? Why do you say that?

Do you think beyond a reasonable doubt is too high? If you have any doubt, you need to look at the holes in the evidence and you should go back and look.

Who has the burden of proof, and do you think it is fair?

Is there any way to prove a negative?

In your questionnaire, you put that someone in your family is in law enforcement. Are you close to them?

Do you feel that law enforcement officers are more credible than laymen?

Do you think experts always give opinions on what they know or study or do they go further?

Could you base your decision on the fact that someone is probably guilty?

Do you watch Nancy Grace, Geraldo Rivera, Discover ID, 48 Hours, Dr G or truTV?

Have you ever been in the position of smelling something terrible?

Have you ever trained a dog other than just your personal dog?

Would you like to be a juror on this case?

How many people have approached you wanting to talk since you have become a prospective juror?

The prosecution makes the charges; do you understand they must prove the guilt?

When you see a person who is in the back of a police car do you say, "what did they do" or "they are innocent"?

Sitting here now, do you think Casey Anthony is 100 percent innocent? (The Judge steps in to explain the fact that at this moment and until the evidence in the trial proves differently, the defendant is 100 percent innocent. The judge tells the juror that the defendant is cloaked with the cloth of innocence until proved guilty to the juror. After that, the prospective juror, who has previously said that she must have done something wrong to be a defendant, says he feels that she is innocent and could base his service on this fact.)

Would you base your decision on anger over the graphic nature of the evidence?

Do you have a Facebook, Twitter, or any other social media accounts?

Do you write or read blogs?

Do you believe in the concept of mercy?

Can you consider life without the possibility of parole?

Can you consider imposing the death penalty?

Out of over 200 possible jurors questioned, twelve jurors and five **alternate jurors** are selected. The alternate jurors may come into play in the event one of the twelve cannot complete the trial due to illness or the like. All seventeen will listen to the case together and share experiences outside the courtroom. From the time they leave the hotel until they return, they will be together. They will even eat all of their meals together. We know which are the first twelve jurors and which are the alternate jurors, but the jurors themselves do not. That, we assume, is to make sure that every juror pays close attention to the testimony and evidence, because they do not know which among them will be called to deliberate at the end of the trial. Of course, we cannot be sure either - none of us can predict what may happen during the course of the trial. What follows is a description of those who will decide the fate of Casey Anthony, based upon their responses to questions asked in the courtroom. Would you want them to decide your fate?

As jury selection proceeds, the **State** (the prosecution) suggests to the judge to begin death qualifying first to save time. Judge Perry is considering this and goes away from the bench to review case law the lawyers have submitted on another issue. The question he is considering is whether the jurors can be asked if they are willing to consider mercy as a reason for imposing a life sentence instead of death. Both sides have cited cases on this issue. The defense wants to ask this question of potential jurors. The judge rules that the case law prevails on this issue and the judge states, that he will not give a jury instruction to that effect, that jurors cannot be stricken for cause if they cannot give mercy, however the lawyers can ask the question. (It really cannot hurt to ask.)

We will try to maintain the integrity of the words of the judge, prospective jurors, lawyers, side events and sideshows as we believe we hear and see them. However, this is not verbatim testimony or quotation from a court transcript. We are writers interpreting and analyzing the trial of Casey Anthony as the events occur.

Chapter 6

THE JURORS

Juror 1 - The Counselor: is a female sixty-eight years of age who is now a counselor. She has two children and three grandchildren. Counselors are trained to listen to both sides of an argument, and hopefully give some solid advice. She mentions that she does not really listen to the news or get the paper, but it seems she does watch some CNN and international news. She is cynical of media and does not believe all that she hears. She also was a pediatric nurse, and she has seen and smelled dead bodies. This may lend to a unique viewpoint of life and death, especially the death of children, for she has experienced it first-hand. She is pro-life (relating to abortions), and she says she accepts that the death penalty must be given at appropriate times. Her life is busy, and she does not see the potential for others second-guessing her decision as an issue. She has experience as a juror; she was a juror in a high-profile mafia murder case, and she served as a juror in a drug case, as well. This juror may have a difficult time sentencing someone to death based on any medical mitigation such as mental issues. On the other hand, she may have already sentenced someone to death in her prior murder trial jury service! The lawyer in the family says that the attorneys are not allowed to ask about that. She may be more inclined to give a sentence of life without parole. We believe her inability to see the "gray" areas of this case is concerning, and that she is unlikely to hesitate in imposing a death sentence if Casey Anthony is found guilty of premeditated murder.

Juror 2 - The IT Worker: is a black man, married, about forty years of age, who lives what some would consider a middle class life. He works as a information technology trainer and application designer for the county. He is familiar with computers and how they operate, and he holds computer certifications. He has two children; one is four and the other is nine. He has never been the victim of a violent crime, only a car break-in. He has no interest in talking to the media after the trial. He is hesitant to say that he could impose death on another person. On one hand he says he cannot, and yet he feels in some circumstances he could consider death as a sentence. The contradiction seems alarming, but the judge intervenes, and the juror stated that he could impose death in certain circumstances. This juror seems uncomfortable being asked the questions by both sides. His wife is a heart nurse dealing with both adult and pediatric patients. So, we should assume he has heard all kinds of stories of children dying from her. This could make it difficult for him to look past the more gruesome evidence the prosecution gives at trial. He was raised by a single mother and has been on his own since the age of twenty-two, and he was the defendant in paternity litigation. He says that he will give no greater weight to the testimony of law enforcement witnesses than the testimony of any other witness. The juror seems reluctant to give a death penalty but does not want to be disqualified from the case. In the end we believe he would not give the death penalty no matter what the evidence, but he seems to be good for evaluation guilt phase evidence.

Juror 3 – The Weaver: is a female about thirty-two years of age. Her hobby is weaving. She is a nursing student at St. Pete College and has no children or financial burdens. She is the youngest of five, and was raised by a single mother and appears to have no idea where her father is. That statement strikes us as odd – possible but improbable. Something in her voice sounds off, but maybe she is just nervous. She claims to know nothing about the case, and first heard of it within the last week. The juror feels she has a high emotional maturity for this case. We think she comes off a bit arrogant and naive. She says she really hasn't heard much about the case but does have a Facebook account, and has posts on her wall relating to the case. She claims she told her friends she does not want to discuss the case. She has watched the Dr. G television show about a dozen times. That is significant because Dr. G is Jan C. Garavaglia, M.D, the Orange County Medical Examiner, and she will testify in this case. The feeling we get is that she is being untruthful – she knows more than she is letting on about the case but does not want to be disqualified. She can impose a death sentence based on the evidence and feels the punishment should fit the crime. This sounds more like an "Eye for an Eye" perspective when she says it, despite her denial of feeling that way. Her attitude is even clearer when she says that the law gives jurors the "opportunity" to impose death in some crimes. We do not think she could really set her emotions aside in this case and objectively make a decision. We believe that the defense does not want her but the prosecution does. We are surprised that the defense does not exercise a peremptory challenge, but perhaps the attorneys feel that she is better than the alternatives available.

Juror 4 – The Unassuming Lady: is a middle-aged female. She does not watch the news much but had heard that a child was killed. She is genuinely unaware of the facts of the case. She watches westerns and does have a Facebook account to play online games such as Farmville. She does not communicate much with other people in person and says she does not really have friends. She does not watch any shows like 48 Hours or mysteries. She says that she does not like to judge based on what people say, but when asked about what witnesses say, she distinguishes testimonial evidence from talk outside the courtroom. This juror believes she could be fair and listen to all the evidence before making a decision. When she is asked about whether she could impose death she reluctantly responds that given the right circumstances she thinks she can. She seems to be telling the truth - she could reluctantly vote for death, but she certainly doesn't want to. The defense wants this juror and the prosecution does not. They exercise a peremptory strike based on her wavering about life or death. The judge intimates but does not say that the prosecution's challenge is based on reasons other than those announced. The Florida courts have said that jurors cannot be removed with peremptory challenges in a way that is discriminatory, because that affects a defendant's right to a fair trial. We believe the prosecutor was basing the strike on the fact the juror is black, and it seems the judge does, too. By the way, Judge Perry is also black. Since we have no racial biases, we really hadn't noticed until now - it wasn't relevant. The judge refuses to allow the juror to be stricken by the State, and so she becomes a juror trying the case.

Juror 5 - The Housekeeper: is a female between the ages of sixty-five and seventy who is a retired housekeeper. She lives with a retired plumber. She is not all that religious. She completed the eleventh grade and reads books, mysteries, magazines, and the like. She does not go out much and watches TV. She occasionally reads the newspaper, and does not own a computer. Her fifty-two year old daughter is in the Air Force, and a forty-eight year old son who is on disability from a back injury. She was once arrested for DUI but not convicted, although the State announces that adjudication was withheld. She has a son and grandson who have been in trouble for bad checks and drugs. This may be helpful for the defense because she and some of her family members have been defendants. The juror may see the possibility of a person being arrested whether guilty or not. She has heard about this case from the media and newspapers. The juror believes in hearing all of the evidence before making a decision and weighing the evidence in sentencing to determine aggravating and mitigating circumstances. She has developed no opinion about the guilt or innocence of Casey Anthony. She seems sincere in her answers. The defense is not sure if they want her but the prosecution may. She has been a juror before in a criminal case. She is death qualified based on her ability to weigh both sides at trial.

Juror 6 - The Chef: is a married female, thirty-three years old with two children ages six and two. She is a stay at home mom now, and has no issues with leaving to be a juror for long lengths of time. She probably wants a break from the family for a little while, is our take. She moved to Florida in 2008 from California. She was born in DC, grew up in Florida, and has moved a lot. She has no legal background; she reported for jury duty ten years ago, but was not chosen. She goes to Orlando once a week and is back the same day. We wonder why she goes once a week, but no one asks. That seems weird to us. The juror heard of the case but not much, although she says her husband has followed it. She has worked in the restaurant equipment/supply business, as a chef until two years ago, and has been on small-market TV as a chef. She also had computer forensics training, and a business degree from Florida. She mostly gets her news from her phone, and she watches national and international news on TV. She remembers seeing K-9 dogs being trained on her high school athletic field from afar, but had no close contact with them. She says she can weigh all evidence before giving a verdict and is not opposed to life in prison or the death penalty. It seems to us that this juror is being truthful. Neither side objects to her. When she is asked if she would like to be on this case her response is, "No, not particularly." This juror may not be able to set her feelings aside if she does not want to be there. She may be in a hurry to leave and vote whatever way is easier – this may not be the vacation from her kids she wanted. This juror should not be on the jury, in our opinion.

During most of the questioning, Casey Anthony is somewhat in a daze almost looking drugged. We see very little emotion. She does speak to her attorneys.

Juror 7 – The Lawyer's Daughter: is a divorced female who is about forty years old. She has no children and an ex-husband who is an engineer with a defense contractor. She doesn't really use any social networking sites. She has heard about the case on CNN – she describes herself as a CNN junkie, and says she is in withdrawal from avoiding reading the St. Petersburg Times because of her jury service; she does not watch the Dr. G show or 20/20. She has also heard from people about Casey Anthony working at Universal Studios and that Casey said that Caylee was left with a babysitter, but not much more. Her mother was an attorney and she is familiar with how the law works in these cases, although her mother did not practice criminal law. She says she thinks the death penalty has been racially motivated, and that bothers her. She attended college and majored in sociology, but did not get a degree. The juror has worked in accounts receivable at a nursing home, as a university secretary, at a

children's hospital in Atlanta, and as a fund raiser. She
has also helped with Meals On Wheels and with training
people in administrative work. She also worked in the
juvenile justice and child welfare systems. She dated an
Assistant State Attorney, but the way she says "he'll
always be a prosecutor" lets us know that she isn't
impressed with him. She was the victim of a burglary when
she was at home; the burglar was armed with a knife, but
she was not hurt and got safely out of the house. The
burglar was caught and pled guilty. Her deposition was
taken in that case. We wonder whether what she has heard
in the media will color her view of the evidence. This
juror does not have any experience with search dogs. She
is familiar with the system and attorneys and undoubtedly
has heard war stories and horror stories about child
abuse. She was the victim of a serious crime and had her
deposition taken, so she may sympathize with witnesses
and victims. Those things could make her a prosecutor's
dream juror, at least in guilt phase. She says she would
be willing to consider both a life and death sentence
depending on the evidence. She calls a death sentence a
solemn decision, and says that she has done a lot of
soul-searching, so she may be inclined toward a life
sentence if it comes to that. Frankly, although the
defense unsuccessfully tries to have her stricken for
cause, we are shocked that they do not use a peremptory
challenge on her. She says she wishes she couldn't put
her personal views aside because she does not want to be
on the jury. We think she is sandbagging, and has an
ulterior motive to be a juror.

Juror 8 – The Verizon Service Representative: is a female
between the ages fifty and sixty-five who is married with
two children ages twenty-three and twenty-seven. She
works as a customer service representative for repair of
fiber optics and customer assurance. She has worked for
Verizon for thirty-nine years. She has supervised as many
as twenty-five at work, but she is not a supervisor now.
Her husband owned a bike shop but is now retired. Her
oldest son is in the Coast Guard and her youngest son
lives at home and works part-time. This could give her a
perspective sympathetic to Casey Anthony's parents since
she has a son who still lives at home and the juror
probably helps him out with money. On the other hand, she
says that if one of her sons were on trial, she would
want people to consider all the facts and not go in with
closed minds. Her house has been burglarized, but no one
was caught. She has served as a juror twice before - once
as an alternate juror in a criminal case. Her father was
a police officer in New Jersey, so she probably has a
law-and-order perspective. She says that testimony of
police officers does not carry more weight than the

testimony of other witnesses. This juror might have more knowledge than most about how evidence is collected, labeled, and held for trial. Her father lives in Orlando, and one of her sons went there to college, so she is familiar with the area. She has very little understanding of social networking sites and watches some local news, which is where she thinks she heard of the case, and has heard other people express the opinion that Casey Anthony is guilty. She says that her son will kill her for admitting that she doesn't know what blogging is. That seems to us to be an odd thing for her to say in a murder trial voir dire, but perhaps she is getting comfortable in her role of being questioned. She says she believes that a defendant is innocent until proven guilty, not the other way around. She says that she understands that the State carries the burden of proof, and that the defendant does not have to prove anything. She can weigh all the evidence before making a judgment call and has no issues with giving life or death if all factors are weighed. We think she is level-headed and not jaded. Although she has two children, she would not see the defendant Casey Anthony as her child and would hope anyone would consider all the facts before rendering a decision. We believe the prosecution wants her more than the defense.

Juror 9 – The Semi-Retired Mill Worker: is a male, who is fifty-three, single, from Ohio. He grew up in San Francisco and moved to Florida from Indiana four years ago to avoid snow. He went to high school, vocational school for printing, and has an associate's degree in business. He does not watch Nancy Grace, Geraldo Rivera, or 48 Hours; he watches PBS, History Channel and Discovery Channel. He is a book reader, and is reading a Tom Clancy novel now. He is semi-retired and works some as a handyman. He now cares for a stroke victim. He worked for over thirty years for the same company, in a paper mill. He helped set up the computer network at the mill. He has no children. He has two sisters and two brothers; he is close with their children (both young and old enough to be getting married), and describes himself as the favorite uncle. His relationship with his parents was good; they are now deceased. He heard daily about the case in 2008, but says he never formed an opinion about the case. He believes everyone has the right to a fair trial and that the media has been unfair in its presumptions. He seems honest with his answers, and it is apparent he has a dislike for the media. He would be able to take all factors in before determining a punishment. His nephew is in law enforcement and just became a Manatee County deputy sheriff. He is happy that law enforcement is protecting people. He is familiar with Orlando and has done trade shows there selling water purification, so he has experience with public speaking. He has no experience with dogs or forensics. He sees things from different sides and would be able to judge based on facts given and not just opinions. Although he knows about social media networks he doesn't really care what others have to say about the case. He seems sincere and open in his answers, seems to be willing to consider all of the evidence, and is comfortable with imposing either life or death based on the evidence, if the trial results in a first degree murder conviction.

Juror 10 – The Verizon Retention Specialist: is a male, approximately fifty-seven, single, never married, no children, two siblings, a brother and a sister. He lived in Knoxville, Tennessee, left there 16 years ago and moved to Florida after he lost his job. Both of his parents still are living and he takes care of them. His father was an educator and his mother was a secretary. This would lead us to believe he has some kind of connection with his parents and may be able to understand the relationship between Casey and her parents some. When he first moved to Florida, he became certified as a corrections officer, but never applied for that kind of job. He has worked for his current employer for fifteen years. He works as a retention specialist for Verizon, and he may not appreciate Casey lying to everyone about having a job she does not have. He seems like the kind of man who knows how hard it is in the working world and would take offense to Casey's partying and immaturity. That is especially true because his sister "was all messed up" seventeen years ago, and was convicted of breaking into his parents' house with her boyfriend, tying up their father, and stealing money; the juror is not sure if that man was ever caught. His sister was sentenced to prison, but is now a certified nursing assistant and has a lovely family of her own, so he also can understand that immaturity in early life does not mean immaturity forever. His brother works for the government, and just returned to the U.S. from an assignment in Syria. He has no connection to social networking sites and watches TV but not true crime. He has not been to Orlando and only remembers hearing about this case in 2008 from local news. His answers seem sincere and would be able consider both guilt and punishment deserving of the crime, based on facts and not speculation. He seems to be a reasonably balanced juror, but his sister's history may be a concern for both sides.

Juror 11 - The Phys Ed Teacher: is a male, approximately thirty-five years old, who has two siblings, two dogs and teaches Physical Education to tenth graders. He is working on a master's degree in special education.

Because of this we can assume he likes children and may have a somewhat hard time seeing Caylee's death pictures. He admits that he has heard a significant amount about the case, both from the media and from other teachers, and that he concurs with other teachers that Casey Anthony is guilty. He says he can set aside his opinion and judge the case based solely on the evidence adduced at trial. This juror may want on this case for more personal reasons. Perhaps he feels that if he can convict Casey, he can get some justice for Caylee and be a hero. This is just one way to view it. He was a burglary victim. He does have a Facebook account. Although he says he has no presumption of guilt, we don't believe him fully faithful in tone. Something in his voice leads us to believe he has a hidden agenda. Maybe this goes back to our theory of him wanting to punish someone for Caylee's death. He has no children of his own but has two dogs which he loves. The only good thing for the defense about him is that when initially asked, he says that he cannot impose the death penalty, but ultimately says that he guesses he could consider imposing a death penalty, and would not automatically vote against it. This juror is a defense lawyer's nightmare. The defense will not want him but prosecution will, unless the prosecutors are truly adamant about seeking a death sentence.

Juror 12 – The Publix Employee: is a female, approximately sixty years old, who has been married for fifteen years in her second marriage. She worked in a day care center in Michigan, and now works at Publix supermarket. She adopted two children as infants, a daughter who is thirty-eight, a teacher, and a son, thirty-three, who runs a repossession business. She has one grandchild, a boy two years old. Her husband retired from General Motors, and cuts stones for a jeweler now and teaches his technique to others. Both are blue collar workers the same as Cindy and George Anthony. She has been around young children Caylee's age and this may result in a tremendous amount of sympathy for the victim and prejudice towards Casey. She feels that she could weigh all evidence before giving a true verdict. We are not completely convinced. She does wear a hearing aid and during questioning she has had to adjust it a few times. She states this would not be a problem and can hear just fine. She seems sincere and we believe wants to be on the jury as a matter of duty. Her hearing issues may cause problems understanding all the evidence presented at trial. She does not have a computer nor does she have a dog. She does art, crafts, and quilting in her spare time. This juror is an old fashioned lady who will likely side with the prosecution. Her answers sound deliberate, "If she did it, she deserves the punishment." That is especially concerning for the defense attorneys, because during death qualification she tells the defense that on a scale from one to ten (with ten being for imposing death) that she is a ten. Her emotions regarding the death of a girl not much older than her grandchild could color her view of the evidence in the guilt phase, and her stand on the death penalty would likely result in her rendering an automatic death vote in penalty phase, should it come to that. This is understandable but not someone who can be unbiased, in our opinion.

Alternate Juror 1 – The Surgical Tech: is a white female, forty-eight years old, who has been married twenty-eight years. She is a surgical technician. She has two sons; the younger is age twenty-two, and he is going into the military as a Second Lieutenant, and the older son is twenty-five, and works for a clothing store. She is from New Jersey, but has lived in Pinellas County, Florida since age nine. Her husband was a butcher for Boar's Head client distribution and is now unemployed. She was a nurse's aide at age sixteen and achieved a surgical tech degree 28 years ago. She has seen bodies cut open on operating tables, blood, bones and most likely dead bodies before. Because of this she would be able to sit through the evidence presented at trial. She has a Facebook account for family to stay connected, and watches shows on the History Channel, the Military Channel, and some local news and sports. She has previous experience as a juror in a civil case, and found the experience interesting. She has not heard much about the case since 2008. Because of her job, she feels she could be objective as a juror. She understands that in her job, prior knowledge of the patient is important to a successful outcome, but is willing to set aside what little she recalls about the case and consider only what she hears in court for a successful outcome here. She has an understanding that each situation is unique and may have different results. Several times, she likens herself to a sponge ready to absorb information; only then can she render a decision.

The authors notice that Casey is going through files and paperwork, she wants to appear in control, it is like she is pretending she is a lawyer now. When the lady lawyers try to communicate with each other she acts like it is her they are talking to. Casey is looking at their cell phones and the like. She is seated between the two lawyers. The bottom line is that she is playing pretend. We find this unappealing. She is a defendant, not a lawyer.

Alternate Juror 2 - The U.S. Government Teacher: is a high school government teacher who is in his fifties. He is who has been married for four years. His wife is a seventh grade math teacher. He was married twice before, for fourteen and seven years. He has a grown son and two teenage stepchildren. He has a college degree in history. He worked in labor relations for the Postal Service for 20 years before becoming a high school government teacher; he also teaches dropout prevention. In his work for the Postal Service, he presented cases in federal court, both with and without counsel. He says he has the ability to weigh both sides before coming to an opinion. He watches Fox News and does not watch Nancy Grace, Geraldo Rivera, Jane Valdez or 48 Hours. He watches NCIS and Dancing With The Stars. He loves to read spy novels and murder mysteries. He heard about this case on the news - that a child was missing, and then found dead by a utility worker. He does not use Facebook or Twitter. He has never been a victim of a crime or witnessed one. He has never been a juror, and looks forward to it as a civic duty and a great teaching tool. He was pulled over and arrested for DUI, but the charge was reduced to careless driving. He has mentioned that he teaches seniors in high school about the steps of law but does not feel he will bring any special knowledge to the case. We believe he is either being very humble or thinks the court naive. The high school he teaches in also has a criminal justice academy and sometimes he would bring in lawyers and police officers to talk to the children about the process. He has already arranged for a substitute teacher, and prepared lesson plans. He has been an elementary school teacher. This we feel could be a bias. He may have dealt with young children who may have been abused by a parent and or guardian. If a child he taught has been killed in a violent way, it could seriously affect his mindset. This was not brought up in questioning, but it is a concern for us, as is his courtroom experience. He says he has no issues with either life in prison or the death penalty, and would vote for a life sentence without proof of aggravating circumstances.

We authors are still watching Casey in the courtroom. We are looking forward to the trial, and trying to put all of our opinions behind us. We see a woman, almost without remorse, enjoying her 15 minutes of fame and it is quite unpleasant. As we told you when we enter the trial she will become an unnamed defendant and it is our intention to try to base our verdict only on the evidence we can see.

Alternate Juror 3 – The Young Widow: is a female who is thirty-seven years old. She is a widow; she was married for fourteen years but separated for eight. After her separation, her husband went to prison for drugs and died there. She was born in Michigan and moved to Pinellas County, Florida seventeen years ago. She moved to Florida with her parents when she was four. She has a son age twelve, and they have lived with the help of her parents for most of his life. She has left him with her parents. She has worked as a car dealership cashier for seven months; before that she worked for Home Depot. She has an eleventh grade education. She has been in trouble with the law about some checks a few years ago. She thinks it will be a hardship to be gone for the time of the trial, but the judge decides that the hardship would not be so great that she should be excused for cause. She has watched Nancy Grace but not after Caylee's body was found. She recalls a lot of detail about the facts leading up to Casey's arrest. She has heard other people talking about the case. She does watch CSI, Dr. G, and Bay News 9. She does not want to be on this case. Emotionally she feels she could not handle it. She does not have any opinion on guilt or innocence, but she hopes Casey didn't do it. She believes that whatever the evidence shows is what she will base her decision on. She has used social media before. This juror seems uncomfortable and does not want to be there. She can vote for the death penalty or life. She is pretty good with computers and can retrieve files from a hard drive if needed. This means she can understand the process when given as evidence in the case. She does have a dog, a Labrador retriever, but has not been involved in searches with a dog. The defense is okay with this juror, and we bet that the State thinks that she will not be called to deliberate.

The Defense has one back-strike left, and the prosecution has three. Watching Casey, she really looks like she is playing a game and she is the star. This is sick. She is counting jurors on the juror list. We think the lawyers are happy that she is clearly giving active input in her trial.

Alternate Juror 4 – The Carpenter: is a male, twenty-five years old and single. He lives with his parents and has no bills. This would mean there would be no real hardship for him to be on this jury. He has never served on a jury, and seems to be blasé about the prospect of serving on this one. He got in trouble for marijuana and paraphernalia when he was sixteen or seventeen. He has partied in Orlando at college parties at the University Of Central Florida (UCF) over five years ago, and

27

attended Orlando Magic games last year (Amway Center, the Orlando basketball stadium, is only a block away from Church Street Station, a nightclub area that plays a role in this case). He has been to a few amusement parks. He does not got to "too many bars". He also has a background in child daycare for three year olds. He has heard about the case from 97x Radio (an alternative rock FM station) and some from family and friends. He does not have a Facebook account – he says he had a Facebook "problem," but no one asks the nature of the problem. He does help take care of his step siblings' children who are three and one. He does not watch the news much. He watches the History Channel and Cake Boss. He believes that the death penalty should be imposed for rape as well as murder (no non-homicide offenses can carry the death penalty since a 2008 U.S. Supreme Court decision), but says he can vote for a life sentence in a murder case.

Alternate Juror 5 – The Former Coast Guardsman: is a married male, thirty-nine years old, who has no children. He works as a water reclamation manager, and works both inside and outside in that job. He previously worked as a trucker. Before that, he was in the Coast Guard for 12 years, first as a mechanic, and then as a border officer. His wife works for HSN. He had plans to fly to Baltimore with his wife to see a Red Sox game with his grandmother, but has cancelled the trip and gave away the seats to the game after he made it through the first round of questioning several days ago. The judge promises him that he will arrange to provide the juror with good seats to another Red Sox game. He has no Facebook or Twitter accounts. He has no cable TV, watches DVDs, avoids the news, and listens to the radio. He has been careful about limiting his exposure to media coverage of the case since being told he was in the jury panel. Since then, he has realized how much news he hears on the radio and how often he looks at the St. Petersburg Times online. He listens to Bubba The Love Sponge (a shock jock) on the radio. He heard some things about this case from that show, and has heard The Parity Song (a sarcastic song derogatory of Casey Anthony) on that show a number of times. A girl was missing and a smell was found in the mother's car. They also mentioned a pizza box may have been in the trunk. He knows that the girl was found in a wooded area near her grandparents' home with tape on her. He has not discussed the case with others – it is not big news in his circle of friends. He has concerns about the death penalty, and is aware of cases where people were sentenced to death and then proven innocent through DNA tests. Still, he says he would not automatically vote against a death sentence, despite being against the death penalty. He also says that his feelings about the death penalty would not affect his verdict in the first phase of the trial. He does use a computer and reads the St. Petersburg Times online. He has been to Orlando on overnight trips five times since 2008. He goes camping at Disney World's camping facilities. His Coast Guard assignment involved law enforcement and he says he has witnessed crimes too many times to count, made arrests, gathered evidence, and written official statements. He has been in a deposition twice. Despite (or because of) his experience, he says that he is generally distrustful of law enforcement officers, and asks to speak more about that off the record. A bench conference is held with the attorneys and the court reporter, but we do not know what was said. Although he is challenged peremptorily from the first twelve jurors, the prosecution and defense agree to keep him as an alternate juror.

Once the jury and alternate jurors are sworn, Judge Perry releases them to go home for a couple of days to pack and make any final preparations for their long adventure in Orlando. He reminds them that they are to have no contact with any sort of outside influences regarding the case, and he assigns law enforcement officers to guard them and protect them from the media twenty-four hours a day until they are taken to Orlando. Once the jurors are transported to Orlando, they will be guarded whenever they are outside the courthouse. They will also be kept together as a group, so that their experiences are all the same while they are trying the case.

After the courtroom proceedings are over and the jury is sworn, Judge Perry does something else unusual. He meets with the jury, presumably so that he can accommodate their needs and desires, and so he can explain to them the procedures that will be employed for them. He tells the lawyers that he will not discuss the case with the jurors. He invites the lawyers to be there if they wish, and tells them that a court reporter will attend and take down everything that is said, so that there will be a record to review.

Jury selection is like a chess game with three players…

Both sides want to see everyone available in a panel of prospective jurors before exercising challenges. The reason is that for each juror who is struck, another comes in to take his or her place. Neither side wants to replace a juror with one who will be less favorable to their position in the trial. The lawyers know the order in which alternate jurors will be seated as replacements in the primary panel of twelve. So, like chess players, the prosecution and the defense look to the jurors beyond the first twelve to favorably adjust the primary panel for their side. They not only look to the next juror, but several beyond that one, and try to predict the other side's challenges (like moves on a chessboard). Judge Perry becomes a third player in this game of chess when he announces that he intends to swear the first twelve jurors as the primary panel, and then choose alternates. That limits the prosecution and defense to using up all of their challenges on the primary jurors without knowing who will be coming next. If he does that, it also means that each of the jurors will know whether or not they are an alternate. After much maneuvering by the defense throughout the days of jury selection, Judge Perry ultimately decided to allow the lawyers to challenge based on a panel of finalists larger than twelve. We think he made the right decision, since both the defense and the prosecution should be free to pick a jury that is as bias-free as possible.

Jury selection is only part of the story during voir dire, and other weird stuff that happens...

During breaks in the jury selection, but outside the presence of any prospective jurors, the judge hears the issue of evidence from Casey Anthony's trunk and the smell in the trunk. Will the Judge allow questioning about such items used to get juror's responses?

There is another related issue on which the prosecution wants a ruling. That is whether the State will be allowed to open cans of preserved air and a piece of tire cover from Casey's car truck for the jury to smell. Judge Perry is ruling on if this evidence will be admissible. I believe this could be important evidence for the prosecution. Have you ever smelled an old container from your refrigerator? His ruling is that the State cannot allow the jury to smell the cans' contents. Judge Perry rules that the jurors become witnesses when they smell, and they cannot be cross-examined. The prosecution is citing cases to the judge, fighting to get the smell evidence in before the jury. As of now, his ruling is they cannot open the cans for the jury to smell. That is a good ruling for the defense... our house criminal lawyer likes it. This fight will undoubtedly continue.

Even a lawyer is not exempt from jury duty – A lawyer is now AWOL for jury duty. He was present in the central jury room for the morning session, but failed to return from lunch, according to a jury clerk. The lawyer has not been called to the courtroom for questioning – at least, not yet. Judge Perry issues an Order To Show Cause for contempt of court. The judge says that the lawyer/juror can come back and explain why he is not here and I will listen or I will have a subpoena issued. The lawyer returned promptly after being notified. It seems that there was miscommunication in the jury room, and the lawyer believed he was excused from further service. The judge asks if anyone wants to talk to a lawyer as a juror for this case. Of course, neither the defense nor the prosecution wants a lawyer on the jury. The judge decides that the lawyer/juror's error is inadvertent, and the lawyer is excused as a prospective juror. He is free to return to his office and resume his own practice of law.

If you plan to write a book, better not post it on Facebook – The questioning of most jurors continued over a period of days. One potential juror had the audacity to post the judges rules on Facebook. He denied reading the posts to his page since, but admitted posting, "they ain't sending no young black male home. They probably all over my Facebook making sure I do not give out anything, book coming soon, lol… title, cover and all." That juror is excused for cause for violating the court's order about avoiding social media and for his inability to be upfront and honest. We think he's lucky that he isn't found in contempt and fined or sent to jail.

One bad apple can spoil the whole batch – An entire day's **venire** (panel of prospective jurors) is tainted and dismissed because of a prospective juror who claims to have been a Texas EquuSearch volunteer. She says that she helped to search for Caylee in the fall of 2008. She talks to or within hearing of every potential juror about the case, about the background and facts of the case, while loudly voicing her opinion about the guilt of Casey Anthony. She starts as soon as she hears what jury is being selected. We are convinced that she is looking for her fifteen minutes of fame. She gets a little of it, being interviewed on television, but her story is merely a flash in the pan. Thankfully, the prospective jurors who already have been questioned are not present, or the whole process would have to start over. Still, there go fifty potential jurors, discharged from jury duty because they are all tainted by one self-aggrandizing loudmouth. The day is lost for jury selection, although the judge and the attorneys deal with other matters.

How can a spectator end up in jail? Jury selection occurs in a courtroom that is open to the public. That is because every defendant has the right to a public trial. One morning, as the jury selection is nearing its conclusion, but while one alternate juror was in the courtroom being questioned and another was waiting just outside the door, a woman enters the **gallery** (the area where spectators sit) and takes a seat. Shortly after, she yells, "She killed someone anyway!" The proceedings come to an abrupt halt. The woman is surrounded by bailiffs and restrained. She is brought to the podium, after the prospective jurors are sent to a holding room, Both prospective jurors are later excused – they both heard her, and neither can be on the jury after that outburst.

Judge Perry tells the spectator (now a defendant) that he is going to conduct a **summary** (on the spot) contempt of court hearing. He tells her that he can sentence her to jail for as long as one hundred and seventy-nine days. He orders her to explain why she should not be held in contempt. The woman is distraught, apologetic, and crying to the point where it is difficult to understand what she is saying. The judge questions her, and she tells him she is bipolar. She is at the courthouse for a first appearance hearing for her boyfriend, who had been arrested for domestic battery on her. She says that she came to get her boyfriend out of jail. She initially says she came into the courtroom because she had never been in this courtroom before, but later admits that she knew what case was being heard. She tells the judge that she is on medication for her mental disorder (one of the medications she names is an anti-psychotic drug), and she also takes methadone for her drug addiction. She says she had her medicine today. She really can't explain why she said what she did, but she says she didn't mean to say anything – that was just what she was thinking. She says she can't go to jail because there is no one to take care of her young children. It is clear to everyone that this woman has significant mental health problems.

The judge finds her in contempt and sentences her to two days in jail. He appoints the Public Defender to represent her and says he will reconsider the matter after lunch recess, so that someone from the Public Defender's Office can speak with her and present any additional evidence. In the meanwhile, the woman is taken into custody. After lunch, an experienced Assistant Public Defender appears with the woman for her hearing. She testifies that, although she went to the methadone clinic today, she forgot to take her mental health medication. She is still distraught and crying, and she again apologizes numerous times for her outburst. The judge announces that he took her obvious mental health issues into account when he imposed sentence, and that his sentence of two days in jail will stand. We believe he was right.

Word travels fast. The courtroom gallery, which had contained only a few spectators in the morning, has filled to about 50 spectators now. We suppose it could be because the judge is getting ready to swear the jury soon, but we expect it is really for the contempt hearing. Scandal sells.

Being a writer can be dangerous – One of the writers began having the nightmares while writing this book, after searching the internet for how to make homemade chloroform. One formula is bleach and acetone. It sent our minds spinning about the pain and suffering that could cause if used on a child.

Jury selection began on Monday, May 9th, 2011, and the jury is finally sworn late in the day on Friday May 20th, 2011. The judge, the lawyers, the court reporters, the bailiffs and some of the jurors worked eleven of the twelve days they were in Pinellas County. We are sure they are exhausted, but we are also sure that no one will get much rest between now and Tuesday, May 24th, 2011, when the trial gets underway in Orlando.

PART Three

Chapter 7

PROSECUTION'S OPENING STATEMENT

State of Florida v. Casey Anthony
May 24th, 2011, in Orlando, Florida

The Prosecution:

1. Linda Drane Burdick (Lead Counsel)
2. Jeff Ashton
3. Frank George

The Defense:

1. Jose Baez (Lead Counsel);
2. Cheney Mason (the old dog with forty years experience trying murder cases);
3. Ann Finnell (the penalty phase expert);
4. Dorothy Clay Simms;
5. William Slabaugh (a lawyer who works in Baez's firm);
6. Lisabeth Fryer (a dark-haired lady lawyer who does complicated case law arguments);
7. Michelle Medina.

Today we leave the court of public opinion, and we venture forth into the court of law and the evidence

33

presented at trial. Casey is keeping her head down as they prepare to start the proceedings. We have moved from Clearwater to Orlando, where the remainder of the trial will be held. The jurors are now sequestered. The judge asks the clerk to call the case. The clerk says, "State of Florida v. Casey Anthony." The judge asks if the State is ready. An Assistant State Attorney responds in the affirmative. The judge asks if the defense is ready. A defense lawyer says that they are. A **sidebar** occurs. (This is where only the judge, lawyers and court reporter hear what is being said. It is sometimes referred to as approaching the bench.) The judge arises from his seat and walks to the part of the bench farthest from the jury box, and all the others huddle around. We do not know what was said at the bench conference.

The judge begins by telling Mr. Baez that there is a portion of the instruction on the defendant's right to remain silent that must be read, and then he tells a bailiff to bring in the jury. Everyone rises. The jury enters the courtroom and is seated in the jury box. Everyone takes a seat.

The judge asks for the first time, "Do the defense and prosecution recognize the presence of the jury?" Both sides reply, "Yes, your honor." This procedure will be repeated each time the jury enters the courtroom, so that the court reporter's record is clear that the jury is present. The judge addresses the jury, and asks if they heeded all of his instructions about not discussing the case, not watching news, media, or doing any Facebook, Twitter or social media. The jury, as a group, responds that they have. This is how the judge will begin each day with the jury, and he will ask the jury the same question each time they return from a lunch break or recess.

Judge Belvin Perry announces the charges against Casey Anthony. He begins with, "This is a criminal case and the defendant is charged with: First Degree Murder, Aggravated Child Abuse, Aggravated Manslaughter of a Child, Providing False Information to a Law Enforcement Officer, Providing False Information to a Law Enforcement Officer, Providing False Information to a Law Enforcement Officer, and Providing False Information to a Law Enforcement Officer."

The judge then reads the indictment, which sets out the dates and particulars of each charge. He explains to the jury that the definitions of the crimes will be explained later. He tells the jury that it is their responsibility to judge the case only on this evidence and the law. The judge will be the one to make decisions on the law and procedure, and he will relay that information to the jury as needed. He also explains how this procedure will work.

He then tells the jury that opening statements give the lawyers a chance to tell the jury what they think they will prove, but that the jury should not considered what the lawyers say as evidence. He tells the jury that witnesses and evidence will be presented, and cross-examinations of the other side's witnesses will be allowed. He warns the jury that they should not discuss the case among themselves until the case is over and presented to them for deliberations as the complete jury. He tells the jury to report if anyone tries to discuss this case with them. Judge Perry tells the jury not to conduct any investigations or research of their own. He tells the jurors that they must not talk about the case using an electronic device, nor send or receive any messages concerning this case on the internet. He tells the jury that the defendant has the absolute right to remain silent and that the jury cannot consider Ms. Anthony's exercise of her right to remain silent as an admission of guilt or draw any conclusions from it. He tells them the jury cannot in any way consider Ms. Anthony's choice not to testify.

He tells them that they must not speculate on his rulings to objections. He tells the jury that they may take notes, but they are not required to do so. He says that the notes must never leave the courtroom, and a court deputy will hold their notebooks during recess. He tells them that if they choose to take notes, they should not get so involved in note-taking as become distracted. The judge emphasizes that notes are not entitled to any more weight than the jurors' memory of testimony and evidence in this courtroom.

As the writers begin this journey with you, it will be our attempt to bring you as much as possible from our viewing of this trial from Courtroom Twenty-three in Orlando, Florida. We are multiple writers viewing live video streams on many monitors. All of the coverage of this trial is from pool cameras that give different views of the courtroom action. These streams are provided nonstop from multiple media sources whenever court is in session. Our trial notes, taken as the action occurs, will be our guide.

We will try to maintain the integrity of the words of the judge, witnesses, lawyers, side events, and sideshows, as we believe we hear and see them. However, this is not verbatim testimony or quotation from a court transcript. We are writers interpreting, analyzing, and expressing our opinions about the trial of Casey Anthony as the events occur.

Our Interpretation of the Opening Argument for the Prosecution by Attorney Linda Drane Burdick.

Good morning. This is the case of Casey Anthony, but it is the story of Caylee Anthony. She lived every day of her life on a quiet street in Orlando. Her doting grandparents filled her life with stuffed animals; in the back yard was every little girl's dream – a doll house with her own mail box.

In 1989, with Casey Anthony three years old and her brother Lee age seven, the Anthony's moved to Hopespring Drive in Orlando and have lived there ever since. George Anthony was a retired police officer, Cindy Anthony a nurse. In 2005, Casey told them she was pregnant. They were concerned, but excited. The Anthony's were committed to them financially and with love.

After her maternity leave, they believed their daughter returned to a job at Universal Studies. They believed their daughter was a hard working single mother. Caylee was loved, lots of photos were taken, and she was the apple of the Anthony's eyes. With a lovely home, its swimming pool in the back yard, she watched Sponge Bob with JoJo, as she called her grandfather. Casey Anthony appeared to all outside observers, just as her parents thought, a loving single mother. That was an illusion. Casey Anthony was not employed. Casey dressed in work clothes and went who knows where for two years after Caylee was born, although the cracks began to show in her ruse in the weeks and months before Caylee's death.

June 15th, 2008: started out as a typical Sunday. You will hear during the course of this case that George Anthony worked the three-to-eleven shift and Cindy worked for eight to five most days. George worked that Sunday, Father's Day. Cindy Anthony took Caylee, her granddaughter, to see her great grandfather in a nursing facility. Cindy recorded the event on video and with still photos. Cindy, unknowingly at that time, took the last known photo of her granddaughter Caylee. On that Father's Day at the nursing facility in Mount Dora, Caylee colored as she sang and had fun. Eventually, the afternoon grew longer and Cindy decided to leave for home. She returned to the Hopespring Drive home with Caylee. Casey Anthony spent the day with her new boyfriend, Tony Lazzaro.

That evening, they went to bed to ready themselves for a typical work week. On Monday June 16th, 2008, Cindy went to work between seven and eight AM, which was typical. George was up early, and had breakfast with Caylee. He noted that Casey began to get ready for work shortly before noon. At 12:50, Casey Anthony left with Caylee. Caylee was wearing a pink shirt, shorts and sunglasses. JoJo kissed his granddaughter goodbye and never saw her again. No one but Casey ever saw her alive again. We have already shown you the last photo of Caylee alive. This is the next photo from December 11th, 2008, when the dead skeleton of Caylee was discovered. This story is not about Casey Anthony, it is about what happened between June and December. What happened to Caylee Anthony?

You will hear witnesses during the testimony in this case. No one had any idea that anything had happened until July 15th, 2008. Where was Caylee? Thirty days passed between the time anyone but Casey saw Caylee and when she was reported missing by her grandmother.

June 16th, 2008: cell phone records show she did not leave the area of her home until 4:00 PM, despite that she left for work at 12:50. She told her father and mother that she and Caylee were spending the night with the babysitter, named Zanny. Like Casey's job, the babysitter was a figment of her imagination. June 16th, 2008 Casey appears on a store video at Blockbuster with her boyfriend in the evening; no Caylee.

The defendant's June 17th, 2008 cell phone records show she was at her boyfriend's apartment until 2:00 PM and then traveled to her parent's home between 2:00 and 4:30 PM, while they were at work. Her car was seen backed into the garage. No one saw Caylee. Casey again told her parents they were spending the night with Zanny. Tony Lazzaro will testify that Casey was at his house and Caylee was not there.

June 18th, 2008: Casey was in the area of Tony Lazzaro's apartment until 12:20 PM. From 12:30 until 1:15 PM., she is attempting to call her parents. Then a neighbor sees her again, backing the car into the garage between 1:30 and 2:00 in the afternoon. Casey asks a neighbor to borrow a shovel and then returned it after about an hour. George worked from 3:00 to 11:00 PM. Cindy inquires about her granddaughter, who had never spent more than a day away from her grandparents. Casey tells her mother that she is in Tampa with Caylee, Zanny and Juliette. There is no Zanny, no Juliette. Casey spends the night with Tony Lazzaro, without Caylee. June 18th, 2008 where is Caylee?

June 19th, 2008: George does not work on Thursdays. There is no indication in Casey's cell phone records that she came to the area of her home. Casey Anthony was looking for apartments for her boyfriend, Tony Lazzaro. Casey was at Tony Lazzaro's by 9:00 AM, Caylee was not. Where is Caylee?

June 20th, 2008: George is not working. Cindy wants to know where Caylee is. Casey tells her she is still at a conference at Busch Gardens and it is going over to Saturday. Casey went to Club Fusion that evening and participated in a hot body contest. Caylee was not with her or Tony Lazzaro or her grandmother or grandfather.

June 21st and 22nd, 2008: Casey did not return to the area of her home on Hopespring Drive. Sunday, Casey tells her parents the conference event is over and she went to the park, and Caylee is with her.

June 23rd, 2008: Cell phone records show the defendant is at Tony Lazzaro's until 1:30 in the afternoon. Casey heads in the direction of her parents at 2:30. Phone records show she calls her boy-friend Tony Lazzaro, telling him she had run out of gas. He comes to help her, and Casey breaks into the shed and takes her dad's gas cans. Cindy is still inquiring about where her granddaughter is. Casey speaks to her mother and says Zanny is in a hospital, and Casey is taking care of Zanny at hospital with Caylee. She is out with Tony Lazzaro that night.

June 24th, 2008: George decides he is going for a walk. He sees the lock on his shed is broken and calls police. George also goes and tells neighbor to look out, that someone is stealing in neighborhood. He was normally at work but he stayed home this day. At 2:30, Casey shows up at the Hopespring house, no Caylee, no Tony Lazzaro, just Casey and her white Pontiac Sunbird. George asks where Caylee is. He tells his daughter that he would like to see that little girl, and that he and his wife miss her. Casey dismissively says that she has ten minutes, then she needs to get back to work. George thinks Casey may have the gas cans, and he is going to look in the car. Casey rushes past him, gets the cans from the trunk and tosses them on the ground in front of George.

June 25th, 2008: Casey calls Amy Huizenga and says that there is a smell in her car that seems to be coming from the engine. She says it smells like a dead animal. Cindy is still asking for her granddaughter. Cindy is told Casey and Caylee are still out of town. Cell phone records show Casey was at Tony Lazzaro's, but not Caylee.

June 26th, 2008: Casey reveals that Zanny is still in the hospital and they are spending another night at the hospital.

June 27th, 2008: At 11:00 AM, Casey is in the area of her house for about half an hour. Shortly after this time she texts Amy about a dead animal being plastered to the frame of her car. Within minutes, Casey's car runs out of gas at an Amscot on University Blvd and is pushed into the parking lot next to a dumpster. Casey calls Tony Lazzaro to come get her. Tony does and she has grocery bags with items from a refrigerator at her parents' home, but no Caylee. Video was taken of Tony Lazzaro and Casey at a store where she bought shoes, and they went out to Fusion Nightclub. Cindy is continuing to press Casey, "Where is Caylee?" Casey tells her they are back in town and she has a late meeting, so we are going to stay with Jeff Hopkins at the Hard Rock Hotel. Casey was not in Orlando and had no contact with Jeff Hopkins. She tells Jesse Grime that Caylee is with the nanny. She tells Amy that Caylee is at the beach. Where is Caylee?

June 28th and 29th, 2008: Casey continues telling her mother she is at the Hard Rock with Caylee. Cell phone text records show she is going to rent a video at Blockbuster.

June 30th, 2008: Tony Lazzaro goes on a trip to New York. Casey takes him to the airport and he gives her use of his car. Her car is still at Amscot, where Casey left it and told Tony her father would handle the car. The manager of Amscot calls a tow company. They tow the car to an impound lot. The car stays there until July 15th, 2008. Casey goes to Target, a video store, no Caylee, to JC Penney, no Caylee. Cindy is pressing, "Where is Caylee?" Casey tells her she is working late. Caylee is with Jennifer, a roommate of Zanny's. Casey tells her mother we are staying with these people until July 3rd, 2008, and Jennifer is taking Caylee to Universal Studios. Cindy is on vacation and she wants to spend time with her granddaughter, Caylee. She has not seen Caylee in two weeks. Cindy makes repeated calls to Casey. Now, with Tony Lazzaro in New York Casey has no place to stay, and shows up at former fiancé's to take a shower. Casey is out at the bars and Cindy is calling and texting. Casey is telling her Caylee is at the park. Multiple attempts to call Casey from Cindy continue. Casey gets a tattoo, buys new clothes and dances at nightclubs. She ends up spending the night with Amy.

July 3rd, 2008: Cindy has had enough – she is on vacation and making multiple calls to see her granddaughter. Cindy drives to Universal Studios and calls her daughter from the parking lot, and tells her that she wants to pick up Caylee. Casey says that they are in Jacksonville. Cindy is bedside herself. She returns home and in pure frustration, creates a My Space account and posts to Casey's account, "My Caylee is missing." Casey sends texts to her friends, if my family tries to contact you, tell them nothing. My family is crazy. At 8:00 PM, Cindy contacts her son Lee for help. Lee tries to find his sister on people's Facebook pages. He finds out his sister is going to be at nightclub that night. Lee searches for Casey and cannot find her. Lee sends a message to Anne, a friend of Casey's, and she alerts Casey that her brother is in the area looking for her.

July 4th, 2008: Casey keeps lying, saying that they are in Jacksonville. She tells her former boyfriends that Caylee is at the beach. Casey partied on the 4th at Lake Eola for the fireworks, and there are photos of Casey having a good time.

July 5th, 2008: Casey is caught on video at IKEA, no Caylee. Tony Lazzaro comes home from New York and they go out. Casey tells her mother that her car broke down in Jacksonville and they will not be home until July 12th. She tells Cindy that Caylee is with Jeffery Hopkins's mother.

Day 21, 22, 23, 24, 25: no one knows where Caylee is and Casey is gallivanting around town, no Caylee on any video.

July 11th, 2008: Casey is at Fusion nightclub.

July 12th, 2008: Cindy gets texts that they are still in Jacksonville, but Casey is in Orlando. Casey tells Cindy they are staying longer do to a wedding.

July 15th, 2008: Over the weekend, George Anthony gets a certified letter on the towing of Casey's car. The car was titled in George and Cindy's name and the tow company sent a letter. George and Cindy drive to the company and while Cindy deals with people at desk, George and Simon, who works at the lot, go to retrieve the car. George is telling of the problem that he has not seeing his daughter or granddaughter in weeks. As they approach the car, an overwhelming smell comes and he says a silent prayer that it is not his daughter or granddaughter. The tow driver says that he had been doing towing for years; Simon Birch will give you his opinion on the smell.

Simon, hoping they are not going to find a body in trunk, is relieved when the trunk is open and a bag of garbage is inside. Simon throws garbage over fence and then places it in a dumpster later. George drives the car home. When they arrive home, Cindy has her first contact with car. Her words to George were, "Who died?" The Anthony's are frustrated about the car being towed and Casey not being in Jacksonville where she said she was. The car had been at the tow yard from June 30th, 2008.

They knew Casey was lying, and George had to be at work at a new job. Cindy goes back to work and tells her co-workers, who tell her to call the police. Cindy texts Casey at 4:40 PM. Casey now has Amy's car, because Amy is taking a trip to Puerto Rico. Casey has taken her to the airport. Casey makes an appointment to get another tattoo. On the way to the airport again, she gives Erica the impression on the telephone that Caylee is in car with her. When she picks up Amy, she tells her that Caylee is with friends. They drop her at Tony Lazzaro's. Amy goes to Florida Mall with other friends.

Cindy is trying to figure out a way to find Casey and Caylee, as her car seat is in car that has been towed. In the car were dryer sheets, items in a bin, along with items they thought Casey used for work. Cindy finds Amy's contact information. Cindy calls Amy and asks if she has seen Casey and Caylee. Cindy has had enough and she is not going to be denied access to her granddaughter any longer. Amy, because of the concern, allows Cindy to pick her up from the mall. Amy takes Cindy to Tony Lazzaro's apartment, knocks on door, and gets Casey out of apartment. Caylee is not there.

Cindy takes Casey out of the apartment without her phone or belongings. They drop Amy off and return to the home on Hopespring Drive. Cindy wants access to her granddaughter, who has been gone a month. Casey tries the same old any story. But Cindy will not be denied access. Casey tells her mother that she will bring Caylee tomorrow, since she does not want to upset Caylee's routine. Cindy drives Casey to a police station, which is closed, and makes her first 911 call. She wants her daughter arrested.

Dispatch is trying to find out if a crime has been committed and if so, in what jurisdiction. Cindy can wait for the deputy or go home and make a call to the correct department. Cindy is threatening to take Caylee away from Casey. Cindy calls the police again. George calls Lee from work. Lee arrives at the house, just before Cindy and Casey arrive. Lee notices an overpowering smell from the car in the garage. Cindy tells Lee to get information from his sister, and that she wants Casey to take her to Caylee now. Cindy makes the second call to 911. She tells 911 there is a missing three years old. Her daughter will not tell her where Caylee is. Lee is trying to take his mom to Caylee, and Casey will not tell where she is. Lee asks Casey what the problem is, because they are going to get Caylee whether Casey wants them to or not. Lee pretends to be the police officer trying to get Casey to talk. They will tell you to take us to the child.

Lee Anthony failed in his efforts to get Casey to tell Cindy where Caylee is. They were all going to see Caylee that night one way or the other. When her back is against the wall, Casey comes up with a new bigger better lie. Casey tells them that Caylee was kidnapped by the babysitter, a babysitter no one knows, Zanny. Lee goes into panic mode and is trying to solve this problem. Cindy now knows her daughter has lied for 31 days. At that moment, she had to believe her daughter, although her first response to Casey was to ask what Casey had done. Mother and brother are now in her face, trying to find Caylee. Cindy calls 911 for the third time in a panic. Hysterical, Cindy wants Casey to speak to the 911 call operator and Casey gets on the phone like nothing is wrong. During the call Cindy tells the dispatcher, that she cannot find her granddaughter, that Caylee has been kidnapped, and that it smells like a dead body in the car.

911 keeps a second by second record of calls. When the officer arrives, he is not completely apprised of the seriousness of this call. Eventually he realizes after the three of them tell him Caylee is missing. They start looking to locate this kidnapper. Casey tells them Zanny lives at the Sawgrass Apartments. Deputies ask Casey to show them the last place she saw her daughter, 31 days ago.

Casey directs them to the last apartment, which is where she dropped Caylee off on June 9th, 2008. Management or maintenance advised on July 16th, that no one has lived there since February 2008. Deputies return to the Anthony's home and Cindy insists on something being done. She demands that deputies arrest her daughter, because she needs to tell where Caylee is. She tells the deputies that Casey says she has contact information in her phone. The deputy sends someone to Tony Lazzaro's apartment to get the phone. They ask Casey to tell them everything on paper about the person who she claims kidnapped her daughter.

Casey wrote that on June 9th, 2008, she took Caylee to her nanny's apartment. The first words she wrote are a lie. Deputies decided they needed a detective and to have him follow up. While waiting for the arrival of the detective, the police officer talked to Casey, and asked her if this is just a domestic thing, and that Casey did not want her mom to have contact with the child. He is left with the impression that Casey thinks it is not a big deal.

In the early morning hours of the following day, detectives arrive. They talk to and record a statement from Casey. The detective asks if it is correct and if Casey wants to change anything, She tells him no, that the statement is correct. She takes the detective to the same place at the Sawgrass Apartments where she took police the night before. No one knows anything, so they return to her home. Casey goes inside and the detective contacts Universal Studios about Casey's work and the people Casey said she talked to about Caylee being missing. He discovers that Casey was lying and does not work at Universal Studios. The detective calls Casey and verifies information on her work at Universal Studios. Once she confirms the same information, he has Casey brought to Universal Studies.

At the security gate, she is denied access because she does not work there. She says she forgot her badge. Detectives and park security allow her in and she is to show them where she works. Casey walks with purpose, then suddenly at the end of the hall puts her hands in her back pockets and admits that she does not work at Universal. They talk to her in a conference room. She admits she was lying about working at Universal Studios. But she will not wavier in her story about the nanny.

Detectives talked to her and showed her driver's license pictures of women named Zanny from a database. None are her Zanny. Casey is arrested for lying during an investigation. By necessity, this investigation takes two paths, locate Zanny, who supposedly has Caylee, and find Caylee. Because there is a tip line, there are sightings all over the United States, tips police have to follow. No Caylee, no Zanny.

July 16th, 2008: With the permission of George and Cindy, police seized the Pontiac Sunfire.

July 17th, 2008: Orange County Sheriff had a cadaver dog examine the car, and the dog alerted on the trunk of the car for the odor of human remains. The dog was taken to the Anthony house, and the dog alerted in backyard to human decomposition. A second dog was brought in and later detected the same odor, in the same place near the playhouse. They dug but did not find Caylee. Evidence samples of hair, carpet, air, and a tire cover are taken. DNA from Casey, Cindy, George, and sample from Caylee's hair brush are sent to the FBI. They discovered that the hair found in the trunk only occurs in a body that had decomposed. The smell was confirmed by persons who had smelled dead body before.

An expert in a biochemistry laboratory for the study of decomposition says the chemical odor of human decomposition was present when he opened the can that contained the sample of the spare tire cover. He immediately recognized it as human remains odor. He performed chemical analyses, and the compounds he found are consistent with decomposition. They found the highest concentration of chloroform he has ever seen, in the tire cover. It was thousands of time greater than he has ever seen with human remains. Different sections were sent to FBI and their analysis confirmed the presence of chloroform.

We contacted a forensics computer department, with a desktop from the Casey Anthony house. Dr. Voss had found chloroform and they searched the computer hard drive for previous searches for chloroform. On March 17th, 2008 at 1:43 to 1:55 PM, that computer was used to perform searches for chloroform, acetone, peroxide, and 21 different searches on how to make chloroform, self-defense, neck breaking, and on shovels. These were done by a user using Google on March 17th, and included inhalation, chloroform, and death. Twenty-one Wikipedia searches were also done for making weapons from household products and chloroform. Cindy was working. George was working. After these searches, no other user was logged into the computer that day.

Despite the mounting evidence, in September of 2008, many police and people continued to search, hampered by the passage of time and a tropical storm. Efforts to find Zanny continued. George and Cindy held out hope that Caylee would be found alive.

On a rainy December 11th, 2008, 911 received a call from a dispatcher at Orange County Utilities. They reported a tiny child's skull had been found. It was within walking distance of the Anthony home and on the grounds of the school Caylee would have attended. She was wrapped in a Winnie the Pooh blanket, black trash bags and a laundry bag. Caylee was tossed away like garage into a swamp-filled area. For ten days police, CSI, and FBI collected the evidence of the remains. They would not be left in a swamp. Caylee spent many months in that swamp; roots had taken effect, which consumed her skeletal remains. Duct tape covered the nose and mouth of the skull; the back of the duct tape was placed on the skull before decomposition. It was tangled in her hair and the killer never planned to have it removed. On July 23rd, 2008, they found a piece of identical duct tape on the gas cans the Anthony's owned. FBI confirmed that the tape was created at the same time. That same tape was used on a poster for the search for Caylee Anthony.

Caylee's Winnie the Pooh blanket was missing from the house, and the laundry bag found in the house was the same as the one with Caylee's remains. The three pieces of duct tape could be the only cause of death. These were placed in an attempt to kill this child, as difficult as it is to think that a mother can kill her child. It is the only explanation. No one but Casey had access to all the evidence. Blanket, duct tape, laundry bag, and Caylee.

(A photo is shown of the beautiful Caylee. Then in seconds, a photo of the tiny skull replaces it.) The State of Florida is asking the jury to return a verdict that reflects the truth of what happened to Caylee, first degree murder.

Linda Drane Burdick leaves the podium and returns to her seat at the prosecution's table. Everything is surreal in the courtroom. It is packed and intense. Casey and her attorney Jose Baez talk a lot. The jury took no notes, just listened intently. The prosecutor talked softly and only to the jurors. George held a Bible and Cindy was clutching Caylee's bear in her hands. The judge was clear that there would be no ribbons, pins, t-shirts, or the like in the courtroom, but they are letting them keep these items. It appears the jury cannot see what they are holding. We are not crazy about the parents, but they are victims who lost a granddaughter they loved, and now have their daughter on trial for the murder. Cheney Mason, another defense attorney, and Casey are developing a relationship at the defense table.

Chapter 8

THE DEFENSE'S OPENING STATEMENT

Our Interpretation of the Defense Opening Statement by Jose Baez:
(George and Cindy Anthony are not in courtroom for Jose Baez's opening argument.) Baez thanks the jury for their

service. He tells them that they had to leave home because of an onslaught of publicity and media coverage while Casey Anthony stands trial for her life.

I would like to tell you what happened. You sat through the opening statement of prosecutors who did not mention Roy Kronk. They did not tell you what if any role Kronk will have in the evidence. They did not tell you that the investigation was exclusive, purely focusing on only Casey.

The problem with this investigation is that it reached the level of desperation. At what point do you stop guessing? Suburban Drive is where the body was found, near Casey's home. Who put it there and for how long is the question. The car, a tow lot had a lot of time to deal with this car. The amount of contamination around this car may double or triple, after so much time. It is relevant? Does it tell us how Caylee died? Not about Casey's actions - but about how Caylee died? You may get distracted by emotion. You are here for a first-degree murder case, a death penalty case.

However, this is not a murder case. This is not a manslaughter case. This is not a case of aggravated child abuse case. This is none of those things. There is no alleged child abuse, no neglect. We picked you because we believe you could remain focused. We are not the media. We are not speculating. Forensics, what is reliable? Some forensics is not science, but science fiction. You will see that as the prosecution reaches that length of desperation.

Everyone wants to know how in the world a woman can wait thirty days before ever reporting her child missing. It's insane, it's bizarre. Something's just not right about that. Well, the answer is actually something relatively simple. She never was missing. Caylee Anthony died on June 16th, 2008, when she drowned in her family swimming pool. You're gonna hear that Caylee loved to swim and Caylee could get out of the house very easily, and did so on that day. The reason we're all here is not because of the commonality of this tragedy. It's far too common. In fact, in the State of Florida, it is the number one way that children die - drowning in swimming pools. What makes this case different; what makes it unique? What makes the reason we're all standing here today is not because of the commonality, but because of the uniqueness of the family that it happened to.
You will hear stories about a family that's incredibly dysfunctional. You will hear about ugly things, secret things, things that people don't speak about; things that

Casey never spoke about. Going into that dark corner and pretending that she does not live in the situation that she's living in. She went back to that deep, dark, ugly place called denial to pretend as if nothing was wrong. And you'll see as the evidence comes in, that is the most likely conclusion of the evidence – that something's not right here. Something's not right with this girl.

What you did not hear is that Casey was an excellent mother. She took care of Caylee. That child never went without food, without clothing, without shelter. You won't hear a single person come up here and testify how she was neglected or abused. There are no broken bones; there are no trips to the hospital. There's no moment that that would help you determine that this child was abused, or anything but loved. Caylee was loved by all members of her family. Casey loved her child. If not for a common tragedy we would not all be here today.

Casey's father George is accused molesting Casey at 8 years old. What does a sex abuse survivor look like, a sign here and a sign there? What makes Casey behave the way she does? She did not run, she did not hide. She acted as if it did not happen. Casey pretended she had a job and a nanny. She would get dressed up and pretend she would go to work. Anything Casey could do to protect her child. She forced herself to live in the world she wanted, and not the world she was forced to live in. When Casey told her family she was pregnant, she was told to keep quiet. It was seven-and- a-half months that the outside world did not know she was pregnant. The family went to a wedding together. Cindy and George denied she was pregnant; they said Casey was retaining water and maybe had a tumor. The entire family wanted to keep it quiet. Note that the whole family lied to protect their reputation.

If they had hid the pregnancy, she would hide the death. Cindy's co-workers questioned the pregnancy of Casey. Cindy had to admit that she was going to be a grandmother. Everyone hid this child, this pregnancy. Lee also attempted to touch his sister, just like the father but it did not go as far. The FBI even did a test to see if Lee was the baby's father. You're gonna hear about all kinds of bizarre family behavior that just doesn't make sense. How parents should stand by their child, but instead are throwing them under the bus, making bizarre statements and accusations. And that's what this case is gonna be about. You're gonna hear about all kinds of interesting behavior from all parties, not just Casey. And once you see some of this behavior, you'll realize that the apple doesn't fall very far from the tree. We are what we are because of who brought us in to this world, and how we were raised. Casey was raised to lie.

At thirteen, she could have her father's penis in her mouth, and then go to school. Sex abuse does things to people in a way that some may never understand. This is a sad tragedy. Casey was home with Caylee and her father. George approached Casey and started yelling. They searched the house and could not find Caylee. This is a mock-up of the Anthony house. You'll see that both came outside. Casey came around to the left of the house, and George Anthony went that way, towards the pool. They had an aboveground pool, with a ladder, and we'll talk about the pool and the ladder in just a moment, but what happened next, just as Casey came around this corner and went back, she saw George Anthony holding Caylee in his arms. She immediately grabbed Caylee and began to cry. George said look what you have done! Casey asked for her father's help. She should have called 911, but she did not. George covered it up and did not call 911.

It was the pool Cindy and Caylee went swimming in the night before. They were religious about making sure the ladder was down, but did Cindy forget that night before Caylee died? Caylee could get out the glass doors. On June 17th, Cindy goes to work and tells them someone is swimming in our pool, and someone left the ladder up and the gate open. You will find that professional police work was not done. Within 24 hours of the report that Caylee was missing, Cindy told police that someone was in the pool area. Police did not investigate.

George took certain steps to see that he was as far away as possible, so Casey could be blamed. He took steps to throw his daughter under the bus, not to protect her. She takes the gas cans all the time. George knew she was not working, yet nine days later, he reports the gas cans and calls the police. Who would report gas cans missing? The reason will come to life six months later.

On July 17th, the detective comes around and George says nothing about the gas cans. He took a trip to the police department to tell the FBI about the fight with Casey over the gas cans. Two weeks after he had talked to detectives and did not tell them. A photo of the gas can with duct tape is before the jury. Caylee's remains are found with the same duct tape. There is more to the story. George is passing out flyers and the media interviews him. Behind the donation jar is the same role of duct tape. Casey is not the only one who had access to the duct tape. These gas cans will lead you to the evidence. While at Publix passing out flyers about his

48

missing granddaughter, he met a woman and had an affair. Was he grieving or multitasking? Krystal Holloway, the woman he had the affair with, was at the memorial for Caylee. He will deny that he had an affair and that he told this woman it was an accident that snowballed out of control. He carried this secret and eventually tried to take his own life. We are not nor will we ever say that George had something to do with Caylee's death. It was an accident. This is not a murder or manslaughter case. This happened to a family with unresolved issues.

Roy Kronk is the person who found Caylee's remains. Interesting circumstances around this discovery, Mr. Kronk had nothing to do with the death. There was a $225,000 reward for a live Caylee. Mr. Kronk did not read the fine print. Caylee had to be found alive for that reward. His first statement had to do with getting the reward. His second statement is, "Will my ex-wife find out about the reward, if I get it." In the wooded area, closest to the home, the first search party should have found her, not after she was missing for six months. Caylee was twenty feet from the street. There were many searches, none of which found the body. On December 11th, 2008, the sheriff announced that they were all over the area and how much underwater this area was. That was for ten days, but the rest of the time it was dry.

Kronk stopped there on August 11th, 2008 with two co-workers. One worker says this would be a good place to hide a body. Kronk goes in to relieve himself, and then the others walked into the area. They all see a snake and panic. He does not mention it again to his co-workers. He calls 911 later and says, "I am not saying it was Caylee, but it was white and round." He calls again, and this time the description is different, round with a vinyl bag, near a tree that was down. Then he comes out and meets a deputy. It is a bag, not just a skull, it is a bag of bones, but the deputy finds nothing. Kronk again has the route, and he calls his son and tells him that he has found Caylee's body and he will be famous. He goes into the woods and finds the body. He has control of Caylee's remains for several months. Where he found the remains we will never know. He kicks the plastic bag and the skull rolls out. He says he called police and they told him to keep quiet. The duct tape is all they have. Skull rolling out of the bag, he clearly says it rolled. He now asks if he still gets the reward if she is dead. He wants to know if his ex-wife will know if he gets it. They ask him to stay quiet, and Orange County pays a lawyer to represent him. He licenses a photo of a snake for $15,000 and an exclusive interview. He gets his reward, his interview and becomes famous.

In August, police get a tip. They see the tip and officers says it has already been searched many times. Kronk is all about the fame and he is not reliable. There is not one piece of evidence that Casey is smart enough to deceive the FBI, the police and the like. They did a snake autopsy in this case! We would love to have more than just George with duct tape at Publix. They took everyone's phone records in this case, but not Kronk's. They just subpoenaed his records, and he refused, so they found his son. He said that his dad told him that he is going to be rich and famous. They did not look for anyone else. This case is about the fact that Casey did not act right. It takes an elegant prosecutor to stir you up, but there is no evidence.

The prosecutor said Casey was at Blockbuster, but there is nothing in the evidence. The officers were within five feet of the body. They found two store videos, only after the defendant brought it up. The police went to all witnesses, and they all said that area was under water. A psychic dog handler does a video, and the dogs walk about thirty feet and it is dry right around the area Caylee was found. Two private detectives who worked for George and Cindy were on the phone with the psychic. Cindy Anthony introduced the detectives to the psychic. As for the car, the air samples have never been admitted in a court of law, the hair has never been admitted in Florida. You are going to hear from a dog, well his handler. Everyone talks about the smell of this car. June 16th, 2008, Caylee drowned. On June 20th, Casey runs out gas. She calls her boyfriend, Tony Lazzaro. They break into the shed and take the gas cans. This young man cooperated with law enforcement. He spoke to us only in deposition, and wore a wiretap.

Casey opens the trunk and puts the cans inside, and he did not smell anything in her car. George does not smell anything in the trunk and was next to it, if you believe the argument happened. Casey is tossing out the garbage, she was carrying, taking garbage to the front of the apartments by carrying it in her trunk, and Casey forgot to toss out the garbage; wet, sticky garbage. The police dried it out and it cannot be tested. It has been air dried by police.

George did not pick up car until the July 15th. They will say they did not see the notice they received in the mail. George tells everyone he has found his daughter, not his granddaughter. He asked someone else to open the trunk. He tells everyone this is a dead body. He does not pick up the telephone and call Casey. He made zero attempts to contact his daughter. He also had access to the car. How did he know to show up with gas cans when picking it up? Why does he not call Casey or Caylee? Cindy called Casey and sent a text. She went back to work. Some friends at work told her "Cindy, you need to call the police." Cindy answered, "No, I will call Casey later." Cindy goes back to work, and a supervisor tells her to go home. This is how Casey learned to deal with her problems - just to leave. Cindy finds Casey and confronts her. Casey blames the babysitter. Cindy turns to George while on the 911 call, which was taped, and he does not say a word. He knows what happened. He says he was not there when she called. We do not believe any part of this. He is with his mistress, and she is paying him so he can pretend he is working.

Forensics: the car has a possible hair found in it. The FBI analyst was telling everyone she cannot say if it was Caylee's. Dr. Lee, our expert, found 17 more hairs. The banding has the discoloration. This type of analysis is rarely done on one hair. The car, a retired dog came back the next day and did not alert. He broke every rule in the book, no car line-up. The police took this dog out to Suburban Drive, and the dog never alerted where they found remains, and there were still some left at the spot.

A thirteen-year-old who had her father's penis in her mouth and then she went to school like nothing was wrong. This is where she learned to lie. Air samples are taken out of pure desperation. This guy is some type of inventor and he has a copyright on the device, and he stands to make millions if you validate this evidence. They searched all of the clothing Casey had, but nothing was found. Casey's shoes were searched for soil samples matching those taken on Suburban Drive - nothing. On the duct tape, no finger prints, no DNA of Casey or Caylee. The DNA from the duct tape was contaminated by an FBI analyst. Another profile they do not know. Was Casey dumb enough to leave a body at the side of road, but smart enough to leave no DNA? George lied and did not get arrested by law enforcement. There is no evidence in this case. Thank you.

Baez takes a seat at the defense table, sitting next to his client. There was shock in the courtroom as Baez announced his theory of defense, that Caylee's death was an accident. It deepened to being palpable when he alleged sexual misconduct involving Casey's father and brother. Everyone is reeling from the punches and counterpunches in the opening statements. Time will tell what the evidence actually shows.

PART FOUR

THE STATE'S CASE IN CHIEF

Chapter 9

THE STATE'S CASE IN CHIEF - WEEK ONE

May 24th, 2011

The judge now states, "Prosecution, you may call your first witness." The State is about to call its first witness in its **case in chief**. The State has the opportunity to present its evidence first in the case, since the State must be able to prove the charges made against Casey Anthony. Then, if it chooses to do so, the defense can present its case in chief. If the defense puts on a case, the State has the opportunity to present **rebuttal evidence**, which is used to call into question evidence presented by the defense. Rebuttal evidence cannot be a rehash of evidence presented in the State's case in chief, and it is limited by the defense's evidence. Some judges permit the defense to present **surrebuttal**, which is limited by the State's rebuttal case. We shall see what happens in this trial. We have decided to omit most of the questions asked and include only the approximate statements of the witnesses. When the witnesses' stories appear to be fragmented, that is because of the order in which the questions were asked.

The State's First Witness

Background of witness George Anthony: He is the father of Casey Anthony. They came to Florida from Warren, Ohio. George was in law enforcement for 20 years and met Cindy at a local hospital in Ohio, where she was a pediatric nurse. They married in 1981. George was a police officer when they married. He worked as an undercover drug agent, auxiliary officer, in road patrol, as a detective, and in homicide for Tremble County Sheriff's Department. They have two children, Lee a son who is 29 and Casey, their daughter, who is 25 now. She is on trial for her life for the murder of their granddaughter.

Interpretation of Testimony - George Anthony: (Direct Examination by the State) I left law enforcement because I was hurt on the job and returned to the family business. Casey was born after I left law enforcement. The family was in the car business then. I started my own used car agency. About a year after Casey was born, I started out on my own. Both of our parents were in Florida, so we both decided to move here. Cindy worked full-time when Lee was born, but mostly part-time to raise the children. Lee was seven years old and Casey three years old when we moved to Florida. Cindy went to work right away. I did go to the police and inquire about police work in Florida. After thinking about the drawbacks, I decided not to go into law. My wife was part of that decision. She did not want me to go back into law enforcement. I worked private security for the City of Orlando and other security work. Cindy's work has been consistent.

My daughter and wife told me that she was pregnant. We were excited but concerned. I did not know who the father was, but I thought we would talk about it later. I really was not sure who she was seeing. We went to ultrasounds, and we were excited. Casey has always lived at home. She had already finished high school. She was working as a subcontractor at Universal Studios taking photos. We knew that Casey and the grandchild would be living with us until Casey wanted to leave and got a promotion. Cindy found the realtor and our home on Hopespring Drive. Casey worked during the pregnancy, up until two or three weeks before the child was born. Tell us about Caylee's birth. Cindy, Casey and I were all at home, Casey began showing signs of labor, so we took her to the hospital, and in a few hours Caylee was born. In the delivery room, amazing, but embarrassing at the same time. It was brought up about the father and I felt he had an obligation. There was a name that Casey thought could be the father. Casey has also been seeing a man named Jessie, and he could have been the father. I met Jessie on the day the child was born. Casey and Caylee returned home and he became part of the family group.

DNA revealed that Jessie was not the father. I was Caylee's grandfather, and like a father to her as well, since I was around. Cindy cared for Caylee both as a grandmother and a caretaker. Caylee called me JoJo, and sometimes she called Cindy Grammy. In 2008 Caylee was advanced, very vocal, and could put many words together. She could turn on the TV and put her own DVDs in. She could get a spoon and peanut butter. She did puzzles well; she was bright. She would hear a song once and remember it. In 2008, I believed Casey was employed. She said she was. Also that she had a part-time job too. I always wanted to give her the benefit of the doubt. I wanted to believe it. She worked early afternoon to evening.

Cindy was working eight to five, and I was working three to eleven PM, Sunday through Thursday. When Casey was at work, Caylee was with Zanny when we were not available. Another picture of Caylee is placed into evidence. It was taken in early 2008, and it does look like her. On June 16th, 2008, I woke with my wife and had coffee, and then Caylee came out and spent time with me in the morning. I took her to brush her teeth and wash her face, and I fed her. She likes the movie Lady and the Tramp, and 101 Dalmatians on the TV. I saw Casey about nine to ten AM, just getting up and getting herself around for work. I just let her go and I played with Caylee. It was a normal morning. I will never forget, Diners, Drive-Ins and Dives was on TV. I watched the show and a commercial break came. Caylee was in a pink top and jeans shorts, sunglasses, and a backpack. "I am going to Zanny's," she told me. Casey said she was going to work, and then they may stay over at Zanny's for the night. I watched Casey put Caylee in the car. I have never seen her since that moment on June 16th, 2008. I have never committed an act of sexual molestation on Casey. I was not present when Caylee died. I did not dispose of the body of my granddaughter. I never obtained duct tape and place it over the mouth of my granddaughter.

George Anthony - Defense cross-examination: I found out Casey was pregnant about six months in. I was confronted by Cindy's brother and told him that we would handle it. I had a feeling, but it was not confirmed to me yet. (A photo of pregnant Casey is put into evidence.) I did not know at that time. The first time I heard about it was when Casey and Cindy and told me. I suspected, but I did not know for sure. Six months earlier, she did retain water like that, but she would put on weight now and them. I was in the delivery room, and observed my granddaughter being delivered. At some point, I thought I knew who the father was. The day we were confronted with this news, we did not have a party. I thought my daughter was working. I recall speaking to the FBI. I felt responsible because I know her, and I had had a feeling that she was not working. I believed she was working, but I never saw a paycheck. She seemed to pay for gas and insurance on the car. We wanted to make sure she was responsible. We never asked to meet the nanny or speak to her on the phone. We never saw or heard anything about the nanny. She had someone who was helping when we were not around. That is what we were told she was doing. As far as I know, for two years. Most of her life, Casey dropped her off at a nanny when we were not available, which was not often.

I went to see if she was working at Sports Authority, and
to take her to lunch if she was working. Sports Authority
is not the same as Universal Studios. Just to check and
see if she was working part time. On June 16th, 2008, we
had breakfast, just like numerous times. Caylee would
swim most days with me or Cindy would take her with her
if she was not working. She would wake me up sometimes to
swim, so Casey could get out of the house. We had marital
problems. After Caylee was born, I moved out. I moved out
when Caylee was about 4 months old. She was an infant.
Lee was out of the house and on his own at that time. The
issue with me moving out was not because Casey did not
want me around. We have financial problems. I had gambled
on the internet and was a victim of a Nigerian bank scam.
There was tension because of this, and I moved out. I
took a few months, and I had gotten back my confidence.
On June 16th, 2008, I just spent time with Caylee. Casey
and Caylee left the house at 12:50 PM. I left at two PM
for work. I do not know what Cindy wore to work that day.
I do not know, maybe slacks and a top. Nobody asked for a
month what Caylee was wearing, but I know because it is
the last time I saw her.

On June 24th, 2008, I reported a break-in of my shed and
stolen gas cans. Caylee did not drown in the pool that I
am aware of. If I knew that, we would not be here. I have
heard this drowning story before, just when we discussed
how I would be questioned in court. I was told it looked
like I would be the first to be called and we discussed
what it would be like in general. I was not prepped with
the questions I would be asked. (An objection was
sustained; the judge ruled that the witness should not be
discredited for talking with a lawyer. When an objection
is sustained, the judge agrees with the attorney making
the objection that the law precludes the question or
evidence, and when it is overruled, the judge disagrees
with the legal basis stated by the lawyer making the
objection.) The witness responded that Paul Kelly is a
workers' comp attorney. I did not retain him; he just
talked with me. He just helped us go in the right
direction. I understand there was duct tape. I understand
the issue. I have had many duct tapes and I may have had
this one. Were you in possession of the duct tape at
Publix? (Objection sustained.) I first found out that the
car was towed by a USPS notice. On Sunday the 13th, I
found out the car was towed. When I saw the car had been
towed, I did not say she was missing. When I smelled the
car, I hoped this was not my daughter or granddaughter.

At the Sports Authority, I was met by a younger man and I
asked if Casey was in. When I was told she did not work
there, I got concerned and asked to see the manager.

Knowing Casey was not there, I got in my car and left. I told Cindy it was not the best conversation. Cindy was not happy that I had checked up on Casey. I just let it go. Maybe this happened around the end of 2007. Mr. Kelly, the attorney for my workers compensation, we had become great friends. We have been to dinner and to his home. He is our friend and helps us with legal matters. Cindy and I did not know where to turn, so we talked to him. What were my emotions that day, July 16th, 2008? I was tired, on edge, running on fumes. My whole world was to find my granddaughter.

We notice that George Anthony has had training as a witness. He looks at the jury when he answers questions, especially during direct examination by the State. Police are taught that trick, because if the jury sees your eyes, they think you are being truthful. On cross-examination, Mr. Anthony is antagonistic, and often talks around the responses to questions rather than simply answering them. We suspect that he has heard that the defense has accused him of being involved in Caylee's death and of molesting Casey. He seems to have forgotten that the defense is defending his daughter, and is bristling because he feels his character is being attacked.

As the first full day of evidence begins, the prosecution prepares to call its second witness. The lawyers are in chambers with the judge. Casey is crying. The Judge returns to the bench. He is obviously irritated. He announces that it would be very helpful if the State gives a list to defense of the order of the witnesses they intend on calling, so they can get their files ready. He says that he cannot make the State do that, but he can take only thirty-five minutes for lunch and will go late in the evening and work half days on Sunday if they do not. If the State is going to play games, then the judge will play. He says that he will not have the jury waiting every time a witness is called. He announces a ten-minute recess for the defense to prepare its file for the witness.

The State does not have to give the order of the witnesses they plan to call, only the names of people who have knowledge of the case and any written statements or reports they generated that are in the State's possession. That is the law, and it is an advantage in a big case with hundreds of pages of files on each witness to be called, and even more files on potential witnesses who will not be called to testify. This judge is good. We are not sure what we expected from him. So many of us have heard and seen the judicial robes disgraced by tales of judges abusing their power, and using penis pumps or playing computer games while presiding over a trial. Casey is still wiping tears, off and on. Now she is smiling and batting her eyes. We are not sure the jury is going to like her. We think the judge was upset by the defense in this case as well; his voice changed yesterday. The judge brings the jury in, then a side bar with lawyers then the statement; "Member of the jury, have you have you adhered to all my admonitions?" We shall assume they said yes.

May 25th, 2011

The State's Second Witness

Interpretation of Testimony – Cameron Campagna: Mr. Campana was a roommate of Tony Lazzaro. He attended college in Orlando and lives in Cleveland. He attended media school and had a Bachelors of Science in music. He lived at the apartment in Orlando. He was Anthony Lazzaro's roommate in a two bedroom, two bath apartment. Roy "Clint" House slept on couch, and others were also roommates off and on. At one point there were four men living there, sleeping on the couch and the floor. (Lawyers take a side bar for a moment.) This young man looks like a perfectly respectable young college student. He attended classes and did not work. He had a different schedule from Mr. Lazzaro. He got ahead and they did not take any classes together.

Cameron Campagna begins his testimony: In 2008, I met Casey Anthony through my friend Tony after a birthday party on May 24th for Mr. Howard, a mutual friend. When we first met Ms. Anthony, she appeared to be a happy, normal, average twenty-two year old. After May 24th, Ms. Anthony started staying with us in June 2008. She was inside the apartment daily. She had a daughter Caylee, who I met three or four times. Caylee was watching TV or in Tony's room. Caylee never spent the night, but Casey did. She said she had worked for Universal Studios, and I understood it was her job then. She talked about it, like picking up tickets, or saying that work is stressing her out. She told Tony that she had red carpet tickets to a Batman première. That never happened. Casey started staying with us at the end of June. We never discussed her moving in. She told us she was looking for an apartment with Amy. I think I met Amy once. I went to school from one to nine PM. I did not see her get ready for work.

After she started living with us, I think I saw Caylee once. She was with her nanny, according to Casey. She ever appeared anxious about seeing her daughter. She would say she had talked to her daughter. She talked on the telephone while she lived with us, but she would step outside and walk around the pond. One time, she said she was speaking with her mother. I asked why she goes outside, and she said it was her time to vent. She never told me what the discussions were about. Everyone cooked and when she moved in, she cooked and bought groceries. She did laundry and bought food. She did Tony's laundry and my laundry once. She cleaned; she helped keep the apartment clean. We all had computers. Casey had a computer. She had a laptop and I never used it. She used it.

Casey's demeanor was the same. She was happy, excited about life. We socialized at the apartment of a friend and at Fusion nightclub over food and drinks. I never spent time with Casey at that club. I drank some. Casey never drank at the apartment. One time, I saw her come home to the apartment drunk. She had a swimsuit for Caylee, and Caylee swam some at the pool. Caylee had a book or video at the apartment. Casey never told me her daughter was missing or kidnapped. She never said she was looking for her daughter or asked for my help. I was told by Tony and Nathan that Cindy was at the apartment. I also met Lee Anthony that same night. I told him I was sorry to hear what happened, and we would help if we could. I gave Lee a bag of Casey's clothes and he seemed calm, but upset. I was not in the Anthony home on June 16th, 2008.

The State's Third Witness

Interpretation of Testimony - Nathan Lezniewicz: He was another roommate in the Lazzaro apartment. I live in Fort Pierce, Florida. I moved back about year ago. I was in Orlando, going to school for audio engineering, from 2007 to 2009. I did not get a degree. I play in a band, keyboard and percussion. I played in a few bands in Orlando. Tony Lazzaro and Cameron Campana had the apartment at the end of May 2008; I slept on the couch for about a month or so until Tony's lease was up. I played music on road. I traveled, and I would leave town a lot. I met Casey Anthony with the drummer Daniel Howard on May 24th, 2008, that is where Tony and Casey met. We all met that night. She seemed like a normal 22 year old, outgoing. I became aware of Caylee at the apartment two or three times. During this time, Casey spent the night, just Casey. The third or fourth week of June, she began staying over quite a bit. She said she was an event coordinator at Universal Studios. She told us about the Batman première and that she could get tickets for some

of the guys. She did not complain about anything. I saw
her get ready, she would leave when we left. I assumed
she was getting ready for work. She left when we did and
she did not have a key. I hung out alone with her watched
TV sometimes too.

She was easy to talk to. She seemed normal, seemed like
everything was fine. I saw Caylee Anthony but not after
Casey started living at the apartment. Cameron and I had
a conversation about not seeing Caylee. While she was
living with us, Casey did talk about her parents, like
when she had telephone conversations with her mom. She
would leave the apartment and then say they were fighting
and she did not want us to hear. She had a white car. I
was never near it. She had broken down at Amscot and Tony
picked her up. Tony was gone fifteen to twenty minutes.
She cooked and cleaned at the apartment. At the Fusion
Nightclub, we socialized, mostly on Friday evenings. Tony
and Roy 'Clint" House had a production company, trying to
bring people in to Fusion. I have been there two or three
times with Casey. This is a photo of the two of us. Casey
entered the hot body contest in June. The dress she is
wearing in the photo is Casey at Club Fusion. I am not
sure which night at Fusion. This photo was taken in 2008,
when I was at Fusion with Casey. She looked like she was
having a good time. When she was living at the apartment,
she was never scared, distraught, upset, or depressed.
She never told me Caylee was missing, kidnapped, that she
was looking, or asked for help

Tony, Casey, and myself were waiting for the All Star
Game to start. Nothing was strange about her demeanor.
There was a knock at the door and Casey answered. A blond
girl was there and Casey walked out. It was Amy and
Cindy, her mother. Cindy came in, Cindy and Casey argued
and Casey did go outside to talk to her. She said she
would talk but was not leaving. Casey went outside with
her mother and then left. We were confused, thought it
was something between mother and daughter. We were not
worried. Lee Anthony came by later that night. Lee felt
bad for us and said if he had known we were involved with
his sister, he wished he had known us, so he could warn
us. He gathered a few of Casey Anthony's belongings.
Before Lee arrived, the deputy had been there and Tony
gave law enforcement a cell phone. They did not question
me. They were there just long enough to get the cell
phone and leave. The law came back after Lee was there.
They searched the apartment and we had no problem with
that. No clothes, no stuffed animals or the like were
left at the apartment. I saw Caylee two or three times.
She looked well cared for and Casey attended to her and
did not hit her. I found out later that at the time Casey

was living with us, Caylee was dead. Casey showed no signs of the trauma. We were all parked near each other. I was not present at any time Caylee drowned in a pool. (The witness is excused.)

We, the writers, do not buy the defense so far. The only reason George would have hidden the body would have been because of sex abuse to the child. He would destroy the evidence. Although, we think they could not prove if somebody sexually abused a child after drowning. We see no evidence of any sex abuse to anyone in this case, as of yet. We are not there with the defense on this one. Also, the way the defense has presented this in the opening statement, they have put themselves in a position to prove the opening statement. That was backing them into a corner. Only George and Casey would have seen the child the last time. Our question will be answered by the cell phone of Casey and what time George was at work or gone from the home on June 16, 2008, we think. Although at this time we are not buying the defense, we think the prosecution could have problems poking holes in it, because they will be trying to prove a negative.

The State's Fourth Witness

Interpretation of Testimony – Roy "Clint" House: He lives in Orlando and attended Full Sail College, studying recording arts. He works for his parents' company cleaning carpet. He did not receive a degree.

I lived with Anthony Lazzaro and Cameron from April 2008 to the end of June, sleeping on the floor. The guys were planning to get a new apartment. School hours varied. In June 2008, I think, me and Tony met Casey at a party a friend was throwing. This was the first time Tony met Casey. She seemed like a fun party girl. I knew at the first meeting that she had a kid; Tony told me. I met Caylee at the apartment four or five times. Caylee did not stay the night at the apartment. Casey started staying at the apartment in the beginning of June to end of June. It was a small apartment, but we did not mind. While she was staying, she said she worked at Universal Studios. I saw no credentials. I would see her get ready and say she was going to work. She never really talked about her work. When I first met Casey, I saw Caylee. When she started staying at the apartment, we never saw Caylee, and Casey said she was with the nanny, a local nanny. She never said Caylee was anywhere other than Orlando. I asked her why I hadn't seen Caylee in a while, and she said she was at the nanny's. Her demeanor never changed from the time I met her. I have a laptop. Casey had a laptop and I never used her computer. I do not believe Casey ever used mine.

When she spoke on the phone, she walked outside to talk and she told me it was her mom or the nanny. There was no change in her demeanor; she was not nervous or scared. I saw her daily at this time. I also saw her at Club Fusion. Every Friday night, we had our own DJ promotions. Tony and I were partners and Casey helped to bring people to the different clubs, including Club Fusion. I never saw the texts bringing people to the clubs, but I did see the Facebook and Myspace messages. None of her friends ever came. She was in a couple of our contests, and mingled with the crowd. She was in the hot body contest. Every Friday in the month of June, we would have something at the clubs. Casey was not a shot girl and they were not paid. She had nothing to do with shot girls. She would give tidbits, and I gave the girls instructions on what to wear. She never worked at home on outfits; she only made suggestions to the girls, as Tony's girlfriend. Maria Kissh was my girlfriend. She attended Fusion with me. (Sidebar, Casey is calm and whispering to one of her attorneys.) During the nights at Fusion with Casey she was partying and having a good time. Drinking, dancing, and never displayed any emotion that anything was wrong. She was happy. Tony and Casey seemed happy with each other. I never saw Casey and Tony fight. She was not sad, angry, nothing like that. Casey was the same as when I first met her with Caylee. I moved out two weeks before and had no other contact. Tony and I had a falling out and she was trying to be the good friend and get us back together. She tried to stop the beef and get things back together. I had no other contact with her. Casey never told me her daughter was missing, kidnapped or that she was worried about Caylee.

It was the end of May, the 21st or 22nd, and it was a friend's birthday. That's when we met Casey, and then I moved out July 1st. In the month and a half, I saw Caylee three or four times. She came with a backpack and flashcards with colors. Casey would flash and tell them to Caylee. No other learning tools, but some DVDs. She would have diapers and snacks. I never saw the child hungry, unkempt or abused. I think she was a good mother. I never saw them go to the pool together. We were aware that Tony, Casey, and Caylee went to the pool on June 2nd. Everyone had a computer and I did not keep a close eye on her computer. A promoter will help get people in and get a percentage of the door. We got no discount or revenue from bar sales. We would contact everyone and sell the atmosphere at Fusion. It is a sushi bar and then it turns into a martini bar. Because Tony was dating

Casey, she would post and text friends to come to the bar. Casey was not a shot girl. She was not managing the shot girls. She took an interest in helping us be more successful, and she was living rent free. She cooked and cleaned, the guys took out trash. I do not know if Casey did. She seemed nice and cared about me and people. She cared for her child. I found out that Caylee was missing after the other guys did. I saw no change in Casey's behavior the entire time I lived in the apartment.

The State's Fifth Witness

Interpretation of Testimony – Maria Kissh: She is the ex-girlfriend of Clint House. She is 26 and has worked as a Central Florida sales manager for a retail company for about a year. She graduated from University of Florida in political science. In 2008, she was employed at the county, campaigning for man who was running for office in May and June, 2008. She worked nine-to-five, and sometimes later. She lived in Kissimmee. Clint Roy House and Maria started dating in May. In May, June, and July of 2008, they dated but did not live together.

In June of 2008, I met Casey Anthony. I do not recall where, but we were out somewhere in a party atmosphere. She was the girl Tony was seeing at the time. I knew all the guys, and Casey was new to the group. I met Caylee at Tony Lazzaro's apartment. I was meeting Clint, and Caylee answered the door by herself. I just said hi. I knew who she was; I had been told by Clint. I did not see Casey. I spent less than a half hour at the apartment that time. Casey came out of Tony's room for a minute, and then she went back into the room. My boyfriend and I were sitting out on the balcony of the apartment with Caylee. We started to leave and I knew Caylee would be alone if I left, even though it was a screened balcony. (Sidebar) Caylee and I were on the balcony and everyone was getting ready to leave. Tony, Casey and Caylee were going to leave as well. Casey and Tony came out, and Casey told Caylee to get ready. Caylee was struggling to put on her shoes and I helped her. Caylee was verbal. We were not going out with them.

After that visit, I saw Caylee again in June 2008. I was at the apartment two or three times a week, and stayed the night a few times. I would talk to Clint, and he said that Casey had been there all day. I would stop by to see Clint after work sometimes, and Casey was there. We saw each other several times. We were polite, but not friends. She told me she worked for Universal Studios as an event planner. I saw no identification on her. I never questioned that she worked there. We would all go out at night to a bar or club, or grab a bite to eat. Casey and Tony Lazzaro got along together well. It just seemed to be a beneficial relationship for Tony. I think they liked each other. I never saw them argue. Fusion is a restaurant nightclub and I have been there with my boyfriend and Casey one time. The time I went, June 20th, 2008, was a hot body contest. I met everyone there. I saw the hot body contest. Casey participated in the contest. She was wearing a thin knit blue dress. (A photo of Casey and Nathan is shown to Maria and placed into evidence.) That is the outfit she was wearing on June 20th, 2008. I did not participle in the contest. Casey was supposed to be in charge of the shot girls, and I heard her talking to them, telling them what they were supposed to do. She never appeared angry or upset. I was there until closing and I stayed at the apartment. I saw Casey the next morning in the kitchen of the apartment.

I asked where Caylee was, and she said that Caylee was with the nanny and she paid her four hundred a week to care for her. I asked about Caylee's dad and Casey told me Caylee's dad was deceased. She was going to move into her parent's house. They were moving out and giving her the house in the next couple of months. She never told me her daughter was missing, kidnapped, or that she needed help to find her. I rode in her car while she lived at the apartment. It was Casey, Tony, Clint and me in the car. I cannot remember who drove; I was in the back seat. I smelled no foul odor. I did not have a friendship with Casey; we were acquaintances. It did not bother me personally that she stayed at the apartment. It did not bother me at all that she was dating Tony. The witness is excused, and steps down from the stand.

The jurors have their notebooks open today and take a few, but not a lot of notes. Casey Anthony is distraught. The friends she had at the time seem stable, and they have gone on with their lives. No witness made eye contact with her. The attorneys are building the timeline for what happened. After June 16th, the friends did not notice a smell in the car and the boys say she was a good mother. The female acquaintance does think Casey was a very good mother. Will we believe the story of Casey Antony being abused and Caylee drowning, after all the lies she has told? We need evidence of sex abuse and proof of what George and Casey supposedly did with the body. George appears to be telling the truth, but he is a law enforcement officer and is trained to testify. Outside the jury, the defense is renewing a **motion in limine** (to exclude or limit the use of evidence) about the shovel, and the argument is that this is not relevant to the case. The defense argues that the shovel is

misleading and not tied to the charged crime. This issue
has been argued before and the judge has already made a
ruling. He confirms his ruling – the shovel is
admissible. The lawyer in the family says that pretrial
motions have to be renewed at trial to preserve issues
for appeal.

The State's Sixth Witness

Interpretation of Testimony – Brian Bruner: He lives in
Orlando, and knows George and Cindy Anthony; they are
neighbors. He lives in the house to the south of theirs,
next door. In 2005, he moved into the neighborhood. The
Anthony's already lived there and he saw Cindy, Casey and
George the most, Lee not as much. The relationship was
that of cordial neighbors. They did not eat dinners
together; they were just neighbors.

I am a truck driver. I've been doing that for more than
24 years. I am married with two sons aged 21 and 16, and
a daughter who is 10. My children are not good friends of
the Anthony's. On June 16th, 2008 – we had been on
vacation, and returned home the evening of June 16th,
2008. I had another week off and was home on June 17th,
2008. I noticed Casey's vehicle backing into the garage.
I have seen Ms. Anthony drive that car before and I have
not seen others drive it. I saw her back into the garage
from the window of my home. It was pulled into the garage
and the car was already in when I noticed it. It did not
seem strange, but I had never seen Casey back in the car
before. I also saw her do this on June 18th. I do not
know how long the car was in garage on June 18th; I was
doing yard work. Casey approached me later in the
afternoon, about 1:30, to borrow a shovel to dig up a
bamboo root. I can see the monitor (which displays a
picture of a garage); that is my garage and that's my
shovel. It is the one I loaned to Casey. (The photo is
moved into evidence, over defense's objections.) When Ms.
Anthony borrowed the shovel, I was in the street blowing
off grass. I do not recall her asking for anything
before. I walked to the shed and gave her the shovel. She
followed me to the shed, and we both walked back and she
walked into the garage.

I finished blowing off grass and did not see the
defendant, and then I walked to the front to see if she
was finished. The garage was still open. I told my son
that Casey had borrowed a shovel and if she returned it,
he could take it. About an hour after that, she returned
the shovel to me. I put it in the garage. I did not see
her leave. The car was backed in the garage when she
borrowed the shovel. I saw the car on the 19th or 20th

again, early in the afternoon. I was in the house on the
couch, and the car backed in again, but I did not see
anything else. I had no other contact with Casey. I did
have contact with George in July. We had police in the
neighborhood. I did not speak to George or Cindy about
what was going on. On June 18th, Casey did not tell me
that her daughter was missing, kidnapped or that she
needed help. She was not sad or happy, just normal. I did
not see Casey during this time in other cars. I first
gave a statement to law enforcement on July 17th, I
think, when the media began showing up around the Anthony
home. I think it was two days after. I am aware that I
did not know the dates at that time. I'm not sure of the
date I gave my first statement to police, but it was the
week of the 16th. On July 30th, when I gave a second
statement, I thought of the date when she borrowed the
shovel. Her car was backed in, and I had never seen that
before. She borrowed the shovel in the middle of the day.
She was not sweaty. It was not muddy. I did not know what
she used the shovel for.

That Monday, a week after the shovel was borrowed, I
heard a man and Casey at the shed, but could not make out
the words. I did not see the white car, just a vehicle I
do not remember. It is pretty hard to look back and
recall a month before. My garage faces the front of the
street, and the Anthony's house would be to the right. My
living room is in the front, and there is a picture
window to the right when I'm looking at the TV. When I
watch TV, I also see the window, and I see the Anthony's
driveway and garage through the window. The date I heard
the male voice, it was about one PM. I saw the male for a
second and then Casey. My shovel was turned in to the
FBI, I believe. Media trucks were outside the home for
months. Casey seemed normal when she came to borrow the
shovel.

The State's Seventh Witness

Interpretation of Testimony - Jamie Realander: She is a
female, 22 years old, and is about to begin working for a
hotel in Indiana.

I am moving to Indiana on Monday. In May, June, and July
of 2008 I lived in Orlando. I was in school and working.
I worked for the Rosen Hotel and Resorts at the Golf Club
at Shandle Creek. I met Casey through a friend at Fusion
nightclub; it's a sushi restaurant and nightclub. I met
her with a customer named Jenna Prentice, a friend. I was
not an employee of Fusion at that time. Casey was happy,
seemed nice, nothing odd. I was just introduced at first.
Later, I was employed as a shot girl at Fusion. You carry

shots and waitress. You pay for the liquor you sell at the end of the night. They charged us $40.00 a bottle, and we made the difference from the bottle cost to the shots sold. On June 20th, 2008, I did not work as a shot girl. On June 27th, I did work and I saw Casey Anthony. I understood we would go to her for questions, to get answers to questions like where to be stationed. On June 20th, I did go to Fusion for the hot body contest. This is a photo of Casey and me at Fusion. She is wearing a blue dress. I spoke with her that night, but do not recall any of the conversation. The photo is a fair representation of both of us on June 20th, 2008. I recognize the photo as being taken in the Fusion nightclub. (The defense's prior objection to the photo is renewed and denied; the photo is admitted in evidence and can be published to the jury.) I do not think I was in the contest. I never noticed Casey to be upset or crying. I did work as a shot girl after this, and Casey told me what area to work. I know I was told what to wear but I am not sure if it was Casey who told me what to wear. Casey approved of what I wore, but she did not give me tips on what to wear.

At Fusion on that night, someone tried to grab a shot girl and scratched her stomach. For our safety, she had us leave for the night. I spoke with her on July 15th, over the phone. I did not know she had a daughter. I knew she was in a relationship with Tony Lazzaro. On July 15th, we had a conversation on that day, and she said she had to go to Universal. Casey said she had to pick up her daughter. Her birthday was the next month and she invited me to her daughter's birthday party. I never saw her outside of Fusion. There were no other calls to my knowledge. I received a text message from Casey looking for help to find Caylee, after the police had been notified she was missing. Nothing from that night at Fusion has anything to do with Caylee's death that I know of. Casey was not sad and she was nice. She was also concerned about our safety at Fusion and nice, like a big sister, a protector. I do not know anything about what happened to Caylee on June 16th. Casey never told me her daughter was missing or kidnapped.

The State's Eighth Witness

Interpretation of Testimony - Erica Gonzalez: She is 22 and a full time mom. In January of this year, she had a baby. She goes to school at an online college now.

From May to July of 2008, I worked for Fusion, every Friday. I think I worked every Friday in June. I met Casey at Fusion. I met her through one of the girls that

66

worked at the nightclub, Jennifer. Later, we talked many times. Tony was her boyfriend, and she worked at the club. Kind of like a manager to oversee us. She would protect us kind of. Casey told me she worked at Island of Adventure. I know Jamie Realander. Casey told me in the bathroom that she had a daughter, and made a connection of taking care of her daughter and taking care of us. She did not tell me her daughter was missing, kidnapped, that she was looking for her daughter, or anything was wrong. She appeared normal; she had a great time, was always happy, and treated everyone with kindness. I do not remember when it was that we were all going to meet up to talk about the shot girls and what had happened. She was headed to the airport to pick someone up, and she never called me back. I heard that night Caylee was missing and I called Casey and offered my help. She called me back and thanked me, and said that she was with the nanny. I made flyers over time. Casey was kind, nice, and looked out for the girls. I never saw Casey drunk. I do not know anything that can bring light to what happened to Caylee or how she died.

The State's Ninth Witness

Interpretation of Testimony – Anthony Lazzaro: He is 24 and lives in New York. He was Casey Anthony's boyfriend at the time of Caylee's disappearance. I haven't lived here all my life; I was just here when I went to college. From August of 2007 to 2008, I was in college in Florida. I graduated in the music business. I now work for Best Buy and I am interning at a record label. In May, June, and July, I was living in Sutton Place Apartments. I moved in with Cameron and then other people moved in. Two of my friends have lived on my couch, Roy Clint House and Nathan Lezniewicz. They did not pay rent. Nathan and I were going to get another apartment together. Classes are 24-7 at Full Sail; the college is always open. My schedule was not consistent, sometimes in the morning, and sometimes the evening. I could be in a music studio or learning technology at any hour. I received a Mac Pro as part of my tuition. They wanted you to get involved with other students at the school, since they could be people that you would work with out in the world. In May, June, and July, I tried to set up a small DJ business with Roy Clint House. We had a number of different names, like DBC Entertainment. I started working under the name DBC at Fusion. We met with the owner and planned to do parties on Friday night. That conversation started at the end of May, and the job started in June. I have '97 Jeep Grand Cherokee.

In May, 2008, I met Casey on Facebook and we became friends. Facebook showed you people in your area and I think I sent a request. Our first contact was through Facebook; I do not know how long. We met in person at my friend Dan Howard's birthday; we were throwing a party. I made a Facebook event and was inviting everyone. Casey responded and I expected to meet her at the party. I think I knew she had a child from Facebook. I just knew she was a toddler, a pretty girl. She showed up with two of her friends, and we hit it off. I do not recall what we talked about. We made plans to see each other shortly after that night at the party. She would show up to my apartment. When it first started, it was a couple of times a week and she brought her daughter. We went to the pool, I would say June 2nd. I invited her to a pool party after that. She brought no one. That was the end of May or the beginning of June, but she did not stay at the apartment. She drove a white Pontiac.

June 4th was a birthday party for Troy Brown. Casey, Clint, Maria and me went. Club Voyage was the location. We went to the mall together. I wanted to do some promotion before the Fusion event on Friday, June 13th. I handed out flyers, while Casey and Caylee walked around the mall. I handed out flyers alone. We went to the Cheesecake factory. I believe Casey drove to the mall. She and Caylee left later that evening. Caylee never spent the night at the apartment. That was the last time I saw Caylee Anthony. On June 13th, I went to Fusion with Casey, myself, Clint, and the other two promoters. We worked with the owner of Fusion in the end. Casey wanted to help out, so I told her she could help keep the shot girls in line. She told me she had a daughter. She had a job at Universal Studios as an event planner. She would talk about the job to a couple of the girls at work. I do not remember her complaining about her job. She would walk in with a Universal badge to the apartment. I was told that Caylee was cared for while Casey was working by her mother and a babysitter, Zanny. This is in the beginning of the relationship. She did not say where the nanny lived, or what she paid Zanny. It would be either the nanny or her grandmother taking care of Caylee.

June 13th was the first time Casey went to Fusion with me. (The witness is shown a photo.) This is a photo of me and Casey. We are sitting down. It is in June 2008, and it has to be June 13th because I have a tie on, and I stopped wearing a tie to Fusion. It is a fair representation of Casey and me in the photo. (Defense objects to these photos. A sidebar occurs; the judge overrules the objection; the photo is admitted in evidence over objection and published to the jury.) That

68

night was a success for me, as far as I remember. Casey went home with me and stayed the night. It was the first time she stayed over. After June 13th, she stayed over more and basically lived with me. She came to spend every night with me. On June 16th, I saw Casey late in the evening, 6:30 or 7, and we went to Blockbuster together. I spoke to her right before we she arrived that day. (There is a **stipulation**, or agreement between both sides to something. A written stipulation, signed by lawyers for both sides and the defendant, is filed in the court file in open court. The State moves the DVD into evidence. The judge reads the stipulation to the jury. The essence of this written stipulation is that a video is an accurate depiction of what it purports to show. This procedure is used for every stipulation.)

On June 16th, we went to Blockbuster video and rented a movie. (The video is shown to the jury and the witness.) This is me in the video. I am sure because I recognize the jersey I am wearing; it is me. I have my arms around Casey Anthony on June 16th, 2008. She was the same as every day, happy to see me, having a great time. She did not cry, act scared, or seem nervous. She never told me that her daughter was missing, that anything was wrong with her, or that anything had happened to her. She stayed that night and every night after. I do not remember a suitcase, or Caylee's clothes, or stuffed animals; there was nothing for Caylee at the apartment.

I do not remember Casey speaking with her parents that night. I cared for Casey. It was early in the relationship and it was going well, no fights, no disagreements. She stayed that night, and the next day I played hooky and did not feel like leaving bed. I decided I'd rather spend the day with Casey. She always walked outside to take calls. On June 17th, we stayed in my bedroom and there was no change in her demeanor. She said she was happy to be there. On June 17th, I do not recall that she called anyone in my presence. We spent the day and night together on June 17th. On June 18th, I went to school and figured she would go to work or to Caylee. On June 19th, we went to look at Cranes Landing, to look at an apartment. Nathan and Brian would be my roommates. Only I looked at the apartment, Casey did not have her ID and so she could not look. She lived at home with her parents. She was always talking about getting the Anthony's home and sharing it with Amy or getting an apartment. Amy Huizenga was there the night I met Casey. At that time, did she did not say anything about her mother and father. By June 28th, Casey and I were still not really sharing secrets. June 20th was a Friday. I went to Fusion and Casey went along. The hot body contest would happen, but it was a last minute decision. I had enough people for a hot body contest, but Casey told me she was going to participate. I was not pleased, but if she wanted to, she could. My role was to make sure nothing got out of hand. Kind of like head security. (A photo of the hot body contest is admitted.) That is the same dress she came in. Clint Roy House is singing. I recognize the picture, and it is a fair representation of Casey in the hot body contest. (A defense objection is overruled, and the photo is published to the jury.)

On June 20th, there was no difference in Casey's demeanor, no change in demeanor, nothing about her child being kidnapped, missing, or that she needed help. On June 23rd, Casey called and said she ran out of gas, mid- to late- afternoon. I was home; I had been to class that morning. She just said she ran out of gas and needed to be picked up. She was walking on a main road going south to her house. I talked on the phone to her on my way to meet her. She had a backpack and was walking. She said she had gas at her house. I had never been to her house before. I parked in the driveway. There were no other cars there. We walked to the backyard after we went in the garage. She opened the garage with keypad or a remote. I went through to the back yard. I do not recall if we walked through the house or if I have ever been in it. She said she did not have a key and that she would have to break the lock. I was concerned. She said it was okay, that it was her shed, and so I broke the lock with a crowbar from my car and took two gas cans. We returned to her car. She put the gas in, and then she put the gas cans in the trunk. When she opened the trunk, I could not see inside. There was no concern from Casey for breaking into the shed. Her mood was the same as always. We spent the rest of the evening together. When she took a call, she always went outside. I found it odd, but I figured it was a private conversation with her mom. Sometimes she told me that. Sometimes she would say she was calling the babysitter and go outside to call. I do not remember her saying anything about talking with her mom. I did not care – it was not my business.

On June 26th, Casey stayed the day with me at my apartment. On June 27th, before midday, she ran out of gas again and I went to get her. I never got out of the car at Amscot. Casey had bags with groceries, I think. She said the car broke down. I asked to look at it, and she said her father would take care of it. We returned to the apartment with the groceries and then we went to a mall together. (The parties stipulated to the introduction of a video from JC Penney.) We were together before I went to New York on June 30th. (The video is

70

published to the jury. Casey is buying woman's clothes at JC Penny, and Tony is with her.) I drove to the mall. I never saw Casey's car after I picked Casey up at Amscot. That night, I went to Fusion with Casey. (A photo of Tony and Casey taken on June 27th is admitted.) I know because I have no tie. A friend took the photos for free, but he was a professional photographer. (The judge overrules a defense objection, and the photo is received in evidence and published to jury.) There was no change in Casey's demeanor on that night, she was not mad; she did not tell me that her daughter was kidnapped. She was not distraught or crying, and she did not tell me she needed help. I left on July 4th for a short vacation home. Casey drove Cameron and me to airport. We drove my Jeep. Casey was to drop my car back off at the apartment. I did not agree to or expect her to use my car while I was gone. I thought her car had been taken care of. When asked, he points to Casey Anthony and says she is wearing a blue blouse. (Tony has identified Casey Anthony.)

I am aware I am here to testify in a first degree murder case. When the photos were taken, Casey had not talked about any murders she had committed; she did not talk about murdering anyone. She did not buy weapons or chloroform that I am aware of. At Blockbuster, she did not talk about murdering anyone and she did not talk about duct tape. I saw Casey with Caylee two or three times. It was okay that she had a daughter. I liked Caylee. She appeared loving and caring with daughter. Caylee was not dirty. On June 2nd, I went with Casey and Caylee to the pool, and I do not recall her disciplining Caylee. (Tony reviews his statement to police, and his memory is refreshed.) Caylee was going near the pool and Casey did not want her going close to the pool and she said "Stop, hey, stop." Caylee liked the pool. Casey did share the secret that she has been abused by her father. (The judge rules it is a self-serving hearsay statement by Casey and not admissible.) I only spoke with law enforcement. I spoke to the defense only by deposition. I gave sworn statements, wore a wire and more. I made no statements to the media. I broke in the shed for her. She could have broken in, I just did it was because I was a guy. I got the gas cans and drove her to the car. She did not tell me to stay away from the car. She did not block me from the trunk. She poured the gas in the car. I was more than two feet way. She put the gas in the car and she put the gas cans in the car trunk. I did not smell anything but gas. I was not in the car. I did not see the inside lining of the trunk. From where I was standing, all I could see was where the rubber meets the edge of the trunk.

She told me she ran out of gas, so broke down to me meant that she ran out of gas again. I have family in Fort Lauderdale. (The defense wants to enter a photo now, so Tony does not have to come back from New York later to testify and there is a side bar.) When I picked up Casey at Amscot the car was parked. I do not remember what is next door. (Tony is shown photo of Amscot.) I do see a gas station in the picture next to the Amscot. I did not notice it that day. I saw Casey looking at a video on her computer. (Objection overruled.) I gave many statements. I do not remember which statement it was, I just told them she ran out of gas. I saw Caylee and Casey laugh, hug, and run; it appeared genuine, a lot of love. I remember a book, a teddy bear and going down to the pool to teach her how to swim. Caylee liked Dora The Explorer and could count to 40 in Spanish because of the show. Casey was always affectionate with her.

I promoted the club online. Photos are made for people to see a party atmosphere. Pretty girls promote the club. The person who took the photos was a friend, and part of it was to show a good time. The defense asks if there was a secret Casey told him before she was arrested. (A sidebar occurs due to a State's objection.) Our relationship became more intense in June and July and we spent more time together and talked. When she would go home, we talked and texted. We talked until we fell asleep and passed out. Not drunk or on drugs. I am one of the people who will pass out talking on the phone - it is not my thing. When this all occurred on July 16th, I was shocked when I heard the news about Caylee. Casey's behavior before June 16th and after June 16th was the same. She did not confide in me. Casey talked to her parents outside and kept it separate from me. The gas cans are red, small hand cans. I cannot remember if they had duct tape. When Casey moved in, we did not talk on the phone as much. After I got the gas cans and went back to the car, I got the gas cans out of my car and gave them to Casey. I gave her the gas and she poured it in. I stood at the front of the car. It smelled like gassing up your car. I handed her the second can, and I walked away to close my tailgate. She poured the gas from the second can in the car. I was in front and I saw her open the trunk, I could see the rubber lining only, where the trunk meets and seals, not inside the trunk. When the police questioned me about this incident at the time I knew it was important and I told them there was no smell. I told them the truth. I could smell nothing but gas.

May 26th, 2011

(Although Anthony Lazzaro's testimony carried over from May 25, 2011, we have chosen to present all of it on that date for the sake of continuity)

The State's Tenth Witness

Interpretation of Testimony – George Anthony is recalled to the stand for additional testimony: On June 24th, 2008, I was home in the morning. My schedule was different, and that day I had banking, house stuff, and a job interview. About 10 AM, I went to the side shed to open the door. I found the lock broken. *(A photo diagram of the Anthony house and yard is presented and there is an objection from the defense, views photo and a sidebar.)* That shed contains lawn equipment. The items at the top of the photo are Caylee's playhouse and an aboveground pool. Other sheds have plant things and bicycles. I found the lock broken and the door open 3 inches. It is a Rubbermaid shed. It has a small Master key lock. The shed plastic was partly broken. I opened the shed, looked to the right, and saw the lock. Then I saw my tools, trimmer, and like was all there, but the gas cans were missing. I found it unusual. I took a step back and I thought, "Why just the gas cans?" I decided to call the Orange County Sheriff to make a report. I called about ten thirty, and within 20 minutes I had a deputy. I explained and made a report and the officer said there were break-ins in the area. The deputy was there five or ten minutes.

I could not do lawn work. I told my neighbor we had a break-in, and went to get new gas cans and gas. I cannot remember seeing Casey from the 16th to the 24th. Shortly after 2 PM on June 24th, I saw Casey. I normally leave at 2:00 to 2:15. I was inside the living room, after being at the bank with my wife depositing a check. I heard the garage door and I saw Casey. My car was inside the garage. I saw Casey come in through the garage, and she seemed somewhat surprised. I asked how she was and how was Caylee. She said she only had 10 minutes; that she had to get to work. I have felt on different times that gas has been used without my knowledge. I asked Casey, and she said she did not know anything about it. I let it go, but was suspicious that she had taken the gas. I wanted to question her more. I have supports in both cars to change a tire. I told her I need something out of her car, I needed the blocks for changing a tire. I told her I would go get it and I started to walk down the hallway. Casey runs past me and to her car. She opens the trunk and reaches in and grabs the gas cans. Then she says

73

"Here are your fucking gas cans, Dad. I needed them. I
have been running low on fuel and money." I did not want
to get upset with Casey, and I said we will talk later. I
was annoyed. Her car was in the driveway. I never looked
in the trunk, and I never smelled anything but the gas.
Casey got in and left. I did not see her again. I told
her I had made a report and she said she knew, and that
mom knows about it.

They are red, old, gas cans with duct tape. The plastic
cap was gone when Casey brought the cans back. So I put
the duct tape on that can. The car is a white Pontiac
Sunbird, and use and possession was Casey's. Yes, Casey
took gas. I suspected it, and we had have discussions
about it. On June 24th, I had not seen my granddaughter
in nine days, and yet it had never been more than 24
hours before that. The last time I saw my granddaughter
was on June 16th, 2008 and on June 24th, I called the
police about the gas cans. I had no idea my granddaughter
was missing at that time. She was not missing at that
point to me. I just had not seen her. I called the police
about the gas cans. The argument I had with her, she came
in was in a hurry and I told her that I needed something
out of her trunk. She opened it, and I did not smell
anything. When she gave me the cans, they had no duct
tape. I could not see into her trunk. (The judge warns
the defense attorney not to speak when not at the
microphone, because the court reporter cannot hear what
is being said.)

I remember speaking to an FBI Agent named Scott Boland. I
told the FBI I could see clothes, I think. I do not
recall if I could see clothes. I know that the trunk of
the car is an issue in this case. I know I did not see in
the trunk and therefore I was not close enough to smell
the trunk. When Casey gave me the gas cans, there was no
duct tape on one of the cans. (A photo of gas cans is
presented to clarify which cans they are speaking about.)
That can did not have duct tape on it when Casey gave it
back. I put it on when she gave it back on June 24th. I
cut grass every week to ten days. It depends. (The
defense is questioning him, and refers to George
Anthony's deposition taken in August, Page 199, lines 12
to 17. The prosecution objects that it does not qualify
as an inconstant statement. There is a sidebar.) I try to
mow every week to ten days. I am not sure. On June 24th,
my lawn needed mowing. So on June 24th, the grass was
high enough to need morning. (The witness steps down to
view a chart of a calendar. When asked, he writes on the
calendar in the courtroom the last date he saw Caylee;
the date the gas was missing and the police report was

made; and the date his granddaughter was confirmed missing on July 15th. He then returns to the stand.)

On August 1st, 2008, a law officer confiscated the gas cans. I told law enforcement of the gas incident involving Casey around July 30th. I do not have a report to review. I am not sure of the date. (The attorney gives him a book with the police report from July 31st to George to refresh his recollection.) I made a report on June 24th. I did not connect Caylee being missing with the gas and tell police about the gas can incident with Casey earlier. I told a law officer about this argument over gas with Casey before July 31st, 2008. On July 31st, 2008, I gave the officer the information about the argument. Between June 24th and August 24th, I mowed my lawn, and purchased other gas cans that I used after. I am probably the one who put the duct tape on it. I think I did. Mine and my wife's lives were lived day-by-day, trying to find my granddaughter. I would have put that duct tape on the can to prevent fumes in the shed. I remember a deposition at the State Attorney's office. The gas can appears to have one piece of duct tape. There were two pieces of duct tape. This is not the photo I was shown in the deposition. The photo in the deposition had two pieces of duct tape. (The judge warns that this image is not in evidence.) This image and photo was not shown to me. It was dirtier and it was a larger piece of duct tape. (This is not the same photo George Anthony was shown in the deposition and there is a sidebar.) When I gave the gas cans to the police on August 1st, one of the gas cans had duct tape. The cylinder gas can had duct tape. It shows it and it had duct tape on it. The twenty-year-old cylinder gas can. (The judge stops the questioning.)

The judge removes the jury and asks if the lawyers heard anything he said at sidebar. The Judge is angry. The can you keep referring to… Defense, do not interrupt me! This is not in evidence; you cannot ask someone about a photo that is not in evidence. Move on to another question. The defense wants a sidebar and the judge says no. The judge is having George Anthony step down from the stand and Tony be brought back. The judge had Tony Lazzaro wait outside. He asks if the State plans to introduce this photo later, as it is authenticated. There appear to be two photos with different duct tape on them. The state responds that they cannot answer the question at this time.

Meanwhile, the jury sends in some written questions. The judge and the lawyers review them, so that the judge can respond to the jury. On Friday evening, May 27th, 2011, the jury wants to watch the Tampa Bay Lightning playoff game and have pretzels in the break room. Some jurors wants to know if they can continue to keep diaries that they have kept daily all their lives. The prosecution's opinion is that if they want to write something about the case in their diaries, then they cannot. The judge says that he will discuss security questions with the jury later with a court reporter. The judge returns the jury. They also asked the judge if the first twelve jurors would be the ones deciding the case. We suppose they based the question on how they are seated in the jury box. The judge tells them that he cannot answer the question, and that all jurors are to pay close attention to the evidence. He says that they will not be told who the final twelve jurors are, and again that all jurors must pay attention. He tells them that no journals or diaries can be allowed with anything about the trial or the case. He tells them that he will see what he can do about the Lightning game, and he'll let them know.

Interpretation of Testimony – George Anthony: Questioning of George Anthony continues.

The round cylinder gas can that I gave to law enforcement August 1st, had a piece of duct tape. On July 17th, 2008, the detective may have searched my home. I do not remember him coming on July 17th. When he was there, I gave him a tour of the yard, but I do not know when it was. I opened the shed up the first few days because we had cadaver dogs, media and police. I have many shovels in the shed. I also have expensive lawn equipment. When I showed the shed to whomever, I do not remember if I told them about the argument with Casey. I did speak to the detective and told him about the smell of the car. (Objection) I am not sure of the dates – I talked to detectives all the time during the first weeks. I do not recall if I told them about the fight over the gas cans and shed in the first weeks. I have been allowed to sit in the courtroom during testimony. (The Judge is getting irritated. The defense is trying to get in that he has been excused from the **rule of sequestration of witnesses** and can be in the courtroom all of the time. The rule of sequestration of witnesses, which keeps witnesses from hearing other witnesses' testimony, is designed to prevent coloring or tainting one witness's testimony by hearing the testimony of others. The rule of witness sequestration also requires that the witnesses, like the jurors, receive no outside influence from conversations with others or from the media. In fact, witnesses are instructed not to speak to anyone but the lawyers about the trial.)

Law enforcement gave the gas can back to me in the next few days. I had no idea that this can might have been involved in the death of my granddaughter. In December, the significance of the gas can became clear. They took them from me a second time in December. I kept it in my shed during the period in-between. The FBI talked to me about a wide variety of things in their questioning. They asked me about everything that happened between June and December. So I mentioned it then. On June 24th, 2008, I believed that my granddaughter was alive and well. I had no reason to suspect that anything had happened to my granddaughter. I thought she was with my daughter or a babysitter. I learned on July 15th that Caylee was not with her. I did not know on June 24th that these gas cans would become an issue. I do now. On June 24th, I did not know that a few weeks later my granddaughter would be reported missing.

The State's Eleventh Witness

Interpretation of Testimony - Ricardo Morales: He is 27, and has lived in Illinois for about a year and half. I have lived in Florida in the past, in Orlando. I worked at a car dealership in the service department, setting appointments for people. I've known Casey Anthony since about June 2007. I dated her in February 2008. She told me she had a job at Universal Studios as an event coordinator - tours and things for out of town people. Occasionally, she talked about people, a co-worker named Juliette and a boss named Tom. I was living in a townhome. I lived with John Chat. I was aware that Casey had a daughter, Caylee; I knew Caylee from February 2008 until April 2008. Casey stayed the night. Caylee stayed almost every night Casey stayed, and the three of us shared a bed. Caylee was to the outside of Casey, not in the middle or next to me. Casey brought clothes and did not leave anything at the house. (A photo of Casey and Caylee at the townhouse, in Ricardo's room, was placed in evidence.) The photo was taken in late January, because Caylee has a bruise under her arm and another on her face. It is a true and accurate representation of how Casey and Caylee looked when I dated her in 2008. (It is agreed by the lawyers for both sides that the bruises are not from abuse, and the judge will announce the stipulation when the photo is published to the jury.) We broke up in mid-April 2008. It was not a bad break up. We remained friends, and Casey would come by. While we were dating, I never met George and Cindy Anthony. She invited me for breakfast at her house and her parents were not home. On June 7th, 2008, she spent the night and Caylee was there with her, as well. They stayed on June 9th and 10th. She and Caylee stayed the night. The morning of

June 10th was the last time I saw Caylee. I had heard the name of Tony Lazzaro. I did not see Casey again until July 1st, 2008.

She might have texted me in that time frame. She did not tell me that Caylee was missing, kidnapped, or that she needed help. On July 1st, 2008, I saw Casey; we had another roommate Amy Huizenga, sleeping on the sofa. Amy got in a car accident and our house was close to her work. She was looking in the area of Orlando for an apartment. She planned to move in with Casey into Casey's parents' home. I was getting up to go to work on July 1st, and Casey was in the living room talking to Amy. I do not know when she arrived. I was surprised; I had not seen her in a few weeks and did not expect her. She appeared the same as always. She did not tell me anything about Caylee being missing or anything like that. There was no change in her behavior. On July 2nd, 2008, I went to Boston for six days, and then stayed at the airport until my flight to Puerto Rico left. I flew alone and met Amy and others. Casey was invited. I did not think she was going. She was still invited. On July 15th, 2008, I came back from Puerto Rico and saw the defendant at the airport. She was expected to pick all of us up. She was driving Amy's car. She was the same as always - laughing, smiling, normal. She said nothing about Caylee being missing.

(Court recesses for lunch. Casey has changed her hair for the afternoon court session, and is fussing with it again now. Tony Lazzaro is coming back to the stand this afternoon. Ricardo Morales, Casey's ex-boyfriend, is back on the stand.)

Interpretation of Testimony - Ricardo Morales (cont.):
Ricardo says he took the photo. (As the photo is published to the jury, the judge reads a stipulation to the jury that the parties have agreed that bruises on Caylee's face and arm in the January, 2008, photo are not a result of child abuse.) I sold the photo to the Globe (a supermarket tabloid) when they approached me in August 2008. I sold to the Globe for about $4000. I did not license or sell it to anyone else. (All photos of Caylee and Casey in the townhouse of her ex-boyfriend are moved into evidence and published to jury.) We dated from February 2008 until the middle of April 2008. This photo is from my Myspace page, about the time I dated Casey. The photo is a creepy advertisement that says, "Win her over with chloroform." Yes, we were dating in March 2008. I think I posted this in the time period we were dating. I posted it because I found it humorous. I never had a conversation with Casey about the photo or chloroform. I

did sell pictures to the media. When the Globe came knocking, I felt it was okay to sell it to them. They wanted to find me because I had dated Casey. Casey and Caylee slept with me, while we dated. Caylee slept next to Casey. Other than the photograph of chloroform and selling the photos, I cannot you tell you anything else about Caylee's death. I do not think that I was intimate with Casey while Caylee was in the bed.

Myspace is how we communicated with friends in 2008. I do not know the date that I uploaded the photo, but it was sometime in early 2008. I know what chloroform is. I did not search on the computer for chloroform. One night, Casey spent the night without Caylee. Casey and Caylee stayed the night on June 9th, 2008 and they both were my bed. I woke up in the morning that Casey was in the bed but not Caylee. (The witness is now reviewing his deposition.) Casey said her mother had called her during the night and asked her to bring Caylee home. I woke up and Caylee was gone but Casey was in bed. I did not hear the call. Caylee never slept next to me. I saw Casey's interaction with Caylee, and from what I saw, Casey was good with her. I do not recall Caylee running to Casey. Caylee appeared happy with Casey. I never saw Casey strike or torture Caylee. She has issues with Caylee going to sleep and she always had to discipline Caylee to get her to sleep. It appeared normal.

The State's Twelfth Witness

Interpretation of Testimony – Melissa England: She is 26, and she now lives in Boston, Massachusetts. I've worked for a software firm for about two-and-a-half years. I know Troy Brown. We dated a couple of years ago. In June and July, 2008, we dated and I lived in Arlington, Virginia. On July 2, 2008, I was in Orlando visiting. Troy picked me up. I did not know Casey, but Troy had mentioned her. I dropped my things off at Troy's and we went to a club call Voyage. Troy had mentioned that is where he wanted to go and meet his friends. I met Casey Anthony there. She was friendly and was asking about our plans for the weekend. Troy was a valet at a hotel. He had taken off, but then he was called in to work on July 3rd. Casey asked about our plans, and we told her he had to work. She offered to take me shopping while he was at work. I accepted her offer. We were at the club late - we were there for about three hours. I can remember us all drinking. She seemed fine - happy and outgoing. She did not mention her daughter, but Troy had told me she had a child. She did not tell me her daughter was missing, kidnapped, or that she needed help. While we were at the club, she said she was going to get a tattoo. I was not interested in a tattoo, so I did not go. We did not exchange phone numbers; she contacted me through Troy. I was staying with Troy and his sister. I went from Troy's sisters with Troy to JP's, and Casey was there.

Her demeanor was happy, friendly, and very outgoing. She did not tell me that her daughter was missing at all. We left shortly from JP's with Casey. It was in a Grand Cherokee. She said it was her boyfriend's car and her car was in the shop. I met Amy Huizenga the night before at the bar with Troy. Casey told me that there was a story that Amy had lost some money while she was sleepwalking.

Casey and I left and went to Target and the mall. Casey received a phone call. I could hear part of the conversation and she was arguing with someone. The call lasted for five or ten minutes. Casey was speaking harshly to whoever was on the other end. She said something about money and the nanny, but she did not say that until she hung up. Casey told me she just had an argument with her mother. The relationship with Tony was new, but she really liked him. She never mentioned her daughter. She purchased a few things; I did not. She was on her cell phone, mostly texting, throughout the day. One text, she said it was her work and that she was on vacation, but they needed her. I asked, and she said she was an event coordinator for Universal. We talked about it, because we do the same work. I did not hear her talk to a nanny or her daughter.

From the mall, we stopped by Troy's sister's place so I could get ready to go out. She stayed with me while I got ready. There was no reference to her daughter. We were there and Troy's sister asked about Caylee. Casey said that she wanted to take Caylee out of Orlando to get a better education. We went to Hooligans for dinner, just Casey and I. We sat in Amy's section. I asked about Caylee. I thought Caylee was fine. She did not tell me that Caylee was kidnapped or missing, and there was no change in her behavior. She was happy at dinner. She talked about her boyfriend. We left and picked up Troy from work. We went to JP's. She made a phone call to her friends and changed plans to accommodate us. She told the friends she had car trouble, then tossed the phone down and said, "I am such a good liar."

We planned to go to bars, Troy, Casey, JP, and me. Amy was to meet us. We went to a place called Chillers. Everyone was drinking. Casey's demeanor was fine. There was no mention of Caylee. Casey received several phone calls or made several calls or texts. She was upset by the calls. I believe she was crying. She was arguing with her brother, Troy told me. (Objection, hearsay) Her mood changed; she was very upset by the calls. There were many calls and she wanted to leave. It seemed she was taking the calls. She was trying to get happy, and every time she got a call she was upset again and wanted to leave. I went home with JP, and said goodbye to her outside the bar. She was still upset. We had said that we were going bowling on Sunday and she could bring Caylee, and she seemed to think that was a good idea. I flew here from Boston to testify. The State paid for my expenses and they are paying for my hotel. I do not know how Caylee died, when or where.

Casey was happy-go-lucky. She did not tell me about her child being missing. She did not tell me about any horrors in her life, since she was age 10. (An objection results in a sidebar. While counsel is at the bench, the camera stays on the witness. She is a noticeably attractive woman, and she presents well. Questioning then resumes.)

I returned to Orlando several times for short visits in the month of July, 2008. I was in Orlando when Casey was arrested. The day before, I was on the phone with Casey, while she was in a car. I thought Casey was talking with Caylee in the car, during our phone call. Later, a friend received texts that showed Caylee was missing. I barely knew Casey Anthony; I just met her. I do not know about how good a mother she was, or whether she loved her daughter, or if her daughter loved her.

The State's Thirteenth Witness

Interpretation of Testimony - Troy Brown: He is 26 and he lives in Virginia. He has been in advertising sales for two years. In 2008 he was in Florida as a student attending Full Sail University.

The Defendant and Ricardo Morales dated; I knew them when they broke up. I know Anthony Lazzaro a little. In May 2008, I met Tony and I also saw Casey that night. I knew Casey before Ricardo started dating her. In June 2008, I saw Caylee and Casey at Ricardo's house. After June 9th or 10th of 2008, I believe it was late June when I communicated with Casey with a text. I communicated with Casey; she sent a Facebook message in late June. This is my Facebook account printout between me and Casey. On the screen is the Facebook entry from Casey to me June 24th, 2008. She was talking about Amy, and she still has yet to move in to the house. "It is hell. I have not even been staying at home. Drama, I will fill you in later." Casey and Amy were looking for a place to live. I did not know where. Based on my knowledge from Amy, she was to move in with Casey. I came back from vacation on June 18th. I saw Casey on July 2nd, 2008, with Melissa England. Melissa stayed with me. We had a trip planned. It had been planned for a month or so. I talked with Melissa, but I do not remember talking about my friends. I picked Melissa up from the airport, and we went to my sister's and Voyage. We were probably planning on seeing the friends that night. I do not know what time I arrived at Voyage. Amy and Casey were there. Casey was normal when I arrived, in a good mood. I never saw her angry, sad, or was told her daughter had been kidnapped or was missing. Nothing appeared wrong with Casey.

We went to Mako's; I believe we all went together. I introduced Melissa and Casey, and they seemed fine. Casey was friendly. We stayed out probably until one AM. I believe Casey and Melissa planned to spend the day together because I had to work. On July 3rd, I saw Casey before I went to work, and I believe she dropped me off at work. She was in Tony's car. She said there were issues with her car, but nothing specific. I got off work at ten or eleven o'clock. We went to Ricardo's and then took a taxi to bars. It was Casey, Mellissa, Amy and me. Casey was upset, because she was receiving phone calls. We were led to believe they were from her brother. She would stop being upset and then start again when another call came, over a short period – an hour or two. She wanted to leave, so we left. Casey did not come with us. I received phone calls regarding the trip to Puerto Rico. We all planned to go. Casey was "a might be going" thing. On July 10th, she said it was official that she was not going. She was trying to find a place to live and a car. She did not mention Caylee. On July 15th, Casey picked us up from the airport. She seemed fine. She did not tell me that her daughter was missing or kidnapped. She seemed normal. I do not know how Caylee died, where she died, or when.

The State's Fourteenth Witness

Interpretation of Testimony – Iassen Donov: He is 27, and lives in Florida. I am a pharmacy recruiter. When they need an executive, they come to me. I have been with the company about a year, and I have a BS degree. I met Casey in January 2007. She was dating Brian Snow, and he introduced her to me. I saw her in 2008. It was the end of the month June, at Ale House. She seemed like Casey, social, happy and talkative. She never told me her daughter was kidnapped, missing or anything. She was happy. I met Caylee at her second birthday party. I never asked about Caylee at the Ale House. We had a good time.

It was a typical meeting. I saw her again at Buffalo Wild Wings on July 2nd, 2008. We kept in contact on Instant Messenger. I believe she worked at Universal as an event coordinator. I had one question about her babysitter in Instant Messenger message, and she told me she had a nanny she has known for six years.

(The witness states that he has reviewed AOL Instant Messenger transcripts, and that they are accurate. The transcripts are entered into evidence. The dates of the conversations between them are June 13th June 19th, June 20th, June 27th, and July 14th, 2008. The defense's objection is overruled. Testimony resumes.)

Casey was moving out, she had been looking for apartments at Winter Park Villas. She plans on moving within a week. Casey said, "I have a nanny, I love her." She had a boyfriend and I knew the picture from Myspace. I was interested in dating her, and she said she was interested. Casey invited me to Fusion by Instant Messenger. I never went. I have known Casey since January 2007, a year and half before she got arrested. I thought she worked at Universal and then Sports Authority. Now that I know that it was not true, I am shocked. She seemed the same all the time. I do not know how Caylee died. I told law enforcement that Casey was not a heavy drinker and left clubs early.

The State's Fifteenth Witness

Interpretation of Testimony – Dante Salati: He is 26 and a mechanic. I have known Casey for eleven years. We went to high school together. I knew she had a daughter. I met Caylee multiple times at the Ford Dealer. From January until June 2008, I lived at the Sawgrass Apartments, number 218. I moved in about 2005, and was there until late 2008 or early 2009. I now live in a country club. Casey was there in 2006 and 2007.

In June and July 2008, I saw her at Miller's Ale House. July 1st, 2008, we all – Shawn, Daniel, Brandon, and me – went to the Ale House. I saw Casey there and she was normal; she seemed like someone free of worry. She did not tell me Caylee was missing, had been kidnapped, or that Casey needed help. I spent an hour with her, and she did not mention Caylee.

I have known Casey for about eleven years. She is nice, caring, and Caylee loved Casey. There was lots of affection. Casey was attentive. It appeared Caylee's affection toward Casey was real. She was well fed and well dressed. I never saw Casey abuse Caylee or torture

Caylee. I did not see a change in Casey before and after June 16, 2008. Knowing her for many years, I am shocked that there was no change in Casey's behavior.

The State's Sixteenth Witness

Interpretation of Testimony - Christopher Stutz: He is 23 years old, and works for the YMCA giving swimming lessons and the like. He has a BS and is working on his MBA. I met Casey at a football game. On May 16th, 2008, or the week of, she came to my parent's house. I knew she had a daughter. She brought Caylee. My parents were not home and she stayed the night. I saw her driving a black Cherokee, I believe on Mother's Day. (The State refreshes his memory with his deposition.) I was mistaken; sorry. I saw her in June, 2008. I saw her at my parents. Caylee was not with her, in mid-June, about June 17th. When she came to see me, she did not tell me Caylee was missing. She told me it was a friend's car and that hers had broken. I saw her again on July 7th, 2008 at Buffalo Wild Wings. I just ran into her. Shawn and Iassen were there, I believe. She approached and said hi. She seemed the same upbeat and happy Casey. I became aware that Caylee was missing by text from her cell phone. Caylee had been missing 31 days. Later that day, I received a call from Lee, Casey's brother. I also received a phone call from Casey from jail.

The State's Seventeenth Witness

Interpretation of Testimony - Matthew Crisp: He is 24. A residential property manager, he rents apartments. In June 2008, he worked for Cranes Landing Apartments.

I have had general contact with Casey from 2002 to 2008. In June 2008, Casey called the leasing office. She said her boyfriend was looking for an apartment and wanted to know if they could come take a look. Between June 17th and 19th, I met Anthony Lazzaro at the office. That day, Casey was with him. That day, Casey did not tell me her daughter was missing. She was joyful. She did not have ID to go into the apartment, so only Tony looked at the apartment. I met Anthony Lazzaro on July 7th at Subway for lunch alone. (The witness is excused, and exits the courtroom.)

The jury is dismissed for the remainder of the day, while the judge and the lawyers take care of other case-related business. Judge Perry is allowing the defense to **proffer** Anthony Lazzaro's testimony outside the jury's presence regarding the secret Casey told him about her father's abuse of her. A proffer is like testimony before the jury, but without them present. It is for screening the testimony's value, with the attorney or attorneys asking questions, and the witness giving answers. The judge will decide if this evidence is admissible for the jury to hear. A proffer is also done for appellate purposes, because the appellate court has to know what the requested evidence would have been, in the event that the judge refuses to allow it to be introduced in the presence of the jury.

Interpretation of Proffer Testimony – Tony Lazzaro: He is called to the stand. He says that Casey told him that George hit her. Lazzaro's impression was that it was corporal punishment. She also told him that her brother Lee tried to touch her breast once. (That appears to be the abuse...)

The judge and the lawyers decide that proffers regarding other known problem areas in the evidence should also be handled. The lawyers know that Cindy Anthony has previously said that Cindy did not think the police were doing enough in the search for Caylee, and that law enforcement initiated her distrust of defense attorney Baez. We assume that she said that in deposition. Cindy Anthony is called to the stand and sworn in for a proffer regarding those issues.

Interpretation of Proffer Testimony – Cindy Anthony: She says that if the police stopped looking for Caylee, I would have continued setting up a command center, tip line and used all means to find Caylee. She says she did not feel the police were doing enough to find Caylee. At no time did I assist in building the case against Casey, not intentionally. Caylee is my granddaughter.

The judge, while remaining calm, cool and collected, reads the riot act to counsel for both sides, but he seems to be directing most of his rancor toward defense attorney Jose Baez. He tells the lawyers that their bickering is costing time and money, as well as needlessly prolonging the trial.

It is costing $361,000 for jurors, hotels are costing $125,400, the jurors' meals and snacks cost $50,000, and there is an additional $44,000 a week for general costs of the trial. Transportation and clerical costs are not included. Most of it is being paid by Orange County, and the Orange County Sheriff pays for security. We thought that you would want to know just a few of the numbers, so we can all recognize how much a high-profile criminal trial costs the taxpayers.

During the same hearing, the defense asks to call Orlando television channel 9 (WFTV) reporter Kathi Belich as a witness for the defense. Apparently, during one of her many broadcasts about this case, George Anthony was captured on video at a Kid Finders Network tent, with Henkel duct tape similar to the tape that was found with Caylee's remains. The defense wants to introduce the video and have Ms. Belich testify about the video. The judge denies the defense's request.

In the hearing, the lawyers talk about a video the State will seek to introduce in the trial. During a video taken while Lee Anthony visited Casey in jail, he tells his sister that he will not reveal what she tells him if she sends him a letter from jail. (We know that he is still trying to find Caylee. We also know that all inmate mail is screened, and would be read by corrections personnel if sent from the jail. We do not know if Lee knows that or not.) There is also discussion about Casey's family trying to convince her to hire someone other than Baez to represent her during jailhouse visitation videos. The Anthonys make unflattering comments about Baez to Casey, trying to convince her to get another lawyer. Baez wants the tapes excluded, or wants those portions of the tapes redacted. The judge tells him that his motion is untimely, and that the judge had issued orders that all such motions had to be filed and argued before the trial began. The judge refuses to entertain any motions regarding the tapes. During this discussion, Baez and Ashton are again bickering.

The judge makes it clear that if the lawyers' decorum doesn't improve, they will not like what he will do. He tells them to address their remarks to him, not to each other. Baez apologizes to the court on behalf of the defense. The hearing continues with proffers of testimony of three more witnesses.

Interpretation of Proffer Testimony – George Anthony: The defense asks Mr. Anthony if there were court next Wednesday, and I told you not to show up and that it would save your daughter's life if you did not show up, would you fail to show up? Yes, if I knew it would save her life, I would fail to appear. When asked about seeing his daughter in jail he said, I just started seeing my daughter at jail, the police told me it was a private visit, and I think it was without your knowledge. You were out of town, Mr. Baez. Then a lawyer from your office was present and prohibited the visit.

Interpretation of Proffer Testimony – Cindy Anthony: A meeting was scheduled at the attorney's office for me and

George to see Casey, but because of security it was cancelled. In August 2008, there was a meeting at the courthouse. I never told George to write a letter to Casey. I did say that all of the answers lie with Casey.

Interpretation of Proffer Testimony – Orange County Deputy Sheriff Reginald Hosey: I arrived about a stolen car and the grandmother told me she had not seen her granddaughter for 31 days. I walked with Casey, and she told me that her parents wanted to take her daughter. She tried to convince me that her mother was just causing problems; that it was a domestic issue. I do not remember Casey Anthony being handcuffed. (After the proffers conclude, the judge announces that court will stand in recess for the evening.)

May 27th, 2011

There is a morning hearing about money the defense needs from Orange County. The defense argues a motion to preserve evidence and for additional forensic testing, if witnesses are going to be able to testify as witnesses. The motion is granted. Depositions of Dr. Wise and someone else have not been transcribed, and the defense needs money to do so. There is a request for money for defense costs for an investigator and a mitigation expert. Those motions are granted. The defense's motion to suppress Casey's statements and 911 calls is denied.

The jury is returned to the courtroom to begin its day's work. There is a housekeeping announcement from the judge before the evidence begins. Although Orlando does not carry Tampa Bay Lightning games, Bright House Networks, a cable television provider, arranged to get a feed of the hockey game for the jury.

The State's Eighteenth Witness

Interpretation of Testimony – Mallory Parker: She is 27 and has worked as a customer service representative for about a year. I know Casey. I am engaged to Lee Anthony; I met him in 2006. Early in 2007, we broke up for a bit, but in early 2008, we were a couple again. Casey and I chatted, but we were not real close. We did not fight. Cindy and I have a good relationship. We were not as close in 2008; we are closer now. It is the same with George – a good relationship. I knew Caylee. In June 2008, I did not notice Casey and Caylee were not at the house. In July, I received a call from Lee Anthony. I tried to text Casey a day or two before July 4th. I was asking if she was in downtown Orlando. I do not recall the date, but I made other attempts with Lee and Danny

Alverez to locate Casey in the Church Street Station area. It is an area of bars and nightclubs.

Lee, Daniel, and I believed she was downtown. We had received information from friends and family that she was going to a club. We went to the club looking for her, but we did not find her. I tried text messages, maybe five or six; some she responded to. I was asking if she was downtown. She did not say she was downtown. She asked if I was with Lee. She did not want the family to worry; she just wanted some space. I asked her if she would be coming and bringing the baby for a family weekend and she said she would try. Lee was focused and frustrated, and concerned. While I was texting Casey, so was Lee. Lee talked with her. I did not try to call Casey. We were at the club for two or three hours. We never located Casey. I do not think I texted or spoke with her after July 3rd, 2008. I do not recall if I spent time with George and Cindy during that period.

I was aware that I was looking for Casey because Cindy wanted to find her. (Objection sustained.) Lee wanted to go downtown, and I went along at Lee's urging and at Cindy's urging, not George Anthony's. I saw Caylee's affection and love for her mother – it was amazing. Casey and Caylee had a very special bond. It appeared genuine. Caylee was cared for and I never saw Casey hit or abuse her.

The State's Nineteenth Witness

Interpretation of Testimony – William Waters: He is 32, and is an unemployed engineer. I live in Florida. I know Casey I met her on the Fourth of July 2008, at a party at my home. I met Casey through Amy Huizinga, who was decorating my home for a party. It was an all-day and all-night party. Amy and Casey came together about 1:30 in the afternoon. Casey was polite, and engaged in regular conversation. She did not tell me her daughter was missing or kidnapped. I knew she had a child; I was told by Amy. Casey also told me she had a child, that evening. It was only a short conversation. She was taking care of my home while I was outside at the party – she watched my belongings inside. I lived in downtown Orlando. (A photo is shown to the witness.) I recognize the photo. It is a picture of Amy and Casey walking to the lake. I took the photo on July 4th, 2008. (The photo is admitted into evidence and published to the jury.)

I did not speak to Casey about her employment. I did talk to her about her child. She mentioned she had a child. We went to the fireworks in a big group. I was near Casey, and she was on the phone with her boyfriend. Casey was talking with Tony Lazzaro, who was moving back to New York. She did not want him to move. She was angry after the call. We went back to my house. The party ended about two AM. Casey was drinking, and watching over the house. She was no longer angry. Casey and Amy left together. I got her phone number, and we planned on going to IKEA. We did not set up a time to do that.

On July 5th, 2008, I saw Casey at seven in the morning. I was not expecting her at my home. She had Amy's car. She said something was wrong with her car - an alignment or tune up. My roommate let her in. She hung out while I got ready, and then we went shopping. She had spunk and was happy. She did not tell me her daughter was missing, had been kidnapped, nor did she ask for help. We went to Target, and got coffee and bubble gum. Next we went to IKEA, I believe for about two hours. Casey said she needed to get a bunch of furniture for a new house. She said that she and a friend who had kids were looking for a stay-in nanny, and they were moving in the next two months. She said she worked for Universal Studios as an event coordinator, and did a lot of the work at home on her computer.

Zacksby's is a fast food place, and we had lunch there. There was no change in her demeanor. We went back to my house. She did not mention Caylee that day, July 5th. It was a fun day for me. After a few days, we made plans to go to dinner and take a helicopter ride. She agreed to go. I had free passes. I was texting her and got no answer, and then she said she was busy and could not come up with a nano. I do not know what a nano is. She did not come around, but she texted a lot after July 10th, while I was at work. I never saw her after July 5th. We were supposed to meet for lunch, but my work got in the way. I was aware she had a boyfriend. I was not really interested in Casey; she was just a friend. On July 15th, I got a phone call from an FBI agent. I do not know if I talked to Casey after that.

I had just met Casey Anthony. I believed she had a job and she appeared to love the job. I realize that turned out not to be true. She did not indicate that she was unemployed, and as far as I could tell, the only thing wrong in her life was the relationship with Tony. That was on July 5th, not in June. She was moving in with Amy, and they were going to bring their children and have a live-in nanny. I believed everything. Baez, who is cross-examining, says, "You believed in her world," and the witness replies that Casey was happy and all seemed true. I trust a lot of people until they prove differently. The statements the defendant made were incorrect or were lies. Based on my observations, Casey is convincing. (The witness is excused, and steps down. The jury is given a break, but the judge and the attorneys work during some of the recess, outside the presence of the jury.)

During the hearing outside the presence of the jury, stipulations are entered between the defense and the prosecution regarding several videos. The defense says they stipulate to the authenticity of the videos, but the state will still need to lay the foundation for introduction of the videos through witnesses. A sidebar occurs. We assume this is done so that the gallery and the media cannot hear what is said. We do not know if the discussion involves the stipulations or other matters.

Casey appears more agitated today. She is more frazzled looking than she was yesterday. She is wearing a while top with a black top over it. Her hair is messy. The lawyers and the judge are talking about a defense motion about the videos. Perhaps that is what they discussed in the sidebar. The judge says that the defendant's demeanor is an issue for the jury to decide based on her behavior. The defense has apparently argued that something in the videos could be construed as lack of remorse by the jury, which could be improperly used as an aggravating circumstance in penalty phase. Apparently, the defense cited Jones v. State, because the judge says that lack of remorse for a murder did not apply in Jones and that Jones dealt with a photo line-up on a kidnapping charge. The judge says that Jones was his case. The defense motion is denied.

There are objections to some of the videos; there are some in which Casey is purchasing beer and alcohol. The defense is objecting because of relevancy and introduction of improper character evidence, improper state of mind, and lack of remorse. They are not objecting because of authenticity or it being Casey in video.

Our house lawyer and your writers debated this motion. He explained there is a weighing process that must occur about a fine legal issue between evidence of lack of remorse (since lack of remorse cannot be considered by the jury as an aggravating circumstance in a penalty phase) and the permissible introduction of evidence by the State about the defendant's state of mind. The judge agrees with the State. They can continue presenting evidence of Casey's behavior during the thirty-one days Caylee was not seen. The court personnel take a recess.

After the recess, the jury is back. A video of Casey at Target on June 30th, 2008, is admitted into evidence by stipulation. The jury is told that it is a true record of what occurred at Target. It is Casey, it is a correct video and it is published to the jury. The video shows the parking lot of Target. The video then shows Casey in Target, at a checkout counter purchasing clothes. She seems normal, is dressed well, and Caylee is not with her.

The next video is from July 1st, 2008, at JC Penny. It is admitted and published to the jury. Casey is at a check-out buying clothes, and appears normal. Her hair is neat. Caylee is not on the video. The next video, from July 5th, 2008, is at IKEA. It is also admitted and published. Casey and William Waters appear to be very well dressed and neat, and without Caylee.

The next video is from July 7th, 2008, from Target. It is admitted and published. Casey and another girl enter Target and check out. Casey looks clean and neat. She is buying something in a small package, maybe chips, without Caylee. The next video is from July 8th, 2008, also from Target. Casey is not as neatly dressed. She appears to be buying food and shampoo. She probably has more than one hundred dollars' worth of items – the cart is full. She is not as well dressed, but still looks put together and calm. She writes a check. These seem to be regular groceries. She is there without Caylee.

The next video is from July 10th, 2008, again at Target. Casey is well dressed, wearing a mini dress and sunglasses. She has a cart full of women's clothes and some lingerie. Casey writes a check. Again, it looks like more than a hundred dollars' worth of clothes. She is there without Caylee. The next video is also from July 10th, 2008, in another Target. Casey is dressed in clothes that she bought early in the day, in the last video. She is buying more food. It looks like one hundred dollars' worth or more, as well as some alcohol. She is calm; she shows no signs of stress. There are some more clothes in the cart. She writes another check. Casey is so calm that she snaps her wallet closed before putting it in her purse. She is there without Caylee.

The last video is from July 12th and 15th, 2008, at Winn Dixie. Casey has another cart full of food and drinks, more than one hundred dollars' worth. Casey is calm, well dressed and again, there is no sign of Caylee.

(The courtroom is full again today.) There are technical problems, and the jury is told that a Bank of America

91

video from July 15th and a Blockbuster video, also from
July 15, will be introduced later.

The State's Twentieth Witness

Interpretation of Testimony – Catherine Sanchez: She is a
well put together woman. She is the district manager for
Amscot. We are a financial institution. I operate sixteen
stores, and in June and July of 2008, I was at the
Orlando location on Goldenrod and Colonial Drive. A photo
of the store is on the monitor and is published to the
jury. A second photo shows only the parking lot with one
car, the Pontiac Sunfire of Casey Anthony. It is also
introduced into evidence and published to the jury. (In
that photo, we see the parking lot, the car, and a
dumpster.) We use the dumpster with two other businesses,
Papa John's Pizza and another. Another photo of the
dumpster to the side of Amscot is published.

On June 27th, 2008, I was working at that Amscot from
seven to seven. I noticed a white Pontiac Sunbird parked
next to the dumpster. The car was pulled straight into
the spot and no one was near the car. I did not see when
the vehicle was parked there. I never went near the
vehicle; I just noticed it. On June 28th, 2008, I worked
from seven to two; it was a Saturday. The vehicle was
still there with no one around. I went up to the vehicle,
wrote the tag, and walked around it. I did not touch the
vehicle. I wanted to report it as an abandoned vehicle
and looked to see if there was a note saying it was a
breakdown, but there was nothing. I looked inside. It was
messy; I remember seeing a blanket. I called the Orlando
Police non-emergency number to make a report. The police
said the car was not reported stolen, and so I called the
compliance officer at Amscot. He told me to wait one more
day, and then call the tow company we use, Johnson Tow
Company. I was off on Sunday. It was still there on
Monday, June 30th, 2008, so I reported it. The car had
not moved. They towed it away. I saw them towing the car.
I did not touch vehicle. The car had no odor that I
noticed over the odor of the dumpster.

The corporate office of Amscot has surveillance videos. I
do not know where the cameras are. They are inside and
out, and visible to the public if they look. There are
two gas stations close to our location. Someone could go
to get gas next door; it is within walking distance. I
smelled trash in the dumpster, but nothing more than
trash.

92

Interpretation of Testimony – Simon A. Birch: He now lives in Madison, Wisconsin. He speaks with an obvious English accent. I did live in Orlando. I was the operations manager for a wrecker service, Johnson's Wrecker Service, Inc. I handled the day-to-day operations of the business. The impound yard is secured by a seven-foot fence with barbed wire on top and a second locked barbed wire fence for inside storage. I lived on the property twenty-four hours a day, in a trailer. I received the car from Amscot, the Pontiac Sunfire. (There is a stipulation announced that on June 30th, 2008, Johnson's towed the Pontiac from Amscot.) The witness reviews Johnson's records and the records are admitted into evidence.

The driver delivers a vehicle, and the office fills out the receipt and runs the tag. We find out to whom the car belongs, and then the car is stored. Vehicles are segregated by why the vehicles are towed, which makes maintaining the vehicles easier. (An aerial photo the storage facility, with minor changes to the front because of widening of the road it fronts is introduced into evidence and published; the witness explains the changes.) The yard is completely fenced. The gate is always closed to the storage yard and locked to the public. We have bulletproof glass between the public access area and the office. People are never happy when they come to a tow yard to pick up a vehicle. A clerk would approach the window from inside and the customer would be outside.

The Pontiac Sunbird was stored and stayed there for about two weeks. We can keep it if the car is not picked up by a certain time limit. We could keep and re-title the car or part it out. The time is between thirty-five and fifty days. On the third day we have a vehicle, a letter is generated and sent by certified mail to the registered owner. It would tell the owner the charges and procedure to pick up the vehicle. I did look at this particular vehicle after a few days. I looked at to determine its condition, to help decide if we would title it if it was not picked up. I looked at the exterior, but I could not enter the vehicle. I pulled the handle and the doors were locked.

I did notice a strong odor. I have almost thirty years in the tow business and I did waste management for two years. I have been exposed to odor. I have been exposed to six to eight dead bodies in my time in towing. I am familiar with the smell of garbage and the odor of a dead body, and the difference in the odors. I can distinguish between the smell of garbage and human remains; the smell of decomposition is distinct. I noticed an odor from the white Sunfire that was fairly well consistent with decomposition. But the car was locked up, so the odor was mild.

On July 15th, 2008, Mr. and Mrs. Anthony came to pick up the vehicle. I had contact with both through the bulletproof glass. I heard the clerk, and I could tell the people were agitated, so I came out of my office. The clerk gave me a look. I spoke with Ms. Anthony, who wanted to know why we did not tell them right away that we had the car. It is normal for people to be upset. The letter would have been mailed on the Fourth of July weekend, which could have slowed the delivery. I explained that we had followed due process and it just took longer because of the weekend. (A sidebar occurs.)

(We think that Casey has a very catty look while chatting with a female at defense counsel's table. She humps her shoulders and smirks like she is getting away with something.) After the sidebar, the witness continues. Our company sends instructions on what the owner needs to bring to pick up the car - proof of ownership, identification, and cash only for payment of the storage bill.

I went to the vehicle with Mr. Anthony. (Photos are shown of the area where the vehicle is stored.) It is behind two closed gates, just to get to the car. We walked together for about 15 seconds and we talked. Mr. Anthony apologized for his wife's outburst. He vented, and said that he did not know where his daughter was. He also stated that he and Mrs. Anthony will probably get divorced over this. At the vehicle, Mr. Anthony had the keys. I assumed he would get in and drive out. Mr. Anthony had no other items. He opened the car door and the smell came out very intensely, a very strong odor, eye opening, like it was released into the atmosphere. In my mind, that smell was decomposition. I did not say it out loud. I had smelled it recently and many times before, and you never forget it, deceased human remains. I did not say it out load and the man talked about his daughter and granddaughter being missing. I didn't want to inflame him or attempt to stir the situation.

He cranked the engine but it would not fire and run. He did not have a gas can with him at that time. I saw the gas gauge was on empty and thought the car might be empty. The battery was healthy, so I thought of gas. He stated that he had some gas with him. He went back to his car and retrieved a gas can. It was an older metal gas can; it seemed really worn. I did not notice whether there was tape on the can. At that point, no one had opened anything but the car door. He put gas in the car.

At some point, we decided to open the trunk to see if the odor was coming from the trunk. I suggested he open the trunk. One of us opened it. We saw a white trash bag, and I thought that I could toss it away. The odor was even stronger, and there were flies. We noticed just one bag. We looked in the bag to see if it was the odor. I can't remember if it was tied tight. I can't remember who opened it. Inside was a pizza box and papers, it was very light, nothing that would have caused that odor. It was just a general look and there was nothing that I could see that was causing that odor.

I disposed of it by tossing the bag over the fence to the garbage, and it landed like a bag of paper. I went around later to toss it in the garbage. We did not make any further comments on what the odor was. The car started and he drove out. I met him at the gate, he apologized again and pulled out of the fenced area. I could see Mr. and Mrs. Anthony conversing outside the car and she got in another car, and they left with both cars. (This witness sounds completely truthful.)

By law we must send out a notice on the fourth day after we tow a vehicle. It was the Fourth of July weekend, and that delayed the letter. Mr. Anthony said his granddaughter was missing. The smell became more intense when we opened it; it was the smell to me of decomposition. Mr. Anthony got the gas and we opened the trunk after he got the gas, but I'm not sure if he put gas in the car before or after we opened the trunk.

I think I am qualified to tell the different between the smell of garbage and decomposition. He had gas cans with him when he arrived at the yard. It's not usual for customers to bring gas. I escorted him to get the cans. We were together maybe five to ten minutes, all together. I would not obstruct justice or destroy evidence. I did not know this car was evidence. Mr. Anthony told me that his daughter and granddaughter were missing. I did not call the police. The car was picked up and never brought to the location again.

I lived in Orlando and was exposed to media. I am not aware that the car being towed was in the media. The following day I saw what was on TV. I am sure I saw something. On July 24th, the police came to take my statement. I knew there was a missing child at that point. I knew it was being broadcast, that there was a foul odor, and the police were the biggest part of our business at that time. We did towing and impound for the City of Orlando Police Department.

I do not know how long the car was at the Amscot property. Mr. Anthony said the car was at Amscot for 3 days. He was upset about the storage charges. I believe the paperwork has an address on where the car was towed from. I called the Orange County Sheriff's Office when I saw the Anthony's were on TV about the child being missing. I thought I'd better call them. I went to the dumpster and jumped in, and did not find the garbage bag then. When the bag was separated from the car the smell did not appear to follow it.

The letter we sent would have had the location of the Amscot where the car was towed from. Mr. Anthony had the key to the car. I called the police and then gave a sworn statement on July 24th. I discussed what I heard on TV with the police. It was in my memory about the car when I called.

I believe I have a recollection that there was a pizza box in the bag. I recalled what I saw in the trash and then what I saw in the media. I am seventy percent sure a pizza box was in that bag. No, it is not hard for me to separate TV, from what I saw. A good portion of my memory tells me it was in the bag.

The State's Twenty-second Witness

Interpretation of Testimony - George Anthony (recalled):
He is recalled for the second time to testify. In the middle of July 2008, I learn the vehicle that my daughter drove had been towed. We received a notice about certified mail. On Sunday July 13th, Cindy found the notice. We use the garage to enter and exit the house. The sender was Johnson and it was addressed to both of us. I did not know who the letter was from. I said I would go see about it Monday, and I ended up going on Tuesday because of work. I ran errands and went to the post office.

I went to the post office about noon on Tuesday to get the letter. It was a notice that our vehicle had been towed. I remember it had something about the address where it was towed from and the date it was towed. I believed that my daughter had this vehicle. I thought it was in Jacksonville, Florida with my daughter, as my wife had told me.

I arrived at Johnson's Towing and inquired about a charge of nearly five hundred dollars. We live within a mile and half of Amscot. I called my wife and told her that I would stop at the bank to get the money, and I would go home and wait for her. Cindy picked me up, and we went to get the car. I had to get proof of ownership at the house.

There were a lot of things that went through my mind. I did bring a gas can. My wife arrived and we went to get the car. We were agitated, because the five hundred dollars charge was a lot. They lessened the bill a bit. I was more irritated about the time we had to spend away from work to handle this.

The gentleman took me to get the car. As we approached the vehicle, I smelled a pretty strong odor. It was the smell of decomposition - you never forget it. I worried that my daughter or granddaughter or both were in the car dead. I did not want to believe what I smelled. We had keys to the car, a spare set. I looked the car over. I could see the vehicle. I unlocked it and looked inside. The odor was more intense, but there was nothing unusual inside. I rolled the passenger side window down and tried to start the car. We went to the trunk, looking for damage. I whispered, "Please do not let this be Casey or Caylee." I saw a white bag with a pizza box and an Arm & Hammer laundry container. The gentleman said that this has got to be the smell. I was relieved when I saw the trash. I could see through the thin plastic bag.

I never touched the bag. The gentleman tossed it over a fence into a dumpster, I think. I drove back to where Cindy and the other car were, and kept the windows down, and then we left. The smell was still there with the windows down. I don't remember what I said to my wife. I was much more concerned by July 15th, it had been longer since I had seen my daughter and granddaughter. We got home with the car about two PM.

I opened the sunroof, windows and trunk to air out the car. It was raining, and I put the car in the garage. I had a conversation with my wife. Caylee, Casey, my new job, I was worried. I maintained the cars for all of the family. I keep the cars clean. I noticed a slight circular type stain on the tire cover, the size of a basketball. It was a circle. The car was messy. There were Casey's high heels, Caylee's car seat, something on the front seat, maybe music, but the car was not that messy. I do not remember what was in the trunk. I had to go to a new job, and we agreed Cindy would try to get hold of Casey.

That is correct, the notice was found in the door on July 13th. I am aware that the registered letter was sent out on July 4th. The tow yard is a mile and a half from my home, but I do not how long it takes to get mail from there. Cindy found the notice; I did not see where it was. We do not use our front door.

I did not see the notice from the street It is yellow. I usually get the mail, because Cindy works days. I leave for work about 2 to 2:15. The mail varies in delivery time from early to late afternoon. I have received these notices before. I believe Cindy was on vacation that week. I was at home all week at night to sleep. I am not aware if a second notice arrived at my home. You can see the front door of the home, but it is back a little. You can see the door a little from the driveway.

I called Amscot after I got home with the car. I did not tell Mr. Birch that the car had been at Amscot for 3 days. Experience told me to take gas. I am not sure if the gas can I took had duct tape on it. I do not remember which gas can I took.

I do not remember, but I do not think I had spoken to Casey since June 24th. It had been three weeks since I spoke to my daughter. When I arrived, I was concerned about Caylee. I told people at the tow yard about not seeing my daughter and granddaughter for a while. This is after the July Fourth weekend, it was July 15th and I was more concerned. I smelled a smell of decomposition. I did not ask him to open the trunk with me. I have given statements in this case. I was concerned about the smell, and I was not trying to distance myself from any evidence.

I did not know at that time my granddaughter was missing, and my daughter was missing. I opened the trunk and the smell was more pungent than the smell from opening the car. Once I opened the trunk, all I found was garbage. I had smelled decomposition before. As a police officer, I had smelled the smell before. I smelled the car, but I did not call my daughter to inquire about Casey or Caylee. Looking back, there are many things I should have done that I did not. I was just trying to get the car out of the tow yard and home. As a police officer, I know that if I moved that car I would be destroying evidence, if I knew at the time that the car was evidence. I did not. I went home and aired out the car and went to work. I did not tell anything about my personal life to anyone at work at that point.

I did go to law enforcement, but did not want Cindy and Lee to know. I was going to do anything I could do to find my granddaughter. When I met with them, I told them about the experience smelling that car. I told police that I had smelled a smell like that in the woods, houses, and cars in my lifetime. That was six months before my granddaughter was found in the woods. (A sidebar occurs. The judge is angry at Baez about his cross-examination. The lawyers are really arguing at the sidebar. Mason is pulling Baez away. Testimony resumes.) I did not know when I drove the car way from the tow yard that Caylee was dead.

On re-direct, he says that he does not know what day the certified mail receipt was placed on the door. The State says that Mr. Baez asked about the witness distancing himself from the evidence. He then asked a hypothetical question to the effect that, "if you took the little girl's body after a supposed drowning and dumped it in the woods, there would be no evidence in the car." The witness answered "Correct."

The State's Twenty-third Witness

Interpretation of Testimony – Anthony Lazzaro (recalled): Yes, L7 Tone is my AOL Instant Messenger name. I had Instant Messages with Casey. Yes, Casey O Marie was her name. (He is shown messages from Instant Messenger.) These are conversations between me and Casey. (Instant Messages dating from April 29th, 2008 through June 12th, 2008, they are placed in evidence. There is a sidebar. It seems clear that the defense does not want this in. The judge excuses the jury.)

The Judge says he wants a proffer of the testimony about the text messages outside the presence of the jury. It seems he has some concerns about this whole thing, and wants to know the purpose of this exhibit. It starts out with April. The State announces it will not seek to publish to the jury any of the Instant Messages before June 10th, 2008. The first message from Casey to Tony that the State wants to use reads, "Only few more days and you can bring your ass over anytime and stay anytime you want." The State reveals at least some of its theory of the case, saying that the message makes it clear that the child and the parents are in the way. Casey is living at home. When she and Tony first dated, Casey was limited by Caylee on what she could do. "Your Honor, the prosecution believes that Casey was planning on killing her parents too." The defense objects because the texts are not relevant and are unduly prejudicial.

Judge Perry wants copies of all texts that they are going to use to review before the jury hears any more about them. The jury is out for the rest of the day. The judge announces that they will discuss the Instant Messages and text messages out of the presence of the jury. The judge sends the jurors to watch the Lighting Game on a 65-inch big-screen TV, compliments of Bright House Networks, and tells the jurors that Bright House worked hard to get them the game, which will not be seen by other Orlando customers. A last-minute witness is added by prosecution. There is one more sidebar, then court recesses for the evening.

May 28th, 2011

The State's Twenty-third Witness

Interpretation of Testimony – Anthony Lazzaro (recall continued): (Anthony Lazzaro returns to the stand. He says that he recognizes an item that is shown on-screen by the prosecution.) It is my orientation sheet from the university, Full Sail University. I used it to register for my first classes. It is in my handwriting, my name, and the address of the apartment. It was my apartment.

I left for New York on June 30th and stayed to July 5th. I stayed in contact with Casey every day. Casey picked me up from the airport in my car. There was no change in her, she was just happy to see me. We went to my apartment. Then went out to Buffalo Wild Wings and we met some of her friends. Casey stayed with me every night until July 15th. I saw no change in Casey.

Evidence of a receipt of Anthony's from Blockbuster is presented. It is from July 6th, 2008 at 7:58 PM. He and Casey rented the movie Jumper. Defense objects. During a sidebar, Anthony is still looking at the receipt.

On July 15th, 2008, Nathan and me were at home playing X Box. Casey was in the apartment and had been there all day. The All Star Game was going on. A knock came at my door, and Casey answered. Amy was at the door, they looked at each other and Casey walked out with her. I do not remember hearing anything said. The door flung open and Casey came running in. Her mother was at the door. I asked her politely to come in. She and Casey were yelling. Casey told her mother something like no, I'm not getting my stuff; I'm coming back here. I sat in shock. They left together. I did not call Casey, I figured they would work it out and I would see Casey later.

I called her phone later and realized that her phone was still at the apartment. So I called Amy, and then a deputy came to the door. I said nothing to the deputy; I gave him the cell phone. It took only minutes to give the phone to him. There were no calls from Casey by that time. The same deputy came back not long - less than an hour - later. I received a call from Lee and he told me what was going on. I let the deputy search my apartment. He took nothing and was there about half an hour. Next Lee Anthony came, after the deputy left. He was concerned, very concerned. I gave him Casey's clothes and a laptop. I think he asked for Casey's things, a duffel bag of clothes. It was a bag; the deputy had already searched it at my home. My reaction was wow; I was pretty taken back, surprised. No one else came that night. I did not attempt to contact Casey.

On July 16th, 2008, Casey text messaged me. (The witness is shown and looks at a printout of text messages between Casey and him.) He says it is a fair and accurate reflection of the texts. He is permitted to read the texts aloud.

Casey texted: I am so sorry for not telling you what happened and we obviously need to talk. I need you and love you more than you know.
Tony texted: Where is Caylee?
Casey texted: I honestly do not know.
Tony texted: I don't know… are you serious?
Casey texted: I've been filling out reports all night and driving around with multiple officers looking at old apartments. I'm the worst fucking mother in the world. I don't know what I will do if something happens to her. Too long let's just leave it at that.
Tony texted: Why would you lie to me of all people? I was your boyfriend who cares about you and your daughter. It doesn't make sense to me. Why would you lie to me thinking she was fine with your nanny?
Casey texted: I lied to everyone. What was I supposed to say? I trusted my daughter with some psycho. How does that look?
Tony texted: I don't know what to say. I hope your daughter is okay and I am going to do everything I can to help your family and cops.
Casey texted: They handcuffed me for ten minutes and I sat in the back of a cop car. The best thing and the most important person in my life is missing and God knows if I am ever going to see her again. I am the dumbest person and the worse mother. The most important thing is getting Caylee back. I will never forgive myself and nor will my family. I am the dumbest person and the worst mother. I honestly hate myself.

Tony texted: Who is Zanny the nanny?

Casey texted: Someone I met through a mutual friend four years ago. She used to be my buddy's nanny. I'm scared.

Tony texted: Are you home?

Casey texted: Yes, almost twelve hours of stuff, finally getting a shower. I feel like hell.

Tony texted: Where did you drop off Caylee the last time you saw her?

Casey texted: At the apartment, bottom of the stairs.

Tony texted: Where?

Casey Texted: Sawgrass Apartments. Have told and shown police the apartment. Told them and drove out with two different officers. If they don't find her guess who gets blamed and spends eternity in jail?

Tony texted: No shit! Why didn't you say something to anyone earlier? Why are you texting and not calling?

Casey texted: I talked to two people who have been directly connected to the nanny. I was scared something was going to happen to my baby. I was upset and angry.

(Tony testifies that he called Casey and asked where Caylee was.) Casey told me she did not know. Tony states that he was angry, felt lied to, betrayed, and it is hard to explain. I asked her, how do you not know where your daughter is. She told me, I just do not know. I was very irritated. I said I had to go to class and hung up. I was getting nowhere with Casey.

Baez continues to question Tony; Baez says that this conversation is pretty bare and a slap in the face on your reality and Casey's reality. In the messages she acts if Caylee is alive and she blames herself for hurting you and concerning for family. In these text messages, you basically do not know what is real and what is not. What happened and what did not. Lazzaro agreed. I did not know anything that was going on. He also agreed that the Blockbuster receipt was placed in the garbage, that the dumpster to his apartment is in the front of the apartment and that he walks or drives.

The State's Twenty-fourth Witness

Interpretation of Testimony - Cindy Anthony: She is Casey's mother and Caylee's grandmother. Our home address is 4937 Hopespring Drive. We've lived in Orange County since October of '89. My husband George, my son Lee, and daughter Casey moved from Ohio. Lee was six or seven and Casey was three or four when we moved here. I had to wait a month for my nursing license to be reset in Florida, so about November I started working. My parents had retired in '89 and George's parents moved back and forth, and we have a brother in Florida.

102

Lee went into school but Casey was too young. Hidden Oaks Middle School is where Casey went. They walked 5 minutes from my house to school. In 2005, I was blessed with a grandchild, the daughter of Casey. I found out on June 30th, 2005. Casey came to work at my quitting time and told me she had something to tell me. So we sat in the car and spoke.

We had been to a wedding about June 8th. We attended with Casey, and I had no suspicion until the day of the wedding. She has always had issues with her periods. Casey and I were always on the same cycle and we both spotted and had a belly from the symptoms.

Casey's face started getting a little fat, and I thought the sedentary work at her new position at Universal Studios was the cause. I think she gained fifteen or eighteen pounds total. We were not hiding it and when she told me, we came home and told the whole family including Lee and Casey's grandparents. We told her we would continue to help and take care of her and the child. That same day, June 30th, we took her shopping for maturity clothes and turned the computer room into the nursery. She was six to seven months along. Casey had already had a Winnie the Pooh bear, and Casey was a fan. So, it was a no-brainer to do a Winnie the Pooh theme. These are photos of Caylee's bed. (Cindy is very upset and in tears seeing this photo.) This photo is one of Caylee's bears; she had many. (The Pooh theme was throughout the room. The baby blanket, sheets, and curtains, all were Winnie the Pooh. Casey is emotionless during this testimony and her mother is in tears.)

This is a diagram of our house, and the nursery is next to Lee's bedroom. Lee was still home at the time. Now Lee's room is just a spare bedroom. Casey's room is next to the nursery as well. The master bedroom is on the other side of the nursery. There is no significance to the locations of rooms; that is just the way it worked out. You can get to the back yard from the kitchen, living room, and master bedroom. We have locks on the sliding glass doors. We keep the doors locked all the time. We do not use the front door, we have triple locks, and unless someone came to the front door, we would not use it. We use our garage to enter and exit.

This is an aerial view of our home from the air as it is today. Since 2008, we now have no grass in the front; last fall we took the grass out. We have been unable to grow grass, so pavers and cement were put in. Out of frustration, George and I did cosmetic changes. In 2008, we had grass and now we have pavers and bark chips and an area for the dogs. The back is completely fenced. Through the gate, there is a complete privacy fenced back yard. The fence is five feet tall. You can enter the back yard on the side of the house, but the gate is locked. The inside has a latch and padlock. Caylee's playhouse is in the photo. Also, our aboveground swimming pool. We have had it since 2002. It is about 4 feet high, at least. This is a photo of the front of the house in 2008. (We see that Cindy is truly upset at seeing the photos of Caylee's playhouse and more in the back yard. Now, Casey is wiping tears, twenty minutes into this.)

Lee and I purchased the playhouse. We all had looked at it, and we were fitting it into our budget. (A photo is presented that shows the inside of the home; it is lovely and well-kept, with glass doors to a screened patio.) The lock is a latch that goes up and down. You flip the lock up and down and then there is a screen door to the yard. (Cindy continues describing the screen doors, how they are kept open or closed, depending on their use, and whether it is summer and the air conditioning is on.) On a cool day, we would leave the door open with the screen. There is a lock on the screen but we do not use it. Once out the sliding door there is are two doors in the screened area and they have locks on the handles. Those locks are at my hip or waist in height. There are three sets of sliding doors in house. All have the same locks. The master bedroom enters to the screen porch as well. The living room is the main door we use to access the back yard.

We childproofed the house. Casey purchased doorknob devices that are hard to turn even for me, and rearranged things for safety. In June, 2008, Caylee was 34 months old and very mobile. She slept most of the time in Casey's room and napped in her own room. She was very verbal, speaking in paragraphs I could understand. She lived with me from the time she was born. Casey always lived with us as well. Lee lived with us and moved out later.

Caylee was home almost every day. I do not think I went more than 24 hours without seeing her. In June, 2008… I usually take my birthday week off. So I took the entire week of my birthday off. I spent some time with Caylee, not as much as I wanted. On Father's Day, 2008, I had Caylee. George was working and the kids had plans, so I took Caylee to see my father at the nursing home. Casey was working and Lee was already out on his own. I went to Mount Dora with Caylee from the morning, about 11:30, until 3:00 pm. I took photos and video of Caylee.

The photo that is showing is our Caylee at the nursing home. It is a fair representation of Caylee. The coloring books are items I brought with me for Caylee that day. She was over 3 feet tall, above my waist, and about thirty pounds. She was a little hard to carry. We went to visit my mom at her home when we left the nursing home. We arrived before five o'clock back at our home. It was just Caylee and me. We put our things away, and I told her she needed to eat and then she could go swimming.

There is a ladder and you need to attach it to climb into the pool. Part of it is attached with bolts, and the steps are attached to that. There is a detachable ladder to get in. We took the exterior ladder off as Caylee became a toddler, and we kept the ladder off and put it on when we wanted to swim. It is chest high to get into the pool for me. The detachable ladder is taller than me. It is a heavy ladder, and a small child could not lift it.

On June 15th, 2008 I put the ladder on the pool and then she could climb the steps. I would stand behind and make her sit on the platform and then she would wait until I got in and then jump into my arms. I held her because I did not want her to fall from the ladder. We were in the pool for at least an hour. She had on a life jacket we put on over her swimsuit. Casey came home, but did not get in the pool. We took Caylee in the house. I told Caylee she had enough swimming. Casey came out with a towel. I took Caylee's suit and life jacket off and handed her to Casey in a towel. I took the ladder off and placed it on the side of the pool, and then I got Caylee's bathing suit and lifejacket.

That evening was a very special and emotional evening. Hospice was called in for my father and I wanted to document that day. I told Casey about the pictures and videos. I was excited to show Casey, and so the three of us sat at the computer and watched the video and photos and we cried. Caylee did not understand why. It was special. We thought it would be the last time we would see my dad and Casey's grandfather.

George returned after Casey, Caylee, and I went to bed. On Monday, I had to go to work early and left about seven that morning. After June 15th, 2008, I never saw Caylee again. When I left that day, I believed Caylee to be in the house. I believed Casey had a job at Universal Studios as an event coordinator. Her hours were sometimes during the day and mostly evenings, she told me. I saw her neck lanyard identification badge, and text messages and e-mails from her boss.

Sometimes the identification badges had names other than Casey's on them, and Casey said the employees switched for fun. I had seen Casey at work before, before Caylee was born. I believed that Casey went back to work at Universal Studios after Caylee's birth. I continued to believe she worked, all the way to July, 2008. Casey was not employed for a few months there, but then she went back to work, I believed. E-mails from Hard Rock Café came to her and she said she had a relationship and they were from a supervisor. Casey printed and showed me the e-mails in 2008.

I watched Caylee. It depended on the day of the week. I would be the babysitter, or George would. George would watch her if Casey and I wanted to do something. On June 16th, 2008, I believed she had a baby sitter. I believed it was Zanny, a friend of Casey. She was one of the primary people she would leave Caylee with, I believed. Casey had talked about Zanny since 2006. Someone at work had offered to be a fill-in if she needed a babysitter. Jeff Hopkins and Zanny were associated. (Cindy made a request to take the photo of Caylee off the screen. The prosecutor hadn't realized it was still up, he said. He removed the photo from the projector.)

I believed Lauren Gibbs was one of Casey's best friends at that time. I know her, have met her, and I knew where she lived. Zanny I never met, I've never seen a picture, and I have no knowledge of where she lives. Casey said there were different places Zanny lived. Casey had described them. Zanny moved around quite frequently. I never had a need to go get Caylee from her. Casey did not have to pay anything at home, but she pitched in with laundry, cleaning, cooking. No money, but pitching in. I was more lenient with Lee.

Some days Casey would come to my office and she would be fully dressed or have clothes in the car for work. I never ever found Zanny, even after we looked for her. I looked for her from July 15th, 2008 until about six weeks ago.

On June 16th, 2008, I left for work and worked a normal shift. I talked with Casey throughout the day. We left messages. I think we had a brief conversation about 4:00 PM. She said she was going to spend the night at Zanny's. She was going to take Caylee to Zanny and she would just stay there too, and she had late meetings. So it made sense. Mondays can be bad for me, and my husband was working three to eleven. I could have watched Caylee later, but it made sense to let her stay with Zanny and Casey. I expected her to return on June 17th.

On June 17th, 2008, they were in a lot of meetings and negotiations at Universal, and Caylee and Casey stayed at Zanny's again.

On June 18th, part of the day I expected them home. Then Casey called and the Hard Rock negotiations were going to take Casey and Caylee to Tampa. Zanny was going along and taking Caylee to Busch Gardens with Juliette and her daughter, Annabelle. She thought they might come home Saturday evening June 21st. I talked to her once or twice every day, we always checked in with each other. I asked to speak to Caylee, but there was always a reason Caylee was not with Casey. She was at work and Caylee was with Zanny or at Busch Gardens. Casey told me work ran over and they were going to stay a day longer. She would be home Sunday or Monday.

On June 23rd, No Caylee and Casey, and I waited all day at work to hear they were home safe. I called and left messages, "Are you home yet?" I talked to a co-worker and said I was worried that they were not home from Tampa.

Casey called and said there was an accident, they were following Zanny's car and Zanny had an accident. Therefore she had been at the hospital all day with her. Casey and Caylee were fine; just Zanny's car was involved in the accident. I asked to talk to Caylee and Casey told me Juliette took Caylee and Annabelle to walk around and Casey was in the emergency room with Zanny.

On June 24th, I remember a break-in of the shed and George calling me before he called the police. I told Casey on June 24th. I spoke with Casey to find out what their plans were and how Zanny was. I told her in casual conversation about the break-in. I thought it lightened the day. I learned later that my husband had seen Casey on June 24th at the house.

I talked to Casey and told her I thought she was in Tampa. Zanny did not have any insurance information and Casey said she had volunteered to drive back to get her documents. She told me she slipped home to get some things. I asked why she did not bring Caylee back. I would have taken off from work. She said it did not occur to her. She said that she had taken the gas cans to Tampa and that she thought something was wrong with her car's gas gauge and wanted to have them on hand.

I asked her why she had to take care of Zanny, and she said Zanny had a sick mother and no family to take care of her. Casey felt obliged and wanted Caylee close to her. I missed Caylee from the first day and I was really missing her by now, so I began sleeping with her teddy bear. I missed them because Caylee and I or Caylee, Casey and I would cuddle up at night together. (There is an objection, followed by a sidebar.)

A few days later, I found Caylee's teddy bear that I was sleeping with was missing. It was after 4 or 5 nights. I think I told about it after all this happened in mid-July.

June 25th, 26th, and 27th, I do not see Caylee or Casey. The situation did not get resolved on the 27th, and Zanny had a concussion and was bleeding. They were going to stay at a hotel at the Hard Rock and come home on Friday. On June 27th, I was hoping she would surprise me at work with Caylee. That did not happen. Sometime in the early afternoon, they had gotten back and she was called into work for a few hours. I was to see them at home later that evening. Casey called later that day and said that her friend Jeffery and she had begun dating again. Casey still liked him a lot. She was going to see Jeffery and his son and I am just the granny, so that was that.

I have never met Jeff or his son. We were supposed to meet them many times, but it never happened. We were supposed to meet Jeffery's mom and son Zack at the mall for Santa. Caylee, Casey and I ended up the only ones there. Zack supposedly had an asthma attack and could not make it.

So, Casey was meeting Jeffery and Zack with Caylee, and then coming home. She did not do that. My impression was Jeffery was well off and he had a suite, so she was staying a few days. From Casey's description of him, he seemed stable, and Casey is a grown woman and I had no control over Casey or her daughter Caylee. I was not interfering with her life.

On June 30th through the 4th, I was on vacation again. That weekend before my vacation, I expected she would come home and get clothes. George and I spent the weekends together. I was not sitting home waiting for my daughter and granddaughter to come home. I had daily communication with Casey. I thought I knew where she was. I believe she was headed back to work on Monday, and I was expecting to watch Caylee on my vacation. I cannot remember what excuse Casey gave me. I told her I would watch Caylee that week while I was off from work.

Casey was working on events that were set up for kids and sometimes the Make a Wish Foundation. So Casey wanted to keep Caylee for that event. I ask if I could come to the event, and she said no, it was by reservation only and Caylee would be watched by an organized group there. It was a pool party at Universal. Universal Studios is twenty to thirty minutes from our home.

On July 3rd, I decided to drive out to Universal. I had some issues and I wanted to talk to Casey and see Caylee at least one day of my vacation. Those were money issues to discuss with Casey. I left the bank and called Casey from Guest Services at Universal. Casey told me she was not there at Universal; she was in Jacksonville. That came as a complete surprise to me. She said that she took Caylee and followed Jeffery to his home to rekindle their relationship.

I was upset about 3 PM on July 3rd. I had no idea. I did not know what to think, and then I realized that she had been lying to me the last few days. I had my doubts she was in Jacksonville. I reached out to Ryan, a friend who was in Jacksonville, and thought maybe he could confirm she was in Jacksonville. Ryan thought she was coming to see him. So now I think she is in Jacksonville. At some point on July 3rd, I called Lee, and he had not spoken with her.

I opened an account on Myspace and posted a message to Casey. I was upset. I had never been on Myspace before and Lee had the impression from entries online that Casey was not in Jacksonville. Casey had mentioned that she would be in downtown Orlando on Myspace, and Lee said he would check and see if she was in town. I was upset, betrayed and I was just venting, and I posted and thought she would be the only one to read it. It was my way to say how she made me feel and I hoped that Casey would contact me. This photo was posted later the text date and time are correct. (There is an objection and a sidebar.) After I posted that message on Myspace, it was a few days before Casey called me. She said that she was mad because everybody saw it. I thought it was just between Casey and me. I still do not know how that works. We briefly discussed my posting. (There is another sidebar.)

We see that the courtroom is almost full again, and the spectators seem to be mostly women. The judge decides to break for the weekend. Cindy Anthony will return to the stand to resume her testimony on Tuesday, May 31st. The jury has communicated that it would like to work on Memorial Day, May 30th, but the judge explains that the cost of opening and staffing the courthouse just for this trial is too prohibitive, but that he has made plans for the jurors to be involved in activities on Memorial Day. Thus ends the first week of testimony in State v. Casey Anthony.

Linda Drane Burdick, representing the prosecution, gave her general theory of the case in opening statements, as we have summarized. On Friday, March 21st, 2008, between the hours of 2:16 and 2:28 p.m., Google searches were conducted for how to make chloroform, how to make chloroform with a different spellings, self-defense, household weapons, neck breaking and shovel. There were also, Wikipedia searches for the words inhalation, chloroform, acetone, peroxide, hydrogen peroxide and death.

Jose Baez, attorney for the Defense, followed with their theory of the case in opening statements as we have summarized. This child (Casey Anthony) at 8 years old learned to lie immediately. She could be 13 years old, have her father's penis in her mouth and then go to school and play with other kids as if nothing ever happened. Nothing's wrong. That will help you understand why no one knew that her child was dead.

Chapter 10

THE STATE'S CASE IN CHIEF - WEEK TWO

May 31st, 2011

Caylee Anthony's manner and cause of death is listed as Homicide by Undetermined Means. The media provides blogs and tweets with continuous minute-by-minute coverage of this case. This is a sample of what they say.

Blog postings:
- I think she was more than jealous of the love Caylee had for Cindy.
- So far we know Lee and Cindy will take the stand, who else?
- You get front row seat to see Casey die.
- They say Baez does not look good at the state bar they have files of complaints against him. (However after your writers checked this for truth at the Florida Bar website, we see no disciplinary history at this time; it's likely just blog talk.)

- Baez and his team have body guards when they walk into court.
- Like to see Casey in the slow speed chase on the freeway.
- Who thinks Baez objects to everything too much?
- The defense has no case… just trying to give her a trial and they know it… she is entitled to this and Baez knows he surely can't be stupid enough to get her off with all this testimony. He just needs media attention and it's not to his advantage.
- Justice for Caylee!
- I am glad we got to see this woman get the justice she deserves.
- Someone needs to file a complaint for Casey not paying taxes on all this defense money.
- I love it, Casey listening to all her lies.
- Baez and Casey did what they set out to do…take the focus off Caylee.
- Kill her.
- Where will we all go when the trial is over?

This atmosphere challenges the justice system to provide a fair trial. Those who listen to media personalities for coverage of hard news run the risk that the biases of those personalities become the biases of the listeners. The danger to the justice system is that listeners become jurors – jurors who have been infected and influenced by pre-trial publicity that is not necessarily factual, but opinion. Even when prospective or sitting jurors hear factual matters, those may be facts that are not trustworthy or reliable enough to be presented as evidence.

This case is being tried in the media, on most stations, magazines, newspapers, Facebook, blogs, tweets, and in video streamed on outlets as diverse as YouTube and ABC. Opinions about this case range from mild dislike of Casey Anthony or her lawyers to pure venomous hatred of the defendant and the defense. In the modern court room, the evidence includes text messages, tweets, videos, blogs, cell phone messages, cell phone tower pings, hard drives, SIM cards, Google, computer search histories, Wikipedia, 48 Hours, Nancy Grace, Dr. G, Geraldo Rivera, and more. Welcome to the brave new world of the justice system. The thing that stands out the most to us is that the media coverage is reasonably true to the testimony, although some of the commentators put their own spin on the evidence. Sometimes, there are only a few words added for media zing. However, in many cases, a few words change the content of the evidence and statements completely. We thought you should hear just a few words of our ponderings.

Casey's brother, Lee Anthony, has filed a motion to be present in the courtroom during all testimony, just as his parents have done. The sequestration rule, designed to insure the integrity of a witness's testimony, must be weighed against the victim's (in this instance, Uncle Lee's) statutory right to be in the courtroom under Florida law. In a previous ruling, the judge has sided with Cindy and George Anthony, as grandparent victims and allowed them to be in the courtroom prior to giving their courtroom testimony. The judge stated that their testimony was taken many times in depositions and is written, therefore the possibility of taint is less. Casey has just entered with a new mauve top and her bangs down to play with again today.

The judge takes the bench for motions. He addresses Mr. Mason by saying that bench conferences are all public record and he can get a transcript. Judge: Mr. Lippman (attorney for George, Cindy, and Lee Anthony), you may proceed. (Mr. Lippman argues the same motion regarding Lee Anthony's presence in the courtroom that he did for George and Cindy Anthony.) The judge inquires: Mr. Mason, have you deposed Lee Anthony? Mason replies that the defense has not. The judge announces, "The defense opted not to take his deposition and prosecution chose to take his deposition. The defense was present when the prosecution took Lee Anthony's deposition. Mr. Lee Anthony has also given written statements to the police." The state announces that it does not object to Lee Anthony being granted an exception to the rule of sequestration.

Mr. Mason for the defense *does* object with a witty argument: "There is a presumption that the legislators know what they are writing when they do it" (which provokes a hearty laugh from everyone in the courtroom). "However, in good faith, I believe that there is a case where an uncle of a victim was shown to be next of kin. However, at some point it has to stop. What about cousins, or Mr. Lee Anthony's fiancée? We have already seen an impact from George Anthony being in this courtroom and hearing witnesses before he testified. A line has to be drawn somewhere. In my humble opinion, it should have been drawn before with Cindy and George Anthony not being allowed in this courtroom. I cite the cases of Avis, Gore and Rose as **case law**. We strongly object." The lawyer in the family calls this the 'slippery slope' argument, or sometimes, the 'parade of horribles'. (Case law is appellate court decisions. Cases are cited by the name of one or both the parties involved. Case law is **controlling** if it is from an appellate court that has direct supervision over the trial court where the case is being cited or **persuasive** if it is from any other court.) We love the old school lawyer in this house. These lawyers are usually from the days of honorable advocates in the court, although a very few are the most evil of dragons. With Mr. Mason, we are pleased to say we see the former and not the latter. Great argument Mr. Mason, but we think the judge will follow his previous ruling involving George and Cindy and let Lee Anthony in the courtroom.

Judge Perry continues: As to the coloring of Lee Anthony's testimony, when Lee Anthony's deposition was taken, Mr. Baez and other attorneys were there. Mr. Baez cross-examined him in the deposition, although I see it was not that long of a cross-examination. "Has Casey ever told you she killed Caylee? No. She never told you Caylee died by accident? No." That appears to be the entire cross-examination that was done. What testimony do you think will be colored, Mr. Mason? What happened the night the police came? Mason replied that he does not know what the prosecution is going to ask the witnesses. (Attorney Lippman has cited a case to the judge in which a blood relative, a brother, was included in the immediate family for an exception to sequestration. Based on that and the fact that the judge has already allowed the victim's grandparents in the courtroom, the judge rules that there is no evidence to suggest that Lee Anthony's testimony will be colored, so he is exempt from sequestration.)

The ruling of Judge Perry to allow the rule of sequestration to be waived for George, Cindy, and now Lee Anthony may be the very mistake that gets this case overturned in a higher court. It is the one ruling that we all strongly disagree with. All three are critical, central witnesses for the State in its prosecution of Casey Anthony, and now all three are free to hear all court proceedings. Depending on how far Judge Perry's order can be stretched, they may also be free to talk among themselves about the case, coordinate their stories, and watch as much infotainment coverage as they can stomach. We believe the judge already opened the door with the ruling that Cindy and George could be in the courtroom, and he has now followed his own ruling with Lee Anthony. Perhaps Mr. Mason could have added to his argument that the defendant's ability to effectively confront and cross-examine other witnesses is being chilled by defense counsel's realization that the Anthony's will hear answers and therefore adjust their future testimony, as it seems that each will be recalled numerous times during the trial. We're just saying Mr. Mason, next time you might add this one into the mix…

Judge Perry also rules in on **in camera review** issue. (An in camera review involves the judge reviewing documents that are reviewable by the judge but that are unavailable to one or both parties.) This involves the defense's request for the judge to unseal a transcript of the grand jury testimony of George Anthony and give it to the defense for use in cross-examination. Since grand jury proceeding are secret, grand jury records are not public records, and may only be reviewed by court order. The judge reviewed the grand jury transcript in camera, and he has decided it is the same as the trial testimony given by George Anthony. Therefore, the judge chooses to keep the testimony sealed.

Judge Perry grants a request from Baez: **Permission to lead** the witness in this delicate area. (Permission to lead means to feed information to the witness and then let them answer. A question like, 'Who did you see?' becomes, "Did you see Casey at the car?' when it is a leading question. It is an odd request, since **cross-examination** is generally a series of leading questions. Cross-examination is questioning of a witness called by the other party; direct examination is questioning by the party who called the witness to testify. Direct examination seldom can be leading, but cross-examination usually is.

The State's Twenty-forth Witness

Interpretation of Testimony – Cindy Anthony (cont. from May 29th): (Prosecutor Burdick resumes the questioning of Cindy Anthony.) On the evening of July 3rd, 2008, I posted on Myspace. I discussed the post with Casey in the following day or so. When I posted that Caylee was missing, I was speaking metaphorically, because I hadn't been able to see my granddaughter. I still believed that Caylee was with Casey and fine. I was feeling that Casey had betrayed me by just taking off with Caylee after years of George and me caring for both. Casey told me she just needed some time away, that she was seeing Jeff again and it just kindled old feelings. Casey also told me that I was going to have deal with Caylee and her moving out at some point, and that I needed to adjust to that. I realized that I was being selfish about demanding so much of Casey's and Caylee's time and attention, and that I needed to give them some space.

When I posted on Myspace, I was expressing just an overall feeling of betrayal. Casey's ex-fiancé had told

114

me that Casey was jealous of me and when I confronted her with that, Casey denied it. I tried to discuss Casey's leaving with Caylee without warning, to no avail. I thought writing my feelings down would have more of an impact on Casey. After posting the comment, I realized the posting did not go only to Casey, but to others. I had never used Myspace before. Next, I decided to learn to text so I could keep in touch with Casey and ask to talk to Caylee. I was told at various times that Caylee was napping or at the beach with Jeff's mother and son, or various places, so I still wasn't able to talk to my granddaughter.

I expected that after the weekend, Casey and Caylee would return from Jacksonville. When that time arrived, Casey called me and told me that the car was broken down. Then it turned into Monday or Tuesday that they would be home. Since I knew the car needed a brake job, I believed Casey again. George was asking me every day about Casey and Caylee. I told George that I had talked to Casey, and just to leave her be. She needed some space. Next, I received a text that Jeff's mother had cancer and was going to get married quickly, and it would be a few more days. Then it was, they were loading the car and would be home soon. They were going to caravan back in separate cars with Jeff.

Within another day or two, George and I were outside the house weeding in the yard. I noticed that there was a postal notice taped to the glass window of our front door. It was hard to see the notice because the house is peach and we get the afternoon sun, so the notice blended in. As I moved closer, I could see the notice. I think that it was put there Thursday or Friday, and this was Sunday. But we used the garage door to enter and exit the house, not the front door. I saw it was about a certified letter from Johnson's, and we had no idea who that was. George decided he was going to pick it up on Monday. George was just starting a new job on that Monday. I was expecting Casey and Jeff in the afternoon, and George was scheduled to work a three-to-eleven shift. George went to pick up the letter about lunchtime on July 15th. He called me from the post office and told me Casey's car was in Orlando, not Jacksonville, and it had been towed. I called Casey and told her that she had a lot of explaining to do; that her car had been towed from a parking lot and had been in the tow yard a couple weeks.

Casey told me she needed to get home to talk this out. George went to the tow yard and they told him it was nearly $500, and that they needed both George and me present to pick up the car. So, I went to the bank to get cash and then met George at the house. Together, we went back and picked up the car from the tow yard. I did not have access to the car at the yard. I was at the office taking care of details, and then I waited for George, who was getting the car with the tow person. I went back to my car. I was near Casey's car when George drove up, but it had started to rain, so George suggested we get the car home. He told me that the car stinks. I followed George home in my car. George pulled Casey's car into the garage. Once the car was in the garage, I went up to the car and said, "Oh my God, what is wrong with the car? It smells like something died in it." George told me they had to throw garbage out that was in the trunk. We opened the car and George took the battery out; we were afraid that Casey would come home, take the car, and we would not be able to talk to her. We opened the trunk and all the doors to air the car. I saw Caylee's favorite doll and backpack, so I took them out along with Casey's work purse, slacks, and maybe some more things. I told George to go to work at his new job.

All of the items smelled like the car. I sat them down in the garage on the dryer, and went to get a Clorox wipe. I wiped the doll's face, and then sprayed the doll's body and the car with Febreze. The smell in the car was like something I had smelled before. I just took what George said about garbage being the source. I'm a nurse; I work with amputees and I've smelled rotting flesh before. However, at that point I did not consider the possibility that someone had actually died in the car. I was in the garage with George most of the time, until he got his things and left for work. (Photos with views from all sides of the Pontiac Sunfire are placed in evidence. Cindy acknowledges that they are fair and accurate depictions of the car on July 15th, 2008.) It was the car we got back from the tow yard, minus what we took out to clean. A steak knife from our house was on the car seat, and it is missing on the photo. (A sidebar occurs. The judge orders the jury to disregard the testimony that one of Cindy's steak knives was missing in the photo. It appears Cindy found and removed the knife. That is what the sidebar was about. The photo that is already in evidence shows the back seat.)

(They are talking about missing items that Cindy took out.) I took slacks from the back seat; they had the same odor, so I put them in the laundry in the garage. I also put a dryer sheet in the back seat because of the smell. (The prosecutor uses Cindy's deposition to show that she gave an inconsistent statement in deposition in July, and to refresh her recollection.) At that time, I could not remember. (There is another sidebar. Meanwhile, Cindy is reading her deposition.) I made the statement that I did not know if I put the dryer sheet in the car, and I was under medication. Since then I have had flashbacks. I said I did not know of a reason I put the dryer sheet in the car. I was medicated, tired and more, at the time and you knew that. I remember you asking if I could go forward with the deposition and I told you yes, it was the best you were going to get from me.

(Another photo is presented; it is the bin from the trunk of Casey's car with the doll, purse, and other items that were turned over to the sheriff.) I went through the purse and found a yellow envelope and found a résumé of Amy Huizenga and Amy's identification. I looked through the back pack, but that's all. (A photo of Caylee's back pack is introduced.) I took out Caylee's toothbrush. Then I put it back. The backpack was in the trunk on the floor, I believe. The bin was in the back, as well. It had hangers in it. I did not vacuum the trunk. I sprayed Febreze and maybe used my hand to brush some debris away. I went back to work and I left the car with all the doors, trunk, and sunroof open, but closed the garage door. I was there about one or two hours all together. I tried to call Casey, but I could not reach her. Everybody knows I do not leave work in the middle of the day. I went to my desk and spoke to a couple of my coworkers about the car and Casey. My supervisor told me to go home and I told him I needed to get some things done on my Coumadin levels. Then my director told me to just go and they would handle it. They knew; we talk about family and they all knew about Caylee and that I did not get to see her over my vacation. I told them that the car smelled really bad and I told them it smelled like something died, but George found garbage. I went home and tried to contact Casey, but there was no answer. That is when I went through the purse and thought that Casey having Amy's information was strange. I knew Casey was lying, so I contacted Amy. I made arrangements to pick Amy up from the Florida Mall where she was and asked her to take me to Casey. She explained that she had seen Casey. Casey had picked her up from the airport. She knew where Casey was. I drove, and she directed me to an apartment complex, to Anthony Lazzaro's apartment.

I was surprised that Amy knew exactly where to go. I followed her up the apartment stairs. We decided that Amy would go to the door and I would stay in the hallway so Casey would come to the door. When the door opened I heard Casey's voice, and Amy asked her to step out. Casey did and I asked her to come with me; we needed to talk. I asked where Caylee was and she said she was with the nanny. I stepped up and smelled cigarette smoke, and knew

Caylee would not be there. By then, Amy realized I was pretty upset, and she went back to my car. Casey reluctantly agreed to come with me but she did not grab any belongings. She said that she was coming back. I told her not until we resolved some things and I saw Caylee.

Casey, Amy and I got in the car. I questioned Casey about Caylee. With Amy in the car, it was not the time to talk to Casey, and then Amy was dropped off. Before we pulled away I said, I need some answers and Casey said she would take me to Caylee. Then she decided it would not be a good time. She asked me to take her back to Anthony Lazzaro's and I said that she was not going anywhere until I got some answers. I saw a police station and told her if she was not going to give me answers about where Caylee was then I would get someone to help me get them. Then I realized that Substation One was closed. I got back in the car and told Casey this was her last chance to tell me and she did not, so I called 911 at that time. (There is a sidebar.) (The jury is given a morning recess.)

The judge presents additional video and DVDs for the State and defense. He wants them to look at these and give him a response on them. As we watch Cindy and George Anthony, they look like they are being thrown to the lions. We believe this. Cindy was probably controlling and wanted to raise her granddaughter. George was probably militant, being a former detective, and the home was filled with its share of marital discord. That said, Casey Anthony paid nothing to live, eat, or for most of her childcare. Prior to 2008, she was spending the night with boyfriends and partying. She was not being controlled or even made to stay home and take care of her child. If she did not like it, all she had to do was get a job and move out. The issues of Casey Anthony are much deeper than environment; they are deep in her DNA, in our opinion. However, she is far from insane; Casey is selfish. They talk about the recordings of the 911 calls by Cindy Anthony. In July, they had a hearing on the admissibility of the 911 calls and they were ruled admissible based on the prosecution's argument that they were excited utterances. (The jury is still in recess.)

The judge discusses giving a **limiting instruction** to the jury. (Essentially, a limiting instruction says that evidence is to be considered by the jury only for one purpose, but not for others.) The evidence you are about to hear is to be viewed to be excited utterances and the state of mind of Cindy Anthony. Prosecution, the limiting instructions only apply to the first two 911 calls and the third does not need a limitation. The Judge says the conversation about the stolen car and theft of money by Casey referred to in the 911 calls by Cindy are criminal acts that Casey is not being tried for in this case, and are not to be considered by the jury. The 911 calls will have the limiting instructions to the criminal acts. They will be played with text on top of them for the jury to hear and read the words said on the call. (After a recess, court resumes with the jury.)

The judge reads a stipulation between the parties to the jury. On July 15th, 2008, Cindy Anthony called 911 in Orlando. They are fair and accurate representation of the calls. He then tells the jury that, regarding the first and second calls to 911, the evidence you are about to receive in the first two 911 calls is to be only considered by you as it relates to Cindy Anthony's state of mind and as spontaneous utterances. The defendant is not on trial for any crime or wrongful acts not included in the indictment such as a stolen car or a bank account.

(**First 911 call**)
Cindy (extremely upset): I drove to a police department and it is closed. I need to bring in someone the car and I need to bring them in. I need to bring her in for grand theft of my car and money. I have an affidavit from my bank and I want to press charges and I live in Orlando on Hopespring Drive.
Operator: That is the Sheriff's Department's jurisdiction, and I will transfer you.
Cindy: Is the Sheriff open?
Operator: I am transferring you. (*Cindy can be heard talking to Casey during the 911 call.*)
Cindy to Casey: The thing is, we will have a court order to get Caylee! I am not giving you another day, Casey! I have given you a month!

Cindy Anthony's testimony continues: I did not stay there at the station. They told me to go home or go to the side of the road and call. I did not call George or Lee at that time. I went back to my home as I was almost there. Lee called and he said his dad had called him… that something was wrong. Lee was already at the house when I pulled into the driveway. Casey jumped out of the car and ran in past Lee. Lee followed Casey into the house and I followed them. I explained to Lee that I need some answers from Casey. I needed help. I needed her to take me to Caylee. Lee thought if we sat down we could get answers. I wanted to call the police. We were all together in Casey's room and the hallway. I continued to insist that she take me to Caylee. Casey kept saying no, that Caylee was sleeping. I did not care; I wanted to get Caylee even if it meant I would stay home from work the following day, because Caylee needed to be cared for. Lee kept trying to reason with his sister, but it was no use. I called 911 again.

(**First 911 call from home**) (Cindy gave the operator her address on Hopespring Drive)
Dispatch: 911, (inaudible) what's happening?
Cindy(agitated): Umm…I have someone here, umm, that I need to, umm, be arrested, in my home.
Dispatch: They're there right now?
Cindy: And I have a possible missing child. I have a three-year-old that's been missing for a month.
Dispatch: A three-year-old?
Cindy: Yes.
Dispatch: Have you reported that?
Cindy: I'm trying to do that now, ma'am.
Dispatch: Okay, what did the person do that you need arrested?
Cindy: My daughter.
Dispatch: For what?
Cindy: For stealing an auto and stealing money. I already spoke with someone, they said they would patch me through the Orlando, umm, Sheriff's Department… have a deputy here. I was in the car, I was going to drive her to the police station and no one's open. They said they would bring a deputy to my home, when I got home to call them.
Dispatch: So she stole your vehicle?
Cindy: Yes.
Dispatch: When did she do that?
Cindy: Umm on the 30th. I just got it back from the impound. I'd like to speak to an officer. Can you have someone come out to my house?
Dispatch: Okay, okay. I have to ask you these questions so I can put them in the call, okay?
Cindy: Okay.
Dispatch: The 30th of June?
Cindy: Yes
Dispatch: Okay, how old is your daughter?
Cindy: 22.
Dispatch: Okay, what's her name?
Cindy: My name?
Dispatch: Her name.
Cindy: Her name's Casey Marie Anthony
Dispatch: And you said you have this vehicle back?
Cindy: Yes. And I have the umm statements.
Dispatch: She's there right now?
Cindy: Yes I got her. I finally found her after a month. She's been missing for a month. I found her, but we can't find my granddaughter.
Dispatch: How tall is she?
Cindy: Umm, five foot one and a half.
Dispatch: Thin, medium or heavy-built?

Cindy: Thin.
Dispatch: Color hair?
Cindy: Brown.
Dispatch: What color uh shirt is she wearing?
Cindy: White.
Dispatch: What color pants?
Cindy: Oh, they're shorts. There umm, plaid. They're like pink and teal and white and black. Plaid.
Dispatch: Does she have any weapons on her?
Cindy: No.
Dispatch: Is she not telling you where her daughter is?
Cindy: Correct.
Dispatch: Okay, we'll have a deputy out to you as soon as one is available. Okay?
Cindy: Thank you.
Dispatch: Thank you.
Dispatch: Bye.
Cindy: Bye.
(Call ended)

Cindy Anthony's testimony continues: The car is the Sunfire and Casey had permission to have the car. The police arriving seemed like it was taking forever. I popped into the hallway and watched for the police. I was getting more and more upset. Lee was in the room with Casey. Casey was on her bed and Lee was leaning up against the dresser. I heard Casey on the floor crying and that Caylee had been gone for 31 days. Zanny the nanny had taken her. I lost it! I started yelling at Casey what do you mean she has been gone for 31 days? I swore at her and hit the dresser. I ran out and called the police again.

(Second 911 Call from home)
Dispatch: 911, what's your emergency?
Cindy(nearly hysterical): I called a little bit ago. The deputy sheriff's not here. I found out my granddaughter has been taken! She's has been missing for a month! Her mother finally admitted she's been missing.
Dispatch: Okay. What is… What is…
Cindy: (inaudible) someone here now.
Dispatch: Okay. What's the address you're calling from?
Cindy: We're talking about a three year old little girl. My daughter finally admitted that the babysitter stole her. I need to find her.
Dispatch: Your daughter admitted that the baby is where?
Cindy: That the babysitter took her a month ago. That my daughter's been looking for her. I told you my daughter was missing for a month. I just found her today. But I can't find my granddaughter. She just admitted to me that she's been trying to find her herself. (pause) There's

something wrong. I found my daughter's car today and it smells like there's been a dead body in the damn car.

Dispatch: Okay. What is the three-year-old's name?

Cindy: Caylee. C-A-Y-L-E-E Anthony.

Dispatch: Caylee Anthony?

Cindy: Yes.

Dispatch: Okay. Is she white, black or Hispanic?

Cindy: She's white.

Dispatch: How long has she been missing for?

Cindy: I have not seen her since the 7th of June.

Dispatch: What is her date of birth?

(George returns from work during this call, and Cindy can be heard talking to him.)

Cindy to George: Umm. 8… 8-9-200… Oh God, she's 3. She's 2005. George, Caylee's missing.

George: What?!

Cindy to George: Caylee's missing! Casey says Zanny took her a month ago. (inaudible).

Dispatch: Okay. I need – um… I understand. Can you… Can you just calm down for me for just a minute. I need to know what's going on. Okay. I'm going to try and…

Cindy: (inaudible)

Dispatch: Is your – is your daughter there?

Cindy to George: I'm on the phone with them.

Dispatch: Is your daughter there?

Cindy: Yes.

Dispatch: Can I speak with her? Do you mind if I speak with her? Thank you.

Cindy: I called them two hours ago and they haven't gotten here. Casey finally admitted that Zanny took her a month ago and has been trying to find her.

Dispatch: Ma'am, ma'am.

Cindy: It's the Orange County Sheriff's Department. They want to talk to you. (inaudible) answer their questions.

Casey (calm): Hello.

Dispatch: Hello.

Casey: Yes.

Dispatch: Hi. What can you… can you tell me what's going on a little bit?

Casey: I'm sorry?

Dispatch: Can you tell me a little bit what's going on?

Casey: My daughter's been missing for the last 31 days.

Dispatch: And you know who has her?

Casey: I know who has her. I've tried to contact her. I actually received a phone call today. Now from a number that is no longer in service. I did get to speak to my daughter for about a moment. About a minute.

Dispatch: Okay, did you guys call and report a vehicle stolen?

Casey: Umm. Yes, my mom did.

Dispatch: Okay. So is the vehicle stolen too?

Casey: No. this is my vehicle.

Dispatch: What vehicle was stolen?
Casey: Umm, it's a 98 Pontiac Sunfire.
Dispatch: Okay, I have deputies on the way to you right now for that. So now your 3 year old daughter is missing? Caylee Anthony?
Casey: yes.
Dispatch: White female?
Casey: Yes. White female.
Dispatch: Three years old? 8-9-2005 is her date of birth?
Casey: Yes.
Dispatch: And you last saw her a month ago?
Casey: 31 days. It's been 31 days.
Dispatch: Who has her? Do you have a name?
Casey: Her name is Zenaida Fernandez-Gonzalez.
Dispatch: Who is that? Babysitter?
Casey: She's been my nanny for about a year and a half. Almost two years.
Dispatch: Why… why are you calling now? Why didn't you call 31 days ago?
Casey: I've been looking for her and have gone through other resources to try to find her, which was stupid.
Dispatch: Can you… can you give me the name of the baby… nanny again? Like spell it out for me?
Casey: Zenaida. Z-E-N-A-I-D-A.
Dispatch: Last name?
Casey: Fernandez.
Dispatch: Fernandez?
Casey: Hyphen Gonzalez. I think the officers are here.
Dispatch: The officers are there?
Casey: Yes.
Dispatch: Stay on the line.
(Call ends when the officer speaks.)

Cindy Anthony's testimony continues: On that call, you can hear I am addressing someone else. It was my husband George, and I saw George pull up and he got out of the car. His reaction was shock. Visibly, I could not see any more as I collapsed in his arms and George was trying to hold me up. The police arrive very shortly, within minutes after George arrived. Much later in the evening, I gave the police a written statement. When they first arrived, Casey was on the phone with 911 and then the call ended when the sheriff started talking to her in her room. I turned over the car and the items in it, in an attempt to locate my granddaughter. Later, I turned over the desktop computer. It was taken about July 17th, a few days later. I also turned over a laptop with the items from the car.

We gave them my laptop and other items that I believe the nanny might have touched, or things in Caylee's bag, to help find Caylee. I turned over my cell phone on one visit. So while at the sheriff's office, they took my phone and were trying to retrieve messages. I later gave samples of my DNA and hair in an attempt to find Caylee. I sat up a tip line to try to find Caylee. That was really my son trying to find Caylee. We set up a command center by our family in a Publix shopping center to try to find Caylee. Casey had been arrested on July 16th and we received a call from her.

The judge announces a stipulation to the jury that Casey Anthony made a recorded call from the jail to her home and the recording is a true and accurate record of that call.

(Call from Casey to her parents from jail)
Jail: Hello, free call from Casey, an inmate from the Orange County Jail. It is subject to monitoring and recording.
Cindy: Casey?
Casey: Mom, I just saw your nice little cameo on TV.
Cindy: Which one?
Casey: What do you mean which one?
Cindy: Which one? I did four different ones, and I haven't seen them all. I've only seen one or two so far.
Casey: You don't know what my involvement is in (inaudible)?
Cindy: No, I don't know what your involvement is, sweetheart. You are not telling me where she's at.
Casey: Because I don't fucking know where she's at. You are kidding me!
Cindy: Casey, don't waste your call screaming and hollering at me.
Casey: Waste my call sitting in the jail?
Cindy: Whose fault is it you're sitting in jail? Are you blaming me you are sitting in the jail? Blame yourself for telling lies. What do you mean it is not your fault? What do you mean it's not your fault, sweetheart? If you would have told them the truth, and not lied about everything…
Casey: Do me a favor and just tell me what Tony's number is. I don't want to talk to you. Forget it.
Cindy: I don't have his number.
Casey: Well, get it from Lee. I know Lee is at the house. I saw Mallory's car was out front. It was just on the news. They were just live outside the house.
Cindy: I know they were.
Casey: Well? Can you get Tony's number for me so I can call him?
Lee: Hello?
Casey: Hi. Can you get me Tony's number?
Lee: I can do that but I don't know what good it's going to do you at this point.

Casey: Well, I'd like to talk to him anyway because I called to talk to my mother and it is a fucking waste, by the way. I don't want any of you coming up here when I have my first hearing for bond and everything. I mean don't even fucking waste your time coming up here.

Lee: You know, you are having a real tough year and making it real tough for anybody to want to try to, even if it is giving…

Casey: See that is just it, every…

Lee: You are not even letting me finish.

Casey: Go ahead.

Lee: First, you are asking me for Tony's phone number so you can call him and then you immediately want to start pressing toward me and don't even worry about coming up here for all this stuff and trying to cut us out.

Casey: I'm not trying to cut anybody out.

Lee: I'm not going around and around with you. You know, that is pretty pointless. I'm not going to put everyone else through the same stuff that you've been putting the police and everybody else for the last 24 hours and the stuff you've been putting mom through for the last four or five weeks. I'm done with that. So, you can tell me what's going on. Kristina would love to talk to you because she thinks you will tell her what's going on. Frankly, we are going to find out, whatever is going on is going to be found out. So, why not do it now?

Casey: There is nothing to find out. Not even what I told the detectives. I have no clue where Caylee is. If I knew where Caylee was, do you think that any of this would be happening? No.

Lee: Anyway, you only have a couple of minutes with this so I'm not going to let you completely waste it. Here is Kristina.

Casey: No, no. I want Tony's number. I'm not talking to anybody else.

Kristina: Hello.

Casey: Hi. I'm glad everybody is at my house, but I'll have to call you later or I'll have to call to get somebody to get your number. Do me a favor and get my brother back because I need Tony's number.

Kristina: Okay, is there anything I can do for you?

Casey: I'm sitting in jail. There is nothing anybody can do now.

Kristina: I'm just trying to be a…

Casey: I know you are, honey. I absolutely know you are and I appreciate it and everything you are trying to do but I'd like to call Tony. He's not at my house is he?

Kristina: No. It's just me and your parents and Lee.

Casey: Well, can you do me a favor and get my brother back so I can get the number from him, please?

Kristina: Does Tony have anything to do with Caylee?

Casey: No, nothing.

Kristina: Okay, so why do you want to talk with Tony? You probably don't want to tell me, do you?

Casey: Tony had nothing to do with Caylee.

Kristina: Oh, then why do you want to talk with him?

Casey: Because he is my boyfriend and I want to actually try and sit and talk to him because I didn't get a chance to talk to him earlier. Because I got arrested on a fucking whim today and because they are blaming me for stuff that I would never do. That I didn't do.

Kristina: Well, I'm on your side, you know that?

Casey: I know that, I just want to talk with Tony and get a little bit of...

Kristina: Casey, you have to tell me if you know anything about Caylee. If anything happened to Caylee, I'll die - you understand, I'll die.

Casey: Oh my God! Calling you guys (was) a waste - a huge waste. Honey, I love you. You know I'd never let anything happen to my daughter. If I knew where she was, this would not be going on.

Kristina: Then how come everyone is saying that you are lying?

Casey: Because nobody is fucking listening to anything that I'm saying. The media misconstrued everything that I said. The fucking detectives pulled fucking shit. They got all of their information from me, but at the same time they are twisting stuff. They already said they are going to pin this on me if they don't find Caylee. They've already said that. They arrested me because they said...

Kristina: They said that the person you left Caylee with doesn't exist.

Casey: Because, oh look, they can't find her in the Florida database. She is not just from Florida. If they would actually listen to anything that I would have said to them, they would have had their leads. They maybe could have tracked her down. They have not listened to a fucking thing that I've said.

Kristina: You know that whoever has Caylee, nobody is going to get away with it.

Casey: I know, nobody is going to get away with it but at the same time, the only way they are going to find Caylee is if they actually listen to what I'm saying and I'm trying to help them and they are not letting me help them.

Kristina: So, how can I help them find her? The best thing you can do baby is to listen to me.

Casey: They need to look up her information in the New York database and a North Carolina database. And other places that she's lived outside of Florida. That is what I told them, even again today. I told them that four times today. I sat up at the police station. The county police station...

126

Kristina: Does she have Caylee, or did she transfer Caylee to someone else?

Casey: Honey, I have not talked with her. I don't know. I have not talked to her.

Kristina: How come everyone is saying that you are not upset and that you are not crying and you show no caring of where Caylee is at all?

Casey: Because I'm not here fucking crying every two seconds because I have to stay composed to talk to detectives, to make other phone calls and do other things. I can't sit here and be crying every two seconds like I want to - I can't.

Kristina: Okay, Casey, don't yell at me, I'm on your side.

Casey: I know you are on my side. I'm not trying to…

Kristina: Nobody is saying anything bad about you. Your family is with you 100 percent.

Casey: No they're not. That is fucking because I just watched the fucking news and heard everything that my mom said. Nobody in my own family is on my side.

Kristina: Yes they are.

Casey: They just want Caylee back. That is all they are worried about right now is getting Caylee back. And you know what, that is all I care about right now.

Kristina: Casey, your daughter, your flesh and blood and baby girl…

Casey: Kristina, please, put my brother back on the phone. I don't want to get into this with you right now. I love you honey and I'm glad that you are there. Thank you for your help. I will let you know if there is anything that you can do.

Kristina: You can't tell me anybody who can find Caylee?

Casey: No. No because everyone that I've tried and every number that I've called is disconnected - nothing. I can't get ahold of anybody.

Kristina: But that girl was the last person to have her?

Casey: She was the last person to have her. That was the last time I saw Caylee.

Kristina: Lee said he doesn't have Tony's phone number.

Casey: Yes, he does. He has Tony's number in his phone. He needs to stop fucking lying. He just told me a second ago that he'd give me the number.

Kristina: So, if I go and get you Tony's number, are you going to finish talking to me?

Casey: I will call you tomorrow. I want to talk to him really quick. I wanted to actually try and call. I haven't slept in four days. I have not slept in four days.

Kristina: Listen, if you are going to talk to anybody, you can talk to me.

Casey: I know I can talk to you but at the same time, I know that I can talk to Tony and that is who I want to talk to now. I have not gotten the chance to talk to him since this morning. Since all of this stuff happened with trying to set up the Myspace and I made the Myspace.

Kristina: Do you know the password?

Casey: I made all of it.

Kristina: What's the password to Myspace so we can see if anybody has written any leads of where Caylee might be?

Casey: You can go online and see it. As far as messages, I don't know if anybody is going to be messaging.

Casey Anthony gives Kristina her log-in information.

Kristina gives Tony's phone number to Casey.

Kristina: Can Tony tell me anything?

Casey: Baby, Tony doesn't know anything. And, I have not even talked with him since this morning.

Kristina: Has Tony seen Caylee?

Kristina: Tony has not seen Caylee since the beginning of June. What's Tony's number again?

Kristina gives the number again.

Casey: Thank you. I will find a way to call you later. Leave your number at my house with my mother and I can get it later tonight.

Kristina: How can I get a hold of you?

Casey: I'm at the jail, you can't.

Kristina: You don't have a way to write my phone number down?

Casey: No, I have no way of writing it down. I have to remember Tony's number. I have to try to memorize his number right now. Just leave your number with my mom and I will try to call you in the morning if I don't get a chance to call you tonight.

Kristina: So, how can I find information about that girl?

Casey: Have them look up a New York license for Zenaida Fernandez-Gonzalez. They've just been looking up the last name Gonzalez or the last name Fernandez. If they look up her entire name, they might actually find her. They have not done that. They haven't listened to anything that I've said.

Kristina: "How do you spell Zenaida?"

Casey: Z-e-n-a-i-d-a

Kristina: Where does she live? Because they went and looked at her place, and…

Casey: Baby, you are not telling me anything that I don't already know. Again, I've only been in jail since about 8:30 tonight. I was with them all day. I know that. I was with officers pretty much since 9 PM last night up until this evening when I came up here.

Kristina: But you are telling the whole truth and nothing but the truth?

Casey: That I have no clue where my daughter is? Yes, that is the truth. That is the absolute truth.

Kristina: They'll find out and whoever…

Casey: Okay, Kristina, I'm hanging up. I need to make this other call before I forget the number. So, I'll call you later.
Kristina: Okay, bye."
(Call ends.)

The authors are dismayed. Wow, she has not talked to Tony since this morning and she *must* have his number to talk to him. Yet, she has not talked to her daughter in over 31 days, with no concern. This woman is a piece of work! We think the psychiatric reports the defense must have had done on Casey Anthony are going to be mind-blowing. We should hear about the reports if she is found guilty of anything. Even if there is no penalty phase, when the judge sentences Casey, there will probably be some mitigating evidence presented – for instance, the psychiatric reports. She certainly does not seem to be legally insane.

Cindy Anthony -- Defense cross-examination (cont.): It is fair to say Casey and I are alike in most ways. I raised Casey to be caring and loving, and I raised her to tell the truth. I tried. I got to see what kind of mother Casey became. She was loving and caring and had a natural maternal instinct. She reminded me of myself. Caylee adored her mom, her eyes would light up and she did not want to sleep without her mom. She pretty much followed Casey most of the time. She did not cry after her all the time if George and I were there. I never witnessed Casey abuse or torture Caylee. Caylee had everything. The first time Casey went to the doctor was a few days before she told me she was pregnant. On June 7th we went to a wedding with Casey. (A photo is shown to the witness of Casey and Cindy at the wedding.) At that time I did not believe Casey was pregnant. I was confronted by my brother. We were at the dinner table and Casey had flown in, and she was not feeling well. My brother asked if she was pregnant and we said we did not think so. Previously, she was walking the park at Universal Studios and she had taken a sedentary job in Human Resources. (The defense attorney says that Casey has been in jail for three years. She spends twenty-three hours a day in a jail, and asks if that is sedentary.) Yes, that is sedentary. No, she does not have a belly that I can see now. I know she is not eating. (The defense attorney tells Cindy to stand and look at her daughter's belly. There is an objection and a sidebar.)

Cindy Anthony's testimony continues: (The judge asks the defendant to stand.) I can see just from her chest up. (Cindy stands down from the witness stand. She motions to Casey for her to turn and pull her shirt back some so that Cindy can see her stomach. Cindy returns to the witness stand.) She is not as big as she was at the wedding. Casey was having bloating pain and told me she had more periods than normal and we thought she might have a cyst. From the age of ten to nineteen, she did not go to a gynecologist. Yes, going to a gynecologist is traumatic to a child. The irregular problems had just started. She finally went to a doctor, and was referred to a gynecologist for the first time. Casey told me the father was Jessie. I asked right away. I found out Jessie was not the father. Casey gave me the name of Eric Baker. I have never met this person. Casey said he was two years younger than her, and he was an old friend. She had seen him about the time she was seeing Jessie. They spent one night together and he was in North Carolina and back with his girlfriend. I made no attempts to contact Eric Baker. After Caylee's second birthday, Casey called me at work and told me that Caylee's father was in an accident and died, and that Caylee has a half-brother.

Casey was engaged to Jessie in 2006. She told me about another young man who worked for the IT department at Universal Studios. Casey was confiding in him about her relationship with Jessie. She would talk off and on about him. He had a child named Zach. I saw a picture of Jeff on Casey's phone about a month later in 2006. She had him listed as boyfriend. After all of this started, law enforcement looked for him. He has never worked for Universal. I never spoke to Jeffery Hopkins. We were supposed to meet up at the mall with his mother and son, but they she never showed up. I had no phone number for Jewels, his mother, so I never called. Later in July, Casey told me Jewels had cancer. Casey told me she was attending the wedding and that was keeping her from coming back from Jacksonville with Caylee. I believe Jeffery was older than Casey. Both of them had toddlers, and Jeffery took custody of baby Zach when his old girlfriend died. Casey wanted to move in with Jeffery and Zach. There were lots of plans to meet him and his family, but something always came up and we never met. Always the day of the meet-up, they would cancel. I made plans, bought food and then it would cancel. I shared with friends this wonderful possibility of this great guy for Casey.

I did not know they were imaginary people. I thought they were real. As for Juliette Lewis, I never spoke to her and never saw her. I waited for Juliette, at Universal Studios with Casey. Casey called Juliette and it canceled. When I asked Caylee about Annabel, Juliette's daughter she would repeat the name and her eyes would light up. I never saw any photos. (The authors wonder if

Casey used the name of the actress and singer.) Rocker Farrell was her roommate and I have never seen ether one. (One of the authors knows that the front man for the alternative rock band Jane's Addiction is Perry Farrell, also referred to as being "zany" by people. Is it possible that Casey's imaginary friends are named for musicians?) I never spoke to Rocker.

I never saw a photo of Zanny the nanny. I never spoke to her. Casey first mentioned her in 2006. Casey called her Zanny, she was Jeff's girlfriend and Jeff offered her as a babysitter for Casey. Until then, Casey's high school girlfriends had been babysitting Caylee. She told me that Zanny had gotten her hair cut, and that she was a very attractive girl. She said she was a beautiful person inside and out. I don't think that I ever asked if she was Spanish. Casey spoke some Spanish. Caylee learned Spanish from Dora the Explorer, Casey and Zanny. I really never talked about how Casey and Caylee spent the day. Caylee had some scratches on her leg once. I asked Caylee about it, and she said a dog scratched her. She said Zanny got a puppy. Caylee did not stay with Zanny much. Casey dropped Caylee off at my office. George and I took care of her most of the time. Casey talked about Zanny's mom being sick and other changes in Zanny life. Zanny's mother has heart issues and her name is Gloria, according to Casey.

Zanny had a sister I heard of in July 2008. I never saw photos of Gloria or spoke to her. (The defense attorney announces that none of these people existed, and asks if Cindy has any information over the last three years that any of these people are anything but imaginary people.) I just found out that they are imaginary. I looked for Zanny ever since Caylee was missing, tip lines we sat up, and looked up every combination of Zanny's name in Florida, New York, and North Carolina. We even went to an apartment in New York and we followed a lead to find Zanny in California. It was your detective, Mr. Baez, Dominic Casey, who when you had a falling out with him, he decided to help us for free, and kept looking. When Casey's high school graduation arrived, no one knew until the last day she was not going to graduate. (An objection was sustained.)

I trusted Casey and I believed in her, because we had no knowledge these people were imaginary. I did not tell law enforcement that I thought Zanny was Amy or Jessie, but I thought maybe it was Ricardo, and I told the FBI that. It was the agent who put it together that they might be the nanny.

On July 15th or 16th, 2008, I gave law enforcement what I thought was Zanny's number. That number was not to Zanny it was other friends of Casey. (The defense attorney asked if Cindy believes Caylee is alive. A prosecutor's objection is sustained.) (They are showing the photos of the inside of the Anthony home on the monitor.) I have cream carpet. There is no bar that would keep Caylee from the pool. Caylee had trouble with the door. I have testified that Caylee could get out. (Jose Baez asks Cindy how many times she told law enforcement that Caylee could have drowned. An objection is sustained.)

I told the detective that the ladder was up in climbing position on June 16th, 2008 and the gate was open. I let the dogs out in the backyard and the side gate was open. The dogs alarmed me that the gate was open. I called George to ask if he left the gate open. I thought maybe he had cooled off in the pool. He said no. So I assumed someone else was swimming in our pool and leaving the gate open. I told co-workers about the ladder. I thought someone was using our pool. Caylee loved to swim. In June 2008, Caylee swam every day with me in a life vest. I do not know if I told law enforcement that maybe Casey left the ladder up. In June, the last night I saw Caylee, I swam with Caylee and I recall taking the ladder down. I'm as sure as anyone can be.

I let Mark Furman and another man in my home. Mr. Furman wanted to offer any help he could. The other man was not a detective, and after speaking with him, I found out he worked for Greta Van Susteren and Fox News. I did not know that when I invited him in my home. I did not tell them I forgot to take the ladder down on June 16th, 2008. Casey tried to call me about 4 PM several times that day. That was an abnormal amount. I was very busy. When I came out of the meeting, at that time, about 4 PM there were numerous calls from Casey. I know that now. I did not realize that there were that many missed calls from her while I was in the meeting. On July 13th, 2008, I found the notice that alerted us to the certified letter. We have a community mail box that is a few doors down. So they taped the notice to the door. I have never received one before. I found it on the door. (Baez asks why, on July 15th, when she called the police, she told them that she received the notice that day.) I was referring to the letter we had picked up and then the car. When we got the car and it was in the garage, I said the car smelled like a dead body to 911; I was upset and it just came out. I used the car as an excuse to speak to the police. I referenced the smell as a dead body because I wanted the police to get there. I never picked up the letter - George did. (There is a sidebar - there sure are a lot of

132

them! Is the judge serving drinks at that bar? Of course, we know that's not true.) On June 15th at 4 PM, there were six missed calls, a phone message, and the office told me Casey had called. I worked for home health care on July 15th, 2008.

(They are now playing a small part of the third 911 call. George pulls up and Cindy yells to him: Caylee is missing! George: What?! Cindy: Casey says the nanny took her a month ago! The recording stops.) I was yelling to George as he was getting out of the car. That's all he said. When Lee and I questioned Casey, George was not home. Everything happened at once, George came home, the police arrived immediately, and they separated us. I told them Caylee had been missing since June 7th, I did not reference Father's Day, and I was just upset. Again, I made the statement that it was the Sunday before Father's Day and that was wrong. It was Father's Day. (Cindy reviews her statement: She said June 8th in the statement, which was the Sunday before Father's Day. On the 911 call, Cindy said the 7th, and in her written statement Cindy said June 8th, 2008.)

Again, Mr. Baez, I was hysterical and later realized it was June 15th. The police took a look at the video of Caylee with my father. They wanted to verify the nursing home and I was concerned they would upset my father, who was ill, and my mother. I am a registered nurse. I'm on disability now. I do not have a financial interest in this case. I have filed a trademark application for Caylee's name. We have not made money – we have lost money. I sold photos to pay my attorney and received $20,000. He got $6,000. (Baez asks if she has discussed a book deal or flown to New York about a book deal.) I went with my attorney, Tom Lippman, and my husband. My son and his attorney were there in New York. I do not know what they were doing there. I have not attempted to earn a living as a director of the Caylee fund. I have not had fundraisers. I do not have any media deals for this coverage. (Baez asks her how many networks she has flown to New York for.) We went up when Caylee was missing for a 48 Hour interview. (Sidebar)

(The prosecution questions on re-direct.) Caylee always had food. I provided it and most of her clothing. We provided the house. My daughter's weight has also fluctuated while she's been in jail. When Casey told me that Jessie was the father of Caylee, I told George. When the Greta Van Susteren show was in my house in August, I did not tell them the gate was open and the pool ladder was on the pool. The pool ladder was before the gas cans went missing. The gate is locked and can only be unlocked from the inside and it is usually locked. (The State asks if the gate was unlocked on June 15th, 16th, 17th or 18th.) The only day I found it open was on June 16th. You called George? Yes, he said he did not unlock it. Caylee cannot reach the gate lock, and neither George nor I opened the lock, so that only leaves only Casey in the house to unlock the gate.

I told the people that George and the tow driver had pulled out garbage from the trunk. I used words dead body at work, to law enforcement and 911. I said the car smelled worse than rotting flesh at work. I do not remember what George said when I told him Caylee was missing. He was very upset and had a reaction similar to mine, and then I collapsed in his arms. Law enforcement separated us immediately. We are trademarking Caylee's full name to prevent abuse by strangers. (The prosecutor asks if the lies that Casey was telling started after Caylee was born, and immediately describes them as the elaborate lies you have detailed for us, centering on who was caring for Caylee, her employment, or why Casey was not home.) Yes.

(The defense asks questions on re-cross.) The closest thing to the smell of the car is rotting flesh. I did not call the police about it, because I thought it was garbage. George was visibly upset and crying, and weeping as much as me. You did not hear George's reaction because George was far away at the car. When Casey was about to graduate from high school, I had planned a graduation party and we got word Casey was a quarter of a credit away in mandatory credits and she had more other credits. The counselor called and we knew the day before. She said Casey could graduate but could not walk in the ceremony. (The witness steps down and the jurors are taken out for the judge to hear a matter outside their presence.)

The prosecution wants to introduce evidence of Casey's prior felony convictions. The Judge states a composite exhibit of six felony convictions for Casey Anthony is at issue. The defense objects. The prosecution argues that the defense opened the door. The State argues that the defense has placed out-of-court statements by the defendant about the paternity into evidence, and once he opened the door to the character of the defendant, it is wide open. (It is sometimes possible to get things into evidence that were not previously allowed. There had been a pretrial ruling that the defendant's convictions would not be admitted unless she testified, and maybe not even then.) They are arguing the Huggins v. State case on this. There are six felony convictions the prosecutions want to show the jury. Since it does have a devastating effect, the judge will permit argument in the morning. The Judge tells the court reporter to prepare a transcript of Mrs. Anthony's testimony for the day. The judge says that the testimony has to be looked at surgically, and not in a shotgun approach. Before the six felonies will come in, they will analyze and argue before the judge tomorrow morning. The State says they are going to call Amy Huizenga as the next witness. The defense is arguing they do not have a file for this next witness; the file is in Kissimmee. Judge Perry tells the defense, I offered file space to you for the files and you have not used it. Have you stored any files in this hallway? We will take her direct testimony and stop and the cross will be tomorrow. If you want files, you better put them in this courthouse so you can access them. You are not sequestered, the jury is, and they are going to keep working. We will take all the time we need to try this case, but we will not waste time.

The State's Twenty-fifth Witness

Interpretation of Testimony – Amy Huizenga: I am 26 and work aboard a cruise ship backstage. I met Casey on New Year's Eve 2008. We were close friends. I know Ricardo; he is one of my best friends. In January, February, and March, 2008, I was working in Orlando and I was under the impression that Casey was an events coordinator. We spent a fair amount of time together, maybe once or twice a week, when she started dating Ricardo. We texted and talked daily. We hung out after work. I was living with Troy Brown and another friend. I saw Caylee, and most of the time she would be in bed at Ricardo and JP's. There were times when Casey could not go out because she did not have a babysitter. Casey would put Caylee to bed and we would hang out at Ricardo's. About once a week, there would be a problem because Casey did not have babysitter.

When she broke up with Ricardo, it was messy. Casey and I talked. I was still living with Troy Brown. I had planned on living with Casey in mid-May. We talked about getting an apartment and then about a house. We planned to look at an apartment, but we couldn't go for some reason that day. Casey decided it wouldn't work. Then Casey told me she was going to be taking over the mortgage payment soon at her parents' house. Maybe June or July, we could move in. I wanted to meet her mom, because I was going to live with her daughter and granddaughter. During the month of May, Casey was upset when Cindy could not watch Caylee so she could go out.

In May, it became more frequent that her mother couldn't babysit, and Casey was very upset about it. (The

135

prosecutor shows the witness a transcript of text messages. She recognizes the messages.) After July 15th, 2008, I gave my phone to the police. This is a text from Casey on May 3rd to me, 11:10 PM "Downtown tomorrow, my mom owes me." Then at 11:12 PM, "Nothing is stopping me." That is her mom babysitting she is referring to. Many times, she cancelled plans because her mom was not watching Caylee. Casey said her mom was continually agitated, and her mom was saying she was unfit.

I overheard many arguments. Casey said her mom was crazy. She was frustrated and she needed space, and her mom did not understand that. In June, 2008, I moved in with Ricardo so I could walk to work after I had wrecked my car. JP, Chad, and Ricardo lived there. Casey was going to give me a ride to Jacksonville, so I could buy a car from my uncle. She was to pick me up early in the morning on June 13th. I texted her, and she said she was having family problems and she was going to the hospital with her dad. I looked for a rental car or some other way to get to Jacksonville. We spoke on the phone and she told me what happened with her dad. Then she called me later she and wanted me to come to Fusion. I did not go. I work in theater so I am always looking for jobs, but not necessarily looking for work. I asked if she could get me into Universal Studios and I e-mailed her my résumé. I do not think I saw her on June 13th.

About three weeks into June, I did not see her but we talked and texted. She had gotten a few flat tires, she had run out of gas twice, and the car had a bad smell. (More texts from Casey are shown to the witness, and she says they are true and accurate.) On June 27th, "There is part of a dead animal plastered to the frame of my car." We had other conversations about this smell. She said maybe when my dad borrowed the car he hit something. Maybe a week later, she talked about the smell in her car. This is another text about her car running out of gas. She did not ask for assistance. Two weeks in a row on Friday she said her car ran out of gas, the second is at an Amscot, and she said she left it and hopes that it doesn't get towed. At the end of June, June 30th, early in the morning, Casey knocked on the door, came in, and did not leave.

I knew Tony was out of town. She did not say she had not been home, but it was implied. She talked about problems with her mother but not more than usual. She was frustrated with her mother. Most of it had to do with Caylee. Cindy wanted to see Caylee and there was stuff going on at home, and Casey wanted to keep Caylee away from her mom. There was drama with George and Cindy; they were considering divorce. Her dad had cheated on her mom and Casey was keeping Caylee away from her mom.

It was the unhappiness at home that Casey wanted to keep Caylee away from. It was time to move out of her parents' home with Caylee. She was frustrated and they had problems. I do not think it went as deep as resentment. (The prosecutor asks if she was still planning on moving into the Anthony home at this time.) It was cancelled and I even had movers and a truck. Then Casey said it needed landscaping, and George wanted to fix it for us. There were twenty workers in the house and we would have to wait. Then she told me that Cindy took back the deal. The paperwork had a thirty day clause that could be undone and it was not happening. That was in July. She called her mom crazy. It was a lot of normal child complaining about parent stuff, and a lot to do with Caylee. It seemed there were past relationship problems.

On June 30th, she shows up and stays a week. She did not ask. She had stuff in Tony's car. The only problem was, it was not my place and I could not allow her to stay. I invited her a week before to a party. Casey said she could not go because of Caylee and I suggested she bring Caylee. Caylee was always on tour of Florida according to Casey, Busch Gardens, beaches and more. She told me at the party that Caylee was at Sea World with the nanny. I got woken up by tapping fingers on the computer, Casey was happy on July 5th. Tony was coming home. She said her car was in the shop.

On July 8th, I left for Puerto Rico. Casey was planning to go. We all traveled separately. She told me after I left for Puerto Rico that she was not coming. She needed someone to watch Caylee. I was not surprised. On July 15th, when I returned from Puerto Rico, Casey picked me up at the airport in my car and I took her to Tony's. Then I went back to the airport to pick up everyone else from the trip, and then went to the Florida Mall. I received a call from Cindy Anthony and she was very scared. I was cautious about speaking with her, because Casey told me she was crazy. She needed me to take her to Casey. She picked me up at the mall and I took her to Tony's.

I knocked on the door and they said it was open. I walked in and Casey was on the couch. I told her to come out. Cindy waited just outside in the hall, on the landing. It was very confrontational, angry, a massive explosion of mother and daughter, with lots of confrontation and defensiveness. Where is Caylee, Cindy asked? She is with the nanny. Casey agreed, with a big amount of persuasion,

137

to take her to Caylee. Casey was confrontational and holding her own with Cindy. Casey did not want to leave Tony's. We all went to the car; I was in the back seat. Casey got in the passenger seat and was defiant. She would not speak unless asked a question. The questions were mostly where is Caylee? Casey appeared like she was sixteen and she looked like she was caught doing something bad. She said she and Caylee needed their space. (The witness steps down for the day, and the jury is excused for the evening.)

The judge and the lawyers begin talking about tomorrow's hearing regarding the State's contention that the defense opened the door to Casey's character and introduction of evidence of her prior convictions. Judge Perry says that the lawyers will get a direct (not final) copy of the transcript tonight by e-mail. The State says that the defense was supposed to proffer the testimony but didn't. The judge wants the State to tell him whether the exculpatory hearsay statements relate solely to collateral matters, rather than being exculpatory statements regarding the charged offenses. He says that if the exculpatory hearsay statements of the defendant relate only to collateral matters, we need to talk about the balancing test (whether the probative/impeachment value of the convictions is outweighed by the danger of unfair prejudice). Once that bell is rung it cannot be un-rung. Each side has 10 minutes each in the morning to argue, so do not waste time with speeches. (The Judge will review the transcript before tomorrow mornings hearing.)

June 1st, 2011

The day begins with a hearing regarding admission of Casey Anthony's prior felony convictions. (Casey is not wearing a good choice of clothing; her shirt reminds us of prison stripes.) The State says that the Jeff Hopkins statements were going to be offered in the same vein and not for the truth of the matter asserted. He is not waiving any argument for the future. The paternity of Caylee has never been determined. He decides not to push for introduction of the defendant's convictions at this time. Judge Perry tells the defense, to please read Florida Statues 90.403. He tells Baez, that when a hearsay statement has been admitted in evidence, any evidence to counter it, may also be admitted. The judge tells both sides, to just be really careful when if they elicit hearsay statements. *The aftershock can have devastating effects.*

(The admission of her six previous felony convictions for bad checks involving the time period of this case could taint a jury. There are only certain ways that they can get into evidence. When a lawyer opens the door with a question or evidence that needs to be rebutted by previously inadmissible evidence, that evidence can suddenly become eligible for admission by the other side. Opening a door is a big no-no for lawyers. The old boys know that one. Defense lives and prosecution will fight another day on this one. We think Baez will be very careful now.)

Interpretation of Testimony - Amy Huizenga (Defense Baez cross-examination): I was friends with Casey for not very long, maybe 5 months. I did not spend a lot of personal time. It was more of a text or phone calls type relationship. These are my text messages. I gave them to law enforcement freely. They mostly cover the period I knew her. We texted a lot and I had a lot of time at work, so text, Myspace and more. It shows a good picture of our friendship and my life as well. Only one refers to Casey's mother watching Caylee. There are numerous ones where I ask Casey to go out. She says she is sick or gives other excuses. I don't know her motivation for not wanting to go out. I spoke about the relationship and what I was told. I had limited knowledge – what I was told by Casey about her relationship with her mother. There were many phone calls as well. I only knew one side of the relationship.

(She is shown a text.) This is one of my texts on June 27th, 2008. It is about her car smelling. When asked if her memory during that time period might be fogged, she said I drank with friends, but not more than other friends. It was not every night, I could not afford to. I drank but not heavily, maybe went out 3-4 nights a week, like most people my age. When I crashed, it was on a long dark stretch of road and it is boring. I had dosed off during the day on that road before. I had stopped drinking three hours before. (A text message from Amy to Casey is shown). I hit a guardrail and thank God, I did not get a DUI. (Sidebar, objection sustained.)

In the accident, I totaled the car and the airbag blew. I do not remember having a head injury and I guess I did send out a text for people to call me in ten minutes. I do not know if I hit my head. I had never been hit with an airbag. No one had to call me and I did not see a doctor. So I guess I cannot say what happened. Casey dated Ricardo then Tony. I moved in with Ricardo and met Jessie after that. He was Casey's ex-fiancé. I admit I told Jessie I wanted to meet a good Christian boy. It is

139

the truth. I was not at the Anthony home on June 16th, 2008. I do not remember if we talked or what was said. (The witness is excused subject to recall. There is a sidebar including Amy, probably about the possibility of recall to the stand; she appears to work for a living.)

The State's Twenty-sixth Witness

Interpretation of Testimony - Lee Anthony: He is Casey's older brother. He is graying and looks older than his 32 years. He is not working. He lives in Orlando, but not with his parents.

In June and July 2008, I did not live with my parents; I lived five minutes away. I had contact with my sister every couple of weeks on Myspace to say hello in the middle of June and spoke with her numerous times on June 23rd. In the beginning of July, I went to my mom's because she asked me to come over. She needed to see me. On July 3rd, 2008, I knew that neither Casey nor Caylee had been home for a while. On July 3rd, 2008, I talked to my mom on the phone. I did not help her set up her Myspace. On July 4th, 2008, I looked for my sister. I went onto Myspace and eventually through Facebook figured out where I thought she would be that night, at the Dragon Club.

I decided I would go and ask a friend to go with me. Malory Parker met us down there; she is my fiancée now. I arrived at nine or ten PM, and I even tried to reach Casey by text and calls. When it became clear she was not at this club, I texted. I probably invited her to meet for a drink, no response. Then I asked Malory to text Casey, but not to tell her that she was with me. I only went to the Dragon Room. I texted Casey for about an hour, off and on, with no result. Then I called a half dozen times and probably left some messages. She picked up on a few calls. I asked where are you? Do you want to meet?

"I am busy," was Casey's response. I am out with friends and doing my own things. She hung up on me a lot. I had numerous conversations. I asked where she was and she said Jacksonville. I knew it was a lie, so I just kept questioning her. Casey told me, I am at a country western bar and I called her out on that. I knew she was in town. I asked if they were coming to the Dragon Room and where is Caylee? I do not recall who she said Caylee was being watched by, while she was out. I do not believe I asked who the friend was at that time. She insisted she was in

Jacksonville the entire time. I told Casey she needed to talk to mom, that mom was worried, and she hung up on me. I told her that her family was worried about her and you guys. I was worried about her too. She said everything is fine and she would talk to mom tomorrow. She hung up and I tried numerous more calls. I do not think that I talked again, maybe texted. I continued to look for her on the bar strip of Church Street. I never found her and I left after 2 AM.

I came to learn that no one in the family had seen Casey or Caylee for weeks. I made no future attempt to locate her because my mom asked me not to. I thought everything was under control. I do not think I saw mom between July 4th and 15th, but I talked to her after the 3rd and she said do not pursue this any longer. She felt she had it under control. I gave a deposition in this case and I was asked how my mom was acting during this time. (Witness is reading to refresh his memory. It does refresh his recollection and it is the same.) I next saw Casey on July 15th, 2008. My dad called me and asked that I go over to the house. I arrived about 8 PM. No one was home. I used the garage door and I saw my old Pontiac Sunfire in the garage. I noticed a smell and the windows were down and writing was on the window of the car. It was very poignant and strong. It was offensive. I walked by to get inside, but did nothing else to the car. I was there for less than 5 minutes when Mom and Casey arrived.

My sister went into her room after entering the house, before she said anything. (The State is refreshing Lee's memory with his deposition.) Casey said that she was not sure why she bothered; no one was listening to her. Her demeanor was combative and mom was equally or more combative. I followed Casey into her room. Mom and Casey were continuing a discussion that probably started before they arrived home. Where is Caylee, was the topic. She, Casey, said Caylee was with a nanny. I did not know she had one or used one from time to time.

She said Caylee was with a nanny and was already asleep for the evening. She did not want to disturb her. Casey said she had a routine and that she did not want to change that. Sleeping routine, I thought she was talking. It made some sense as a routine, but not as an appeasement to my mother and a means of getting Caylee back. (Again, the State refreshes Lee's memory with his deposition.) It was referenced that her routine was only about three weeks of routine, so let's get Caylee. Mom and Casey were arguing, a couple of minutes the first time. It was a lot of arguing, but a few minutes at a time. Casey said she would get Caylee tomorrow. I offered

141

to go get Caylee or my roommate could go get Caylee. She said okay then no, I do not want to disturb her, or I do not think mom would allow it.

(Lee Anthony looks very much like a man. He does not appear crazy. He is not willingly giving up anything that could hurt his sister. The prosecutor has to drag everything out of him. At this point, we believe he is afraid his testimony could help send Casey to death row. This is understandable to us. In the beginning, the family told the police everything to try to find Caylee. Now Caylee is dead and his sister could be put to death, and the prosecution wants him to help them do it. So we understand why since we come from a family with siblings.)

I asked, why won't you allow us to see Caylee? I do not recall, maybe she said she was asleep, I think. I gave a taped interview to the police. (The prosecutor is having Lee review a transcript.) I recall now. Yes. (Sidebar) When I asked why we could not see Caylee, I told detectives that Casey said, paraphrasing, "Because maybe I am a spiteful bitch." Mom would come and go, and I tried to talk and reason with Casey when mom was out of the room. I asked what is going on? What is happening? She said that Caylee was missing and someone had kidnapped her. Before that, I do not recall what Casey said about mom. (Lee's memory is refreshed with his deposition again.)

I told the detective that when mom would leave and I would ask Casey to talk to me she would express. (Objection, hearsay and sidebar requested. The Judge will allow it.) I have no memory of the statement. (The State asks, "Do you remember, not paraphrased, what you told the detective? Do you recall exactly what you told the detective that Casey told you?") She told me that my mother has numerous times thrown it in her face that Casey was an unfit mother and Casey said, maybe I am. My mother references Caylee as being a mistake, but the best or greatest mistake that Casey has ever made.

I was getting very frustrated with Casey; nothing was making sense. Why could we just not go get Caylee? There was no reason to fight. I asked her what is in this for me. We just want Caylee. (Lee is reviewing his recorded statement again. Casey and Baez appear not to be in the courtroom while Lee is testifying, which we find interesting.) I role-played with Casey. Why do we need to get the police officer involved? So I told her to follow me, this is going to happen. The police show up and the officer is going to say, where is your daughter? You say at the nanny's. He is going to say okay, let's go get her. She said that she had not seen Caylee in 31 days and she had been kidnapped. The nanny took her.

Within a couple of minutes she said the nanny was Zenaida Fernandez-Gonzalez. She was very specific about the number of days. Mom was not in the room, but she was close enough to realize what we had been talking about and she was upset. Mom says to Casey, What did you do? We could have found her! (Objection, motion to strike. The judge strikes those statements as hearsay.) My father is not home at that time. I talked to Casey, and asked the last place she remembered seeing Caylee. She said, at the Sawgrass Apartments. Where have you been staying? She said, at Tony Lazzaro's apartment and she had been trying to find Caylee herself.

Later, she said she camped out in her car at the last place she saw Caylee, looking and watching for Zanny for a couple of days. She said she would go to places that Caylee could be, like a store or a park. She said she had a call that she had received and that she talked to Caylee on that day, July 15th, 2008, for a minute. She said she talked to Caylee and I do not remember any more. Casey asked Caylee to put an adult on the phone and the call ended.

When I heard that Caylee had been missing, I asked her the questions we discussed and went into search mode and got her boyfriend's name. Casey told me her boyfriend's name. I called Mr. Lazzaro and went to see him late on July 15th or the early hours of the 16th. I told them what was going on and I got Casey's belongings from him – a laptop, clothes, a backpack, and the like. The computer was on, but it was a blue screen. A virus, something was wrong, and I tried to reboot it and it went to the same screen. I just turned it off and took it with me. (The prosecution hands Lee an envelope to review) I recognize the items; most of them. (There is an objection, and the Judge reviews the items in envelope. The envelope is given back to Lee from the judge.)

I recognize what is inside, receipts, movie tickets, stubs and a photo of a note. (All of it is put into evidence. There are nineteen receipts.) I never had possession of the receipts. They were in one of the bags I recovered from Casey's stuff at Tony Lazzaro's. I became aware in a few days of their existence during a family sit-down with law enforcement. I recall I received a laptop and three bags including the laptop from Tony. I was present when the bags were emptied. These receipts were in the backpack. That is the only time I have been to Anthony Lazzaro's apartment.

The police arrived, came in to my sister's bedroom and started asking her questions. I was in the next room then. Dad was home by then. Dad came home shortly before the police, by minutes. I talked with Casey in the garage and it still smelled bad from the car. I just asked her additional questions and she told me she had talked to Caylee that day. I asked about Anthony Lazzaro and mentioned how bad the car smelled. It was difficult to stay in the garage with that odor. I did not see anything that belonged to Caylee in the items of Casey's I brought from Anthony Lazzaro's.

Lee Anthony - Defense cross-examination: I received a phone call from my mother and she did not say Caylee was missing. I left for Chicago and stayed for a week. I think it was in June. From June 15th to July 3rd, 2008, I saw mom about once. On July 15, 2008, I was present when my mother called the police. The Sunfire had white shoe polish writing on the window from the tow company. That car was the one that Casey drove, and my father had a set of keys to the car. When I was talking with Casey, we whispered and she was crying. My father arrived but did not go into Casey's room and question her. Prior to the police arriving, there were no questions that my father asked me. During the conversations between mom and Casey, I tried to mediate.

My mother was more, instead of trying to fix it, she was more on how could you do this. The way my mother behaved and talked to Casey, Casey did not really have a chance to respond. At Anthony Lazzaro's, the bags were already packed. (Sidebar) When my sister and I pack bags, we shove stuff in, and these bags were folded. Casey did not pack the bags. (The defense asks if the opinion that his sister did not pack the bags is a firm opinion.) (Objection) The bags had no odor. My father cleans and details the cars. He did it all the time, every other weekend. The laptop with the blue screen was on at Mr. Lazzaro's when I got there, and when I got it. (The defense asks if it is correct that he cannot say who caused the screen to become blue.) (Objection sustained)

Lee Anthony - Prosecution re-direct: The phone call of July 3rd from my mom was about Caylee and Casey. It was mentioned that Casey and Caylee had not been home, but not that Caylee was missing. (Sidebar) Dad arrived shortly before the police and we were eventually separated. Casey told me Caylee was kidnapped and my focus went to finding Caylee and not on Casey. My sister

144

told the police that Caylee was kidnapped. I spoke with the police and talked about what my sister had told me about the kidnapping. My conversation was with the detective about what Casey had told me. When I had a substantial interview with the law enforcement, it was about the kidnapping and the Zenaida Fernandez-Gonzalez story. (Witness is excused, subject to recall.)

The State's Twenty-seventh Witness

Interpretation of Testimony - Brendan Fletcher: I am a Corporal with the Orange County Sheriff's Office. In July, 2008, I was a Patrol Supervisor. I was hired in 1999. I was the first officer to arrive in a patrol car and in full uniform at the Anthony home. I was alone. I was responding to a stolen car. I was under the impression it was a stolen vehicle and a confrontation between the mother and daughter. Someone answered and I went into the house. I began to gather information from three adults, Cindy, George, and Casey. George and Cindy were in the living room. George did not say too much, but Cindy was very upset and telling me information. Cindy was the caller. I asked why the call and then was told about her granddaughter being missing. I spoke with Casey maybe 10-15 minutes. She did not say much. I asked questions and Casey was not forthcoming. She was not reasoning at all at first, and then she told me her daughter had been missing a month. Casey had seen her with the nanny last and she was conducting her own investigation. I did not understand this. Other officers arrived. Once my superior arrived, he took over the scene. At the time, Casey did not know the location except by showing it to us, and she was willing to show us. I drove my marked patrol car and Casey went with another officer in her car. We went to Sawgrass Apartments and Casey pointed out the last location where she dropped Caylee off. (He is reviewing a supplemental report). I went to the apartment and it appeared empty. No lights, no answer. Casey left with the other deputy.

Brendan Fletcher - Defense Cross-examination: When I arrived, the car was open in the garage. The car was in the garage and we went through the garage once on the way into the house. I did not notice a foul order, but I was not near the car. None of the other officers told me that there was a car with human decomposition inside. (Object sustained) In my report I put down my observations, not necessarily what other officers told me. Some do, the officers' reports are all different reports. There is a main report and supplemental reports. I gave a supplemental report. I only noted it if it was something they told me, and I did not always interact with

145

everyone. My report contains facts that I observed or was
told. Facts of things people told me, but not what other
deputies said. (The witness is excused. The Judge is
advising the defense attorney that impeachment with
police reports is not easy to do.)

(We knew from the outset that this was a circumstantial
case. No one saw Casey kill Caylee. We know there is no
smoking gun. At this point, the prosecution needs some
powerful evidence. Unless Casey has the genius IQ to set
this up in way to destroy all possible evidence, we need
some scientific evidence. We are sure it is coming. We
are still holding to our original theory, spawned by the
media coverage. We suspect that Casey Anthony tried to
sedate Caylee with homemade chloroform and killed her.
Then she put the tape on Caylee's face to cover the burns
from the Clorox and acetone Casey used to make the
chloroform. So far, there is no proof of that, and
suspicion is not proof. We will also say that Casey's use
of the name Zanny has reminded us of the drug Xanax.
Could that be the nanny she was really using? Juror 4 is
now standing out to us. The jurors are facing Casey. This
juror stares at Casey, and the other jurors glance at her
and look away. She is the juror who said that she does
not like to judge people.

A motion in limine is requested by the defense. The State
is seeking to introduce audio video evidence from the
jail. Defense: We are trying to find out what part they
are seeking to introduce and we can speed along the
process. Prosecution: They have had three years to file a
motion and we are planning to introduce all of the video.
The defense has refused to mark what he objects to.
Defense: There are things contained in the video that
this court has ruled not admissible. Prosecution: The
defense has had all of the videos and had opportunities
to file motions. The judge offered to hear all motions
before we went to Pinellas County to pick the jury. There
were no motions filed objecting to those videos then. The
defense feels in the course of defending this case many
issues have been litigated and they have had to
prioritize the issues. Later they realize that there is
an issue they are trying to resolve, so they are bringing
it up to the court. The Judge says that his pretrial
order provided that all evidence that was not scientific
or required testimony should be heard before the start of
trial. Judge: If you failed to file a motion to suppress,
you have waived this objection. We are not going to wear
the carpet out with objections. You can make your short
objections. At this date, the motion in limine is
untimely, and there is not time to redact the portions of

the video you are asking about. You have five lawyers who have had ample time to do this.

The State's Twenty-eighth Witness

Interpretation of Testimony - Adriana Acevedo: I am a Deputy Sheriff. I have worked for the Orange County Sheriff's Office for five years. I was on road patrol in 2008. I responded to the call at the Anthony home. I arrived after Corporal Brendan Fletcher. We have a record of the time officers arrive and the time I arrived was 9:52 PM. Corporal Brendan Fletcher was already in the house. I met with him at the door and asked for specifics on what was going on. Then I took written statements from all in the house. Cindy, George, Casey, Lee. I gave them witness forms. Sergeant Hosey arrived and directed our activities at 11:50 PM.

I was asked to escort Casey. I did, she rode with me in a marked patrol car. She was in the back seat, but not under arrest and not handcuffed. I asked her to go voluntarily and she did. I was taking her to the last location where she had seen her child. I communicated with her that she could leave at any time. She did not object to being with me in the car and I drove to Sawgrass Apartments. We arrived at five minutes after midnight. Casey advised us which apartment it was by pointing to an apartment. Casey is the one that directed us to the apartment complex and apartment. Casey told me where to drive and where to stop. I asked her if this was where she had last seen her daughter and she said yes. I returned to the house with her after 12:25 AM. I let her out of the vehicle and she went back in the house.

Adriana Acevedo - Defense cross-examination: When I arrived, Mrs. Anthony was upset. Mr. Anthony was calm and quiet. Casey was quiet like Mr. Anthony. I did not observe her to be handcuffed. I was in the house about two hours before we left. I saw the car but did not see the trunk open. I smelled an odor and I did not know if it was coming from the garage or car, like garbage. I never advised that CSI should be called. I did not notice if the car trunk was open? I went through the garage, but I was not close, I just passed the vehicle. (The defense asked if she described that as a garbage odor) Based on my little experience with decomposition, I could not give an opinion. I spent another hour after we returned. There were a total of four officers that night.

Interpretation of Testimony – Amanda Macklin: I am the manager of Sawgrass Apartments. The apartment has a shared staircase with one other apartment and the apartment in question was empty in July, 2008. However, Zenaida Fernandez-Gonzalez had filled out a card and she was looking at an apartment, but did not live there ever. (The witness is excused, and leaves the courtroom.)

Zenaida Fernandez-Gonzalez really does exist, but not in Casey's life. Casey is being sued by Zenaida Fernandez-Gonzalez for involving her as the nanny. She has nothing to do with this case. This is a woman with two daughters. She did not know Casey or Caylee. Casey could not identify Zenaida Fernandez-Gonzalez from a photo for police and she does not fit the description Casey gave.) Ms. Fernandez-Gonzalez has been well checked out and cleared by police, and it is believed that Casey found her name on a visitor's form or other paperwork at the Sawgrass complex. Casey's lies have just destroyed this woman's life. Casey had her name, car description, and her children's names. Based on media interviews, Ms. Gonzalez has been threatened, received vicious e-mails, and her daughters have been threatened, all because people thought she had done something to Caylee. (Over twenty e-mails a day plus telephone calls.) She believes a card she filled out to look at an apartment at Sawgrass Apartments was how Casey got her name. That card had her children's names and car information. She was contacted by police. She immediately cooperated by telephone and told them she did not know Casey or Caylee. She even rushed home to meet the police to help. They were looking at her as a suspect and she was scared.

She was afraid that she would lose her children. She has lost her job, lost her car, and was kicked out of an apartment, because people thought she was a kidnapper. (This says a lot about Casey's intent to lie about a nanny. She was prepared to start using this name as the nanny. This name was so usual that the police could follow the lead easily and find Zenaida Fernandez-Gonzalez.

The State's Thirtieth Witness

Interpretation of Testimony – Lt. Reginald Hosey: I am a 13-year veteran of the Orange County Sheriff's Office. The first call that night was for a stolen car. I did not follow up after that, and I had other calls. Later, I did respond to the scene. I do not recall if Casey was handcuffed. I do not recall telling anyone to take the cuffs off Casey. I have discussed this with the State Attorney. Were you advised she had been handcuffed? Yes. However, I do not remember her being handcuffed. I directed the drive to Sawgrass Apartments. I was present when Casey got out of the patrol car. Casey was in the back, and there is a cage in the car to protect the officers.

When I first arrived, the garage was open and the car trunk was open. I went up to the car and I smelled a foul odor. I do not believe I talked to CSI about it. I did not write a report about it. I decided to separate Casey from the other people to talk to her. She walked with me about 40 yards away, and we talked. I am not aware of anyone giving her Miranda Rights. She could have asked to get out of the car. I was present when she returned from Sawgrass. Casey was led into her house by a deputy. She was kept there until the next deputy arrived. She was inside with at least three deputies, waiting for a detective. It was a couple of hours until the detective arrived. The deputies were not inside all of the time. They were in and out, taking calls or statements.

I was present when the detective arrived, and he took over the scene. We were just the preliminary investigating officers. I was done except for reports, and so I left. On July 15th, 2008, I was advised by Casey that her child was alive and well, and with a babysitter. She did not want her mother to have contact with her child that evening. I did not make any effort to stop Lee Anthony or George or Cindy or Casey from leaving. They did not tell me they wanted to leave. They appeared to be cooperating to locate Caylee. Casey was free to walk around the house. I did not tell her she could not go anywhere. I am not aware that anyone told her she could not leave. She appeared to stay of her own free will. George Anthony was calm, but voiced the same concerns about Caylee as Cindy. Cindy was not calm. She was tearful, but she was also calm at some points. Casey was flat all the time when we walked and talked.

The State's Thirty-first Witness

Interpretation of Testimony - Detective Yuri Melich: I have been with the Orange County Sheriff's Office for about 10 years, General affairs. In 2008, I was a detective corporal in the Criminal Investigation Division, assigned to the Child Abuse/Missing Persons Unit. I worked in the Homicide Unit for over two years before 2008. On July 16th, 2008, I received a call from Lieutenant Hosey about the Casey Anthony case. I arrived about 3:30 in the morning. I met with Casey Anthony. I became aware that she had given a written statement. I reviewed the statement of Casey to the patrol officers. I was provided with the statement when I arrived. I believed I showed it to Casey and referred to it as we talked. She said it was her statement, that she had written it, and she adopted it as her own to me. I see the statement document on the monitor.

It reads in general, on June 9th between 9 AM and 1 PM, I, Casey Anthony, took my daughter to her nanny's apartment. She is nearly 3 years old and is 3 feet tall, medium brown hair, wearing a pink shirt. On Monday, I took Caylee to the Sawgrass Apartments. Zenaida Fernandez-Gonzalez has watched her for the last 2 years, and we met through a mutual friend Jeffery Hopkins. On June 9th, 2008, I went to my job at Universal Studios and went to work. I had worked there for 4 years. I went back to pick her up from Zenaida Fernandez-Gonzalez and they were not there. I had called Zenaida that morning and she was there and then in the evening the number was disconnected. I was worried and I stayed with my boyfriend where I felt safe. I continued for a month to stay there. I have lied, stolen, and cheated family and friends to hunt for my daughter. I have not been able to locate her. I have contacted Jeff, who now lives in Jacksonville. Today, I have received a call from Caylee and that is the first time I have talked with her in a month.

I reviewed this statement with Casey Anthony in a spare bedroom. I asked if she would speak to me about the statement and she agreed. I recorded the conversation on audio, and I have reviewed it. It represents what was said. I have also seen the transcript, and it is accurate. (The recording of Detective Melich and Casey is played for the jury.)

(Taped Interview of Casey Anthony on July 15th, 2008)

Detective Melich: I was called in on a missing child, and I am with Casey Anthony. I reviewed her statement together with her before I began this recording. I told her if she wanted to recant this statement she can before I make a recording. Casey told me, that is my statement and it is the truth.
Detective Melich (reads written statement): My daughter's name is Caylee. On June 9th, 2008, I took Caylee to a babysitter Zenaida Fernandez-Gonzalez and I dropped her at the Sawgrass apartment number 210. I had known Zenaida Fernandez-Gonzalez (Zanny) for four years. I met her through Jeffery, who worked at Universal Studios. He is no longer employed there. I spoke with him a week ago. I

have two cell phones and I got them from Universal for work and personal. If we get the phone I have numbers for Jeff and Zenaida Fernandez-Gonzalez. The phone is lost and I had taken the SIM card out and it was stolen from my desk at work. I reported it to Universal nine days ago. Jeff's son Zack was watched by Zanny. Before Zanny, Caylee was watched by Loran a middle school friend. I dropped the child off and for a few months I would drop Caylee at Jeff's and Zenaida Fernandez-Gonzalez watched both children. I started taking Caylee in 2006 to Zenaida Fernandez-Gonzalez at Sawgrass or Glenwood apartments or her mom's house on Michigan Avenue in the downtown and then she moved to Sawgrass apartments this year.

I dropped Caylee off at that apartment the last years, before that she lived with her mom. Zenaida Fernandez-Gonzalez lived with two girls at Sawgrass. I dropped Caylee off and went back to get her after work and no one was home. I called Zenaida Fernandez-Gonzalez and the phone was out of service. I waited and no one came, so I went to a park looking for Caylee until after seven. I was getting upset, and I did not want to go home because I did not know what to say about Caylee. So I went to Anthony Lazzaro's, my boyfriend's, house. I talked to a couple of friends of Jeff and the mother of Zenaida Fernandez-Gonzalez. I did not tell my boyfriend Caylee was missing. I do not have numbers stored and I lost my other phone over a year ago. If I could only find that other phone number… I tried to call Zanny's mom, Jeff, and Juliette, who I work with. I do not have any numbers. None of these numbers are in my SIM card. Juliette moved to New York a couple of months ago and no longer works at Universal. I went to bars like Fusion and the like looking for Zanny. So the only people I told were Jeff and Juliette, and I do not have numbers for them. I talked to her after she left for New York about 3 weeks ago.

Detective Melich: Why did you not call the police before today?
Casey Anthony: I think part of me was naive enough to think I could handle this myself or fear of the unknown or Caylee getting hurt.
Detective Melich: Is there anything about this story that is untrue and did you hurt Caylee?
Casey Anthony: No.
Detective Melich: Caylee has no medical conditions?
Casey Anthony: No.
Detective Melich: Do you do any drugs?
Casey Anthony: No.
Detective Melich: Is there any reason Zanny would have taken your child?

Casey Anthony: No.
Detective Melich: Will you drive with me to show me these places?
Casey Anthony: Yes. Caylee had very distinctive features and a birthmark on her shoulder. (Tape ends.)

This statement was taken and then we went to 301 North Hillside. She pointed out at the windows. She claimed that Zanny and her family had lived there at one point. I discovered later that there are individuals who are friends of Casey and live near this building, directly across the street. Casey did not tell me that they lived there or that she had spent time there with those friends recently. Then we went to Sawgrass Apartments and she directed to me apartment 210, followed by the Crossings Apartments. Then she took me to another location. By then it was light, and I got out of the car to investigate. I had a marked car follow us in case I got out of my car. She said no one looked familiar at any of these locations. After all of this, it is 6 AM, and once that process was completed, I drove Casey home. I did not have her cell phone. I dropped her off and she went into the house. I told her I would keep looking to find Caylee. I left and began an investigation into the things she had told me.

Detective Yuri Melich – Defense cross-examination: Do you go by any other names? Do you ever go by Dick Tracy Orlando? (Sidebar, the jury and the detective leave the courtroom.) I do not have the document Baez is talking about, states the prosecution. (Baez is making copies for the judge and prosecution. Looks like they have something on Dick Tracy Orlando...Sidebar) There is a hearing outside the jury's presence.

The judge says, Mr. Baez, why you think this is admissible? Baez tells the judge that this detective is promoting himself and talking about this case. It goes to his credibility and bias, the engagement of his conduct. The judge says, Mr. Baez, this goes more to unprofessional conduct. Judge Shafter imposed a death sentence where a defendant claimed that it violated his rights to not to cross-examine an officer on his professionalism. In that particular case, the defense wanted to bring out the detective was not professional and it was considered not a proper method. These blogs you have provided to me, is there anything in the content that would affect his testimony based on bias? Not his professionalism. Baez replies: Your Honor, on September 29th, 2008, at 2:50 PM, the date is above the avatar of Dick Tracy on the blog. The blog states, a true missing person is akin to a murder without a body. Your Honor, when faced with information that this was an accident, Detective Melich took it to a murder. Cindy had told him that the gate was unlocked and the pool ladder was attached. The judge replied, Mr. Baez, what evidence would one glean from a pool if a body was not found in the pool? Your Honor, there could be blood and hair. If you do not look you will not know.

The judge says, Mr. Baez, there is no evidence that the victim drowned. What counsel says in opening statements is not evidence. Purported evidence of bias that is not probative of bias is not admissible. In the evidence thus far, Mrs. Anthony has not testified that the pool had been tampered with. Do these blogs show a bias? No. (Objection sustained.) Add this to the record for appellate use if we get that far, but no, not in this court's evidence.

Baez says, Your Honor, I think there is a case called Memphis v. State and I will look later at that. The judge tells him, no other blog material, Mr. Baez. The judge asks about the reprimand of Melich that Baez brought up at sidebar. Baez tells the judge that Melich's supervisor reprimanded him for blogging. I think the activity would be frowned upon by any detective during an investigation. He made it clear he could not discuss the case. Thanks, I cannot talk about the case. In a Sept 20th, 2008 blog, he says thank you for keeping Caylee on the front, so we can find her soon. (The prosecution requests an entire set of the blog documents, in case Baez brings it up later.)

It seems to us that the judge is trying to help Baez, but Baez does not listen, in our opinion. To connect that information on the officers, it is presumed under law that the knowledge of one law enforcement officer in a case is imputed to all that have been involved in an investigation. If one officer was told that the pool ladder was up, Caylee loved to swim, and the gate was open, then Melich knew that information, because another deputy did. So, if Cindy Anthony told any of the deputies about the pool and the ladder, then Melich, as lead investigator, should have investigated Caylee's disappearance as a possible drowning from the outset, even if only to exclude that possibility.

The State's Thirty-first Witness

Yuri Melich - Defense cross-examination (cont.): I arrived about 4 AM. I met with the other officer to be briefed with the situation report at that time. When I arrived, it was a missing person case and maybe a theft of a car or money. I was made aware that Casey Anthony had been taken to Sawgrass Apartments. I cannot recall if they told me that it was to look for a suspect, or if they just handed me the defendant's statement. I was informed when I arrived to look for a missing child. I do not recall the car or garage. At some point, I was told that there was a comment about an odor coming from the car. I was told the child was missing and then about a car and I did not go look or call CSI to look at the car. I did not look that night. I did not find a need to secure the car. When I arrived, Casey Anthony was the mother of the missing child. I never knew she was handcuffed. I did not read Miranda rights to Casey at that time. She was just a mother of a missing two-year-old. But I had not talked to her yet. I read her statement and I asked her if she was adopting the statement. I cannot recall what I thought at the time, but I did eventually put it in the report that she was suspect.

In my opinion, at the time I arrived, she was not a suspect. I read the statement over carefully. Baez asked if Melich noticed that there was a portion in quotations, the words "at home?" I cannot answer why she put quotes on the words. I did not ask her why she did not feel at home. I later documented that she went somewhere she felt "safe." I did not ask why she did not feel safe at home. I think it was in the statement, and so I placed that in quotes. (Objection. Your Honor, this is inquiring about the truth of Casey's statement.) (Sustained; move on.)

Before I get an official statement, I give one last chance to the person to change what is written on the statement, before I record. I did not find her story to be a fabrication; she had a lot of detail. Casey gave enough detail that I had to investigate before I could go on. Casey said she had lost a phone and then had the SIM card. She told me Juliette was one of her coworkers at Universal Studios, and that she was an event coordinator. Then I asked for a number and she could not think of the phone number. Then she said that Juliette just moved up north in the last two months. Then she said that Juliette is not at Universal. She does not have a phone number.

Melich is asked if it occurred to him that what Casey was saying did not make any sense. I cannot tell you what I was thinking. I was just trying to get information to locate a missing child. I eventually went to Universal Studios to try to locate these people. I asked if she had a drug problem or was on any medications. I inquired if she has ever tried to commit suicide. I also asked if she had ever been taken to the Lakeside facility to get treatment for mental health problems. I cannot tell you why I asked these questions. Baez asks if Melich made inquiries to Cindy and George about any medical problems, seizures? (Objection) (Sustained) (The witness is excused and is subject to recall) (Court recesses for the evening.)

June 2nd, 2011

(There is a hearing before the jury enters the courtroom.) Judge: I will inquire of the State when they will be wrapping up their case, so the defense will have an idea when they will start their case. Prosecution: Your Honor, it will probably be a week or two more. However, I do want to alert the court that we are going to play the jail videos; we will begin playing them tomorrow. We do not find much that we do not think is admissible. We have transcripts of most, but not all. We expect to have the last transcript ready on Friday. Judge: Mr. Baez, if there are objections that are *not untimely* it would help to have transcriptions and if the defense would let the prosecution know if they have anything in those videos that is *timely objected to*. Prosecution: Your Honor, the prosecution is going in chronological order of the videos, so that will make it easier if the defense has any timely objections.

Baez: Your Honor, the out-of-state witnesses for the defense needs five days for the clerk to pay their expenses directly. Judge: Mr. Baez, do you have the motions and orders ready? Baez: No, Your Honor, but they will be forthcoming. Judge: The defense can approach the bench and give them directly to me as soon as they are ready for me to sign. (Baez is talking with Casey and does not seem pleased. He reverts to the lawyer's thinking position now as the jury is brought in, and then the next witness is called.)

The State's Thirty-second Witness

Interpretation of Testimony – Jeffery Hopkins: (The party is on! This witness should be interesting… Well, he is presentable, 26, and has known Casey since middle school. They are more or less acquaintances, not good friends.)

I worked at Universal Studios in 2002 and 2003. I do recall Casey working there. I never introduced her to Zenaida Fernandez-Gonzalez. I have no children. I have never lived in Jacksonville or North Carolina. I have not seen Casey in years, except I ran into her on July 2nd, 2008, at the Ale House. I did not plan on seeing her. I did the hellos, and exchanged numbers and that was all.

Casey text messaged me in a mass text message about going to Fusion. I did not go. My middle name is not Michael. I knew Casey in middle school, but I cannot remember her having a crush on me or me having a crush on her. She was attractive and nothing more. I was contacted by law enforcement, and I told them that I do not have a child named Zach. No children, no Zenaida Fernandez-Gonzalez, and no trust fund. I never met Caylee. I never told Casey any of this. I was not moving in with Casey or Caylee and I do not have a son. All of these stories are great fiction and not me. I have no information about what happened to Caylee. Law enforcement first contacted me the night they came to the Anthony home, I believe. I spoke to them once at my house and once at the police department weeks later. I know no one named Zenaida Fernandez-Gonzalez. (Mr. Hopkins seems like a nice young man who knows nothing about this case and little about Casey Anthony.)

The State's Thirty-third Witness

Interpretation of Testimony – Leonard Turtora: I am the Assistant Manager of Loss Prevention at Universal Studios. I do the internal and external theft, as well as the security of the resort. I had contact with the Orlando Police at security. Detective Yuri Melich contacted me asking about an alleged employee. I advised that Casey Anthony was not an employee. From the database we have, I advised she was not currently an employee. However, she was employed by a third party business not owned and operated by the Universal Studios a long time ago. A third party, Colorvision, took pictures of people who come in to the park. She was not employed by Colorvision at this time. April 2006, was the last time she worked with photos. I also checked Jeff Hopkins's name and he had been an employee in 2001-2002. Juliette Lewis was not in our database, and Zenaida Fernandez-Gonzalez was not, either. I also tried to validate an e-mail address later for a Cheryl Davis. I could not validate such an address.

On, July 16th, 2008, I met with Detective Melich in my office at the park. I also met Casey Anthony after we could not verify anything. When the detective put her on speakerphone, I searched the database with the information she was giving. Then he and other detectives brought her to my office at Universal Studios. I met them outside the security gate with all the officers. The detective explained to Ms. Anthony that I was an investigator with Universal Studios, and was helping them with the investigation. I asked Ms. Anthony if she was an employee. She said yes and I asked for identification.

She said she did not have it. She did not know her employee number. She said she worked for both marketing and events. Again, one of our staff whispered to me, and said she was not an employee in our database. I said I knew.

I then tried to contact the name of her claimed supervisor, Manly. I offered to bring her on the property to locate her office. She pointed to a building that had nothing to do with the events department. However, we walked in and looked around. Then she looked at me, put her hands in her pockets, and said, "I do not work here." I guided them to a conference room and left her with the detectives for about 45 minutes. The detective came out and used his cell phone, and went back in. Then two other detectives came out and sat down to make calls. Then I escorted everyone back out.

Leonard Turtora - Defense cross-examination: (Mr. Mason for the defense:) You already knew that Casey Anthony was not an employee and this meeting bringing her out to Universal Studios was a sham? The witness replies, No sir. I was not pretending that she was an employee, but the detectives brought her anyway. I had verified she was not an employee, except years ago for a subcontractor. I do not recall her demeanor. She was not crying. Mason asks, even though you and the detective knew she was not an employee, you let her through? Turtora replies, I was not sure of the other detectives' knowledge, and even though I knew that she did not work there, we all walked with her. About two hundred yards in, she pointed out a building and we went along. I knew she did not work there. As soon as we walked in, I believe she knew that I knew she did not work there. I offered a room for them to talk. I did not see her advised of her Miranda rights in the conference room. Three detectives went in with the accused, Casey Anthony, but I did not go in. I do not recall how long they were there - between thirty and forty-five minutes. I do not know if it was taped. Thomas Manly is the person she claimed was her supervisor. He is not a real person to me. Mason asked, based on Casey's prior statement to you, and at the gate… you knew she was not an employee, so all the while she walked the 200 yards, you knew that she had lied to you. Turtora replies, this is based on her ultimate statement to me. She was not handcuffed to go in the room, and she did not appear to resist. When they emerged, she asked if they had looked in other states for found children. Even as she left the room, there was a missing children conversation.

Interpretation of Testimony - Detective Yuri Melich (recalled): After dropping Ms. Anthony off at six in the morning, I began an investigation that sent me to Universal Studios. I arrived around 9 AM. Casey had given me a witness with no phone number, so I went to get information. Ms. Anthony had stated that Zenaida Fernandez-Gonzalez was a part-time employee and I wanted information on the suspect. I also wanted to locate this lost cell phone. I am investigating where Caylee is, and the suspect is Zenaida Fernandez-Gonzalez, and this was the lead I had. I called Casey and spoke to her by her cell phone and I think she was put on speaker. I told her I was planning on going to her employment and I wanted to verify the information was correct. I did not tell her that I was at Universal Studios and that the security was inputting the information as she gave it over speaker into their data base, to try to locate these people.

We had a conversation, at least one conversation and I asked if she would come out to Universal. Clearly, Casey agreed, and I did talk to a sergeant. I asked if he could bring her to Universal Studios if she was willing to come. They did. I believe I told her, but I do not remember. I do not remember her refusing to come. She arrived within the hour. I first saw Casey at the employee's gate with officers, she was not handcuffed, and no hands were on her. We wear shirts and ties, and wearing badges and guns. No threats were made to her. (The prosecution does not like the detective calling her Casey and corrects him to call her Ms. Anthony.)

Ms. Anthony kept saying she worked there and she did not have identification; she was very convincing. Casey was leading as we walked, we did not know where. She said that she worked there. (The prosecution shows photos and the defense does not object to them being admitted into evidence. It is photos of the grounds of Universal Studios by satellite, among others.) I used the satellite image and drew the path we took. We were led by Ms. Anthony to this building marked in the photo. We had small talk on the way and she turned left, and halfway down the hallway turned and said, "I do not work here." This is a photo of the hallway. We walked following Ms. Anthony, and at the middle of the hallway, it was getting dark. That is when she said that she did work there.

This is a photo of a conference room at Universal Studios. They gave us a small room. I told her we needed to talk. She agreed to speak and we went into this room to conduct an interview. The room size is the same but the furniture is moved into his photo. In the room were Adam Wells, another detective, myself, and Casey. Casey and I sat on the couch and the detectives were in chairs. I had a tape recorder with me. Did you tape it? Yes, except for the small talk coming in. She was not under arrest, and I did not tell her that she could not leave and she did not leave. I recall I placed the recorder on the couch between the two of us. I have reviewed the audio and transcript of the audio. It is accurate. Prosecution: Your Honor, the statement is just over an hour. Can I sit during the audio? Mr. Baez: Objection - just kidding! Prosecutor Burdick: I will come sit next to Mr. Baez and then he can object! (They are all tired.) The judge says a little levity is always good.

(The audio from the recorded interview of July 16th, 2008 at Universal Studios, the interview commences and then the tape begins to play. This is the Interpretation. At 1 PM Casey Anthony and three detectives are at Universal Studios in a small conference room and the door is not locked.)

Melich: We just need to ask some more questions. Everything you have told me is a lie. I have gone to addresses, checked phone numbers and employers. We are in a bad position, so this is the time to tell me. Everything you told me is a lie.

Casey: Not everything.

Melich: We have about thirty years of experience including homicide, and I can tell you for certain everything is a lie. I know that what we need to do is get past this, and you know where Caylee is. We need to find Caylee. I understand that Caylee may not be in good shape, not the way you or your family remember her.

Casey: I do not know where she is or this would have never happened at all.

Detective: The apartment of the nanny had been vacant for months. The other house is across from your boyfriend's apartment. This can go a couple of ways. I can help you, or are you afraid of something that happened, or a cold-blooded killer? Are you scared about what happened or cold blooded? You are bright and you are willingly here. No one is forcing you to talk to us. You are here to find Caylee. You called us in an attempt to find your daughter and you have driven us around. Now taking us to the place you really do not work.

Casey: I understand how all this looks.

Detective: You can carry the weight around or tell us. Everyone makes mistakes and you can lie, bury it, and it never goes away. Stop and think about what is going on. At this point, we can explain you are scared, but at some point, it biases a person who does not care and lies, because they did something bad. You called and asked me

159

to help. You have given me bad addresses, walked me to a place you do not work.

Casey: I understand.

Detective: By burying this, you are not going to get to a better place. At some point this is all going to come out. Go to your parents and tell them some horrible thing happened. You are going to let this drag out and we will figure this out. When someone had hurt you in the past and says I am sorry you forgive them. Someone who lies, it is harder to forgive. Your best bet is to get it out in the open and get past it. There is nothing you can tell us that is going to shock us. I have sat down with mothers who have rolled over on their babies or **they drown in the swimming pool.** I have also sat down with people who have done horrible things and then people who have lied and lied. They are bad people and people have no sympathy for them. So far the only thing we can say is you have lied and brought us here.

Casey: The one thing that is true is that the last person I left my daughter with is Zenaida Fernandez-Gonzalez.

Detective: That is not true because of the rest of the lies you have told. We know that you know what happened to Caylee. **If this was an accident, tell us.** If you are a person who is a young mother and something terrible happened. There is a person who makes a mistake and the person who says I have no idea what you are talking about. I have found all these people you gave me and everything is a lie. Tell me the truth and we can work with that. If you continue this, everyone including you is going to get hurt. On June 9th, you dropped her off at the babysitter. You have dropped her off a bunch of times and her name is Zenaida Fernandez-Gonzalez. So far is that is true?

Casey: Yes.

Detective: You know your parents found your car towed and you tell your parents that you have not seen your daughter for 31 days. Then your parents called the police to bring her home safely. You give bad addresses and take us where you do not work. Then you say that you dropped your child off five weeks ago and you made an attempt to find her on your own.

Casey: So the only reason the police are called is that my parents are trying to find my daughter.

Detective: So you lie to police. So does it make sense that you lied to the police when we are trying to find your daughter? So explain to me how coming here is helping to find your daughter, to look for clues or evidence. We are here because we are trying to find your daughter. Wait. You have three experienced detectives here to find your daughter. You brought us here and you do not even work here. Why did you do this?

Casey: I wanted to come here and pass around a picture.
Detective: Jeff has not been an employee since 2002. What about Juliette? She left two months ago? She has never worked here. Where is the baby's dad? Did you give her to him?
Casey: No, he is dead.
Detective: Zenaida Fernandez-Gonzalez never worked here.
Casey: She had an ID.
Detective: Just like you?
Casey: I have an ID at home.
Detective: We have put a lot more together than you think. Why are we here? There was no purpose. I am trying to help. We are here because…
Casey: Because I lied.
Detective: It is not going to help.
Casey: Because I am scared.
Detective: Of what?
Casey: I am scared of not ever seeing my daughter again.
Detective: How is your lying going to us help?
Casey: Since I just talked to the officer, everything else is questions. I talked to Caylee today and she started talking about books and shoes. She seemed happy and fine. She could not tell me where she was. She was excited, but she did not get upset when she talked to me.
Detective: The last time you saw Caylee, someone took her and you did not see her for five weeks, and she is not upset?
Casey: She has always been like that. She has never not seen me for five weeks. She calls, you ask where she is, and she just wanted to talk about a book. This is the first time that I had been away for more than the day, and she was fine. When I asked to talk to an adult, she was willing and then the phone disconnected.
Detective: I am a parent. I would have called the police immediately.
Casey: I thought I could find her and track them down. Maybe I just missed a call or a text.
Detective: After not seeing or knowing where your daughter was for five weeks. She is calm, and you ask to speak to an adult and the call is terminated. But you still did not call anyone yesterday, and you did not think it was odd.
Casey: I thought it was extremely odd.
Detective: My officer is telling us, he pulled a surveillance camera where you spent the night. It was not at this place you were staying, it was at another friend while Anthony Lazzaro was gone. We drove by the old folks home, one of the places you were saying Zenaida Fernandez-Gonzalez lived. You were staying across the street with Ricardo. We have these people talking with detectives now on video. You are treating us like we are stupid, and unless we start getting the truth, we have

two choices. You gave the child to someone, or she is dead and buried or in the trash. Everything you told us is lies, everything. This needs to end.

Casey: The last time I saw my daughter was on the 9th of June.

Detective: What happened to her? She is out there somewhere and her body is decomposing. You are lying! We will find Caylee alive or not alive, it might still help you. No more lies, no more bull! What happened to Caylee?! I do not know where she was the last time you put her.

Casey: The last time was at the apartment when Zenaida Fernandez-Gonzalez took her.

Detective: If you know, maybe this was an accident; or are you a cold blooded person? You are giving us no choice. This is the opportunity to tell us the truth, the only opportunity. We are trying to prove your story and everything is a lie. Tell us what happened to Caylee.

Casey: I dropped off Caylee, and that is the last time I ever saw her. I gave her to Zenaida Fernandez-Gonzalez.

Detective: Did Zenaida Fernandez-Gonzalez give you any money?

Casey: No, I would not have sold my daughter.

Detective: What about her father?

Casey: I have not seen or talked to him since middle school.

Detective: People are at the police station telling us this is all lies. Your parents are calling trying to find out where is Caylee. Let's get past being at Universal and talking to your daughter yesterday and your mom's reaction off the bat. You are more afraid of your mom's reactions than finding Caylee.

Casey: I know my mom won't forgive me.

Detective: Is there something more important than finding Caylee?

Casey: I purposely mislead you. I am coming back to familiar places and because she is with someone else and maybe they can bring her. She could be anywhere.

Detective: Why would a person, who had hid your daughter for five weeks, then let your daughter call or bring her to this office that you do not work at?

Casey: Maybe they have something on video of Caylee coming through the Universal Studio turnstiles. I told you about the other places, or where I think that they might be at those places. I am sending you where I think she might be, but lying about some.

Detective: It is not helping find Caylee.

Casey: If I knew where she was I would tell you.

Detective: Is your daughter in a better place?

Casey: No. She is with someone I do not trust the minute her phone was cut off and I did not call police. I went to no one.

Detective: I cannot think of anything else I can say to convince you to do the right thing. Do you want water?

Casey: No I am doing everything to find my daughter. My mom puts pressure on me. It is rough being a single mom. I would never do anything or let anything harm her.

Detective: I can see the tears in your eyes. I know what it is like to have pressure from parents.

Casey: It is not constant and I took advantage of them by using credit cards or buying material things and was very selfish, and my mother was right. Then my car ran out of gas. I bought it from my brother three years ago. It ran out of gas after Caylee was missing. It was at the corner and it ran out there. Two guys helped me push it to the lot. The car is in their name for insurance purposes. It just ran out, and my boyfriend picked me up.

Detective: If you were in our shoes, what would you do to help find Caylee?

Casey: I do not know. I instant messaged Zanny.

Detective: If we can take your computer, with your permission, and have it searched.

Casey: Yes, I am okay with that. Zenaida Fernandez-Gonzalez was at other locations. Yet another house, but she was renting a room not in her name, with roommates and I have two names but I did not know the roommates. I did not meet them. This is so hard – there was never a sign. Zenaida Fernandez-Gonzalez is Puerto Rican and is black. I take no medicine and Caylee has had one cold in her life, and Dr. Solos is her pediatrician. My mom, dad and I took her at different times. She likes parks, the playground. There was a jogger killed, and my mom did not want me there because of it. Caylee plays at both, usually the bigger one. She was there the last time in April. She was there with Zenaida Fernandez-Gonzalez in end of May. On June 9th, 2008, I last saw her. Mom took Caylee to see her parents at Mount Dora on June 8th, and I was with my boyfriend.

Detective: So the baby was with mom to see her great-grandparents and they are in their eighties. You are the biggest help to find Caylee. Zenaida Fernandez-Gonzalez does not have children?

Casey: She could, it did not come up. She always said how much she loved Caylee and that she was being raised well. Then this just happened and she was fine in the morning when I dropped Caylee off with her. I always called and sent text messages and IM's. The phone only saves twenty calls and only saves the messages I receive and not the ones I sent. I had the bills for July that I printed and my SIM card last night. It just showed that one was sent not what the text or messages said. She has lived in Orlando since I met her, but in different places. I dropped Caylee off on the steps. I had friends there and she talked about people and never used names. It did not seem strange then, but does now, the changes in addresses and phone numbers.

Detective: If we found the nanny and the baby, what is the biggest concern in your life?

Casey: Just finding Caylee. That next hurdle is not my mom. It is me that I would need to prove to me I am a good mom. Even if my car was in perfect order, what was I going to do? Drive around? I would never hesitate talking to my parents if this happened again. I will offer up my computer in a heartbeat, just like my phones. I have done this to my daughter by failing to notify someone, by not notifying someone.

Detective: Okay, we will head back. I am going to put Zenaida Fernandez-Gonzalez in the DAVIS system. Swear everything you told me is true about the lies and everything else.

Casey: I do.

Detective: Appling Wells and John Alan were on the recording with Detective Melich.
END.

Interpretation of Testimony - Detective Melich (cont.): I believe other detectives were following up on things. No video really existed. I was just trying to get information. We spoke to the manager of Sawgrass Apartments and there was no Zanny. I knew that the Anthony car was towed and no surveillance was available; they are all dummy cameras. Mrs. Anthony had given me a zip drive, the phones of Casey and cell phone records from her ATT site. I was there when she downloaded and she used the desktop computer to locate them in the same room, as we were talking.

At the conclusion of the interview, Casey went into the front seat of the police car and the officer was going through pictures of Zenaida Fernandez-Gonzalez in the database. Ms. Anthony said Zenaida Fernandez-Gonzalez had a silver Ford. The Orange County Sheriff received tips, and we received over 6000 tips. Several had to do with Zenaida Fernandez-Gonzalez and Caylee. We never located the Zenaida Fernandez-Gonzalez that Casey gave us.

I never found any evidence that Caylee was with a Zenaida Fernandez-Gonzalez after June 16th. Mrs. Anthony gave us more records of the cell bills, and we collected Casey's cell phone. This pack has our evidence tape and stickers. It says cell phone from Casey Anthony and more. We obtained a court order to get the text messages and download the friends and any information we could. I believe I gave it to Officer Stinger or Officer Osborne, our forensics experts. We got records directly from ATT. (Records are stipulated as true and correct records of

ATT.) I collected items of Caylee's from Cindy Anthony at the home; four toothbrushes, a comb and brush, and a thermometer belonging to Caylee Anthony. Casey was in the front seat of an unmarked car looking at photos of Zenaida Fernandez-Gonzalez. She was placed under arrest upon return to the police station for lying and child neglect.

Yuri Melich - Defense cross-examination: I talk to the jury because that is what I am taught, to look at the jury because they decide guilt or innocence. Sometimes, this is appropriate and I do this to assist them. Baez: On July 16th, you referred to Zenaida Fernandez-Gonzalez as the suspect. This after hearing the child was missing, you could not find Zenaida Fernandez-Gonzalez, finding an odor, and Casey is lying about working and her office telling you she does not work there. No Juliette Lewis, all of this time Casey is not the suspect? Casey had lied and she was very adamant that Caylee was with Zanny. I could not understand why a mother would go through this if we were trying to find her child. I suspected that she was hiding, but no, I did not suspect foul play. I suspected right after Universal, we just did not before. We did not know. A missing person investigation is close to a murder investigation, and we need to presume that something has happened. The investigation can be akin to a murder, but not in all cases.

I have gone to Hopespring Drive, read a statement from Ms. Anthony. I have information and I went with Ms. Anthony to a number of locations and got no answers and even to an old folk's home where Zenaida Fernandez-Gonzalez lived with parents. Later I found Casey's friend lived across the street. (Baez: You briefed your sergeant on the bizarre events, like a child missing 31 days, and you and others have gone to the apartment.) Detective: Then I went to Universal, Sawgrass and then senior's apartment. There was a guest card that had been filled out with that name. (Baez: You cannot put your fingers on all the stories and they are confusing?) Yes, I think I talked to Sergeant Allen after Universal. I found out she does not work there and these people are just more stories. I asked her if she had ever been to Lakeside or had thoughts of suicide. (Baez: After hearing she did not work there, you called her so Leonard Turtora can hear.) So she could give me an extension. (Baez: Leonard tells you that it is not a real extension, and you have her come to Universal and ask if she can tell where she works?)

I would have told her about what I had found out. Ms. Anthony was calm and clear when she told us. I wanted to see where she was going to take us. Yet she attempted to get in even then. It was beyond me why she would come to the gate with two officers. I cannot figure out why she is doing this if she does not work here. It sounds very convincing; she was walking with purpose. She lead us to the building and into the building. She looked like she knew where she was going, and then she stopped and told us she does not work there. Throughout the morning, I was verifying things and they were not true. As an officer, I deal with drugs, mental illness, and other things. I had to make a call during an investigation. I did not lump her in a category. (Baez: A hypothetical, as you are to sit down, if Casey told you "don't sit down, Zenaida Fernandez-Gonzalez is sitting there… ") (Objection) (Sustained)

(The judge says to the lawyers) There are two cases I have made reference to at the sidebar. Good faith basis for asking questions and we will have some brief statements, but we must have a good faith basis for asking a question. (Casey is talking to Mason behind her hand and he seems like he is uninterested in what she is saying.)

Yuri Melich - Defense cross-examination (cont.): I was at Universal questioning Ms. Anthony with two other detectives. It was a pressing matter, and I was doing all I could to find Caylee. I was talking to the last person who saw Caylee. It was an opportunity to question her again. This allowed me to confront her with why we were there and about these other people she claimed. I have attended workshops in how to question; I have both school and on-the-job training. I use different tactics in questioning in order to get the truth of the matter. We afford opportunities to tell the truth. To make them feel comfortable to open up and get concrete information and in this case where the child was missing. (Baez: These tactics did not work.) I am trying to get her to tell us the truth. (Baez: Despite all the tactics, did it get us closer to truth?) She did not tell us where the child was. She still claimed that the child was left with the nanny.

(Baez: You mentioned in your transcript that you had been getting all kinds of calls, Cindy calling, but it did not say George called.) I left with Detective Allen to talk, but not necessary to call them, but I did call her when we were outside. Cindy told me about the pool ladder being up sometime in June and the gate being opened. I had the opportunity to go in and ask Casey about the pool. (The detective reviews his deposition to refresh his recollection.) (Baez: Did you find the pool incident to be important?) I do not doubt it to be important. But, it was not critical, and all information was important. I had the opportunity to confront Casey about the pool. Unfortunately… (Sidebar)

A majority of the information was verified as not true by the time we had gone through the Universal interview. Video was done after June 9th, but I did not verify the date of June 9th as being incorrect until after I got a date on the video with her great grandfather. We determined many lies after Universal in the following weeks after her arrest. I got her cell phone and she volunteers her computer in the interview, I think. I collect a hairbrush. All items were tested for DNA.

Detective Yuri Melich – Prosecution re-direct: Cindy gave me a date when this pool ladder being up; it occurred sometime in early June. I was present and *it was suggested to Casey, a pool accident with* Caylee. *She said no.* After the tape was turned off, she never adopted any other theory other than the kidnapping. The scenarios that we gave to Casey included the pool drowning and other things like rolling over on a baby or boyfriends beating a child. She stuck to the Zanny kidnapping, no matter what we said. (The witness is excused, subject to recall.)

(A jail recording of Lee visiting Casey at the Orange County Jail is introduced into evidence.)

(Jail Video)
Casey: hold on, turn up the volume.
Lee: How are you?
Casey: Laughing, I do not want to start crying.
Lee: Heads up, we have an hour together and mom and dad are coming at one. Baez would or could not do it for us. I am sure you know everything inside the jail is being recorded, except if you write a letter and that is not monitored. I will write a letter so you can have a line of communication. Do you have access to paper and a pen?
Casey: I can get that.
Lee: You already know how you can reach out. Baez works for you and anything you say is attorney-client and if you say to deliver a letter to us, he is not obligated to send the letter. He has his best interest. If you try to reach out, he may not give us the information. He has told us that his number-one focus is you, and then Caylee. The most important thing is him; it is a business for him. I cannot speak to anyone else's focus. My focus is Caylee, then you, third mom, then dad, and then me. I don't care about Baez, the police or anyone else. I need you tell me, should my focus be anything different?

Casey: That is the same as my focus.

Lee: The police are only going off information that gets to them. They have been reaching out to Baez and they left two messages and he had never returned a call. He faxed a letter saying you were willing to cooperate. He is not communicating with the police and the bond stuff I will leave it at that for now. How did Baez become your attorney? His name was given to you by someone in booking?

Casey: Yes, an inmate.

Lee: How do you feel about him as an attorney?

Casey: I think he is doing whatever to help me. I am his priority and not Caylee.

Lee: We think it is best to get information out and help us find Caylee. Use the letter from jail to help us. Do you want to talk to law enforcement?

Casey: Yes and no, I know they are looking at me, so the family or Baez is best with the police.

Lee: When you gave your statement to the police about dropping Caylee off on the 9th, it was the 16th, Father's Day, or after. I figured you knew it after and you have not been able to reach out and correct your mistake.

Casey: At the same time, they have misconstrued and put words in my mouth. I would rather not. I am not dealing with it anymore.

Lee: If you wrote a letter through Baez and he could decide not to give it to the police. Send a letter through the jail mail and copy us and Baez. This way you can get the truth to the police. Now the information they are going on, they have, is correct?

Casey: I have been giving the information to the police. They were looking at Universal employees, not Kodak.

Lee: We need to figure out the best way to get the information to them and remember you write me a letter from the jail, too. I am the only one, and I will do what you want. Baez is going to decide. I need to know who I can trust. If I can trust them do not say anything. Anne?

Casey (responds anyway): No.

Lee: Melissa?

Casey: No.

Lee: Amy?

Casey: Yes.

Lee: Ricardo?

Casey: do not know,

Lee: Tony?

Casey: not sure, I do not know.

Lee: Jesse?

Casey: No.

Lee: Mom?

Casey: Yes most definitely.

Lee: Dad?

Casey: Yes, most definitely.

Lee: Ryan?
Casey: Yes.
Lee: Will?
Casey: Maybe - barely know.
Lee: Is there anyone who you do not trust that you want me to look into?
Casey: Not that I can think of.
Lee: As far as any area or places where should I focus a search or tips?
Casey: Check things locally, things that are close to the family and ask mom. Try to go through mom. If not, I can give it to you, places more than people. I have no idea - this is my first contact other than Patrick Beasty from high school to connect with anyone. He had a whole group we can trust.
Lee: Mom and Dad and I have been trying. We have been on telephone hold trying to see you. We were instructed by Baez and the police that we could not see you for seven days after the arraignment. This is what I am telling you, information is not getting to us and people have their own agendas.
Casey: Melich read me my rights and said he is going to hold me as long as he can.
Lee: We have had a lot of communication. They prep their witnesses, just like Baez. I knew how the bond hearing was going to go. We ask every day and you have not gotten a letter from Mom or Anne, and we have been giving them to Baez. He is reading them or not, and he is not giving them to you. You have to realize that. We do not have any say in your representation. If you want to change jockeys in this race you can. You are an adult; we cannot do anything about the people who represent you. You, I, the family, and if they are not effective resources, we need others. I have been talking to people who have missing kids. I have learned from them how to manipulate the media, police, and lawyers, so I am learning from them how to do it. The focus is not on Caylee. The only way to get information out to the media is through Baez. If you send me a letter, I can get out any information you want. The media calls me every ten minutes. If you want it known or corrected, send me a letter. Are there any clues? Myspace, Facebook or Photobucket?
Casey: No. My telephone records, I just opened an account at Wachovia, Mom has POA.
Lee: That does not matter; the POA means nothing about getting information on this account. Bank, credit cards records of mom or friends?
Casey: No.
Lee: Any clues at the house, stuff on the computer?
Casey: The family computer one disk of pictures we have, only one I think. Nothing stands out in the pictures. My password is RICO234.

Lee: That password does not work Casey; I tried.
Casey: It's the one I used before I left the house. Mom was there when I logged in. Log in CASEYOMARIE@yahoo.com and cays234 for Myspace.
Lee: The laptop?
Casey: No.
Lee: Houses to look for clues?
Casey: Tony's, just my blow dryer and shirts.
Lee: Ricardo's?
Casey: No.
Lee: Jessie's?
Casey: No.
Lee: Fusion?
Casey: No.
Lee: Text messages?
Casey: Yes. There really was a different phone and I do not know where it is. We have five minutes, if you can find the other phone.
Lee: What numbers are on the missing phone Casey?
Casey: Jeff.
Lee: Casey, I have your complete list of your phone records. Is there something, maybe a date or time?
Casey: No.
Lee: Is there meaning behind the Facebook and Myspace accounts? Your tattoo, is that Caylee related?
Casey: No clue in that. Speak to the media and express my concern for Caylee and I love my daughter and my family, and Caylee is my only concern and nothing else matters. I want them to hear it from me, her mother. You have everything that I feel comfortable giving now.

(The jury is in recess.) The defense is asking for a mistrial based on the video statements from Lee that the counsel may withhold evidence and more from his client. It is the prosecution's obligations not to present these videos and misstatements of law and facts as it relates to the representation of Ms. Anthony. The prosecutor says, I think they should not be prejudicial to the point of confusing the jury as to what the law is. The State of Florida requires the pleadings to be specific to an issue, but the motion does not raise such an issue. This is untimely. The judge announces, the deadline was December 31st, 2010 to bring evidence issues to this court. Mr. Baez broached the subject and did not file a motion to redact this video. The prosecution says that we were never approached on redaction on or by the deadline. Baez concurs, saying, I agree with the prosecution. We did not file this among our hundreds of motions. We did not, but I believe we can object. The defense chose a higher priority. The judge tells him that the defense received these videos in 2008 in discovery, and one about three weeks ago. No, 2008 and 2009 and the one three weeks ago is a duplicate. Time can be harsh, and there must be some finality. We gave December 31st, 2010; and January to April, we had time for motions. It is untimely and your motion is denied, Mr. Baez. (The jury returns from recess.)

The State introduces a jail video of George and Cindy Anthony's jail visit to Casey Anthony in 2008:

(Jail Video)
Cindy: I love you, Casey.
Casey: I love you too. I saw you sitting down. I was talking with one of the doctors.
Cindy: We forgive anything you have said and done.
Casey: I did not say anything.
Cindy: Casey, are you okay?
Casey: I talked to Lee. We got cut off, but we got to talk. **Cindy:** Look, a t-shirt with Caylee.
Casey: Lee showed me.
Cindy: The whole United States is looking for Caylee. She is going to be the cover on People.
Casey: Oh, good.
Cindy: Are we going to find her, Casey?
Casey: I hope so.
Cindy: It is okay to cry, Casey. I want to ask you a couple of questions. Is the picture of Caylee with drums in Zanny's apartment? I know whose apartment that is Casey.
Casey: Mom, it is Ricardo's apartment.
Cindy: I can't get in to Myspace.
Casey: I gave Lee everything.
Cindy: We need to show her personality in video. Look at me.
Casey: I cannot look at you and the camera.
Cindy: Do you think Zanny is acting by herself or with others?
Casey: I do not know. I have nothing to go over. I am extremely upset. Baez has given me nothing. I read the one note and that is all. That is the only note I have been given.
Cindy: A lady at the airport said she saw Caylee and the child said she was Caylee Anthony.
Casey: I do not know. I just want the police to look into it, and I want you and Dad and Baez looking into it, as well. Zanny had roots in North Carolina, New York and Miami. Her mother is Gloria, about 55.
Cindy: Is it possible that Zanny's mom could be with her aunt?
Casey: I do not know.
Cindy: Does Josephine sound familiar to you?
Casey: No. I'll ask if they are going to let us have more time, since we started late.

George: Hey gorgeous, how are you?

Casey: I look like hell.

George: Keep your spirits high.

Casey: I have not been crying, dad.

George: We have to get that little girl back.

Casey: Dad, Lee has a quote for the media. I have not taken Caylee out of town. I went to Cocoa in May. I am staying away from the TV and newspaper.

Cindy: What message do you want to give Zanny through the media?

Casey: She needs to return Caylee. My only concern is that she comes back and is smiling and happy. Tell Caylee I love her and to smile and be brave. I truly love her and miss her. I miss you guys.

Cindy: We miss you too.

Casey: I know that Caylee is on top of everyone's list. I am on the bottom of the list. I am protecting our family, not from anything I have done.

Cindy: Is someone threatening us?

Casey: Just leave it at that.

Cindy: I know; do not try to protect us, we all have to protect Caylee. There is nothing to protect us from. Why did you not go get the car?

Casey: Because of this being recorded, I cannot say. Lee and I are finding other ways to talk.

Cindy: Has someone else been in our house?

Casey: Possibly, I told you a long time ago Zanny had a key. How is the rest of the family?

Cindy: Grandmother is not doing well and I cannot talk to her. She is not doing well at all.

Cindy: We all know you have done nothing to Caylee.

Casey: I get it daily here.

George: What can I do?

Casey: Keep talking to the media and be positive and focus on Caylee.

George: We are all just given a lot and we need to be strong. We know where you are, and we are sure you are safe; and once we get Caylee home, then we will get it taken care of with you. Mom and I worry about you being in here.

Casey: I am watched at all times in protective custody.

George: I talked to Mr. Baez on Wednesday. Have you thought about talking to the police?

Casey: Dad, they misconstrued everything. I think there has to be money in my account, so you need money to make outside calls even collect. Tell Amy I am sorry. Tell Ryan I appreciate all his help. And ask him to visit.

George: What about Tony?

Casey: What is there to say? Tony has not made any effort and will not even talk to Baez. Jessie needs to stay away from the family. I do not know if I can trust him. Jessie may know Zanny, but I do not trust him. I think his parents are okay, but I do not trust Jessie. Jeff gave me my heart ring; I have not seen it in years.

Casey: Dee from Kodak sent her best. Tom Frank and Tom Maly both, Mike Cusack might know lot of these people. I know the Myspace password. I will give it to you.

George: Mark Hawkins, the workers' compensation lawyer I trust him to talk to. I talked in passing with his mother at Target. Tell us about Zanny's car.

Casey: Silver Ford Focus 2008, four doors, very basic with a pink floral car seat. Zanny had everything Caylee could need, so I did not need to give her the car seat for Caylee or things. I do not know who else other than Jeff she was a nanny for. I never took Caylee anywhere to get her hair cut. I've never had my hair done since 2006. June 16th, was the last day I saw Caylee. You mean Mark's psycho ex-wife, I have not spoken to her since the end of May. It has been months. The babies never spoke to each other. You have my phone records. I am fine and I am eating to the best of my ability.

Cindy: If I list names, is there anyone who might have insight?

Casey: Lee and I went over this and he has it. I was thinking about going to Puerto Rico and we were all buying our tickets and staying at his apartment. Nothing pre-scheduled months in advance. I picked her up from the airport. The menu was for me. I wanted to start working out. Baez has asked me a number of times. I love you and I miss you. Stay as strong as possible.

Cindy: Our whole life is turned upside down looking. We are going to find that little girl. Everybody wants an end to this. Did Caylee ever stay at Tony's? Tony admitted to Lee there are drugs in the house and his roommate smoked weed and it had nothing to do with this?

Casey: No. Patrick Beway from middle school just came for support from high school. He is going to write and try to get people to write. I appreciated his visit. I have not talked to him for years. Tia Toris, do you know her? She told someone that I was hospitalized with a mental condition. People want their face on the news. Everyone knows you are the mom of the group. They say your mom is a real spitfire.

Cindy: I am just trying to find Caylee.

Casey: I know. Me too. I would lie, steal, and cheat to get her back. I want her to be found.

Cindy: I think once she is found you can tell what you know and then you can tell the truth and be released.

Casey: I do not know. Yuri thinks I have done something.

Cindy: What the hell is that? (Casey just hung up and left. Casey returns.) Casey: They have to take me away when other inmates come in I have to leave. I am in protective custody. I am speaking to the psychologist. I am not opening up to someone I do not know, just Baez. We have open meetings and he can get my cuffs off in the private meetings. I can only see police and my attorney.

George: Did you borrow or take something from someone and Caylee is being held for that.

Casey: No. Lee advised me to write.

George: Tell me what I can do for you. I want to get you out, but not until the bond can be reduced. I want Caylee back too. I want to take your pain away; you can tell me everything.

Casey: You are a great dad and the best grandfather; Caylee **was** so lucky and she still has both of you.

George: Our house is empty without you. I wish you could have come to me sooner. I wish I could have said something and at least spent a moment the day of the hearing. It is hard to be away. We are trying everything to get the little girl back. I got threatened by Melich to send a squad car to see grandfather because of the video. So I know some of what you are going through.

Cindy: Do not worry about protecting me or dad or Lee, just Caylee.

Casey: I ate coleslaw. I eat baloney and cheese and grits. Visit with Baez, you and Dad and Lee, so I have some contact. He was putting in the appeal for the bond, maybe a week to know.

Cindy: Describe Zanny.

Casey: Short brown hair 5'7, very thin, maybe 140 pounds, brown eyes, no tattoos. I would think anyone who knows me and Caylee would come forward.

George: They said you could not pull her out of a line up.

Casey: I have told Gabriel and Baez to get a sketch artist for me. They only searched by part of her name, not both names. I think her dad or stepdad is Victor. Her parents have a lot of money. I think it is Fernandez. He legally adopted her. Her sister is Samantha and was a student. I do not know her last name and she is older, a year or so.

Cindy: Did Zanny ever talk about taking Caylee to the beach?

Casey: She would take her to Coco and the places over the last month I told you I was. I do not know who she could be with.

Cindy: Could Jeff look preppy?

Casey: I do not think he has ever worn glasses, fitted jeans and a polo shirt maybe. I do not know his sister's name. Rocker Farrell and Jennifer Rosa are roommates of Zanny. It has been a month or two. I do not know where they are originally from, but they lived here. I think Jennifer worked at a Friday's. It is good to see you guys smile a bit.

Cindy: We had a flat tire. Trenton's father has been helping us. There is a $225,000 reward to find Caylee.

174

Casey: That is almost half of my bond.

George: I get many calls of support. If you think of anything that can help, do not be afraid. You do not need to protect this family, we just need to find Caylee. Think of your hand as the family that needs to be together. We are missing two fingers – you and Caylee. We are trying to find that little girl. Share it, write it down. Will you talk to the FBI?

Casey: I will talk to who you want. I do not want to talk to Allen and Melich. I will talk to Happy Wells, who was at the house, with or without Baez. I think he will go out of his way to help you guys. He was at the house – a big guy, no glasses. He picked me up Wednesday. They are just going to tell me, I am lying. I do not want them if they are going to take information.

George: I think you should have an attorney. We are going to leave out the back before the media follows us.

Casey: Just look locally. Post pictures.

George: The quicker we get Caylee, the quicker we get you home. But if we do not find her, they are building a case against you.

Casey: Bring in the FBI and I will talk to them. I just want her back.

George: Just stay positive. Do you think after this long they would still be local?

Casey: I know in my heart she is not far, I can feel it. I do not know if they have any leads in Jacksonville. I have a long history with those guys, big brothers trying to help like Ryan.

George: Once we get Caylee, everything will figure itself out, where she has been.

Casey: Tell Lee I love him.

George: What your brother and the family has been doing for you, the officers tell me is unconditional love, darling.

The State introduces a jail video of another of Lee Anthony's jail visits to Casey Anthony:

(Jail Video)

Lee: Hi, Sis.

Casey: How are you?

Lee: I made it here through the media; to get in and out is hard. So I just wanted you to be able to talk, before I start asking questions, Sis. Do you have anything from me?

Casey: Did you get my messages from Baez? Yes?

Lee: I look forward to a personal message from you. On Caylee went missing, am I correct that you had spoken to three people over the phone?

Casey: I had talked to three people before reaching out to mom. Are any of those people involved? My gut feeling is they could be involved.

Lee: Two out of three you had texted before reaching out to mom. One you talked to first.

Casey: As far as the order, I do not know.

Lee: Out of the two, was there someone you spoke to on a more frequent basis and it could be either? Do any of those three people – would they have talked to each other?

Casey: Yes, they were all intertwined as friends.

Lee: On June 17th, you had called a place that would deliver food.

Casey: I was out and about in the day looking. Not at night.

Lee: During the day, would you have reached out to any of these people that you might be interested in? That other cell phone; was it purchased for you by someone else?

Casey: I do not remember when I bought it. In the last three months.

Lee: The person would have contacted you on that phone, no preference. The three on June 16th, you talked with. The other person, I know your feelings on this person it is noted, but you had a long conversation with that person. It appears a lot of franticness. Would she have any information, would she open up to me?

Casey: I hope so.

Lee: I am going to reach out to her. The Fossil crew. When would they have first met Caylee?

Casey: The last week of May, first of June. I brought Caylee to the apartment and that is where they met her. We went to the pool a couple of times, around the first week of June, maybe after Mom's birthday.

Lee: If I were looking for the nanny's place, would it be advantageous for me to look in an area of the other friends of yours in the complex?

Casey: Yes.

Lee: Would that include any of the people I referenced earlier?

Casey: No.

Lee: Zanny had used a few different phones to call.

Casey: Yes.

Lee: Is there any other area codes I should add to that list? Miami maybe, throughout Florida, or on the east coast?

Casey: That is Mark Hawkins; there is nothing to follow up.

Lee: I already talked to someone who confirmed these people exist.

Casey: Zanny called from the three area codes.

Lee: Did you get text or calls or both?

Casey: Varied. Most of my communication is text.

Lee: Is it safe to assume the person who took Caylee has resources out of the State of Florida?

Casey: Yes.

Lee: As far as places I have been recently, Casey? I wanted you to keep into consideration based on the contact you have had and what I know right now. It has all changed from a month ago. We have been following a certain way and I need to know if we are still working off the same time, the same people and the same area. Has any of it changed? Let me know what you have been stressed about and reacting to. Maybe someone else needs to stress, too. Reporters are following me, and there is a certain level of respect for us to continue that relationship with them. Baez set up a place for one interview. That is not going to happen. We have news vans twenty-four seven. Is there anything that you think will be helpful to me and the things you were told this weekend?

Casey: Nothing I can think of at this moment. I see Baez this afternoon, and will send a message. If you guys are able to probe Orange County, that might be good.

Lee: Can you ask Baez to check?

Casey: Absolutely.

Lee: The jail calls account I sat up, those calls can only come to me. So do you know when you might call?

Casey: Yes, nine-to-four.

Lee: Call any time you want to reach out. Do not worry about the money, and call if you have something. We are working on keeping the focus on Caylee. The media photo is just nationwide. Mom and Dad and I are working real hard with places for flyers, volunteers on a massive level, and donations to the reward. We have a great deal of support and reference of the Lord a lot and to lean on that. So many old friends, strangers, and more through prayer. Regardless of what you hear, there are good people trying to help and give resources to find Caylee. Anything you think of, let us know. Caylee being missing is on Myspace, profiles to mirror the other profiles to let people know how they could help, helpfindcaylee.com and more. We take tips, volunteer information and a hub to communicate with everyone. We have had charities in the form of billboards, flyers, mobile billboards, t-shirts, fundraisers with donations from coca cola and more, to get the charities helping funds. We are in the thousands of the support. This is how we can get the word out about Caylee.

Casey: I want to thank our family and friends for their unconditional love and support. I want to thank all the charities for their time and resources. If there is anyone who had any information about Caylee, please come forth without haste. Publicly, tell them I miss her and I love her I want her to come home and be safe with her family. I know with every ounce of my being we will be with her again. I did not thank you for all the help. I love you and thank you so much, and Mom and Dad, too. I will be with you soon and we will have our family back. Dad gave me an analogy and there are two fingers missing. I know we will be together. Mom said we are stronger than we have ever been, and we will all make it through this and be okay. I love you too, Lee, and we are going to find Caylee. (Video ends.)

(The jury is in recess for the evening.) Judge Perry asks, Mr. Mason, did your defense team serve this motion that you want to be heard tomorrow morning? Mason has a quick comeback that provokes a laugh from everyone. "Your Honor, I have an alibi! I have been here all day!" The judge asks Mason to take a look, and Mason agrees to do so. The judge wants to know the difference between the new motion and similar motions the judge previously heard. Mason tells him that he does not know the difference, other than that this one is signed by Finnell (Ah, the old, 'I'm just the messenger' defense!). My understanding about what might be outstanding is limited. I do not think we need to have a hearing on that motion.

The prosecution announces that they just received a new witness as an expert from the defense, and that they have been given a one-page web download and a CD with George Anthony's hospital records. The prosecutor reads from a document that Dr. Sally Karioth, PHD, RN, teaches courses in professional nursing and holistic medicine. This is an expert who has not interviewed the defendant. The defense tells the judge that in light of all the evidence that has been introduced, the defense wants to present evidence of some kind regarding different times of reaction in the grieving process. Much of the evidence that the defense felt would be inadmissible has been admitted. The witness's testimony would not require her to see the defendant. The defense attorney says that he gave the State what the defense has. I think it would be malpractice not to explain the different reactions to death and dying. I had no knowledge this would be an issue, and so I sought out someone as well. She is available for deposition, as well, as I am going to be taking Dr. Vass's deposition. The prosecution tells the judge that the court heard evidence on all of the witnesses, and Mr. Baez's claims that he was surprised is disingenuous, and that the defense has said the same thing in previous motions and claims. Baez tells the judge that he just thought of this, and it should be exempt. (It appears to us that his claim is not genuine.)

Judge Perry says that testimony on grief and bereavement is not automatically admissible, and that for him to rule he will need a deposition and reports of the expert, just like all experts. He tells Baez that he will not even consider letting her testify until Baez produces a report, qualifications, outline, and a statement of all of her opinions. He tells Baez that if he does all that jumping, then the judge will decide. The Defense and prosecution will speak with them this evening.

The prosecution says that the defense had first brought this up in a motion of some form, but now they claim they just got the witness. Baez says it is true that they just got this witness, and the comments of the prosecution are disparaging. The judge says that he does not think the comments were disparaging, and that even if the defense jumps through the hurdles, it still may not be admissible. The judge then turns to George Anthony's medical records, and says that he does not know what the late delivery is all about, what portions will be admissible, or the good faith for the delay; the good cause for late disclosure. He announces that there will be a hearing on Saturday at 1 PM on the medical records. He requires that the depositions be taken early next week of the expert. The State says that as soon as they get the report, they will set the deposition very quickly.

(We close this day with this writer's message. Based on Baez not objecting timely to the jail visit tapes being edited and removing the content about his representation of Casey by the visitors, he has almost guaranteed Casey a Florida Rule of Criminal Procedure 3.850 motion for post-conviction relief after the direct appeal, if she is convicted. That kind of motion addresses issues that cannot be addressed on appeal, like ineffectiveness of counsel, and if it is granted, Casey gets a new multimillion dollar trial.

June 3rd, 2011

Good morning world! We hope the prosecution presents some science today. We think at this point the jury (and we know the shadow jurors) are waiting. We expect that the first video today should be the last of the jailhouse videos, since the prosecution is presenting them in chronological order. We were just thinking, lawyers work with the evidence and witnesses they have, they cannot choose the facts. Baez is working with what he has, but it's not pretty. The prosecution is working with what evidence was left after Caylee's body was missing and underwater for months, also not pretty. So it is a fair sword fight, a duel of the law. The referee, Judge Perry, seems to be doing a very good job in the middle of the fight. Although we disagree with some of his rulings, he may try this case cleanly enough and without bias… sadly, that is not always the case in the courtrooms. So, if the mistakes in this trial are minor and do not afford issues on appeal, the verdict will not be overturned by a higher court. No trial is without error. But if the errors are considered harmless or minor in the scope of the entire trial and the appellate court feels the errors would not change the course of the case (that the verdicts would be the same without the errors), they can let the lower court's verdict stand. This is our system, and how it really works or does not. The court deputy announces, "All rise!" Judge Perry strides in.

(The jury returns to the courtroom, and the evidence commences. The State introduces a jail video of another of Cindy and George Anthony's jail visits to Casey Anthony. This one is from July 30th, 2008.)

(Jail Video)
Cindy to George: Casey is not here again, they told me she was going to that hearing. Casey enters the visitor's room with cuffs.
Cindy: Good morning, honey.
Casey: Good morning.
Cindy: Can you see our shirts? Anne had them done; we just got them last night.
Casey: Yes. I was catching up on my sleep and I got some rest. I woke off and on.
Cindy: It was good to see you yesterday in court at the hearing. It was good to see you in person.
Casey: How is Dad?
George: It is so good to see you and to see you yesterday. I love you. The house is so quiet. It gets harder and harder each day. The outpouring and everyone's focus is on Caylee. I wish everyone's outpour community was this focused. Our focus is finding Caylee. How is your focus? We need all the help we can get, getting her back.
Casey: Lee was telling me about the charities.
George: People Magazine is doing a story on missing children and Caylee is the cover.
Casey: I know, you told me that.
George: Is there anything else you want me to tell Caylee through the news?
Casey: Just tell her I love her and I miss her. We are not talking here. I am being as strong as I can, considering the situation. I just want to go home, and every day I wake wanting to go home. I want to help you find her. Every day gets harder… (crying) I am glad you were on Larry King. He is insightful.

180

Cindy: Harley went on Nancy Grace. Everyone is helping. Lauren; I saw her and the baby. She had a boy.

Casey: I knew she was going to have a boy. I want to see her (still crying). Every day I am worried about Grandmother, is there any change?

Cindy: I know it is hard for her; she can barely talk.

Casey: My heart is aching because I want to be with my family. I know Caylee is coming home. I feel it in my heart. I know I am going to be home with you, and so is she. One day last week, I was with Baez, and there were two people at the table and they were from church and we talked. One of them said, one night he went to bed and had a heavy head and he woke in the closet. Then he laughed a lot and he told me laughter can get out the things you are feeling.

Cindy: I know you are consumed with Caylee.

Casey: Yes, but I have to keep myself up. They woke me at 4:30 and took me to holding. They thought I had morning court, and there is no room for me because I have to be by myself. The time was for the wrong hearing and they knew me by name. It made me smile and giggle. I expected what happened at the bond hearing. I was not surprised. We have to be careful about what we talk about. I just want to talk about other things. I was glad to see you live yesterday. I rode in the vans three times, and so I got out. It was uplifting. It just put a lot into perspective. I saw the outside world and got to see you both. I am sure you did not hear about the court until you were sitting here at an empty screen. I did not know about it until 10 PM the night before. Dad wants to talk.

George: Grandparents send their best. They are not doing too well. I nearly had to call the paramedics. They want the best for you, but they want Caylee. They feel that they were not around enough. Every time they ask how is Casey, Caylee and Lee, and they are concerned. We miss you a lot. I wish I could have been a better father and grandfather.

Casey: Dad, you have been the best father and grandfather. You and Mom have done everything to be the best parents and especially the best grandparents. We are coming home. Take care of Mom and make sure Mom eats. All this is going to work itself out. It is what it is. I just want you to keep your focus. I want to talk to everyone, but I think I need to wait and not let everyone's rights be violated talking to me. I missed two visits, and I so do not know who they were last night.

Cindy: Casey, I love you, and I want you home. I am trying so hard, and it is getting harder every day.

Casey: I know better than anyone how hard it is.

Cindy: I just want Caylee to come home, then you. Caylee does not see us. She is not going to hurt Caylee is she, Casey?

Casey: In my gut I feel she is okay and I – we are going to get her back. We will figure all that out when I come home. I am thinking about the jobs and all that.
Cindy: You will not have to work, just take care of her.
Casey: I used Dad saying on the hand and it makes everyone smile. Tell Dad be strong, I can see him. You are doing the right thing looking for Caylee. I need to get out of here. I talked with Baez last night it was more on a business angle. I still have not had time to make the calls to friends who ask. I am declining all visits from anyone but family and Baez. I need to keep things in the family. I have been crying every day inside. But I am able to calm myself, but considering where I am…
Cindy: I could curl up into a ball, but with Caylee I am being her voice out there. Dad is the strong one and processes things before he says something. He has always been like that.
Casey: It is so good to see you all.
Cindy: Do you want us to make another appointment as soon as we can?
Casey: Yes.
Cindy: You have only so many times we can see you.
Casey: Will cancelled. That is good. God bless you Dad (with a laugh). I am glad you were on Larry King, Mom.
Cindy: I would have liked to talk more about Caylee and not the 911 calls.
(Video ends. Defense requests a sidebar regarding this video in evidence.)

We, the authors, were wrong. The State is introducing another jail video. This one is of George Anthony's solo jail visit to Casey Anthony, from August, 2008.

(Jail Video)
George: Good morning beautiful, how are you? I love you and I miss you. Mom loves you, Lee loves you. Everyone loves you and wants everything to work out as soon as possible.
Casey: I love you too.
George: We want Caylee back.
Casey: I want her back.
George: I want to have that party.
Casey: I want to be home so we can do that.
George: A lady here used to work with you, she is a great person. I know what they are saying is wrong. Have you talked to Baez?
Casey: Last night.
George: I called him last night.
Casey: How was the charity's thing last week?
George: It was great! All about Caylee and other children, everyone is working so hard to bring Caylee

home. This little girl, my granddaughter, your daughter, has captivated the world. I got a call from a man in DC who made his own shirt. They just want to bring her home and if we can get Caylee home, then all the other stuff will work out.

Casey: But I want to be home when she gets home.

George: When you get home and Caylee is home, with this, we are going to be more proactive in finding other children. I know she is close I can feel her every night. I go out and pray to the stars. I am doing everything I can for her and for you. It is destroying your mom. Maybe we have all been too domineering and we could have been better to let you be a good mom. Would you speak to someone else about Caylee?

Casey: I would.

George: A man named Scott and he is with an agency. I think you could talk to him about Caylee.

Casey: I want to be home now and I want to be home when Caylee comes home, not three or four days later.

George: We have done everything financially we can. When I did the thing I did, it was handled in the judge's chambers before court and yours is the same way. I would do anything for her and you. Are you eating? I know – doughnuts and coleslaw. Do you have pen and paper?

Casey: I wrote with Baez last night and I called him this morning. He has been giving me stuff to read.

George: The place and the outpouring of support were amazing the other day. They do it for all missing children. They had a video with Caylee, and songs they sang, and other children. They played SpongeBob Square Pants.

Casey: (crying)

George: Realize we love you and we want you both home, whatever you can do to help us.

Casey: I am doing everything.

George: We can go into protective custody and they can get Caylee back, just help them.

Casey: I can only do so much from where I am. They are going to the Supreme Court to get my bond lower.

George: I hope he is concerned for Caylee and not just you and himself. Everything has happened. It is all about getting you all back.

Casey: The media is going to spin.

George: Is there anyone who had threatened our family?

Casey: I do not know. I have just been here.

George: People Magazine, we thought it was to be about Caylee and it was spin.

Casey: Caylee should be everyone's concern and I want her to come home and us to be left alone.

George: You are a good mom and you will always be. The people that matter know.

Casey: The people are going to feel dumb when this is all over and Caylee and I are home.

George: Our faith and compassion has changed.

Casey: It has always been our choice. You, Mom, and I did not want to sugar-coat the world.

George: Having you and Caylee is all that matters. Your brother is a genius in the media and getting things out. There are a lot of doors and positive things in spite of this terrible thing. Do you need money in the commissary?

Casey: I do not need anything; they go through everything. I did get a Bible and I read it. I miss you and I love you. I want to meet in person and I want to hear her laugh - be with my little girl.

George: It is a few days to her birthday. We were going to have a small party for her. Now we want a big party. We just need our lives in check, and to be straight with each other. Your mom and I have opened up more to each other. We all need to do that. I have a different t-shirt today. They are making more, flyers, billboards, Tampa, everywhere. There is no expense not being used to help find Caylee. The photos are beautiful, and in person, such a personality.

Casey: She had the best in all of us and she shows it all the time. She is the best of the four of us.

George: Parents give children the best of them. You have your mom's good looks and personality. From me, maybe always watching out for your car. I never thought I would have anyone in my family going through this. I would trade places with you. Can I set up a phone account for you to call? It would be nice if you could call.

Casey: I tried this weekend and it just rang.

George: It could be a private number and we are not picking up. Is everyone being good to you? Not screaming at you?

Casey: No, I am in protective custody.

George: We are going at it 24 hours a day, no stone unturned. Going into Caylee's room, I wish I could have brought something for you to see. Caylee is going to be home soon. We will all be together soon. It is clear there is a lot of love. I miss the hug and squeeze for papa Joe. I am sorry I have been so tough.

Casey: It is not a bad thing. You will always be my buddy, besides my dad. I love that little girl more than anything.

George: I got a card from a teacher and she was very kind. I do not want to say her name and the media get it.

Casey: They made me file something about visitation, and then it was on TV the next day. It is not fair for anyone else to be put through this. I am so strong from the love of you, Lee, and Mom. I am glad to know there are so many people offering support for our family and Caylee. I get letters of support from all over the country.

George: I am just worried about you. If something pops into your head that will help find Caylee.

Casey: I will. I told Lee, Baez, and you, I will call.

George: Yes, this will assist with John Walsh. I have reached out to John Walsh to help find Caylee. He lost his son. This is a club for missing children and that none of us wanted to join. Caylee did not want to join. Do you have any ideas besides what we are doing?

Casey: HelpfindCaylee.com is just for her.

George: Mom and I are trying to get you out. Your mom hit the barrier, she was sick last night.

Casey: She is tough.

George: When I leave here, I have the media outside and I want them to concentrate on the finding Caylee. We all love that little girl more than I knew possible. I hope wherever this person or persons who have her, are feeding and letting her watch videos. I am looking. That is why I need to know everything.

Casey: I want to do everything I can. I want to be out and help. They think we are speaking in code. I am giving whatever information I can, when I can.

George: That is being released by the sheriff stuff. They want to release all of the calls and visits.

Casey: Just know how much I love and miss her. I know we are all going to be together.

George: I want to hear her say Jojo mail, Jojo wagon, Jojo swim, Jojo walk. I love you.

(Video ends.)

The last video is about to be presented, and Mason has already cancelled the 8:30 hearing. The judge gives a proposed instruction to the lawyers about the videos. (The attorney is in charge of strategies in a case, and decisions are made in a vacuum.) The defense says that none of it is relevant and it is highly prejudicial. The judge tells the lawyers, these tapes have been out there since the beginning of time. The statements in the video about the attorney by the Anthony family – concerning them, we do not have an agreement. Now, you guys can wade through and dicker with language later, or I will craft a jury instruction over lunch hour. Not now. No stipulation.

(The State introduces a jail video of Cindy and George Anthony's jail visit to Casey Anthony from August 14th, 2008.)

(Jail Video)

George: Casey, good morning. I love you

Casey: Why is Mom crying already?

George: Because we have not seen you.

Casey: I was asleep.

George: What else is going on?

Casey: Nothing, waiting around. Those are new shirts. The Never Lose Hope Foundation made them.

Cindy: Hi, sweetie (crying).

Casey: Hi Mom (crying).

Cindy: None of us is doing well, none of us. Lee is sick and Dad blew up at the media. And someone just said Caylee was dead and she drowned in the pool.

Casey: Surprise, surprise (with an eye roll). I am reading the articles.

Cindy: We get hate mail, threatening letters. We need something to go on, Casey.

Casey: I don't have anything.

Cindy: Did Baez ask how you wanted to meet with us?

Casey: Yes; Dad - I had to pick one. I had to pick and I picked Dad. I have given everything to the police and I have helped in every way I can. I know you guys want Caylee and I want Caylee more than anything. I want to talk to you, just you. Baez keeps me updated.

George: It has to be focused on you and Caylee.

Casey: Baez is focusing on me and then Caylee, and you are focusing on Caylee. You want me to talk. I am not in control over any of this and my entire life has been taken from me. I have no answers. I have no one to talk to but Baez. Baez and I agreed to keep the media from me. I have contact with no one. I have no answers. The first week and a half I backtracked. I cannot backtrack on anything. You guys are not understanding my side. The opportunity was there. I could have helped, and now I cannot. I can do nothing but focus on my case. Your focus has to be Caylee.

Cindy: I thought about everything that you have told me, and I was in Lake County two weeks ago, is there anything there?

Casey: I am angry and frustrated with all of this.

Cindy: We are all going in so many directions we just want to go in the right direction.

Casey: Random people have more of a point to look on this. You still have family and friends and house. I have no one to comfort me. I am pushed away from everything.

Cindy: They have to honor your wishes and Baez is in New York.

Casey: I know. He is doing business for me.

George: In his absence, Dominick is a good person I have set up who you can see and talk to.

Casey: He is telling me what I am up against. The opportunity was there and it passed. You could have got me out. I was pissed off, and now I am really mad. This is the most aggravated and frustrated I have been. Even when I watch Nancy Grace, I am more frustrated. You have to understand where I am coming from, a month out of the loop and you expect me to come up with something new. It is hard; you and us and we are trying and sticking together. You guys have each other and I only have me and my attorney and what they can do for Caylee.

George: It is taking a toll on Mom and me.

Casey: Nobody can see my side and I have to keep my mouth shut or the media and the police will throw it back in my face. I had to pick, and Lee would interrogate me. That is how it has been. Mom would dominate the conversation. I wanted to see the person that I had been so disconnected from, and that was you.

George: Thank you. I appreciate it. I know it was a tough decision. I am so honored on the decision. Let me see if I can get in sooner. Through the people who are with you. If you mention to the corrections people you want to see me…

Casey: I tried that and it did not work. I have asked every question.

George: I will do what I can, and I will do what I can to get together quickly. How did you get through last Saturday?

Casey: I spent the day under the covers with my Bible. I was so upset and broke down, Caylee's birthday. Hearing Mom making chili and there was a bunch of people at the house and this is what I was hearing.

George: It was just close family, not a big party. Just a young guy who was alone, it was not a big party.

Casey: The Bible says love thy neighbor. I am eating so they leave me alone.

George: The area you are in is a good area.

Casey: There are others in this area, not in media seclusion like me. I wanted to talk to you, but I did not want to upset Mom, but I can only hold so much back.

George: I am praying it does not go out on the media. Only the one with Lee has and our conversations have not been out.

Casey: It is personal. So it does not feel like another business transaction. I am by myself sleeping.

Cindy: Casey, I am sorry that I upset you.

Casey: I cannot hold in my frustration.

Cindy: I know. Each day is getting harder on us. You do not know. You are secluded. I am trying to stay calm.

Casey: People need to shut up, and they are not going to look at it, and it is all fabricated. It is going to blow over and I am not giving the media anything. I just want my family back together.

Cindy: Do you still think she is okay?

Casey: I know it.

Cindy: What can I say to Zanny?

Casey: I forgive whoever has her and I just want my baby back.

Cindy: Do you think they would do that?

Casey: We know what it is to have our family back. I do not want to be one of those parents that do not know where my child is and that she is alive.
Cindy: Do you think they will?
Casey: I do not know. I cannot talk to you. This is what happens and why I chose Dad. You and Lee just ask questions. I can't help you, I have been here!
Cindy: It is hard to go into Caylee's room now.
Casey: I know, I saw in People.
Cindy: At least I know you are okay and I do not know about Caylee.
Casey: I may be here, but I am not safe.
Cindy: We do not know where Caylee is and if she is being fed.
Casey: I know she's okay, I can feel it. Even on her birthday. Nothing can describe what I was feeling. I am glad you have had so much support, so have I. It has to be checked through security books and Bibles.
George: Can you ask for something to write with? Attention Kevin Perry and tell him you want to speak to me or Lee or Mom.
Casey: Okay, I will do that.
George: It can be in a place not recorded and it can be done with only you and me or Lee or Mom. They want us to have that time.
Casey: If it came from the police, I do not trust them. I will do it today.
George: All I want to do is tell you I love you. They can set it up. All right sweetie, I love you.
Casey: Tell Lee I love him, and I am sorry I missed our visit. I am sorry Lee is sick. The only reason I want home is so I can help get Caylee home faster. I am being told what to do when. I will get that note to the sheriff done.
Cindy: This is hard on everyone. They are not releasing stuff with me. Only the phone calls with Lee and not the video. The Sheriff's Department picks what they release.
Casey: I put in a plug on the sheriff, so they will not want to release the video. If they came in attacking me they will not get a shot. I am just as much of a victim as the rest of you and it has not been portrayed that way. Give everyone my love and I will see everyone soon.
Cindy: I hope so, Casey.
Casey: Put Dad on, I want to say goodbye.
George: Just know you can trust Mom, Lee and me.
(Call ends.) (Sidebar)

(Judge Perry reads an instruction to the jury.) The statements in the video expressed by others about Ms. Anthony's counsel, you are to disregard those opinions as to Ms. Anthony's counsel.

The authors note that Casey's eye rolling to Cindy's drowning comment is her response to the very defense they are claiming in the courtroom. Maybe Baez did not watch the video. Or maybe that's where he got the idea for his opening! Whether you look at the videos from the defense's position or the prosecution's, it seems clear that in June, Casey knew Caylee was dead. Yet, she kept telling her distraught parents (who were leading searches all over the world to find their granddaughter) that Caylee was still alive. Millions of dollars in resources that could have gone to other missing children were wasted. The only thing that is clear in these jailhouse videos is that Casey lies, and she appears to be manipulative and narcissist.)

The State's Thirty-fifth Witness

Interpretation of Testimony – Charity Beasley: I am employed as a detective in Orange County. I have worked for the Sheriff's Office for seven years. I assisted Yuri Melich in obtaining evidence in the Hopespring Drive case – a vehicle, a laptop, and miscellaneous items. The car was towed to the forensics garage. I sealed the doors, windows, and trunk with evidence tape before it was towed. I followed the wrecker the entire way and turned it over to another detective at the location of the forensics garage. The other items were given to me in a blue plastic crate. There was a doll, a backpack, a child's toothbrush, a black leather bag. Also a laptop computer and it was unplugged and off. I provided the other items to the same officer, except the laptop went to the Computer Forensics office.

I knew there was an active investigation regarding a missing child. I was requested to go to the Anthony residence to pick up the car and evidence. I was the one sent to collect, and it was my job to seal the car. When we see the car photos here, I put a small piece of tape across the door openings and windows. I do not recall if I smelled an odor. The computer – I did not open it. It was completely down to my knowledge, and I turned it over to Ms. Kahn in Computer Forensics. I was requested to handle the items, and that was my part in this case. (The witness is excused.)

We think that Mr. Mason is not happy today. This poor woman just picked up evidence. What we cannot figure out is why Mr. Baez (who is lead attorney and controls this case presentation) is not using Mason to cross-examine more important witnesses in this case. He appears far more skilled at the art of cross-examination and believe me, this is an *art*. Books are written on this one area of law.

Mason announces that the defense has not been provided with witness logs. The prosecutor says that they plan to have witnesses to lay the predicate. They are here in an abundance of caution.

The State's Thirty-sixth Witness

Interpretation of Testimony – Awilda McBryde: I am with the Orange County Sherriff's Office; I have worked there for 10 years. In July 2008, I worked in Missing Persons as an investigator. We look for missing children, adults and runaways. I am not an officer. I only assist and do background work. In July 2008, I met with George Anthony and accompanied him to the location of a tow yard. It is when Caylee had been reported missing, and I was told by Detective Yuri Melich, to go recover a trash bag. July 16th, 2008, is the date I went. It was dark, the gate was closed, and we called the company. A company driver opened the gate to let us in. I had to give identification to gain access. I gained access, and George and I went to the dumpster. I had my camera. A photo of a dumpster is shown.) That was taken prior, before we looked in the dumpster. I took a picture of the dumpster.

The dumpster had sections to the lid. They were closed, and George, the employee, and I opened the lids then took the photo before we reached inside to touch anything. (A photo of a trash bag with a pizza box is shown.) We took the picture before we touched the bag or anything inside. I did not open the bag at any time. No one but me touched the bag. I wore gloves, and I put it in a brown paper bag. I used two to completely cover the plastic trash bag. After, I put it in the trunk of my agency vehicle. Then I took it to the Orange County Sheriff's Office. George was with me in my car, and I dropped him at home before I took the bag to the Sheriff's Office. I met with a CSI officer and turned the bag over. I did a property form and handed it over to Yuri Melich when he came down to the evidence room. I was also asked on July 17th, 2008, to retrieve a computer tower and digital camera from that same Anthony home on Hopespring Drive. We brought them to the Orange County Evidence Department and gave them to Detectives Allen and Melich. I had another woman with me when I picked them up, but I took custody of the items. (The witness is excused.)

Interpretation of Testimony - Christine Narkiewicz: I am a Crime Scene Investigator with Orange County. I have been so employed for three years. I have a Bachelor's of Science degree in Forensics with minor in Chemistry. I was trained by the Sheriff, and I have three hundred and twenty additional hours in training. I worked just a few months in 2008. I assisted Yuri Melich in 2008. On July 21st, 2008, I was asked to go to the jail for DNA samples of Casey Anthony. I arrived at about 10 PM with hair and buccal swabs. They are sterile cotton swabs and I rubbed the swab in her mouth to collect cells, two swabs to the left cheek, and two to the right. I used gloves and a mask. I recognize the sealed package and the swabs I took from Casey Anthony. I turned them over to the lead Crime Scene Investigator. I had sealed them that night, before turning them over. I obtained hair standards. I requested Ms. Anthony turn her head over and I retrieved the loose hair on brown paper and sealed that. Then I pulled Casey Anthony's hair out from the root to obtain root samples on separate paper and sealed that one separately. The plastic tweezers did not work, so I used my gloved hand. Both packages are identified by the CSI on the stand. It was turned over to lead investigator Gerardo Bloise.

On July 28th, 2008, toothbrushes, a hairbrush, a comb, and a thermometer belonging to Caylee Anthony were received by me. I received them from Yuri Melich and I packaged and sealed them all separately. I can identify Casey Anthony in the courtroom as the person who samples of hair and buccal swabs were taken from. I wore gloves to protect from any cross contamination. I take extraordinary precaution when collecting DNA. For the most part, we try not to speak when we take DNA. I am not a DNA specialist. The packaging used is specifically designed to protect the sample. If properly packaged you could go back 20 years, if the sample had not been used up.

The State's Thirty-eighth Witness

Interpretation of Testimony - Gerardo Bloise: I am a CSI Level 2, and have been with the Orange County Sheriff for 11 years. I was a police officer in Puerto Rico, and then a Forensics Scene Investigator in Puerto Rico. I trained with the FBI and have a BA and Master's Degree. I process crime scenes, notes, processing, photos, protecting, and providing evidence to the Sheriff Office as needed. I do not perform analysis of the things I collect. I received a Pontiac Sunfire. Detective Beasley turned it over to me and it came in on a tow truck to the Forensics garage bay. All the doors and the trunk were sealed.

(A photo is shown.) The vehicle, with the correct tag number, is in the photo with seals intact. I also received evidence in a black garbage bag, the items in the basket, the doll, backpack, tooth brush, black leather bag, papers, and clothes hangers. Photo and evidence verified. I have had the opportunity of being around people who have been deceased and smelled the odor of decomposition about thirty to forty-five times here and in Puerto Rico. I have experience in getting fingerprints from dead bodies. I have experience at different levels of decomposition. I have searched dumpsters and landfills. I broke the seal on the door and opened the driver's door. My observation immediately was that I smelled the odor of decomposition coming from inside the car.

The first thing I did was photograph the car's outside, and then the inside. I documented the report. I take notes and I utilize the notes to write a report. I attempted to determine if the gas gauge was working. I photographed the gas gauge, then I put some gas in, and then I photographed the gas gauge again. This was several months later, and it was working properly. (A photo of the gas gauge is presented.) I photographed the interior of the car, sunglasses, CD case, a brown belt, the back seat with a car seat and shoes on the seat. The car seat was closed up. This is the condition of the car. (Photos showing shoes, an air freshener dryer sheet in the back seat, and a photo of the undercarriage of the car while it is on a lift are shown.) There were no foreign objects, just dry leaves near the transmission and near the front tire. Just dry leaves. There were not any animal parts under the vehicle.

(Photos of the inside of the trunk are shown.) The spare tire well is plastic. I removed the spare tire to inspect it. The marker "A" is a different dryer sheet, "B" is residue of dirt. The processing took several days. This is a photo of the reverse of the tire cover after it was removed. The section removed is the fiberboard material. It is normally covered with carpet. I removed the carpet. This is a photo of dry leaves in the trunk and marker "C" showing the dry leaves in the trunk. The spare tire would be sitting in the wheel well, before I removed it. The fiberboard and carpet would be on top of this wheel well. (We see this man as a reliable witness.)

I tried to document the condition at every step as I removed everything from the trunk. The liner of the trunk

192

of the Pontiac was removed and I took it to the forensics laboratory. We are looking at the trunk liner in this photo and I placed two markers to show the left and right of the liner of the cover well. This package contains a piece of carpet that lined the trunk. (Photos are introduced. They are from all sides of the vehicle with a pointer pointing at a piece of suspected human hair on the trunk carpet, and a close-up to show the hair.) There was a red fiber in the trunk, and the hair was over it. It was found on the left side of the trunk carpet. This is a photo of the basket with the doll, and the like. I reviewed and secured everything in a box in my evidence room inside a locker. I opened the backpack. I took pictures of its contents while the pack was open and preserved it. I collected other evidence from the trunk: more hair, an air freshener dryer sheet, and residue, and preserved it. I can I identify the evidence packages. They were then submitted to the lab for analyst.

(The defense is objecting at nearly every word the witness utters. You know, lawyers fight like cats and dogs in the courtroom, and when it is over, some of the lawyers for opposing sides go out for drinks together. Even if they are not friendly, most are at least social to each other in public. Still, the reality is that the defense and the prosecution typically are very different creatures who do not much like each other.)

(The witness reads aloud an inventory list of evidence presented to the witness for identification and gives a description of the contents of each package.) He reads: A package containing samples of the left and right side dirt and particles from the car trunk in Petri dishes; a package containing the spare tire cover and another with a Petri dish with hair; a package containing samples from the bottom of the radiator of the car - dry vegetation; a package containing samples from the seat under the black shoes; a package containing a dryer sheet from the back seat; a package containing samples from the right side of the trunk liner; a Petri dish with hair; a package containing samples from the middle of the trunk liner in a Petri dish with hair; a package containing samples from the left side of the trunk liner - a Petri dish with hair… (He continues to read from the list about samples taken from the vehicle for several minutes.)

(The witness steps down from the stand. He identifies a large box with four items enclosed in the box. He looks at the entire package and recognizes the large box; he also identifies it by the date he put on the box with his initials.) I can verify this box was the one I used for items on the right side and left side and the remainder since I had to cut the carpet for evidence samples. But all is in the box. The prosecution opens the box in the courtroom. The witness puts on gloves and begins to pull out pieces of the trunk liner and show them to the jury. The box also has a plastic bag that contains a can with a piece of the liner. These packages contain samples from the spare tire cover – two swabs. These packages are samples from the trunk and a piece of spare tire cover, placed in the box by me. These packages contain more samples from the trunk and another piece of spare tire cover, placed in the box by me. He has verified all evidence from the car, identified the packages, and verified the **chain of evidence** as to his handling of those items. (To prove an unbroken chain of evidence, the State has to produce every person who handled or had custody of the evidence and show every step in the recovery and processing of the evidence since it was discovered. The defense will try to show a break in the chain if they can.)

When the car first arrived, I did an exterior inspection of the car. Then I did an interior inspection. Upon opening the car, I smelled decomposition – human or not, I do not know. It could be animal, meat, or human. I have smelled various bodies at basic stages of decomposition. It could be a common thing to see maggots when it is fully decomposed. That would not be my expertise – different stages of decomposition. In the Medical Examiner's Office, I have smelled formaldehyde. That is in a different area of the Medical Examiner's Office. This area does not have chemicals. I know the difference. The smell of decomposed body is something that you never forget. I know from my first time smelling it in Puerto Rico. The only difference in the smell is whether it's weak or strong. I can smell it. When it is full decomposition, you have different smells. When a body starts to decompose, it smells different from when it is completely decomposed.

The gas gauge is something that I did. I did not drive the car, I can just tell you the gauge worked when I did that test in the garage. The leaves, I believe were sent out, and I believe were tested and I do not know if they were of any value. I did vacuuming of the car. I use it is hand held device, and it catches evidence. I used an alternate light source to identify stains. I found a stain, and that is not uncommon. I use a chemical called Blue Star to identify blood. It's better than luminal. I received negative results with Blue Star. I did a presumptive test on the stain, and it was negative for blood. I swabbed for DNA. I do not know the results of the DNA test.

194

As for hairs in the trunk, I found twelve by hand on July 17th, 2008, from the edge of the vehicle. I did observe the first hair was longer, but I cannot say if they were different colors or sizes. I do not remember the color. I cannot say if there were any animal hairs. I am experienced in trace recovery, the recovery of the small amounts. I wear a net, white suit and gloves when I collect, and sometimes a mask. To find hair in the trunk is very common. In the example of other items in the trunk transferring hair, it is possible - like a sweater. It depends on the owner; how clean the car is. I sent it all to the laboratory and I cannot say if they tested every hair or did every kind of test. I send evidence to laboratories all the time. A bullet goes to ballistics, a fingerprint to a fingerprint expert. I submit hair for DNA, and I do not know what the laboratory does, what kind of DNA test. Twelve hairs were found by hand, and eleven by vacuuming. A total of twenty-three hairs were found, after inspecting the car twelve times. I searched the trunk to my best, and I did a thorough job. I was present when the defense inspected the car. Who inspected the car for the defense? Dr. Henry Lee. (Sidebar)

(The authors know that is the famous Dr. Henry Lee from the O.J. Simpson case and others. However, this famous expert is more infamous to us because of a fingernail that disappeared in a case. It really damaged his reputation. The judge in the Phil Spector murder trial ruled that the world famous forensic scientist Henry Lee removed and hid evidence from the crime scene. After hearings outside the presence of the jury, Judge Larry Fidler said he was convinced that Dr. Lee removed the evidence. A witness who said she saw Dr. Lee pick up the white object was at the time an attorney working for Spector's defense team, Sara Caplan. Judge Fidler said she was the only witness who testified during the hearings that he found "completely credible." The judge said, "If Dr. Lee has this object, he is to produce it forthwith.")

(The State moves to strike the question from the record. The judge says no, but I am advising the jury to disregard the last question.) While inspecting the trunk liner, an additional hair was found. I destroyed my handwritten notes after writing the report. The report dated is January 1st, 2009. I wrote the report. That is the date my supervisor reviewed my report and signed it. That is not the date I wrote it, but the date he reviewed and signed it. The trash - it was trash. On page 23 and 24 of my report, there are 37 items of trash, including a box of Copenhagen chewing tobacco, an empty Crystal light bottle with brown liquid. I do not know what the liquid was. Three empty boxes of Velveeta cheese. (Objection) Those items are not in evidence.

When I referred to the negative results from the Blue Star, I was referring to the fact that the test was negative for only blood. A Blue Star test is only positive for blood, not other bodily fluids. I handwrite the notes, and then when I complete the processing of the evidence, I complete a report. Then I destroy the notes, in accordance with Orange County Sheriff's Office policy. I turn the report over to my supervisor and he reviews and signs. When the defense inspected the car, they did not wear hair nets or suits, no, just gloves. The odor was of a particular type of decomposition. Yes, it was human decomposition, based on my twenty years of experience and smelling thirty to forty fully decomposed bodies, it was the smell of decomposition of a human body. Everything that is reflected in this report is accurate to my handwritten notes, and again everything from my notes is in this report. It is possible that I did not say directly that my opinion was based on my experience. In the report, I said based on experience. (Baez asked if the witness was referring to someone else's opinion.) In my opinion, it was decomposition. (Baez tried to trip him up a little bit, but the authors think the jury knows what he smelled. We think it is more a language barrier that caused the slight slip. The witness has a heavy Hispanic accent. However, he appears truthful.) (The witness is excused, subject to recall.)

Karen Korsburg-Lowe, an FBI analyst will be testifying for the prosecution tomorrow. The judge asks, and the prosecution estimates their case in chief will end around June 16th or 17th. Then the defense will or will not present their case. The defense has a choice. If they think the prosecution did not prove a case, they may not present a case (testimony or evidence) for the defense. Then, the jury deliberates only with the evidence they have from the prosecution to prove murder. This is risky, sometimes very effective, but risky nevertheless. We think the defense will put on some kind of a case in this truly ugly trial. There are stampedes every morning to get one of the fifty seats in the courtroom. This case has captured the public's attention and the news has covered the trial non-stop. It seems nearly impossible, but the media coverage is even greater than before the trial began.

June 4th, 2011

The morning starts with all the boys and girls on the defense and prosecution heading back toward the judge's chambers. Casey sits in an unremarkable striped shirt with the lady lawyer Sims next to her. They are back. The judge walks in. The court deputy says, "All rise!" After the judge sits, the same court deputy intones, "You may be seated." The judge starts with, Let the record reflect that the State, the defense, and the defendant are all present with the court reporter.

A pretrial Frye objection by the defense is renewed regarding Karen Korsburg-Lowe's testimony. (The lawyer in the family says that Frye was a case that set the standards and procedures, now modified slightly, for how new or novel scientific evidence can be that is introduced in Florida courts.) The defense asks to voir dire the witness regarding her qualifications to testify before the jury hears her testimony. Judge: I have already done that at the Frye hearing. Defense: We are entitled to voir dire the witness. Judge: Unless the prosecution does not get her credentials, this has been ruled on. There will be no mini-Frye hearings during trial. (This fight is about the postmortem banding on the hair.) Defense: We just think that we are entitled voir dire of the witness under [Section] 90.705 [Florida Statutes]. Judge: The ruling is no. Defense: I am clear that the court is not allowing us to voir dire this witness? Judge: No you cannot; we did that a Frye hearing. You did not object to her qualifications at the Frye Hearing. Your objection was that this is new or novel evidence in the Frye Hearing.

(Judge Perry knows his law. He can pull cases out of his head on many different subject matters.) Judge: I have ruled that the prosecution must lay a foundation as to credentials, and if they do, she testifies. We have wasted enough time on that this morning. Bring the jury in.

Good morning, jury. Did you heed my many warning? Yes, Your Honor.

The State's Thirty-ninth Witness

Interpretation of Testimony – Karen Korsberg-Lowe: I work for the Federal Bureau of Investigation in trace examination at Quantico. I have been with the FBI for 15 years. I have a Bachelor of Science and a Master's of Science degree. I have taken several post-graduate classes at George Washington University in Washington,

DC. Those classes relate to microscopic analysis. I have also had additional training in that area. I have looked at thousands of samples of hairs and fibers. I have taken many classes. I have been qualified forty-four times as an expert to testify all over the country in federal, state, and local courts. The majority of my testimony has touched on hair examination.

(The defense asks again, and receives permission for brief voir dire of the witness.) When Baez asks if this is the first time she has testified on hair root banding, she replies that it is. (Sidebar; the defense does not want this woman from the FBI testifying, and we are sure that Baez is arguing that the witness does not have sufficient experience or expertise in hair root banding to testify.) (Voir dire continues.) The topic I am going to cover… the amount of training I had in hair was six months of a year-long course. The root banding training was a portion of the six months. I have taken three courses on this topic, all there are, plus a year of on-the-job training and experience in case work. Whenever I conduct an examination, I render an opinion. I have been accepted as an expert on microscopic analysis and hair analysis. (Objection) (Overruled)

(The voir dire is over, and the judge finds that she is an **expert witness**. The only real difference between an expert witness and any other witness is that an expert witness is allowed to give opinions involving the area of the witness's expertise.) (The State resumes questioning her.) Hair analysis has been around since the late 1700s, and it has been used in the U.S. by the FBI since the 1930s. There are three steps: collection – how hairs are removed or recovered, identification, and comparison. For comparison, two hairs are compared under a stereoscopic microscope, really two scopes with a split screen effect. It is then possible to compare whether the two hairs are from the same source. I can conclude that the hairs come from the same source, or I can exclude a source. If there are racial differences, I can identify that. The root will tell me how the hair was removed, and can be used for comparison of hairs to determine if hairs came from the same source. This is done all over the country.

Are there signs that point to decomposition on a hair? In 1988, there was an article that looked at hair in all growth phases. It defines a postmortem hair root band as opaque, elongated and there are other factors. The keratin would be at the soft and the hard. Then in 1998, they looked to see if nuclear DNA was there. The hair comes to a point at the root, and more articles have studied this. In 2001, they looked at samples from 22 postmortem cases, to see the differences, and found that hair root banding occurred from two days to fifteen days postmortem. They compared these samples to hairs from non-decomposed hair that had been placed into the woods for forty-five days. None of the hairs from a live person mimicked the hairs from the decomposed person. We do not know what causes it. The appearance of decomposed hair has never been duplicated in any other way. Hair banding does not occur in every case; it is among the least common of the characteristics of postmortem hair.

(A chart with hair is presented.)

These are different roots in difference stages. After birth, during life, and post-mortem stages are shown for hair that is both forcibly and naturally removed. These hair roots are clearly distinguishable. Decomposition is seen only in hairs that have been forcibly removed. The appearance of decomposition on a hair root has never been duplicated by a hair of a live person. The determination of these articles we talk about is a visible assessment to see decomposition. Some of the articles mention a math formula for the length of decomposition. I am looking at it in three dimensions, also enlarged to a big image. We have hairs in different periods. A number of cases involve known hair samples of hair from a decomposed body.

I have examined hair in over two thousand cases. Not all involve decomposition, but there are a fair number in my cases. I would not guess how many. Samples usually come from a deceased when I look at them. I have seen postmortem root banding. In cases where there is decomposition, I have seen postmortem banding. This is the first time I have been asked to analyze a hair sample from an unknown source to determine whether the hair is pre or postmortem. I did the tests on the hair in the Casey Anthony case. I had items from known individuals in this case for comparison. (Several packages are shown to the witness to identify by packaging, labeling, and initials. She identifies known samples of George Anthony, known samples of Casey Anthony, known samples of Cindy Anthony, and known samples reported as being from Caylee Anthony's hair brush.)

Upon examination, did you know if there were human hairs in the unknown samples that were submitted to you? I will refer to my notes. There were at least ten or more human hairs in the unknown exhibits. One of the hairs showed the characteristics of decomposition. What I examined was a decomposed hair, and I saw postmortem root banding. I examined this hair on different microscopes; on three different scopes. It is light to medium brown color and it was nine inches long. None of the other hairs had the banding. I did not compare the known hairs to each other. I compared the hair with decomposition and the hair from the hair brush. I also compared the hair sample from Casey Anthony, and her hair was not similar. The unknown hair was similar to the hair from the hair brush. I had only one unknown hair, so I can say it is similar to the hair from what is believed to be Caylee's hair brush and I can say the hair was apparently on a decomposing body. The darkened band is consistent with apparent decomposition, and it has not been shown to be found under any other circumstances. (The prosecutor wants to introduce photographs of the hair that shows the banding, and the defense succeeds in keeping the jury from seeing it.) I reserved the root portion that showed banding on a fresh microscope slide and sent the remainder to another part of the laboratory for DNA analysis on the hair. This package contains two tubes that were sent to the lab for mitochondrial DNA analysis.

Karen Korsburg-Lowe - Defense cross-examination: You refer to apparent decomposition? It has not been shown to be duplicated under any other circumstances, but we say apparent to be conservative. This history of microscopic hair analysis in the FBI has been done since the 1930's. We have learned more about the science, and the equipment and records have gotten better since then. I have read four articles on hair root banding. I am familiar with the National Academy of Sciences report. The National Academy of Sciences is not all scientists. Legislators are involved, as are others. (Sidebar) (The jury is excused.)

(The defense is presenting the National Academy of Sciences article to the judge. Baez wants to use it.) Judge: You need to establish if she considers this an authoritative source. Defense: I point out that Justice Scalia used this report. Judge: In what way, Mr. Baez? I recall. (The judge pulls up the case.) Baez: The Committee's Report states that, "testimony linking microscopic hair analysis with particular defendants is highly unreliable. We now know that hair comparisons without mitochondrial DNA are highly questionable. A number of people whose convictions were based in part on faulty hair comparisons have been exonerated by DNA testing. An FBI publication reviewed by the Committee stated that subsequent DNA testing proved that hairs did not match in 11% of cases in which hair examiners previously declared two hairs to be "similar." Surely, this new data on hair comparisons would be highly relevant under existing law in any judge's assessment of the admissibility of such evidence. Judge: Until the witness recognizes the article as authoritative, you cannot use it to impeach her. Besides, she did not say this hair is identical. She was clear.

Karen Korsburg-Lowe, Proffered outside the jury to prevent taint: I have seen part of the National Academy of Science Report. The National Academy of Sciences is recognized by some scientists and is ordered by Congress. When asked if she agrees that the report is authoritative, she says that not all participants in the report were scientists. She knows the article is critical of hair analysis. She says the criticism of hair analysis in the article was that it is really at the limit of the science and more research is needed, and it did point out the limitations of analysis but the article found the methodology was sound. (In other words, she never answered the question, and Baez did not push her to answer.) Baez asks her if she agrees that there have been cases where the FBI lab has identified someone through hair analysis and been wrong, and the witness says that she is not aware that any cases where identification was made through hair analysis. He asks her about Michael Malone (a former FBI lab analyst who exaggerated to assist in obtaining convictions, and who was caught at it). I know Michael Malone. I do not think he works with FBI now. I am familiar with the Gates case and a 1991 case in DC. It is not microscopically indistinguishable. I think his testimony was, the words were "microscopically similar," and I do not believe he went beyond that. The judge steps in, Mr. Baez, I am not allowing any testimony about another case in this court. Just so we are clear.

Baez: It states that hair cannot be one hundred percent. It can only be similar and not indistinguishable. The study says that this testimony should not be permitted without both microscopic comparison and mitochondrial DNA. The witness says that's what the FBI does. In the proffer, the State asks the witness if she accepts the report as an authoritative scientific treatise. I do. Then the State asks if her methodology matches that in the report. It does. The judge tells Baez that if he wants to bolster the witness's testimony with the report, he can do so, but that he has not heard any impeachment. The judge also says, I know it is Saturday morning, and I think I have made myself abundantly clear, Mr. Baez. You will not discuss any other cases. (The jury returns.)

Karen Korsberg-Lowe – Defense cross-examination (cont.): Ms. Lowe, we were discussing the history of microscopic hair analysis, and the report of the National Academy of

Sciences. It was commissioned by Congress, and it was put together in part by the courts and in part by scientists. They were highly critical of microscopic hair analysis. Parts of the report dealt with the limits of the science. The witness responds, Hair is never a means of identification unless there is also DNA. As I have said, it is a limit. We require nuclear DNA to say this hair came from only one person. Nuclear is more discriminative to an individual. Mitochondrial DNA can only test maternally - a mother and daughter have the same mitochondrial DNA. Nuclear is one person, and would exclude the daughter. That is why I do not testify that one hair came from one person in a mitochondrial DNA examination. This is the first time I have testified on banding. The studies show postmortem banding can occur in as little as eight hours. Not all deceased persons have root banding. There are some cases known with samples of deceased persons who do not have it. I can testify the characteristics are apparent in some postmortem hairs. I cannot say for certain that banding only occurs in postmortem hair, but I have never seen this in any live person, and so far, no one has been able to replicate it with live hair. The other cases where I have seen hair banding have been directly from the dead body. I requested that if there was vacuuming from the trunk, if I could get more hairs. If we find more hair, it is just like any other trace evidence, more is better to make the case stronger. I have no doubt. I had no doubt. I would have liked more hairs to make more studies.

I got more hairs. (She is reviewing her report.) I was given 12 hairs from a vehicle; some had different characters. The only hair I compared had signs of decomposition. There were no others hairs with apparent decomposition. They sent the hairs in August, from the trunk liner and none of the hairs had the decomposition. They sent items of clothes from Casey Anthony. (Objection; not in evidence.) In October, I was given more items and the vacuum sweeping; there were no hairs with decomposition. In October, I was given a single item. (Objection) There were no hairs with banding that came from the car. There were no hairs with decomposition. In November, I received items from a trash bag; although there was hair, it showed no signs of decomposition. Were there any other hairs that showed apparent signs of decomposition from the car? No. I cannot say absolutely that decomposition is the reason the banding is present. My conclusion was confirmed by another examiner, and it is my opinion that the banding is decomposition. On July 31st and August 1st, I did a comparison of this hair. The postmortem banding is at the root portion. It is consistent with the hair in the chart; in the range for decomposition. (Sidebar.) This is a photo of evidence item Q12 and in the photo it shows… (State's objection) The judge says that he ruled that the State could not admit it over defense's objection, but if the defense wants to put it in evidence, they can do so.

(Baez shows her a series of photos, including the one she examined in this case, and tries to get her to say that the banding on the hair in this case has banding in the wrong place.) I prefer to look under a microscope to see if the banding is in the correct location for decomposition on a hair. It is hard to photograph without a microscope. It is difficult to view changes in the hair from a photo. It is less difficult with some and with hair that is in the anagen (growth) phase. The articles you use give you photos of the hair. I failed my first proficiency test in 2000. I did participate in the Stephen Stall Study regarding hair banding, but the purpose of the study was not to further the science of hair banding to the point that hair banding would be conclusive. This topic may have been addressed. I do not know that the science will ever get to the point where someone could say definitively that a particular hair comes from a dead body. It will always be consistent with a dead body. This hair has the root. I would make a decision on where it should go to for more examination. I made a match to the brush of Caylee. I was told the brush belonged to Caylee. Yes, she was still missing. The examination would not have been meaningful considering the common environment has other hairs. I can do nuclear DNA if there is no tissue on the hair. Without tissue, I cannot send it for nuclear DNA. I am not a DNA analyst. I make a call to see if it would go to nuclear or I ask for a conference with a DNA analyst. An analyst is the one who decides if nuclear DNA could be taken from that hair. In this case, there was no tissue, so the hair was tested for mitochondrial DNA. It could be Caylee Anthony's hair, or it could be from anyone in her maternal line. Finding hair in cars in not uncommon, the average person loses one hundred hairs a day, mostly in grooming. Hair from one person to another is transfer. I never really know how hairs got to where they are collected, but I consider it. If there were a large number in one location it would probably be primary transfer, directly from a head. Because we have only one hair, I cannot say if it was primary or secondary transfer. It is consistent with transfer, but I do not know how the transfer occurred.

Karen Korsberg-Lowe - State's re-direct: The National Science article is consistent with FBI policy. Hair analysis is not a means of positive identification. My report contains that, and notes that the hair had the root band. This hair was not naturally shed. It was still in the growth stage. You looked at a lot of hairs in this case and found one with decomposition? Yes. The source was anyone who is maternally related, you can eliminate others. The defendant was eliminated as the source of the decomposed hair. Her hair is not a match; a relative with blonde hair could not be a match. The defendant's mother's hair was dyed, and this hair was not. The hair from the brush did not have a root band. Whatever happened to the hair I inspected from the car, it was not taken out the same way as the naturally removed hair from the brush of Caylee. I do not know how long that hair had been in the car. It is consistent with hair from a dead body, but I cannot say for sure.

The State's Fortieth Witness

Interpretation of Testimony - Michael Vincent: I am an Orange County Sheriff's Office CSI. I retired from a police department in Pennsylvania, also as a CSI. I was in the Air force as a law enforcement officer. I have attended crime scene schools - thirty or more courses. I was the supervisor of Gerardo Bloise. I assisted in processing the car. There were different kinds of samples taken, stains in the trunk were tested for blood with three tests, and air samples were taken, as was the spare tire cover with the stain that was on the carpet. On July 21st, 2008, the air samples were taken with the University of Florida assisting. The first time the doctor from University of Florida was assisting and he tried to insert a needle through the rubber. So we opened the trunk slightly and removed a small amount of air out and transferred it to a plastic bag and then hung a filter. The doctor performed the sampling and I observed. I collected an item sent to Oak Ridge National Laboratory (We, the authors, would believe this laboratory's work. The history of this laboratory is excellent, since it was created for the development the H-bomb in the 1940s) I can identify the package of evidence. I placed the Tedlar plastic bag in this package.

I also took a sample of the stain from the spare tire cover. My label and initials are on this package. I transferred the can with air to the Oak Ridge National Laboratory. We attempted more than one way to preserve air with Dr. Michael Sigman. We put a carbon filter and other kinds of filters in the trunk for forty minutes, then opened the trunk and collected the samples. These are my labels and initials on the can, and my label and initials on the package. I sent them to Oak Ridge National Laboratory. I collected them with a special kit that Dr. Vass at Oak Ridge National Laboratory sent back.

It was a portable air pump, nine test tubes, along with instructions on how and where to collect the air samples. I did the test air from the vehicle and from the trash. I also took air samples of the garage the car had been kept in, for comparison and control testing and the samples from the car, as requested.

These are nine separate packages with my labels and initials on a package; one for each test tube that was to be sent back to the lab in Oak Ridge. After taking air samples from all areas of the car inside and out, the trash, the forensics laboratory garage, I also sent one test tube back clean in the package, to make sure there was no contamination in shipping. If any contamination was there in shipping it would show up in this clean one, when the samples were tested by Dr. Vass. I also collected an item from the wheel well and sent it to Oak Ridge later. There was a substance on the inside of the wheel well, and it was scraped off and sent to Dr. Vass. Later, pieces of the spare tire cover that were stained, and another that was not stained (for control testing) were sent. In October, an item was placed in a can and shipped to Oak Ridge, it was a six inch by six inch stained carpet sample with my initials, and a two inch by two inch piece of the spare tire cover without my initials as a control sample.

I assisted in other aspects of the investigation. I took pulled hair from George, Cindy and Lee and placed the hair in Petri dishes, and took buccal swabs from George, Cindy and Lee. These are the packages (and the collection and storage were verified). I responded to the Anthony home and collected two gas cans. The cans are shown in the photo and identified by time and date. They were collected on August 1st, 2008; there has been no alteration to the photo. I swabbed the cans for fingerprints and DNA, but found nothing. I returned the cans to the Anthony's. (All items are admitted into evidence the first time each is used in court.) When I was processing the car, it was not on TV. I had the garage door open in the forensics garage when using Blue Star chemicals. There was a TV crew that filmed. I could not see the camera lights. I did not call the media.

Michael Vincent - Defense cross—examination: As far as the air samples, this is the first time I have ever heard of it or done it. It was new to me, but it was not an experiment. We did multiple samples. They were done by Dr. Sigman. I observed the process. Multiple filters were used to collect the samples. I collected the samples for Dr. Vass at Oak Ridge National Laboratory, but only observed Dr. Sigman. The air in the garage was not the same air. I cannot tell you the quality of the air when the samples were taken, and the air would come and go. No air samples were taken at the tow yard or in the Anthony's garage. I took many samples to get a control. I also collected samples in the bay of the forensics garage in this case. These tests were not conducted for control, but to test for the air from the car getting into the air in the forensics garage.

There was an odor from the area and items. The air sample of the trash was taken on August 29th. The odor of the trash could have been different on the July 16th. I do not know if the trash was taken to a dry room immediately. I was not there when the trash was received, so I cannot answer. I was not present when it was received and the items in the trash bag look different in the photo, as well. I was not present to dry or store those items. When I took the trash air samples, it had already been in the dry room. I am not sure if it had the same odor. Trash would smell different dry than wet. The trash was stored in brown box and the box was not moist.

(Defense Exhibit - a photo of a metal gas can) The can was completely dry. It could be a stain, but it was not gas, and it was not wet. There were no prints of any kind. It did not appear to be wiped down. I collected the cans using gloves and people normally carry cans by the handle. Between July 16th and end of August, the car was kept secured in our garage. The car still had a strong odor. It did not appear that it had diminished. The trash was not handled by me. The trash was stored separate from the car at all times. (The witness is released subject to recall.)

The prosecution makes a request of the court: We have a consultant to assist me with the computer expert. We would like to excuse the witness regarding computer forensics from the rule of sequestration of witnesses to the extent that the consultant for me be allowed to talk with the witness when I do. (No objection, so the court gives permission.) (Court stands in recess until Monday morning.)

Chapter 11

THE STATE'S CASE IN CHIEF - WEEK THREE

June 6th, 2011

Good morning, readers. Well, Casey looks rested, playing with her hair and laughing. The defense has an objection to Dr. Vass who will be taking the stand today, and they renew all other objections.)

Defense: We took Dr. Vass's deposition on Friday, and we have questions on a database. It is in his office in Oak Ridge Laboratories. It can be turned over to the defense. Although, his database could contain exculpatory information for cross-examination, we do not have the database he is going to use. This is the database at the Oak Ridge National Laboratory. (No way is the defense going to get this database from Oakridge… but they have to ask.)

The State's Forty-first Witness

Interpretation of Testimony - Arpad Vass, PhD: I am a Senior Research Scientist at the Oak Ridge National Laboratory, and have been with them for twenty years. Research scientists have many areas of expertise, including biology and microbiology. I have a Master's Degree in Administration of Justice (Forensic Science) from Virginia Commonwealth University. I also have a Medical Technology degree. (I am Board certified in Clinical Pathology and Clinical Laboratory Science - ASCP/CLS) from Fairfax Hospital. While I was at Virginia Commonwealth working on my PhD, I was offered a position at Oak Ridge with Dr. Bass. I worked on decomposition for my PhD dissertation topic. The media refers to the location where I worked as the body farm. I began my discussions with Dr. Bass in 1988 for my Ph.D. It was a specific area for determining a biochemical way to discover the length of the postmortem period - the time someone has been dead. It is an anthropology research facility, and in 1988 the only facility to study whole body decomposition in the world. It began in 1972. There have been eleven hundred donated bodies in various conditions. There are subjects in the trunks of cars at the facility. I was looking at the study of time of decomposition since death and the chemical breakdown of human skin. The skin becomes fluid, and at different stages, different viscosities of fluid.

I will try not to be too morbid, but the when the skin is fresh, the fluids are different from when the skin is in decomposition, because it bloats. In a fresh stage, there are two processes at work in early human decomposition. There is a self-digestion, or autolysis process. There are at least one hundred trillion cells in the human body. Suddenly after death, the cells of the body do not realize the body is dead. The cells continue to act normally – cell metabolism continues, and the byproduct of that metabolism is carbon dioxide. Cells are made up of very complex things. As cells of the body are deprived of oxygen, carbon dioxide in the blood increases, the cell becomes acidic, and wastes accumulate which poison the cell. At the same time, cellular enzymes begin to dissolve the cells from the inside out, eventually causing them to rupture, and releasing fluids. Self-digestion is readily apparent by the liquid. It is nutrient-rich, and you begin to see skin slippage as a first sign. As the blisters rupture, the liquid makes the body look wet, and it is wet. That leads to the second stage; the organisms and bacteria begin to liquefy the body and break it down into smaller molecules. A bloat stage is when microorganisms in the digestive tract go to town and create gas. As the bacteria utilize the nutrients available, they make different gases.

When the esophagus becomes blocked, the gas builds up in the abdominal cavity and causes bloating. Wherever the gasses are trapped, they will eventually find a way out. Active decay is forty to sixty percent of the major liquefactions of the body, and that leads to the dry stage or mummification, or the skeleton. The most important things are the environmental factors. Temperature: higher temperature accelerates decomposition. It is the most important, then water, the environmental pH – acidic surroundings speed up decomposition, and the presence of oxygen. Oxygen also speeds it up. There are only a few fatty acids in a body that are useful in discovering the time of decomposition. There were examined in the early publication of the fatty acid and other inorganics, like calcium, studies. We discovered that the inorganics are more useful in later decomposition. That study in the Journal of Forensic Science was in 1992, and included all the others. The first ten years was in the development stage of the studies, and since homicides never occur the same way twice, we needed a lot of different ones to view. I was employed at Virginia and then Oak Ridge National Laboratory. I completed my PhD based on my work at the body farm.

Oak Ridge National Laboratory is run by the Department of Energy, and it is the largest of the DOE laboratories. It has many areas of studies – very large, complicated studies. Things like climate change, bio-fuels, and materials science. We have the second and fourth largest and fastest supercomputers in the world. We have a broad range of equipment, and many things beyond 'energy' items. I have to have expertise in many fields to even be in the Oak Ridge Laboratory. We are looking at new plants that produce fuel. We study microbiology, chemistry, physics, and more.

There was a time that I felt I had done all I can on human decomposition. The study was complete with the cutting edge work determining, by the hour, how long someone had been dead. Early in 2001 the work ended. Determining the time since the death was the most difficult. It was the most important thing that an anthropologist can do. The graves study and the ability to find a way to identify where a body had been buried was the next most important. The most common and accurate way at the time was cadaver dogs. Hand probes and machines, none were very effective, so we were looking for a more universal way to find a body. Cadaver dogs locating bodies was most promising, so we went to odor identification for a location.

We buried bodies then used a tube system at different depths. And we began to analyze the odor coming up through the soil and which compounds made it from the deep body odor to the top of the soil. This would allow us to create a machine to analyze the compounds released, in order to locate a body. I have smelled the odor at different decomposition times. I have smelled fifty individuals from start to finish, and a hundred at any single time point. It is a unique odor. There are publications that describe the chemical components of decomposition. It has been studied in Greece as well, and they use pigs and humans for comparison of the different odors. At the decay facility, we have both humans and pigs. So there is a difference in the two. We also have deer, dogs, cats, and there is difference between the odors. Animals have a musk scent and pigs have sweet scent. Both are very different from humans. After 2004, our paper was on the establishment of the graves, the chemicals and environmental impact. Ground is breathing, and high pressure pushes it down. Low pressure sucks the odors up out of the ground. As for rainfall, some chemicals are water solvable and some are not. So the environment is important. My next paper… (Baez has been objecting to try to interrupt this testimony as much as he can. The judge calls a sidebar.)

The authors think Baez is upset that Dr. Vass is brilliant and very interesting, really quite captivating

209

even on this subject of decomposition. I cannot wait to hear him on chloroform. Sorry Baez, this witness is very bad for you! Shut up! We want to hear what the witness has to say, and I bet the jury does too. The defense, including Mr. Mason, is fighting with all they can against this witness. He is so good, he knows his stuff, can explain it simply yet thoroughly. We expected no less from someone at the Oak Ridge facility; we have been there. Many years ago, while passing through Oak Ridge late at night. We eluded the first line of security at the Oak Ridge facility grounds, to get close enough to see some of the facility from afar, after a few tries. We were pushing being arrested, and we were still far away from it. However, it was late and the visiting hours were over, so we took our chance to see the amazing facility from a distance. We had a mission. We picked a flower from the grounds at Oak Ridge National Laboratory and placed it in our Aristotle on Ethics book. The reason was that the scientists who built the H-Bomb to save America from Japan in WWII had only ethical questions when they completed their work. This place, hidden in the mountains, we will tell you this place is cool… We are back from our reverie, and the court reporter is telling us where we were.

(The prosecution continues.) In 2004, the research continued, with the buried bodies and in-surface bodies. I worked with above-ground bodies as well at the research facility. In-surface, some bodies were wrapped with plastic tarps and body bags. We contained samples of the air containing the odor on a triple absorbent trap. These are filled with carbon. Filter systems have three types of carbon. It catches the odor on the active carbon. We dangled it close to the bodies on a string on some, and we used an air pump on others. We remove the tube and they are then sealed. It goes through a process of heating and you get a flow of gas and the activated odor compounds go into the measuring machine for analysis. Also we use cryofusion. It freezes all the gas into a pellet. All the components of the odor become viable again. I studied the above-ground remains for two to three years. In the initial stages we take samples every week, then biweekly, and then monthly, the surface more weekly and biweekly. Then we updated the 2004 paper with a 2008 paper. (The doctor is accepted as an expert by the judge.)

In 2008, I was contacted by Detective Yuri Melich. I had a discussion, I believe. They sent items to me in Oak Ridge. First was a metal evidence can (witness is viewing). I received a box. I am not sure I recognize your box. (The prosecutor opens the box so the witness

can look at the can inside.) I will look at the can, but
I will keep it where the jury cannot see it. (There is
some obvious confusion and it looks like the State may
have managed to get Dr. Vass to identify the wrong one of
the two cans initially.) I recognize the can. (Sidebar.
The judge wants the court reporter. The defense does not
want the jury smelling this can of decomposition air.
Mason is fighting hard, and the prosecution lets them
look into the box but not touch it. The prosecution has
moved the cans into evidence.)

The prosecutor asks if at some point the witness received
a plastic bag with hair and fibers from Dr. Sigman. Dr.
Markus Wise received it and we were not sure about how it
was collected, so we may not even have run the test. We
did not use the first bag samples they sent us in this
case. We asked for air samples from them using our
equipment, triple filter traps and a pump. We asked for
samples from many different areas. This pump is portable
and it pulls air. It is the same style of pump we used in
our studies. We received back a number of items for
testing, along with the equipment we sent for use in
taking samples. I recognize the packages in which the
samples were returned to me (about ten to twelve
envelopes). Yes, my initials are on all of them. The
items are introduced.) Analyzing the various items, some
were done by Dr. Wise – it was his laboratory. He is an
analytical chemist. Markus Wise has a PhD in Physics. A
gas chromatograph was used in his laboratory. The can lid
was cracked, and a small amount of air was taken out by
syringe. Dr. Wise and I looked at the chromatograph
results. The sample of air was taken from the space above
the sample in the can. Only a small amount was removed
from the can.

(The defense wants the entire lab brought into court,
which means every person who worked on these tests. So
they want about three to five scientists from Oak Ridge,
Tennessee, each of whom who had a machine used in his lab
or read a result with Dr. Vass, to be brought here. That
is burdensome. These scientists work together, and we
cannot spend thousands of dollars to bring everyone who
has a lab machine used to conduct Dr. Vass's studies on
the samples. We want the prosecution to open the can of
air before this gets to be a bigger fight, and they lose
the ability to open the can. The prosecution is fighting
back hard at the sidebar. The judge is ruling for the
prosecution; I can see the prosecutor agreeing with the
judge. The defense is fighting, but their heads are not
shaking in agreement with the judge. The defense has Ms.
Fryer, their case law lawyer, at the sidebar with Baez.
By the way, the gallery is packed today with spectators.)

Arpad Vass, PhD - State's direct examination (cont.): I went over the results with Dr. Wise. They showed one large peak and it was chloroform. I have had experience and it is a decomposition product in human decomposition. The reason we processed further was that gas chromatograph results regarding chloroform were shockingly high, abnormally high. I decided to use the Cryotrack. I was in the room with Wise when he did the next test. We removed the carpet from the metal can to do that test. We removed the carpet out of the can and put it in a Tedlar bag. Tedlar is used for containing air samples because it will not react. We incubated it at body temperature, at thirty-five degrees centigrade, for two days. We knew the trunk temperature would have been warm, and incubation also speeds up the elevation time.

We wanted to release that carpet air itself with no interference. We extracted ten milligrams through the cryotron and used the Gas M machine. I believe I was present at every step. We identified fifty-one chemical components in the ten-milligram sample of air. GCMS output is called a chromatogram. Large tall peaks mean a large concentration of an element. The largest peak is called the base peak, and it was an element in chloroform. Other high peaks were consistent with the elements in chloroform. Based on the GCMS, it was chloroform, and it was the highest concentration of chloroform I had ever seen. We were seeing a concentration of parts per trillion. We shot a standard of chloroform - we had a known standard to compare. We tested other samples from the carpet air. The rough approximation of the average chloroform in the carpet air samples was part per million. So that is million, then billion and trillion. It is a lot. We considered that the part on the carpet was a minimum amount; chloroform has a high rate of evaporation. So chloroform was in the trunk and it is had had time to evaporate, and we were still in the parts per million. We could not get closer to an exact concentration.

We obtained a sample of another similar vehicle carpet for a control. Both Dr. Wise and I conducted the test, and we reasonably rely upon this equipment and procedure in testing. (Dr. Vass is looking at his graph from GCMS.) Sixteen parts per million is a rough estimate on the peak from the cans. The incubated carpet samples were well above the sixteen million range, in this case. There are a number of other peaks. They represent gasoline and the compounds that make gasoline. The odor of decomposition has the same elements as gasoline, but I would expect the odor of gasoline in a car. This graph is from the sample of two vehicles used as controls. The samples were taken from vehicles in a junkyard in Tennessee. The cars were the same make and model. The chloroform peak in the sample carpet is five thousand, as compared to sixteen million in the Anthony carpet sample. We are talking about control samples showing trace amounts, and shocking amounts in the Anthony car samples.

We also used LIBS analysis. We chose these two tests because they do not destroy the sample. LIBS analysis uses a YAG laser, one that creates green light and is a crystal laser. It is directed onto the carpet elements that are composed of atoms, and we measure the ground state and the excited state. When the laser hits, it creates an excited state of atoms and when it is shut off, they fall, creating a ground state. The energy that is produced is released as a photon of light and picked up by fiber optics. Every element has its own light signature. I was not present when the test occurred. I reviewed the results and used it in the results of the testing in my report. We were looking for elevated components as is consistent with decomposition without destroying the sample. (The defense is objecting on all issues and wants to voir dire the witness. The jury was removed for this voir dire.)

Arpad Vass, PhD – Defense voir dire of the witness: I am not a physicist, and Dr. Martin conducted the test; it is her laser lab. I have used lasers and I am laser qualified. I was not present but the procedure is well established. The judge says that Chapter 90.704 of the Florida Evidence Code says that the facts or data upon which an expert bases an opinion may be either perceived by or made known to the expert to support the opinion. Professor Ehrhardt on Evidence, 2010 states the intent was to explain the result in the same way as they would in their lab or their office. The purpose is to allow nurses, tech people and hospital records. Mr. Baez, Dr. Vass is able to rely on reports of others in forming his opinion, if they are the type reasonably relied upon in his office.

(Defense voir dire continues. Baez asks Dr. Vass if the results of the LIBS examination showed the inorganic chemicals that were present in high volume.) These were calcium, magnesium, sodium, carbon, iron and more. I personally do not regularly conduct LIBS exams, however our lab does, and I utilize them. These elements are found in everything known to man. I am not a physicist. However, I know which elements are liberated in the tests, and the compounds those elements form in certain ratios. This is just another form of verifying what my nose already knows. My organic work was done on surface bodies. Dr. Vass you cannot compare the output? Mr. Baez you do not understand. I can compare anything that is equal, soil to soil, water to water, and air to air. We compared what was in the trunk to control samples of two similar pieces of carpet from two different, yet the same year, make, and model carpet samples using LIBS and other techniques. The judge overruled the defense. The evidence is admissible. (The jury is brought back.)

This chart shows every element as a wave length. A trace sample of all the elements was higher in the Florida vehicle. We cut off a few fibers and placed them in ethyl alcohol, then injected into methyl alcohol. Head space air is the air above where compounds evaporate. On the carpet sample, we saw butyric acid which is one of the first compounds of decomposition, and it was in the carpet itself. When I first obtained the can, it was sealed. When I first opened it the odor was overwhelming. I jumped two feet back. I was shocked that the can could have that much odor. It was human decomposition. After twenty years of experience, I knew it. Also, among the samples, there was a glass vial containing a scraping from the spare tire well. We decided to open and analyze it. The vial is plastic, not glass, but I do recall that vial. I examined this item for chemicals. Acetic acid is a byproduct of human decomposition, and so is chloroform. Both were present in significant concentrations in the sample from the tire well.

I also was given napkins for examination. I remembered them being in a white bag, but it was fully sealed, absolutely. (Baez wants to inspect the box before it is introduced. It is conditionally received into evidence at this time.) I did a chemical extraction on the napkins. GCMS results were that of fatty acids. Those acids are a byproduct of the breakdown of fat in decomposition. The trap samples from the garage and the car were tested. We wanted to confirm that the carpet sample was the source of the odor. We also tested the trash. The carpet was the source of the odor. The car interior, trash, and garage samples contained less than the carpet. None of the components found in the trash and garage were the same as the carpet sample. Each odor is comprised of chemicals, and it is the compounds of chemicals that make odors unique. A rose may have 12 chemicals that make up its odor; trash may have 20. There will be some interaction, but it is the total that makes the odor unique. The car trunk had fifty-two compounds, and forty-two of those were related to human decomposition. We have an overlap with gasoline, so we removed the gasoline chemicals from our analysis. That left twenty-four compounds. Then we started looking at control samples and the garage samples and subtracted those compounds. That left sixteen compounds. Of those, seven are significant.

Decomposition involves thirty compounds. Those thirty compounds occur based on many different parameters early or late in decomposition. It is cyclic. Early decomposition compounds are different than late. We have seven compounds left in the carpet sample that are exclusive to that sample, and could not have come from any environmental source. They are the most relevant of the five hundred we originally started with. It is my opinion that the odor is consistent with human decomposition. The scraping from the tire well, it is consistent. In the examination of the tire cover extraction, butyric acid is very consistent with decomposition. The napkins included every one of the elements we can expect to find in human decomposition. By taking all of the examinations and adding the smell I had, I do have an opinion that there is no other plausible reason other than a decomposing human body in the trunk of the Anthony car.

Arpad Vass - Defense (Baez) cross-examination: I am not a chemist. That was an omission and I sent an update. My PhD is in anthropology. The forensics report shows Wise is a chemist and Martin a physicist, and I am an anthropologist. Probably, I took chemistry in the 1980s. I have never done anything on Facebook or Wikipedia. I do not have a financial interest in my testimony in this case. I used the same data that I used in the publications that I wrote in 2004 and 2008, in this case.

In the grave testing, you bury four bodies and set up the measures to see what the chemicals below ground were, and take measurements from above, and wait for the chemicals to migrate up from the source. It took seventeen days for the compounds to get to the surface. They have been seeping all along underground before making it the surface. Baez asks if the witness refused to give the database to the defense. Yes, it is owned by and deliverable only to the organization, the grant organization, in this case, the U.S. Government, and it is not mine to give. I apply for, and get grants or products, in this case, it is research grant. I do not hold the patent for the Labrador machine. It uses the compounds in my 2008 paper. The goal is to file, and I am required to file invention disclosures. This was a grant from the DOE. Because of that project, a decision was make to disclose the machine. Baez asks if the goal is to sell this to police departments. My goal is not to sell it at all, so if a patent is licensed, someone could use it to make the machines. My goal was simply to find and create a way for the machine to help find dead bodies. I do not understand the formalities of the patent process. I understand that if it is licensed, fifteen percent of the licensing proceeds will be divided between all of the inventors. It is Oak Ridge that applies for the patents, not any individual scientist who worked on the project. This work on the Anthony case was done voluntarily on my own time.

When I published a report in this case, I did not disclose that I had a financial interest. The differences between labs are that one develops, and the other deals with the protocols and procedures. For this case, the protocols are published in the 2004 and 2008 papers. We used all the procedures in this forensic report that we did in the publication. If you want to review the report, Mr. Baez, it is in the 2008 studies we used for surface bodies. We use quality control at the laboratory. I did qualitative analyses, and included quantitative analysis. This was to give an idea if these were big amounts or small. As usual, I issued a preliminary report in August, and that report gives what I was looking at so far. Baez: You were aware that decomposition had been found in the car was reported by the media before your report? (Sidebar.) In August of 2008, or shortly thereafter, it became public. I am not sure how. I did not release the information. I was upset that any preliminary results were released. I think fifty-four was the number of chemicals in the carpet sample in the second report. (Dr. Vass is trying to review with the reports, and Baez is flipping the pages so Dr. Vass cannot see his report. That's tacky, Baez!)

The report had fifty-two chemicals. The reason for overlapping names of chemicals is that some compounds occur in multiple sources, and we eliminated the duplication in the preliminary analysis. In my second report, I had seventeen overlaps with gasoline. The conclusion of the final report is not based on those numbers. The final report is always the most accurate. I list three samples in the preliminary, and two in the second report. We considered a new car would not be fair. I took two samples for one, but it was corrected in the second report. I do not review Dr. Wise's bench notes. (When asked if he was aware that there were three cars selected, the witness says there were only two, not three.) I do not know the history of the cars in the junk yard or the car from Florida. We did both qualitative and quantitative analysis. There was a piece of empty plastic, and I did not see the garbage. I can sample the air of the composite of all these in the garbage bag. I used multiple air samples from the trash, air samples from the passenger area of the car, air samples from the forensics garage bay, and trip blanks. At my table in the lab, I did not use the trunk air, because everything had been removed from the samples we retrieved. That is because the samples were for different uses. The point source sample was from the trunk liner. It is not a valid comparison after the liner is removed to use the trunk air.

We only considered five chemicals because we were being very conservative. Three out of the thirty that you consider is an unfair statement. If the trash was in the car, and then in a large amount of air, you are still going to get some trace amounts. The original thirty chemicals have to do with bodies in graves and unburied, so I had to reduce the number of compounds that we searched for in this case. Assumptions are sometime relevant in conclusions, and are as well in common sense. If you would like to review the LIBS results, I will need my report to identify the compounds found. These items are found in the body, but I have not done an inorganic analysis of common trash. The car could have been there in the junk yard for years. We considered the worst case environment to get fully contaminated cars as the junkyard samples. I was told the trunks were unlocked and open.

(We wish you could see Dr. Vass, he is probably, not that old, maybe fifty. He is extremely interesting, and obviously knows his work. Baez is not putting a dent in his testimony. This lab clearly did what we would expect of a great science facility. They tested and tested in different ways, giving the benefit of the doubt that they were wrong, and then worked back to the only conclusion possible: that they were right, and a dead body in early stages of decomposition was in the Anthony trunk. This is really good science and a good scientist. We expected no less from a facility of this status. We do not doubt a word Dr. Vass has said. We are now convinced that Caylee's body was in the trunk in a state of early decomposition. It is very sad…)

I do not recall asking for any Blue Star (like luminol) control samples. The spraying of and running a sample of Blue Star was not done. A chemist looked at Blue Star and Febreze, and said neither could have contributed. Our chemist at Oak Ridge reviewed the printed data sheets on these products, and said they would not affect our chemicals, and could not interact to cause our chemical analysis results. The paper towels had different fatty acids. My report says they are like adipose, or are adipose; it is semantics. It takes only a few days for fatty acid to occur. I do not think you can find these acids in hamburgers and chicken. The formation of adipose is favored by a number of environments. There was THC and cannabinol, marijuana. The marijuana was there. I do not know how it got there; we just tried to be thorough. In March, 2008,

I was asked to analyze some soil samples for the Barker Ranch. (Baez says, They were analyzed using a GCMS and you said decomposition.) I used several instruments, along with a Magnetometer and ground penetrating radar and dug, and did not find anything. At the depth we dug, we did not find anything. It was a search for finding bodies buried 40 years ago. We did not understand the environment. This is not the only place we have looked for bodies. You cannot use error rates for this. We did not understand the environmental parameters for a search. Time is one, and it was an exploratory dig. The Barker Ranch is a ranch where Charles Manson murdered and buried people forty years ago. The conditions are completely different. There are protocols I have, instructions on collections of samples. We wrote those protocols in a large area. You do not want to collect a control sample next to the dump. Those instructions were written for collection in a forty-acre field. Unless the trash is part of the crime scene, then you collect and use that in the study as we did here. A crime scene is where the evidence of a crime is. Baez asks, can you tell us what divining rods are? (Sidebar.) Divining rods are antennas that can be made by coat hangers of the right material.

Baez asks, is this the first testimony of this sort in a court of law? I do not know whether it is or not. Another database could have it, but I do not know. Are there any other paper and studies? I identified four of the five elements we used. There are a number of studies by people who used pieces of tissue. I was looking at a single time point and we looked at a four-to-five year study. My opinion is the smell of human decomposition is similar to rotten potatoes, but the chemical composition is different. I did not find fluoride. I do not know anything about the manner of death of that child. It did not matter for the study. Mr. Baez, you are twisting things around. This experiment was based on items delivered to me. We did a chemical analysis, so I know the makeup of the items. I do not know what was in the trunk of the Florida car. I do not know the history of the cars. (Baez questions about a blanket in a child death in the mid-west that the witness mentioned during direct examination.) A dead child was in this blanket that I was able to obtain as a control sample. It was the best we could do. Thank God, we do not find that many children in car trunks for samples. I am not a member of a professional organization; my background is so diverse that I would not know which one to join. I am paid to think outside the box, and I think far out of the box. I have no prospect of financial gain from this case.

Arpad Vass – State's re-direct: I was asked about the patent in deposition; I had no clue at the deposition, and I had to ask people at the lab so I could answer these questions here today. I did try to find the most contaminated sample, and that is the reason I asked them to go to the junk yard. Odor diffusion is when an odor goes from a higher to a lower concentration. This is why I looked for the highest concentration and the spare tire cover sample had the highest concentration and was the source point. The MDSS (Material Data Safety Sheet) is a source of information from manufacturers. Neither the Blue Star nor Febreze had chloroform – we checked. Meat would cause the same thing, if it is raw, large content, mammal, it would have to be loaded with bacteria and a large size, perhaps a pound, rotted. The other study we used was two bodies found in the sea. We search for a positive control, and found a child in Montana about three years dead and left in the trunk of the car for three months. Four compounds were present in the control subject, but not chloroform as in the Florida Anthony car. In a small child, it is assumed it is a small child, they have not consumed enough fluoride in water or the like in the few years they have been alive to have it in their bone and tissue. Fluoride has not been studied in children. Bioaccumulation is well-known in science. Fortunately, we do not get a lot of children. Mine is an opinion based on something that has not been studied in a well-analyzed study of the biochemistry. Something attracted the flies to the paper towels. There was no meat or residue of meat on these paper towels, just fatty acid. (Dr. Vass is here on an interstate subpoena from the prosecution. He has been served a **subpoena duces tecum** (a subpoena to produce records) from the defense since he arrived to testify, attempting to get the database. The state moves to quash the subpoena from the defense because subpoena is invalid. The defense withdraws the subpoena duces tecum, but says that they will probably call Dr. Vass during the defense case in chief, and ask that he remain available in Orlando until that time. The judge says that if they want to recall him, they can handle that through the court. Dr. Vass is free to return to Oak Ridge. The witness is excused. Court is in recess for the remainder of the day.)

Casey Anthony was stoic for most all of the day, until the jurors left the courtroom. Then she smiled, and was laughing as she left for her jail cell. Baez fought hard against Dr. Vass's testimony today. It was to no avail. As intelligent as all the lawyers, judges, and experts are in a courtroom, it is fair to say Dr. Vass is a rocket scientist in his field. He stood up to all the cross-examination the defense threw at him. Then Dr. Vass gave it back to them with slaps on the face, like, "Fortunately Mr. Baez, we do not have many children decomposing in the truck of cars." We also think that Baez, who we assume makes the decisions as the lead attorney for the defense team lawyers, made a mistake. It might have been better to let the old dog Mason cross-examine Dr. Vass. We are not sure it would have helped, but it could not have hurt to have a more experienced lawyer with witnesses like Dr. Vass.

We have not seen the defense case, so for now it is one-sided. The prosecution is presenting a solid cumulative case of circumstantial evidence with about another week or more to go in their case in chief. We do not think Baez will risk not putting on a defense, so we expect a defense case of some kind. However, we also do not expect Casey will get up to bat… We do not think it would behoove her to put hand on a Bible and swear to tell the truth, with her history of lies. Judge Perry is keeping a tight hold on decorum in his courtroom, and demanding good sportsmanship of the swordsmen as much as possible. Although there have been a few rulings that we did not agree with, overall he has been fair to both sides to date. Interestingly, if Casey is found guilty of anything but first degree murder, Judge Perry will decide Casey Anthony's sentence.

June 7th, 2011

Judge: Good morning. (Sidebar) (While we wait, we believe today will be a chemistry course. Now you see why we write books, it is all about the education we get on our journey. Hopefully, we can effectively pass that on to you. Hopefully, all of this will get us closer to the truth about what happened to little Caylee.)

The State's Forty-second Witness

Interpretation of Testimony - Gerardo Bloise (recalled): I am a CSI in Orlando, Florida. I received a trash bag from CSI McBryde on July 16th, 2008. I took possession from Ms. McBryde. I removed the trash from the bag, did a visual inspection and took photos of the items. I can identify the photo of the plastic bag. (It is placed in evidence and published to the jury.) We are looking at the paper bag that covered the plastic bag. The paper bag had liquid in it. It was a little wet on the paper bag and the outside of the plastic bag, and the handles of the plastic were not closed tightly. Then I opened the plastic bag and pulled out the items inside without cutting the plastic. I did a visual inspection and placed all of it in a dry room in order to dry the items out for handling. Some items were wet and it smelled like normal trash and different from the car odor. It is standard trash: paper, bottles, wrappers, hanger, a dryer sheet, a box of detergent, and the like. These were empty cans and packages. (He is referring to his notes on this evidence.)

On July 18th, I removed the items from the dry room and placed them into a box and put them in the evidence locker. So they dried for two days. (More photos of the trash are introduced in different stages with bag open and more photos of the contents: napkins, cans, cigarette pack, aluminum foil, a beer can, tobacco, a Pepsi can, a Mountain Dew can, a Crystal light bottle with brown liquid inside, a Crystal light mix can, a broken pizza box, a broken box from a pack of soda, a receipt from Fusion lounge, an empty Velveeta cheese box, and documentation from Full Sail University.) The napkin I collected and placed in the plastic bag. I did this on July 16th, when I received the trash. I placed the paper items in one area and photographed them and the like. The photographs show all of the contents. The box that I put all of this in for the evidence locker has my identifying initials and seal. The napkins in the plastic bag have a separate box and my identifying initials and seal. (The defense wants to wait for one more witnesses to verify the chain of custody before they admit the napkins in the plastic bag into evidence.) I did a written inventory of all of the items in my report. There were thirty-seven items. I placed each item in a separate envelope and then into the box for the evidence locker.

Gerardo Bloise – Defense cross-examination: (The defense is cross-examining on the trash.) The trash was some wet and some dry. When I received it I placed it in a dry room and they were dry when they came out. (Baez showed photos side-by-side; one of wet trash and the other of the dried trash.) They look different because of the drying. I did the inventory before they came out of the dry room. I just received it like any other evidence. I did not know it would be a disputed item in this case. There is no destruction of the evidence by drying. When I received the items, I received trash and I preserved the

items and went by protocol. I do not consider that I
destroyed anything, I preserved it. There is no
alteration of the evidence. The photo is of the packaging
of paper towels. They were moist when I received them,
then they were dried in the room and placed in a plastic
bag. That item is not of value for DNA at that time, I
would not attempt to test it now. I just placed it in the
plastic bag. I did examine it when securing it, and I did
not see anything in forensic value in DNA such as blood
or other sources of DNA. You can get DNA from semen and
the like. It was not my intention to alter the evidence
in any way. The purpose is to dry then to re-inspect. If
we let it get wet, it could become moldy. The car carpet
was dry when I inspected it. The defense questions the
witness about Dr. Vass's testimony that the air samples
were taken of the dry garbage and I do not know about
what air samples of the garbage would have shown before
it was dried.) I do not remember if the items had bug
larva. The witness admits that he is not a DNA expert.
(The witness is excused.)

The State's Forty-third Witness

Interpretation of Testimony - Dr. Arpad Vass (recalled):
State: Are these States exhibits IR for identification?
Yes, I believe so, I see my initials on the can and I
want to make it clear that I showed you the correct can
yesterday. This is the correct can I was sent. (They are
entered into evidence.) Prosecution: Yesterday you
testified about a piece of evidence - that can identified
by you. (Sidebar. This line of questioning involves the
mistake made by the prosecution in showing the wrong one
of two identical cans sitting on the evidence table to
Dr. Vass yesterday. Is this is an opening for defense to
fight the air in the cans? What a mistake for the
prosecution! I was wondering why the prosecution brought
Vass back when he had done a great job yesterday. It was
to cure their error. The prosecutor has no choice.)

Arpad Vass - Defense cross-examination: Yesterday, you
mistakenly admitted the wrong piece of evidence as you
were handed the can by the prosecution and looked at a
label. Yes, we are not a forensic lab, and we do not
handle all that much evidence in court. (The witness is
excused.)

Ouch! That hurt the prosecution, but we still trust the
doctor and the laboratory's work at Oak Ridge. The
prosecution made the mistake; do not blame the witness.
These men work in laboratories and they are not in
courtrooms as professional witnesses identifying
evidence. The lawyer should know when he has two

identical cans that were sent to the laboratory to be careful. In a laboratory, the very nature of science would be control of samples to prove or disprove a theory. Well, the defense saw the opening and took it. It is hell to make a mistake and have to cure it in the courtroom, but to be honest, it has happened to any real trial lawyer. We suspect that will be the last one from the prosecution in this case. The prosecution will not be sloppy again. Welcome to the real courtroom, a tough place.

Let us sum up what we heard from Dr. Vass. He seems to be an honorable man, telling the truth about what he discovered. He found shockingly high levels of chloroform and clear traces of human decomposition still in Casey Anthony's car trunk months after Caylee was last seen. With the help of some of the best scientists in the world, he has stepped up to become the voice of Caylee Anthony, echoing through the air in that trunk.

The State's Forty-fourth Witness

Interpretation of Testimony – Michael Rickenbach, PhD: I work for the FBI forensics laboratory examiner. I have been with the FBI for fifteen years. I have two bachelors in Forensics Science, a Masters in Chemistry, and a PhD in Chemistry. I have testified as an expert in most federal jurisdictions. In August of 2008, I received items in this case. Earlier, during the break, we examined the items, and I recognized my initials over the heat seal and recognize the evidence items submitted to me for examination. (They are admitted into evidence. All of the samples of the car trunk liner from the Anthony car were admitted.) I examined these items for chloroform, from fabric reported to be a piece of the tire cover. I did a visual inspection, took a cutting based on stains, placed the samples in sealed vials, then did a gas chromatography test on the head air in the vial. Did you smell an odor? (Sidebar.) The results were residue of chloroform. This is another fabric material cutting from the tire cover. The results from that sample were residue of chloroform. I repeated the same test on additional spare tire cover cuttings, and again, the results were residue of chloroform. I tested this, the fabric, not the cardboard. The results were residue of chloroform. On samples taken from the left side of the trunk liner, I did same test. The results were residue of a chemical consistent with chloroform.

There are two different testing techniques. When it is consistent one test gives a positive, I need two positives to say for sure it is chloroform. Tests on the right side of the trunk liner were consistent with chloroform. So, the tire cover was chloroform and other areas were consistent with chloroform. We use GCMS for separation and identification of the chemicals. Our machines are very sensitive, and I can find chemicals from water. It can break it down and detect it in small amounts. The second test is a different way of detecting the chemicals. Residue of chloroform is usually found in a liquid state, but when subjected to testing, it can be found in small amounts. It has been detected in household items. I do not know if you can find it in swimming pool water. I have no knowledge if it is in soda. Usually, I find it in cleaning products, small amounts like in these items. If detected, the level goes up and we read it on a graph. The item does not tell you exactly how much. There is a qualitative analysis, which identifies the substance as chloroform, and a quantitative analysis, which would tell exactly how much is there. The quality gives you a range. I did dual tests. In the internal test, we also tested negative and positive control samples.

Michael Rickenbach – Defense Cross-examination: The questioned sample was significantly less than the standard I provided. No, it was not the most I have seen in twenty years. It was not shockingly high. Shockingly high levels? No. It was lower than my positive control. The left side was consistent with chloroform and the right was consistent with chloroform. The first test picked it up and the second test did not. On the two spare tire cover pieces, residue of chloroform was significantly lower than the positive control I chose. I have tested other items, and I am not sure where they came from. This is all from this batch I received. Baez asked, did you test the steering wheel cover? (Sidebar) These residue levels of chloroform have been detected in cleaning products. Low and high limits are relative. I have never before been called upon to look for chloroform in a fabric like this; it is usually tested in a liquid state. What might be high or low in a carpet sample? I would need to do a laboratory study. The sample was packaged inside a cardboard box. The package would seep out the chloroform, and I was surprised I got any chloroform from it being packaged that way, and not in an airtight container. The positive control was a known amount of chloroform of one hundred parts per million in water. That was the standard. This is a very rough estimate. The piece of spare tire cover was in a can, and that was a better way to keep it – in a heat sealed container is the appropriate way to do it.

It was significantly less. (The witness refreshes his recall on the range of percentages in his report.) It was about five percent of the positive result in the control sample. This is a very rough estimate of the control sample. Some were one percent. They can contained a much higher level of chloroform. Another sample in a sealed container was between one and two percent on the next sample. The highest is on the sealed sample in the can. However, the samples were not the same. This is not the best way to relate the numbers. An open atmosphere will result in less chloroform remaining. It would have evaporated a lot. I have never tested air samples; I have no firsthand knowledge. I test with liquid samples for chloroform and not normally analyze these kinds of samples. I would not want to give an impression of a physical amount of chloroform, based on the tests I did. I do not have any experience with testing chloroform from a solid object before this case. I have knowledge about the way this should have been packaged for testing. Based in qualitative analysis, if you can test cleaning products, you can test this, which is all I was saying. I was not comparing the two things. (The witness is released.)

The State's Forty-fifth Witness

Interpretation of Testimony – Deputy Jason R. Forgey: I have been with the K9 Unit now for seventeen years, with the Orange County Sheriff. I have worked with dogs since 2001. I cross-trained with the unit. I received a dog in 2001, as a part time handler. I was a part time Bloodhound handler. These are dogs that will track an individual. They have five weeks of training and then testing. Garrett was the first Bloodhound I worked with. I did follow-up training with a minimum of two training tracks a month and the supervisors watched the dog work. I worked with Garrett until we had to put him down. Then I got Ike, a scent-discrimination and tracking dog. I gave him to another handler. I trained multiple dogs. I had Bones in 2002, a cadaver dog – single purpose. That is all he does, obedience and human decomposition. I did one hundred and sixty hours of specialty training and he is certified.

I was chosen for this dog because our dogs after 9/11 were utilized as bomb dogs. The training is much different. You introduce the dog to the odor to see if it agrees with him. Then you take him straight to this odor over and over. That imprints the odor, and you train him to sit when he smells that odor. Then you train him using multiple cans and stop only at that odor. You will notice changes in his body as he is headed to the odor and smells it, and then he sits when he finds the source. Bones was trained to sit at this final source alert. We used rags with decomposition and bodies with decomposition to imprint the smell. I also have pills to put in water that simulate drowning victims, to help recognize the drowning victim odor. We use blood and tissue as well. We give the dog direction to begin smelling. All these things are used to train him.

The Sheriff's Office went to full service dogs, dogs that do all kinds of searches both of the living and the dead. He could not be retrained to full service and they wanted to retire him. I was given a full service German Shepherd. Garus came from Germany. He was twenty-one months then. He will be nine this October. He was trained in a program with me for four hundred hours of basic schooling, scent and tracking. He is certified by DFLE after being evaluated by two outsiders. I am the only person who works with my dog. He is tested and I am tested. Then he worked and went back to an additional one hundred and sixty hours of human cadaver work. This dog lies down at the source. The same items are used to imprint the odor for him, like human remains and water pills for drowning victims. We distraction-proof the dogs to other odors, so the dogs will not be distracted from the odor they are trained to locate. We train them not react to pizza, hamburgers, ham bones, dog urine, feces and other scents. They will not alert to any of these items or any other distractions. I exposed him to everything I could think of.

Garus goes with me to special schools and we trained in places where neither the trainer (me) nor Garus knows where the odor to be found is located. We go to great lengths to avoid any cueing of the dog to alert. Garus went to an independent cadaver school in Sarasota. This school was led by a recognized trainer of dogs. (An exhibit is shown; it is a composite of documents.) I recognize them as my and the dogs training and experience records. (Defense objects. Prosecution is asking more questions about the exhibits.) The first set of documents is certification for basic human remains. Next is the copy of a memo in reference to the dogs' certification. The evaluator evaluated the dog for certification, and he passed. I keep the business records of the dog. The next is the original document for the Sarasota school, then documents on cadaver search school, on advance cadaver search school, on team certification for K9 Garus, this is his FDLE certification, documents showing lots of cadaver dog training logs and more. (These are accepted into evidence.)

(Defense wants to voir dire the witness.) I keep the records so if I ever go to court, I can show the training and logs of the dog and his certifications. These are training logs. (Baez objects and argues that the records are inadmissible.) Judge: The supreme court says differently, and they are admitted into evidence. Forgery resumes, the information on the log tells the name of the dog, if he trained all day, the location and the quantities of searches, the locations, different environments and if the target was found. Total false alerts: if he had a false alert that day. On this form, Garus found all targets on that day in this log. There were eight targets and eight finds. I note the weather information, and whether there is wind, fog, or anything else. He has had a few misses and one false alert in his career. Mostly those happened when he was over-tired after a number of searches, like thirty-one in the same day. It is in my log. In the real world, it is one search a day. He does maintenance training regularly.

(The father of one of the authors trained family dogs to find children, just as a hobby or for protection of the kids in the family. At first, when were young, they were to find us if lost. When we were older, father would play with us by sending the dog to find us when we were playing in the neighborhood. He would come walking behind the dog. We had great parents and grandparents. Well-trained dogs are amazing. We were raised with dogs, including a Labrador named Jake, who liked us to read books aloud to him.)

These are photos showing a dog in action at training. When his hair sticks up and turns in, he is on the scent, then he sits when he finds the source. These are many photos of the dog in different locations and the dog finding things against other obstacle odors. The dog sits on final find of the odor, and then he turns and looks at me while seated. He makes eye contact. These photos include vehicle searches. (Sounds like a good dog.) He has trained in situations where a body was in an area and then removed. A deceased man was near a pond, and I requested permission to train my dog. We found the body. Ten day later, after the body was removed, Garus and I went back. We searched from two different directions, and Garus found two additional bones. This was a training aid. We have done other similar "removed body searches" for training. He did not miss or false alert on the areas. I have done two hundred real-world searches and five hundred training exercises.

We always work together, eighty hours every two weeks. I am usually called by detectives on fresh cases, on cold cases, or I hear dispatch, and go to the scene. In a typical call there is no alert, nothing to be found. We did no searches in 2005, in 2006 six calls and one alert on a body. In 2007, there were nine calls, and no alert for a body. In 2008, we had seventy-one cadaver searches, with three alerts for a body or a part of a body. This was because of the Anthony case. We had an increase in calls of possible leads. After July 15th, 2008, I had several calls on tips looking for Caylee Anthony. We had hundreds of tips on this case to follow. Two cases looked like a recent shallow grave, an indented area or grass disturbed. Garus did not alert, and they found animals. In 2009, he had twelve searches and one alert. It was a drowning victim, still under water.

In 2010 we did eleven searches. Garus is retired now. A male called the sheriff's office in 2006 and said there was a female shot, and her body was near a retention pond. The police had searched and they were looking for her body. They called for a helicopter to search and then the helicopter fueled and searched again. The helicopter called and said there was a large alligator in the area. I asked them to stay and watch the alligator while I searched with Garus. It was dark, and they videoed this search because of the alligator. Video of the 2006 search is available. (Defense objects that they have never seen the video, and it was not included in discovery.) Prosecution: We just discovered it from the Sheriff's Office. (Sidebar. The video is received in evidence.)

(Casey seems more upbeat today, in front of the jury. Probably because the defense got a few strikes at the prosecution experts. It is going to take more than a few strikes to save her from life in prison or death. There is a lot of circumstantial evidence in this case. The defense is still objecting about the video and the officer testifying. They are holding a motion to suppress in front of the jury. The jury is hearing things that should be argued outside their presence. The effect is improper bolstering of the witness. Twelve individuals will soon be asked to evaluate the believability of this testimony. So the reliability of the dog, the trainer, and the certificates may be an important part of the jury deliberations regarding the facts in this case. This evidence will help the jury determine the value of the K9-related evidence that will follow.)

The video shows Garus searching high grass near a body of water in Florida. The dog is in the dark, heading for the search area and arriving at a body floating in the water. It is good infrared video. It is a wooded area with high grass, with a very steep incline to the water. It is very dark, and Garus is jumping through the high grass. There is trash all over. The dog finally arrives at a sink hole with the body below the surface. When Garus got to the body in the water, he sat down. It really shows the dog in action in a pitch black, high grass search. The helicopter above caught this video at night on its infrared camera. (Defense stills objects to the video.) (Judge puts it in evidence. And another sidebar happens.)

This is the way it works, every expert or piece of evidence must be brought into the courtroom in very specific ways and accepted into evidence. It would be hard to imagine the hours that go into prepping a murder case, except we have seen it. It is hundreds, sometimes thousands of hours for each attorney and their assistants. At this point, millions of dollars and thousands of hours of time have been spent to bring this case to court and try to find out what happened to Caylee, and by whose hands she died. This is happening in part because the last person responsible for Caylee's safety, Casey Anthony, led the world on a wild goose chase for a missing child. Then, once Caylee's body was found, Casey refused to tell them the when and how about Caylee's death. She exercised her right to remain silent. At the end of the day, it is really all about the legal system attempting to use justice to get a very simple answer to one question. "What happened to Caylee when she was in Casey's custody?" Unfortunately, all that will be achieved at the end of the trial is the punishment of Casey if she is found guilty. With her history of lying, at this point we could never believe what she said. We could not believe her, for even if she did tell us what happened to Caylee that ended her life, at thirty four months on this earth, how could we know it was the truth?

Testimony of Deputy Jason R. Forgey resumes: I was called to assist in the investigation of Caylee Anthony on July 17th, 2008, just before 4 PM. I use the collar to let Garus know that he is doing a different job; a collar over his head is a sign to look for human remains. A body leash is for searching. I arrived at the forensic bay, and they said they wanted me to search a car with the dog. Having had numerous prior searches for human remains, I recognize the smell in the garage as that of human remains, and Garus was kept in the car. I asked to have the car bought out of the bay before I brought Garus out, and had it placed in the parking lot. I wanted it in the open air away from biohazards, and they put it in a clean area. I had the car sit a short time. I moved my vehicle with Garus to the back of the area near the car. I swept a blue car on the right side, it see if he alerted on the unknown vehicle. He did not, and went to the subject vehicle. The doors were closed on the Pontiac Sunbird. I told the tech in at the bay that if I needed to open the car, I would have him do it. The dog picked up on the scent, and when the door was opened, he jumped into the backseat and was trying to get into the trunk. The tech opened the trunk, and Garus jumped into the car trunk. He came out and gave me a trained alert.

The next day, I was asked to go to the Hopespring Drive address. They had a couple of concerns that the father was not familiar with in his back yard. (Objection. Judge: The jury must disregard the part about the father having concerns about two areas.) I brought Garus out of the car and performed a search of the backyard. He was off a lead, since the area is fenced and I told him his command, "Find Fred." We passed sheds made of Tupperware and a swimming pool. Then the area of concern was near the other side, but nothing near the pool. It was in the play area where a doll house was and in the sand box and picnic area of the doll house area. I suggested a second dog come and search the areas. I gave minimal information to the other dog handler to see if they had any alerts. Bones arrived, it was a little while later and Garus was back in the car. Bones had been with the other handler a few years, so they handled Bones. I did not.

I was in the back yard; the lot is not that large, and the grass is less than the area of the courtroom in size. The only alert was in the doll house area. My dog is trained with residual odor. I have had real odor older than thirty days. Residual odor, something being there that is no longer there, it could be decomposition or a body. It could be there or nothing there; dogs are not perfect, just like humans. He worked over six years as a find dog. When I went to see the car, I was told it was the suspect's vehicle. I brought out the car because there were other things in the bay and I want to get a clean look. I had a car that did not have anything to do with it and the suspect car. I did not videotape the find.

If we could have predicted where we would be today, we would have videoed that search. We do not do video on a live search normally. Doesn't one of the books suggest videotaping? Yes, but we cannot video all of the searches. I knew there was no body in the car. I do not have anything that is in my policies or procedures that would have me video every search. When we train our dogs, the log is an indication of our work as a team. If I train my dog, it is not blind testing but there are also unknown finds. The dog's real finds are unknown finds. Part of the motivation is that the dog wants to please me. The sergeant who has Bones was found, and then CSI was called. I do not think they dug in the area. I did not get any alerts the next day after they moved the surface ground. I have six searches and a report for the find; we do not file reports on non-alerts. On all of the other searches, there was one when I reached a non-alert and there was a shallow grave, then they dug and found animal remains.

I was called out after they removed the body from the area on Suburban Drive. We did not find the missing girl's remains on Suburban Drive. I did not want to find the bones that they already knew about. I did not want Garus to get to that area. I wanted to remove him from the area to look at other areas for the bones that might have been spread from animals. Garus was alerting, and I pulled him away from the area. But we were looking for really small bones in other areas. I wanted to keep him moving to another area. I was not letting him go to the spot where the body was located. I wanted him looking in the surrounding area. They told me a couple of small bones were missing. My work is subject to scrutiny every day. Over three thousand calls. Very few searches are videotaped, if a helicopter was there, it was taped. When the CSI scraped the ground by the doll house, whatever was there was probably on the surface and was destroyed. That is why I believe the dog did not alert the second day.

Baez told him, I do not think a dead body in the backyard of the Antony's home is in dispute. You do not know why the dog alerted one day then not the next. Forgey said, I could not tell you exactly why the dog alerted and then did not. I believe it is because CSI had disturbed the ground searching and the odor was only on the top of the ground. I can only tell you from experience. It is my speculation, based on my training and experience. I smelled the odor of decomposition in the car trunk of the Anthony car on the day I did the search, before I got the dog out for the search. Mr. Baez, you are jumping around from the car to the backyard. I smelled it clear as day at the car. I have been present at body scenes with my dog, and I have worked many dead body calls without my dog. (The witness is released.)

The defense renews all previous objections to the next witnesses; the judge states that these are matters for the trier of fact, and that the jury has a right to know the reliability of the dogs and their handlers. If the defense wants to accept the evidence as fact, we need not do this. The defense does not want to do that.

Cindy Anthony has been in the courtroom today without George. Our guess is that George is either working or is too emotionally drained to come to court. This case has surely eaten them alive in dollars, as well as the emotional toll it must surely have taken.

June 8th, 2011

The State's Forty-sixth Witness

Interpretation of Testimony - Kristin Brewer: She is a Supervisor of Patrol with the Osceola County Sheriff's Office. I am the current dog handler of the dog Bones: I have been with the K9 unit since 2005. Primarily I am the supervisor of patrol, and my secondary duty is as the K9 backup. I know Bones's background and training. It was a hobby of mine to train dogs before I got Bones. (Sidebar) (*We are really jealous - she got Bones, sounds like a cool Bloodhound. Okay, we admit it. We are dog people.*) In 2005, Bones was given to Osceola. I received him and he was already trained. He came with all his training paperwork. I then trained and maintained the records from that day. Training records are reviewed and identified. (Judge views the records… Have we mentioned that this lead prosecutor is very good? She is detail-oriented.)

I bonded and got to know the dog and met with the previous deputy trainer for information. Then we trained sometimes several hours a week. I wrote the training results in the log and we attended outside training schools with authorities such as Andy Redman, on cadaver dog training. I do not recall any misses or false alerts and Bones found all targets on land and water. He is exposed at all searches to urine and feces and does not alert. He does not alert to food or animal remains. The results are recorded in the school logs you have. Bones and I have attended Country Class K9 with Lisa Higgins another dog trainer specialist training events. Bones final training alert is a sit. He has been trained to alert to body that has been removed from a location. Bone's reward is a tennis ball and he gets food and treats just for being a dog. Real world records are in the log. In 2005, Bones searched and did not alert. A deceased dog was found later. In 2006, four calls no alert, dead dogs and animals located. Bones only alerts on human remains. In 2009, call, no alert animal remains again. No false alerts under my handling.

In 2007, we received a call. Bones alerts on human remains, and a couple of small bones of a skeleton were found. A body buried in the woods two to three weeks, Bones searched and alerted on the exact area the body was later dug up. There was an elderly female that had not been seen, Bones alerted on the outside wall of the house and she was deceased inside. At a landfill, Bones deployed into the landfill for several days, and alerted to a comforter that a baby had been born on. In 2008, we had calls, human skull was found and Bones alerted on other bone parts he found. A water search of large lake and Bones alerted. We dropped a buoy and divers found the body there. A burned body, he was within a few feet when he alerted to the spot. Two bodies buried in the same hole, he alerted in the area and both bodies were recovered. He is a single purpose cadaver dog who does a lot of searches inside and outside the State of Florida.

In 2008, with the case of Caylee Anthony, who resided at Hopespring Drive, I arrived and found out it was the grandparent's home. We were there on July 17th, 2008 at 8 PM. It was pretty dark, but that does not stop Bones. I met with Deputy Forgey and he told me they wanted the back yard searched, so we walked back. He told me his dog had searched, but nothing else about where. I got Bones and took him into the back through the gate and I put on his search collar and set him off lead. He did a quick search by the swimming pool and porch and he kept going to an area of interest and finally sat at one location for a final alert. That final alert was at the doll house area. (A photo is shown to her, and the deputy marks the same areas as where Forgey had marked, the area that Garus had alerted. Deputy Forgey told me his dog had alerted within six to eight feet of that spot. I returned after the yard surfaces had been moved by CSI – they were in the backyard. Bones had no alert the following day. My opinion is it was because the ground had been dug up and it was either the surface odor or buried deeper.

Kristen Brewer – Defense Cross-examination: The dogs can alert to a drop of blood that is then decomposing. We do not know why the blood scent is there, because the strongest odors are of the body fluids. I cannot say exactly where Garus located, but it was in the area. It could be in any direction. The swimming pool is behind us. I never deployed the dog inside the house. I deployed where asked. No, I was not asked to search in the screened porch. I do not know of any house search was done, because it was not my case.

The State's Forty-seventh Witness

Interpretation of Testimony – Sandra Osborne: (The authors note that the witness is followed by someone who looks suspiciously like a lawyer. He is carrying a briefcase, and after being stopped by a court deputy, he is permitted to be seated in the front row of the gallery. Does she think she is in trouble, the kind of trouble that might lead to criminal charges against her or trouble with the Sheriff's Office?) I have been doing computer examinations for 21 years with the Orange County Sheriff's Office. I was in patrol, CSI, sex crimes, child abuse, homicide, and computer crimes. I have a business degree through Columbia College and seven hundred hours of computer forensics training and a certificate through IASIS and another one. I learned the basics of computers, how to find and document those things. In the real world, I have done several hundred exams on computers, Iphones, cell phones, anything that carries a digital file. (The witness is accepted as an expert in computer forensic analysis.) I received items in the Anthony case. The first was a cell phone that was reported to have belonged to Casey Anthony. (She identifies the package as initialed and sealed by her containing a Nokia cell phone, which is admitted in evidence.) There are applications that can be used to retrieve information. The Cellebrite application was used for the fields such as contacts, call history, video, text, logs, and more. The limitations are imposed by the phone, and in some cases, we cannot retrieve it all, but we do receive updates that allow us to retrieve more.

I attempted to find anything on Zenaida Fernandez-Gonzalez, and the contact list and several music files. They are limitations of Cellebrite; it could only retrieve so much, and it could not retrieve all of the information on the phone. The SIM card is a card that allows the phone to connect to the network. That phone had a SIM card, I removed the SIM card, and it plugged in to the Cellebrite. It contained the same information as the device. It is not my function to analyze the data, the detectives do that, but I did not see any information on Zenaida Fernandez-Gonzalez. The Cellebrite makes a nice data report. I received computers. There was a laptop; Detective Beasley brought it when she brought the cell phone. I was able to identify it by a serial number from the laptop. I also received a floor model computer, (the serial number was identified) from McBryde. I received two cameras, a Polaroid digital, and a Nikon digital. I use forensics tools for the cameras, Encase. I pulled the SD flash card which stores the files and viewed the card. I found video of Caylee Anthony, dated June 15th, 2008. I reviewed the video of what appeared to be a nursing facility.

The file imbeds the make, model, date and time a photo was taken, and some GPS coordinates are in some cameras. Nikon gave me information, the camera model, date, and time of pictures. I compared the date and time with the current date and time shown on the camera; the camera was correct to within two minutes. The laptop, I do not remember if it was off or on when I received it. In a lab, I power the machine off and remove the hard drive to retrieve data. It was a desktop computer with a 160GB hard drive. That was powered off when I received it. I use different tools to examine a computer; I used Encase software, which is a standard in forensics use. I have been using it since 2006, and it has been in use maybe a decade or more. It is an industry standard and a reliable software tool.

Encase can look at every single bit on a hard drive whether the user can see the information or not. We protect the hard drive as original evidence. I attached it to a right blocker that prevents making changes or writing to the hard drive. It becomes a read-only drive at that point, then I duplicate it and work from my copy, and the original goes back into evidence. We eventually returned the hard drive to the family. The files were stored on a server as well as a duplicate hard drive and the original hard drive was then stored for evidence. I have the information with me on a hard drive. Cell phones have less information, and I give it to the detectives to work with. The computers have a great deal of information and I analyze it.

When you look at a hard drive, it shows what the user sees, the user systems, and deleted files, as well as more. A computer records the date and time everything is entered on the computer. On July 18th, 2008 at 12:13 PM, I viewed many applications such as, Windows XP operation, Explorer, Firefox, applications for Office, Facebook, Myspace, Peer-to-Peer, Yahoo Messenger, and many others. The Windows application was installed in 2005. The HP came standard loaded with Windows most often. Some of the browsers were loaded from the internet and Safari was also located. The HP computer had 2 users; 1 owner, and 1 Casey. I was asked to find any information on Zenaida Fernandez-Gonzalez and asked if there is any information in this computer that will lead us to Caylee. With an examination of that type, I look to see how the users are using, look for current items, internet history, temporary files, phone numbers, resumes, what, and who are using it for work, games, and searches.

I located references to Zenaida Fernandez-Gonzalez in the temporary files. They are all dated and timed. The internet pages save themselves to the hard drive on your computer, as a cache for fast access. When I go back to an internet page, it reloads more easily because of the cache. The cache saved to the hard drive was Zenaida Fernandez-Gonzalez. It was several searches going to people and someone searched Classmates pages for people aged 22-29, was what they were looking for. On July 16th, 2008, no other references to Z were on that the computer. The computer was on and running a good period of time. There was not too much office work, resumes, or schoolwork. Lots of internet history, the longest was 4 plus years. You can right click on properties and it is deleted, but that does not clear all browsers. It gets saved to deleted space, but until that space is overwritten it is still on the hard drive. It depends on usage and how full the hard drives are. That information could stay for years. Key word searches allow us to sort a lot of information fast. The Rico password was set up for the Casey user in 2008, I believe.

The internet history is a record of websites and the temporary files are the actual pages. I examined the history with another software program spreadsheet, and I can sort information. I used net analysis, which is a forensic tool. I can tell which user account is using the computer to search. It can only know what user account is used at that time. I did a key word search for chloroform. It was put it in spelled correctly an incorrectly. The key words appeared in deleted space on the hard drive. I can view the information. I can see some of the record. We are able to recover a complete history from Mozilla, Firefox, everything. I turned it over to my supervisor, another expert. What it found was the word spelled correctly or not, and I recognized it as an internet search. I was not able to determine which software was used for the search, and turned it over for analysis. We are a few feet away from each other, and we copied it to another source, and examined it on his machine and created a report.

Ricardo Morales's computer was turned over to me in October 2008, by Sergeant Allen. I preserved the data the same as the other computers, removing, write blocking, and copying after removing the hard drive. I asked for key words and pictures of Caylee in a pink shirt with certain writing. I found it in the graphic files on his computer. Once an image is located in the graphic file, it is embedded with the date and time from the camera in the computer. (A picture of Casey and Caylee is introduced.) (Sidebar) The Judge gives the jury a caveat: The photo that is currently displayed, please remember the bruise on the eye is not a result of abuse or anything of that nature.

The photo was given to me on a thumb drive originating from the Globe; it was also on Mr. Morales's computer and thumb drive. According to the information on the drive, the embedded photo was taken January 28th, 2008, but I could not verify the date and time without the camera, to make sure it was properly set. I did not have the camera to analyze the time and date on the camera. Another photo… (The defense objects to the date and time being stamped on the photos. This is because she did not have the camera to verify the date and time were correct. (Sidebar) The photo appeared on a thumb drive and the computer of Morales. The Canon camera took the picture. The camera was set to the date of March 19, 2008.

Sandra Osborne – Defense cross-examination: There are two user-created profiles. I found internet searches on both profiles. There could be multiple users using one profile and anyone who has the password could use the profile or if the computer is not turned off after use. The owner profile, that profile had a password. If the user with the password logged off, or if the computer goes to sleep then they can be required to re-enter the password to log back on. I did not determine the settings on this computer, so if someone used the computer logged on as the owner, as far as I know, anyone else could use that profile on the computer as long as the owner did not log off. I did a key word search for chloroform around August of 2008. My supervisor has the information on the date the searches were done by users. I did not see the Canon camera that took the pictures, and I do not know if the time was correct. Not every camera and computer has the exact time set. I ran searches on Ricardo Morales's computer for chloroform and I found no webpages or pictures that referenced chloroform on that computer. (The photo of Morales's Myspace chloroform posting, the "Win her over with chloroform" photo is shown to the witness, and she is asked to read and describe it.) The photo is of a man and a woman in a black evening gown. They are having dinner and the man is behind her with a white napkin, reaching around her shoulder. I am not aware that Morales posted it on Myspace. I did not find that photograph on the computer. (It implies sedation of a woman with chloroform. Bad taste, Ricardo, bad taste!)

There are several ways to upload this from Myspace, another computer, a phone, and so forth. At the time I examined the drive, it was not there. It is possible that it could have been deleted and overwritten on the drive before I received it.

Sandra Osborne – State's re-direct: The pictures are digital and are not readable with the software we use. Embedded words are a part of the picture and will not be revealed with a word search. The computer had no keywords for chloroform, no references to it, and no photos that I found. (The witness is released.)

The prosecution looks tired and the defense looks perky. This is probably because the defense may be presenting most of its case in chief during the prosecution's case, or perhaps because the defense scored more points with this witness. A really petrifying thought just crossed one author's mind. At 34 months, Caylee was just starting to talk in concepts. Could Casey have murdered her because in the foreseeable future, without malice, Caylee would have busted her mother on all of the lies she told to her friends, parents, grandmother and grandfather? Could this have been Casey's motive?

The State's Forty-eighth Witness

Interpretation of Testimony – Detective Kevin Stenger: I have been in the computer forensics crime unit of the Orange County Sherriff's Office since 2002, when it was formed. I have a graduate certification in computer forensics, and I have a master's certificate in computer digital forensics. I belong to IASIS. I have attended every conference since 1996, and presented at many conferences. I have testified in state and federal court as a computer forensic expert. In 2008, I was the supervisor of Detective Osborne in the Casey Anthony case. An HP desktop computer was given to me, and it came from the family. I reviewed all of Osborne's work and assisted in any additional problems she might have. A keyword search for chloroform on the HP was one of the active roles I took. I assisted in analyzing the deleted files. They are similar to the Dewey decimal system of locating a file, just like finding a book in a library. It looks it up, and then goes and locates it. Once deleted, there is no reference to the files, but the files are still there and the record from Firefox was there.

Firefox is an internet browser. I am not aware that it clears any records; normally the user must delete the record. Even if dumped, it is still on the hard drive. Firefox does not store the user name of the deleted file in the search history. Firefox does not record the user name. I found where the files started and ended, and then I began to use other programs to read the information. The file starts with header and ends with footer. I have a tool to extract the data and I save it through Encase. Once I create it, I use other tools to read the information. I had a problem with the history time due to daylight savings so I used another tool to even the time

238

balance. This history of the chloroform searches span from, March 4th, 2008 through March 21st, 2008. I used the CacheBack. In that program, I would have the ability to view the date and time it was created and not just based on my computer. I also asked the creator of CacheBack to review the files and asked him to give a statement to his findings. I filtered the information for March 17th and 21st. Those dates contained the information of chloroform searches and other searches done in that same time frame. (He reviews and recognizes the March 17th report and March 21st report he generated. They were admitted into evidence. Mr. Bradley of CacheBack was given a copy of the file in the unallocated space of the computer.)

Kevin Stenger – Defense cross-examination: Unallocated space was deleted in the internet history, wasn't it? It was, but I do not know when or why it was deleted. If your computer is slow you may have deleted your history. The search for chloroform shows up at 1:43.41 PM that would have been 2:43:41 with the hour off for daylight savings. At 2:43:48 there is an advertisement. The records are appearing from another site, so even though you have not navigated away from the site, the time of the ad is downloaded. From the address, they did not leave the website of the chloroform. That photo of the chloroform was on Ricardo's Myspace.

Where you went is stored and the rest of the page is placed in the cache so your computer can store it and then retrieve it quickly. I can recover the history and may not be able to recreate the page. You can tell where that keyword search is from, like 'this was from Google' for an exact search for chloroform.

The State's Forty-ninth Witness

Interpretation of Testimony – John Dennis Bradley: I have been self-employed since 2001. My company is called SiQuest. I am a former Canadian law enforcement officer. I led the crimes unit in Computer Forensics. In 2000, I was transferred to major crimes and promoted to sergeant and I was back in uniform. I left law enforcement and took a position at a bank in crimes investigation. During that employment, I started a computer software company. I left banking, and went into arm data for law service for litigation. The increase in demand made me do more software and training. I have testified in Canada as an expert. In criminal defense, I have testified about issues relating to my software. I am an expert in computer analysis.

239

I have developed CacheBack to retrieve information. Cache
is the information stored or hidden in your computer. The
cache makes it easier or faster to retrieve information.
The software extracts and extrapolates the information
for law enforcement. My software compensates for time
changes. I am an instructor, both in the private sector
and for law enforcement. I taught the course in 2009 at
UCF for the US Secret Service. I was asked to take a look
at a data file on a thumb drive that was recovered from
the hard drive. Detective Stenger explained that the
block of data was from Firefox Two and the body of the
information was the word chloroform contiguous related to
where it was retrieved from. There was deleted
information, and this information had the header,
content, and footer all intact. Numerous amounts of
clusters of data were there.

I copied it onto my workstation laptop and returned the
thumb drive. I reviewed in visual mode; I scrolled
through the file and located the keyword chloroform. It
was a complete file. The file was about 3.2 megabytes. A
byte is about one character. Based on the information, I
was impressed it was recoverable. I cannot say when it
was deleted. The browser of Firefox did not come with an
auto-delete or privacy mode. The file would have had to
be deleted manually.

I ran it through a number of tests, for three days. I
needed to decode it, and I worked around the clock to
decode it. I was able to decode it and wrote functions in
the software. I used third-party reliable software to
confirm and CacheBack generated a report. (They are
viewing the report in evidence.) On March 17th, 2008,
March 21st, 2008 and one entry appears for March 20th,
2008, appear to be a CacheBack report. (These are
accepted into evidence.) The first entry on the report of
March 17th, 2008, has column headers which tell us the
index, URL ID, type of browser, the number of visits,
times, action date is the local time and date, user, and
IE for Internet Explorer. This is the only one that
stores the user.

It appears it is a web address from Google on March 17th
at 2:43 and number of times it was accessed from the data
I extracted. You enter keywords and it will filter the
results. You click search, and the keyword is submitted
and anything related to the search is sent back to your
computer. History stores this information and the where
and when. The search was on Google, and the keyword was
chloroform. The Google searches the keyword query for
chloroform. The exact value of the time stamp was a
different spelling of the word chloroform. Chloroform was

240

misspelled with an "a", and Google offered the correct result. If the time stamp is different, they are in correct order as searched. This is an entry that tracks the user for advertising; it is in the background. You can see the background information is applying tracking information while the user was searching. It would not appear to the user that they are being tracked.

This is a bookmarked URL for Photobucket. There was activity on the Photobucket site. This is an entry for a Wikipedia search for chloroform that was selected from the Google search. This entry is on the computer log, another search ending in alcohol was selected. This entry was on the computer log, it is another search ending in alcohol and was selected. The user was querying chloroform and alcohol in Google. A Wikipedia result at 2:58 PM was "inhalation, death". "Self-defense" may have been auto created. At 2:59 PM a search for "hand-to-hand combat" resulted in a link being selected. At 3:00 PM, a selected Wikipedia word was "injuries, head injury". At 3:02 PM, the search was for middlemen in jail. At 3:30 PM, a search for "ruptured spleen". At 3:40 PM, a search for chest trauma and at 3:40 PM, there was a search result from Wikipedia for "beating".

At 3:05 PM, there is a link to an article, "internal bleeding". At 3:05 PM, "hyperborean". Myspace seem to be created automatically by a stored cookie. This is a Facebook entry, an item that was accessed by a hyperlink from the user, and there is a bookmark during the time of these searches. There is an Index as a default of a Myspace profile; that is something that could have been user-selected. This Profile on Myspace is of the user view profile and friend ID. The View album on Myspace supports that the user selected the items for Myspace. There are visits to Facebook by a cookie or bookmark user activity. There is another visit to Myspace, and there is possible user interaction. Facebook activity is user generated and that is someone sitting at the computer on Facebook. (They looked up who was using the computer to search chloroform and by the searches and visits to Facebook and Myspace by Casey.)

On March 18th, 2008 this is an item from a Google Chrome search. This was a user generated search result for the website sci-spot.com, "chemistry/chloroform". That page would be what it is today, some pages could be unchanged or they could be different. These are how to make chloroform, the next how to make chloroform and it was a search request to Google that the user, at the time, typed in how to make chloroform. I believe some of these items were bookmarked. This is a result for a search for the word "chloroform" by a user at the computer. How to make chloroform from household products, selected by the computer user. This was selected, typed or bookmarked by the user. The items appear that the user selected them in relation to the two preceding URLs. A Google search, "neck breaking by person" was on the computer. Wikipedia was used in this search, and could be a saved bookmark or manually typed in.

Myspace is next as a bookmarked item used. Facebook is a path that shows the user went to an inbox in order to read messages. This is a Facebook profile ID or transaction. The user generated the item or possibly used a bookmark. On March 21st, 2008, this appears to be Facebook activity for the balance of the report. The Facebook ends at 3:37 PM on March 21st, 2008, for this report.

John Dennis Bradley – Defense cross-examination: I stayed up all night for a few days to fix the program and change it in order to work on this file. I am here today for free, and then they could pay me later based on a state set amount. On my website, I have a link to an article in this case. Firefox was recorded in obsolete software. It was advertising, it has been two years and I have not promoted anything. I am not overwhelmed with calls, so I put a small article on my webpage. In the chloroform search, the user is on the site Google, on the home page at 2:43 PM for seven seconds until the next page with results appears on March 17th, 2008 at 2:53 PM. Wikipedia then one second later – another page. The reference is on Wikipedia and it is self-defense. In my own common experience, it describes an article and link within Wikipedia. At 2:59 PM the search is "hand to hand combat", "head injuries", and "chest trauma", those searches are longer times than was spent on the chloroform search. On March 21st, 2008, the first chloroform search is at 3:16:13 PM on sci-spot for 17 seconds, then there is a Google search for chloroform. At 3:18 PM, a sci-spot page, "chloroform" and that is for 2.27 seconds with nothing in-between. At 3:19 PM, there is a drug library search for chloroform for 21 seconds. That page is about the chloroform habit. The page is talking about someone having a chloroform habit in the 1800s.

The next search is in Google, for neck breaking. I do not see any references to a book. Making weapons out of household products – I believe we are referencing two different reports. All of the searches we have covered so far are surrounded by other searches. Then you have the search for the word shovel. Are you aware of any other uses for this word shovel, a movie maybe? No. The link only gives so much information, they could be jokes, chemistry, or kung fu. A computer can never testify that someone is reading what is on the page unless there is a security camera that shows exactly what the user is doing while the webpages are displayed.

I think the information that has greatest importance would need to be taken in context – it would depend on the person. I cannot tell you if this other cache or history is on the computer. There was just a little time that we could recreate. I was not asked to do any more testing on the computer. I looked at the data for December 2009. All I have is what I worked with. I think that this is what took place with the Firefox browser. The three minutes on chloroform is not evaluated on this the basis of how much time was spent on this computer. The issue that Sergeant Stenger ran into was decoding the history of the deleted files. There was little documentation. So I need to write the program into my program in order to decode this. It had happened some time before I received the information to work with. It has been eighteen months, and websites change during that period. The word was typed and seconds later search options return, and then the user selects their choice. Wikipedia is the link, and it tends to keep on the site, and sometimes it will send you to another site. I cannot tell if the webpages were printed for later review. I cannot tell exactly what was on the site on a given day eighteen months later. I was only asked to decode the file. The entire search time was an hour. This sci-spot chloroform was visited 84 times by this computer. This is not my report; it appears to be from someone else. It is a not a CacheBack report. (Sidebar) (The judge dismisses the jury for the day. This witness is returning tomorrow.)

It appears there are at least two reports to us. The defense will have a field day if this is true. The defense is fighting; you must work with the evidence you have. It is a victory if they get her off the first-degree murder charges. One of the authors thinks if she is convicted of a lesser degree of murder, the judge is going to nail her in prison years. She is twenty-five now, and even on a lesser, we doubt she will see the light of day before fifty. I hate to tell her it is harder to dance at fifty…

June 9th, 2011

George Anthony is back in the courtroom gallery with Cindy today, and he looks tired. After court ended yesterday, the media found someone else looking for their fifteen minutes of fame. George Anthony's ex-wife says he is a liar. It appears she did not take the information to the defense or the prosecution, but to Dr. Drew on TV. Maybe the defense will put her on the stand. After all, she is a reliable ex-wife with no motive to lie, except for getting revenge and her fifteen minutes of fame. I hope everyone is seeing what it really means to be a lawyer. Seeing just how much work it really is will chase a few away from the legal system – those who believe it is a cushy job. The reality of law is much different from the image. (Witness, John Dennis Bradley is back on the stand this morning. Defense is resuming its cross-examination.)

Interpretation of Testimony – John Dennis Bradley: Defense cross-examination (cont): We left off discussing the internet history. I had the header and footers, and I believe I captured the entire history, mostly in the month of March. Orange County had run a history and was not able to analyze the files. I was only provided one file, the deleted file. (He reviews his report.) The 84 visits were to the sci-spot site about chloroform. This is the report in evidence from March 21st. This report was created by someone else on June 3rd. All I can testify to are the results I tested. A history keeps track of how many times you visit, not separate URL address. It only maintains the last time it was visited and each time was refreshed. It depends on the website set up. There are no other internet searches that have any other chloroform, based on the files I received. I do not know if the pages were printed. The scope of my focus is the data, not the computer. The data I was given did not include any printed pages. This is a data history file only.

The data file was from March 6th to March 24th. The counter will only automatically refresh if there is something in the files of the page that says please refresh, but for most part, the user must refresh. If one tab is opened and if you select a new page, the first page stays open on Firefox and a new tab opens. (He is excused, but subject to recall.)

The State's Fiftieth Witness

Interpretation of Testimony – Lee Anthony (recalled): I am Casey's brother. I was on the family's home computer on July 16th, 2008. I deleted no records. In August of 2008, Casey came home from jail. I had private conversations with Casey and she told me a different version of Caylee being missing. She met Zanny and

Zanny's sister and her children at a park, and during that meeting, Zanny held Casey down and told her that she was taking Caylee with the help of her sister. Casey was held down by her wrists and body. She told me why, but I do not remember why. (His deposition is used on screen to refresh his memory.) She told me that Zanny took Caylee because Casey was not being or would not be a good mother, and Zanny was taking her to teach Casey a lesson and she warned Casey not to go to police. Casey said Zanny was normal height about five-eight, with a good complexion, long hair, and around 100 pounds. She had a dark tan complexion and was Hispanic. Casey told me she could not believe it when it was happening, that it was surreal. She did not tell me she tried to stop them from taking Caylee; she was scared and did not know what to do. Zanny was controlling her movements through Myspace; she had Casey's password and was sending her messages and she said she would go to the places Zanny told her to go. Timer55 was the Myspace password. She told me she did not create the password but she explained it was the days between when Caylee was taken until Caylee's birthday, and then she would get her back. She told me Zanny created this password. I do not know how Zanny changed the password. Casey told me that Zanny the nanny would contact her through Myspace and tell her what to do and she would go places and hope to see Caylee. She would look around and look and look for Caylee. Casey was never successful, and Zanny has never materialized to this day. (The witness is released, subject to recall.)

(The prosecution has to pull the information out of Lee Anthony. He gave a great deal of information in an attempt to find Caylee. When Casey was released from jail for a short time in August 2008, Caylee's remains had not been found. Lee was still searching for Caylee. This information is damaging to Casey, but it is not his fault. It is the fault of Casey Anthony. Casey was setting up all possible defenses, and it is Casey who may end up putting herself in prison for life, or on death row.)

(There is a sidebar and Baez does not look happy again. A stipulation with the defense on Dec 11th, Orange County made a recorded call to 911 and the recording is true and accurate.)

(911 Call)
Operator: Emergency dispatch.
Spare: This is meter reader Rusty Spare. One of my meter readers has found a skull at Suburban and Chickasaw, the Casey Anthony area. It is near the school, the road that dead ends into the woods. Roy Kronk, an employee, is

there and he is not touching it. I will tell him to stay
there, away from the item, and not draw attention.
Operator: I am sending a sheriff.

The State's Fifty-first Witness

Interpretation of Testimony – Edward Turso: I was a
deputy on patrol on December 11th, 2008. I responded to a
call that was on Suburban Drive at 9:32 AM. (He reviews
his report.) It was on Suburban Drive near the
intersection of Chickasaw Trail, in a much wooded area. I
met with Roy Kronk and he took me into the woods. He told
me he was relieving himself; he led me into the woods,
and we walked past the bag and skull by five or ten feet.
Then he looked around, wondering what happened, and he
sees the bag on the ground behind me, over my shoulder. I
looked at it and left the area immediately. We did not
touch it. I had to wait to start taking a statement from
him, because we put up crime tape and waited for other
officers to arrive.

Edward Turso – Defense cross-examination: Mr. Kronk did
not advise me he had called. (Hearsay, move on Mr. Baez.)
I was in the woods and found the skull within twenty
feet. All I remember is a wooded area, and I do not
remember if there is a mowed area. We passed it by about
5 feet in the woods and he was looking confused, like
where did it go? Then he saw it behind me over my
shoulder. I just focused on the skull and the bag next to
it. (Sidebar, Baez is fighting at the bench. The judge
has called whatever they were fighting about.) You
directed Mr. Kronk to his car and then went to write a
statement. I told him to write down what he told me. I do
not recall telling him anything else. (He is excused but
subject to recall.)

The Judge is speaking to the gallery of spectators in the
courtroom outside the eyes and ears of the jury, and
tells the gallery that the next witness will testify as
to the crime scene photos. Judge Perry tells them that if
you cannot control your emotions or facial expressions,
exit the courtroom until after she (the witness) leaves.
Please govern yourself accordingly. (We like this phase
in law, it means look out... I will be watching you or
coming for you.) If you do not control yourselves, the
deputies will be assisting you. (Sidebar) Judge: The pool
camera is to pixelate and blur any image that contains
subject's skull. No electronic devices shall be used to
try to capture a photo. No one is to pull out a cell
phone, or it will be confiscated. There will be no
pictures of the skull. (We agree with the judge on this;
we know it is there and we have no desire to see it or

have others see it. The vultures should not make a profit on images of Caylee's remains.)

The State's Fifty-second Witness

Interpretation of Testimony - Jennifer Welch: I have seen the crime scene photos. I have worked with the Orange County Sheriff's Office Forensics Unit for over five years. I am a CSI. On December 11th, 2008, I was called to a location on Suburban Drive in the eighty-nine-hundred block. I arrived at about 11:25 AM. When I arrived, it was raining. There were a lot of law enforcement officers present. No one was in the woods. The crime scene area was taped. The law officers were in the street but not in the wooded area. I took initial photos before any recovery of evidence. I took photos of the scene upon my arrival. Photo 1 is a picture of a wooded area where the grass goes from the edge of the road and heads into immediate dense vegetation and woods. Photo 2 is the same dense wooded area from the street. There are tall trees with vegetation growing up the trees; it is dense woods. In the beginning, there is a path leading in to the wooded area, but the path is covered in foliage and hard to see. In Photo 3, the path is covered and the picture is taken as a panoramic viewpoint in a series of photos from right to left. In photo 4, the path is a little clearer here, and is to the left or the east of the woods and then the crime scene tape begins. With photo 5, the path is along the wooded part of the street and the woods begin immediately to the right. It shows the area from where the cars are parked and the entire crime scene, taped from the road to the path that enters the wooded area. It is clearly deep foliage and trees.

This is a sign advertising KinderCare on the ground, tossed away onto the path. You can see the path that leads into a wooded area. Rain drops are on the camera lens on some photos. The path leads to the woods. No one would want to walk in, it is highly overgrown and there are dangerous vines, vegetation hanging off trees, and it is a snake haven. The medical examiner was with me and recovered a skull in this area, and I took the photographs of the skull. This is the top of the skull and you can see part of the right side. This is another picture of the skull; the view is pulled back for scaling to the wooded area. You can see a light pole on Suburban Drive in the distance, and for this photo, I was in the area of the body looking out toward the road; there was a lot of foliage in between. This photo shows a log; the skull is located to the northwest of the log, and there is a black plastic bag to the northeast. There is also an off-white canvas bag. In the northeast location is a plastic Disney bag. The vegetation on the west obscured my view of the skull. The plastic Disney bag shows with the canvas and the black garbage bag.

The photo of the log shows the skull, plastic bags and a pair of shorts. A small section of a beer bottle and a small section of the plastic bag, the black plastic bag, clothing remnants, and a collar with a tag were still present. A close-up of the clothing remnants is shown. This is the front of the skull with the duct tape showing. This is the off-white canvas bag, the plastic bag and the skull. I could not tell what was inside the bags. These photos show vegetation, which hid the items. I cannot tell if the skull is in the photo but I can see the duct tape. This duct tape was on the skull. I had to lean over the log to take this photo. This is a close-up of the duct tape on the skull and clothing remnants. I thought a towel was in the photo, but I was later advised it was a blanket. This is how I found the scene that morning, and it is how the medical examiner found the scene.

(The authors can see the photos. The black plastic bag, a red Disney bag and the skull with duct tape are shown as the medical examiner is removing the skull from the scene. The photos show us the skull; it is the small, round, cream-colored skull of Caylee Anthony, with her long brown hair now a mat, still attached to the base of the back of the skull by tape and roots. The duct tape around the mouth is holding the hair to the skull. Vegetation is growing out and around the skull and clothes. Older brown vegetation is on the bottom layer surrounding the skull, and then more fresh vegetation is at the top layer. It is clear these items have been there a long time and not moved. Everything is wet and dirty. The blanket is a rust color and almost unrecognizable as a Winnie the Pooh blanket. This area that the remains are found in is best described as a tropical plant vegetation area overgrowing the trees. It is more of a jungle scene. The bags are crumpled up, and everything is grimy and dirty, including the scant remains of her shirt and shorts. Those things, her skull, bones, and some clothing tags are all remain of Caylee to help her tell her story to the investigators. This is a horrific scene for anyone to view.)

(The witness continues.) As a CSI, one of the first and most important things to document is the scene. I am trained to do this. It is rare to get a second chance at a scene. If the scene is tampered with, it affects everyone, the medical examiner maybe, and investigators.

I look to see if a scene is staged and I am careful to look for that evidence. People may try to steal things, or make it look like something else happened. It is important that the scene not be tampered with in any way. (The duct taped area in the photo is circled by the CSI.) The duct tape is somewhat in the air and it appears you can see the entirety of the duct tape. I cannot tell if it is flat on the ground in this photo. Here you see the duct tape and not the skull. You can see the width, and the end piece of this is the duct tape. This is a close-up of the duct tape, and you can see the width of it and the end. It appears to be a section of the tape.

Investigator Hanson and I collected the skull and the duct tape. He had to apply force to lift it, because he is lifting and grabbing vegetation. We have to be careful because they can be stepping on other items of evidence at the scene as they are collecting evidence. (She is excused but subject to recall.)

The State's Fifty-third Witness

Interpretation of Testimony – Steven Hanson: I am an examiner for the Medical Examiner's Office. Jan Garavaglia is the Chief Medical Examiner. I have been here 7 years; I have also worked for medical examiner's offices in Palm Beach County, Florida and Texas before I came here. I work cases and collect evidence for examination. On December 11th, 2008, I was advised of remains about 11 AM and arrived on Suburban Drive. This is a good picture of how dense the woods are, and it was raining hard. I take photos of the area when I arrive. The scene was inside the woods. These are more pictures of the opening in the trees and vegetation, kind of a path. (It appears to be even deeper woods in these photos.) The path curves into the woods. It would be easy to hide a small body in these woods without going very far off the main road. The fallen log is deeper in, and the body is on the other side of the log. This photo was taken with a flash; the area is overgrown, dark, wet and it was rainy. Some of the pictures were better than what I could see then. It was raining and cold.

The area I arrived at was heavily overgrown woods with undergrowth. It took a while to familiarize myself with the crime scene, as the remains were difficult to see. This photo was taken after we had begun the clearing. I was on the other side of the rotten log and I was looking over to take this photo. I am above and behind the skull. I am not sure that I could appreciate the duct tape at that point. I wanted to make sure we took pictures. It appeared to me to be duct tape on the skull. Once this photo and additional ones were taken, we cleared more so we could get a better look at the remains. In the next photo, the vines are cleared and we can see the remains better. I put a blue line where I removed the log. We had only cleared what was blocking us from seeing, not the remains. The next photo is a close up of the skull after the vines had been removed from the ground. We had not moved the remains yet. This photo was taken from the opposite side from where the other photos were taken, and we did it in a way not to step over or disturb anything.

The camera is about two feet off the ground. You can rotate the screen so you do not have to get on the ground. I can see the duct tape now in this photo, but I cannot tell at this point if it is more than one piece. The tape was bound up in matted hair and it was hard to tell. We see a portion of the duct tape under the leaf debris and it was below, but we did not know that until we moved the debris. We had to clear stuff to see. It appeared to be hair, and it was later proved to be hair. The hair appeared on the skull, as well. We are responsible for providing details to the medical examiner on how the remains were found. We focus more on the scene as it bears on the remains, not evidence of the crime. Law enforcement has the crime scene and we have the remains. We thought the remains were all in the bags and we were in control of those items. Later, we discovered they were not all there but scattered into the woods.

Portions of the skull were imbedded in the vines and leaves, about the middle of the eye sockets. The entire lower part of the skull was in debris on an angle. We decided to remove the skull and tape together, lifting extra foliage to see we got both at once, and placed it in a paper bag. I was reaching to get all the foliage, skull, and tape at one time when this photo was taken. I took about six to eight inches to each side of the skull, and scooped down and lifted up the entire area. I attempted to keep the hair and tape in the best representation of how they existed at the site where I collected them.

We also collected the bags of trash, plastic and canvas, taking a large area around them, as well. We took long bones in the area. I took items of clothes and cloth as well. I turned it all over to Gary, the pathologist. I continued to go back to the area and the CSI people, as they found items, and I collected things that were possible human remains. I would sign for them and return with them to the ME. There were one or two times the CSI may have brought something to us. My first trip was on December 11th, and my last was December 17th. Some items had to be reviewed by Dr. Shultz, an anthropologist. He was at the Medical Examiner's Office on the afternoon of December 11th. (Mason is cross-examining this witness about the photo of the street to the wooded area.) Mason: There is a machete in the ground and the other item is maybe an arrow? Hanson: It was nothing that I put there. It looks like someone cut a path through some of the underbrush, but that is how I found it. I do not know how it got that way. There were several CSIs and deputies. The media was down the road and not near the area.

A log was beside the remains, and I removed the log and the items after I photographed the log. (Mason is not tech savvy with the court monitor system; he's having trouble showing what he wants on the screens.) I see duct tape that seems flat. There is a portion that looks flat. I am not sure if that is the end; it looks like it is coming apart from decomposing. I did not measure. The skull was imbedded in the vegetation. The person who found it may have kicked it. (Motion to strike – hearsay) I have no firsthand knowledge of this. I took the foliage with the skull to get the duct tape and hair, to preserve as much as possible. The duct tape could have changed position some when I lifted it. Dr. G took over the remains from the other medical examiner a few days later. I no longer was involved. There were other people in the room while the bones were assembled into a skeleton, to make sure that no bones were missing. Other processing of the remains was also being done. I did not handle this part of the investigation, as the medical examiners were in charge. I moved the log; I do not know who photographed it. I tried to move it out of the way of the evidence field. I never saw anything like a white two-by-four.

The State's Fifty-fourth Witness

Interpretation of Testimony – Gary Utz, M.D.: I am the Chief Deputy Medical Examiner, and I have been since April, 2008. I have a BS and MD from the University of Cincinnati, training in surgery, pathology, and I have been licensed to practice medicine and pathology since 1997. We were all aware of the missing child, and I was in a deposition in the office. It was interrupted. I was told that the child's remains had been found, and Dr. G was going out of town. I was asked to take charge until she returned. She had already sent Hanson out to the scene. I looked at the reports, received the remains, and examined them primarily to identify them and send them to the FBI lab. Several bags came in, one large bag came in with fabric and small bones, another bag contained a skull, hair and tape. We photographed the items at the morgue. I believe this is the first photo of the items in the morgue taken at my direction.

You can see two plastic bags and a partially torn piece of paper advertising mixed with debris and a leg bone. The leg was near the top of the bag. There is an off-white fabric laundry bag mixed in with the garbage bags. They were separated and photographed. This is the skull with hair and tape. You are looking at a human skull upright facing the observers. Over the jaw and facial area are several pieces of gray tape and hair extending over the skull. I photographed from all directions; there are strands of hair hanging down and a hair mat is there at the bottom. You can see the tape, and it appears to come around to the side of the skull. There are plant roots within the hair on the skull. One of the doctors is supporting the skull to photograph it to show the face, cradling the head. The hair is partially covering the eye sockets, and right below that is the tape. The pieces of tape were attached to each other. I think there were three. I do not recall exactly, and I did not separate them. It is unusual that the mandible stayed in place, because in this stage of decomposition the mandible separates. The hair will mat, but the plant material is holding the bones together. The tape was no longer adhesive, but it was still sticking to the mandible. It was the fabric of the tape and roots that had grown into it that was sticking to the mandible. Some of the hair and fabric had to be cut to maintain the integrity of the tape as evidence.

We took photos of the mandible and removed the tape from the skull. The bottom of the back of the skull is covered with the hair mat. I had to tease apart the hair to remove the mandible. I have never seen a mandible that was found with the skull when the skeleton was found above ground. We see the skull is tilted on its left side and the right side of the mandible is showing, still attached to the skull, and we are lifting the tape to show how the fabric of the tape and the plant roots have adhered it to the skull. So the tape goes across the entire mandible. It is a circular band of tape. This is a large amount of tape that would cover a tiny head all the way around the mouth. It is a gray silver tape about a total of maybe ten inches or more, made up of multiple pieces. (It has been identified and is entered into evidence.) The tape has a label on it, and there was no attempt made to clean the tape. The canvas bag is still completely intact, but with some holes. It is a heavy canvas, and it is dirty. It has a hard ring designed to keep it open, and was a water resistant laundry bag. This is a tough, expensive laundry bag. It was made in China and is a Whitney Design designer bag. The black garbage bag is wrinkled and ripped. It has yellow handles that are still knotted, with about a two-inch opening at the knot. There is a second plastic bag. I cannot tell from the photo which of the plastic bags was inside the other, but this canvas item was in the plastic bags brought to the ME. The photos are not in order, but the removal of the items was documented sequentially, but I cannot tell you today which bag contained the shorts. (The witness steps down, and the jury is excused for the evening.)

Mr. Mason gives a try at objecting to the photo of the shorts the State is seeking to admit, since the witness does not know which of the bags things came out of. No luck. Good try, Mr. Mason, but you lose! It is admitted into evidence over objection. If Mr. Mason had kept this piece of evidence out, it would have been a coup for the defense. He has not been objecting to everything, so he took his shot on this piece. Nice try, Mr. Mason, but we agree with the judge's ruling. If the photos were put back in order, the witness would know which of the bags the item came from, but that would take hours more. Since they are all in evidence, it really does not seem to matter at this point. However, Mason's objection was well thought out and had a factual basis, unlike many of Baez's seemingly random objections. Good old dog... Good lawyers are a beautiful thing to watch. The courtroom is not an arena for mediocrity. (Court stands in recess for the evening.)

Casey was just led out of the courtroom, and she appeared weak and slow moving. Casey has looked like she is feeling sick, holding her mouth and deep breathing all day with her head down, not looking at the pictures. We were not surprised that she has fallen ill and court was recessed for the day. Because we have been watching her all day, we noticed a lot of her rubbing her face, pushing on her nose, and wiping her eyes with a tissue. We have been unable to see any tears. Something was bothering us, so we asked our house lawyer. Would Casey have seen these pictures before court? He said that he cannot imagine that she has not been shown these pictures before the trial. So, how sick is Casey? We do not think it is very serious. She has been making her face red all day by rubbing. Casey has had her head turned away from the photos or down and not viewing them. That said, the verbal descriptions are very bad. As the court deputy informs Casey that they were ready to leave the courtroom for the day, Casey appeared to us to have a moment of recovery in her eyes before, weakened, she hobbled out of the courtroom. Maybe it is real, maybe it is an anxiety attack, or maybe it is theater. We think the performance of Casey Anthony continues… playing to the jury.

The problem for her is that the jurors had their heads focused on the monitors all day, looking at the pictures and taking notes. They got through looking at some pretty gruesome photos. To Casey's chagrin, the jurors were so busy looking at the evidence photos on their monitors that they were not watching her performance.

June 10th, 2011

A ruckus broke out this morning when people in line were trying to get seats in the gallery for the trial. Firefighters were called to break it up. You receive a golden ticket to get in the court room, (well it's really a white slip of paper). Will Casey be back in court today? We think so. I just saw Ms. Fryer (the defense case law lady) in court…hmm. We wonder what the fight will be about today. Is Casey is too sick to be tried on charges of murdering her daughter? Is there case law on the defendant being too sick to be tried as a result looking at pictures of the crime they are alleged to have committed? If the defendant is involuntarily absent they cannot proceed with the trial, but if the defendant is voluntarily absent, they can go forward. It is up to the judge to decide, but we think he would require it to be established by physician or Casey's hospitalization. If the illness goes on long enough it could result in a mistrial. The defendant has a constitutional right to be present at trial, unless the she waives her right to be present. There is Casey, walking in this morning, looking upset at having to return to the reality of the courtroom. It should be interesting today. (The judge takes the bench. Both sides are ready to proceed.)

The State's Fifty-fourth Witness (cont.)

Interpretation of Testimony – Dr. Utz returns to the stand: This photo is from the crime scene with Caylee's shorts which have a Circo label. This is prosecution Exhibit 233. The shorts are intact, with most of what damage I can see coming from decomposition. I cannot be sure all of the damage is from decomposition. There are also labels from what appeared to be a child's shirt. I have reconstructed the letters on the shirt to make sense, and they appear to read, "Big Trouble". The tag from the remains found shows size 3T. Once I identified these items, I released the tape to the FBI for evaluation and my work ended except for some work assisting Dr. G, and a couple of visits to the scene. Dr.

G returned and took over the following day, to take over responsibility for the case.

Gary Utz - Defense cross-examination: I am a board-certified pathologist. Clinical pathology is the study of disease, and forensic pathology is the determination of the causes of suspicious deaths. Both physicians and pathologists do autopsies. I was aware of the missing child; it was discussed in the office. Before the remains are found, the ME's office is just a spectator. After the remains are found, there is more discussion and the ME's office takes an active role. The CSI arrived before me, and then I was in charge upon my arrival. Dr. G was gone when the remains were discovered. She returned, and I believe she became involved because she has established relationships with different agencies to assist in the investigation, and I was new. I do not think the high media profile of the case had any influence on her decision. The duct tape extended but did not completely encircle the skull, and there were points of adherence from left to right. I cut it from the skull, looked at it, but did not swab for DNA. I suited up and used gloves the entire time. I then packaged the tape for release of the evidence to an agent from the FBI.

I did a preliminary exam. My goal was to provide material for the identification of the remains and to remove the duct tape so we could give it to the FBI for analysis. There were portions of bones that were disrupted. I did not see bone fractures. If the body had been found earlier, I might have had more evidence. That is certainly possible. I recovered clothes from the bags and I believe the shorts were size 24 months. I was involved with Dr. Schultz on that day. He is a PhD anthropologist from UCF. I did not jointly sign the autopsy report, because I did not have involvement with Dr. Goldberg, a toxicologist. The mandible was held in place by the hair and roots. I held the skull and the mandible did not fall off when moved around. A medical examiner's job is to determine the cause and manner. I do not know the cause of death. The manner of death was determined to be homicide by Dr. G. I did not render an opinion on the cause of death in this case. (Mr. Mason is doing the cross, and considering what he has to work with, it is good thing he's the one asking the questions, and not Baez. Mason's approach is surgical, but Baez seems to always use the scatter-gun approach.)

Gary Utz - State's re-direct: The tape was on the right to the left side as seen in the photo. (The witness is excused.)

Interpretation of Testimony - John Schultz, PhD: I am an associate professor at UCF, and I have been so employed since 2003. I have degrees in forensics, anthropology and archeology. I have a bachelor's degree from Stony Brook in anthropology, a Master's in Human Anthropology, a PhD from the University of Florida, and five years' experience, at a human identification laboratory. That is a laboratory that provides services to medical examiners and law enforcement agencies. Forensic anthropology is the study of human skeletons. I am a forensic archeologist in the field collection, site inspection and recovery along with the study of after death onsite disbursement of the remains. I also use a remote sensing tool, ground-penetrating radar, GPR, to locate a site without disturbing the ground. I was able to work with Dr. G at the recovery site, and I assisted her as needed. There were some other anthropologists who were involved, but they did subset studies. There are not a lot of local anthropologists, so I was on call if they needed an anthropologist at the Medical Examiner's Office.

I received a call from Hanson and Dr. G to go to the scene and assist in the initial recovery. The first day, I was not available. I was in finals. The initial recovery had been done, and so I went straight to the medical examiner's office. I reviewed the evidence at the ME's office and I held the skull for photos. I saw the tape and the jaw. To see a mandible still attached was surprising. This exam showed the hair and roots which helped the mandible stay attached. I think the tape was adhered to the hair. I provided a recovery assist from the area, I screened for items in a mesh screen to locate the bones. The Sheriff had set up a secondary area at the recovery site, and that area was sifted twice with a small mesh screen because the bones were so small.

The sheriff took the photos, and I was there as an advisor. We set up a protocol to photograph every step. They put a canopy over the main area. One of the crime scene persons was on her knees searching. We tried to document the spaces between the different areas for evidence for the police, and bones for the ME. Ron Murdock was in charge when remains were found. I would assist. I could tell them if they were human or not, because of the environment and the search area. This search area was increased, and additional CSI persons canvassed a larger area. We started with a small area and expanded out. The flag was placed at the location where we found these small bones. It is important to understand how the bones were placed and separated from their original position. Photos show the process. Lanes were established for mapping purposes. They mapped everything; every bone and all evidence found. I told them what was human. Some of the non-human remains could have been transferred to the Medical Examiner's Office and I would have sorted them out there. We can see in this photo the vertebra, and they are separated. All of these vertebrae are separated. The vertebra to the right tells you that this was transported to the site when all the bones and skin were together, and then the body decomposed at the site. A photo of bones would be packaged for evidence with the bone, and then later we would have information of where it was found in the sifting. These photos are from lane five of the mapped area, and show the largest bones of the body, the leg bones to the pelvis. These bones relate to each other; they have been chewed on by animals and the fragment fits back onto this piece of leg bone. (Sidebar)

(Casey appears upset again, maybe… She has her head down, and is pinching her noise again with tissue. She has on a black shirt and I think she has been instructed to keep her head down and a tissue in her hand. Again, she is rubbing her face and making it red but we see no tears. A close up shows no tears, and Casey is wiping her eyes so hard that she is moving the skin on her cheeks. We just went to break and as soon as the jury leaves, Casey raises her head up and is talking, still appearing mildly upset at best. It seems there is a lot of interest in the crime scene photos of Caylee's body. (Court reconvenes.)

Dr. Schultz continues on the stand. (Slip screen transparencies show that the small piece of bone fits into the area of the leg bone.) This photo represents the hand bones. (The judge is handling all publishing of photos from his computer, to ensure that only certain photos are visible to the gallery.) These photos are taken with a quarter next to them to show size. The recovery effort took from December 11th until the last mapping finished on December 20th. (All of this witness's items so far are introduced in evidence, and the judge publishes them.) This is a child we are looking at, the top part of the pelvis. One of these was completely buried in the muck and that is significant. This is the photo of the skeleton; all the bones are laid out in order after the recovery. Generally, we do not get this much of the skeleton when they have been out and subjected to animal predation. We collected almost the entire spine, teeth, body and foot. There are a few pieces missing, but this was a very successful effort in terms of what was recovered and the mapping. We use this information to come to any conclusions on this crime scene and the death.

(The survey of the mapping is placed in evidence.) It is clearly a map showing the locations of where the bones were found.) Area A is going to be the primary place the body was placed into the woods within bags and where the initial separation occurred. We can follow along in area A, B, and so on as we expanded the search based on our finding of remains. When the area was searched, we discussed where things were found. When we completed one area and moved to the next area, we expanded in all directions, from the known until we found nothing. Surface debris was searched, and a trowel was eventually used in a final search. This map shows only where bones were found. Area A was the initial area where the skull was in bags along with bones, arms, hands, lower legs, and left foot. Area B is where part of an upper arm bone was found. Area D had only one bone, a right foot bone with animal damage. Area E had one hand bone. In Area F, we only found the trunk of the body with the pelvis; the lower legs were dragged to this area. This was the trunk connected with both legs and the pelvis attached. We saw multiple areas of animal damage. In Area G, the ribs and the bottom of the spine were found, and damage is consistent with animal damage. In Area H, there were more ribs; and in Area I, we found most of the spine here in this location. Twenty of the twenty-four vertebrae were found here. This is consistent with animals dragging the body. Some of the vertebral segments are in two parts; they have not fused due to the age of the child.

There was tissue there when the body was moved to the site, because it needed to be there in order to hold the bones together for the move. My opinion is that the body was deposited as a relatively intact unit, because it was in the bags. There is no indication that the body was dismembered, it was just natural decomposition. The hip bone was buried in the muck and this helps to tell us how long the bones had been at the site. (Sidebar) This was a swampy area, and the leaves tell us that water covered the area and the body sunk into the mud and at a lower level than the leaves. The plants and water move the leaves and ground, and that process would have buried the bones. I believe the remains were in the area for months - the bones were dry of marrow and the skin was completely decomposed. With the rough evidence, it would be a possible period of six months in this area.

John Shultz - Defense cross-examination: The dispersal was primary animal activity; the bones had been chewed. This area was processed very well; and as for the missing bones, an animal could have eaten them completely. As an anthropologist I examined the bones, the bones were x-rayed. I found no evidence of perimortem trauma. There was no evidence of fractures, torquing, or twisting of this child. There was no evidence that this child had traumatic injury at any time in her life. I think this site is about 25 to 30 feet from the edge of the road. The measurements were provided. I cannot tell you without a ruler. If you give me a ruler, I can tell you. (Mr. Mason says he is fresh out of rulers.) The bones were in bags when deposited at the site, I believe. I saw the laundry bag. The majority of Area A had the main part of the remains. We processed the scene at the same time in other area. The initial find was in Area A, we separated the people and searched in different areas simultaneously.

I cannot provide you with a specific time of disbursement of the remains. I could not answer how she died; I can just tell you there was no perimortem trauma. I looked at the duct tape, but I did not analyze it. Mason said, when you removed the duct tape it was not covering nasal aperture; it was in the area of the mouth. The nose was gone, so I could not tell if it covered the nose. The majority of the bones were found in area A: the skull, the fibula, and a few more. Area B was the humerus, and it was the closest to area A. Area F was the largest area on the diagram and it is larger because the dispersals and the other bones such as the collar bones, pelvis, both femurs, ribs, and vertebra were found there. (The witness is excused.)

The State announces Jan Garavaglia as their next witness. (Jan C. Garavaglia, M.D., aka "Dr. G", is the chief medical examiner for the District Nine Medical Examiner's Office in Orlando, Florida. That office serves Orange and Osceola County. She is Dr. G. of the Dr. G: Medical Examiner show they were asking about in voir dire. Welcome to the courtroom of 2011, just another case odyssey.)

The State's Fifty-sixth Witness

Interpretation of Testimony - Jan Garavaglia, M.D.: I am the Chief Medical Examiner for Orange and Osceola Counties. I have worked here since 2004. I was a Deputy Chief ME in Texas and in Jacksonville, and my education is from Saint Louis University School of Medicine in 1982, I did an internship and specialized in anatomic and clinical pathology. I did a fellowship at the Dade County Medical Examiner's Office in Miami, and obtained certification by the American Board of Pathology in combined anatomic and clinical pathology. I am also certified by the American Board of Pathology in forensic pathology. (The witness is tendered and accepted as an expert witness.) I became involved in the Casey Anthony case on December 11th, 2008. I learned of the possibility that they may have found the body of Caylee Anthony. I was late for the airport, and I ran back into the office to find something I forgot. That is when Mr. Hanson told me that they had found remains. I contacted Dr. Utz and Dr. Schultz to handle it until the next day when I returned. I did not think my absence for the night would matter. I returned the following evening.

I reviewed all the photos from the scene and from my laboratory assistants when I returned. I continued to investigate; I went to the scene, made suggestions, and I brought in more consultants. (The photo of the hair mat is admitted into evidence by the prosecution.) The hair was returned to me upon my request from the FBI. This is a photo I reviewed. We are looking at the hair mat of the decedent. A lot of plant roots are growing through the hair, shown in the photo. We are looking at the hair mat and the roots growing through the mat of hair. This is a photo of the hair teased out from the hair mat so we could remove it for toxicology. I have a six-inch scale beside it, and the hair is longer. This photo was taken at my direction. It is the scale next to the roots of hair. I examined and photographed the items found with the body. This is a baby blanket, and the photo taken at my direction or by my staff. We took many photos. This photo is clear; the blanket is dirty. I detected figures on the blanket, and took photos close up. The photo clearly shows Winnie the Pooh with Piglet on his back.

The blanket had plant material growing inside the weave of the blanket. There was massive weed growth in the weave of the blanket along with roots and vegetation. The black plastic bags had root material growing through the holes in the bags. The canvas laundry bag was vinyl inside, and there was only growth on the inside of the bag. Plant roots were growing in bones, bags, and the blanket, but not in the shorts. The shirt collar was completely disintegrated. The best DNA is nuclear DNA. We hoped for a nuclear DNA result or at least mitochondrial DNA, and sent a bone off for analysis. They have to remove a small piece of the bone to test for DNA. The FBI identified the remains as Caylee Anthony. A medical examiner's job is to determine manner and cause of death. Manner of death is based on science, reviewing all the history of the case and all tests conducted, to come up with an opinion. (Court stands in recess for lunch.)

Casey just looks angry today. That is the look we are seeing most of the time. She is fine and cannot wait to get out of the courtroom. Jail must look better than reality in this court. During this lunch we have been beating our brains. At this point, there is a great deal of evidence that points to Casey Anthony killing little Caylee. The question of why is driving us crazy. If she no longer wanted the responsibility of raising Caylee, these grandparents would have assumed it. That seems clear. At one point Casey appeared (at least publicly) to care about Caylee. Why kill this child? It has to be one of two reasons, cold blooded murder by an emotionless killer, or a history of drugging this child that went awry and caused her death, if Casey is the killer.

Now, the criminal lawyer in the house is used to not knowing the whys. Your writers are not. It is driving us to keep going in the hope that at some point, we can enter the mind of Casey and discover the answer. When that day comes if it does, may it be a short stay in her mind. One of us still finds the nightmares unending as we write this book. Just a note as we come back from lunch the laptop has been moved out from in front of Casey; we suspect it is so the jurors can see her in full as she performs. We really do not know what to think of this defendant. Casey was overheard telling her lawyers that she cannot do this – she cannot be in the courtroom. The judge wants her in the courtroom, and will only tolerate so much of her being upset. (Court reconvenes, and the jurors return to the jury box.)

Dr. G is back on the stand. Defense attorneys call her testimony, "death by one hundred cuts." She is personable, as well as highly educated and skilled in her field. Mr. Mason will have his hands full with Dr. G., when it is his turn to cross-examine her.

Jan Garavaglia, M.D. (cont.): The prosecution continues, with Dr. G. identifying all of the necessary evidence packages from her medical examiner's office.) Manner of death is the classification of death based in all evidence, the scene, the skeleton, photos and more. The manner of death in this case is homicide. We know from experience, when a child is not reported immediately to authorities for injuries or as being missing, the body was hidden, and when the body is in some kind of container like bags or when there is duct tape located on the head of the child, it is a homicide. There is no reason for duct tape being on the face of the child, and duct tape should not have been placed on the child after death. It is a homicide. The cause of death is the specific injury or disease that causes the person's death. In this case, I picked homicide of underdetermined means. We can reliably say it was a homicide. I do not know the means by which this child was murdered. The items that would cause death that were found with the body, could cause death by suffocation – either with the tape, or in the bags.

Jan Garavaglia – Defense cross-examination: It is true that there is nothing that shows exposure to chloroform. On the other hand, if the bag contained chloroform, then the child could have died from the chloroform. We have enough to say it is a homicide, but we do not have the means of the homicide. The body was very decomposed, so from the skeleton, I cannot rule out anything, a gunshot could miss the bones. There is no antemortem injury to the bones that could show case of death. The child had no history of illness or disease. I live in Orlando. I was aware of this being a big case. I knew there was a lot of speculation about this case. I was hoping the body would be found in Lake County, not my county. I came back from my business trip to handle this case; I had only planned to be gone overnight. I was told by investigators that there was a question of chloroform. It may be a reason, and I was asked to examine that possibility. I brought in a toxicologist, Dr. Goldberger, who had dealt with bones, because it is hard to get information from bones. The left femur was sent to him to look for chloroform and other chemicals. He also examined for alcohol, isopropanol, and any other chemical that might have contributed to the death. He checked for volatile organic compounds, but it is very limited with bones. The results were negative.

Doctor, were you present when Dr. Spitz came to the ME's Office as an expert for the defense? (Sidebar.) No he did not participate in the autopsy. I was informed there was a request for him to participate, but our policy is for us to come up with the cause of death. I explained that once we did, we would make the evidence available to him. Dr. Goldberger is a PhD. He tested hair, soil, bone and the scraping I made on the skull and in the cranial cavity for drugs. Benzodiazepines are also known as Xanax. I did not cut the cranium open. There was no trauma to the bones prior to death, but there was after-death… animal activity on the bones. There was no pre-existing trauma. The means of the homicide could not be determined. The only reasonable scientific and observational conclusion is that this is a homicide. It is true that drowning cannot be excluded as a cause of death, but that does not necessarily make the death accidental. Observation studies are important. We looked at every drowning in this area, and never has 911 not been called for a drowning or drowned child. So by my experience and evidence, a drowning not being reported, tossing the body in a bag, with duct tape anywhere attached to that child's face, and disposing of the body in a wooded area, those factors show homicide. Accidental deaths are reported, as we know from behavioral science. Accidents regarding children are reported one hundred percent of the time. They call 911 in hope there is a chance the child could be saved. No matter how stiff the body is, the data show that they call 911 with the hope the child can be revived. I cannot explain away the red flags surrounding this death, and that led to my conclusion that this was homicide.

I felt that the manner of death was scientifically homicide. If these remains had been found earlier, it would have helped us with a cause of death. Duct tape was in the vicinity of the lower mandible. I attempted to keep the body in the same condition for the defense, except what we had to use for DNA and drug testing. We would not expect to find anything in the bones, but we had to try. If Caylee died on June 16th and she was found four months earlier that would have helped a great deal. The closer in time remains are found to the time of death, the more information we can obtain, such as tissue samples, DNA, and the like, and the less likely that animals will disturb the remains. After two months, the remains would still have been skeletonized. The organs would still have been completely gone. We packaged the remains up very nicely to deliver to the defense for their examination. (The witness is excused, and the jury takes a recess.)

Mr. Mason tried to shake her, but she is good. He made her more credible. It was a bad day for our old dog. He had to try to damage her testimony. The judge is excusing the jury for a while. No cell phones are allowed, or they will be seized.

Witness Dr. Michael Warren shows a videotape in a proffer outside the presence of the jury. Baez is not happy watching the video. The video is the anthropologist's work using a computer to technologically superimpose a photo of Caylee over the skull and the duct tape, from photos in evidence. It shows that the tape could have covered her mouth and nose. The issue is that the duct tape can take a child's life by suffocation. This video is the only way to display the results. The defense is stating that the duct tape cannot be shown to be the cause of death, and so the video is pure speculation. The proper way is to use his testimony to state how the skin relates to the skull without the tape, as an

263

anthropologist. Not this demonstration on video with the skull and tape. The judge tells Baez that he is thinking of McDuffy v. State. He says he is rereading it, and suggests the lawyers do, too. The judge says the case is 26 pages. He reminds the lawyers that he is the referee of this case. Baez argues that the probative value is clearly outweighed by the prejudicial effect and the cumulative nature of the testimony, and there is no testimony establishing that this duct tape was ever in this position. (We think the judge wants the jury to hear Dr. Warren's testimony and this is a proffer to determine whether he will take the stand in front of the jury.)

Interpretation of Proffer Testimony - Michael Warren, PhD: I am a forensic anthropologist employed at the University of Florida as an associate professor with the Human Identification Lab. I agreed to go with Dr. Schulz to examine the remains. At some point, we wanted to see if the duct tape could be the cause of death. I saw photos from of the FBI, outside labs, and internet pictures of the child. The face has no scale, so we need to first match the face scale to fit onto the skull, and then we superposed the tape over the soft tissue of the face. There are some measurements out there, and we feel that was the only way to show the ability of the duct tape to cover her mouth and nose. (The video is shown to the jury.)

Michael Warren - Defense cross-examination in proffer: The question is can this tape cover the mouth and nose? I was not present when the duct tape was found. The tape is attached to her hair and the hair mat was nestled to the bottom of the skull, according to the photographs. There is no scale on the photos. I would have to have knowledge of the skin and the photo I selected appeared to be a recent photo. The purpose of the demonstration is to show that the tape could cover both the nose and mouth. The skull photo is taken with a scale, the tape photo is taken with a scale, and we enlarge the images to make the scale, skull and tape actual size. I can scale the facial photograph to fit the skull and superimpose the tape to the face and skull. This animation will aid me in explaining my testimony to the jury. The disadvantage is there is not an illustration to explain the science and technology employed.

The defense again argues that the use of the video in this testimony poses a substantial risk of unfair prejudice that outweighs any probative effect, and also argues that in his deposition, this witness defers to Dr. Shultz, and others for introduction of the unfairly prejudicial and speculative video, this witness is being called solely to bolster Schultz's testimony. Having two experts testify on the same topic is merely cumulative.

(The use of technology in the courtroom is still in its infancy. We think we will avoid committing crimes; no payoff is worth the risk of being caught, and the scientists and police are getting better and better at catching criminals.) The judge announces a fifteen minute recess, so he can think about whether or not to allow the video to be used. The proper application of the law is that if the risk of unfair prejudice outweighs the probative value, then the judge should not permit the evidence to be introduced. The defense also argued that the witness is merely speculating on the location of the tape relative to the skull, since the tape was no longer attached and the skin was gone; since it was the plant material that held it to the skull, there was no way to tell whether the tape was ever attached to the remains, and if so where it had been attached, since it could have moved or been moved prior to the roots growing and adhering it to the skull. The evidence is basically a superimposed photo of the victim over the skull, to show the possible placement of the duct tape. Casey's head has been up and she has not crying while the jury is gone, she does not appear upset, she just has that angry look on her face. The defense and prosecution have both brought up the placement of tape. The jury has seen several pictures of the skull. Dr. Warren has stated that the video would help. Unfortunately the evidence in a homicide is not pretty. Both sides have debated the relevancy of the duct tape in this case. We are sure they will continue to do so.

(The judge returns to the bench and announces that he will overrule the defense's objections. The video comes in. The jury is now being summoned to return.)

The State's Fifty-seventh Witness

Interpretation of Testimony – Michael Warren, PhD: Dr. Warren and his video are in court before the jury. I am the Director of the C.A. Pound Human Identification Lab at the University of Florida. It is the UF's forensic anthropology laboratory. The C.A. Pound Laboratory performs analyses of skeletal remains for many of the 24 medical examiner districts in the State of Florida. I am a Fellow and past Chair of the Physical Anthropology section of the American Academy of Forensic Sciences. I am a diplomat of the American Board of Forensic Anthropology and I am currently serving on the Board as a board member of the Scientific Working Group for Forensic Anthropology. I received my Master's degree in Forensic

Anthropology, and my PhD in Forensic Anthropology under Dr. William Maples at UF. I was a visiting assistant professor and I am now an Associate Professor at the University of Florida. I have joint appointments in the Departments of Pathology, Immunology and Laboratory Medicine, and I am a founding affiliate of the William R. Maples Center for Forensic Medicine at UF. I am an annual lecturer at the Armed Forces Institute of Pathology's Forensic Anthropology course. I have been qualified to testify as an expert on about 16 to 18 times in two states in addition to being qualified in Florida. My doctorate was on the bones of children in the fetal period and identification of the age of children at time of death.

I was contacted by Dr. Schultz on December 15th, 2008, to assist in the analysis of the remains. I also examined photos of the remains as they had been found. The mandible was attached. This is very unusual. I have had cases where the mandible was intact and fully attached to the skull in skeletal remains. All of those cases were in Bosnia and Kosovo, of people who died as a result of ethnic cleansing. All of the remains were victims of genocide who had tape over their faces that was applied perimortem. I have never seen any other cases where the mandible was still attached to the skull in skeletonized remains, nor am I aware of any others mentioned in the literature.

I attempted to discover if a single piece of tape could cover the mouth and nose. I used literature. I was interested in the bottom of the nose, mouth and the bottom of the teeth. I could get estimates using the research. I used a method using video supervision. I usually use this technique to exclude the possibility that the remains are another person where that is suspected or is a possibility. You use a picture of the person, and superimpose it over the skull and use anatomical landmarks to determine whether the skull is the person in the photo. Typically, the landmarks are the bottom of the teeth and the edges of the eye orbits. In this case, I was not addressing the identity of the skull. I used that same technique to scale the photo of the skull and the photo of the tape and a photo of the victim in this case. The video shows the process, and helps me to explain this to the jury. (The video is admitted into evidence.) The judge tells the jury that this evidence is to be used only to illustrate the expert's opinion. An expert's opinion is reliable only when you believe him to be an expert.

(Casey is having no reaction to the superimposed video of her daughter and is looking angry, that is it. Maybe she is mad because the judge ruled against her and let this be introduced. Dr. Warren states that the reason he moved the tape up and down in the video is so we can see exactly where the tape was. However, what it really shows is that the single piece of tape could be applied to the nose and mouth. It would have covered them both and made breathing impossible for Caylee.)

Michael Warren, PhD - Defense cross-examination: I never saw the duct tape before it was removed. The image, if scaled, should be exact. The defense asks if the only reason he has shown this to the jury is to show that it is possible that a piece of duct tape could have covered her nose and mouth. Dr. Warren says, it is a form of demonstration to form a possible way it could have happened. Is it speculation? Yes. (Baez goes on for a while. Caylee was found in the mud and the hair mat was below the mandible. When alive the hair is on top of her head, and the duct tape was found across the front of the skull. Baez draws a chart.) The duct tape is attached to her hair. I understand her remains were once in three bags. Yes, I saw photographs of the bags. (Baez asks, you have no idea if this duct tape was used to wrap her body, do you?) Yes, the duct tape was over some part of the mandible and the hair. In order for the hair mat to be underneath the skull something has to be put there. The duct tape made its way to the surface.

(The jury is removed for a short voir dire of the witness.) In the voir dire, Dr. Warren says that it was his suggestion that the movie be made. It was not to get the jury angry, or to be of such a graphic nature as to upset the jury. It was not to appeal to the emotions of the jurors, but to explain the method used.)

(The jury is back. Cross-examination continues) I am not aware of more duct tape in this case. This video just demonstrates one possibility. In terms of the position of the duct tape over the face, there are no other possibilities. I have an opinion it was placed on Caylee before decomposition, based on the mandible still being attached. The tape was stuck to the soft tissue and the duct tape stays in place and supplies support. The hair is under the base of the skull not under the mandible and when tissues decompose, the hair slips. Hair preserves fairly well and lasts a while. There is root growth under the mandible. The roots could also contribute to keeping the mandible in place. Does active decomposition inhibit root growth? No. Are you familiar at all with plant growth in decomposition and remains? Yes. Roots would keep the mandible in place, but not after the hair fell off. By the time the hair slips, the mandible would no longer be attached. Only the tape could keep the mandible in place in this case. I am not a botanist. Duct tape stuck to hair is what we have.

The State's Fifty-eighth Witness

Interpretation of Testimony – Michael Vincent (recalled): I recovered certain insect evidence from the trash bag once located in the Pontiac Sunbird. (He is identifying the evidence and it is admitted.) I collected it, but it is not my initials on the envelope. Inside there is a vial of maggots that were in the trash upon opening the package. It is pupa. It was sealed by the investigator and shipped off by me. These items were taken from the garbage bag. They were collected on August 28th, 2008. I am aware of insects being of use in an investigation. I have some training in insects. I know there are different stages, and they can even give you a time of death. On July 16th, 2008, I did not see insect activity in the trunk of the car.

The State's Fifty-ninth Witness

Interpretation of Testimony – Robin Maynard: I was a CSI for the Orange County Sheriff's Office, but I no longer work there. In December of 2008, other CSIs and I assisted at the site where Caylee Anthony's body was found. I collected the insect activity present in December 2008 at the site. They were pupa. As I collected them with Dr. Neil Haskell, I documented the location of the finds and I packaged and turned the packages over to Dr. Haskell. (She identifies all packages of insects and other items from the search site.) In the search area, we found a piece of mesh that had a heart shaped sticker on it. It was brought to me in a bucket by another CSI. There were multiple people doing searching and sifting; there were all kinds of items of evidence in the lanes, such as beer bottles and cans. I was the lead in charge on sifting. I cannot say this was a common dumping area. It is not directly across from the elementary school. I saw no children. (The witness is released, and the jury is released for the evening.)

After the jury leaves the courtroom, Baez moves for a mistrial based on the superimposing of the video. He says it was a highly prejudicial image of the beautiful child, shown with duct tape. The judge denies the motion for mistrial, and court stands in recess until tomorrow morning. (We realize that both the State and the defense have put forth arguments about the location of this duct tape, when and how it was applied, and whether it was or could be the cause of Caylee's death. The witness said it was a possible method of death, but that there were other possible methods. We believe that at some point, that beautiful child did have duct tape over her mouth, her nose or both.)

Saturday June 11th, 2011

Last night, we again reviewed Casey's cell phone logs during the thirty-one day period between when Caylee was last seen and when she was reported missing. We awake today with a discussion of the time window on June 16th, 2008. At this point in the case, we think the evidence is mounting against Casey. So we look to aggravated child abuse, the other degrees of murder, and first degree murder. Casey seems to be a "mommy dearest" personality to us. She came off great in public; in private, she was mean-spirited, but she was not so abusive to Caylee that she left physical scars. We wonder about emotional abuse. Casey appears to be a great mother in front of other people, and we believe "loved" Caylee to some degree. A few things are clear. Because Casey had been lying to everyone about everything, the walls were closing in on her. Amy was expecting to move in with her, she had been caught stealing money, had no work, and Tony was going back to New York after graduation. Casey was stressed to the max, and most of the stress was induced by her own lies and behavior.

It seems likely that Caylee spent most of her waking hours, un-napped, riding around with her mother in the car to stores, parks and whoever's house was available, for nearly two years. With the exception of evenings and some days when her grandparents were home to babysit, Caylee was with Casey. Casey was realizing that Caylee was near the talking and comprehension stage and she would be communicating with everyone soon. This would reveal their daily whereabouts over time, and even more questions would arise. Tony was all Casey wanted to see and do. Something happened in a two-hour period on June 16th, perhaps a sedation of Caylee that went wrong and/or tape to keep her quiet. However, we cannot rule out the possibility that Casey decided to get rid of her baggage, Caylee. Hopefully, the next weeks of trial will guide us more and our review of this work before final release will bring the insight we seek.

(Today, Casey is in a light blue sweater after her black mourning shirt yesterday. She is looking up and talking with Baez, who has a sour look on his face. He laughs as Casey whispers to him. She listens intently as someone talks to Baez. She has moved tissues into place while chatting with one of the female lawyers. Casey smiles and quickly covers it up with her hand.)

The State's Sixtieth Witness

Interpretation of Testimony – Neil Haskell, PhD: I am a professor of Entomology. I received my BS in 1969 and a MS in Forensic Anthropology in 1989 and a doctorate, all from Purdue University. I have worked on more than 850 cases worldwide. I am qualified in 25 jurisdictions in the U.S. and Germany, Canada, Spain. In Florida, I have testified as an expert in forty cases. I am a farmer and I was a rancher. (He is accepted as an expert.) Forensic Analysis has been a standard practice for over one hundred years. The study of insects and the forensics aspects are associated with certain groups of insects. In 2008, around August or September, I had contact with law enforcement officer Michael Vincent and had conversations about the insect evidence in this case. I received evidence that he sent me. He wanted to see if there were important insects, larva, maggots, and pupa that would assist in the investigation.

In September, I received evidence from the case, the trash bag from the car, which had been sealed and stored. If it is sealed, the adults should be there in paper towels. In the trash bag, we found fifteen to twenty adults. I found hundreds of these very tiny flies. I contacted an expert at a museum in Los Angeles, and I sent him samples of the adults for positive identification. He told me that these insects would be found in human and animal decomposition. I have had thirty cases involving these flies, and the museum provided confirmation for what I already knew.

They were a number of paper towels, and I started pulling them apart and there were a number of the dead flies. They were at the cocoon stage. I notice all three stages in the towels, and placed them into a white porcelain pan. They are very small. The flies were attracted to the substance on the towels. I believed the substance to be decomposition fluid, and I requested it be tested. Dr. Vass tested it at Oak Ridge and it was adipose tissue from the breakdown of fluids. I deal with these fluids all the time. We had some time lines as to the whereabouts of this bag and paper towels. We see these flies based on environment and more. There was a leg of a blowfly, which was in decomposition. There are regionalized and it was a southern species. None of the flies are partial to human decomposition. Some feed on anything.

At the time of death, decomposition begins. The insects attracted by decomposition change, depending on the different stages of decomposing. So the insects feed at different times, based on the decomposition. Blowflies are usually first, in seconds to minutes if the temperatures are high. The blowfly leaves, and another insect comes to feed a few days later. They are very small, gnat size. They can enter into very small openings, the size of a tiny crack. This pattern continues, and they all leave eggs. The greater number of the small flies instead of a higher number of blowflies appears in the trunk. That means the decomposition in the trunk was advanced to the point that blowflies were no longer attracted. That is also consistent with the partially decomposed blowfly leg I found. The small flies would have deposited eggs very quickly into the trunk, and remain at least a few days. If a body is wrapped in a plastic bag or two, that will lessen the number of flies. It can delay the flies getting in. The source of the decomposition would not have been in the trunk very long, because of the heat in Florida. I was able to make an estimate of three, four, maybe as much as five days in the trunk would have caused the number of flies I found. These are cold-blood creatures and their activity depends on the heat. Heat will drive the flies to work faster.

In December 2008, I planned to inspect the vehicle and where the little girl's body was found. So, I consulted with the person who recovered the items to save evidence. When I arrived, I went to the recovery site, the ME's office, and the tow yard where the vehicle was stored. I had a large number of specimens at the recovery scene and at the ME's office. Chain of custody was maintained. I checked samples, and followed protocol. I conducted microscopic examinations to attempt to identify the groups of insects. Then we begin to sort the species into groups by known time of activity and temperatures. Then we analyzed. Decomposition and insects are both temperature driven. I found a number of species and groups I would expect on a decomposing body. I found different groups of insects. I found a long grower, a black fly. They had hatched and left. All were consistent with long-term decomposition in samples from the recovery site.

Since they had gone completely through their life cycles, all were established by time to a range of decomposition. No blowflies were there. That shows that the remains initially began decomposition elsewhere for a few days, because we did not see thousands of blowflies. When the body was placed in the woods, we probably had initial decomposition elsewhere and then the body was in the woods for many months. In June and/or early July, the body was deposited there in the early stages of decomposition and it was not a skeleton when placed there at that time. The body was purging fluid and bloat but still with small areas of tissue. The car and the scene tell me decomposition began in the car and a few days later the body was placed out of the car; it could have been placed where it was found.

Neil Haskell, PhD - Defense cross-examination: I was talking to Dr. Vass about another case and he told me that Michael Vincent told him that there were fruit flies. Dr. Vass and I have known each other for a long time; we go back to the body farm 25 years ago, and I have had dinner with him. I knew he was an anthropologist. I know he studies chemistry, although I am not sure if his degree is in biochemistry. The statements I made to Dr. Vass were before I saw anything in this case. It was just a hypothesis. I received items from the trash. The flies look like fruit flies to the average observer. Velveeta cheese would not attract the same insects as leftover food, because it is processed food. I wanted adult flies to make the identification. It is more difficult to identify the other stages. Vincent looked in the trunk and did not find any, so he sent me the trash bag evidence and I found adults for my identification.

I mentioned we looked at the paper towels with the material on them, which I believe was products of decomposition. You can get DNA from flies, and they are doing research to remove human DNA from flies and more. I sent them samples to Dr. Vass, my trusted colleague. I trusted him to the do the right tests. I cannot testify to his actual testing, just the results. We did have some filters from the vacuuming of the trunk. There were some flies of that species from 2008. That would be consistent with the decomposition; they do not fall out of the trash like a roach motel. (Objections.) If flies get in the trunk, the vacuuming collection would be of flies from the trunk that had not made it into the trash, and they would not have left the trash in the adult stage.

I do a postmortem timeline on every study. I do that in order to find out how long an item had been deceased by the flies attracted. I was able to determine how long a range of time because of the biological material. Because I got insect evidence that was collected on July 16th, I could track it within a range of dates. I was not contacted until September. I got these items and then came in December. It was the most well processed scene I had seen in years. I was there; I observed the collection protocol, the sifting methodology, and the documentation as it was being done. They were doing a really good job processing.

There are a couple of other specimens from my report, from the site or ME office. There are certainly not tens of thousands of insects. The early maggots leave sometimes. They do a change of form, a metamorphosis. I have seen maggots to up to one hundred yards away, and sometimes you may not find them at all. The body decomposed elsewhere. It began the decomposition process elsewhere, and then finished decomposing at the site. Initially it decomposed elsewhere, at least some. The majority of the insects found at the remains site are later colonizers. I saw how thoroughly the scene was processed. Water would not account for the presence of only late colonizers if the water was rising and falling. I wrote three reports, the car, the recovery site and the vacuum sweepings from the trunk. I began in September, and then came here in December to the site and see the car. In September 2009, I submitted the final report to the prosecution. The reports are about a year later. The result of my investigation was my opinion, and I have testified to it today. I am retained by the prosecution, and I have been paid twenty-two or twenty-three thousand dollars. Mr. Baez, I have not received payment from you for the deposition you took. Baez tells him, the check is in the mail, Mr. Haskell. (This prompts a chuckle form everyone except, perhaps, the witness.) Dr. Haskell says that his fee is between $150 and $400 an hour for testimony, and that he will be paid for his testimony after his involvement in the case is concluded.

Baez asks the difference between trash and garbage. Garbage is decomposing material, versus trash is nonorganic. Insects do not go to an empty box or can, they go to a food source. There was no food in the trash bag, and they were not decomposing. There were some flies loose, but the majority of them were on the paper towels. I think they could have picked up the fluids when they tried to clean up the material. If the paper towels were used to clean up the trunk, they would have picked it up from the carpet. There was an usually low number of blowflies; the food source was gone after decomposition. A portion of the decomposition, three to five days, would have been elsewhere. This body was not put there as a skeleton.

I was not present when the trash or garbage was collected. I inspected this trash in the garbage. I had these photos of the trash items, plus the bags and the paper towels. I cannot tell from a photo if the items were wet or moist. I did no tests on the ease of access to the trunk for blowflies. I see no organic material in the photo. You have to have organic material, to a large extent, for decomposition and there needs to be a large amount of garbage for blowflies to be attracted.

(Now do you see the how millions of dollars can be in this case? All because Casey Anthony would not tell what happened to her daughter Caylee. We really are not upset at the cost to prosecute her; Caylee's death should be resolved. We are angry with her for causing the expense by lies no one can comprehend. Caylee, you are worth it to us, and we just wish she would have dropped you at our door that day and driven away. So many other choices could have been made. We are sure you did not drown in the swimming pool. The duct tape tells us so. Peace be with you, child.)

The State's Sixty-first Witness

Interpretation of Testimony – CSI Jennifer Welsh (recalled): On December 11th, 2008, I processed photos at the scene. Investigators were there a total of ten days. It was my responsibility to photograph things as they were discovered. Fifty people or more were there processing the scene. We set up baselines, lanes, grids, and then each piece of evidence was flagged and photographed by me before removal. It was dense vegetation, trees, hanging vines, roots, and deeper roots. It is difficult to walk on the path because of large vegetation and then it was even more difficult with the roots. We have certain instruments we use such as a machete, and a sheath or cover for the machete is standard issue to CSI. The machete may belong to the Orange County Sheriff, because it was not there when I first arrived. The tree roots that needed to be walked on are over 8 inches in diameter, and there are palmetto trunks. A flag is near the trunk for a piece of evidence.

Someone called my attention to a bone and needed a measurement of the distance the bone was embedded in the ground. It is a three-inch piece of clavicle bone. I collected 390 pieces of evidence. I collected bottles, trash, black plastic, and duct tape. The duct tape was near the area of the skull to the southwest. (Casey has her head buried, even though there are no graphic photos. She looks up with great curiosity at a package as the prosecution shows the exhibit to the defense. It is six inches away from her, but she cannot look at photos on a screen?) The package contains duct tape. It is over six inches long, and an inch and a half to two inches wide,

274

with markings from Henkel, an Ohio company. I also collected letters from a piece of material, pink wording with a strip. I recognize what is contained in the bag. The lettering I collected was at the scene where the remains were located. (Casey has no reaction to Caylee's clothing letters, a pink plastic letter from the t-shirt. We wonder if she really feels anything.)

CSI Jennifer Welsh – Defense cross-examination: This is the photo of the wooded area with the street – a street view. The distance from the street until you get into the wooded area is ten feet, but that's a guess. From the street to the skull was written up by another CSI to be 19 feet, 8 inches south of Suburban Drive. That duct tape was found to the southwest, and I do not know how far away this is from the body and bags; it was documented in another CSI's report. It has the same impressions as the duct tape near the skull. Stones were also there, and one was near a piece of evidence. The stones could be consistent with pavers.

The State's Sixty-second Witness

Interpretation of Testimony – Ronald Murdock: I am a forensic supervisor. I have been employed by the Orange County Sheriff's Office for eleven years. My duties include going to major sites to ensure that all work gets done, and I oversee evidence. I was the supervisor of the Caylee Anthony site and arrived on the 12th of December. I assisted another supervisor in clearing the area and getting equipment. I used a computer and a total station at the scene. A total station is also used by surveyors. It's like a surveyor's transit, but it requires only one person to operate. The total station downloads data to a computer program that generates a diagram. I took the measurements after photographs of the evidence were taken, and I obtained the measurements from the street and the like. I grouped the bones in locations. I marked other evidence items. I marked the duct tape that was recovered. I had my laptop at the site with the total station program loaded on it. I can print the screens from the Total Station. In the evidence is the diagram of bones in an area and a light post. You cannot make out every tiny bone. The second diagram makes the bones more visible in the diagram. The areas are circled some, with many bones in a group, including the skull. The actual distance is nineteen feet from Suburban Drive to the area of the bone discovery. The cut grass area between the road and the tree line is about five feet. There was duct tape with the Henkel brand name, and there were three different areas of duct tape. I supplied the measurements and diagrams to the company, to get as much information about the tape as possible.

In addition to my responsibilities at the scene, I participated in executing a search warrant at the Anthony home, and I collected evidence from the home. This photo shows a shed filled with items, balls, water toys, a bike, and more. I collected a red metal gas can with duct tape on the can. This photo is a variety of children's heart-shaped stickers on a sheet with some missing; they were collected at the Casey Anthony home. A plastic red heart-shaped sticker is clearly seen on the duct tape mesh found at the scene.

(Baez is fighting to keep the heart sticker evidence out of court. Baez is making the record for appeal. Should Casey be convicted of anything, the record includes what the court reporter is taking down. Much of the procedure, and much of what is said, is to preserve the record for appeal. Baez is a fighter, but just does not do a good job on some things. During his cross-examinations, he often seems to keep asking questions after he gets a response that is favorable to the defense… until the witness ends up hurting the defense. You would think he would figure it out after a while, and quit when he is ahead.)

This is a photo of Casey's bedroom at the Hopespring Drive house on the day of the search warrant. (Objection from the defense. Overruled, and received in evidence along with a photo of Caylee's room also taken during the December 11th search warrant.) We collected evidence from those rooms. (The Winnie the Pooh bedding from Caylee's room is introduced into evidence.) We collected other Winnie the Pooh items from the guest room/office dresser. We also collected items from the garage on December 11th. This is a photo of the garage on December 11th, 2008. Photos were taken, and I was responsible for collecting the items such as black trash bags with clothes inside from the garage. In one of the trash bags, I found and removed two canvas laundry bags with the brand Whitney Design. They and the garbage bags are duplicates of the bags at the remains site where Caylee's body was found. (This is a home run for the prosecution.) We also collected various garbage bags from the home.

The items taken from the garage wall were from suitcases and other locations in the garage, such as the black garbage bags. Black garbage bags with yellow handles were taken into evidence from a cooler, from shelves from inside the garage and sheds, and from other areas of the home. The laundry bag photo is shown, and it was in a garbage bag. They were placed in evidence in one package. The diagram shows a piece of duct tape away from the skull about the distance of 6.27 feet away from the skull. I knew the brand name of the duct tape, and it was one of the items we were looking for. We did not find any of the Henkel duct tape except on the gas can. We had other people there, including the FBI and another ten to fifteen people from various agencies. I believe there was a lock on the shed, and I do not know who opened it. I found rolls of duct tape in the cars at the home. None of the rolls had the Henkel name on the tape.

The State's Sixty-third Witness

Interpretation of Testimony – Gerald Johnston: I am an owner of a land surveying firm in Orlando, and I was asked to provide a survey and a three dimensional animation of the site. (Introduced in evidence is an overhead animation of the area.) We stripped the trees in this animation to see the ground. The road is several feet from the wooded area. Much of the ground cover was stripped when the area was searched. The purple markers are where the bones were found.

Chapter 12

THE STATE'S CASE IN CHIEF – WEEK FOUR

Monday June 13th, 2011

(Casey is in the courtroom having a conversation with Cheney Mason (the old dog). I am sure he has told her the reality of her situation. He is reviewing case law. Casey is smiling and happy, as though she hasn't a care in the world. She almost looks smug. The jury is not in, and we are waiting for her demeanor change. Will they keep her off death row? George and Cindy are in the gallery, trying to get through another day of their granddaughter gone and their daughter being tried for the murder. Could Casey create a worse nightmare for her parents?)

The State's Sixty-fourth Witness

Interpretation of Testimony – Stephen Shaw: I work for the FBI doing examinations of hair and fibers. I have been employed by the FBI in that capacity for the last six years. I have a BS and MS from North Carolina. My additional work has been as a research assistant. I have one year of training with hair and fiber examiners from the FBI. (He is qualified in courts of many states, and is qualified as an expert in this courtroom, as well.) In

2008, I was working at the FBI lab, and confirmed the hair evidence as a second confirmatory opinion. I was the quality control examiner. Whenever we have a positive identification, we have a second examiner review it. I already knew the results of the first examination; it was an examination for matching and decomposition.

I also was the first examiner who did the hair mass. (He admits it into evidence with identification.) I performed the tests microscopically, and compared hair from the hair mass to hair recovered from the trunk. I found decomposition at the root in one hair from the trunk. The mass was a later stage of decomposition. The hair from the trunk had a root, and it was in an early stage of decomposition. I compared it to a hair from the hair mass. The hairs were microscopically the same. The hair in the trunk and the mass were the same. I cannot say that the hairs come from one person, just that they are similar. I do not know the source of the hairs. We have an ongoing research project on the decomposition of hair. The study involves groups of six hairs stored in various conditions from live humans. Each person donates six hairs. The preliminary results are that upon examination of the hairs, none have banding. We have not been able to recreate hair banding with environmental exposure in hair from living donors. I then included postmortem hairs and a blind study of examiners. On the preliminary test, each scientist confirmed one antemortem hair as post-mortem. Then when they did final analysis together, they both eliminated the antemortem hair and identified only the postmortem hair. (Sidebar, Baez walks back, looking unhappy.) Baez wants to proffer this witness's PowerPoint presentation. The State says that all of the PowerPoint photos have been given to the defense. Baez responds that none of the photos we received are in color, and the defense received some just this morning, and the State is seeking to publish a PowerPoint presentation on hair banding research. The judge decides to allow the defense voir dire of the witness before the PowerPoint is shown to the jury as part of the State's case, but I will not grant your request for a proffer. The jury remains in the courtroom.

Steven Shaw - Defense voir dire: Mr. Shaw, please describe the exhibit. These are hairs that were used in the study and stored in different locations and times. Hairs look extremely different under magnification; there is a color difference. There are three parts of the hair that you see in the photos. It shows hairs before and after being stored in a trunk, being stored outdoors, being underwater, and being stored in woods. There are also hairs showing decomposition, from deceased donors, subjected to the same conditions. All of these hairs look extremely different in color and filaments. The pictures show the hairs under different conditions, before and after. A band has to be above the root point, opaque, and a certain thickness. There is decomposition shown with and without root banding.

Baez: There appears to be a difference in hair underwater, it looks different. Yes, the hair was submerged in water for 100 days. The soft tissue on the root is smaller and straighter than hair that was not submerged. Apparent decomposition is broader than the postmortem banding. In the analysis, I would note that I recognize decomposition because of banding. (Baez is complaining about the location of cadaver hairs in the study, climate and location.) In this study, the examiners are completely qualified and not trainees. (The State starts to interject.) Judge: Just let Baez cross this expert before the prosecution even presents its evidence.)

The climate can affect the rate of decomposition. Hairs in warmer climates will produce bands earlier. All the hairs, I believe, are from thirteen adults and two children. Depending on the age, there is little or no difference between the hairs of children and adults under a microscope. The children's hairs were not in the water part of the study. (Baez objects to the PowerPoint and is arguing with the judge.) This study was provided to the prosecution and defense in March of 2011. It was provided in a written report and with photos in color. In early May at a deposition, the photos were sent to the State and defense, then followed with the written report. They were e-mailed in color. In March, both the prosecution and defense were told of the study and it was described. Then in May, I was in deposition, and arrangements were made for the State to view the photos in color and the defense arrived. On the weekend, they opened the FBI office for them and we copied and sent the photos on to the State. The FBI has gone to great lengths to provide the defense this study in its preliminary form and photos. I have provided color copies of the last four photos, and I was never told by the defense that there was a problem. (Baez tells the witness that he went to the FBI and reviewed the photos, and then he went back to the FBI again and he was not permitted to see them.) Because this is an ongoing study, the FBI cannot allow copies, and they have allowed great access to review the photos and studies.

Baez is done with the witness's testimony in voir dire. He argues that in March, the defense brought this to the court's attention. Here we are. The FBI has supposedly been cooperating with us and we are still arguing for discovery, here in the middle of trial. We are still dealing with FBI's refusal to cooperate near the end of the prosecution's case. The FBI had offered to transfer the files to the local office for our expert to examine, but they did not. The deposition spurred the inspiration, but this study was done because the need was there, and the FBI persists in refusing to allow independent investigation of their protocol, procedures, and results. Judge: The defendant is charged with first-degree murder, and the prosecution is seeking the death penalty. The State of Florida is to provide discovery to the defense; it is not the sole responsibility of the FBI. The Accused is given the opportunity to cross. The color PowerPoint was not provided to the defense, and the court will not allow the PowerPoint. It is in the FBI's study and they can give it out whenever they choose. However, they cannot expect to be able to use it unless they are willing to disclose it to the defense. The witness can testify but without the PowerPoint. The flip side is that if the defense opens the door on the photos, I will revisit this ruling. Baez: We could not depose him after the study was turned over. We want to be able to inquire and ask more questions about the study. What we do not know is almost unending. We would not have been able to duplicate the study, because of what we don't know. Judge: If we go back in time and think this out, our country's scientific studies go on every day, and the fact that you cannot duplicate a study is not an objection to admissibility. The testimony comes in, but the PowerPoint does not.

(You cannot un-ring a bell, and this is a hollow victory for the defense, since they were forced to question the witness with the color photos on the screen in the presence of the jury by the judge's refusal of a proffer. The judge struck the exhibit at the defense's request, but he did it in a way that the jury already saw what he ruled that they should not see. So it ends with the defense showing the jury the color photos that are not deemed admissible. Bell rung… There is no way the defense could have foreseen this; sometimes things just happen in the justice system.)

Interpretation of Testimony – Stephen Shaw (cont.): I started this study because of a thesis that I saw on hair decomposition under different environments. The study said additional research was needed, and so that is what I did. The study became more of a priority because of this case. This study was trying to recreate hair with banding in hair from live persons. I got the hairs for

280

the studies from live volunteers for a permission study. I received samples from eighteen people and used fifteen of them. They were hairs that were pulled from live individuals, male and female, the youngest was three, and oldest was fifty-three. They all came from different environments and conditions. This was a controlled study. I checked the hairs at intervals and then again at the end of the time I had set as the maximum period. The difference between postmortem banding and antemortem decomposition is major, not slight. None of the hairs from live people had postmortem banding. The two examiners worked together to match the results, and in the end, all of the postmortem banding was identified. The final result was that there was banding only where postmortem hair was involved. This is the real world of how examiners come to conclusions. Hairs with decomposition and hair banding would be another, more precise study. The hair in the photo of Caylee is admitted in color on the monitor for the jury. The banding is clear, and there is a clear example of postmortem banding above the root that occurred in none of the live study subjects.

Steven Shaw – Defense cross-examination: I did not do a side-by-side comparison of the hair from the car and hair from the hair mat found with the remains. The root portions were dissimilar. I was prompted to do this study by another thesis. The hair mass did not have much of any root left to examine. Apparent decomposition is an umbrella, and postmortem banding is a part of apparent decomposition. In my study, the two examiners gave different opinions and realized through further examination that they actually excluded the live hair. They realized they were wrong, and then they re-did the examination before I was even aware of their results. They were examiners not involved in my initial examination of the hairs, and had less experience. The result was different from mine only on initial examination, but their conclusion agreed with mine. There is still research being done and it is not well established yet.

I ask for expedited results in the study. I wrote my report, testified, and then did a validation study. Postmortem root banding is based on experience in doing examinations. That was already established, so I did the study for more information. I received only one hair and the hair mat. Most of the hairs we shed are non-root. Hairs are found everywhere at scenes. I cannot tell how the hair arrived at the scene. Finding any hair separated from the scalp is called transfer. It is a transfer whether it is one hair or more. The environmental conditions of the study were at Quantico, Virginia between August and April.

Steven Shaw - Prosecution re-direct: Heat will speed up decomposition. The hair from the trunk was taken out by force. I have never seen a hair with decomposition root banding from a live person in the many thousands I have tested. (Sidebar)

Steven Shaw - Defense re-cross: Based on your studies and experience something pulled the hair out of Caylee. Yes. A brush is a possible reason, and moving a dead body could also pull the hair out.

The State's Sixty-fifth Witness

Interpretation of Testimony - Elizabeth Fontaine: I am a FBI physical scientist and I deal in latent fingerprints. I have a MS from University of Florida in Chemistry and BS in Biology. I have had 18 months of training at the FBI and learned process and control, and I have processed hundreds of items. I have done seventy-five thousand comparisons. I was certified in 2008, before I was involved with this case. At the time of my involvement, I was still on probation with supervisors, because our work is still reviewed for months after we are done with the FBI Academy. In December 2008, I received items from the Caylee Anthony scene, duct tape in three pieces. My initials are in the seals and tape. I received them as numbers 62, 63, and 64. 62 was in a separate package, and 63 and 64 were in a single package and packaged separately inside. The tape was six to eight inches per piece in length, and the glue was nearly gone and no longer sticky. The glue and strings were hanging onto the plastic. I was told the remains in that area were subjected to water.

I expected not to find latent prints from underwater. I still examined 62, 63, and 64, and there were no latent prints on any of them. I did find one thing on 63; an outline of a heart appeared on the duct tape. I was using an alternate light source after super glue. It shows as a flat image. It was the size of a dime, and looked similar to the glue from a removed bandage. At the time I saw it I did not think it was that important, but I noted it and called a supervisor, who also viewed it. Then it was turned over to the investigator. When I found this outline, I continued on with my examination and I did not attempt to photograph it at that time. After I completed the exam, I decide to try even though I had used chemicals to dye the stain on the tape, and I had used black powders, all in order to try to get prints. I could not find the outline after I used the chemicals. All I can tell you is that it was heart shaped and the size of a dime.

Elizabeth Fontaine - Defense cross-examination: It first went to evidence control for inventory purposes, and then it was sent to trace evidence, and then to me. Upon the initial inspection, trace evidence contacted me to help them view it. We can look visibly, and then use a laser to help, and then ultraviolet. Then trace looks for hair and fibers. When I received it back, I did the first three tests again. Super glue is attracted to moisture, and so it is used by heating it and exposing the item to the fumes to enhance fingerprints that might otherwise be missed. Then the RUBIS system which allows the monitor to show the items and to eliminate reflection, shows them on screen and blown up. After the RAM, a dye stain, is applied, the black power was put on both sides of the tape.

Elizabeth Fontaine - State's re-direct: I saw this heart shape in the RUBIS system and it was gone after all the further testing was done when I went back to photograph what I had observed. No fingerprints were found. (The witness is released, and the jury is excused for the evening. The lawyers and the judge stay for argument and housekeeping details.)

In argument to the judge, Baez says that the item was contaminated by someone else. (Sidebar.) We are sure she followed protocol, but we would have stopped and photographed it at that moment. A heart-shaped outline? We definitely would have photographed this before continuing, even if we had to stop and get six supervisors! This was a child victim, and the duct tape that was on her remains. We are not happy with this work by the FBI lab. We believe the witness when she says that she saw the heart-shaped imprint, but come on! She could have at least printed from the monitor or photographed the monitor. There is a new witness, who should be here at 1:30 tomorrow to testify. The State says it will wrap up its case either tomorrow or Wednesday by noon. The trial is ahead of the schedule Judge Perry anticipated. By Saturday, we will have an idea how long the case will continue. We think maybe the evidence will be concluded by the end of next week, and the jury will start deliberating by the 25th or 27th.

June 14th, 2011

The State's Sixty-sixth Witness

Interpretation of Testimony - Catherine Theisen, PhD: I am Chief of Quality Assurance for the FBI. I have been employed by the FBI for over twenty-three years. For six years, I was a research scientist and for five years a quality assurance specialist. For the past nine years, I have worked in forensics dealing with mitochondrial DNA. I have a BA from Virginia Tech and a Human Molecular PhD from Johns Hopkins. I have taught graduate school classes around the world. I have testified twenty times in federal, state, and local cases. The lab does nuclear DNA analyses from both parents and mitochondrial DNA analyses only from the mother and siblings. Mitochondrial DNA can only identify genes from the maternal side. We cannot identify a person with mitochondrial DNA. The DNA is subtracted and copied, or amplified, so we have enough to test with. Then we type it and look at the DNA's building blocks. We can then compare mitochondrial DNA from known and unknown sources. They can be searched in a mitochondrial DNA search. If DNA is different, it can be excluded. If two are the same, it can be concluded as a source. If an individual cannot be excluded as the source, we can compare it to a DNA database and find the numbers of probability that a sample and the known individual are from the same donor.

Hair and skeletal remains may not have enough DNA for nuclear analysis and/or enough mitochondrial DNA for analysis. In July 2008, I received the evidence in this case. It was a piece of hair, and was identified as hair from the trunk of a car. I also received a DNA sample from Casey Anthony. (She identifies the samples of the hair and buccal swabs as those she received.) My initials are on the items. (Both exhibits are admitted into evidence.)

I did a mitochondrial DNA test on the part of the hair from the trunk of the car. I did get a profile from it, and I also got a profile from the swab sample. The types are the same and therefore I can say they came from one maternal family group. The characteristics are in less than one percent of the population. They include Casey, her brother, her maternal grandmother, and maternal aunts and uncles. In December of 2008, I received an additional sample for analysis profiling for mitochondrial DNA. It was a hair mass. The result is the same as for the single hair and hair mass. I could not exclude Caylee, Casey, or anyone in their maternal line.

284

Catherine Theisen, PhD - Defense cross-examination: I am the quality assurance manager of the entire FBI laboratory. I oversee a group of quality assurance people who oversee and analyze the work. We conduct standard tests for the police and have standardized procedures. I develop the rules of how items are processed, to a general degree, and then the others have procedures to follow, depending on what is being tested and what sort of analysis is being done. We do not use a checklist, a set procedure. All casework has at least two levels of review. Evidence examiners are subject to review and testing. As for mitochondrial DNA, the entire family line on the mother's side cannot be excluded for any sample analyzed. As part of my duties, I get the communications and see the chain of evidence. I do not use the information in my work. All of our case files are required to have communication in the file, and we read it, but we do not use the communications in the examinations. Information on the names may have been in the files, but I do not recall a mention of Lee Anthony in the file.

The State's Sixty-seventh Witness

Interpretation of Testimony - Alina Burroughs: I am CSI with the Orange County Sheriff's Office. I have been so employed since 2003. In 2008, I worked as a CSI with the Caylee Anthony remains and I assisted in execution of a search warrant on December 2008, at the home. This is an aerial picture of the home, and it shows a nice subdivision. The area where the remains were located is a heavily wooded area about a mile away from the home. I facilitated the collection and documentation of the evidence removed from the home. I saw items before they were collected; in some cases I might see them in the location and in some, after they were moved and brought to me. There were heart stickers found located in the bedroom of Casey Anthony. (Sidebar.) They were located inside a yellow box in a dresser inside Casey's room. The box contained other items. When the item was located, the note was just a background in the box and the heart sticker was not affixed to anything. (A close-up of the heart sticker is admitted into evidence; it appears about dime-sized in the photo.

I packaged and sealed the sticker and the sticker was placed into evidence. There were other stickers that had been cut. The sticker sheet had been cut in half, and that item was located in a black binder in Casey's room. This photo is clearly a half page of dime-size heart stickers. (These are admitted into evidence.) Another set of stickers, mostly removed, was located and removed from

Caylee's room. (These are admitted into evidence.) This is the metallic red heart shaped sticker sheet with three stickers left. (These are also admitted into evidence.)

Alina Burroughs - Defense cross-examination: The photograph of the letter in the box has a thirty-seven cent stamp. I do not know when the letter was dated. There are heart and star stickers, I do not know if the other items like Disney characters are stickers. I do not recall seeing scrapbooks for children or children's art on the wall. I also searched the other rooms, and I do not recall if any of them contained stickers. We searched Cindy's and George's items, but did not recover any stickers from there. (When shown a photo of the sticker found with the remains, she says…) The photo has a sticker-like item, but I do not recall the item and do not know if it is a sticker. I do not know this item, and not to my knowledge, we are not holding the item.

Suburban Drive was in the vicinity of an elementary school, but not directly across from it. The school is not very close to the remains site. It is not present in the photo, and I do not want to attempt to estimate the distance. I do not know what was at the end of the road or whether there were any houses. I did find this item at the Anthony home - it is a beveled raised heart sticker. (It is admitted into evidence.)

The State's Sixty-eighth Witness

Interpretation of Testimony - Cindy Anthony (recalled): When Caylee was found on December 11th of 2008, we were in Los Angeles and we were not present when a search warrant was issued on our home. I noticed that on July 3rd, Caylee's teddy bear was missing. Caylee also had a blanket with Winnie the Pooh, and I noticed it was missing, too, and realized that I had not seen it since the end of May. There is video of me in July of 2008, and my hair was the same style but a little longer than it is now. I cut it regularly, but in the winter, it grows longer. In the July videos, my hair is processed. I have been coloring my hair since 2002. Before that, I just highlighted and I was a brunette in 2002. From 2002 until the present, it has all been dyed and not highlighted. This photo of Caylee was taken early in 2008, the first couple of months. The hair had grown and I trimmed it. Caylee's hair was not processed. In 2008, Casey started dying her hair after Caylee was born; she cut it shorter too. Casey has brown hair naturally. (A 2007 photo is admitted of Casey and Caylee. Casey's hair was very short, and Caylee was chunkier.)

286

Caylee's second birthday was August 9th, 2007. (Cindy is reviewing her deposition.) I remember making the statement that this photo was taken around Caylee's second birthday or a little before. Lee shaves his head down and lets it grow no more than an inch long. Lee does not process his hair. My mother lives in Mount Dora, and I believe she was in the Pontiac Sunbird. I cannot say when my mother was in the car last. Her hair is shoulder length or less. Her hair is a blondish-brown with gray and white. I recall duct tape in black, blue and possibly silver. I am not aware of the duct tape being kept in the garage. I do not think that our duct tape was used in the searches; the search group had purchased duct tape, and I do not believe it came from our house. I couldn't say if the duct tape at the command center came from my home.

I recall George telling me about putting a piece of duct tape on the gas can after the police returned it. I remember telling you about using the duct tape at the command center, and I do not recall if it came from our house. I recognize Caylee's sign from the Kid Finders, the missing children's organization. Kid Finders made the poster of her. There was a tent at the command center and we had small tents and then Kid Finders had a larger tent and I do not know which tent is shown. These are photos of laundry bags similar to the one we had at home. The bottom one we had, but the other I am not sure about. I can see the size now and they appear to be similar to the laundry bags we had in the home. These bags were kept in the sheds and we stored balls for Caylee, then the bag was put in the garage over the laundry area, on the shelf. I had not used it for months in 2008. I also had removed a bag from Caylee's room and replaced it with a hanging one. I placed the laundry bag in the garage along with the others.

I made the statement in July 2009, the last time I saw the laundry bag was in Caylee's bedroom, but I was wrong. I had replaced it with the hanging bag in Caylee's room. When they issued the search warrant, I thought it was still in her bedroom and I was wrong. This photo shows where the canvas laundry bags were stored in the plastic garbage bags in the garage. After the execution of the search warrant in 2008 I did not see the items again. I recognize the shirt that Caylee is wearing only from seeing it at my deposition. I had never seen it before. It says Big Trouble Comes In Small Packages. I did the laundry at home most of the time. I never remember seeing this shirt or a photo of it until after July 2008. (The witness stands down, and a recess is announced. Cross-examination will be after the recess.)

Cindy Anthony mouths to Casey as she leaves the stand, "I love you." Casey does not acknowledge her mother. The jury sends word that it wants to see Exhibit 313, because they did not see it when it was introduced. The judge will get the exhibit for them to see. They also want an exhibit list during deliberations. The judge agreed to supply this list at the time of deliberations.

The defense objects, as the sticker has fallen off the cardboard during the passing around. The prosecution says that they can call the person who collected it and ask if it was stuck on the cardboard. The judge says, the jury asked for 313, and they are going to get it. Put it on the document viewer and then if they want it, they can have it passed around. Defense: I want to know if there is record evidence that this heart was attacked to the cardboard. Judge: I will have the court reporter pull the transcript and tell me. I am going to let the jury look, and I am going to see if they want to hold it and review it. The heart is number 313 in evidence, a raised heart-shaped sticker)

Interpretation of Testimony - Cindy Anthony (Defense cross-examination): Caylee was found on Dec 11th, 2008, and the police executed a search warrant and I was not home. We went home the next day. Then went back a couple of days later, and we saw what the police had done. Then on December 20th, they executed another one. I am not sure at what time we got a copy of the items taken. It was a difficult time. There was a confrontational moment. I do not know when I told them about a missing blanket. I am not aware if I made a statement at that time about it. When I came home after December 11th, my house was a mess and the police had not put anything back after the search. At some point Caylee's bedding set was taken. They opened and looked in and under everything. (She is reviewing the deposition.) I do not remember if I was asked if Casey removed any duct tape while she was home. I recall giving a deposition on July 23rd, 2009. Defense: Okay, did Casey remove any duct tape when she was out of jail, during the two periods of time? As far as I remember, no. I think we only had one roll of duct tape and George was using it. During that time we had only a black roll and we used it for signs and it is not correct that I used it to affix the signs up of Caylee. This is photo of Casey and Caylee when Caylee was about two. I think we have owned the Pontiac since 2000, and all of our hair has changed. My mother's hair is only 5 inches max and Lee's is short. Caylee is less than two months maybe 18 months, in this photo. She had grown a lot since then, and she might have outgrown the shorts. They appear to be 24 mounts and she was in a three. (The witness is excused, subject to recall.)

Exhibit 313 has been located and is displayed to the jury on the document camera and is passed around. The heart on the cardboard was taken in pieces and the cardboard matting with pink heart-shaped material is attached. It has separated in evidence. (This is the matting from the duct tape, we believe.) It appears to be from the remains site. It has a red metallic looking beveled heart on it. When it was taken into evidence, it was attached to the cardboard liner. (The jury is excused for a recess, while the lawyers and judge work on.)

Defense: This is the affidavit of the journalist who took the video and or still shots on the July 20th, 2008 at the command post manned by Lee Anthony on behalf of the child Caylee. WFTV has provided them as discovery to the defense. The photo is of a Caylee Poster, and the duct tape on the poster is silver duct tape. They were at Publix when they were searching for Caylee. It appears to be the same duct tape as was found at the remains site, the Silver Henkel tape. There are stipulations and an affidavit to the items. The parties agree that they are accurate.

Stipulations are read to the jury, and items are introduced.

(By stipulation.) In 2008, Cindy Anthony was employed by Geneva Health from January to July 16th, 2008. A business record is attached and a time card history report is included.

(By stipulation.) In 2008, George Anthony was employed by Security Forces, Inc., and the employment records of George Anthony from January 16th to July 4th, 2008 are included with weekly time reports of Mr. Anthony. (There is a sidebar for the next stipulation.)

(Stipulation.) The attached documents are from May 2007 to July 2008 from Photo bucket.

(Stipulation.) The identity of the remains found Dec 11th, 2008 are agreed that they are skeletal remains Caylee Anthony.

The Identity of the defendant is confirmed. All witnesses who referred to Casey Anthony were referring to Casey Anthony the defendant in court.

The State's Sixty-ninth Witness

Interpretation of Testimony - Jenny Welch (recalled): I am a CSI investigator with Orange County, Florida. On August 13th, 2009 I came in contact with Casey Anthony to photograph a tattoo on her back. I took twenty-three photos. The photos accurately depict the defendant and the tattoo as I saw it at that time. (The photos are admitted into evidence.)

The State's Seventieth Witness

Interpretation of Testimony - Bobby Williams: I am currently employed at Cast Iron Tattoos as a tattoo artist. I have been with them eight years. I have known Casey about seven years. I saw her on July 2nd, 2008 at the tattoo shop. She came in; she had an appointment with me to get a tattoo. She made the appointment a few days before by telephone. She told me on the phone that she wanted *Bella Vita* in a feminine font. When Casey arrived, I ended up doing the design and putting it on her body. It took about thirty minutes. This photo is the tattoo I put on Casey Anthony that day. (Sidebar, the defense does not want this tattoo artist testimony and photos of her tattoo in evidence.) Casey agreed to the tattoo and she was acting normal. (It is placed in evidence.) She was doing fine, and she was on the phone. It cost $65.00 cash. Then we ordered pizza. On the 15th of July, she made another appointment and her mood was normal. She made an appointment for two for the 19th. It was for her and her friend from out of town. It would be something different with the friend. On July 15th, she said Caylee was with the nanny and would be in on the nineteenth with her. People do get tattoos to remember their loved ones. (Sidebar that shuts down the defense's questioning of the witness. The witness is excused, and the jury is taken out of the courtroom for the remainder of the day.)

The defense wants to renew all motions to dismiss based on the skeleton issues video, remorse, Casey's behavior, the heart shapes, the testimony adduced from the last witness about the tattoo (that it is inflammatory and unfairly prejudicial with no probative value), and other things. The State responds that as to the video, there are no new arguments, and the tattoo is only evidence and it would be relevant because it states Bella Vita, the good life.

The Motion for Mistrial is denied. The prosecution wants the court to take judicial notice and instruct the jury on the meaning of Bella Vita and they need a dictionary definition. The judge says that if he takes judicial notice we will include the definition. The State moves the cans of air into evidence. Then the prosecution will rest. The defense says it will be prepared to present a Judgment of Acquittal (JOA) motion tomorrow. The jury does not hear the JOA motion, the judge does. The prosecution urges for them to do it tonight. (If that happens, the JOA motion will be waived, according to our lawyer. The State must rest its case first.) That is a failed attempt at a dirty trick. Mason is not happy. The defense was told to be prepared by Thursday; they have arrangements made for their witnesses to be present on Thursday, and they cannot move witnesses to Wednesday. The judge tells the defense to plan to continue working on Saturdays, and maybe past 1 PM. Mr. Mason got a little snappy with the prosecution, probably because he saw through their game of having the JOA tonight before the prosecution rests. The old dog caught it! Mason won't give them his cases until tomorrow morning. The judge says the law is the law and the facts are the facts. We will hear their argument for the motion for acquittal in the morning. The judge is giving both sides the cases upon which he expects to rely.

What about the grief expert? The judge gives both sides a case of interest. They are deposing her on Saturday. The prosecution is planning to rest its case in chief today by placing the cans containing car tire cover samples in evidence. When and if these cans are opened, they will probably reek of decomposition. We expect a fight from the defense, since the prosecutor's mistakes handling the cans may have confused the jury. The defense will claim that the identification is not trustworthy.

By the way, Geraldo Rivera is in the courtroom today. He is just one of the many media celebrities that have been mentioned during the course of this case. The coverage is now on most major stations for anywhere from a few minutes to round-the-clock live coverage of the trial. Some shows and blogs have attempted to provide intelligent and interesting information, but many have emphasized only the sensational aspects of the case. Some of the coverage is complete with commentary from lawyers, including a lawyer formerly on this defense team. This is troubling. What about that lawyer's ethical obligation to maintain confidences and secrets of clients? Even though she claims she will not talk about the defense strategy or anything Casey said, much of it has colored her commentary. How much of this legal "expert opinion" is driven by lawyers' need for acclaim?

June 15th, 2011

Today, the prosecution will rest its case in chief, and the defense will make its JOA argument. A JOA is a standard motion that is based on the evidence and the lack of evidence, and presented to the court at the end of the prosecution's side of the case. The defense will say that the prosecution did not show that Casey killed Caylee, and there was not enough evidence presented to even allow the jury to deliberate. In our lawyer's twenty-nine year career in criminal law, he has tried many hundreds of cases. He says he has won a JOA maybe two or three times. They are almost always denied by the judge. That said, we know Cheney Mason will fight for the JOA this morning. Then we expect he will lose. At that time the defense has a few choices left. They can present no defense case and send the case to the jury, believing that there is not enough evidence from the prosecution to find Casey Anthony guilty. We do not expect this. It is too risky; there has been a lot of evidence in this case. So we believe they will present a defense over the next week or so, and it will go something like this: Caylee drowned and daddy hid the body after the accident. We do not buy into this one. Dr. G was correct, if a child drowns and even if the child is completely stiff when found, people call for help in hope that the child can be revived.

We thought it would be the thirty-one days that sealed Casey Anthony's fate. Now we believe that the defense tactic of throwing George under the bus has sealed her fate. Once Dr. G brought clear logic, the defense position that George hid the body after a drowning, the body of a grandchild he worshiped, this case was over, at least in terms of George's involvement with his granddaughter's death. The biggest question is will they put Casey on the stand? At the end of the day, it is Casey's choice to testify or not. We believe the lawyers will advise her not to take the stand and she will follow that advice. Who knows? The day starts in about twenty minutes. Today is June 15th, 2011 and it is the three year anniversary of the last time Caylee Anthony was seen alive, June 15th, 2008. On that day, her grandfather George kissed Caylee goodbye as she walked out of her grandparent's home and got into the car with her mother Casey Anthony, never to be seen alive again. Caylee was wearing a pink shirt that said "Big Trouble Comes In Small Packages," shorts, sunglasses, and her backpack. The next time Caylee was seen was on December 11th, 2008, when her skull was found with duct tape still stuck in her hair.

Court begins with Judge Perry saying, before we bring the jury back in there are two issues, evidence and judicial notice. The state and the defense have come to an agreement on the judicial notice. On July 2nd, 2008 Casey Anthony received a tattoo which reads "Bella Vita" that translates to "beautiful life." The prosecution's sample in the cans, the spare tire cover pieces and (the smell) are placed in evidence as long as the prosecution is not opening the cans of air. They say that they are not at this time, and they agree to proffer the items if they plan to open the cans. Cheney Mason is rightfully concerned that the jury is discussing the case, because they asked to see Item 313 in evidence immediately after a recess yesterday. The prosecution says it is no different than saying they cannot see the monitor when an item is published. The judge he agrees with the State, that they just missed a piece of evidence and brought it to our attention.

The Court reads the stipulation for the jury: On July 2, 2008 Casey Anthony received a tattoo. "Bella Vita" translates to "beautiful life".

The cans are also received in evidence. Then, lead prosecutor Linda Drane Burdick stands and announces, "The State of "Florida rests it case." (Sidebar) The judge tells the jury that legal matters will be discussed outside the jury's presence, and that they may return to their quarters until tomorrow. We will reconvene at 9 AM tomorrow. Do not discuss this case among yourselves, do not read any newspaper, watch any news, social networks, twitter, read any texts, or any other communications or discussion about this case. (The jury is dismissed for the day.)

Judge: I received from the defense a number of cases and a memorandum of law. I have only done a quick scan of the memorandum, and I am familiar with all the cases cited by the defense except one. I can review this now, or you can go straight into the argument without me reading that case. Since the prosecution gave me their cases a few days ago, I reviewed all of them. So if you would like, I will review that case. The choice is yours. Mason tells him that he prefers to argue the motion first, and then the judge can take the motion under advisement and read the case before ruling. The judge assents.

(Mr. Mason, it is well established in the justice of this country and at the end of the prosecution's evidence the defense is entitled to seek a JOA. If the evidence is insufficient then the court is to step in. For a JOA, the

evidence is to be viewed by the judge in the most
favorable light to the prosecution.)

**Cheney Mason arguing the Motion for Judgment of
Acquittal:**

Most recently, the Florida Supreme Court a few months ago
stated that the court in this type of case, a capital
case, that there is a special standard of review. A JOA
should be granted in a circumstantial case if the
evidence fails to support any direct evidence. The state
has the burden and the evidence is clearly
circumstantial. It is not inconsistent with other
reasonable possibility other than that the defendant
committed the murder. By circumstantial evidence, the
crime may be proved by a well-connected chain, but the
chain is only as good as its links - those circumstances
deemed themselves to be proved beyond a reasonable doubt.
(We recall that Dr. G said the preponderance of the
evidence showed homicide, but not that the evidence was
conclusive.) They have established Casey Anthony has a
history of lying to family and friends. They have
established by stipulation the child is dead. There is no
evidence regarding when, where, how, or who was there
when she died. They have failed to rebut that there was
accidental death and a cover up. For a first-degree
murder, the evidence fails to support premeditation. The
determination of premeditation must be inconsistent with
every other hypothesis. There has been no evidence of
premeditation in this court, just a stacking of
inferences. In the Smith case in Tampa, the body was
found in chains, wrapped in a blue blanket and taped. The
husband did not call the police to report his wife
missing immediately. Even though premeditated murder can
be proved by circumstantial evidence, it must be
consistent with every other logical inference. In this
case, the cause of death was known, drowning, and the
court overruled to second degree. Dr. G made claims that
one hundred percent of people report these things.

In the Serrano case, the circumstances of the case show a
world of difference in its set of facts. This was a case
of four murders over millions of dollars. There was no
question as to the cause of death; the victims were shot
on their knees. The circumstantial evidence in Serrano
was regarding who committed the homicides, not whether
there even was a homicide; followed by, if there was a
homicide, who committed it. Every reasonable hypothesis
must be eliminated.

Brooks v State, 2006, is the current law, and states that
the underling felony of child abuse cannot result in a

charge of first degree murder. Absent an independent act of child abuse, the underlying felony is merged with and precludes the felony murder. We have no evidence of violence and/or child abuse to this child before. The first eighteen witnesses all said Casey was a loving mother before they besmirched her character.

The judge steps in, Mr. Mason, are you aware of Lewis v State, pending now at the Florida Supreme Court, with claims in Brooks? How would you square Lewis with Brooks? Mason concedes that the Attorney General in Lewis is trying to undo the Brooks case, but there is no ruling yet. What is new about that? This goes on all the time. Brooks is the law today, Your Honor. Mr. Mason continues, in Kennedy v State, the court made an error in not identifying what is child abuse. Perhaps the chloroform and duct tape are subject to contest, but all of the witnesses have stated that she was not abused or tortured.

As to the aggravated manslaughter of a child charge, Caylee is dead, caused by intentional or culpable acts of Casey, and Caylee was under 18. It is our argument to this court that what has been presented to you, the mere presents of duct tape on or near the skeleton, is not enough to convict Casey on either a theory or intentional act or a theory of culpable negligence.

Culpable negligence is lack of care that shows willful and wanton disregard for the safety of another. There is no evidence whatsoever that could be considered at that standard, and none as the cause of death.

The other counts, there are not any supreme court cases on lying to the officers. These were pulled out of the old statute closet to use in this case.

The judge asks, Mr. Mason, shouldn't these issues have been brought up to the court earlier? Mason tells him, we did file various motions before I came on this case, I believe. The statements are troublesome to the defense, and if you find that they were involuntarily given, then they are to be ignored. Witnesses such as Detective Melich admit that Casey Anthony was never given her Miranda rights, while surrounded by police, interrogated and placed in a police car and driven around the area.

I have cited other cases for Your Honor to read. The state is required to prove every element before it can go to a jury. We will rely strongly on the Reynolds case. Two women were murdered and it was a circumstantial evidence in that case. At least the State had a cause of death. The victims had broken necks and spinal cords. If you go through the last eighteen days of testimony in this courtroom, you have to ask, "Where is the evidence in this case?" Despite the notoriety, outcry, publicity, media and more, there is not a case here.

That circumstantial evidence has to establish no other reasonable explanation for the death. The case law is talking a lot about hair, but the supreme court reversed a hair case for acquittal. That case was reversed, and it was not just speculation as we have here in the prosecution's case.

In Cox, the defendant was sentenced to death, and the Supreme Court reversed for acquittal. They said the circumstantial evidence in the case was insufficient. In Randall v State, the supreme court reversed yet another case, because of the absence of proof on the issue of premeditation.

A reasonable hypothesis in this case is accidental drowning, based on the absence of a history of abuse. There is no confession, a piece of cardboard is found nine to ten feet from the body with a heart shaped sticker that is nothing like anything else in this case. The only thing close to that thing was the FBI examiner who claimed she had seen an image on the tape that they could not photograph and did not preserve, at the FBI lab in Quantico Virginia. The only evidence we have of duct tape is near the body in the hair. The only person shown to have access to the duct tape was the grandfather.

The judge interjects, Mr. Mason, you have mentioned accidental death and what record evidence is there of any accidental death? Mason responds, Your Honor, there is none at this time, but it is a reasonable hypothesis of innocence.

In all of the cases relied upon by the State of Florida to justify denial of a JOA, there is no mystery as to the cause of death. In this case we do not have a cause of death.

(Mason is arguing a lot of case law and doing a great job, before he loses. He is really hammering home the point that there is no cause of death. So if you murder, then destroy the evidence by exposing it to months in a swamp, maybe you will get off. We do not think that is how it should be.)

Your Honor, I have tried murder cases for forty years, and all the speculation - could have, may have, might have been, we have no evidence to exclude there was no murder - no premeditation, no aggravated child abuse. These first three counts are not just ripe for, but screaming for acquittal. Thank you.

Assistant State Attorney Linda Drane Burdick presents the State's JOA Argument:

Your Honor, the law is the law, and in a recitation of what the law is, Mr. Mason spent a long time trying to distinguish those cases from this case. All inferences must be given to the State and the State is not required to rebut conclusively all contravening evidence at this time.

The Serrano case was only given to the court to establish that the defendant's ability was in question. In this case some Zanny has the child and Casey did not know what happened. So we have considered the available information, and this is not a reasonable hypothesis.

This drowning claim, which was tossed in this case by the defense, was refuted by Dr. G., the medical examiner, who has told you this case is not an accident. The suggested witness to this so-called accident has rebutted it; George Anthony was not there when Caylee died.

Jackson v State. The defense stated that because there is not a definitive cause of death, that a JOA must be granted. In Jackson, Dr. Beaver, the medical examiner, testified that because the body was decomposed he could not find a definite cause of the death, and stated it was homicide by undetermined means. In Jackson, there were multiple hypotheses that were propounded, and all were rebutted. Dr. Brewer expressed his decisions was based on the location where the body was found, examination, and common sense, as did Dr. G in this case. The supreme court upheld the murder conviction and death sentence in that case, and found that the circumstances proved by the State presented competent, substantial evidence consistent with the defendant's guilt. That is exactly what we have done here.

It is our opinion that a reasonable jury can conclude that Caylee died by duct tape or chloroform or the two, based on how her remains were found. The relationship between Cindy and Casey did provide a motive for the murder, and Casey began a plan in early 2008, with internet searches. The state does not have to prove the method of murder.

In a circumstantial evidence case, Brooks has ongoing litigation at this time. The first was the supreme court's pronouncing it in 2006, and it came out of Dorsey v State. Dorsey does not address the language between first degree and felony child abuse. The mechanism required to result in the death of the child. This is more than a single act. The substance of Lewis is in the First District Court is that it held that the supreme court's language in Brooks was dicta and was therefore not binding precedent, and that there was more than a single act of child abuse, so even if Brooks was not dicta, that the State had satisfied the requirement of Brooks. In this case, application of the three multiple pieces of duct tape is more than one act. At this stage, the question is based on this evidence.

Could a reasonable jury determine that this was an intentional act to cause the child's death? There is no fixed period of time that must pass, just sufficient time for reflection. When she decided to place not one, not two, but three pieces of duct tape on Caylee, she had sufficient time to realize that those act would kill Caylee and it is therefore premeditated.

Mr. Mason responds for the Defendant:

Your Honor, the State is suggesting evidence by chloroform poisoning. There was no evidence of chloroform being used on the child. And there was no chloroform. The duct tape, despite speculation and argument, there were two pieces of duct tape attached to the hair and one found feet away. There are no fingerprints, no witnesses, nothing else.

The only person having the control of duct tape was George Anthony. I want to talk you about the Jackson case. It has nothing to do with our case. Lewis suggests that the drowning by holding a child under the water was one act. There is no evidence Casey Anthony used duct tape and chloroform. I ask the court to read all these cases before you rule.

The Court:

Mr. Mason, I have read most of these cases, and I have spent a great deal of time reviewing cases and the testimony of this case at night and over the weekend, to date. We will recess for 45 minutes while I make my decision. (Court stands in recess.)

Cheney Mason argued for the judge to acquit Casey Anthony based on many cases already decided and pending in the appellate courts. He argued well, but this argument was not as elegant as some. Mason had to intentionally sacrifice some beauty to quote the case law, and this argument is heard by the judge, not a jury. His was a good solid argument for JOA. The prosecution lined up their multiple pieces of duct tape, no evidence of drowning, and the State's having proved the crime sufficiently to have the case go to the jury, short and sweet. Drane Burdick did another good job.

Now the judge will make a decision and he could acquit Casey and walk her out of court, never to be charged again in the death of Caylee. We are sure that is not happening. He can reduce first degree to second-degree murder, and remove the death penalty from this case, then send it to the jury. That is possible but not likely. He can remove the aggravated child abuse, leave first-degree murder, and send to the jury. That is a little more possible. Lastly, the judge can deny the JOA and send this case to the jury as charged in the indictment. That is the most likely outcome.

The case the supreme court is currently hearing involves the question of whether felony child abuse be used as the basis for first degree felony murder that happened as a result of the child abuse, where there is only one act of aggravated child abuse and no other abuse incidents. It seems that they already ruled on that issue, but a lower appellate court case is giving the Supreme Court an opportunity to rethink its ruling.

The judge has a decision. He begins reciting the facts of cases upon which he relied. He says that he relied on a case where the evidence of the case is circumstantial and the defendant was the last person seen with the victim, and the defendant had some motive. There was an eight year old victim. The evidence showed that the defendant left with the young victim and he had dated the mother and had not been dating since. He had only a spot of the victim's blood on his shirt, and there was hair and fiber in this case as well.

In the next case, the evidence showed that the defendant met the victim's mother and he was the last person who was seen with the victim. He was sleeping next to the victim and then she disappeared. The supreme court cited a case out of Virginia. In that case, the victim disappeared on a night after leaving a hotel and went to a lake house with the defendant. The victim disappeared and her body never being found. This case talks about premeditation and what premeditation meant.

I also used these cases on the Anthony JOA for persuasive value. On the first floor a couple heard moaning sounds in the basement. They checked and found a boy, they got law enforcement assistance. He recovered and was later discharged and then was taken back to the hospital, where he remained to his death.

In this case, the victim has been last seen with the defendant before the disappearance, on the porch of his residence by two witnesses. The victim was later found in the basement. Since the victim had been found after being earlier seen with the defendant, the court upheld the ruling on first degree murder. A Supreme Court case says in another case that the defendants were the last two persons to see the victim alive, and again upheld the conviction.

The defense brings up whether under the rationale of the Brooks and Lewis cases, the defendant can be charged on the doctrine of murder and felony child abuse. Felony murder requires that the aggravated child abuse be charged and the defendant convicted of both regardless of the number of abuse events. That law is the law at this time, and the key argument is whether there is more than one single act of child abuse in this case. Duct taping the nose, the mouth, the chloroform in the trunk, the evidence that the child was placed in a trash bag, and the statements during this time period, the defendant's statements that the child was alive. It is quite clear there is more than one act of child abuse in this case, which meets the test of Brooks. The Motion for Judgment of Acquittal is denied; these are specifically questions for the jury. The court finds the prosecution has presented clear and convincing evidence to go to the jury.

PART FIVE

Chapter 13

THE DEFENDANT'S CASE - WEEK ONE

The writers had planned to rest tonight, until a story leaked late today. It is not hard to decide who leaked this story tonight, the day that the judge denied the defense's JOA motion. The Casey Anthony defense team wants to depose a new witness. He is a man convicted of kidnapping, whom defense attorneys say had contact with their client's father on July 14th, 2008. According to Anthony's attorneys, Vasco Thompson, who currently lives

300

in Orlando, had unexplained communications with George Anthony. The defense claims that the communication occurred before Caylee was reported missing. The attorneys said there were four communications on July 14th, 2008, a day before the Anthony family learned that Casey Anthony's car was towed from an Amscot parking lot. It is not known who contacted whom, or if Thompson and George Anthony talked to each other. In 1987, Thompson pleaded no contest to a kidnapping charge. He was sentenced to prison, according to jail records. He was released in 2004.

Mark Lippman, the attorney representing the Anthony family, issued a statement Wednesday afternoon about the matter, saying that his client does not recall communicating with Thompson in any way. He said the defense has not identified who initiated the calls or how long the calls were. The Casey Anthony defense team recently sent an investigator to talk to Thompson, but defense attorneys said he would not cooperate. The simple, although unlucky explanation for these calls is that George Anthony had just gotten a new job that he was to start the next day. The Lexus Dealership telephone number might be close to the telephone number of the paroled ex-convict. In Florida, we have many ex-convicts, so what were the odds. Now, will the defense change the story they told in opening arguments, that Caylee drowned and George hid the body? Maybe Casey lied again and what really happened is the ex-convict with a phone number similar to the Lexus Dealer that George was stating he work for, kidnapped Caylee. I cannot imagine that Judge Perry will allow this before the jury if there is a similar phone number to the Lexus Dealer or some other reasonable explanation. We think that the defense is looking for taint, anything to get a reasonable doubt.

Orlando Attorney Mark Lippman
Issues Media Statement on behalf of George Anthony

Regarding the Recent disclosure of Casey Anthony Witnesses

Orlando, Florida. Orlando attorney Mark Lippman issued the following statement on behalf of his clients regarding the latest speculation that George Anthony had anything to do with the untimely passing of his granddaughter Caylee Anthony.

In the State v. Anthony case, the defense has listed two new witnesses from an incident that happened in 2008 involving George Anthony. This incident had nothing to do with Caylee Anthony or the case in chief against Casey

Anthony. Unfortunately, because of the nature of this case, speculation has been publicly reported as to George Anthony's involvement with the death of Caylee Anthony. This is simply speculation or an attempt at interpreting the actions of the defense and certainly nothing that has been reported about this speculation is a news fact nor should it ever be construed as a news fact.

While we continue to be sensitive to the important role of the news media in informing the public, and we do not wish to dissuade or prevent news media representatives from fulfilling their responsibilities, this line of speculation has necessitated an immediate response. George Anthony had nothing to do with the death of Caylee Anthony. He has been investigated, deposed, examined, and cross-examined by both the prosecution and the defense and neither the defense team nor the State of Florida have maintained that he is at fault in any way. We assert that we will not engage in idle speculation regarding either the defense strategy or the state strategy but make no mistake that any factual fallacy stated contrary to my client's well-being will be vigorously defended to every extent allowed by the law. (End of statement.)

Yesterday at the close of court, George and Cindy rode 23 floors in the elevator leaving the courthouse. They sobbed in tears, holding onto each other. When is it enough for you to tell the truth, Casey? Casey is at the counsel table talking with Mr. Mason in what appears to be a serious conversation. She smiles at times, and then buries her head to hide the small grin, followed by shaking her head no. She is fully animated, appearing unstressed and unfazed at the start of the trial today.

Today is the third anniversary of the day that Caylee Anthony was last seen alive. She was seen leaving with her mother, Casey Anthony, alive in the car and never seen again alive. The judge takes the bench. We do find a huge difference between what is being admitted into evidence in court, and what is on the internet. We read internet stories about Tony saying Casey was having nightmares and sweats after he returned from New York. Or Cindy saying to Tony at his front door, "You had better be rich, because she will take all your money." None of this is in evidence. Tony was on the stand, he did not say any of this. This is not evidence; this is the new media of the worldwide web. Although many things in the media and on the web have become evidence in court, and are correct, a tremendous number are not.

June 16th, 2011

The Defendant's First Witness

Interpretation of Testimony - Gerardo Bloise (recalled):
Mr. Bloise is a CSI from Orlando County and is recalled
to the stand by the defense. On Wednesday, July 23, 2008,
I was asked to inspect the vehicle of Anthony Lazzaro. I
did an inspection of the interior, exterior, and trunk. I
utilized an alternative light source to check for stains,
and it was negative for blood. The light source checks
for body fluid. Then I did a presumptive blood test, and
the results were negative. I photographed the interior
and exterior. I moved the Pontiac vehicle to the lift and
inspected under it. This was the Anthony car on the lift
and not for Mr. Lazzaro's vehicle. Mr. Lazzaro's vehicle
yielded no items of evidentiary value. On August 6th,
2008, I executed a search warrant at the Anthony home. I
was to check the bedroom that belongs to Casey and to
inspect the clothing with the alternative light source
and collect clothing from the area. We checked the living
room, garage and the cars. I did just a visual inspection
of George and Cindy Anthony's room. I went further in
Casey's room.

(Photos are being shown of Casey's bedroom and the
witness says that all photos appear fair and correct. The
prosecution has no objections to the photos. They are
admitted into evidence and published to the jury. It was
a single bed, a nice dresser, several pictures and the
closet is shown. Nice clothes, nice room for Casey.)

I was there to collect clothes from the closet and check
with light sources. My goal was to inspect with light and
if I found stains, I would collect the items. I just put
black covers on the windows to make the room dark and
then turned the light on the clothes to see if I saw
stains. I put the items in a paper bag and marked them
for evidence. Some pieces of clothing from other areas in
the room were also examined. I found the brown pants in
question and no stain was found. I was informed that she
was wearing those pants on June 15th, 2008, but I found
no stains on the pants. I inspected one piece at a time,
and I photographed stains as I saw them. When I see a
stain, I collect and submit it to the FBI for analysis.

Gerardo Bloise - Prosecution's cross-examination: Light
sources show small and medium stains. This is as detailed
as we can get in the photo image. I wore a lab jumpsuit,
gloves, foot covering, and a hair net. I do not speak
while I do it. I took the pictures in the lab by myself.

I collected the items in Casey's room, with another CSI and Detective Melich in the room. Then, after I collected and photographed it at my lab, I prepared a letter to the Federal Bureau of Investigation and submitted the clothing with a property slip to the FBI. I sealed the evidence in a bag and placed my initials. The scope of the search warrant was to locate clothes of Casey. Cindy informed me she hah washed the brown pants we were interested in examining for stains. Mr. Lazzaro's car did not smell like a dead body.

Gerardo Bloise - Defense re-direct: I did not find a bag of garbage in Mr. Lazzaro's car that had been in there for three weeks.

The Defendant's Second Witness

Interpretation of Testimony - Witness Heather Seubert: I am the Unit Chief of the Firearms Department of the FBI. In 2008, I was one of the FBI supervisors at the FBI's DNA unit. There are three sections, the mitochondrial DNA typing, nuclear unit for biological fluid and National DNA processing unit. The national DNA unit does not receive evidence, but manages the data to match with known samples. I have BS in Forensic Science from Michigan State University. I am enrolled in Florida for a Master's program. I started as a biologist in 1998 with the FBI and have had specialized training. Serology is the science of identifying body fluids. I belong to many organizations. I have testified in DNA and serology eighteen times in different jurisdictions. (She is admitted as an expert and the prosecution has no objection.) I was assigned the Casey Anthony case when it arrived at the FBI lab. I have the October 8th, 2008 report in front of me. There is a process at the FBI in assigning, and it helps to identify where an item was collected from. An item of evidence from a crime scene is listed as a Q, and my buccal swab would be listed as a K. I received items from the Pontiac Sunbird. I received it in the lab under a cover of communication that describes the items and the crime scene.

(Objection from the prosecution, they want to know whether the evidence Baez is questioning about… is in evidence.) There is a sidebar. The sidebar ended with the judge excusing the jury from the courtroom for a legal fight. We are all wondering if Mr. Baez is going to jump horses in the middle of his defense. The first witness fell flat for Mr. Baez. If anything, we think the testimony helped the prosecution. Their cross-examination was excellent. It took Baez about forty-five minutes to question and the prosecutor two minutes to destroy his work. In addition, when the prosecutor said, "Were you told by Cindy that she had washed the brown pants?" Baez did not object. Therefore, when Mr. Bloise responded that he had been told that the pants were washed before the examination for stains, it made it in before the jury and wiped out the defense's argument. You cannot miss a chance in this sword fight; the blade is sharp.

Heather Seubert (Testimony resumes): I was given items from the spare tire cover of the Pontiac. (Witness identifies the cans of spare tire covering cuttings for Mr. Baez. Baez just moved the prosecutions cans of air in for this witness to identify. That is shocking, after all the fighting to keep the cans out of evidence!) They were looked at independently, examined in the laboratory, and then tests were performed in the laboratory by a biologist of the FBI unit. It will detect possible blood with phenolphthalein. The test for blood was negative. Also another piece of spare tire cover was tested for blood. The label on this evidence is correct. It would have been opened and then resealed, then the next item opened, and there were brown and yellowish stains. They were tested using a swab and distilled water. The chemical test was performed, and all where negative for the blood. It is a particular type of cardboard backing and carpet. The left side of the carpet liner was tested, it was dark gray with multiple color fabric. It was negative for blood. The next item is on the right side and it was tested for many brown and yellow stains. All stains were negative for blood. The swab is not retained after testing.

I also tested all the items next by taking a swab for DNA typing, and no profile was generated from the items. This is the next test for different types of cell material. You can get DNA from anything that has a nucleus, not from red blood cells. I also received clothing from the Anthony home, Casey's closet. I checked them with a visible test; there were no stains and therefore no testing was done. There was another pair of slacks that had stains on the visional test, and chemical tests were negative. The skirt tested for blood was negative. Another skirt had red spots but was also negative for blood. Another shirt had stains and was tested for blood, it was also negative. A beige shirt was negative for blood. Another shirt, pink, had no stains, so no testing; and the shirt that was pink with a collar, had no stains, and no testing. A green shirt was examined – again no stains and no testing. There was no blood from the items received from the home.

The two spare tire covers had stains, but were negative for the presence of blood. The next thing was DNA testing on the spare tire covers. A swab was taken of the two items, on separate areas and the results for DNA were negative on both. In my report of October 9th, 2008, I examined a shovel and a label from the shovel blade. It was examined visually, and it was tested for blood and was negative. DNA was not generated and a sex typing was generated but it did not meet the minimum for reporting in my laboratory. When you touch something - DNA - you expect to have very little DNA such as a piece of paper you hold for a minute, you may leave some. It depends on a lot of factors whether we can get a DNA profile. Levels of DNA are measured in RFUs - Relevant Florescent Units. (Baez is having a moving microphone pinned to his coat, so he can roam around for the jury, witnesses and camera.)

A low copy number DNA is a type of DNA process when we know there is going to be a limited amount. We can make more copies of the DNA to enhance the DNA process. Yes, to make copies, and there are certain evaluations that account for this. The low copy number DNA process occurs when a swab is put into a tube and there are chemicals added that break open the cells and get to the nucleus. We subtract it from the sample, and then we mark thirteen locations and make multiple copies of the DNA to be tested. The DNA is put into a capillary column and we can then detect the smallest level. It is sent through the computer, then it passes through a laser, and you get a result similar to the heart EKG test graph at your doctor's office. The peaks are markers. They are viewed, and we have cut off levels for typing, which is 200 RFU. Above that, we would make a match and below we would not make a match in our laboratory. That was based on the instrument and the kit. Other laboratories will have different threshold levels. Fewer than 200 can be used to exclude a person; it is a conservative threshold. The lab sets 50 as the peaks for identifying, based on the scientific thresholds. It says something is there and unless it is 200, it has limited value that we can report. We can report sex and the like from the peak starting at 50, but not a profile match. (Sidebar, and the jury has been excused again while the legal fight continues.) The judge says, we are going to proffer the witness now.

Heather Seubert Defense Proffer Testimony: The analog peak that was derived from the shovel was an X, for female, at 55 RFU. I cannot draw any conclusions from this limited result. (The prosecution objects and defense wants her to say there is something there. To what end?

306

Is defense counsel going to say later that this DNA could have been amplified, and the FBI did not do it? We suspect the defense will later argue this without any scientific evidence, or argue that the absence of proof is reasonable doubt.) Considering it is 55, which is over 50, and then there is a peak of potential that could be either male or female, there was no conclusion. I can draw no conclusion from this evidence. (The judge is going to let it in, and the prosecution can cross-examine her on this item. Proffer ends, and the jury returns.)

Heather Seubert - Defense Testimony (cont): I saw something that was above the 50 level and it did not reach the 200 level. The best way to summarize this peak is a result was not obtained at any level. For the sex typing, there is evidence there but it does not meet reporting criteria. (Baez is going toward the lack of evidence for reasonable doubt now.)

My March 19th, 2009 report stated these items were reported. Duct tape from the medical examiner's office. There were three pieces of duct tape. The first exam was on the silver side and it was swabbed with a wet swab for biological material. I have a description of the duct tape, and it had Henkel written throughout the tape. I got DNA typing from the tape, but it was below the threshold of the reporting policy. The top side sample was obtained at six of the nine locations that were tested. There are two typing tests for DNA. They are very different on individuals, 22 markers from the mother and 23 from the father. Nine markers are tested with one kit, and six are in the other. This is the profiler location kit. You do not need all fifteen to have a profile; thirteen markers are enough. As it relates to the duct tape, a typing was obtained, but there was not enough for reporting thresholds. It could take only one marker to exclude. All of the Anthony's were excluded from this tape sample profile. We checked our DNA sample of employees, and it did not match our staff. I knew it was a female, so I checked other examiners from other units. It turned out to be Lorrie's, a documents examiner from the unit. Hers was the profile. Obviously, a mistake was made. Her DNA should not have been on the sample. It was a small deposit of Lorrie's DNA. I would expect to see another profile with her profile merged in with this profile, if it was there. If the presence of a large amount were deposited on an item and a small amount had been on an item, it could override it.

We were the last unit to handle this evidence. It would have not been altered in any way when we tested it. The fewer people who handle it, the less likely it is to be contaminated, but it did not change my work. It was necessary to go through many units, for many tests to be completed. It was collected from the outdoors, in a swamp area, with sunlight and humidity. Other things can influence the amount of DNA on an item. Because this was left on the victim, we wanted to try to get DNA. It is possible to get DNA from something under water, but it depends on how long it was submerged, the type of DNA, and the amount of the original DNA left. I do not have all of an item's history before it arrives at the lab. It depends, but if there is some identifying visible stain, I expect to get a profile. (Sidebar)

I would expect to get a higher chance of a profile of the victim, from the inside of the tape. Just the contact from the tape being placed and it's like pulling a bandage off, it hurts and DNA from skin cells remains on the tape. The information that was generated was inconclusive. There was a peak of 17 at the D3 marker. At D3, Casey is a 14 and so is Caylee, a 14. On July 24th, 2009, I received an item, a pair of shorts from the medical examiner's office. I examined them for blood or semen. The results on the shorts were negative. Another item was identified as clothing with letter stitching and was a stretch material. There was no blood on that item, I did the chemical test for the possible presence of blood. It was DNA typed, but there was no DNA.

The blanket was the next item. It was chemically tested for the possibility of blood. There was no DNA profile. The item was looked at for semen; there was no semen. The laundry bag was the next item, it was positive for the possible presence of blood, but there was no DNA. A second blanket is removed from evidence; the blanket did have possible blood, but no semen results. (It was moved out of evidence by both the prosecution and the defense in agreement of no relevance to this case.) A doll was the next item. It was from a vehicle, the Pontiac Sunbird, and it was located in the car seat that was in the back passenger area. It was swabbed for blood, and there was no blood. On December 16th, 2008, my report states that I was given the profiles of Cindy, George and Lee Anthony.

Baez asked if she was requested to do a DNA paternity test of Caylee for Lee being the father. (Baez slipped this in.) (Objection is sustained, and the jury is sent out for lunch recess.) The prosecution argues that there is no good faith basis for that question. Mr. Baez knows that the FBI laboratory does not and did not do such a test; Mr. Baez found that out in depositions. The judge requires voir dire of the witness.)

Baez: Were you ever asked by the State to run a paternity test, or the Orange County Sheriff Office? Witness: On September 12th, I told them I could run samples and send it to the laboratory and if Lee was potentially the father, they could send it out to a lab who does this testing. The judge steps in. Judge: You are not to ask questions that lead to *inferences for the jury without proper evidence*! You can call a law enforcement officer to answer if he had a question about the paternity. Please read those cases about **good faith questioning** that I gave you. The court reporter is to mark the question for me to review, and I will rule on a motion to strike and a jury warning after lunch. (There is a lunch break for courtroom personnel.)

This is where the media comes in. The media implied that Lee was the father and we think they implied George was the father as well, since Casey appears not to have known which boyfriend flavor of the week got her pregnant. The press was so bad that Lee and George submitted their DNA to a non-FBI lab to prove that neither was the father. This is Baez being dirty. They do not want to have to put their client on the stand. She is the only person who will testify to her imaginary defense that this all originated in abuse. Casey had a good life, free food, rent and childcare. She is a disgrace to all abuse victims. According to the psychiatrists that have been in the media, she does not show the signs of abuse, and if she were abused, the abuse would need to be massive… even get to have some kind of a defense for killing her child. There is no evidence of sexual abuse, if any abuse of any kind existed.

Judge Perry seems to be bending over backwards for Baez. The judge should have already fined him for these sleazy stunts. He puts out inferences, with no evidence to back it up. This is not clever legal work. It is sleazy. If I were the judge, Baez would have to deal with a bar complaint after this case, regardless of the verdict. The man is tainting and confusing the jurors with non-evidence inferences. We are not happy with Judge Perry right now. We want him to stop worrying so much about the record for appeal. We have all seen this kind of lawyer in the legal community; they are a disgrace. They are the reason that people have such a low opinion of lawyers, in our opinion.

Baez is scoring some points, but is losing this shadow jury. The official jury was taking notes this morning, and then closed their notebooks when the DNA became too technical. This is going to cause a strong rebuttal case to be presented. More people will be hurt, like Lee Anthony who just wanted to find his missing niece, who he loved. Now remember we have an in-home defense lawyer, who questions a lot of what Baez is doing, but also knows the fight to try and save a defendant's life. Still he finds many of Baez's behaviors unprofessional at best, and often ineffective as well. Of course, the lawyer found Baez's constant pre-trial media interviews appalling. Baez caused a great deal of the media hype himself, in these authors' opinions.

The conversations are interesting in the writers' lair, to say the least. That is among the many reasons we chose to write this book. With our ability to hear the perspective of a defense lawyer in the home and us valuing children more than the air we breathe, we could not forgo writing this story.

(Lunch recess is over.) Casey is all smiles after lunch. She moves into Baez's chair next to Mason when Baez is at the podium. As soon as the jury comes in, her demeanor changes. Nothing about the woman shows sincere grief over losing a child; she appears only to be acting. We have seen the devastation that stays forever in the eyes of a woman who has lost a child. Did we mention that three years ago today, June 16th, 2008, based on the opening arguments of the defense in this case, *Caylee died*? Baez has said that Casey was there when her daughter died. Shortly thereafter, Caylee's body was discarded like trash or garbage, words they have debated in this murder trial.

Interpretation of Testimony - Heather Seubert (Direct examination cont.): Based on the STR typing… Lee Anthony is **not** the father of Caylee Anthony.

(This is just another sideshow to distract the jury from the real issues, but maybe they will pull it off and Casey Anthony will walk. It has happened before, as we all know.)

(The photo of the car seat is now presented to the witness.) I did testing, no blood. The steering wheel cover from the Pontiac Sunbird is presented. Through the visual examination, no stains were found and therefore no chemical tests were done. These are the packages for the car debris and swabs for the spare tire wheel. We began with swabbing the spare tire cover with phenolphthalein. Phenolphthalein reacts to the cells of the blood by changing color. DNA is normally found in healthy blood, so when the body decomposes you lose the cells for DNA. If the blood cells have decomposed, you are much less likely to get a result. As to the stain being from decomposition of the human body, I cannot speak to whether there was decomposition, because it was not possible to tell.

The stain could still be from decomposition. I will just say it was not blood. When cells decompose, the DNA is going to diminished and loses the information that allows analysis. With decomposing cells, the likelihood of getting DNA as the body begins to decompose demises. Fifty is what is referred to as the minimum for any peak of a DNA test. Fifty RFU is when the computer shows a peak of any kind in a DNA test. We do not evaluate until the peak is at least two hundred. A peak at fifty-five, a sole peak, is inconclusive, and I cannot give any information on what that means. That same sample would not mean anything, even if it were enhanced. The duct tape was an RFU of seventeen, well below the threshold that provides results and there was other contact with the tape in our lab. (Sidebar)

During the sidebar, the judge, defense, and prosecution are all huddled over the court reporter's computer, looking at testimony. George, in the gallery, he has a notebook with a picture from a missing children's pin of Caylee. It is hidden in his lap, where the jury cannot see it. While Casey shows no sign of the pain of losing her child on this, the anniversary of her child going missing, and according to Casey the day she died, Caylee's grandparents do show emotion. We are beginning to understand more about these grandparents. Like all of us who are parents, they are not perfect. However, it is clear to us that this is not, we repeat, not an abusive family. Cindy is the ruling force in the family, and we are sure she could be the disciplinarian. She also appears to have pampered Casey until Caylee came for her to pamper, then Casey took a back seat. This is the order of things when a grandchild is born. We believe Cindy excused Casey's behavior for years. George, on the other hand, could not criticize Casey without being faced with Cindy's wrath. They have all been manipulated and abused by Casey for years, in our opinion. We believe Caylee was the last of Casey's victims in this family, one way or the other. Well, maybe not. She, through her lawyers, took a good last shot at the entire family in this trial. (Sidebar is over and back to the trial.)

Interpretation of Testimony - Heather Seubert (Direct examination cont.): Baez is clarifying the D3 marker with the witness. It had an RFU of seventeen, and was on the sticky side of the duct tape. I then compared it to all known samples of DNA; the top had six markers and only

311

one peak. I looked at known samples Caylee, Casey, Cindy, and Lee, as well as known samples from our staff. I did not draw any conclusions in that report. It does not meet a threshold for reporting. One had a sixteen-seventeen at that marker. Only seventeen was at the peak of the sample from the duct tape. People can have one or two peaks. The lab person had two peaks at 16 and 17, and we had only one peak from the tape. This is an inconclusive peak, and at those low thresholds, it is not possible to tell what might have resulted in the next level. At the D3 marker, 14-15 is Caylee and Casey is 16-19. Ms. Casey Anthony has no peak at seventeen at D3. If someone is killed by a method of non-bloodshed, this means nothing.

I was not involved in the discussions for the order of the examinations of the evidence in our laboratory. If DNA survived, I thought it would be on the sticky side of the tape that was stuck to the face. I did not have any expectation of getting DNA, after the tape was exposed to this environment for six months. It was described as an area with water coming in, and a swamp-type area. The probability of there being cells would quickly start to diminish and degrade for all items of the clothes and tape. The FBI does not do paternity tests. In the samples that were tested for the identity, there was a toothbrush known to be Caylee's, and a tibia bone that was used to get a DNA sample of the remains. I compared it to Casey and Lee. Lee Anthony **could not** be the father of Caylee.

I can only tell you the samples are not blood. From the outdoor scene, other than Caylee, the only DNA sample generated from the laboratory was from an employee of the lab during testing. If you are trying to get identification, then you can use the bone to get a sample. As the body decomposes, the other items with body fluids diminish, and all of the factors of environment make a difference in how long I can get a sample. If the body decomposed in a trunk, and was placed there contained in a plastic bag with a hole, body fluids could possibly leak out. I am giving my opinion based on standard practices of our laboratory, and I cannot provide a conclusion on the peak below our standards. As I said, if the duct tape was placed around someone's mouth, if there was DNA in the area, there would more likely be DNA on the sticky side, if DNA was ever there. When body fluid is spilled on a surface, the fluid continues to decompose.

(As mad as the judge was making us bending over for Baez, it could be that the judge is giving him enough rope to hang himself. However, will Baez have tainted the jury with inferences before he succumbs? Baez has wiped out any of the points he had scored today with us. The in-house lawyer says Baez is required to defend his client zealously. We think the best defense might have been a plea deal. Casey would have been too self-centered to take a deal, is our thought. Therefore, Baez is doing whatever he can to represent his client, zealously. We are not sure that he realizes that zealous representation should also be effective representation within the boundaries of the law and ethics. At this point in the trial, the presumption of innocence is fading fast under the weight of this evidence, at least for the writers. He has helped us reach that point.)

The Defendant's Third Witness

Interpretation of Testimony - Robin Maynard (recalled): I am the founder and executive manager of a breast cancer foundation. I was a CSI investigator at the Caylee Anthony remains site. Yes, I can identify this; it is a cardboard mat with a heart. A photo of it is also shown. I was in charge of the sifting station at the remains. Buckets come to the station, I would record the lane, bucket identification number, and how many feet away from the baseline of the skull it was located. This was lane six and it was 45 feet west of the baseline. It is published in evidence with the map of the area, not to scale. These were the bones that were found in sifting, and we cannot be more specific than that. Thirteen bones were found in sifting and there was a bone found on lane six, as well as this cardboard and heart. (Witness excused. Looks like Baez did not know the answer to the question before he asked.)

The Defendant's Fourth Witness

Interpretation of Testimony – Ronald Murdock (recalled): I work for Orange County Sherriff as a supervisor in the forensic unit. I have my mapping system of the remains site with me. From Area A where the skull was found, the heart sticker was found approximately thirty feet away. (Witness excused.)

Well, Baez moved the heart fifteen feet closer to the skull with this witness and the crime scene mapping. That doesn't seem to be a good thing for the defense, at all!

The Defendant's Fifth Witness

Interpretation of Testimony - Jennifer Welch (recalled): I am a CSI with the Orange County Sheriff's Office. (Exhibits are admitted by stipulations of the defense and prosecution.) I was in charge of documenting the scene of

313

Caylee's remains. Some items were trash and many were collected. I am familiar with the scene. I am viewing a paper copy of the mapping, and it appears that there were no bones collected past the forty-five mark of lane six. I did not find these items; they were found through sifting, and through general clean-up of the area and vegetation. These are more of the same kind of items, they were not sent for testing, and they are miscellaneous items from lane four and items in lane one, such as beer bottles and cans. Miscellaneous items were found in lane three and I do not recall these items being sent for testing. They were items like a tripod from near a wooden fence. It is fair to describe the area where Caylee Anthony's remains were found as a trash dump. (Witness is excused)

The Defendant's Sixth Witness

Interpretation of Testimony - Lorie Gottesman: I am with the FBI, the laboratory division. I am a supervisory document examiner. I have been with the FBI since 1992. I have a BA and MS from San Diego, California. I compare questioned items with known items. I have taken many courses, classes, testing and oral boards. I have worked under other document examiners, in training, before I moved into the area. I have been admitted as an expert more than 20 times, in state and federal courts. (The witness is accepted as an expert.) An item does not have to be on paper for me to examine it. An item would be in different subject areas, such as writing on a wall or a package that needs to be put back together. I work with many tools and machines in my work; lights, filters, computers and more. I have my report from December 2008, in this case. I received three pieces of duct tape. I understood that they came from the victim through correspondence from the medical examiner's office.

I was looking to determine if I could find a heart-shaped sticky residue. I used the Video Spectral Comparator, the VSC, which uses lights and a filter, and allows us to see things that we cannot normally see. It takes us into the infrared spectrum and more. I was unable to see any sticker residues, fragments or remnants, and so I went on to the VSC and tried all the light wavelengths and filters. I could not see any remains of a sticker on the duct tape. After I conducted my examination, I was asked to submit a DNA sample. The DNA lab had an unknown sample and it was not from their unit. It turned out to be my DNA on the sample, and I have no idea how or when it happened. I did not sneeze on it. They were in plastic and I exercised great care. I do not know how it happened.

314

Lorie Gottesman – State's Cross-examination: Based on my report of April 2nd, 2009, I was given a number of pieces of plastic and I was to give an overall assessment and compare some of the pieces of plastic to others. Some I eliminated from the others and with some, my findings were inconclusive. I received the tape after the print unit had already examined it. I viewed the item then continued to process with chemicals. They had seen something and went back to photograph it, but could not find anything after the chemicals had been put on the tape. I attempted to locate it again under VSC lights to be photographed, but it could no longer be found after the chemicals had been put on the tape. There are machine impressions on bags and some of these bags. I can't say whether there was a match, some maybe or maybe not. (Witness is excused)

The Defendant's Seventh Witness

Interpretation of Testimony – Cary Oien: I am the current Section Chief of the laboratory. I have been with the FBI fifteen years in Biology and Entomology. I do hair and fiber examinations. (She is accepted as a hair and fiber expert.) I was managing all of the departments in 2008. I did an examination on this case. On September 12th, 2008, I received the sample. I conducted the analysis. The item was a shovel. I did a mineral test that was requested, there was hair on the stickers, a hair, and a fiber test was done. On one of the stickers, I found a small hair, Caucasian. I could not do any more tests on the hair fragment and sent it to mitochondrial DNA. We have quality assurance in each department and laboratory and then we have additional quality control supervision from the FBI's quality control department, we are accredited. I found a quarter of a hair in the sticker. I do not know where it came from, who it was from, or how the hair got there. (Sidebar) (Witness is excused)

The writers spoke this morning concerning this. Why would the grandparents of a child, a single mother parent, living at home, not have contact information on the caretaker of their grandchild? Wouldn't Cindy want to be able to talk to her granddaughter on the telephone while Casey was at work and Caylee was in someone else's care? Our final thoughts are this; it all comes back to Caylee becoming of age to communicate, on her own. Cindy would have been asking to talk to Caylee on the telephone more and more frequently, because Caylee was becoming verbal. Casey would have been under more stress to hide her unemployment. The lies were catching up. Cindy said the opportunity never came up to pick up Caylee from the nanny. We do not know if she ever called and got a disconnected number, confronted Casey, or was told something like Zanny moved.

For two years, Casey had been lying and stealing, probably from her parents and everyone else, to support her daily outings, which required money for gas, partying, shopping, and food while she was out with Caylee all day and many evenings. The Anthony's had dismissed the initial signs of trouble because of love, hope, and denial. Then the bank records started showing thefts and as Caylee started communicating with people more, the walls began to close in on Casey. However, we think to some degree, the blind eye of denial, that had been turned to Casey's behavior by her parents, was opening, and it would fully open with Caylee becoming communicative. They did not act fast enough to see the danger Caylee was in, at the hands of her mother. Hindsight is 20/20. This is no longer a case of who did it to your writers, but why. We believe Casey Anthony is responsible for the death of Caylee Anthony. At this point, short of a miracle by the defense combined with a tired and confused jury, we expect the evidence has proven her guilt, of some degree of homicide, beyond a reasonable doubt.

June 17th, 2011

Court is in session. Baez announces, Your Honor, Dr. Huntington is our next witness, and he is a diabetic and needs to check his blood level. I expect him to be on the stand about a half hour. The judge says to let him know when the witness needs a recess.

The Defendant's Eighth Witness

Interpretation of Testimony - Timothy Huntington, PhD: I am an Assistant Professor of Biology at Concordia University Nebraska in Seward, Nebraska, and a professional, board-certified entomologist. I have consulted in police investigations since 2002. I have a BS in Biology, a Master's Degree in Entomology, and a PhD in Entomology, all from the University of Nebraska. Forensic entomology was my PhD topic. I am a member of the American Board of Forensic Entomology, American Academy of Forensic Sciences, Entomological Society of America, North American Forensic Entomology Association, and Nebraska Chapter of the International Association for Identification. I have done several papers and book chapters on entomology. I have conducted studies on decomposition forensics, consulted with law enforcement,

316

and I am a reserve deputy sheriff. There are no awards in forensic entomology. I have testified for law enforcement and the prosecution sixty-five times.

I sometimes go to the scene, because it's better to go look and collect my own evidence, but sometimes the samples are sent to me for testing. I have lectured and I am an adjunct professor. I am a diplomat of the American Board of Forensic Entomology, and you must submit papers and take an exam to become a diplomat. There are fifteen members of American Board of Forensic Entomology. (Sidebar)

The authors see it coming. Baez will use this witness in an attempt to cancel Dr. Haskell's testimony. He has very good credentials and we know he withstood cross in the deposition via Skype. Yes, Skype has now entered the legal arena with Facebook and Twitter. Baez wants to cast doubt on the testimony that a body was in the back of the car. (Dr. Huntington is accepted as an expert.)

(Testimony resumes)I received a call from Linda Kenney Baden (a defense lawyer on the Baez team) and I flew down to Florida. The items I received were the Entomology Report from Dr. Haskell, evidence, and samples. I viewed the car and received a box of insect material. Dr. Haskell received sweepings from the trunk and I have not been given an opportunity to review them. The field of forensic entomology deals with estimation of the time of death, when a period of time has passed between the death and the discovery of remains. During the postmortem period, insects discover the human remains.

(We will not go through another explanation of insects in this book; we wait for Dr. Huntington to say Dr. Haskell is wrong. Baez has to lay the foundation for this evidence; however, we are sure the jury is as bored as we are. We will wait for his conclusion that Dr. Haskell was wrong. Baez seems to have abandoned the defense he promised in opening arguments; he is now utilizing the standard attack of the prosecution's evidence, for possible reasonable doubt.)

(Testimony continues) I became involved in this case **on December 11th, 2008, because Linda Kenny-Baden called me and she said there was**…

Baez stops his own witness from saying anything else. The defense contacted this expert on December 11th, 2008. This was the day of the remains discovery, and seven days before the body was identified as Caylee! To us, the only way the defense could have known that this was Caylee's body, would have been if *Casey told them it was Caylee's body... when she heard of the discovery of the remains*!

Dr. Huntington then flew to Florida on December 13th, 2008, five days before the Medical Examiner, Dr. G, announced that the next of kin (Casey Anthony was in jail) had been notified and that the remains found on December 11th, 2008, were in fact Caylee Anthony.

The prosecution has a video of Casey in jail on the day she heard the about the discovery of the remains. They could not put it in evidence, unless Baez opened the door and he just opened it wide, we think. The attorney-client video will not be admissible, because there is an **attorney-client privilege**. The attorney client relationship is a private and confidential one. (There is a sidebar. Now, the jury is out for a proffer of the witness's testimony.)

Timothy Huntington, PhD - Proffer: It appears Dr. Haskell believes it might have been possible for him to make a postmortem interval estimation of the date of death. If you assume the maggots are from the trunk's trash, you might be able to identify the time the body had been there. Then if you make that assumption, you could tell... (Objection) Prosecution: I will withdraw the question, and I have no more questions. Prosecution: Since I know the defense is talking about the car, we can resume his testimony in front of the jury. (Court stands in recess.)

The jury spent a good deal of Friday morning out of courtroom while attorneys argued over whether Huntington could testify about a stain in Casey's car, comparing it to his test on a dead pig. Judge Perry ruled the witness could testify about stains and decomposition fluids, in general, but since Huntington did not examine the stain in the Sunfire, he could not give his opinion on that, since it was also absent from his previous deposition testimony.

Well, we the shadow jurors know what our last line of closing argument would be. "On December 11th, 2008, when neither you, nor I, nor the rest of the world knew that the remains found on Suburban Drive were those of Caylee Anthony, it seems the entomologist Dr. Huntington had ESP in Nebraska." Our house lawyer thinks this would certainly lead to a mistrial, since it is an indirect comment on the defendant's right to remain silent and an invasion of the attorney-client privilege. However, the only person who could have known and we believe told the defense lawyers that the remains were those of Caylee's, was Casey Anthony.

A news conference has just started on the steps of the Orange County Courthouse during this recess. Attorney Matt Morgan of Morgan and Morgan, who represents the "defense claimed witness," Vasco Thompson, held a news conference. Vasco Thompson is going to tell us what his involvement was in this case, which is nothing. Vasco "I do not have any idea who George Anthony is; I just saw him on TV." This phone number became my number in February of 2009. Morgan and Morgan attorney Matt Morgan says, we believe the defense thought that they found a golden ticket. Just to clear this up, the kidnapping that Mr. Thompson was convicted of, that has been played out in the media, was a five-minute domestic dispute. Mr. Thompson and the girlfriend involved are still friends today. He did not have the money for representation, and he was sentenced to a long prison term. He is married to a teacher and is a church-going man. He has paid his debt to society, and this is causing a great disturbance in his life.

Timothy Huntington, PhD – (Defense Testimony resumes): (Dr. Huntington is back on the stand before the jury.) He explains that maggots are larvae – specifically, they are baby flies. Their first focus is to eat, and they will crawl anywhere from ten to sixty feet to find food. According to my findings, Caylee could not have died in the woods where her remains were eventually found. If she had died there, I would have found dead blowflies, which are the first insects to flock to a decomposing human body. It all has to do with the temperature where the remains were. If I knew the stage, rate of development, and temperature, I might be able to tell. I also conducted another test, in which I put the body of a dead pig in the trunk of another car, and monitored its decomposition.

Timothy Huntington, PhD – State's cross-examination: Huntington admits to prosecutor Jeff Ashton that wherever Caylee did die would smell of decomposition, supporting several State's witnesses' claims that the trunk of Casey's Pontiac Sunfire, smelled like death. The State then tries to poke holes in the doctor's pig decomposition study, noting key differences between the study's protocol and Caylee's remains. "Why didn't you wrap your pigs in a blanket?" asks Ashton, drawing laughter from the gallery, the witness, and even Casey. Huntington says that the study was for his broader research, and not specifically designed to mimic the conditions of Caylee Anthony's death. Ashton's other questions are not as light-hearted. He aggressively grills Huntington, and even gets him to back up two key points of the prosecution's case. Huntington admits that the car still smelled when he examined it two years after Caylee's death. He initially says it could have been from trash bags Casey left in the trunk, but later admits that there were very few food products in the trash. He also says the bug evidence from the woods suggests that Caylee had probably been dead for just two to three days, before her body was placed there. Huntington admits that he received his doctorate in 2008, the same year Caylee died, and Friday marked the first time he was ever asked in a court of law, to testify about a photograph of a stain.

Timothy Huntington, PhD - Defense re-direct: Baez quickly fires back and gets the witness to say, I am the youngest certified forensic entomologist in the country. Although I have never before been asked about stains in a court of law, it is common in my field to review photos related to decomposition when samples cannot be produced. (The witness is released. Court is in recess until tomorrow.)

Casey seems at times to be almost flirtatious with her attorneys. It appears that she is playing ringmaster of her circus. She laughed when the pig in the blanket statement was made, and then hid her face from the jury. It was a few seconds late; at least, we saw it. Casey still shows no signs of pain or remorse for Caylee. That remark was funny, except to the mother of a child who died in a trunk, if she had any remorse or pain at the loss of Caylee.

We close this day with this, another physical fight outside the courthouse this morning to get a seat in the courtroom. Media and spectators accost the attorneys each time they leave the courtroom. EBay has now joined the Casey Anthony frenzy by selling a used ticket for a seat in the courtroom, item number 180682802211. Currently there are five bids, and it stands at twenty-five dollars, with one day and twenty hours to go. This is the new world of American justice. On Monday, the Orange County Courthouse is restructuring how people can get into this trial.

June 18th, 2011

The Defendant's Ninth Witness

Interpretation of Testimony - William Rodriguez, PhD: I am here as an unpaid consultant. (Objection) I have been a Forensic Consultant and Medical Examiner for 23 years and I work for the US government. I have a BA, MA, and PhD from Knoxville, which I received in 1985, as a

Forensic Anthropologist. (He got on that stand and said he was testifying unpaid before being asked and the judge has already told him just to answer the questions.) I am a co-founder of the body farm. It was Dr. Vass's idea to make the study, and we discussed how we could get a better understanding. He suggested it and recruited me into this project. I put up fences, helped lay concrete, and brought in the first bodies. I have extensive experience in decomposing bodies, in a subtropical climate. In twenty-three years with the government, I have traveled all over the world.

Taphonomy is the breakdown of an organism after death. I had two publications from body farm and others. I have given numerous papers on cases involving decomposing bodies. The roots of entomology began in Europe. It became more prevalent in the US with the body farm. I have extensive experience. I have been admitted on the topic more than one hundred times. Taphonomy and entomology... (Objection. The prosecution objects because the witness has never been accepted as an expert in entomology and anthropology. They want more about his experience in entomology.) My primary work early on at the body farm was insects. I have worked extensively with entomologists. I have worked hundreds of cases for police. (He is accepted in all areas by the judge.)

In this case, I received the doctor's records, records from the Medical Examiner's Office and the reports of the anthropologist, the entomologist report and photos of the recovery scene. I examined photos of the skull at the Medical Examiner's Office.

The collection at the scene appeared very thorough. At the scene, with a child's remains, it is difficult to find the multiple of bones in a wooded environment; it was a fairly good recovery job. However, the problem is that I did not see them attempt to locate where the body had been originally placed. The bones may be spread out. However, it is very important to find the exact area the body was placed before being spread by the animals. We would look for trace evidence at that location. We would locate it and leave that area marked at the scene. The investigators should... (Objection) (Sidebar The prosecution wants to voir dire the witness outside the jury's presence.)

William Rodriguez, PhD - State's voir dire: What would you look for to discover the original body site? We would look for soil stains, killed plant growth and insects dead on the soil along with environmental changes. I did not see any photos of the soil changes in the reports. I have a lot of experience with duct tape. I have looked at numerous cases where duct tape or other tape was employed. When the body still has soft tissue, we look for the position of the tape. When they are at mummification, we can still identify that location. In skeletal remains, because of decomposition, the adherence of the tape will be affected. (Sidebar)

It is testy in the courtroom. All we have gotten so far is that he is critical and he was made aware of the work that was done on recovering the remains. He has no firsthand knowledge of the site. He has just read reports and viewed photos.

Ashton is accusing Baez of soliciting another opinion that he has not disclosed at sidebar. The defense does not follow the law on the rules of court. (Sidebar) The jury is out and the judge is not happy and neither is the prosecution. Ashton makes his objections: The opinion that is being offered by the witness is not in his report and he does not have a factual basis for that opinion. He says the word duct tape appears in this case and nothing else appears. Judge: Mr. Baez, pull out and read the Court's order.

The judge questions the witness. Dr. Rodriguez, what opinion were you about to express? The witness says the positioning of the duct tape as it was found was in two different positions. In a complete skeleton, one cannot make a finding as to the exact location on the body or the restriction of the body. The movement of the remains excludes anyone from making any estimate of where the duct tape was on the body, which can be determined only in a case of a burial or with soft tissue. When did I formulate that opinion? When I first received the pictures earlier this year, I formed that opinion, before my report of February 21st, 2011. Why is it not in the report? It was not an issue to me. I was not asked at that time about the duct tape. I noted it in my examination and told Mr. Baez about the tape in February of 2011. I was not informed that it was required to be put in a report. I was not made aware and Mr. Baez never informed me about that requirement. I got e-mails from Baez to the give a report. We met two nights ago, and at that time the determination was made that he wanted me to testify to the duct tape. It was to rebut the super-imposed slide of the duct tape. Doing the super-imposing is to identify the remains, but for duct tape, there is no way you can tell where it was located. The duct tape was most likely around the head is all that can be said.

Baez: This was all done and I told the expert about the duct tape exhibit, but the defense has been busy. We did not expect this opinion. Judge: So the doctor is mistaken when he says that he told you this in February 2011? Baez: Well I am not saying that. In an important case like this, they should have deposed him. If this is an issue that so concerns the State, then they should have taken his deposition. Judge: Mr. Baez, are you saying that you can pick which orders of the court you follow and which you do not? Both sides have game-played, and this is not a game. The reason that the order was entered… was because I did not want to be in this position. We have experts with major opinions that are not contained in their reports. The easy thing is, if an opinion comes about, you disclose it, even if it is at the last minute.

Judge: The exclusion of a witness is not to be done except in the most aggravated of circumstances. This it appears – this was an intentional failure to disclose this information to the court and the prosecution. The case law offers contempt and/or instruction to the jury concerning the violation. What other opinions is this witness going to give in testimony that are not in his report? This witness is stepping down, and you can take his deposition. He can testify next week. I will entertain a possible instruction to the jury on this violation, and I will decide whether to do it. I will retain the **contempt hearing** to the end of this trial. We were scheduled to talk about a violation of the rule of sequestration.

Baez: I said that he would rebut information. Judge: Mr. Baez, this is not my first rodeo! I have tried a few cases. They raised an issue that you couldn't rebut until they had done it. In a case I prosecuted, my investigator located four or five experts, and I filed a supplemental list and set depositions so there would be no surprises to the defense. All my order tried to do was to find out what experts would testify to, so we have no "got you" moments in this trial. We will take a ten-minute recess. Dr. Rodriguez, be prepared to give a deposition this afternoon and we will figure it out. Just remember, Mr. Baez, lighting does not strike twice! If there are other opinions you know he is going to give, they have to be laid out and if it doesn't happen that way, you do not want to know what I will do. I do not want Ms. Anthony suffering because of this. Court is in recess.

Much of being a lawyer is all about playing by the rule of law and following procedure, while still going to the line and sticking your toe over then pulling back in time. The term chosen for what just happened is sleazy. Justice does not work if the honor of truth between the lawyers and court is lost. This has been lost in the last twenty years, more than we can say. They are debating what to tell the jury. Mr. Mason said, "I will tell them." The Judge says okay, and then the prosecution can tell what they want them after you! Mr. Mason, okay, as long as I get to go last! The judge will tell them something about what happened. The jury is told that Dr. Rodriguez will be back on Monday and we will accommodate another witness from out town now. (Although that is true, we know it is not the whole story.)

The Defendant's Tenth Witness

Interpretation of Testimony - Werner Spitz, MD: I am Medical Doctor and a forensic pathologist. I went to medical school at the University of Geneva Switzerland from 1946-1950. I transferred to Hebrew University of Hadassah in Jerusalem, before it was the State of Israel, when it was Palestine (That is covering both bases with the jury - clever!). I graduated in 1953. I did a one-year internship at Hadassah, and my residency was in pathology and lasted for another five years. Pathology in a hospital is analyzing tissues and body fluid for disease; and when a person dies, that same doctor can perform an autopsy. This is for understanding the disease. Forensic pathology is to do an autopsy pursuant to the state law and does not need the next of kin's permission. It is also done in police cases where someone died and we do not know how.

In 1959, I came to the USA on a grant from the State of Maryland and worked for them. I was appointed. In 1969, I left America, and worked in Berlin on appointment. Then I returned to the USA, to the medical examiner's office. I was an associate professor at John Hopkins and the University of Maryland, and a Medical Examiner in Maryland. In 1972, I went to the Medical Examiner's Office of Wayne County in Michigan to become a Chief Medical Examiner. At the same time, I was a professor at Wayne State and in Winsor Canada. I am still associated with the University in Windsor, only in name, since I have not taught there in ten years.

I was Chief Medical Examiner for Macomb County in Michigan. Their medical examiner was not a pathologist, and they appointed me to do that work. Then he died and I became the Chief Medical Examiner. I have a fellowship in pathology and there are adjunct appointments. I was on the Board of the American Medical Examiners. I am no longer. I am a fellow of the Association of Forensic

Sciences. I am licensed to practice medicine in America, in Michigan, Virginia, DC, and Maryland, and most all of the European unions. Yes, I think I received awards from the Medical Examiners in 1972. I think so, I do not remember. I have received awards from law enforcement, local police, the FBI, and more because I give courses and consult in many police departments, they are not all listed, so you do not need to bother. I have consulted for the Rockefeller Commission when he was Vice President, and worked on the Kennedy shooting reconstruction of what occurred on the day the president was killed, I testified to the U.S House of Representatives on the MLK and JFK assassinations.

I have published various things. I wrote four books, the last in 2006, and many publications. I have published fourteen articles on the subject of drowning. I published ninety-six other articles. I have testified as a witness in the USA, in all fifty states and in foreign countries, the Middle East, Canada, and Europe. I have done work for the United Nations. I testify as an expert about thirty times a year in court. (He is admitted as an expert in Forensic Pathology.) I first became involved in the Casey Anthony case when I received a call, I think from the Baez Law Firm. I was asked to possibility consult on this case. I requested to attend the postmortem examination, the autopsy performed by Dr. G. (Sidebar) I wanted to attend the autopsy because it is useful to see the body at that time. There is an advantage to having four eyes instead of two, and the findings can be discussed. This is a custom that pathologists do, and we also send samples to other pathologists, to see if they concur with our findings. In a dead person, there is no life-saving reason, but what can be done is to make a reasonable determination of the cause of death. When the autopsy of Caylee Anthony was over I was given the body, and I conducted a second autopsy. I do not think Dr. G had completed her report at that time. I came here to Orlando, and I did not bring a saw. When I came and looked at the body, the profession dictates that there should be an examination of the interior of the head. That had not been done and it should have been, so I opened the skull and did it. (He shows the skull to the jury.) This is a skull, not the skull of Caylee, but an adult skull. (Objection) When the skull is removed, the top is sawed off. In autopsy, I took photographs of this. The skull is in evidence. This photo of Caylee's skull is what represents the base of the skull and the top is taken off by sawing. The spine is connected to this area, at the back. This is the right side and left.

(Photographs of Caylee's skull are shown to the jury.) What you see in this area, the left side, you see black flakes of material that result from the permanent end of decomposition. The brain, which filled this space, has dissolved. This is the dust that remains of the brain. It is less than an ounce, and some has been removed or lost. It could have been by altering, or it was lost. These flakes indicate the skull position over the period of decomposition. The brain has disappeared, and those elements sunk by gravity to this position. The position was with the left side of the skull down. Here, in the base of the skull the specks are localized in the left side, maybe with the face a little up. I reviewed the report of Dr. G. The problems I detected were little bones missing and only small parts at most. The entire skull was there, and Dr. G did not open it. There were things that could have been there, like some discoloration of the skull, in the ear area. There could have been some but there were no factures, no breaks. The skull was undamaged; there was some damage to some long bones on the legs, damage from animals. There was an area of the thighbone that had been opened by those who did the autopsy. They probably opened it to take marrow, for removing material. But I learned that this was not the case.

The cause of death is unknown, and for me to some extent as well, it is unknown. There was not a shred of soft tissue. The skeleton was in pristine condition and had been totally cleaned. I understand that there were some sections of duct tape on the lower part of the skull. The tape in the pictures shows it to be on the right side of the lower face, hanging on hair, roots and vegetation. In the report of Dr. G, the duct tape was clearly placed prior to decomposition and the tape became loose on the skeleton. The only thing that held the tape was roots and hair. There was nothing on the bone that would suggest that the tape was placed on the body. It was placed there to hold the jaw in place. I would have picked this up and the jaw would have dropped. The duct tape would have attached to the skull and would have held it by the hair and jaw. I would have expected DNA if the tape was attached to the face, there would have been some. I put duct tape on my arm and I when I removed it, pulled hair and skin, DNA. There is a firm connection between the tape and the skin. There is less decomposition where there is no air coming in.

It is my opinion that the duct tape was not put on the face before death. It is a later event and not an early event after disposal. Adipose is a stage in decomposition where the tissue breaks down and becomes slimy and smelling. It is like soap. The tissue is broken down to the consistency of wet soap. Adipose develops. (Sidebar) It develops under conditions in warm environments within ten to twelve days. We found no adipose. I reviewed all of Dr. G's reports, including toxicology reports. There is no evidence to the cause of death. You can rule out some things. You can rule out skull fractures or suicide. You cannot rule out accidental death. The manners of death are homicide, suicide, natural cases, or accidental. They are the only cause-of-death possibilities. The duct tape did not have anything to do with the killing; it was put on after decomposition. (This is a very well-credentialed man and he is giving Baez something.

Werner Spitz, MD - State's cross-examination: A medical-legal investigation in determining the manner of death requires more information. I was told about the first autopsy, I went to the scene and the house, the Anthony home. That is about it. To do a manner of death and legal autopsy you need to know the background. I asked for information, sufficient information. I asked Baez, I asked Mr. Mason and I think I spoke to the people in the home. I do not remember who they were. I read police reports. I do not know which ones. My understanding is there was some time lapse before the disappearance and a police report was made. The facts of the last time someone saw the person, and who if anyone the person was with, have to be evaluated. It all needs to fit together. I knew the circumstances of the last time Caylee Anthony was seen alive and was alleged to have been taken to the babysitter. I do not know if I had any information on when she was alive. I do not know what happened when she was alive. The State asks if Dr. G had the information when she made her decision in the report, whatever she wrote in the report. Doctor: I do not recall. Prosecution: It is common to summarize the investigation in the report. Doctor: Some do and some do not. I do not. It is essential to read the reports and police reports. I recall facts I consider important to form an opinion. Prosecution: What do you recall about when she was last seen alive? I thought that there was a pool in the yard, which creates a possibility of drowning. Prosecution: A month went by before the defendant informed the police the victim was missing. Doctor: I do not recall other facts. Those are the facts I found sufficient. The failure to open the skull was a violation of protocol in an autopsy. Especially when it is a child that is under examination in a case that made national news. The protocol is, the head is opened in any individual. This is for possible involvement in the brain or skull examination. The head is part of the body, and you examine the whole body. The body is a complete structure. There are all kinds of things that could be in a body. Prosecution: There are no publications that state that opening the skull is protocol, are there? Doctor: I have trained and I have trained pathologists, and I have been out of practice. When the head is not open, it tells me about a shoddy autopsy. It upsets my better knowledge. A skull is opened in a newly deceased to see the possibilities in the death. I would never have known how this head was positioned if it was not opened. Prosecution: There are protocols that are done on skeletons and non-skeletons. You do not open the chest on a skeleton, because you can see it. (The State gets the witness to acknowledge a book as a learned treatise, so he can use it to cross-examine) Doctor: I wrote most of the trauma chapters in that book. Dr. Haskell and Dr. Vass wrote parts. This is an authority used on the medico-legal determination of death. This is not a book on how to do an autopsy; it is how to read the results.

The chapter by Vass does not contain a protocol that the skull must be opened. It probably does not say the head needs to be opened; it talks about injuries and findings. (the prosecutor tries another book.) This is a United Nations document model protocol for disinterment and protocol for the human rights committee. This is written for and by the lawyers. I do not understand the document, the model protocol for the autopsy. (The doctor is reviewing this book.) I have never seen that part. Prosecution: When you said Dr. G was wrong, she was not violating protocol; did you mean that it is was just not your way of doing it? Doctor: No, I think in a national media case, one must be exceptionally thorough. Prosecution: You have said this was a high profile case twice, is this in important to you? Doctor: That is not the only reason you open the head, you open because it is part of the autopsy. I have given interviews in Tampa, one in Detroit, and a TV station out of Detroit this week. I gave it and it was broadcast all over. The Detroit paper learned I was coming down and called me. I think I did give another; there was not a lot in that interview. I do not remember what I talked about with the reporter. Prosecution: You did talk about facts in this case, on the Today Show and 48 Hours? I do not remember any of this. Prosecution: You like high-profile cases, and you were in the Phil Specter, O.J. Simpson, and other high profile cases. When you opened that skull, you broke it. Can you see a crack? Doctor (looks at skull photo) I did not know that I broke it. I did not do any chemical tests and I gave the substance to the defense to keep it for possible testing. Then I was told it was tested and found its way to the police and they tested it. I do not remember who told me that. Prosecution: You do not know if that is brain dust or dirt? This skull of Caylee Anthony is not the first decomposed skull that I have opened.

Prosecution: But without analyzing the substance, you do not know if it is brain dust or dirt. No, this is brain dust. Were you given the information that this area was underwater? Are you telling us that this could not be sediment from dirty water that infiltrated the skull as it sat underwater? Doctor: This sediment is so common in remains that have been subjected to intensive decomposition; it is almost as definitive as this lower jaw. I do not need more than that. Prosecution: You do not need to bother to have the sentiment tested by any biologist or a chemist? Until someone analyzes this, that is my opinion. I am aware that the medical examiner took salty water and put it in this hole and swished it around, and removed whatever came out. Prosecution: Are you sure that is not the reason there is not any on the right side? Doctor: I was asked to examine a buried skull and found that it had this same sediment and when checked it, it was full of drugs. Prosecution: You sent that sediment for chemical analysis? If I had been there with Dr. G, I would have told her to take this and send it to the laboratory for analysis. If you had it analyzed, we would not be discussing it either. I am not a laboratory.

Prosecution: Your theory is that the body decomposed on the left with the face elevated. Doctor: At the time of decomposition, the brain is relatively intact and everything is decomposing, and the hair is falling with the gravity. The hair is kind of clumped together, and much of the tissue has the consistency of soap, which causes the hair mass. Prosecution: So you are saying is that if everything was completely decomposed the hair on the left would fall but not on the right. Yes. (A photo of skull and remains at the Medical Office of Dr. G is presented.) Prosecution: You would agree that the mass of hair had fallen back and not to the side. So the water displaced the hair, but not the residue. Doctor: I have examined other hair, not this hair, but I knew how it was from the picture. Prosecution: This photo does not support the position in which you said the skull was found. Doctor: You said it was underwater.

The duct tape was stuck on there after the skin had discomposed. How would this person in your hypothesis put the duct tape on the skull? Doctor: Well it comes in a roll and they tore off a number of sections and connected the jaw to the face. Prosecution: So it decomposed where it was found, on the left side and then someone comes

329

over and put duct tape on the skull. If the skull is on
the side, someone has to pick it up and put it on. If the
skull is picked up, the mandible would fall off. This
person picks up the skull and mandible, and then would
have to put it back in position. They would have taken a
piece of duct tape and put it on each side. I do not have
a picture that shows it on both sides. You would need to
attach it on both sides, right? Yes, if your purpose was
to connect the jaw on both sides. Prosecution: Why would
it take three pieces of duct tape? Doctor: Maybe there
were two on one side and one on the other. Prosecution:
They were six to eight inches long. So, this person would
have taken duct tape and then he would have put the duct
tape directly on the skull. Doctor: The duct tape was not
stuck to the bone when found. There was interjection of
water and it will usually remove the stickiness of the
glue.

Prosecution: So if this person put three pieces of duct
tape on the skull, why would it be stuck to the hair? Do
you recall the medical examiner had to cut to remove the
tape from the hair? So, under your theory, the person who
picked up the skull, attached the mandible with the duct
tape and then put it back would also then put the hair
back on the skull? Doctor: The medical examiner took this
hair and put it on top of the skull just to take a photo
and this is not identical to the placement of the hair in
the photos taken at the scene. The medical examiners at
the scene took this photo by someone rearranging this
hair for a picture; you can see a fracture inside the
skull and not outside. Discoloration occurs with
smothering and asphyxiation. If there is suffocation, the
blood pressure alone will sometimes show color. I did not
send the dust for analysis. I read that it was sent to
Dr. Goldberger, and he found no presence of poison. There
was no chloroform in the dust and matter. As far as the
duct tape, I do not know how many persons handled the
skull, no. It had to be manipulated to take a photo and
was put there by hands. That is why the scene photo looks
different from the other hair photo. (The witness is
released, and the court is recessed for the remainder of
the weekend, so that depositions can be conducted by the
attorneys.)

When this witness took the stand, we thought he might be
useful to the defense. However, he seems to us like a
highly credentialed, bitter old man because when he asked
to be in autopsy, he was refused by Dr. G. How dare you
refuse my request! This is the feeling we get and we
would discount his entire testimony. This was a surprise
to us, but that is what we took from his entire
testimony. We all ran out of hands after we reattached

330

the mandible; forget tearing and placing the duct tape on the skull. He lost all the ground the defense has picked up.

His opinion on placement of the duct tape after decomposition was ridiculous. We were surprised that this man did not do better, but even he can only work with the evidence. He made very inflammatory comments about the medical examiner's office. He is trying to say Caylee decomposed lying on her left side. In Florida, during this period, we had Tropical Storm Fay. Anything could have moved the body around in the swamp, even before the animals. If it were not for Caylee's hair, which held on to the tape, almost all evidence of her life and death could have been destroyed. Caylee fought to tell us this story, even after Tropical Storm Fay.

Chapter 14

THE DEFENDANT'S CASE - WEEK TWO

June 21st, 2011

Mr. Mason wants a matter heard before the jury comes in, and they approach the bench. The judge again warns the lawyers to bring matters up before 8:20, but allows it at the nine o'clock start. There is a sidebar. The judge returns to the bench; he does not appear happy.)

The Prosecution begins: The court has left a sanctions package on the table regarding Dr. Rodriguez. I have just gotten a transcript of the Saturday deposition of this witness. I need more time to review this deposition. He is supposed to give an opinion that people cannot decipher decomposition and other odors. This is one opinion again not given in his report. I cannot prepare for cross-examination. Another witness, Dr. Eikelenboom, we received a half page report with no opinion. We asked the defense about him when we saw the witness outside the courtroom. I received a forty-five page slide. I am willing to depose Dr. Eikelenboom on Tuesday evening, if the defense presents him to my office. He has said his opinions are on DNA and trace evidence. He is proposing to give a number of opinions. I have not deposed him and I will on Tuesday at 5:30. There will be more requests for sanctions from the prosecution against the defense. The defense responds that the witnesses were listed timely, and that the defense immediately instructed the witness to put something together. Despite the law not requiring them to put up every opinion, they have completely complied. The court's order was either to provide a written report or a deposition. The prosecution is refusing to take the deposition. I say there was sufficient time for him to take the deposition. The State has violated this order on two occasions with no threats of contempt.

The defense continues, Your Honor, I think that the court has made it clear that this is not a game and that both sides have played games. Mr. Ashton is an experienced prosecutor, and he has used these depositions as both a sword and a shield in this case. Dr. Rodriguez is simple; he is saying that no one can tell where the duct tape had been on the victim, based on the remains site. Dr. Eikelenboom is being raised as being a problem because of the failure of the prosecution to take his deposition. The State was given notice, and this is a common issue. Their argument is that there is no DNA because of the elements and we have someone who can testify there should have been some DNA left despite the remains site of woods and water.

The State: We will be wishing to exercise our right to depositions. Baez: I had Dr. Eikelenboom show up to the State on Saturday. This prosecutor himself, Mr. Ashton, turned him away. I told him to prepare a report at that point and the exhibits are to explain DNA. To me, Mr. Ashton's argument is to have more time to take and review depositions. That is because of his intentional omission in taking them, and now he wants more time. The court orders are clear, one option is written reports and the other one is depositions. I notice Mr. Ashton is intentionally not taking the depositions. We did not look at this order and say we were intentionally going to disobey this order. Even though the rule of law does not require reports, this court has, and I think it is lack of due process. He does not just want only to take the defendant's life; he wants to go after her lawyer. He is doing this in an unreasonable manner. These are obvious opinions and obviously trouble for their case.

Judge: What time is it, gentlemen? The prosecution says it is 9:25, Your Honor, and Baez says that it is 9:26. Judge Perry says, "That shows me that the two of you will never agree on anything. Therefore, all attorneys are to be here at 8:30 every morning from now on." The judge continued, This Saturday we will work a full day. So, Mr. Baez, have your witnesses here to work with. This jury has been waiting 25 minutes. This Court has the right to set timelines it feels necessary to try this case. We have an Order dated December 10th, 2010. When experts have not prepared reports, both parties are required to file a written CV, qualifications, field of expertise or medical specialty, subjects of opinions, and the summery of the experts' options. That was done because a couple of experts' reports contained nothing. The Court thought that Order cleared up the situation. Then on January 6th, 2011, the Court entered an Order Granting State's Motion to Compel a statement of the specific subjects of opinion, a summary, and grounds for opinions regarding Dr. Lee, and that was not provided. The Orders require names of all expert witnesses, complete statements as to the opinions of the witnesses, expertise, any data used, and any subject of the opinions. The court in those Orders required both the State and defense to supply every opinion, and depositions are to investigate those opinions. Depositions do not relieve either party of the responsibly of the report. It was never my intent that you could avoid the report and they could take depositions instead.

Judge Perry went on, I have refused to allow the State to use exhibits that the defense did not have. I have been put in a corner, in not being allowed to exclude this evidence because it punishes the defendant. The Florida Supreme Court did not close the door if someone continues to violate the orders. It leaves the door cracked. It can be surmised that if someone continually violates the Court's orders, excluding defense evidence, despite the defendant's right to due process, exclusion of a witness is the ultimate sanction, and it is proper. There has been gamesmanship and friction between the attorneys', and that is something I think the Florida Bar is going to deal with, and this Court will deal with it when this case is concluded. The testimony of Dr. Rodriguez is deferred to give the state time to review the deposition.

The judge continued, Wednesday is a short day because of me. If I were the State or the defense, when we recess this afternoon, they should go through the reports or depositions. Sub-opinions on minor things are going to come up. Enough is enough. Both sides need to be advised of what I will do next, even at the price of doing this trial all over again, which I do not think I will have to. Exclusion is a remedy. The defense has to get a new witness, and it will cause a thirty-minute delay. I am getting very close to starting every morning at 8:30. I have tried to be accommodating with everyone, but I have a sequestered jury that lives under restriction. If you will not behave professionally, you will have a reduced lunch hour. All of this is going to stop, or you will be working fierce days. Be prepared Saturday to go the full day. (Court is in recess while the defense gets a witness as a substitute for Dr. Rodriguez.)

Court is to start again soon, and we notice Baez has the
case law lady in the courtroom. We like calling her that;
she is good, and she just argues case law. We think she
is the bookworm of the defense team. Case law can be
interpreted for either side in many cases, and each side
applies the parts of the case that they feel is in their
favor. She is probably going to argue something on due
process, is our guess. Casey is highly talkative with the
case law lady. Then she looks up and bats her eyes and
smiles. Unlike the lawyer, she does not cover her mouth,
she is just rambling on, but no microphones are turned
on. It also appears Casey is looking more afraid. Thirty-
four days into her trial, she may be realizing that she
is on trial for her life. It is 10:55, and the first
witness is not on the stand. The judge was more than
irritated earlier, and he showed it. We doubt that his
mood is any better now that he has had to keep the jury
waiting an hour longer than he was willing to allow.

Casey appears not to like it when things do not go her
way. Her face is showing it. Now, the other female
attorney has moved into the chair next to Casey; their
talking continues for a minute, and then Casey sits with
her hand at her mouth looking scared. She is highly
animated today. I believe it is a sign of stress,
finally. Guilty or not, a trial would be highly stressful
for anyone, especially when the trial is for their life.
By the way, if Casey is found guilty and this case is
overturned by a higher court and is sent back for
retrial, it we do not think it is to the defense's
advantage. The media that has followed all of this case
will be less interested, and she will probably be
convicted of first-degree murder. The prosecution will
already know the defense case on retrial, and it is not
strong this time around. The defense already knows the
prosecution's case this time around. It will be a blip on
the news should Judge Perry be overturned for using the
ultimate sanction. I also do not expect him to refuse to
admit much evidence, in spite of his threats. Remember a
win for the defense is keeping Casey off death row. A win
for the prosecution is either a life sentence or death.

Judge Perry returns to the courtroom. He announces that
court will be in recess for the remainder of the day due
to a joint stipulation. This is probably because they
found more witness problems with non-disclosure from the
defense. I think they are going to be in depositions all
afternoon. Does anyone still want to be a lawyer after
hearing about this case? We knew going into this case the
reality of a lawyer's world and a murder trial. Just a
note from the two writers of this story, we are grateful
not just for the four eyes, court documents and monitors,

but for each other to carry the load of documenting the story of what happens in Courtroom 23. It is a project for at least two, and we are exhausted!

We noticed something this morning; the door through which Casey enters and leaves the courtroom from the holding cell each day has a piece of silver duct tape across the door and onto the side of the doorjamb, just above the handle. We suppose it is to prevent anyone from opening this door before the court deputy does, or else it is an example of cop humor. We wonder if Casey has ever noticed.

So far, the defense seems to have only strengthened the prosecution's case. To this point, the defense has not presented anything that Baez promised in opening statements. The defense does not have to prove a case, and they have done their best to confuse and create conflict in the facts and opinions of witnesses in the case. However, when the attorney makes damning claims in opening statements, we think all jurors expect him to back up his words, or they will not trust the lawyer. Casey has just entered the courtroom and is beginning to show the toll of a trial. The Judge is on the bench.

June 21st, 2011

Preliminary matters; discovery issues with Richard Eikelenboom: The prosecutor starts with an announcement that upon the State's review of McDuffy v State, they believe a discovery violation has occurred. The prosecution does not request the exclusion of the witness, but requests the judge include this matter in its consideration of sanctions at close of the trial. The witness proposes to provide an opinion that DNA is recoverable from decomposition. Had this been provided, it would have been a subject of a Frye hearing. He has no science to back this up. The deposition also reflects that he formed his opinions on Saturday and he was not asked to provide a report. We ask only that his opinion on the lack of DNA be excluded as a discovery sanction. Ms. Seubert from the FBI was allowed to testify similarly. She could not establish a general principle as to that opinion. All reports of experts were to be provided timely, and Eikelenboom's was not provided until June 20th, 2011.

Defense: I filed a response with the court on December 15th, 2010 on Dr. Eikelenboom. I listed him as being a DNA, trace recovery expert. The facts would be used to rebut any false claims by the prosecution and until that happened, we could not preview what he would say. I would like Dr. Eikelenboom to testify to the degrading of DNA. As these issues came up, I asked him the questions because I wanted them to come up. I want to call Mr. Eikelenboom to testify as to the degrading of decomposition. Mr. Ashton is creating a ruse for the court. I would like the testimony for explaining DNA and issues of degradation. Mr. Mason will address other witness issues with the court. Prosecution: The State did not offer any DNA evidence, so the defense is rebutting its own witness.

Judge: (At some point, the judge granted the defense motion to examine the evidence for DNA and items tested were the shorts and the bag she was found in.) The defense never requested the tape and carpet for testing. The expert was never informed which items were being tested and asked the results. Defense: The testing he does is low copy DNA. He is a pioneer of this new technology. We asked for another type of testing on the items we tested, and that DNA test was not low copy DNA. Prosecution: My understanding is the only crime lab doing low copy DNA is New York Crime Lab, and it is not certified and it is not Frye-tested. It is running it at 30 markers instead of 24 and he did not represent that this is a specialty in his lab or not done in America. Judge: If you chose to have this testimony after a Frye hearing, I will allow the witness by video conferencing. I will fashion the jury instruction on my own from the two of your suggested instructions. Dr. Eikelenboom the witness is **out** for now.

The Defendant's Eleventh Witness

Interpretation of Testimony - Jennifer Welch (recalled):
I am a CSI for Orange County. On December 14th, 2008, at the end of the remains collection, during December 12th through the 14th, my report states that the area had been cleared of leaf litter and vegetation. From 0-4 inches at ground level and around trees and roots from 0-10 inches, as determined with a tape measure. I took photos at the scene, the vegetation around the body was cut and moved to the side but not cut from around the remains. The photos are entered into our database, as call identification numbers. I do have a call identification number; it is 32. I took photos after the end of each day, as well. A photo is shown that represents the scene as vegetation and after having been cleared. (It is admitted in evidence.) It appears to be the scene after vegetation was cleared. In my report, on page five, there is a reference to a log and/or tree. The log was located near the skull during the process of clearing. A CSI and my supervisor then moved the log. This photo, taken on

December 11th, 2008, is a photo of the scene as it appeared after vegetation had been moved away. From what I recall, it is just hanging from trees. I do not recall I needed to move anything off the remains at that time to take this photo.

Jennifer Welch - State's cross-examination: This is photo of the scene and without the full sequence of photos; you cannot tell where this photo is on the scene.

Jennifer Welch - Defense re-direct: There are a series of photos for identification that were uploaded into the system, and the system gives the call identification number. I cannot give you more without going through the photos and my report. 1838 is not a call number in this case. The witness gives the correct numbers for the photos to the defense. (She is excused.)

The Defendant's Twelfth Witness

Interpretation of Testimony - Jane Bock, PhD: I am a botanist. My specialties are in plant anatomy and forensic botany. I have Bachelors from Duke, a Master's from Indiana, and PhD from the University of California at Berkeley. I am retired and still teach a little. I have 80 peer review papers. I have authored three books on plant ecology and one on plant forensics. I do get research support from the science community, parks, and others. I belong to the American Academy of Science. I have given expert testimony in over fifty cases, including depositions. (She is admitted as an expert in Botany and Forensic Botany.) I have looked at photos from the medical examiner, CSIs, and I visited the discovery scene. I have read documents such as the Medical Examiner's report, the description of the recovery site in Ms. Welsh's report, and the report of the Dr. Hall. I visited the site on February 1st, 2009. With me was Patrick McKenna at the crime scene - excuse me - recovery site. This photo was taken when I was at the site. (It is received in evidence.) On the ground is leaf litter, it falls from the trees; stems, leaves, and tree branches. I believe two weeks is the period of time the remains could have been there, because of the leaf litter. I reviewed a report from Dr. Hall, and he set forth items of vegetation that was found on the Pontiac Sunfire. A camphor tree was listed on report as having been one of the leaf sources in the Anthony car. There not one camphor tree at the remains site. (Sidebar)

When I look at the photo, you cannot tell how old the roots are, since the growth rate is different based on soil and water; whether there is a lot of water or a little water. You would need to know what plant it is, and do time-pace studies with a ruler and notebook, or you would have to watch it grow over a period of time. I am from Colorado but Florida was the site of part of my PhD in 1966. I was looking at a semi-marine area. I studied the food habits of tortoises from 1980 to 1990. My parents lived here and I came to see them, and I did research in tortoises on a support grant. I have friends who write books. I use books to learn and become more experienced. It was in general and continues until now. A big piece of my work is in grasslands here and in other countries. Each place has different vegetation. I viewed the scene photos in many stages from the time the remains were discovered to the finish of the removal. The vegetation is characterized in books as swamp and hard wood. The plants that I saw are species that require a great deal of water. They must be wet or underwater.

Jane Bock, PhD – State's cross-examination: You viewed the roots and you say they could grow through the skull in two weeks? Yes. The roots could grow through the laundry bag in the photos in two weeks? Yes. You are stating that they could have grown in the bones in two weeks? Yes. You have never dealt with a decomposed skeleton with root growth, have you? I have looked at the evidence with skeletons that were there for a long time. (The prosecutor shows her deposition transcript to her, and used her prior testimony in deposition to impeach her.) The answer was no when you were asked the same questions in deposition. I use glass, clay, and the like to explain root growth to my classes. I did see roots in a ten-year-old skeleton. I did not remember that in the deposition; my experience is minimal involving bones with roots. There is growth and leaf litter on the skull, which is in its pristine condition and the skull is in leaf litter up to the area of the nose. The medical examiner at the site said that it had collected up to the eyes of the skull. Do you say that it can collect up to that level in two weeks? Yes, to this height. (Photo shown) I recognize that this is a photo of the skull and leaves from the medical examiner's office. Some leaves are green, some brown, and some gray. Some leaves are blown in, and some fall at different times. Doctor, are you aware that the medical examiner put his hands six to eight inches away on either side to dirt level of the skull and then dug down to keep from disturbing the vegetation around the skull?

These leaves are at different level of decomposition. Given your hypothesis if it has lain there all the time, then yes, the leaves would have come at very different times. Witness: Based on the leaves I saw when I was at the scene, they had been there only a few weeks before the soil was removed. Because of the amount of leaves here are within six weeks, some are not completely covering the ground. I am basing my opinion on that, on what I saw when I was there at the scene. The photo shows maybe the same amount as the photos of the skull covered in leaves and roots. Prosecution: No way! Doctor: The photos show that this was a densely overgrown area. This empty configuration would let the same amount of leaves blow as the growth in the swamp. The vines would allow the same amount to blow.

(This is strange testimony.) Doctor: The land is almost barren of leaves in some area of this photo. The people visiting the site and other factors could cause the leaves not be here. I was told where the skull was found by one of the defense lawyers while at the site. You and the man who took the photos for you were not there when the skull was recovered were you? No. I am saying these remains were left there a couple of weeks before being found. Prosecution: In your deposition, you said you could not render an opinion on how the remains were placed there. Please read your deposition so you can see it in context. Doctor: I do not know exactly when the remains were placed there at the site, and this is my best guess. Prosecution: So you are not of the opinion that the body had only been there two weeks and it could have been there much longer.

Jane Bock, PhD - Defense re-direct: Can a root grow into an opening? Generally, no, but it depends on the root. There was no fallen leaf litter on the log and I looked at it. In Officer Welsh's report, she discussed that it took two people to move it. I think if they said more about the leaves in the report, it would have helped me tell how long the log had been there. The deeper you go in soil, the less organic it is. (She draws a photo of Caylee's humerus with leaves and twigs and other things on top of it.) Defense: If you have an item on leaf litter and it is wet, can the item sink? Witness: Yes.

Jane Bock, PhD - State's Re-cross: The skull could have sunk. It could have laid on leaf litter and then be covered with buildup. One bone was buried in four inches of muck, would you not think that bone has been there longer? Maybe a dog or coyote did it. No more questions! (The witness is excused, and the jury is given a recess.)

This woman provided no insight to the writers. She was either not given the full information on the remains site at the time of recovery, or she was given wrong information. It was clear to us that she has no idea when the body was placed at the site.

(Court is in session; the jury is not present.) Judge Perry: Witness Richard Eikelenboom has provided no report and in deposition, he provided an affidavit. I have reviewed instructions proposed by both the defense and the prosecution. All experts were required by the Order to provide a report. This witness did not provide this report until June 20th, 2011. I want to see the witness for a sanction hearing.

Sanction hearing regarding Dr. Eikelenboom: July 13th, 2010, is the official date I talked to the defense and reviewed the evidence. I was not told that I had to write a report, a CV, a description of my expertise, a statement of the subjects on which I would testify, or the facts and summary of my expert opinion. I was never informed of the court's order. I communicated with the defense by phone, e-mail and Skype. Between December 2010 and May 2011, I was never asked to write a report, by either Mr. Baez or Michelle Medina. From May 2011 until now, I was never asked to write a report until last Saturday. Saturday night, I wrote a short report. I communicated with the defense shortly before inspection of the evidence. I did not hear any more for the while. The defense could question us at any time; we were available. Sometimes in the Netherlands, I am asked to write a report by an investigating judge. They tell you what they want. The report could be on the investigation we have performed or on other tests that have been done, as a second opinion.

My wife and Ms. Medina communicated, and it came from them what I was told to do. It was about the evidence viewing. I wanted a piece of the evidence to review and it was denied. I was not told to narrow or shorten my report. I did not speak with Ms. Medina; my wife did, and then later she spoke to me. On Friday, I made a PowerPoint presentation on touch DNA. We discussed the subject, and then we went to the State Attorney's office. He refused to take my deposition and was rather rude. I was then instructed by Ms. Medina to write a report.

Prosecution: Is there any opinion that you expressed in your Saturday report that could not have been done months earlier, like when you were at lunch with Mr. Baez? For me it was new information, and since I did not follow the trial, some might have been new. I needed guidance. I got new information on the crime scene and reports from the FBI. I got the whole folder. I have seen reports before at the evidence viewing and I formed an opinion. I requested more after I knew I was going to testify.

Judge: There was an order entered and clarified by the court in another order, to list experts, subject matter of testimony, and the area of expertise. Where experts have not prepared a report, both the state and defense are required to file documents providing this information. In January, we dealt with his again, going back to the December 10th, 2010 Order with two exceptions that were December 14th, 2010. After the court readdressed its prior order and ordered it again. The court will find that this violation is not inadvertent, and the information should have been provided. It is a willful violation by the defense. DNA is not trivial, but involves substantial issues. The court has delayed the trial to give the State an opportunity to take a deposition and if the report had been done, the State would not have the opportunity to take a deposition at this late date. This court cannot in a short period of time make that opinion. It is in need of a Frye hearing. The court will not allow the witness to testify on the DNA of decomposition fluid in the trunk of the car. The defense can file a motion for a Frye hearing, and the court will hear a Frye hearing at that time. I am unable to determine whether there is even a Frye issue in the testimony. This is a remedy short of exclusion.

Baez: Today we were handed by the State of Florida two compact discs. Judge: We will take that one up on the lunch hour. I have a jury waiting. Does the prosecution want anything on decomposition removed from the PowerPoint? (The State tells him they do not.)

All experts were to be provided to the court with all their opinions that they planned to testify to, their reasons, CV and data. They were due months before the trial started, and Dr. Eikelenboom's was not provided until June 18th, 2011. You can consider this in weighing his testimony.

Defense Proffer of Testimony - Richard Eikelenboom: I am a DNA expert. I worked in the National Laboratory in the Netherlands, and I did all the crime work. I started in Serology and was a front-runner for DNA and trace recovery and in finding all kinds of material for DNA profiling. I went to laboratory school. Then, while working for the laboratory, I followed up with education in luminal. I have worked for twenty years as a DNA scientist. In 2005, I joined my wife's company of DNA experts. I have an engineering degree in Holland. That is something between a bachelors and not a full master's and it was in luminal. I did not specialize in DNA and biochemistry education. I have all kinds of training in DNA and other areas but my final study was in luminal. I worked for the Netherlands Institute but did not do DNA testing. My emphasis was on trace evidence and luminal, and not DNA. I was not certified to do DNA testing. I did a lot of analyzing. In 2005, we opened Forensics Independent Services. I have testified in the area of DNA. We are monitored, and they bring in an independent DNA expert to review our work. I was contacted about a case in the United States. Proffer over. (The witness steps down.)

The lawyers then take up the State's latest potential discovery violation. Baez: I just received evidence from the prosecution, and all appears to be due to unavoidable delay except with the PC computer disc. The report was turned over to the State two months later in 2008. There are internet searches and photos of shot girls. He referred to Ms. Anthony as giving instruction to shot girls, so they must have had it. I am referring to the use of these items on the desktop computer.

Prosecution: The first several items on the Notice of Discovery, apparently a civilian called the sheriff just last week. She was a witness to a statement by a jail inmate who was in jail while Casey was there. April Waylon is the witness. She heard an inmate say that her child died in a swimming pool, her father found the child dead, attempted CPR, and called 911. The last item is a filtered copy of the items on the hard drive that Mr. Baez has had for years. He had more than one computer expert on his team. I decided that if we are going to use it in the cross-examination of Casey or other witnesses, I would give him the redacted copy, even though she has had access to this hard drive since 2008. All items 1-6 have to do with April Waylon, and I was notified of her being a possible witness last Thursday, Friday, or Saturday. The written reports were delivered to me last night. The defense had their computer expert come to the Orange County Sheriff's Office, or bringing a hard drive was an available option. I am providing this disc in an abundance of caution. As this time, we do not expect to call April Waylon, although we continue to get information and that could change. One through six is accepted. Seven the filtered version of the hard drive, there is so much data that we could be referring to that the State has used a redacted disk. It contains all the HP desktop computer activity for June 16th, 2008. Mr. Baez's opening statement was about June 16th, 2008. This activity is proof that his opening statement is wrong.

Judge: It would seem to me as an outsider looking in that June 16th, 2008, was the last time that Caylee was seen by her grandparents. It is clear that day would be important. The defense has had the hard drive for years and could have focused on it. It is admitted. (The judge declares a recess for lunch.)

It looks to the authors like it must have been a long lunch for the defense. Casey has her head down, and Baez looks agitated and upset. We think he did not like the judge's ruling that hard drive can come into evidence on rebuttal. The Judge is back and in a good mood. Baez wants the judge to say the half day tomorrow is because of judge, not the defense. The prosecution wants the judge to explain why the witness Rodriquez is not coming back. They are crafting language for that one.

(The jury returns to the jury box.) The judge to the jury: We have half day tomorrow because I have a long-standing commitment. It is a meeting regarding the state trial court's budget.

The Defendant's Thirteenth Witness

Interpretation of Testimony - Richard Eikelenboom: Touch DNA is transferred through the hands. I touch and leave DNA. There are different factors; if I touch slightly, it is very unlikely to leave DNA of skin cells. The harder you touch, the more likely you are to leave trace amounts of DNA. The (PowerPoint is presented to the witness. It is a disk for demonstrative purposes.) The top layer of skin leaves no real DNA that we can use. The nucleus is below a few layers down and that is where the DNA is. By applying more force, the chance is better to leave DNA. Alternate light source is one test. Sweat also fluoresces. Then the next samples look for places where force was applied. The chance of obtaining a profile gets better. The dying cells that come off rarely give DNA. I formed a working hypnosis, and then use other tests to try to get DNA. The amount of force is the most important thing in trying to get a DNA profile.

In the Netherlands, we use three kinds of tests; clothing with a prolonged time of wearing helps us be more likely to get a DNA sample; a forceful grip yields more DNA, and touching less DNA. Force is more likely in crimes. Some people shed more DNA. Some people, even with force, do not leave a profile. Sticky material will help collect DNA. Let's take a piece of duct tape. You have one impression on the sticky side and one on the non-sticky side. I can sometimes get DNA, if you can see it, from those torn edges of the tape. The sticky one is the best side. If the sticky side is applied to the face, as it apparently was in this case, it had DNA. In the mouth and skin around the mouth, there is a lot of DNA in the area of the mouth. If it was applied to this victim's mouth and then torn off, you would get… likely get a DNA profile.

Even with the elements of the woods, even if the circumstances are very bad environmental conditions, the DNA could break down, but you could still expect to find DNA. We can copy the small remaining amounts of DNA. It takes very little if we had it, and then we magnify it. There were two partial profiles on the duct tape. They were on the non-sticky side, so if you have contamination of 150 RU and this is not high. If you have lower below it, it does not rule out that you can see both. Sticky sides of tape like these are at such low amounts that there is little information you can get. This prolife has an X for sex. It is DNA. I have experienced extracting DNA when maggots feed on humans there is cell material, if they ate blood and if it is soon after they ate, you might find it. The DNA can be extracted with low concentrations of chloroform. I would not say that chloroform would never destroy the DNA. Just a little would be broken down by that extraction process.

Richard Eikelenboom – State's cross-examination: I do not have a PhD, and I am presently a student in the American University. I am under supervision; there is tutelage. My wife and I started the laboratory. Three of us bought a farm and made it into a lab. In 2008, we decided to expand that business to the U.S., and the exposure from this testimony is going to be extremely helpful. When we opened in the United States, we were trying to scale down. We are not really working for the money. We do some cases for free. The lab is not open in Colorado at this time. Other laboratories in America use the same kind of tests. There are large laboratories that use the same kind of testing in the United States. We have more experience than the other laboratories. We know more than the big laboratories in the United States, because I would do all these big crime cases. The protocol and procedures were invented in United Kingdom. I use DNA kits, and I buy the kits from Applied Biosystems, which is an American company. The difference is that American labs usually run twenty-four, and I run more than that. Dirt and debris can affect the cells.

What is it that you do that any other laboratories cannot do? Contact DNA is what we are talking about; it is the same testing equipment. The problem is finding the DNA. If you find a place with suspected DNA, you still could

344

fail to get a profile. We can do other tests and try to find it. The only difference in the copy is running more samples. Have you ever tested a fruit fly and gotten DNA? No. It has to do with the digestion; the more digestion, the less likely we are to get DNA. If the fly died before digestion was complete, we might get it. I have never published any papers on DNA. Moisture and temperatures are the worst things for DNA. Bacteria are also destructive to DNA. When tape is placed on the face, it is on dead cells and if it is not torn off, placed in an underwater environment, in Florida heat and sits for six months, the likelihood of finding any DNA is remote, isn't it? It depends on the circumstances. If you lose all cell material, then it is impossible. On a bone, you cut into the bones to get DNA. You do not swab the outside. During decomposition that is in the late stages, is everything gone? It is possible to obtain DNA, but it is much more difficult. It would be very difficult to get a profile from the remains, if it is possible.

The only thing the 17 wheel would mask is another 17. Another 15 would mass another 15, and so on. It would only mask its matching low. Contamination would not cover the entire profile of another person. With the very small peaks, you might get something by using low copy. Those could be artifacts, or with low copy, it might give you something. Every laboratory has a standard. We use the same standard. You would not call these a peak in the laboratories? I did not ask to retest this tape. Are you aware if items were sent for further DNA tests? I have no idea if any item in this case was retested. My laboratory is called the Crime Farm in the Netherlands. I have been requested to do many tests. I started getting U.S. recognition in a case for exoneration. We did contact DNA, on the evidence, and we did get a lost DNA profile. We got a match from the 20-year-old suspect. This person was found outdoors. In addition, I found something no one else found. Because of this case, we got other cases from America and law enforcement here, and we are working on them. This is not the first high-profile case we have worked. There are kits that are more sensitive to small amounts of DNA, chemicals for more broken-down DNA, and extending the injection time helps, as well.

It comes back to the trace recovery, and it was underestimated in 1990. You need to look for it and then take many samples. Filters to clean and process samples make it so we can try to find it. My machine is better, my chemicals are better. The state laboratories are not as good; they have more cases. We were able to get some partial profiles and full profiles sometimes. I do fewer samples at a time. I have found DNA on exposed items.

(Sidebar) The 17 wheel on the sticky side, just found
that one marker of all thirteen. You would need to
exclude it if you do not have a seventeen, because it
could not be your profile. The original DNA system
required a large amount of blood or semen. The PCR
approached replicated the DNA and made it easier. With
that, you might find a speck of DNA, but that does not
mean that you can use it. If you had tested in this case,
you might not have found anything inconsistent with the
tape being on Caylee's face.

If you found Caylee's DNA, it would have told you the
tape was on her. Next, if you found an unknown result and
it did not match it could be contamination, from it being
such a small amount. You would test it and compare it to
all the laboratory workers and everyone known to the
crime. You can never know if someone had contact with an
item and transferred it. All of it is possible. We find
contamination from laboratory workers all the time. We
sometimes get an unknown profile from low copy and can
never know where it came from. None of my exhibits came
from fully skeletonized remains. If there is DNA on an
item, if they are on skeleton remains, it is more
difficult. If the tape was placed on the nose and mouth
there would have been DNA in the beginning. It is there
or not. The proximity of the tape to rotting flesh would
increase the chances of the DNA decomposing. It does make
a difference if it is near a body decomposing, the
temperature and environment makes a difference in the DNA
deteriorating. Judge: The doctor may step down.
Prosecution: Your Honor, he is not a doctor. Judge: Okay,
whatever he is.

The Defendant's Fourteenth Witness

**Interpretation of Testimony - Lead Detective Yuri Melich
(recalled):** We served search warrants on the Anthony home
in August, and found no evidence of chloroform on papers,
rags, products, and receipts. On December 11th, 2008,
nothing involving chloroform was found. This is the
search warrant of December 11th, 2008? Yes, we looked for
the items in this search. On December 20th, 2008, the
third warrant, chloroform was not included in the scope
of the warrant. On August 8th, 2008, we did not have a
preliminary result of the high levels of chloroform from
the laboratory. Between August and October, Casey was
home from jail for a time. The next search warrant was
December 11th, 2008. Chloroform was very significant, but
I did not get a warrant for just that. At that time, we
were still looking for a live child. We did not stop
looking until we found a deceased child.

The Defendant's Fifteenth Witness

Interpretation of Testimony - Markus Wise, PhD: I am a Chemist at Oak Ridge Laboratory. I have a PhD from Perdue University and I have worked for almost twenty-seven years at Oak Ridge. I do not belong to any organization except the Boy Scouts. I have published fifteen to twenty articles. I have lectured, given presentations, and I have won awards. This is the first time I have ever testified in court. (Dr. Wise is accepted as an expert by the prosecution in Analytical Chemistry.) We push science to the next level. A research scientist can be a forensic scientist. Oak Ridge is a laboratory, and we work on very cutting-edge science. I have not worked personally in a forensic laboratory. I do not know what they experience. We have flexibility in our experiments. We use methods as routine and clear as those you use driving a car.

There are protocols for the instruments. If I have an item I am going to test, how would it become contaminated in our laboratory? It is our job as research scientists to expand the boundaries of science. We are always aware of contamination. I was asked to run the samples in this case to determinate what was in them. Dr. Arpad Vass asked me to do that. The samples were in his office that day, and he left me a key. I do not recall where they were in the office. There was a bag and a metal can. I took it to my laboratory and I ran a test with the gas chromatograph. I ran a qualitative test, which tells you what is in the sample. He asked me to do the quantitative test, and then it showed an abnormal high peak. It does not tell me how much of each chemical, the result is just in comparison to other chemicals in the sample, and it was high. I decided not to do quantitative analysis to determine how much was there. It would have been a meaningless number. Chloroform is a volatile chemical. It is like gas, the odor immediately dissipates and you can no longer smell it.

If you put a drop on a surface, it is going to decrease because of evaporation. The speed of evaporation depends on a number of factors: the chemical nature of the surface, temperature, flowing of air in the vicinity and other factors. If a trunk is closed, it would slow the volatility but it would make an escape. If we would have made a quantitative test on the small piece of carpet, it does not reflect the entire carpet. It would be a little or a lot less than the original carpet. It could be from 2, 10, 100, to 1000 times more when it was originally there. I did not know the history of the temperature in the trunk every day, how the chloroform evaporated, or how many days the body was there. The amount there could

347

have been a lot more. I would not do it, because that number would have been set in stone and it would have never been the true amount of what was there. My experience with many gas-sampling bags is that they leak, so there is no surprise that it was not there. I did not what was in the vapor or the piece of carpet that was the source point for this chloroform. First we received a metal can and opened it a little, withdrew some air out with a needle, put it in my machine and it was positive for chloroform.

I talked with Dr. Vass and the largest peak was chloroform. We ran the air, saw something, and it was from the vapor in that can. To establish where the vapor came from, we took the carpet out of a can and put it in a clean bag. Then we injected air and held it two days in an incubator. Then we analyzed that sample, and we again saw that the largest peak was the elements that make up chloroform. The machine is highly sensitive. I run my machine at the low parts per million. I did not use the standard of chloroform to compare, as it would have assigned an unreal standard. I did use laboratory standard samples of chloroform to test the analysis time. It takes sixteen minutes to get through the machine and make it to the peak. We can examine the mass peak under that and do library searches. It says it looks like this compound: chloroform. Then we purchase a sample of that chemical and compare it for a known result and match it again. These are my hand-written notes in the laboratory. The notes say that the slides are reasonably clean. I used that phrase because there is no standard to determine anything more than reasonably clean; after all, even the air in the lab is not completely sterile, although my lab is designed to avoid any sort of contamination. This is a triple filter in a trip blank; the benzene suggests the sample was contaminated on the trip. The trip filter is an absorbent trap. I purged the water off; that happens frequently. The triple trap is sealed and packed with carbon, and it is a chemical sponge. We heat it, which causes the vapor and the chemicals to stick to the sponge. There is a lot of water in the air, and we drive the chemicals off and pass them through into a loop of liquid nitrogen. The nitrogen freezes the chemicals. Water gets into the loop and ice crystals are formed sometimes. They are melted. It does not mean that the quality of the sample is lessened.

If you fill a glass with water and ice, the glass would have condensation on the outside. This is the way we often receive samples. I had Dr. Vass verify the testing and he is extensively trained in chemistry. If you consider the training, I can perform in other areas, as well. Our training is extensive; he has worked extensively with me building instruments and analyzing chemicals. Dr. Vass is very talented, very intelligent. The trap froze at about 1.3 minutes and we warmed it just enough to get it flowing. The sample froze again, air sample from the passenger side of the car. The "sample slide appeared clean" notation is just a visual observation for my notes. That is for the samples. I was going to run a blank. I realized I needed to change the computer program, and so I stopped and started over. I caught my mistake.

I was running a standard of something that smelled really bad. I changed the way I was doing it, so I would not smell up my laboratory, but that does not change the results. This was sticky and smelly, and it was not coming through the tube well. It was put in a second container because of this. The idea was to get it into the machine as cleanly as possible and without smelling. I chose these adjustments, it would not go through because it was heavy and sticky. This is a closed valve test, the same one as the retention time standard. My machine did not break down. I have quality control. I am the primary one who decides if the machines are functioning. Dr. Vass ran samples; he is highly qualified. I issued protocol for the collection of soil samples. When collecting soil samples, the object is to collect them in the most pristine location. It is to avoid contamination whenever possible. These are soil samples, but not the samples we ran for this case. When running samples, if it is part of a trash heap, then that is where you collect. Sometimes you have no choice but to collect it where it is.

When running air samples, sometimes you cannot separate the two, and sometimes that is what you do not want to do. I recommend storing evidence where there is no gas if possible. I did not decide what samples were given to me. The sample in question was compared to another car carpet from a junk yard. I do not know the location of that car; I did not collect the sample. You said it came from a junkyard, and I am aware they came from Tennessee, but I do not know what yard. I chose to make an addition to the report. These chemicals can come from other sources. I cannot tell you where they come from, just that they are there. I talked about the triple absorption filters. These samples were taken six weeks later. I have no way of knowing how the air has changed over a period of time. These are my notes. Baez wants to put the notes in evidence, and Dr. Wise says that they have been marked up by counsel. (Objection) (Sustained)

I have done extensive testing of air samples. I have looked at many different kinds. I ran the concentration through and it was chloroform. We saw peaks for gasoline, as well. The chloroform was a larger peak, and I have tested many things that have gasoline in them. The high amount of chloroform, which is a cancer-causing agent, you do not expect to find it in the trunk of the vehicle. I saw the amount and it was very detectable at high levels. It was high in the parts per million. When I ran the concentrated sample, it looked very similar. I did research, and the result raised a question. I looked at data safety sheets and could find no reason for this chloroform. With my limited research, I could not figure out what it could have come from. Certain polymers can trap the volatiles, and are in almost every material, like all plastics adhesives. Whatever amount of chloroform I had, I would never know how much more was in this trunk due to evaporation, temperature, and the trunk being opened. It could have been the most stained area or the least stained with the chloroform on my carpet sample. It would have been greater before I received it. It was clear that the substance was in the trunk or spilled on the carpet.

My notes say the air blank was mostly clean, I usually run room air. No room air is completely clean. I put things in my notes so other people can know what happened, and we know what needs to be considered when writing protocols for other laboratories. Considering that it was six weeks later, it is the best I can do. I cannot take a sample from something three weeks before I need it. I have worked with Dr. Vass for about 12 years. We are a national laboratory, and we work together to increase our knowledge and develop techniques. Dr. Vass is a great learner. One project is the Labrador; it is not patented. All scientists are required to report findings and inventions, and only a minimal amount of funds go to all scientists at Oak Ridge, if any inventions are sold for use outside the government. I worked on the Labrador, and I might have billed this to the Labrador Project; it would have its connection. We are people who build technologies. One is the Labrador Project. No one is going to buy an instrument; they are not going to buy it from hearing about it in the courtroom. It must have its own scientific validation to be marketable. I cannot say what I expected to find in a carpet sample. There was a small amount in the sample. I looked at data sheets for the samples. I Googled items. Labrador was designed to be used by military and police. There would be no royalties. The U.S. Government is allowed to use it free. I would get no royalties.
(Testimony ended)

This witness was called by the defense. He worked with Dr. Vass on this case at Oak Ridge. I do not think the defense succeeded in discrediting the work that was done in any way. Just the opposite, the witness reinforced in our minds that a group of the best scientists came together for one reason – to advance the sciences. He helped answer the questions regarding what, if any, chemicals had been in the trunk of the car, and was there a body in the trunk? The answers are that there was chloroform in staggering amounts, and a body was in the trunk of Casey Anthony's car.

June 22nd, 2011

This morning, the case law lady is in court for a hearing before court begins for the jurors. The judge says he wants the hearing over before 8:55, and he leaves the bench. Unless they are arguing in the judge's chambers, we do not have a hearing this morning, after all. The lawyers and Casey are now in the courtroom.

We are waiting to hear about the jail inmate whose child drowned in the swimming pool and the grandfather found the child, tried CPR and called 911 (the normal response to a drowning). It is believed that she did not talk to Casey in jail, but Casey may have heard this sad story and made it her own. We wait for evidence on this. Also, the prosecution has made a redacted disc of the June 16th, 2008 computer activity from the Anthony home PC hard drive. They gave the disc to the defense yesterday. The defense has had the hard drive for three years. Baez looked very upset that this could be introduced in the State's rebuttal case. We hope it does make evidence. We would like to see everything that was searched, as well as what and when the searches were done. Perhaps the State can establish who was home when the searches were done.

Casey's hair is in a ponytail; she has been wearing it up lately, and she looks stressed. We believe the trial alone is stressing her at this point, and reality is setting in. This case could be headed for a first-degree conviction. The entire defense team looks stressed and very tired. Let us all remember, a lawyer can only work with the evidence and defense he has. Pulling rabbits out of the hat, like in the OJ Simpson murder case, are as much a surprise to the lawyers and the defendant, as they are to the rest of us. The reality is usually much different in a first-degree murder case. The prosecutors are good in this case. The lead prosecutor is good in case presentation and law. The second seat prosecutor is an excellent cross-examiner. The third seat prosecutor has been good; he just has not seen much activity. This is how they work. Where you sit at the lawyers table, in general, is the power you have. Court now begins.

Judge: Good morning. Are both sides present? Yes, Your Honor. Let us remember there is something we must do before this week is out. Approach the sidebar; we do not need the court reporter for this. (Sidebar)

The Defendant's Sixteenth Witness

Interpretation of Testimony - Maureen Bottrell: I am a geologic forensics examiner and an FBI trace examiner. I have a BS in Geology and MS in Geology from the University of Georgia. I have taken courses, lectures and trained in geology. I have published articles on soil, mineral, rocks, gemstones, glass, cement and building material. I have testified about forty times for the federal and states, including the State of Florida. (She is accepted as an expert.) I received evidence in this case. For a geologic comparison analysis, we do soil-to-soil comparison. For example, soil from shoes to match a crime scene, or maybe a location of where something came from, or to identify what something is. We use standard procedures, like what does it look like. We collect by color, texture, and so forth. In a comparison analysis, we compare the two colors, and if they are the same, we go on. Then we compare like sand grains in the soil samples. What do the grains look like? Do they look the same, or different? Then we would move on; if they look the same, they cannot be excluded.

We use microscopes and transmitted light microscopes for minerals. We have other instruments. There are three geologists at the FBI. (She refers to her report.) I received items from the Pontiac Sunbird. I received debris that was collected from the trunk, and from around and under the car. I also received a shovel, items from the home, twenty-two pairs of shoes, and a transport bag. I received items and samples from the remains site as well. The soil samples were taken after the top layer of soil was removed. There was not enough soil in the vehicle. The trunk had a mix of material, and because it was mixed we could not tell exactly where it came from. There was no comparison done between the car and the scene. The shovel analysis was stopped because the body was found. The purpose was to look for the location where the body might be, and so this testing stopped. The shoes, some were never warn, some had no geologic residue, so it limited what we could do, which was not much. Three pairs of shoes, reported to be Casey

352

Anthony's, had residue that was different from the crime scene; they could not be matched. The transport bag did not have enough to test. (This is the best Baez has gotten? It is not enough.)

Maureen Bottrell - State's cross-examination: I cannot say that the three pairs of shoes were not at the crime scene. There can be no transfer, or transfer that falls off. It falls off easily, because when you walk you may get soil on your shoes, then walk elsewhere and get a mix, or it could never had been there. Therefore, it is impossible to tell if these shoes were at the scene. I am employed by the FBI as an examiner. I did not find any meaningful geological evidence to connect Casey Anthony to the remains site. Those scenarios are all possible to happen. If I chose which one of the four, it would be speculation. (The witness is excused.)

The State got Baez on cross again. This witness could tell us nothing that either tied Casey to the remains site or excluded her from being there.

The Defendant's Seventeenth Witness

Interpretation of Testimony - Madeline Montgomery: I am a forensic toxicologist with the FBI; I have been employed by the FBI for 15 years. I have a BS in Chemistry from George Washington and training by the FBI. Forensic chemistry is a very broad area, from drugs to bombs. Toxicology is more specific and deals with drugs and poisons in people. We can do specific tests, and the FBI does such investigations. I have published ten to twenty articles. I am a member of different science organizations. I belong to scientific working groups that are trying to set the standards from DUI analysis to coroners' work, minimum of educational levels, and standards for all over the country. (She is accepted as an expert in forensic chemistry and toxicology.)

In my report, I received a hair samples to test. I received the hair mass of Caylee, State's Evidence, Number 271. Hair is complex, we are interested in getting to the inside, so we break it with liquid nitrogen, and put it in a solvent overnight, and then we make an extract. Then we add drugs to the sample. I used a liquid chromatograph machine and I tested for Xanax and chloroform, they are benzodiazepines, which cause relaxation or sleep. That test was negative. We were evaluating a new method in the lab, and I tested with this for the same drugs plus for nine others, valium, roofies, and more. They were all negative results, even with the new tests that were ten times more sensitive.

You do not know how long it would be before these drugs would show up. In testing hair, after limited exposure to drugs, we are not always able to find the drug. We cannot tell you how many times a person would have to use the drugs to have these drugs show up in hair. (Baez again went one question too far.) Hair is not the best kind of sample to test for drug exposure. If someone was given the drug and died immediately, I would not see the drug in the hair. I cannot test for chloroform in hair. The reason I test is to try to answer questions, and in this case, the test was negative. (The witness is excused)

The Defendant's Eighteenth Witness

Interpretation of Testimony - Michael Sigman, PhD: (He is being questioned by Mason.) I went to UCF and I have a PhD in Chemistry. I had a joint appointment for the National Center for Forensic Science, which is associated with UCF. I received a BS in 1982 from Southwest Missouri State University and my PhD in 1986 from Florida State University. I was a National Institute of Health post-doctoral fellow at the University of Illinois and the University of Chicago. I worked for one year at Dow Chemical, then at Oakridge Laboratory from 1990 to 2002, and then I came to UCF. I know Dr. Vass. A peer review is a process where we write a manuscript detailing a study, which we send to a journal. Then it is sent to a scientist who does similar work. They review it and then the journal decides whether to publish or not. I have seventy-four peer-reviewed publications and book chapters, and I have lectured one hundred and forty times. I teach and I am an expert in chemistry. (The witness is accepted as an expert in chemistry.)

On July 21st, 2008, I received a call from Orange County about air samples. I checked and they were to be sent to Dr. Vass. Vass gave them my name, and I was authorized to take the samples. I phoned Dr. Vass and we discussed a Tedlar bag. The Tedlar bag is made of a polymer and was completely used for collecting air samples. Doug Clark, my associate, and I went to the car and used a syringe to pull air. We pulled the air out, using a syringe with a metal needle. This procedure is usually done with a pump, but we did not have one. We drew the syringe an inch to draw air, and then we put it in the bags, two separate samples. We left both samples in the custody of the sheriff. The larger sample went to Oakridge, and they brought the smaller sample to us the next day. We tested that.

We used a gas chromatograph and mass spectrometry analytic instrument, or GCMS for short; the gas

354

chromatograph is like an oven, with a small glass capillary. The sample is inserted into the machine by a needle, and then the components are separated into compounds. The compounds are then ionized. Then they are sent through in the mass spectrometer, the analyzer. We can then read what chemicals are there. This is a very stable test and has been used many times. We analyzed the sample and the result we obtained, we found trace amounts of volatile compounds, but the sample was not concentrated enough to analyze. In the first sample, it was too weak, just regular gasoline. So we took another sample syringe in which a glass fiber coating is contained in the metal needle, We let it sit for a period of time in the sample to absorb, then we retracted the needle and inserted in into the GCMS.

I found the second sample was very similar to the first. It was consistent with the presence of gasoline. In the second sample, we found several components of gasoline, but we knew we could get a better sample. After the Tedlar bag returned, we took a microfiber bag and an activated carbon strip to the vehicle. We took samples from both after exposing them in the trunk for twenty minutes. We analyzed the findings the next day, and we went back to collect additional samples from a bag and strip left for seven and a half hours. We went through the samples for seven and half hours, and the response was better. The primary compound was gasoline, and there was also chloroform in the sample. Chloroform is a solvent used in chemical laboratories, formed from oxidizing agents like beach and other items from the environment. Dimethyl disulfide, it is found in onions, cabbage, soil and decomposition, and tetracholoroethene, which is primarily used in dry cleaning.

It is reported by Dr. Vass. These compounds are produced in decomposition, and they are the top markers for decomposition. Based on the literature, I believe these are related to decomposition, in my opinion. Based on our samples, the three samples, and based on our test, I cannot say that it was from a body. A total of six samples were taken with needles and Tedlar bags, from forty minutes to seven and half hours. In summary, when samples were taken after the car has been aired and the dryer sheets had been inside, before the chemicals could rebuild in a closed trunk, the samples produced less, but these samples were still consistent with chloroform, just with a higher gasoline concentrate. We did not have the pump to collect the sample. It was later sent back by Dr. Vass from Oak Ridge Laboratories for a more accurate collection of a sample. (Sidebar)

Michael Sigman, PhD - State's cross-examination: The date of July 21st, 2008 was the first sample for Tedlar bags. I cracked the trunk an inch or two and used a needle. I did not open the trunk. I did not know that the trunk liner was removed four days before I tested. (Well, that explains their test to the writers!)

A microliter is one millionth of a liter. The first sample was one liter, and the second was a third of that size and placed in Tedlar bag. The next day a CSI brought the sample. Dr. Vass had requested we use a triple absorbent trap, filter, and pump. We did not have that equipment or the capability to do that. Even in my samples, I found a small sample and with the fibers, it does not have as good a signal-to-noise ratio as the pump and filter. I would consider the triple absorbent trap as better. Since the carpet was not in the trunk, these tests are a moot point. With the methods I could use and the trunk liner gone, I still got chloroform and the two other chemicals that are reported in peer review as coming from decomposition.

Chloroform can come from bleach or in very minor amounts in people who swim in pools, and there should be bromine to form a base of chloroform, methane. It would need the other chemical to come from chlorine. We do not know what caused the chemical. When I opened the trunk, there was an odor. I do know what. I found chloroform in sample three, and two others exposed for the longer times. I do not know the source of the air in the trunk. I provided the report on July 30th. I would say, based on the car being in the garage I was not surprised to find gas. (The witness is released.)

The Defendant's Nineteenth Witness

Interpretation of Testimony - Susan Mears: I work for the Orange County Sheriff as a crime scene supervisor. These photos are of items I collected. A red World of Disney bag and inside it was a Gatorade bottle. Reviewing my report, these items were about seven inches away from the skull. The bottle is shown inside the bag. (Witness ended)

The Defendant's Twentieth Witness

Interpretation of Testimony - Michael Rickenbach, PhD (recalled): I am an FBI forensic chemistry examiner. My report is from July 6th, 2009. The items were a bottle with liquid and a syringe. (Objection, not in evidence.) (Sustained) (Sidebar)

Maybe Mr. Baez lost his Florida Rules of Evidence book. This can come in, but it must be done by the rules.

(Testimony resumes, with the witness now reviewing his report of December 11th, 2008.) I received items from my control unit of the Orange County Sheriff; a car seat and steering wheel cover. I was asked to test for the volatile substance chloroform, and it was not on either item. I took a sample from the child's car seat, and no chloroform was found on the cutting that I took from the car seat. I cannot say about the entire car seat. (The prosecution wants all the items he used put into evidence.)

In the report of July 6th, 2009, I was given a doll to check for the presence of chloroform. There were volatile chemicals, but no reportable chloroform. There was an early indication that chloroform may be present in small amounts. I requested a similar doll, but it was not available. A coworker provided a doll, which was different. However, the small quantity on Caylee's doll was not enough to report any chloroform. A negative control is usual and I ran with it. I did get another doll, and I did not find chloroform on it, although it was from the same manufacturer, it was a different doll. Chloroform can be found in water if the concentration is high enough.

With the Gatorade bottle, we were asked to identify what the brown liquid in the bottle was. I inserted a needle inside and drew some of the liquid into the needle. The photo is in evidence. In the bottle, I found the liquid to be whitish and maybe some cleaning compounds and testosterone. The liquid in the needle was a small amount of testosterone and compounds. Low amounts of chloroform were found, and they were at such low levels they could not be reported. I did not report this because the amounts were small and the test was to find what this was. This had all the chemicals included in a cleaning product. Therefore, it was irrelevant. Cleaning products do contain trace amounts of chloroform. (The witness is excused.)

The Defendant's Twenty-first Witness

Interpretation of Testimony - Karen Korsburg-Lowe (recalled): I tested items of clothes from Casey Anthony's closet and they were negative for decomposition. Hairs were found. In my report of October 15th, 2008, this was debris from the trash box of the vehicle, and there was no finding of decomposition. On November 6th, 2008, a hair from the vehicle and debris

from trash was tested. The hair had no sign of
decomposition. The paper towels had no hair. On June
25th, 2009, the first section of my report shows items
from the trash or trunk. I looked for hairs with
decomposition. Some had no hairs and if they did, they
did not have decomposition. Next was from the Medical
Examiner's Office. I examined fibers from the known hair
mass associated with Caylee and then compared them to
fibers in the trunk and car there was no match.

With the items from the Anthony home, I was asked to do a
fabric portion test from the duct tape at the house and
at the remains site. These were woven fabric tapes. These
did not come from the same source. I received samples
from the Medical Examiner's Office for comparison to the
hair mass that we know as a known sample of Caylee. I
also received numerous items from the scene. We compared
it to that hair mass. There was one Caucasian hair. That
was not Caylee's. (Sidebar)

Baez likes to try to short cut, and not identify evidence
in the proper way in the court. It seems a tactic to try,
perhaps, to confuse the jury. The jury is taken out.
Ashton, the prosecutor, is very good, however his temper
gets the better of him, and he yells. If he could do what
he does without the yelling and intimidation, he would
really be great on both cross and direct examination. The
secret is to kill them with kindness, then go for the
throat smoothly, I hear. Baez will be allowed ask the
names of the individuals, but not if everyone at the
scene was tested. There were more than fifty CSI and
police collecting evidence. The jury is back. Witness
continues.

Karen Korsburg-Lowe (Testimony resumes): I found an
unidentified hair from the scene on collection paper, not
the evidence. I then looked to see who was at the scene
collecting evidence. In my 2010 report, the individuals,
Maynard, Cardillo, Coebell, Wood, Bloise, and Welch were
some of the people at the remains scene. This is not a
complete list of everyone from the scene. This did not
come from anyone I have compared so far, or from Casey or
Caylee, and these are the known samples I was given. I
inspected the remains scene, the items, the vehicle, the
home, and those items from each scene were compared to
the hair mass. All other hairs were unidentified, or they
were consistent with Caylee. Out of hundreds of hairs,
some were not testable, and one had human decomposition.
The Anthony residents and the vehicle hair were tested.
The one hair was just on collection paper from the scene.
The hair that had decomposition was found in the trunk. I
do not know the period of June to July that she was

358

living at the house with her clothes, or elsewhere. If the items from the place where Casey was living were given to me, I could have tested them. (The witness is released. The jury is excused, and the trial is over for the day.)

The judge has a meeting about court budgets, and he must attend. The judge inquires of Mr. Baez: On Friday, I would like your best guess on when you will close your case. This is not to rush you. The State is planning to present rebuttal testimony, as we all discussed at the sidebar. I want them to have an idea when they will begin their rebuttal case. Your Honor, I will give everyone that professional curiosity. Okay everyone, court is adjourned. (Court is in recess until tomorrow.)

The media coverage had died down for a few days, but now they are in back full swing as we near the defense's case ending. We have watched the media, the courthouse crowds, and viewed helicopters buzzing over our courthouse as the jury selection began in our home of Pinellas County, Florida. We have watched, recorded, and reviewed opening arguments, every witness, open court hearings, the sidebars to the extent possible, and the sideshows, since the start of this trial. We have researched the court documents available, viewed texts, telephone logs and emails.

June 23, 2011

One of us sees no reasonable doubt that Casey killed Caylee. She believes that second-degree murder is most likely; that it has been proven that Casey killed Caylee in the course of child abuse. Caylee died in her mother's custody, with the presence of chloroform and duct tape. The other is not sure that the State has proven enough through circumstantial evidence to show beyond a reasonable doubt that Casey was responsible for Caylee's death. Considering we are from a defendant's rights oriented family, it is shocking that even one of us is convinced at this point in the case. However, despite the massive media coverage, which in a sense, has been more a benefit to Casey Anthony than a hindrance. Casey would not have the six or more defense lawyers without the media interest. Casey has been given a more than a fair trial. Casey pulled a fair judge, the luck of the draw, and he has bent over backwards for the defense. CNN reported that Attorney Lippman, the attorney for the Anthony's, said the parents no longer believe Casey is innocent. They do not know what she is guilty of, and they do not want her put to death. So, we begin another day. The first witness of the day will be Susan Mears of

359

the FBI, who is being recalled to introduce evidence for the defense: the Gatorade package, the Disney bag, and a syringe that Karen Korsburg-Lowe testified about yesterday.

The Defendant's Twenty-second Witness

Interpretation of Testimony - Susan Mears: She identifies general evidence to be admitted. (The evidence is admitted, and the witness is released.)

The Defendant's Twenty-third Witness

Interpretation of Testimony - Stephen Shaw (recalled): I am an FBI Expert in trace hair and fibers. I am looking at the photos and I recognize them. These are photos of antemortem, live people's hair, used during my study. I conducted the study after my deposition in this case. They are all photos I took and they are a fair representation of the photos from my study. (Sidebar) My study was inspired by a thesis from John Hopkins on postmortem hair. I put hairs from living individuals in different elements and then added hair from deceased people and looked to see if the appearance of postmortem could be recreated. We are reviewing the same chart of postmortem, dead people's, hair.

The hair was in the water for seventeen days; this is one of the hairs initially identified as postmortem root banding, but before the final conclusion, they are eliminated. The other was not and when the analysts conferred, they came to the agreement it was not postmortem banding. They knew it was a test for the study. They examined over two hundred hairs, and they identified all postmortem hairs but initially included two hairs that were antemortem; then before they concluded, they correctly identified all the hair that was either post or antemortem. I see the photos are clearly different and the examiners in my studies did ultimately identify the hair correctly. I do not believe there are three studies on environmental conditions of live hair. This is my report from January 27th, 2009 in this case. I reported on hairs and fibers from the hair mass, debris from the skull, and three pieces of duct tape. There were Caucasian head hairs consistent with the hair mass. All of the hairs suitable for comparison on the duct tape were consistent with the hair mass.

Stephen Shaw - State's cross-examination: (The PowerPoint presentation is now moved into evidence since Baez showed some of the photos from the PowerPoint presentation in his examination of this witness. Once again, he may not

360

have really thought it through. The defense fought hard
to keep the PowerPoint out, and he just opened the door
to let it in.) Yes, it would be helpful to use my entire
PowerPoint to explain to the jury. (The PowerPoint on
hair banding and the study will be played. They will go
in with the jury for deliberations.) There were six
hundred hairs from fifteen living individuals in this
study. These are before and after they are exposed to the
different environments. These photos are all two-
dimensional, but when the hairs are viewed under a
microscope, they become three-dimensional. Without a
three dimensional microscope you cannot fully appreciate
the opaque nature of postmortem banding. Decomposition of
a live person's hair after it is removed and subjected to
the environmental conditions is not the same as
postmortem root banding. With training and the right
equipment, you can see the difference. There were five
cadavers used in this study, multiple hairs from each,
removed from bodies in trunks, underground, submerged in
water, and other environmental conditions. Of all the
slides, of all the various conditions, no hairs from live
persons could be mistaken for postmortem banding.

(The prosecution is now getting to explain to the jury
the postmortem hair for the second time, with the
PowerPoint that Baez fought to keep out of evidence.
Prosecutor Ashton is having a wonderful time questioning
and allowing this witness Baez called to explain his hair
study in color with the PowerPoint. This is the reality
when a lawyer opens a previous closed door on evidence.
Lawyers live for someone to open the door for them to
walk through. Baez is now standing to play clean up on
the witness.)

Stephen Shaw - Defendant's re-direct: Did you have any
hairs from garbage in your testing? No. All of the hair
slides from living people have the number of days before
collected, but the deceased bodies' hair slides do not
have dates on them. They are not on the slides, but they
are in my notes. (He refers to his notes and has the
specific dates of death and collection of each hair.)
Yes, this was in the winter in Tennessee. The outside
conditions are different from Florida. The house test,
you do not know if they had heat? No. The car was
outside. The conditions were colder than the summer in
Florida. Postmortem banding is a well-established
science; the research is to gather more information. We
want to know as much as possible about postmortem
banding, so I tried to get postmortem banding from live
hairs. The goal is to learn about postmortem banding. I
believe it is already well established in the scientific
community. Examiners in our field examine deceased

individuals all the time, and we have to examine hairs exposed to many environments.

Stephen Shaw – State's re-cross: The study is not just of hairs from Tennessee. There are publications from all over the world and in all kinds of environments. At this point, the science says that only a hair that was attached to a decomposing body can have postmortem root banding. It appears these examinations are clear enough for an opinion to be formed, based on the science of postmortem hair banding. (The witness is released.)

The people waiting to testify outside the court are more forensic experts, including computer experts. Some people in the gallery have been asked to leave because they are falling asleep in the court, and their chairs are given to other people who want a chance to see the hearing. It appears that Baez is sticking to the standard defense of trying to poke holes in the prosecution's case; at this time, he has not backed up his opening statement. He does not have to prove anything, but he planted a seed in the jurors' minds and promised to back it up with evidence. Dorothy Clay Simms is questioning the next witness, since Baez has not used the other lawyers, who almost all have more experience than he does. This is interesting.

The Defendant's Twenty-fourth Witness

Interpretation of Testimony – Barry Logan, PhD: I am a forensic toxicologist and analytical chemist. I have a Bachelor's in Chemistry and a PhD in Chemistry from the University of Scotland, and postgraduate work in Knoxville, Tennessee. I am certified by The American Board of Toxicology. Toxicology is the study of drugs and forensic toxicology is drugs in dead persons. I have practiced for 20 years; I now teach at Arcadia University in Philadelphia; before that, I was a professor at the University of Washington. I am trained in the use of Gas Chromatography, the GCMS machine. I have used this equipment thousands of times. I have tested tissues, fluid, and breath. Cryotrapping GCMS concentrates or amplifies the sample. I work for MMS lab in Willow Grove Illinois. It is an independent lab, which does testing. It is the largest lab in the United States. It does coroners' reports, medical examiners' reports, and toxicology for all fifty states. My position there is as the National Director of Forensic Testing. I work with clients, review results, and I consult on medical and legal cases for courts. Money is paid for my work and testimony. It goes not directly to me but to the company. Last year, I also became Director of the Lab. I have published over eighty peer-reviewed articles. I am a reviewer for journals, including forensic science, chemical, and toxicology journals. Analytical chemistry is applied knowledge on how to separate and quantify, or determine how much of a chemical exists, in a sample. I am also a member of scientific working groups. They are unofficial, but the FBI now manages the activity of the groups. Baez asks if there is a group working on decomposition analysis. (Objection) (Sidebar)

My lab is accredited by the American Academy of Forensic Science, and I have held leadership roles in the organization; it is the largest professional organization for forensic scientists, with over six thousand members. I am also a member and a former Director of The American Board of Forensic Toxicology and I participate in ABFT inspections. I performed inspections on workplace drug testing labs. I am also a member of American Society of Crime Lab Directors. (He is tendered as an expert; the prosecutor wants to voir dire the witness.)

Barry Logan, PhD - State's voir dire: I perform analytical chemistry as it is related to toxicology; it is hard to separate the two. When was the last time you performed an analytical chemical analysis for toxicology? Outside of toxicology, what do you do that is not toxicology? I am responsible for the part of the lab that is toxicology, and I supervise people that look for drugs. I am also the director of the crime lab. I am not an expert in every area of toxicology and the techniques that are used. I have not used cryotrapping in twenty years. I am not an expert in all areas of forensic science. I believe my expertise is limited to toxicology.

Barry Logan, PhD - Defendant's Direct Examination (cont.): I served on the boards of other organizations and have done scholarly research I am accepted as an expert in only toxicology. (He is accepted as an expert in Forensic Toxicology.)

We have suspicions about this witness, we will see. He has testified in early hearings about the science of air samples. He works for a private, for-profit company. They are all around, to provide lawyers with hired gun experts for court.

Barry Logan, PhD (cont.) I use a gas chromatograph. I was provided with records from the FBI evidence of the trunk, reports from Oak Ridge science and many other documents, including autopsy records. I have reviewed the published article by Dr. Vass. My lab is accredited by The American Crime Lab. (Sidebar) What is the difference between a forensic laboratory for court and a crime forensics

363

laboratory for research? A crime lab may do educational lab work; they make discoveries in medical, testing, machines, space exploration, and so forth. Research labs just do research. I have no evidence that Oak Ridge has been certified as a crime lab. To be certified, independent validation test or tests are needed to find out what the lab's tests will show, to make sure they do not get false positives. I have reviewed the material of Oak Ridge, the notes of Dr. Vass and Wise and other material, the forensics report from Oak Ridge to Orange County, and their depositions. They are a commenting on the unexpected result, testing procedures, and any problems in the testing. As a result, of what I reviewed, I concluded that… (Objection, this is out of his area of expertise.) (Sidebar)

Barry Logan, PhD (Testimony resumes.) There were no established, published protocols for the testing that was performed at Oak Ridge Laboratory. If you do not have a written procedure, you could get false positives, or be unable to show the test was done the same way each time. It is critical that you have a written procedure. There is no evidence of what might have been something that could cause contamination. I saw no evidence of quality assurance that was relevant to the analysis. When you document the test, the test samples may have the chemicals and a proficiency test, and they perform the test blind. (Objection) (Sustained) A blank sample is a known sample that does not have the chemicals you are testing for. (Objection, not relevant to this case.) (Sidebar) If you do not have the machine set up appropriately to do a test, you will not get a good result. This is why you should have a written protocol. (Objection) (Sustained, the last comment is stricken.) If you are running a blank sample, and you get a result of the chemical you are looking for, you could get a false positive. A closed valve messing up could ruin a sample and sometimes the valve will become stuck and give a wrong result. When I reviewed the notes, the techniques were changed in the middle of the test. They were changed over the several weeks to try to correct errors. A standard is to be run the same day as the testing. That did not occur. There were several times the standard and evidence were run on different days or weeks.

Oleic acid is a fatty acid, it is in all bodies, and I have tested things that have them. Palmitic acid, acetic acid and myristic acid occur in plants, animals, and household products. Some are in dairy meat. If a paper towel had these acids on them, and yes, these were present in the paper towel, they can come from cheese. I have reviewed articles of food, including pizza. (Sidebar)

(It feels like we are watching paint dry while this witness is testifying.)

Barry Logan, PhD - Direct examination (cont.): These four fatty acids can be found in foods. They were found on a paper towel. All four of these fatty acids are found in oily vegetables like plant oil. There is a difference in the carbon molecules in body fluid and foods. All the carbon chains are four carbons long in food, the carbon chains are eighteen carbons long in body fluid, adipose. There are compounds not in food that are in adipose. There are special challenges in testing. Where you have protocols there are fewer, but there are always problems, and the scientist should adjust for them in testing. The steps and procedures for testing are not published by the forensic science community. A blank is a sample of room air that is run through the machine to check for air samples. If the blank shows unexpected results, the analyst should investigate, find the problem, fix it, and then run it again.

Barry Logan, PhD - State's cross-examination: When a scientist forgets to close a valve, he should investigate, find the problem, fix it and run it again? Yes. So this is what Dr. Wise did? Yes.

Barry Logan, PhD - Defendant's re-direct: A challenge is something unusual in a sample in the testing. There are no published protocols on how to collect air? No. There are no published protocols on how to collect carpet? No. I cannot duplicate the tests. There is not enough information, not enough detail in the reports. I do not know if I did the tests, exactly how Oak Ridge did the tests.

Barry Logan, PhD - State's re-cross: Your lab could not do these tests, isn't that correct? Our lab could do these tests. So, here is the evidence and you are telling this jury that you could do these tests in your laboratory? (Objection) (Sidebar) (The jury is excused again for a legal matter.)

When he picked up the cans to confront the witness, Ashton dropped one of the cans against the table and it made a loud noise. Then he did not ask to approach the witness when he firmly placed the evidence in front of the witness on the stand.

Judge: All right, Mr. Ashton before your argument, you may want to look at Hayes v. State. Ashton: Thank you, I am looking at Overton v. State. Judge: I am reading Overton. Mr. Ashton read the head note on Hayes. Ashton: I will proceed with arguments when you are ready, Your Honor. The State's position is that the defense asked if the witness could reproduce the tests. He said, no. That opens the door for us to ask about his ability to perform these tests. The Overton case expands Hayes. Defense: We do not agree; it is not even close. There is no way it could be done again in this case. It is not an issue of whether his lab could do it. We move to strike the comment and ask for a curative instruction.

Judge: The Florida Supreme Court in Hayes addressed a proposition of law on burden shifting. The supreme court said that the defense never has an obligation to test evidence. Any comment by the State about lack of attempt by the defense to obtain evidence for testing is improper. Such a comment could have led the jury to believe that the defendant had an obligation to test evidence, which he did not. The Overton case states that the defense can open the door by making remarks that the prosecution should be able to rebut. I sustain the defense's objection, but it is subject to opening the door. This witness has not been qualified in the area of hair analysis, and he was not qualified in odor. You have been cracking the door, defense. Mr. Ashton is getting ready to run through it, should you open it. I suggest you be careful. I am not giving a curative instruction as to Mr. Ashton making the noise and removing the items. You did not object. (The jury returns to the courtroom.)

Barry Logan, PhD - State's re-cross (resumes.) In my lab, I could put it in a Tedlar bag and heat for 36 hours, then I could extract an amount of air. I could inject that in cryotrapping. Could you set up a machine if you have the notes from Oak Ridge? No. (Objection) (The witness is excused.)

Judge: (This is the curative statement to the jury from the judge, only on burden of proof.) It is well established in the State of Florida, that the State must prove every element beyond a reasonable doubt. The defense has no obligation to prove or disprove anything.

(The defense keeps opening the door to otherwise inadmissible questions and evidence. The judge warned the defense and gave them a break by stopping Ashton. That is why Mr. Ashton did not get in trouble, since the judge did not let him through the door anyway. The can incident was funny; Ashton is highly animated, and clearly has a temper. While Dr. Logan was on the stand, there was a news flash: the Anthony's say that their comments were taken out of context and they do not believe Casey is guilty. In addition, the alleged mistress of George has been outside the courtroom, and is expected to be called as a witness. George Anthony denies the affair or that he told her anything.)

The Defendant's Twenty-fifth Witness

Interpretation of Testimony - CSI Jennifer Welch (recalled): I was in charge of the recovery site on Suburban Drive. There were no socks or shoes, that I recall. It is then your opinion Caylee did not have on shoes or socks when she died? (Objection Sustained, No more questions.)

The Defendant's Twenty-sixth Witness

Interpretation of Testimony - Cindy Anthony (recalled): I used the computer at our home, in the spare room. Everyone used it; even friends of Casey used it. In March of 2008, I used the computer to look for chloroform. I started looking for chlorophyll because the dogs were eating leaves. I thought that maybe they were making the dogs tired. Looking up chlorophyll led me to chloroform on the internet searches. I know, because I was doing other searches about hand sanitizer. I was worried about Caylee and hand sanitizer and its ingredients. That prompted me to look up acetone and hydrogen peroxide. I also looked up injuries of a friend who had an accident. I usually work a regular schedule, but I took off holidays. Why does your work schedule show you were working? It can happen that I am not at work and the time schedule shows me at work.

This photo is the trunk of the Pontiac. George and Lee drove the car and Lee drove it for about 4 years. Then Casey or George drove this car. I see the stain in the photo, it has always been there since we bought the car; there were a few little stains. I think I saw just a gas can cylinder impression; that was all that was new when I picked the car up from the tow yard. Is it your testimony that despite your work records showing you at work, that you were home? It is possible, and if the computer records show those searches, I did them; I had to be at work from eight to five. It is my testimony that it is possible I was home in spite of that. Have you looked in the last three years at your work computer, to see if you were home that day? Only I would know, and no one but me had access to my e-mails and they are gone by now, since I have not been back to work since this happened. I do

367

not know if my company backs up my e-mails. Our e-mails only lasted so long. Do you have knowledge if your former employers backed up these e-mails? I do not think so, since there were so many. You are aware that these computer searches were issues as early as August 2008. I guess in September 2008, the detective came to the house and I told them and then you in my deposition. I asked, and you told me you had only searched for chlorophyll. You testified in the past that you looked at chlorophyll correct? Yes. You suggested that was in the Google search engine. Did you type into the search bar on Google, how to make chloroform? I do not know. I did not search for neck braking or self-defense. Is this something that you are recalling since you changed your medication? Yes. I did not search for a shovel. On another day, did you look up inhalation, alcohol, acetone, and hydrogen peroxide? No.

I use whatever search engine is on the computer. What browser I use is on the desktop and it is always for anyone and whatever user. I do not recall having to choose the user. I did not have to enter a password. Did you search for making weapons out of things from household items? No. I did not search chloroform. Chlorophyll maybe I do not know. In March 2008, I did not have Facebook or Myspace. The stain in the carpet trunk carpet was in the top section. The password protection was on my work computer. There was no password protection at home. I would come home and get on right after Casey. I told the lawyers about chlorophyll in my deposition. (The witness is excused.)

To the writers, it appears that Cindy is trying to save her daughter now. After a debate between us, it is agreed by the writers that Cindy tried to take credit for too much searching, if the State's expert was correct about eighty-four searches for chloroform. It is understandable, but we do not believe she did these searches. Cindy worked as a nurse; we think the company would still have the records of when she was on her computer or really at work. It has been long established in this case that she worked eight to five or later. We are sure the State is checking with her company now on documentation to prove she was not at home. Even if the State does not present evidence to that effect, she was not believable to us.

The Defendant's Twenty-seventh Witness

Interpretation of Testimony - Sandra Osborne (recalled):
I am a detective and computer forensic examiner. I ran a key search for chloroform. It identified as a deleted

internet file, and I turned it over to my supervisor. He handled it and I watched his work, but I was not involved. I used a software program that is widely recognized. It is a different tool from CacheBack; we use both. I do not use the reporting tool incorporated in the program; I export to Excel. I turned it over with the other reports to the detectives, and I assume they went to the prosecution. (Baez hands her a prepared Excel printout.) This is not my handwriting and I have never seen it. I did not work on this item. I believe this is a document Stenger prepared. These are report summaries of findings after August 2008. It says I exported that Firefox file and saved it and turned it over. This refers to what was deleted from Firefox and it was copied to a flash drive. He took it back to work on. What you are showing me is a different format. I recognize some of the content, as best I can tell. (The witness cannot identify this document at this time.) I am showing you the original that was turned over to us. I do not believe I did this, and I cannot verify it. Stenger did it after I copied it to the thumb drive. I did not work on it, and this is not my document. The Anthony computer PC desktop had a user account with a password of Rico23 that was set in March of 2008. (The witness is excused.)

The Defendant's Twenty-eighth Witness

Interpretation of Testimony - Kevin Stenger (recalled): I am a Sergeant with the Orange County Sheriff's Office and a computer forensics expert. This report, after we entered the key word of chlor, chloroform was found. We used two different kinds of software to retrieve the information. Detective Osborne did the recovery. I recognize the report on the screen. I am familiar with this document. (Sidebar)

This may be one of the first things Baez has done in a while we agree with. He is trying to take the steam out of the prosecution's rebuttal case by attacking the computer searches.

(Testimony resumes. Sergeant Stenger has reviewed the computer data.) It is an accurate representation of the data and the four tabbed pages. (Once a foundation is laid, the report is accepted into evidence.) This is a report of the deleted Firefox searches, which in the deleted internet history. It is done on competing software, CacheBack. I asked Mr. Bradley if he could use his tools to examine the internet history that I had uncovered. We had come up with a problem of dates and times, due to daylight savings. He used tools that could report for the two different time periods. I do not know

369

if it was the same number of files. It took a day or two to fix the problem. On March 21st, 2008, the website is shown on the history (scispot.com/chemistry/chloroform). This is the same website that was visited eighty-four times. There is a difference between the software. In the NetAnalyzer program, Myspace.com was visited eighty-four times, according to the NetAnalyzer report. This Myspace is not on the CacheBack report for the same time. The sci-spot was visited once and Myspace was eighty-four visits, just a few columns down on the NetAnalyzer report. The day before, Myspace is visited eighty-three times. The day before that was a Myspace visit on March 19th at 8:36 AM. It was typed in the browser and it shows eighty-two. On March 13th, 2008, someone typed Myspace eighty-one times. You would not see these dates on the CacheBack report, because it is only March 19th, 2008, on this report. The NetAnalyzer report was having a problem with the EST date and time. The reports are different. I prepared the CacheBack report in evidence. I did not testify about the report. It is a CacheBack report for March 17th, 2008, a different day. Do you know why they had the creator of the software testify to that report? (Objection) (Sustained)

Kevin Stenger - State's cross-examination: You may have printed out the report, but the data was collected by Mr. Bradley. (Objection) (Sustained) What process was used for the 17th and 19th reports from March? Their information was generated by the software. If I had a question about Apple, I would ask Steve Jobs. This was the same with Mr. Bradley, who was the creator of the software. He was willing to look at the problem I was having. I do see some of the Google searches for "How to make chloroform" displayed in evidence by the defense. If you expand the columns, you can see "how to make chloroform" in the Google search that was typed in, then an entry for Myspace. The dates and times on these two reports seem to be accurate. Column 141634 tells the date and time of the searches. The search times between Myspace and "how to make chloroform" are twenty seconds apart.

Kevin Stenger - Defendant's re-direct: The visits for chloroform on March 21st, 2008, show in the NetAnalyzer report. According to the NetAnalyzer reports, they were visited once on this day. They spent three minutes of time that day. We purchased this CacheBack software after we already had NetAnalyzer. The webpages show whether the user was done in three minutes, or spent hours until the user closed the tab. That is true whether the user is actively looking at the webpage or not. It tells that the searches were done in a particular sequence, but not if the user printed or stayed longer. (The witness is excused, and the jury is excused for the evening.)

This was a little help to the defense in causing confusion to the jury on these reports. However, the "how to make chloroform" search is still there, and at the same time as a Myspace search. Cindy did not have a Myspace account at that time. We are not sure that the defense gained ground from this in the end.

Interpretation of Testimony - Proffer of testimony - FBI Agent Nickolas B. Savage: I was the lead agent on the Casey Anthony case. It was in the Crimes Against Children and Violent Crime Unit. In February of 2009, I was in a meeting with prosecutors. (Objection, work product) I did try to find photos at the request of the Assistant State Attorney. I may have requested photos of duct tape from the Medical Examiner's Office, because I did not believe the photos of the tape had been taken up until that point. Did you receive an e-mail from anyone in reference to this request? No. This is the first time I have seen this e-mail. My name is not on the e-mail.

Interpretation of Testimony – Proffer of Testimony – FBI Agent Erin Martin, FBI Request Coordinator: She is questioned about an e-mail to Karen Korsburg-Lowe on February 6th, 2009. She is reviewing the e-mail. (The e-mail is about a photo request that some clerk at the FBI does not want to deal with, and tells the forensics case agent something like this: I decided not to give the measurements to Brian, who e-mailed us. I did not want to go into your case notes. I cannot understand why the Medical Examiner's Office did not take a photo with a scale of all three pieces of the tape.)

The defense is alleging that the State, the FBI, or the two in combination were attempting to manufacture evidence, specifically, a photograph of the three pieces of tape together, laying flat with a ruler or some other scale of reference. The Medical Examiner's Office photographed the tape on the skull, and off the skull together without any sort of scale. The ME's Office then separated the tape and photographed the pieces with a scale. The State says that the request was made to locate a picture of the tape, still together, with a scale if it existed, not to reassemble the tape for a picture. Both sides have known for some time that no such picture exists. This was an attorney from the prosecutor's office making a request for evidence, looking for information, and nothing more.

371

Judge: None of this is relevant in this case. The defendant has been charged in a seven-account indictment. The court finds that that this testimony and e-mail do not go to any material fact or impeachment on any relevant issues. Defense, you are assuming this is evidence of an attempt to create evidence and there is none. That would be a Motion to Dismiss. This testimony is collateral to the issues before the Court. As to Nickolas Savage's testimony, it is not relevant in this case. The defense has known for three years that there were no photos of all three pieces of tape together to scale. As for Erin Martin, her testimony is not relevant. Your request to call these witnesses is denied after the proffer of each witness. (Court stands in recess for the evening.)

The judge is not going to allow a FBI clerk to be tried over such a thing. This is just. It is clear the judge feels this is to distract from the issues at hand, the charges, including first-degree murder, against Casey Anthony.

June 24, 2011

Once the defense finishes it case, the rebuttal case of the prosecution will be presented and then there will be closing arguments. The court is in session. The judge is not happy this morning. The defense is still marking exhibits.

The Defendant's Twenty-ninth Witness

Interpretation of Testimony - Cindy Anthony (recalled): The shorts that were found at the remains site were something similar to Caylee's; they were found off Suburban Drive and were a size two toddlers. (Photos are displayed.) Caylee was in three toddlers when the photos were taken that are being shown. (Sidebar)

Cindy tells us Caylee was still growing and on the high end of the growth chart. This is not very useful; all mothers know that the size of size two toddlers and size three toddlers depends on the manufacturer of the clothing; they vary.

(Testimony resumes.) I have reviewed the video of Caylee in those shorts; it is in early 2007. I took this video of Caylee in the shorts. It is a fair representation of Caylee's size and interaction at that time. (It is entered into evidence. It is the video of Caylee and Casey playing on the floor.) Caylee had grown quite a bit from the time it was taken in April 2007. I have watched this video hundreds of times since I last saw Caylee. I remember the skirt I was wearing, and since it is out of style, I did not wear it after that time. (Defense shows the picture of Casey and Cindy at the wedding when Casey was pregnant and Cindy is wearing the same skirt.) (Sidebar)

They have it blown up to a poster size in color. We think they are trying to get a pregnant poster of Casey in the jury room, looking for sympathy during deliberations. The judge sustains the objection. This poster-sized photo will be introduced.

(Testimony resumes.) Next, he shows Cindy the swimming pool in her back yard, in a regular sized photo. This photo has the ladder disconnected. It removes easily, with a hinge, Cindy states. The next photo shows the ladder attached up for climbing access to the pool. These photos are regular size. (They are admitted without objection.) Now he has a picture of Caylee walking up the ladder to the pool with Cindy behind her. (Objection) (Sidebar)

It looks like the judge is taking a look at more photos that Baez it trying to admit. When the jury deliberates, they will have everything that has been admitted. That is over three hundred exhibits from the prosecution and about a hundred, so far, from the defense. Whether Casey is found guilty or not guilty, this evidence should take at least a week to review thoroughly. They can touch, read, and review, while deliberating. Therefore, what goes into evidence is very important. That poster would have been prejudicial to the prosecution. We suspect that Cindy may change her testimony and say that she might have left the ladder up on the pool; since pool photos are being introduced, we are sure she will be questioned about the ladder again.

Cindy Anthony (Direct examination resumes): This photo was taken in the summer of 2007, I believe about one year before Caylee passed away. (This one is admitted to evidence. It is Caylee climbing the ladder with Cindy behind her.) Cindy says she is barely helping, and Caylee could climb better a year later. She could do it by herself if the ladder was up. (There are two of these photos.) The next photo is the same day, when Caylee made it to the top of the ladder. (Objection) (Overruled, and the photos are received into evidence. It continues with other photos of Caylee and Cindy around the pool.) Caylee would sit on the platform and wait for me to get into the pool. Then in the following years, she would not wait as much for us. We always had a life jacket on her. The pool was put up in March or April, and she played in it about four times a week. During June 2008, I had one week off for vacation and we swam every day.

We took numerous precautions with Caylee around the pool. We made sure that once Caylee started walking, we had a pool box near the ladder and we moved it. We took extra precautions to keep the ladder down off the pool. We took the ladder on and off. She had to have someone with her, and we taught her to go up and down the ladder. We kept a life jacket and swim ring on the porch, and this is the second or third life vest for Caylee. These photos were taken after the video, and she had outgrown the second vest in the photo by 2008 and had a third. Next is a photo of Caylee in the screen porch. She is about door latch height. I am ninety-nine percent sure that we always put shoes on her to take her out. The sliding glass door does not have a bar to keep it from being opened. Caylee could easily open the door at her age. On June 16th, 2008, I came home and the ladder was up, attached to the pool, and it was a highly unusual event. I called George and asked him about the pool ladder and the gate being unlocked to the yard. George said that he did not leave the gate open or ladder up. I also told people at work, I remember telling Debbie, about someone swimming in my pool. Everything could be heard in the office, we had cubicles. On June 16th, 2008, were you having marital problems? (Objection) (Sustained) (Sidebar) (The jury is excused for a recess.)

Judge: I reviewed the Mattel case and the issue of the theory of defense. Your theory of the defense, Mr. Baez is that this was an accidental drowning and your client's behavior after was caused by long-term sexual abuse by the father. Baez: Yes, among other things, Your Honor. Judge: Among other things… that is all you said in your opening statement. The Mattel case had to do with police retaliation and more. Mr. Baez what is your theory of defense? You cannot just use a broad blanket to get everything into evidence. That is why I admitted photos of Caylee at the swimming pool. If your theory is ever-changing, someone had better tell me what it is. (Sidebar) (Mason, the "old dog," has stepped in and is requesting and arguing at the sidebar to get evidence in. This was a long sidebar, for one outside the jury's presence. This judge is not going to allow taint for taints sake.)

Cindy Anthony (Direct examination resumes): (The jury is back.) On July 16th, 2008, I advised the lead detective about the pool ladder incident. (Objection) That was within 24 hours. (Objection) How many times have you advised law enforcement of this? (Objection) (Sidebar) (Objection sustained.) No more questions.

(Baez did not ask her the question about the ladder being attached for climbing. She has already testified it was always removed. She told us in detail how she took down the ladder on the last day she swam with Caylee, then picked up Caylee's bathing suit and life jacket to take in the house after taking the ladder down.)

Cindy Anthony - State's cross-examination: Even after your granddaughter Caylee was missing in June 2008, you maintained her bedroom, and kept presents and clothes in the drawers. In the past, after Caylee outgrew the clothes you had garage sales and maintained some old clothes in storage boxes for some other purposes. Yes. She was potty-trained, and we would carry diapers, pull-ups. She wore panties at home. She started wearing pull-ups in 2008. In this photo, the one with Casey and Caylee, it looks like a pull-up or diaper under the shorts. There is something coming out of the back of the shorts. In April of 2007, in testimony you gave before in court, you have said these photos were a couple of months before her second birthday. (More photos are now presented, and the witness seems unsure of the time when the photos were taken, but concurs.) Yes, mostly George and I did the laundry. Casey and I bought her clothes at Target. The brand on these shorts is a Target brand.

These photos are of tops and a pair of shorts of Caylee. They are from her room. Those clothes were in her room in 2008, until they were seized by law enforcement. The clothes in her room are 2T, and I had some 3T. Like all children, Caylee was stocky as a small child, and as she became more mobile, she thinned out. There are clothing items that could last for a year, even if she is growing taller. The shorts in that video, the defense video, were kept in your house? I do not recall Caylee wearing them in a while. Were those shorts kept at my house? (the shorts appear very similar to the shorts found at the remains site.) Sometimes, but they were not always at the house. Is that because they were packed in the diaper bag or in a backpack? Yes, the diaper bag and backpack were placed in my car, George's, or Casey's, as a change of clothes. When is the last time you saw those shorts? Those were not shorts I dressed Caylee in, unless Casey had them. I do not recall seeing her in those after 2007. Those shorts were in the video taken at your house. Yes, they were at my house sometimes.

The ladder to the pool could not be lifted by Caylee. The door in the picture takes a pretty good force to open.

375

Even though Caylee was two or three, she would comply and listen to me. I was very careful to give Caylee instructions about not going up the ladder. The pool is about four feet; we did not fill it all the way. If an object is not at the edge of the pool, you cannot reach it from the side. I would never permit Caylee to be left alone at the house. You discussed the pool and the side gate being opened with George? You testified on a prior occasion that Caylee could not open the gate to the yard? Yes. I testified the gate and pool incident were at different dates other than the sixteenth. I called George when I made the discovery. I had to call him on his cell or his work phone, or he could call me. I called him, and I might have left a message that day. We did talk.

As it relates to dates in June, you have made errors in your statements? You have made mistakes in the initial report as to the last time you saw Caylee? I told people at work about the pool incident, the gas can. Are you sure you were at work on June 16th, 2008? My time card would reflect that I was at work. The entries in your work records show you at work on June 16th, 2008 and on June 17th, 2008, is that correct? I worked every day that week through June 24th, 2008. I had just come off vacation. Casey was home between August and October 2008. Did you have contact with your daughter outside the jail? (Objection) (Sustained) My daughter did not tell me that Caylee died in the swimming pool. Casey continued to tell me that she was kidnapped by a babysitter.

Cindy Anthony - Defense re-direct: I am showing you the photos that the prosecution was just showing to you. Those are just photos of a tag and some of the garments are knit cotton, aren't they? The witness replies, all of the garments are knit cotton but one. That one is cotton and so are the shorts that Caylee was found in. The knit is more stretchable and Caylee didn't grow out of those as fast. We have kept a lot of things she has outgrown. Some things we kept in her room, some in Lee's closet after he moved out, and some in Casey's room. I had not seen Caylee wearing them for several months. There were specific times I would go through stuff, like at Christmas or holidays. I would take out the too small items. Caylee was a toddler, not a baby. She was not disciplined like the military, or I was not strict. She was like the average toddler.

Cindy Anthony - State's re-cross: (The prosecution verifies the material of the shorts.)

The Defendant's Thirtieth Witness

Interpretation of Testimony - Lee Anthony (recalled): I owned the White Pontiac from 2000 until about 2005. (Photos are shown.) This is the vehicle trunk. There were three stains as long as I can remember in the trunk. I do not recall making the stains, but they were there. When was the first time, that you noticed your sister was pregnant? (Objection) (Sidebar) I suspected that she was pregnant early to mid-2008. I lived at home. It was at night and our bedrooms were near the bathroom. I was waiting to get in when she came out. I saw her mid-section and was surprised. I believe I made a comment about it and she waved me off. Then a couple of days later, I told mom. Judge: I do not know what is coming out so approach the sidebar. (Sidebar)

(Testimony resumes.) The next day or so, I confronted my mom that Casey was pregnant, in the middle of 2005. I am referring to 2005. Casey came to pick me up at the airport and it was brutally clear that she was pregnant. She was far enough out that it was not that she was just putting on weight; it was clear. Can you give us a time frame? (Objection) (Sustained) I did not confront my mother. We had no other discussions about it, from the time I first told my mother about my observations. We did not talk about it again until a few days before Caylee was born. This was the only time that Casey's pregnancy was acknowledged to me. Regrettably, no I did not go to the hospital, I was hurt. (Objection)(Sidebar)

(Lee is now crying on the stand while the lawyers are at sidebar.) (Testimony resumes.) I was angry with my mom and angry with my sister. I was angry with everyone. They did not want to include me and they did not want to tell me. I was hurt. I did not want to believe it. (Objection) When I owned the car, it did not stink. I was asked to come to discuss my testimony with the prosecution, and I refused. I had reached out to the defense to talk to them and then we met a week ago. While I was in court the last time, prior to me being called, I sat with my parents in the courtroom. I felt that there was information that the defense should be aware of.

Lee Anthony - State's cross-examination: I made a remark when I thought she looked pregnant. I recall having my deposition taken. I was under oath, and the defense was present. Mr. Anthony, please review line six to line thirteen about the bump. It was not really my place and I did say it outside the bathroom, but it was not directly to Casey. (Objection) (Overruled) In June 2009, I did say that I did not call her out about the bump or bulge. I am not aware if it was then or the airport. I cannot tell you if my parents were excited, they did not tell me. I saw the preparations for the baby in the house. When I questioned my mom once early on when I saw the bump, she told me to never mind and to leave it. Then they never talked to me about it. It was just easier to block it out, since I was not included. Were your parents over the top about the expected grandbaby, excited and preparing? Well, after the baby arrived. And before correct? In your deposition, didn't you discuss the excitement before Caylee was born? I was just supposed to be in the background, my parents wanted to go over the top.

What preparations did they make? They got a crib, decorated the entire room. Your mom did everything, going nuts decorating? I am sure she did all this before. I was aware they had a baby shower. Their friends and Casey's friends were invited. I was not invited and so I do not know. This was something I was not involved in, so I was not an attentive uncle. No, my parents were not hiding this. During your deposition, we discussed the time leading up to the birth and at the birth. What was different about this question now that made you cry before this jury today and not in the deposition? Then, I did not hold the belief that Caylee was dead, and I have regrets. In January 2009, you spoke at a memorial six months before this deposition. Yes.

Lee Anthony - Defense re-direct: You were asked about a stain in this area of the trunk about the size of the basketball. Do you see a basketball sized stain there? I see a few stains, not necessary the size of a basketball. I see the white powdery stain. In this section, I do not see it. I never saw my mother use an entire bottle of Febreze in the car. I did not see the sheriff use Blue Star in the trunk. I did not meet with the defense before the testifying for the state in this case.

In my deposition I said, I think I did not say it to her directly; or I would have said something to my mom or a friend of mine. My mom told me to let it go when I inquired after seeing her come out of the bathroom. The prosecution asked if your parents were over the top about the pregnancy. Were they? My impression was my mom was not thrilled that Casey would have a baby out of wedlock. I do not know when Caylee's baby shower was; whether it was before or after she was born. You were asked why you cried today and not in the deposition. I do not want to be here. I do not want my sister or parents here. I am emotionally at a much different place than I was two years ago. After having a funeral for my niece, I could block out the emotions for six months. I do not know, if

I saw someone who looked like Caylee, I would turn and look a hundred times. It is very hard; at the deposition, I could not believe she was dead, and now I do.

Lee Anthony - State's re-cross: I remember when I testified to the State of Florida. How many times did the prosecution have to step up and show you your deposition? I don't know. Did Mr. Baez have to refresh your recollection? No. However, when we questioned you, we have to refresh your memory with your deposition. You were asked in deposition if you said anything to your mom and you said maybe or probably at a minimum in passing. I do not think I made a big deal. Maybe she was just getting fat. My memory is refreshed, that the baby shower was before Caylee's birth.

(We do not trust what he says. We believe he is trying to save his sister; it is understandable and likeable, but not trustworthy. They are siblings; they may fight day and night between themselves, but will then fight to the death to protect the other from an outside force.)

The Defendant's Thirty-first Witness

Interpretation of Testimony - Cindy Anthony (recalled): Caylee's shower was postponed because of her birth. Caylee was due in September, but she was born on August 9th, 2005. I had to change the date from August 13th, 2005. Therefore, the shower was after Caylee was born. Photos are presented and Cindy recognizes them. Prosecution objects to them being admitted into evidence. (There is an objection and it was sustained a then a sidebar. The Judge says no to the poster size photo. Another photo is presented to Cindy from her brother's wedding.) I did not believe that she was pregnant. (Same objection, but the judge admits a little picture from the wedding, not the poster he had earlier.) Friends, neighbors and family attended the shower. No, Lee was not there, no men attended.

The Defendant's Thirty-second Witness

Interpretation of Testimony - Ryan Eberlin: (Mason questioning) I am with the Orange County Sheriff. I was dispatched on July 16th, 2008, to the Anthony house. I participated in calming the people at the scene. I saw a white Pontiac, but smelled no odor. I put handcuffs on Casey, and I was told to remove the handcuffs. I was the junior deputy on the scene, and Sergeant Hosey was there. I was told to remove them. Casey was handcuffed for two or three minutes. While I was outside, her mother Cindy

had approached me and said that Casey had stolen...
(Objection) (Sidebar)

The judge is in the middle watching the two sides fight.
(The judge just excused the jury to proffer the
testimony.)

Interpretation of Proffer Testimony - Ryan Eberlin: Cindy
approached me outside with receipts while Casey was
inside the home. She told me Casey had stolen her credit
cards and made fraudulent purchases. I then went in and
detained Casey. I placed her in the car to continue the
investigation. Sergeant Hosey told me immediately to un-
cuff her, that we were not concerned with the theft, we
were concerned with kidnapping. This was after Ms. Casey
Anthony made her written statement to me, I believe, but
before the detective arrived at 4 AM. Judge: The door has
been opened for this testimony to come into evidence. I
will fashion an instruction that she is not on trial for
these thefts.

(The jury returns from recess.) Judge: The evidence which
you are about to hear, is concerning the reason Ms. Casey
Anthony, the defendant, was handcuffed. It is only to
show you why the deputy handcuffed Ms. Anthony. Ms.
Anthony is not on trial for those acts. It is to be
considered only for that reason.

Ryan Eberlin - Defense testimony (cont.): Ms. Casey
Anthony was cuffed for a brief period of time, and I had
taken her to sign written statements. Mrs. Cindy Anthony
came to me outside, and told me she wanted to press
charges for the theft. She was handcuffed for minutes,
until my sergeant told me to un-cuff her, that we were
interested in the kidnapping. The detective arrived
later. I was not involved in taking any statements after
4 AM or at Universal.

The Defendant's Thirty-third Witness

Interpretation of Testimony - Corporal Eric Edwards: I am
an Orange County Deputy Sheriff in the homicide unit. I
have been employed by the Orange County Sheriff's Office
since 2008. I assisted a great deal about the Casey
Anthony investigation. I know a Linda Tinelli.
(Objection) (Sidebar) (The judge just sent out the jury.)
Judge: Let the record reflect the jury is out.

**Interpretation of Proffer Testimony - Corporal Eric
Edwards:** I met Linda Tinelli during the investigation.
She was brought to my attention in the December 2008 time
frame. From my investigation, I got Linda Tinelli's name.

She was in charge of maintaining the volunteer tent in
the search for Caylee. I interviewed her concerning duct
tape that Mr. Anthony had brought to the tent. I showed
her the duct tape. She did not specifically say that it
was the same tape. I would have brought it to someone's
attention if she had said it was definitely the same duct
tape. I went to her home in March of 2009. I discussed
putting a listening device in a light at her home. The
Anthony's were asking to talk to her, since she had been
to their home. Our concern was to capture their
conversations if they came to her home. She was
uncomfortable, and she said she would have to get her
husband's permission, and that it was invading her
privacy. I contacted her at Lowes, Sergeant Allen and I
contacted her, we asked her to wear a wire. It was to
catch conversations with George and Cindy. I am aware of
a message that Cindy Anthony left on Ms. Tinelli's phone.

Judge: Okay, Mr. Mason, what material fact does this
evidence prove or disprove? What relevancy does this
evidence have? Mason: It shows that the focus of this
investigation was on others and not just on the
defendant. Judge: What is the relevancy to the purpose of
defense? Mason: It deals with the dysfunctional aspect of
this family. Judge: What happened in the accidental
drowning? Mason: What happened after, and why they were
so interested that they asked a woman to wear a wire.
Judge: Since the next witness is out there, were they
able to get incriminating evidence? Mason: No.
Prosecution: I argued from the proffer and in open court.
This is to invite the jury to speculation on what law
enforcement was thinking during an investigation. The
only thing that is left is motivation, since nothing was
obtained. Defense: They are asking us to believe duct
tape was the murder… (State's objection based on
speculation) Mason: There is no jury; an objection about
an argument is needless. Judge: First, this evidence does
not go to proving a relevant fact. Second, this does not
go to the drowning theory of the defense. This evidence
is inadmissible. Objection sustained.

(The judge is allowing the next witness to testify to
seeing some kind of duct tape at the search tent for
Caylee and that George brought it. She cannot say it was
the same duct tape.)

The Defendant's Thirty-fourth Witness

Interpretation of Testimony - Linda Tinelli: I know
George and Cindy Anthony. When I heard that Caylee was
missing, I went to the tent at Publix and volunteered at
times with George. I observed there was duct tape at the

table and we used it for the tablecloth. The wind would blow, and we would use tape to keep them from blowing off and we used it for putting up posters. That included Mr. Anthony and me.

The Defendant's Thirty-fifth Witness

Interpretation of Testimony - Detective Yuri Melich (recalled): I am the lead investigator in this case, and I have a supervisor in this case. The supervisors have input on how the case is handled. When I was called out in the early morning of July 16th, 2008, I was made aware of the smell by George Anthony. After about an hour's period of time I left, came back to drop Casey off after looking for where Caylee was, and then left again. I talked to George Anthony when I dropped Ms. Anthony off. I noted it in our report. I met with Ms. Anthony around noon the next day. There were two uniformed officers, and I was busy with the witnesses. I would not know if there were seven or eight officers there. Did anyone tell you the car should be taken? (Objection) I had already made arrangements to get the car. This was all one day. This was the sequence of events.

After she was arrested, I decided to look for evidence. I arrested Casey because she had the elements of the crime she was arrested for at the time. One of the thoughts I had was that someone in similar circumstances had been a danger to themselves. My focus was the missing child. The car was evidence. We were going off what we had been told - that the child had been kidnapped. They were all saying June 9th but the video was June 16th. We had some knowledge of Zanny from Casey, but we had to identify and investigate, because Casey Anthony would never tell us anything else. I listened to her jail tapes and she was still claiming that Zanny had kidnapped the child. I did not previously know this family, to the best of my knowledge. I subpoenaed the telephone records of Casey Anthony. We later subpoenaed George Anthony's records. We subpoenaed his records multiple times and gave them to the prosecutor. I believe it was the home records, not George's cell records, as I recall.

You can get calls dialed, calls received, and towers from cell phone records. It would tell me where the phone was and help in tracking a person's movements. The Metro Bureau of Investigation followed where Casey went. We did not do that for George, Cindy, or Lee. Our focus was on Casey. I also subpoenaed records of a person who called when they discovered the remains. I reviewed his cell phone records. His supervisor called 911. Then I ultimately interviewed him. I asked if there was any important information. I recorded the call. When did you become aware of prior calls from Mr. Kronk? (Objection, hearsay) During the month of August 2008, Detective White told me about a tip off Suburban Drive; he approached me. The tip was general and we had a cadaver dog in the area. We were screening hundreds of tips.

I got the records of Kronk. I think, from June to December of 2008. I would have turned them over to the prosecutor and they have the cell tower information. Only the phone company does a report. I used the information to answer questions I had about where the cell phone was during certain times. At the remains site, duct tape was found. I remember there was duct tape at the search tent. It appeared to have the same logo. It was unusual to me. I had never seen duct tape marked. I have never gone to Mr. Anthony to ask about the duct tape at the tent. (Objection) (Sustained) The only duct tape that had the Henkel marking was on the gas cans. There was duct tape on Caylee's remains. At the time of our search warrants in December, there was no duct tape with Henkel imprinted on it at the home. I knew Mr. Anthony had reported the gas cans stolen from the shed. One of the cans had duct tape on it, and I do not see it now.

I interviewed Mr. Anthony on July 30th, 2008. George and Casey had a fight over these gas cans. (Objection) (Sustained) I believe it was August, when they were collected. It is difficult to say when I was informed about the gas cans, but I would have tried to collect them in a reasonable time. (He is reviewing his report.) It was August 1st when they were collected. I collected Mr. Anthony's cell phone records but I did not collect his computer at that time. I only confiscate items, if I believe it would help me with an investigation. A computer can tell about the computer's history. I obtained statements from his co-workers and his cell phone records. There was a tip from Jerald White, but the tip itself was general in nature. It mentioned a swampy area with a six-foot fence. I knew it was near the Anthony home. I thought the tip was near the dead-end wooded area of the school. This area where the remains were found, between Hopespring and Suburban, it is much closer to Hopespring. I thought the tip was at the end of Suburban Drive. We had searched that area and it is not where the remains were found. (The witness is dismissed, subject to recall.)(The jury is excused for the evening.)

Defense: Your Honor, we believe it will be Wednesday or Thursday for the defense to close. Judge: The State's rebuttal may take a day or two, followed by closing arguments. That does bring up an issue. The State wants to have their arguments in parts. I will permit the State's initial closing to be divided between attorneys, but the State's rebuttal argument may not be split. How much time does each side expect to need for closings? (The attorneys are saying that they think each side will need one-half to one day.) Judge: You could choose a half-day, or until the jury goes to sleep, whichever comes first! I will give you an Order on Closing Arguments on Monday. I will e-mail the standard jury instructions and give you an order on what you cannot do in closing argument. Defense: Melich said he got six months of cell phone records, and we only have two weeks. He also will testify he had the phone records of George, and we have none of the Anthony's phone records. Prosecution: The records are on the disks that we submitted. We will check with Melich to see of something is missing. Mr. Baez is the one that provided the records of the Anthony's to me. Melich said it was the home phone, and I will look at Melich's records and get with Mr. Baez to confirm that the defense has everything. Nothing is intentional. Judge: I do not recall the State trying to introduce anyone's phone records that they did not give to you. The only way it is significant is if the records were exculpatory and the State hid them. The bottom line is that if you need records fine, but it is late in the day to go looking for red herrings.

Prosecution: We also need an instruction on Dr. Rodriguez. Baez: The Department of Defense advised Mr. Rodriguez that he would be terminated if he testified. He did not get permission to testify. Defense: We know he began his testimony, Mr. Ashton took his deposition, and suddenly he is shaking in his boots. Prosecution: Let me straighten this out now. I got a call. I have been told that he would be fired by the Department of Defense. He did not get permission, and they saw him on TV. He was ordered to return, or be fired if he continues to testify. We can have him and his superior to testify to that. Judge: I have offered to order Dr. Rodriguez to stay and if they thought he was going to flee, I would have put him in jail. The defense then said that they did not want his job in jeopardy, and you also said you have another witness. I can tell the jury the whole story, or that his testimony is withdrawn and to disregard his testimony. Let me now. In addition, I will have the proposed jury instructions on Tuesday. As for jury instruction, I want to bring the jury in fresh on Saturday for instruction, depending on the Motions for Directed Verdicts. First-degree and felony murder are there now, second-degree, manslaughter, child abuse. There are no lesser-included offenses for providing false information to law enforcement officers. Think, and let me know what you are asking for on lesser-included charges.

(A new motion is filed by Baez, the judge appears to it find it either amusing or irritating.)

Judge: This is a motion to dismiss, and I need evidence for the hearing and not just lawyers flapping their jaws. It can be heard in the morning or at the evening close of court. (Another day has closed in the trial of Casey Anthony.)

June 25th, 2011

Judge: Good morning. Mr. Baez, I have a copy of the deposition. I need a file copy of the doctor's report. You have not filed it with the court. Is this the same kind of testimony that has already been excluded? Prosecution: It appears to cite new studies in the report. Judge: I need a copy of the report. Baez: We will tailor his testimony, and remove any slides the prosecution objects to, within reason. Judge: Mr. Baez, all I can do is review his report, his deposition testimony, and see if his opinions have changed. Then I can decide on his testimony.

(Mason has requested a sidebar on another matter. That sidebar has taken the judge, lawyers, and court reporter inside the judge's chambers. The case law lady is at the defense table. We like the bookworms. She is an attractive, maybe fortyish, brown-haired woman. We have pet names for most all of them. Case law lady is a great name for her.

Casey looks stoic as the day begins with everyone in the judge's chambers. It appears she has waived the right to be in chambers with the judge, attorneys, and court reporter. George and Cindy look like they are holding up well today. The court is again packed. This Orlando Court room is one of the largest ones. The judge is back on the bench.

Judge: An issue has arisen unrelated to the testimony of the doctor we were discussing earlier. It has resulted in us needing to recess court for today, and we will resume Monday morning at eight-thirty.

Chapter 15

THE DEFENDANT'S CASE - WEEK THREE

June 27th, 2011

We have wondered and second-guessed the why. Why did
Judge Perry, a man set on moving this case along smartly,
suddenly dismiss court for the day after thirty minutes
in chambers with the lawyers? Maybe it was a personal
problem big enough to satisfy the need for Judge Perry to
cancel. We hope not, since Mr. Mason asked for the
sidebar that led to court being dismissed for the day,
and we like the old dog. Maybe the defense did not have
any other witnesses ready, since they were not able to
use the one they have been fighting to get on the stand.
Was there a juror problem? Since Casey remained at the
defense table while the lawyers were in chambers, we do
not suspect a plea deal. We think the key words were when
Mr. Mason asked for the sidebar. He said it was on an
unrelated issue.

Well, we are back in Courtroom 23 this morning to find
out. It is possible we will never know, and the judge
will just tell the defense to call its next witness.
These writers were grateful for the extra day off, to
continue writing this book, as much as possible, in real
time for you. The lawyers are beginning to fill the
courtroom this morning. Casey is all smiles and batting
her eyes at all the lawyers and officers in the
courtroom. However, she looks nervous, worn out, and yet
there seems to be some kind of peace in her demeanor.
This could be a plea. The mitigation lawyer Finnell is
behind Casey in the room. Finnell is handling a lot of
paperwork, while seated next to Casey at the table. Mason
is talking to Casey and she looks relieved.

It could be that Finnell is there to question a witness.
The defense plans to call a witness to testify about the
people's differing responses to a death. It would make
sense for the mitigation lawyer to handle that witness.
Casey is seated between the two best lawyers we think she
has, Chaney Mason and Ann Finnell. They are intensely
reading documents. All of Casey's surviving lawyers
appear to be in the courtroom - Baez, his associate,
Mason, Finnell, Sims, and case law lady. Court is
starting late; it is fifteen past nine. Mason and Baez
are now at the defense table with Casey. The Anthony's
appear puzzled in the courtroom. Casey's head is tilting
down and the animation has slowed in her since she
entered the room. It is almost as though she went from
relief to resignation. Baez appears frustrated. He just

tapped Finnell on the shoulder, motioning her into the judge's chambers. The prosecutors, Baez and Finnell went in chambers with the court reporter. Mason is babysitting Casey at the defense table, as she is reading some papers that she has below the table.

The blogs are going wild: Casey wants to testify and come up with a new lie? The defense lowered her chair so she looks smaller. (It is lower). Casey is very different when the jury is out of the room. The judge enters the courtroom.

He says that on Saturday, a Motion for a Competency Evaluation for Casey Anthony to proceed with trial was filed with the court. The Court appointed three independent psychologists. The lawyers agree that these reports can used by the Court in making a decision regarding Ms. Anthony's competency to proceed with the trial. Mr. Mason made this motion on Saturday, and a lawyer must have a good faith basis to make such a motion.

(We have not seen any overtly crazy behavior from her in the courtroom, so perhaps she is saying inappropriate things to her lawyers or saying or doing strange things outside the courtroom. Competency can involve a defendant's inability to understand the proceedings, to understand and cooperate with counsel, to act appropriately in the courtroom, and other things. Maybe it is something like, as bad as this case is going for Ms. Anthony, she turned down a plea deal she had been advised to accept. Maybe she is demanding to take the stand against legal advice. She could be that narcissistic. Those kinds of things with some evidence of deteriorating mental health could do it. The odds are at forty percent in the media for Casey to take the stand, and we wonder about Las Vegas odds. These are just examples of something that might trigger this motion and a lawyer vouching for the need for such an evaluation in the middle of the trial.)

The judge continues, the Court finds that Casey Anthony is competent to continue to stand trial. The Motion for Competency will be filed in the court file along with the court's emergency order for doctors. As required by law, the doctor's reports will be sealed and filed. The motion is denied. The next issue is Dr. Furton; we have cleared up matters and there is no dispute about him testifying. (The jury returns to the courtroom.)

The Defendant's Thirty-fifth Witness

Interpretation of Testimony - Detective Melich: I misspoke about the dates of phone records that were subpoenaed including Roy Kronk's phone records. We did subpoena his cell phone records for June to July 2008. The first time he called police was in August. His involvement was when the body was found. I wanted to see the thirty-one day period. I did not subpoena records from August to December. Mr. Kronk lives in St. Cloud, and his work is a few miles away from the remains site. If I had gotten the cell phones from August to December, they would give me movements of the cell phone. It would tell me the general area of the cell phone within a mile or two. In August, he had this Suburban Drive route, during August and December. These cell phone records would give me an area of the phone. Are there any other items that you misinformed the jury about in your testimony? You are suggesting I misinformed the jury intentionally and I did not. I made a mistake on something that happened in a three-year investigation. In addition, George Anthony's records for the same period in June and July 2008, those do not have cell tower reports. I subpoenaed them in 2008. I did not think that they played a part in this case. We subpoenaed several numbers from Casey's phone trying to find the Zanny who supposedly had Caylee. We subpoenaed telephone records of many of Casey Anthony's friends, but those records were not helpful to the investigation.

I did not think that the person who found the body was relevant. I found nothing suspicious with the earlier calls in his phone records. I do not recall if I got Mr. Kronk's computer. I did get a computer from Ms. Ray, because she claimed to have taken pictures of the site. She was later Baker Acted as mentally unstable. I got her computer for a reason. I got Ricardo's computer, and that is how I found out he was selling photos of Caylee.

In December, FBI Agent Joe Jordon was giving me information. I do not recall when I turned it over. Can I see the e-mail that we are talking about on the monitor? I do not know if that e-mail was turned over before or after the defense found it. (The prosecution wants the e-mail in evidence.) Melich is viewing it on a computer screen. I recall the e-mail. I do not recall when this e-mail was turned over. On December 11th, 2008, before executing the search warrant at the Anthony home, I had an idea of what was found on Suburban Drive. I left a copy of a search warrant in the home along with a list of items taken from the home. It should be listed in the items of the warrant. On the next warrant, I do not know what conversations we had with the Anthony's while we were searching. It is not uncommon to share information with the victims. I do not recall disclosing any particular things to the Anthony's at that time about what was found on Suburban Drive. I would have given a general report of our conversation in my report. I do not believe I deployed a cadaver dog on George or Cindy's Anthony's car. The issue came up that Casey might have driven Cindy's car. George mentioned it. I requested the toll road E-Pass records and found nothing. I do not recall having a cadaver dog in the house. An aerial photo of the area of the Anthony home and the remains site is presented to the witness. (The detective is circling the area where the remains were found and the Anthony home.) Casey was arrested July 16th, 2008 and she was out in late August to October, about that time. She was subject to house arrest and monitoring. There were media trucks outside her house. I believe she was allowed to go to her attorney's and to report to jail. The media probably followed her; I do not know. Since the indictment in 2008, Casey has been in jail.

The e-mail that was referenced, it was received thirty-six to forty-eight hours after the discovery of the remains. We were busy; we had been receiving hundreds to thousands of tips to wade through. I never received a report that George or Cindy's car had the smell of a dead body. The phone records of all the friends focused on June to July and this was the important time between when Caylee was last seen and when her grandmother reported her missing. Even Casey's records were originally subpoenaed for that same timeframe. The initial investigation was based on the information provided by Casey Anthony in an attempt to find this babysitter or any other party with a connection to Zanny. There was no connection to Zanny or others like Juliette or Rocker Farrell. Anything she said that was connected to the babysitter, we followed.

We were busy at Suburban Drive. This person claimed to have information, and he was not a new person. He had sent other information, and a lot of people were trying to tell us how to do our investigation. I do not know who was giving us blogs, or put us in contact with Cindy's brother and gave us information about the wedding. I did not get any information about trash in the Anthony car and had no reason to ask. I was present in July when the dog and handler searched the car. This is a drawing I made for you in court. I put one car, and then you ask me to draw another car. I could only recall him deploying his dog on one car that day. (Excused, subject to recall.)

389

The Defendant's Thirty-seventh Witness

Interpretation of Testimony - Michael Vincent (recalled):
I am with the Orange County Sheriff's Office. This is a
drawing that I drew earlier in court in this case. It is
the Orange County garage bay and the Casey Anthony car. I
testified there was only one car at the garage that the
dog went through. (The witness is excused, subject to
recall.)

The Defendant's Thirty-eighth Witness

**Interpretation of Testimony - Gerardo Bloise (recalled
again):** This is a drawing that I testified to in March of
this year. It is the forensic bay and Casey Anthony's
car. It is a fair and accurate representation of what I
drew. The focus of the investigation for me was on Casey
Anthony's white Pontiac and I was focused on her car.
Yes, I focus on the details of the investigation as a
CSI. (The witness is excused, subject to recall.)

The Defendant's Thirty-ninth Witness

**Interpretation of Testimony - Deputy Jason Forgey
(recalled again):** (Another drawing is presented) I drew
this in a hearing in March 2011. It depicts the garage
and Ms. Antony's car and another car. There were two cars
that I had my dog sniff. I testified that the other car
might have been blue and I do not know whose car it was.
I started with the unknown car to warm up my dog. There
are witnesses that saw me deploy the dog on two cars, my
supervisor and Bloise, I believe, and Mike Vincent maybe.
That is all I recall. I mentioned my supervisor in
depositions to you, Mr. Baez. I believe they were the
people there. I do an unknown car. I do it because… there
was no real reason; it is just something I do to start
working him and to calm him. Training is different from a
real world scenario. Most of the time, you do not have an
opportunity to have an unknown car. I had it moved
outside the bay, the Anthony car. It is evidence. It is
possible I could have had it moved to the lot with
several cars. Regardless of whether there were one or a
hundred cars, I know it was the White Pontiac in
question. (The witness is excused, subject to recall.)

The Defendant's Fortieth Witness

Interpretation of Testimony - Kenneth G. Furton, PhD: (He
looks like Vice President Dan Quayle.) I am a Professor
of Chemistry at Florida International University. I have
a Bachelors of Science in Forensics Science, and a PhD in

Nuclear Science. I focus on separating, identifying, and quantifying chemicals, and on work involving dogs and machines. I have studied decomposition. Since 2003, we have been looking at the volatile chemicals to find live and dead individuals. I have published. My Masters' and PhD students have published work. I directly supervise their research. I just came back from a field trip with the students to California. Most of my research has been on live human scent; but we do some on deceased scent, as well. I lecture around the county and these lectures have been on human remains.

There are chemicals that are used to identify human remains. Have you testified in the area of human decomposition and chemistry? (Objection) That is a compound question. Yes, in Chemistry, no in decomposition. I have a patent for the identification of humans based on the compounds they give off. I am a member of The America Chemical Society. I have testified in grand jury cases, civil and criminal. (Baez requests to admit the witness as an expert in forensic chemistry and in decomposition. The prosecution has no problem with chemistry, but does not agree as to decomposition.)

Kenneth G. Furton, PhD – State's voir dire: Your work in decomposition is what a dog would alert to at a site. Yes. When we say your studies, we mean your student's studies? They are mine too. The one Master's student worked on human remains, and another one on the whole body. Human decomposition is a complicated matter, so you have different stages and chemicals. The State then says, as to forensics science, I agree to admit. (The witness is recognized as an expert in chemistry and forensic science.)

Kenneth G. Furton, PhD: (Direct examination resumes.) I received the records of the investigation, the autopsy report, reports of expert witnesses from Oak Ridge, reports regarding the car, all depositions of the dog handler, Oak Ridge and more. I was asked to focus on the Oak Ridge work. I was also asked to review Dr. Sigman's work. I believe it was the first chemical report that was done. The next report, a month later was from Dr. Vass. I have reviewed the studies of decomposition. Do you have an opinion if there is a unique compound of human decomposition? I do not think there are any tests that could identify the chemicals of human decomposition that are accepted in the scientific community. I have a PowerPoint. (It is entered into evidence as a demonstrative aid, except as it relates to the area outside of his expertise.)

This is a PowerPoint of the GCMS Gas chromatograph, and the chromatogram. The samples go in and then go through the machine, and the machine produces a written report. The smallest molecules move fastest; the larger the molecule, the slower it moves; and hopefully you get the results. A known standard is one you buy from a chemical company in an exact concentration, and you run it in your machine. That is the only way you can be certain on the chemical, and that the machine is properly calibrated. The chromatogram does not tell you the exact amount, but it gives you range.

So without doing another test, you cannot obtain the actual amount, just a range of the amount is found with this chromatogram. (He has just presented a nice, very confusing report, and he is saying nothing new. Baez stopped him because he is losing Baez. He is now looking at a chart of human chemicals and they are different by individual.) You see the most common chemicals and the least frequent. This chart is living and dead people. Dead people's chemicals are more alike. The next chart is the decomposition of animals. The idea is to identify non-human, versus human. There are chemicals on humans and animals that are the same, but some are different. This is another chart, on the thousands of compounds, and then you refine to a hand-full. The charts are the chemicals in categories. In this table, we list eight different studies, including my students, Dr. Vass's studies, and others. (Objection) (Sidebar)

The methodologies are all very different. They all studied decomposition of bodies at different stages and in different conditions. There are various groups working on the ability to find remains, and my study is one. If the majority of the studies agree, then it could be included. From eight studies, the general agreement around the world must be about 50 percent regarding the compounds in decomposition for me to include results in my study. Only four chemicals meet that criterion. They are shown in this summary chart.

(A slide of the trash from the car of the Anthony's is viewed.) I read the report of Dr. Vass that said the paper towels contained decomposition fluid. These are also found in other items, including human fat and animal fat. I do not think the chemicals are unique to human decomposition and, there is no scientific evidence to identify human remains. The chloroform at Oak Ridge, they did not do a quantitative analysis. It is important to do that. This is a normal chemical in low doses and in higher doses in bleach. (Objection) (Sidebar)

You can find chloroform in cleaning products in different concentrations; you even find it in water. Bleach gives high levels of chloroform. The World Health Organization reports other products; foods, cheese, and soda. (Objection) Baez: This is the report we spoke of at sidebar. I object to his objection. Judge: Approach the sidebar, gentlemen. (The jury is sent out for lunch.) Mr. Ashton, do you have that case cite. Yes, and I will have more after lunch. A legal argument is scheduled for a fifteen-minute hearing before the jury returns from lunch. (Court is in recess for lunch.)

(The hearing begins; the jury is out.) Judge: If he has studied and run chemical tests on household products and not just a Google search, he can testify to them. He needs some basis in fact as an expert. Confer with your witness Mr. Baez before you put him on the stand, and find out if he has tested these household products. We are doing a short proffer.

Proffered Testimony - Kenneth G. Furton, PhD: Dr. Furton, can you explain the basis of chloroform? Have you relied on scientist journals and treatises to gain knowledge in chloroform? At the Frye hearing, you testified to a World Health Organization report on chloroform. Yes, it is a thorough review in basic environments. I do not have chloroform in a lot of our results. We don't have it show up much. I did more research on the internet for this case. I thoroughly researched journal articles and websites. They are reasonably relied upon, some of them. Baez: You have been instructed not to use the recent internet research.

Kenneth G. Furton, PhD — State's cross-examination (proffer): Doctor, have you ever done any research into the presence of chloroform in household products? Everything is based on what I have read, and my knowledge as chemist. My expertise and my life's work are in chemicals.

Judge: The witness can give an opinion, but he is not allowed to give an opinion based on what he reads. He becomes a conduit for hearsay. He cannot say he read it somewhere. That does not work. Mr. Mason's friend, Ehrhardt on Evidence says that the Lynn case has resolved the issue, the expert cannot testify to hearsay from what he has read. Baez: He is saying that it is based on reasonably relied-upon research. I want him to say based on his experience and research and not say what research. Judge: The doctor can give his opinion and not say where he is getting it unless it is brought up on cross-examination. (The jury returns.)

Interpretation of Testimony - Kenneth G. Furton, PhD:
(Defense direct examination before the jury resumes.) You
can commonly find chloroform in chlorine reacting with
common organic chemicals like bleach. Chloroform is a
non-polar compound and you see it in butter, cheese and
things like chlorinated water. The Gas Chromatograph
would pick up these chemicals, volatile compounds. It is
my opinion after looking at the five compounds of Dr.
Vass in his report that they are not unique to human
decomposition. They are reported in trash.

Kenneth G. Furton, PhD - State's cross-examination: Have
you ever examined the spare tire cover that was examined
by Oak Ridge Laboratories? (Objection, beyond the scope.)
(Overruled) (He is presented with the cardboard tire
cover.) State: It has no bleach stains, does it?
(Objection) (Overruled) State: The chemicals that you
testified to do not just create chloroform, they create
other chemicals as well. If bleach were spilled on a dark
carpet surface, there would be stains, wouldn't there?
Witness: Yes. State: In addition, there would be other
chemicals present. Are you familiar with the other
chemicals that are necessary? Witness: I know it can
create other chemicals, but I do not know what they are.
State: Did you research if there are articles on
accidental creation of chloroform? Witness: I do not
know. State: Did you look at the Iranian study? Witness:
I never heard of an Iranian study. One study would not be
enough. State: How many articles are you relying on to
testify to this jury? Witness: I put one in my report,
but there are others. I was not trying to come up with a
particular compound. I was not trying to figure out where
they come from. I cannot say they come from bleach; there
are other sources. Each time, chloroform comes with
something else. You have to look to see if other things
are there as well, to begin to determine the source.
Where the chloroform came from in this case, if someone
was mixing it and giving to a child or it was accidently
created by a mix of bleach and organic compounds, I did
not test. Chloroform is in the parts per million and
billion. The government has a limit of parts per million.
In drinking water there are low levels - parts per
million.

State: This slide that you presented - slide three. You
describe this slide as comparison between the difference
in living and dead odor of body decomposition? Witness:
We smell more alike when dead than alive. It tells us
that there is a common scent around dead bodies. State:
Slide four, one of your students performed this study,
published it, and she is the one who went to the morgue?

Witness: She took a machine to collect human scent. This is used by law enforcement. It is not as good as a triple absorbent trap. State: Your student held the device over the middle section of the body for one minute? Witness: She took some control samples but in the morgue, they are going to be residual chemicals. These were not done outside the morgue. State: In this chart, it is not corrected for that failed control of the excess chemicals in the morgue, is it? Witness: No, it is not.

State: This slide is from restaurant food and not a slaughtered animal allowed to decompose. Witness: It does stress a difference in human and animal decomposition. State: Your chart tells us that there is a great deal of difference between human and food decomposition. This slide, The Vass study, covered decomposition for a long periods of time. Of these studies, the one in Greece and Vass used the triple absorbent trap. Of these studies, the Greek and Vass are the only ones that looked at full human bodies. The others were things used for training dogs, bone, blood, and adipose. You have not found that the Greek study and Vass studies found more chemicals, but that the triple traps and long-time studies have. Don't you agree the composition of decomposition changes over a period of time? Witness: Yes. State: How many of the studies look at oxygen-deprived studies? It is possible that some of them do. The more information you have about the human decomposition the better. State: You state the chemical of decomposition is not distinguishable but helps in locating the odor source. The carpet, the paper towels, can all of those have been explained by a dead human body in the car and possibly the presence of some different chemicals? Witness: The chloroform could have come from a different source. I am discrediting these studies. State: Do you question whether Dr. Vass's study found chloroform? Witness: In his study, he did not run standards, he is basing it on that. I am questioning his 2004 and 2008 studies and published reports. State: Do you remember having your deposition taken in his case? Please read the highlighted portions. (Witness reviews the deposition.)

State: It is true in reference to those same studies you said: I am not saying the study was not done properly or thoroughly. It is just my opinion. I am not saying the work does not have scientific merit. In the study you published recently, you used the top twenty and others but did not run standards. You still published the data. What thing other than a decomposing body can explain all of the findings of Oak Ridge? Witness: An animal or trash could. State: You are telling us that there is no odor combination that can explain human decomposition?

Witness: It could be a human body plus other materials. State: You have to ignore the peer-reviewed papers to make the assumption that it was not decomposition. Witness: The same person who did the testing, did those papers.

State: In you deposition on Saturday, decomposition could have explained all of the chemicals in the car. All of the findings could be the cause of and explained by decomposition. Witness: There were other compounds in the trunk, like gasoline could be consistent. State: The decomposing human body would explain these findings and nothing would have to be added. Can you tell the jury any other event, other than decomposition that could cause this event, a single event? Witness: Of the things found in the trunk. State: What could cause all of these chemicals the same as human decomposition? Witness: Decomposing trash could cause the findings. State: That is just speculation regarding the trash. You do agree that something was decomposing in this trunk. Witness: Yes. State: Is there anything in there that could account for all of the findings of Oak Ridge? The slide with the garbage, salami package has no meat. Witness: There could have been residue that is gone, or it could have been something that was taken out of the trunk. From that one thing, I do not think it could it could make the trunk smell like decomposition. State: The Velveeta remnants? Witness: I do not know how much was in that package and it does not look like much. I do know if wet, the item in that package could smell. State: Here are the items themselves in evidence for you to review. They contain no food items. Witness: Not in the dry form, wet there was decomposition going on. State: There is no organic matter to rot. Witness: I am talking about residue. State: As a soiled box, this would not give off the chemical that was found. Let's look at that actual Velveeta wrapper. Witness: There is residue. State: Okay, then I want to show the jury the residue. (Objection) Judge: It is in evidence, Mr. Baez. (Sidebar) (Ashton is walking his "expert" down the garden path; the witness will smell those roses sooner or later!)

Witness: There are journals that are peer reviewed. The chemicals I cited are not in Dr. Vass's study. State: Dr. Vass's studies were a long periods of time over four years and the second a long time. Do you think a body buried a year would help you in this case? (Objection) (Sidebar) Witness: Having chemical decomposition of a body buried over a year would be of limited use, but I think it would be helpful. There are limited publications but there are differences and similarities with each body. The first reading in Dr. Vass test was seventeen days. I have an opinion that the decomposition of human body chemicals is not part of decomposition. (Objection) (Strike from the jury) The bag of garbage and the list of items could be contributors, and additional chemicals are already there. (Objection) (Stricken) I would have to know these things to make an opinion. The garbage in the photo, the difference is the garbage is spread out in the photo. I do not know if the food was removed. This trash appears to be pretty clean. Not exactly that of college students… (Objection) (Sustained)

Witness: This item of trash has a brown slime in the bottle. There is some purple dry residue. I have seen a little maggot activity there. (Objection) (Sustained) On the Velveeta, there is fingerprint powder. The chemical composition of the trash as it was collected wet would have been stronger. State: Has science advanced enough to identify the decomposition? Witness: No. It is the properties of the primary source of the odor that have the strongest smell, and it is from the lowest to the highest concentration. When this moved to the highest level of concentration, it would account for the smell. State: The substantial amount of the odor would go with the source the trash bag? Witness: Yes. State: In all the statements in this case from the reports does it say that the odor went with the bag? Witness: No.

The Defendant's Forty-first Witness

Interpretation of Testimony - Sergeant John Allen: (Interesting; Finnell is up to bat questioning.) I am a Sergeant with the Orange County Sheriff's Office. I have been employed by OCSO since 1981, and I was the supervising officer in this case. I recognize these items; I was asked to bring them to court. Forensics delivered them to the court today. They are from James Hoover. We received two videotapes when we interviewed him in a Publix in December of 2008, and another video from Mr. Hoover's attorney in January 2009. They are 8mm or super 8 tapes. We had them copied to CD. (As they are marked as evidence,) I believe they are complete copies. They are of James Hoover and Dominic Casey, who, from the inception of this case, was an investigator of Mr. Baez. He worked for Mr. Baez from July 2008 to October 2008, and then for the Anthony's after that with some crossover, for a time. He was employed by the defense. Mr. Casey was a person who would mail all kinds of information about a live Caylee. We heard that Hoover was trying to sell the videos to the National Enquirer. He wanted us to look into a woman who claimed to have seen a trash bag on the side of the road near woods.

These videos tapes were supposed to have all the information that Mr. Hoover had, and then we got another from his lawyer. That tape contained different information. Did Mr. Hoover ask you for any money? I do not think he asked but he complained… (Objection) Dominic Casey was originally working only for the Baez Law Firm. On October 1st, 2008, Mr. Casey gave us that information.

The Defendant's Forty-second Witness

Interpretation of Testimony - James Hoover: I am a licensed Private Investigator. In July 2008, I became involved in this case as a private citizen. I provided service for George and Cindy Anthony. I went down to his front yard to volunteer my service. They accepted. I kept people from harassing them at home, like a bodyguard. I followed up tips with Dominic Casey. I understand that he worked for you, Mr. Baez, then there was a falling out and he went to work for George and Cindy, and that is when we worked together. I followed up on one tip in November 2008; I met Dominic Casey at his office and we went to Suburban Drive. I was supposed to go to another place to meet him, but I was redirected by Mr. Casey to Suburban Drive. We videoed the search we did of the remains site. These are CDs of my video. These in evidence look like the tape I turned over. I viewed the first twenty seconds of the tape. Baez: I would like to admit this tape. Prosecution: Okay. The first twenty seconds can be admitted. (Sidebar) (The jury is out for a legal matter. Hoover is watching the full two tapes. He says it is a fair representation of the videos and is moved into evidence.)

This tape was made one month before the remains were found. (The video is shown to the jury.) This is Suburban Drive. I can mark where I believe Caylee's remains were later found. We walked the length of Suburban Drive and we walked from Hopespring Drive. We did not search from the fence, maybe from the first pole. Dominic was walking with a cell phone in his ear looking around. This is more like a random look around. This is two or three blocks away from the start of Suburban Drive. It is behind an old house that is run down. He is looking in black plastic bags, digging in dirt for Caylee's remains with a potting spade. We are also looking around piles of wood at this house, and it is not the remains site. Mr. Dominic Casey said… (Objection) He finds another plastic bag. We are fifteen feet into the woods. That is a blanket we found, a small blanket. The second tape is the next day. I parked closer to where her remains were later found. I parked about the third poll down, out of five poles. (Objection) (Sidebar) (It looks to us like these two PIs were right in the area, found the baby blanket, dismissed it, and never discovered the remains site.)

This is a map of Hopespring and Suburban Drives, the private fence, where I think I parked and looked. (They are in the very area of the site, but closer to the road. They did not go deep enough into the woods. There are a number of blocks of cement, and this is dense woods. Dominic Casey is probing the ground and we think he was about twenty feet away from the remains and walked past the location of the body as he was continuing forward. They are back at the abandoned house.) Baez: Point out where the school is located, and then point out Hopespring Drive.

We went to the area on two days, and we did not report to George and Cindy what we did or did not find. There is a pond behind the abandoned house. I went to both of the locations one month before Caylee was found. After she was found in the area on December 11th, 2008, I did not tell law enforcement. It was suggested that I could sell the tapes, and they might be worth something. I did try to sell some photos from December 11th or 12th; Dominic Casey had still shots. Dominic was going to supply still shots and I was going to sell them. Then I tried to sell them and I planned to give the money to the Anthony's. I thought the video had been taped over. I gave two videos to law enforcement and my cell phone on December 12th. I met with law enforcement that day. I gave them a couple of videotapes, believing they were these videos. Something was on the videotapes I gave them. I did not contact anyone about selling the videotapes. I never tried to sell this video.

James Hoover – State's cross-examination: As it relates to the videos, I was not trying to hold out for the highest price on the video. State: You gave two, one with bad color and one of a Christmas celebration, to the police. You told law enforcement that it had been taped over. Witness: I believed that was the tape in the woods, but I still had it. State: The two tapes that had virtually nothing on them were turned over and you tried to get the detectives to talk to the woman who claimed she saw something. That was the same day you turned the useless tapes over; and then a few weeks later you suddenly found the tapes. Is it your testimony you were trying to sell the useless tape to Fox News? Witness: I think I called Baez, then I contacted an attorney, and they called the police. State: You were trying to capitalize on your relationship with the parents. Witness: You are so wrong.

On November 15th, I parked near Suburban and Hopespring. Dominic told me to wait, and then I filmed him, then changed my camera film and backed up the car to him in the area of the woods. This is the area where, I believe, he was in the edge of the woods and was talking on the phone the first time. We returned the next day and came back to the spot. I am not sure where he went in the woods. We were looking for three pavers. The second day, we parked at the third light poll, I think. What post are you counting from to show where you are? We went in a little closer to Hopespring. I do not know where the remains were found. I did not see a red Disney bag. Was it a bathmat, not a blanket according to Mr. Casey on the tape? I do not remember. We were forty to fifty feet apart. I saw water about fifteen feet in, and we had more suitable clothes that day, but our shoes got soggy. It was like a marsh. I was not there in July, August, September, or October.

James Hoover - Defense re-direct: I never gave the video to you or tried to sell it. I gave it to law enforcement. We were there looking for Caylee's remains. (He is excused, subject to recall.)

The Defendant's Forty-third Witness

Interpretation of Testimony - Dominic Casey: I have been a Private Investigator in the State of Florida since March 2008. On October 1st, 2008, I was employed by Cindy and George and before that I had terminated my relationship with the Baez Law Firm. There is an overlap in services. I was following up on tips through the tip line and acting as security for them. There were protesters. They would come in the late afternoon and stay to all hours. It started about the first week of September, until the end of October. As security, I parked on Suburban Drive when I would leave the Anthony home. I would go out the back way and then I would park up on Suburban Drive and wait to see if the protesters returned. I would go get coffee, come back to Suburban Drive and look for protesters sneaking back. I did this most every night. It would have been more likely than not that I would have parked there most nights for a little while. This photo is the area where I would park my car during that twenty or thirty minute time. I wanted to see if the protesters returned.

I would see other persons in the area during this time. A Sheriff's car was there most nights and one or two media cars, down past the school. Law enforcement would be around the bend, and media was anywhere. My car would have been turned off. The windows would be down. I noticed no odor. At the end of the September, I facilitated the sending of a teddy bear to Luke Philips. He requested an article of Caylee Anthony's. I acquired his address for Cindy, and then asked Cindy if she could mail something of Caylee's to him. She sent a teddy bear and Cindy told me it was a bear. I do not know if it was returned. Yes, I received a package for Cindy. I met her I think, and I gave it to her. I was a sealed box and I gave it to Cindy. She opened it, and it was a teddy bear. It was referred to as, "Teddy". This was maybe the end of October. It was after Casey was jailed.

Luke Philips is a person who contacted the family and offered help. He represents psychic people and aids in searches. On November 15th, 2008, I was at Suburban Drive and James Hoover was a volunteer and had offered to assist with security. He did not work for my company. I was on the cell phone, and I was talking with Ginette Lucas; she is a psychic. I went into the wooded area on November 15th. (The map photo is the area and it is published to the jury.) It is the map of Suburban Drive. The first time we went to this area, I have marked on the map where we looked. I received another call from Ginette Lucas the next morning. I went there again. I was still looking for the possible location of Caylee Anthony. We pulled up, I got out and it was in the middle of the road. I told James Hoover to stay in the vehicle. I walked far enough to talk without being heard, and called Ginette Lucas back. Then I entered into the woods.

Initially, I went twenty to twenty-five feet into the woods and stayed in the area less than five minutes. I noticed James Hoover standing about ten feet into the woods. I had no idea he was videotaping and I gave him no permission. I asked what he was doing. I came out of the woods and I went to another opening in the woods, where it was easier to get into the area. I went into that area, no more than twenty to twenty-five feet from the curb, and the property went down and it was sandy then there was water about a few inches deep. The water was twenty feet in. I stayed maybe ten minutes. I was looking for three white paver stones, to follow up on what the psychic told me, and I was not looking in particular for garbage bags. I stayed ten to twelve minutes. I came out of the woods into the parked vehicle. Then I went to the vacant house down the way. Because of speaking to Ginette Lucas, I went to that vacant house. I stayed ten to twelve minutes. I was looking for the three stones. I am just cutting open the garbage bags to see what is inside them in the video. I cut just a few, and there were many. We then went to a hotel to pick up someone who was going to attend a "meet and greet" hosted by Cindy and George.

I went back on the sixteenth to prove the psychic wrong.
I think we parked in the same area. We went through the
same opening and went in to just pan around and look. I
saw no remains of Caylee, and that was the purpose of our
being there. I was there about twelve to fifteen minutes.
It was just me; Hoover is videotaping and I am probing.
The ground conditions were soft. I did not want to stick
my hands in the water. There are plenty of snakes and I
put it my probe down in certain areas for resistance. I
did not find what I was looking for. I returned to the
abandoned house and probed there. I went back a third
time alone. I was on the way to the Anthony residence and
it was the 18th. I was in the area and feeling happy
about it, proving a psychic wrong. It is highly possible
I did not go in an area that had that opening. I do not
believe that I handled any evidence. I did not see any
bags that contained human remains while I was in the
woods.

Dominic Casey – State's cross-examination: I was working
for the Baez Law Firm and then the Anthony's, with some
cross over. I had contact with Casey when she was out of
jail and my job was to investigate Caylee being missing.
(Objection) (Sidebar)(The jury is removed for a few
minutes.)

It appears to the authors that the whole woods were
either under water or debris-filled all over the area,
and they missed Caylee's remains. Tropical Storm Fay was
in Florida during this period. This is a large, densely
wooded area. You could be on top of something and miss
it. The prosecutor is looking very tired tonight. Dominic
Casey talked to Casey Anthony a lot while she was home,
and he was looking for Caylee. It seems like the
prosecutor is going to try to elicit from him what Casey
said to him. So, this sidebar could be a few minutes. I
am sure the defense wants the witness to be very careful
about what he says.

Dominic Casey – State's cross-examination (cont.):
(Testimony resumes before the jury.) I had regular
communication with Mr. Baez after I worked for the
Anthony's. A woman named Ginette Lucas directed me to
that area. Cindy's mood in November of 2008 was
traumatized, distraught. She was missing her
granddaughter and her daughter, and so was George,
absolutely. I went to Suburban Drive at the direction of
psychic who called me. George and Cindy did not send me
to those woods. This photo is of Suburban Drive, I think.
(He marks where he was parked on November 15th.) It is an
aerial view. I see a curve and a fence line. Where we

402

parked Mr. Hoover's vehicle, I can approximate with a mark at that spot. (He marks where he thinks he walked into the woods.) I came out the same way I went in. I went twenty to twenty-five feet from the curb. I may possibly have said forty to fifty feet before.

I can see it better on the screen. I would like to remark my location a little more to the left. I saw the broken toilet on both trips, each day. (The authors saw no broken toilet at the remains site in any of the photographs introduced into evidence.) I saw numerous black bags with trash, containing leaves, maybe lawn cuttings. I cut some open and I saw a bath mat. I did not see a Disney bag there. This was not an exhaustive search at all. I was on the phone most of the time, with a couple of breaks between calls. Then I came out and went to the abandoned house. There was ankle-deep water, and the elevation drops about six feet. The water travels toward the dead end of the street; you can see the current, and it was the same amount the next day. It was not like a river, wet then dry with a flow of water; it was more like a swamp with water flowing in it. I never dug or got down to look. This is a photo of the same area on the next day. I went into the woods in the same area. We parked the car approximately here.

I was on the phone again that morning with the psychic, and she told me to go back. I got hold of Luke, and told him she was full of… I talked to her, and told her what I saw and what I did. Then, the next day I went back and I was on the phone with Ginette Lucas again, while I was on Suburban Drive. I can mark where I went back in the woods the second time. I believe I exited it the same way I entered. I did not walk straight; I turned west toward Hopespring. There was still water on the ground and I had a probe and a potter's shovel for planting. I think I did not use the planting shovel in the woods, just like maybe to turn something over. The x with the square is where I went into and came out of the woods, give or take ten feet. James was hanging out about ten feet back. James Hoover came in behind, and he was videotaping. I approved the video with no audio, and he had audio on this video. I heard the audio today for the first time. I had heard a rumor that it had audio before. I told him not to tape. Whatever he filmed belonged to my investigations company. (This cross-examination is by the third-seat lawyer, and he is getting the witness to identify precisely the places he is talking about.) The third day, I parked on Suburban and just walked down the street. I never entered the woods.

Dominic Casey - Defendant's re-direct: I put a 1 and 2 on the entries into the woods. I circled the wooded area that I was in, and these are estimations. Between 2008 and today, maybe March of 2011, I was asked by the State Attorney to explain where I was in the video, I made some circles for them. (Sidebar) Mr. Casey, this event in March of 2011, it was a normal deposition? Yes, it was. Did you do circles for the prosecution at any time before? No. I did not have a tape measure when I was in the woods. I took pictures and the video. The State's exhibits are my best guess, three years later. (He is excused, subject to recall.) (The jury is excused for the evening.)

Judge: State and Defense, are there any additional matters? Prosecution: No. Baez: We can do the Motions. Judge: Notice the State, and we can do them Wednesday or Thursday. (Court is in recess until tomorrow.)

June 28, 2011

The courtroom is full this morning. The gallery is packed with tickets to the macabre circus in their hands. We have all participated. Casey began the show believing she was the ringmaster, only to discover that thirteen others stole the show, twelve jurors and the man on the bench. The lawyers are the circus acts, and she can only sit by and watch. The morning begins with a sidebar. The judge is shaking his head and waving his hands. Someone got a big "no," to what they wanted. Still, he manages to maintain a smile. Power is comforting, but we are sure he wonders at times if he can retain control over the lawyers and their constant sniping. The judge takes a pill to start the day, probably a prophylactic Advil for what is likely to come.

The Defendant's Forty-fourth Witness

Interpretation of Testimony - Joseph Jordan: I work for a dental supply company in Central Florida. I volunteered to work with Texas EquuSearch. They search for missing people, and this was my first time. I became a team leader. I led searches of areas; of groups of between ten and thirty persons. I searched the Suburban Drive area in Orlando. I was given Suburban as one of the areas to search for Caylee. (Witness steps down to review an exhibit. State objects to the poster as it had been marked on by another witness, and an unmarked one is provided on the monitor. The witness returns to the stand.)

I recognize the scene. This photo is a fair representation. I do not recall how many times I searched in this area. I led a team. I believe probably more than ten searchers were in the area at the end of the road. Everyone was searching for Caylee. We would park along this area (indicating to the monitor) and search near the road. There was no fence, so we could search that area. There was a path and we entered there (indicating to the monitor). I do not know if I made it to the abandoned house. There were probably five people then. I did go with a few others into the area. We had been briefed on how to do the search. We went only five feet, and there was water. We found a pink blanket and a red cooler. I noted it in my report to EquuSearch. I do not know what they did with the information.

The second time, I had a dog handler from another team come and bring their dog. It was the same day and same team. They were to check the baby blanket and cooler. There were two dogs brought in. I do not know the qualifications of the dogs. I told the police that I was there with a police officer from Panama City and a cadaver dog. He did not search, he just sniffed the two items that I found. Both dogs sniffed the two articles of interest and did not search. I did go back out to see where the remains were found. I do not know how far from the road it was that the remains were found, maybe about 45 feet… (Objection) (Mason is questioning, and is using a tape measure for the witness to identify the distance.) It was further down than you are with the measuring tape, sir. The tape is not long enough between us. I do not recall how many times I went down there. I do not know if I went to this area a third time; there were many other areas of interest.

On December 13th, 2008, I sent an e-mail to detectives Allen and Melich. (Witness is viewing the e-mail.) It refreshes my recollection. I conveyed that I had been searching in the location where her remains were found and the dogs were there. I think the remains were moved after my search. In the area from the fence and to the school and path, I had about five people who walked along the side of the road, because the brush was heavy. I did not see any other people search along that area. Yes, I was placed under oath, and provided a video statement to police with my attorney present. Was there a mass of one hundred people that were searching that area? The path that you pointed out was only five feet, and this is a big area. There were not a hundred people searching that area when I was there. The area was near the Anthony home, and we drove by the Anthony's home; many media trucks were around the home. I have no idea what the police did with the e-mail I sent.

Joseph Jordan - State's cross-examination: Yes, I volunteered in late August or early September. I had begun to e-mail members of the police several suggestions. I told them about individuals that they should look at, before I volunteered with EquuSearch. I believed Caylee was missing and deserved to be found. I was required to keep paperwork on the individuals who went with me and maps of the areas we searched. The maps had space for items of interest, and it was my responsibly to be debriefed by someone who worked for EquuSearch. This is my paperwork. I took very detailed notes of what I did, and what I thought was of interest. It is a five-page report. The five people are listed that were with me. There are maps with the documents and assignments I was given. My notes reflect where I searched, a church area near Suburban Drive, then at the end of Suburban, dogs were behind the school and the dogs were not fresh. They had been searching. Danny, the dog handler, told me his dog was not fresh, it was the end of the day. Anything that is not highlighted is an area where we did not complete the search. There were two bones, not human. I looked at an anthropology book to find that out. My notes say when water recedes, to re-search; the water was knee deep in that area as soon as you entered. Water moccasins and alligators filled the area. I was also afraid and that we might step on and damage the remains. I marked areas to be re-searched, and that there were black bags in the water area.

We were given such a broad area, and I wanted to make it clear where we searched. We have some confidence that we searched that area that was marked. (Witness refers to his list.) Those were items we found in the area, but I did not highlight the area because it was not searched completely. It was just past the curve and deep water stopped us from getting in very far at all. These documents were created before Caylee's remains were found. When I e-mailed the police about where her remains were located, it was speculation because I had been in the area, but I didn't know exactly where her remains were found.

Joseph Jordan - Defendant's re-direct: Yes, Mr. Churchill showed me where the remains were found. I sent the e-mail on what I saw on TV, and I had not been to the remains site when I sent the e-mail. I thought it was the area. The water was clear when I went to the site. Mason: Now, Mr. Jordan do you have any present reason to alter your testimony in this investigation, in this case? Were you threatened with a felony?" Witness: "On advice of counsel, I exercise my Fifth Amendment right…" (Objection) (Sidebar)

The authors heard the first invocation of a witness's right to remain silent in the case. We wondered which witness would say it first. Our house lawyer tells us that if the lawyers anticipate it will happen, it is supposed to occur outside the jury's presence. Chaney Mason pushed that button for the defense. He can take a bow! Even the judge at sidebar has a smirk.

(The jury is excused, and a hearing ensues.) Judge: Mr. Jordan, you many step down and step outside for a moment. (The prosecutor objects that counsel knew the witness was going to exercise his right to remain silent, because he did in deposition. Mason: I was not present at the witness's deposition, but they discussed that he had broken the law and he says he knew it. Prosecution: The witness's statement was recorded in October 2009, with Corporal Edwards. The witness had recorded a telephone conversation, and admitted that he did it surreptitiously. He has recorded people without their permission. We told him, you broke the law and do not break it again by destroying the recordings, the evidence. He admitted recording it and he said, "Because it is not to your advantage, you are going to go after me." He committed felony wiretapping. He had use immunity for the statement but not for testimony at trial, since he is not under State's subpoena. There is no pending prosecution. Mason: He took the Fifth. He does not get to alter his testimony and not bring it up. I did not expect him to take the Fifth, and his lawyer is sitting there (gesturing to the gallery). His testimony is affected by his credibility. Judge: Mr. Mason was not demonstrating that there has been a difference in his testimony at any other time. Prosecution: The objection is that counsel knew he would be exercising the Fifth Amendment right on the illegal recordings. Mason: I did not intentionally elicit this information. Prosecution: There is no excuse.

Judge: He told Mr. Mason he had been in the area in the e-mail and that he was mistaken about the area he was in at the time. He is trying to elicit the information that someone else did the search, not this witness. Mason: I did not ask him to invoke. Judge: I am looking at David v. Alaska - If there is a pending legal action that could result in prosecution… This is a felony of the third degree, and the taping occurred in October 2009, so the **statute of limitations** is still alive. (Statutes of limitations set out the periods in which prosecutors must charge a crime after the offense or discovery of the offense.) He was granted use immunity for his statement only. This offense has a three-year statute. Mr. Mason, you should have proffered this testimony. Mason: It is fair game to bring up that the witness has been granted use immunity. It would have been up to the State to go into the why. Judge: It may not be a dastardly crime, recording someone without permission, but Mr. Mason, the objection is sustained.

(The judge is thinking... and reviewing the deposition of Jordan. Mr. Baez was at the deposition and knew of Mr. Jordan invoking the Fifth.) The judge repeats Mason's question. "When asked questions in this investigation, were you threatened with felony prosecution?" It does not demand the answer of taking the Fifth; it could have been a yes or no answer. However, it probably invoked a knee jerk reaction from the witness.

Mr. McCollum, Jordan's attorney, is in the courtroom, and speaks up: Yes, Your Honor, for making the recording, my client was given use immunity for his statement, but not for testimony here today. Judge: I will instruct the jury to disregard the witness's invocation of the Fifth Amendment, and the defense can question him on the use the immunity. Prosecution: I will advise counsel for the defense that this line of questioning could open other doors. Judge: One door closes and another opens. Mr. McCollum, talk with your client outside and get back with me. (After a brief wait, Mr. McCollum and Jordan return to the courtroom.) McCollum: Your Honor, I talked with my client and explained the states position on this matter. (Sidebar)

As best we the authors can tell, this witness is a man who sends e-mails to the police all the time and records people without permission. That is illegal in the State of Florida; its wiretapping laws are clear.

(The jury returns to the courtroom.) Judge: Ladies and gentlemen, two questions were asked that are now withdrawn. "Now, Mr. Jordan do you have any present reason to alter your testimony in this investigation, in this case? Were you threatened with a felony?" The witness took the Fifth. The Jury is to disregard the answer to the last two questions as being non-responsive.

Defense: No more questions. (The witness is excused.)

The Defendant's Forty-fifth Witness

Interpretation of Testimony - George Anthony (recalled):
I know a woman a by the name of Chrystal Holiday; I knew

her by another name, River Cruise. She came to our command center. She was someone who volunteered at the command site and at the time was a friend who was going to help us find our granddaughter. She was just another volunteer, and we became friends. I did not have a romantic relationship and the question is funny. (He repeats) I did not have an intimate relationship and that is funny. I have been to her home on two or three occasions, and I can explain that. It is a condominium with a guard. You have to show identification to go in. The first time I went there, we had a conversation. She had a brain tumor and she was going to die. She was giving support to our family, and I went to show her compassion. It was during the day and not at night. (Objection, relevance) (Sidebar) (Overruled)

I did not have an exact work schedule; I went to work later in the afternoon. As I stated, I went there just to console her, and she explained it to my wife as well. My wife knew I was there. I never told Chrystal Holiday or River Cruise anything. There were no conversations with her or other people involving anything about this being an accident gone out of control. I gave information to you, the police, and detectives. (Objection) I never told her that this was an accident that snowballed out of control. I sent a text and said I needed her in my life. Like I did with many other volunteers. I left a letter, something to cheer her up, on her door one day. Did you ever ask her not to tell or for her not to say anything? I did not have an affair, so the answer is no. As to River Cruise, I do not know, I could have talked to her one or ten times, but I do not believe at night. I met her at the skating rink command center while searching for Caylee. It basically ended after the remains of Caylee were discovered. Did you ever tell her that you threw your daughter against the wall and said "I know you did something to Caylee, where is she"? No sir, I would never do that to my daughter.

The Defendant's Forty-sixth Witness

Interpretation of Testimony - Cindy Anthony (recalled again): I never instructed Dominic Casey and James Hoover to search off Suburban Drive or videotape the area. In December, I do not remember if I told Melich anything that day; we were just upset they were back with a search warrant. I do not know if I told him. People searched and nothing was found. I do remember telling him there was a blanket missing, and this was the second search since they found Caylee. On December 11th, 2008, they did not leave a warrant or items list of what they took. On December 20th, I believe our attorney requested the warrant and other items, and we did get it. On December 11th, 2008, they took like seventy-seven items. I do not think I read the search warrant. I never told anyone that I sent Dominic Casey and Hoover to the site and that is because I did not send them. My first knowledge of that search was after Caylee was found. So you never had a conversation with Lee where he asked, why are you looking for a dead Caylee? (Objection) (Sustained)

The Defendant's Forty-seventh Witness

Interpretation of Testimony - Lee Anthony: Did you ever have an argument with you mother about Dominic Casey and Hoover looking for Caylee on Suburban Drive? My mother told me that she sent Casey and Hoover because she got a psychic tip. It was later in the year. I went back to work in October, I believe it was. It created a one-sided argument; it was the first time anyone was willing to look for a deceased Caylee, and I was quite upset. I do not know the exact time frame, it happened before I returned to work, because it fielded my decision to go back to work. So you had this conversation before he went into the woods? If that is the only time he was in the woods. It made my decision to go back to work a lot easier. I was very angry that my parents decided to do that without keeping me in the loop. I could not believe they had given up and were looking for her that way. Before, no one in the family would even think of looking for Caylee dead. At that time, I do not know what I believed, so yes and no. I was sold on the lies that Casey told me.

The Defendant's Forty-eighth Witness

Interpretation of Testimony - Detective Yuri Melich (recalled): On December 20th, 2008, I executed a search warrant. While we were there executing the warrant, Mrs. Anthony stated that she had her people walk that area and nothing was there. Yes, she said something like that. She said it in front of Corporal Edwards, and I wrote it in my report. (The witness is excused, subject to recall.)

The Defendant's Forty-ninth Witness

Interpretation of Testimony - Roy Kronk: (Mason, the old dog is up to bat.) In 2008, I was a meter reader for Orange County; I had worked as a meter reader for Orange County since May 2007. I read water meters. We were assigned routes the night before, and we never knew where we would be. I was assigned to read meters at Hopespring Drive. I read the meters on Hopespring and Suburban Drives. On August 11th, 2008, no one was with me. I started a route by myself, and then two coworkers, David and Chris, joined later. I remember the date. I found a dead rattlesnake that day. Did you stop the vehicle on Suburban Drive in August? Yes, I went into the woods to relieve myself; you have to do this, there are no bathrooms. The shopping center at the end of the road is the closest bathroom. I was aware that Caylee was missing, and I was not watching TV regularly. My roommate watched the recovery of the body from the scene, but we did not discuss it often.

On August 11th, 2008, I went to Suburban Drive. It was the first time I had that route, and I did not know the area. I just went in the woods to go to the bathroom and walked out. I did not go in far. I looked around. I saw an object that appeared a little odd to me. I did not see a black plastic bag. I did not touch a bag. I was never closer than twenty to thirty feet away. I saw something that look like a white object, maybe. Than we found a dead rattlesnake and that got my attention. I did not tell Mr. Dean, my co-worker, that I saw a skull. He did not step on the rattlesnake. He got a shovel and picked it up. I said that I saw something that looked like a skull, but everyone was engaged with the snake. We went back to the office and showed everyone the rattlesnake, and they all took pictures. I called the Sheriff and told Orange County about the possible skull and they told me to call the crime line. I told them I saw an object that looked like it might be a skull. No one talked to me about it.

I worked the next day, on a different route; I do not remember where. I returned to work as usual. On August 13th, 2008, I called again. I was told an officer would meet me out there. Two officers met me. I never took them into the woods. I pointed to the area where I thought I had seen something.

On August 11th, I never called 911. I called the Orange County Sheriff, the non-emergency line. I told them I was a meter reader. Then I told them I was in the route of the Anthony home. I was back behind the school area and I noticed something that was white, and a grey bag. I said, I do not know what it is and I am not telling you it is Caylee or anything. I described the area off Suburban Drive and that there are two path areas, a log, a tree down and it is swampy. I saw something. I had seen a fallen tree, a grey bag and something white. I was never closer than twenty to thirty feet. I said it appeared to be a skull. The following day August 12th or 13th, I called again. I told them I had to relieve myself, and that there was something, like a vinyl bag, and it looked

411

more suspicious. It was a fallen tree and the white board. (Objection) (Sustained) I told the operator about a white board, a tree and I do not remember if I said something round and white to the operator. (Objection) (Overruled) I drew a map for law enforcement of the area that I had seen. I do not remember if I drew in the privacy fence. I recognize the document. It is a fair and accurate representation of what I drew three years ago, on December 17th, 2008. I see where I labeled this fence. I drew in the area, the line represents the water, then the tree and then an X next to the board is where I saw the white object and bag. I cannot tell you how far from the road it was. On the 13th of August the deputies were not taken to the spot, I just pointed to the area. On August 11th and 13th, I did not smell anything particular. I did not in any way lift a bag. I never went to the woods on August 11th, 2008. I just went to the edge to relieve myself. I did not tell the deputies that I found a bag that had bones. I told him I saw an object that appeared to look like a skull. I did not tell him I saw a bag with bones. On August 11th, I never was any closer than maybe thirty feet. I just saw it through the veil of the trees.

The area, on August 11th, where I went into in the woods, it was dry. I believe I was aware of an award like $255,000 or something. I was aware that there were a lot of media trucks in the area. I never said I found a bag of bones to anyone. I never said I found a skull. I said I found something that looked like a skull to my roommate. I said it was white, and looked like the top of a skull sticking out of the bag. The bag I saw in August, I cannot say if the bag found in December is the same one. I recall having my deposition taken. Do you recall being asked the question, "Do you believe the bag in August is the same as December?", and answering yes? I remember the answer. I guess that I thought it was the same bag. I did try to point it out, and I tried to show my coworker, but they got interested in the dead rattlesnake. I tried to get them to look, and they were busy with the dead snake. The calls of August 11th, 12th and 13th, I did not advise the operator that I looked down and saw the skull. (The calls are put into evidence and published.) The judge announces that it is stipulated Roy Kronk made recorded calls on August 11th, 12th, and 13th to 911, and that the recordings are a true and accurate representation of the calls. (The recordings are played for the jury.)

August 11th, 2008: Roy Kronk 911 Call:

Dispatcher: 911.
Kronk: On August 11, 2008, I called a non-emergency line. I had a stop between the swamps near the school in an area. I noticed something white and a bag and I am not saying it is Caylee or anything. It could be nothing. It is like Good Hope Road that the Anthony's live on.
Dispatcher: I do not see Good Hope intersecting with Suburban Drive.
Kronk: Let me look in my GPS.
Dispatcher: Is it the Anthony house on Holiday Drive?
Kronk: No. The road comes up to Suburban Drive then Chickasaw and Lumberton. That is where it is, toward the school. We found a four-foot diamond back rattlesnake, and after I saw that rattlesnake, I am not going in there. The road stops and it is all swamp area. I want to let them know and I do not know what it is. I do not want to waste any of the County's money.

August 12th, 2008: Roy Kronk 911 Call:
Dispatcher: 911.
Kronk: I had the Anthony route and at the bottom of the school area, I called yesterday. I stopped in the swamp area. I went down and there was a grey bag, a fallen tree and a white board and something round and white under it, and I did not touch it. There is no cross streets all the way to the end of Suburban off Chickasaw Drive. You pass Hopespring, there is a wooded area, and I do not know the name of the school. I just read meters. There are two swamps and that is where we found an eastern diamondback rattlesnake.
Dispatcher: I am sending someone. I have a tip line, and I want you to call the tip line.
Kronk: I do not want to call I am a county employee and I do not want to. What if they find a body?

August 13th, 2008: Roy Kronk 911 Call:
Dispatcher: 911
Kronk: Hidden Oak Middle School and I have the Caylee route there is a swamp and they said they would send an officer when I was here and I am here now. I am in a swampy area, no streets.
Dispatcher: Can you go back to the intersection?
Kronk: They will see me when they turn, just past Hopespring.

Roy Kronk - Direct Examination (cont.): After I made the call from home about 9 PM on the first day, I did nothing else. On the 12th, I watched TV and went to bed. That call was also made at night, after I got home. After you made those calls, do you recall making a statement to

Yuri Melich in January? You are being vague; I remember I
made a statement with my attorney to Melich. I was asked
about my crime line calls. I had read meters on the
street. I knew at the end of the day, not at the
beginning of the day. We were all discussing that this
was a suspicious place to look. I thought of it first. He
said it was his idea, I had already thought of it. It may
have been a skull, I said, I was 99.999 percent sure that
it was a skull. It could have been ceramic or a stage
prop. I told him it was a hot day, and I just wanted to
get home. I worked a different route the next day. On the
13th, the deputies responded, maybe a Deputy Cain and a
female deputy. I was many feet away, so I was looking
down at a distance. I pointed in the general area of
where it was. I was not that close. I wasn't going back
in there right after we found that snake!

I remember making the same statement to Melich. I did not
say I got to within six or eight feet. I saw Cain go into
the woods. He went to the water line, turned right or
left and glanced, then slipped in the mud, and came back
up and chewed me out for an half hour. If I was, for the
sake of argument, if I was eight feet away, then the
deputy was six feet. This was the first time I had been
back to that area since the first day. (Objection)

I just said 99.999 percent sure it was a skull. (He is
shown his deposition to refresh his recollection.) Yes, I
see it. I said a hundred percent in the deposition. After
August 13th, and meeting the detectives, I did not work
in any capacity in this investigation. In January, I went
on Good Morning America. I was paid, for my snake
picture, but I knew there would be questions about the
remains find. I was paid $5000 from crime line and Orange
County paid for my attorney, until I was fired. After the
initial involvement, I was not questioned, about
conversations I had with coworkers. (A note from the
authors: according to media reports, Casey Anthony got
$200,000 for an interview, and Baez got $85,000 or maybe
more, of that money.)

I have a son named Brandon Parks. I never called him in
November and told him I was about to be famous. Between
August 13th and December 11th, I was not in the area,
only when I had the route. However, I did not go back to
the area where I had seen it after Deputy Cain met me at
the spot and chewed me out. They never searched my
vehicle or took a cadaver dog in. I was never asked for
DNA. I do not know if any investigation about me was
done. Melich took a photo of my phone, with my
permission. I did not know they subpoenaed my records.

Between August 13th and December 11th, I had no other contact with law enforcement.

On December 11th, I was on this same route at Suburban. I went by myself. I went into the woods, but I was not searching. I found the remains of Caylee Anthony. I had never been to where the bag was before. I cannot answer, it was flooded in August, and in December it was not flooded. The weeds had grown more, so I cannot say it was the same area. I would have no idea if this was the same skull. I was looking at it from behind, and I was not sure it was real. I poked my metal probe through an eye and lifted a little, not off the ground and it was real. I put it back down. I left. I can tell you; this was a horrific thing to find. I called my supervisor. I said I needed him there immediately, and that I had found a human skull. Alex, my supervisor, was in the same area. I do not know if I had to tell him where I was. A deputy showed up. I do not remember talking about… if I mentioned the reward. It is possible. I do not remember if I asked about the reward. I might have said if I get a reward, I want to keep it from my ex-wife. I was doing the right thing. I was chewed out, and I was trying to be a good citizen. I was not angry that I was not believed. I talked to my supervisor; we joked about the reward, or maybe it was said that I should play the lotto. Yes, I could have said I do not want my ex-wife to know, since I was having trouble with her.

I went in the woods to relieve myself. We were discussing the crime line tip and a reward they give. I never joked about finding the body, just the reward money. I did not have -- I told you – conversations with anyone else I can think of. On August 11th, I told him it looked like a skull and it would be a good place to dump a body, and no one would smell it. I never discovered a body, and in August, this area was under water. I never walked in the area in August, and it was not dry.

(When Mason asks why Kronk's son would say that Kronk called and said he was going to be famous,) My son was mistaken about the phone call. What I told him on a call on December 11th, 2008, was that I had found someone, and if he looked on TV tonight, he could see me for the first time since he was eight. I never stood over top of this item in August. I told you that. I talked to my son twelve or fifteen times in 2008. I called from my number. I do not remember his number. I do not believe that I said I was going to famous. I do not remember saying that I was going to be making money. We were talking about when he got out of the Coast Guard and us going into business. I do not recall making any comments to the

detectives about needing money, or "Roy has to eat, too".
I remember my recorded statement with the police. We
discussed several things about the money and me wanting
to stay out of the media. I may have said jokingly, "Roy
has to eat too", probably I did. If it is in my
deposition, then I said it. I told the police I made a
mistake in my original statement, the December 11th,
statement. I told them I poked the bag open and a small
skull with hair dropped out. I lifted the bag arm-length
straight out. I did not put in the statement that I used
my probe to lift it. We had a verbal conversation, and I
told them. Then I forgot to write that down. No, the
skull did not fall out. No, it did not. I lifted the
skull with my stick. After I lifted, I did not know what
it was for sure until I did that. The skull never rolled
out of the bag or dropped out of the bag. If I knew for
sure what it was, I would have done nothing to it.
However, I was not sure what it was; if it was real. On
December 11th, 2008, the statement was made and then I
corrected   it.

After finding the remains, I was unnerved; I just
remember going back to my truck. The skull was there
before I lifted the bag. I do not believe anything fell
out, and the skull was still at my feet. Things shifted
inside the bags and I was upset at what I had found. I
believe I did tell someone about using the probe, and
even mentioned it in my ABC interview. I told the
detectives I had made a crime line tip. No, I was not
told, to keep quiet about my previous calls. I cannot
understand your question. No, the police did not tell me
not to talk about my earlier 911 calls in August. On
December 10th, 2008, I had the day off, because the
clutch went out on my vehicle. I needed over a thousand
dollars for my truck repair. I might have mentioned to my
son or someone about it. Yes, the next day I made the
remains find. This is my car repair bill. (It is admitted
into evidence.) (The defense is looking very silly with
this line of questioning.)

Roy Kronk - State's cross-examination: I do not know
Casey, Lee, George or Cindy Anthony. I do not know
Investigators Dominic Casey or James Hoover. I do not
even live in the area. I moved to Florida. I got my job
in 2008. I had a GPS that took me to the areas. After
training, I was sent to read meters. On August 11th,
2008, I ended up getting this route, and I read their
meter. One time, I was in the area with Dean, and we were
training. He showed me the house. On December 11th, they
were on my route, maybe. On August 11th, I finished my
route and in the afternoon, met with my coworkers. We
help each other, and there are easy and hard routes. We

416

find each other when we are done, and we help each other out. This is when I relieved myself in the woods. I saw something suspicious, and I went to talk to the others. But they started screaming that there was a dead rattlesnake near my foot. That took all the attention after that. I describe it as a swamp, because it is all water in there. There is a grassy area, a hanging veil of vines, and then it drops off and is full of water. I was not allowed to interrupt my roommate until she is done watching TV, so I told her after nine, and then I called 911 after that. I called on August 12th again, crime line and the police, after 9 PM.

On August 13th, I called before 5 PM and asked for a deputy. Then he slipped in the mud and berated me about how I was wasting the County's time. I stayed in the grassy area, and he spent no time looking. He slipped and got annoyed. Prosecutor: Mr. Mason talked about you needing money on December 11th. Witness: I would have needed money in June, July, August, September, October, or November, too. I have never had access to the home of the Anthony's, except for reading their meter. I have never been inside their house, their backyard, their computer, their Pontiac, their garage. I have never had access to Caylee's clothes, diapers, pull-ups or underwear, or the Anthony's garbage bags, laundry bags, Caylee's blanket or the Anthony's duct tape. I have never had access to any of this stuff. (He is excused, subject to recall.)

This man just found the remains. Roy Kronk sounds completely believable. The believability comes in his imperfect but solid testimony. He found the remains; end of conversation. We do not get the impression that what Baez said in opening about Kronk is anywhere close to true. What is obvious is that Kronk wanted to become famous, and he hoped to become rich from his discovery. It does sound like Kronk made some inconsistent statements. Even old dogs cannot always pull a rabbit out of a hat! Still, we will be interested to hear what other witnesses say about him.

The Defendant's Fiftieth Witness

Interpretation of Testimony - David Dean: In August of 2008, I was and I still am an Orange County meter reader. On that day, I was reading meters. I stopped off on Suburban Drive with co-worker Roy Kronk, to help him and rest before we headed in to the office. There were three of us, and we were in two trucks. We checked the meters and we went down the street to park. The Anthony's home and the media were in that area. We did not discuss

417

anything with the media. I said that the little girl's body might be in this swamp here. Roy went to relieve himself and looked in the area. He said he saw a skull. We got up to go look at it. We were headed that way, and I almost stepped on a rattlesnake. Yes, we found the snake more interesting. Then Roy came over to the truck, he looked at the snake and the conversation of the skull just passed. I think if he was serious, he would have pushed it. The snake was on the news and a topic in our office. The snake became the focus for everyone when we returned to the office.

He did not tell me he had called 911 about the skull. He did not tell me he called the police in any of the months. He never told me he met a deputy in the area. I was not aware of anything about the calls or the deputy coming out about the skull until December 11th, 2008. On December 11th, 2008, I heard the radio call, and there was a radio transmission with Roy Kronk. He was excited and explained what he found. He sounded startled on the radio. It was at the time, or near the time, he found the skull, as I far as I can remember. His voice was a normal tone. (Objection) (Sustained) I said to Roy, I told you she was in there! No one else but Roy saw the skull on August 11th, 2008. The snake, I kept it for a while in my freezer. The police took it, and I was told they were going to give it an autopsy. He went in the woods about twenty or twenty-five feet. It was my idea that the child might be in the swamp. I am the one who suggested she might be there. When I told him, I knew she was there. It was not because I had anything to do with it. It was because of something Casey had said to her mother, that Caylee is close by. Hurricane Fay came through this area after Caylee went missing. There are wet and dry areas. Where Roy was, it was dry, but if you go farther, it is wet. This is really dense woods. Did you recall George's statement that she was close? No. Baez flippantly states: That is because no one was looking at George. (Objection) (Withdrawn) No more questions. (The witness is released.)

The authors see Mr. Baez use these bad-faith statements or questions all the time, just to slip in things for the jury to hear. That is one of the things angering Judge Perry. We have become used to them. At this point, they just make him look bad to us.

The Defendant's Fifty-first Witness

Interpretation of Testimony - Alex Roberts: I work for Orange County as the senior meter reader. I worked as a supervisor in August 2008 through December 11th, 2008. I was aware of the area where Roy Kronk was supposed to be reading meters. On August 11th, he read meters in the Anthony neighborhood. I recall my deposition. On December 11th, 2008, he did not read meters in the Anthony area that day. Once he found the remains, I later found him off Suburban Drive that day. He was smoking a cigarette and leaning against the truck. He was shaken. He could not work the rest of the day. I had to send someone else to finish reading his meters that day. (Objection)(Sidebar) (The lawyers are scrapping at the sidebar.)

Alex Roberts (Testimony resumes): Kronk's demeanor was nervous and he was waiting, leaning against the truck. I recall when the workers were back with the snake and after that time I do not remember Roy telling me he called 911. (The witness is released.)

The Defendant's Fifty-second Witness

Interpretation of Testimony - Sergeant Dennis Moonsammy: I am with Orange County Corrections. I am the supervisor of the women's detention center. That includes the area where Casey Anthony has been since October 2008. Baez: Is Casey kept in a more secluded… (Objection) Your Honor, if I could have some leeway, I will tie it up. (Sustained) You may approach. (Sidebar)

(In our opinion, this is what happens when a lawyer does not ask good faith questions; he gets no leeway.) The jury is being excused for the day, with the judge saying, "We have a not short legal matter to take up."

Defendant's Proffer - Sergeant Moonsammy: Casey Anthony is in protective custody. Because hers is a high profile case, we do not put her in with others. She is in the cell 23 hours a day. She can take a shower, go to the recreation room and get a book, or go to the TV room. Ms. Anthony is a model inmate. I speak to every inmate every day, and I record it. Every time I have spoken with Ms. Anthony, she is always smiling without hesitation. She is always pleasant. My job is care, custody and control. I pay no attention to the behavior, unless the inmate is a control problem. She is the same as almost all the inmates in that area. I have spoken to her, and she has engaged me in conversation. She is pleasant and happy despite her current situation. Yes, her mood has been constant. She is never up or down, she is always pleasant. (Objection) (Sustained) The judge says that the proffered testimony is irrelevant to the issue of guilt or innocence.

Interpretation of Proffer Testimony - Marlene Baker: I work for Orange County Corrections in classification. I previously worked in the area where Casey Anthony is housed. I observed her from 2008 to 2009. Her demeanor is pleasant. She is always pleasant, attentive even when someone is waking her. She was under protective custody when I was there. It causes all of the inmates stress, being in protective custody or isolation cells. Casey Anthony would get upset and cry periodically. She would change when she was upset or crying, but that was not often. She was always pleasant. She smiled often, despite the conditions. Her behavior was consistent. (Objection) (Sustained, it is irrelevant to the defense.) (Sidebar on the next witness)

We think the judge has Baez's number and he was right to proffer. His attitude, and ours is for Mr. Baez, leeway - no way! The bottom line of the proffers of these two witnesses is that Casey Anthony is not special, she is not completely emotionless, she is mostly pleasant, and she cries. She is, in our opinion, simply narcissistic.

Interpretation of Proffer Testimony - Jessie Grund: I was engaged to Casey Anthony. Shortly after Caylee was born, I felt uncomfortable around Lee. Casey was uncomfortable with Caylee around Lee. She said she woke with Lee standing over her bed, and once he groped her in the night. I told her that was all I needed to hear. (Objection) Judge: The statement I do not want Caylee around Lee is not relevant, and certainly the rest is not. My research shows this testimony is not admissible, but I will look again tonight. Both sides submit what cases they can.

Baez: Ms. Finnell wants to take up the death penalty motion by phone. Prosecution: We also need the proffer of another witness, Sally Karioth. We have been told by counsel that she knows nothing about facts of the case, and so the defense agreed to proffer. Baez: We had her available and she had technical support ready by Skype. I think all these proffers are ridiculous. Prosecution: The proffer can be by telephone. Baez: We had her scheduled for 2 PM, and Mrs. Karioth had been waiting. Prosecution: I said if she does not know anything about the particulars of this case we can proffer. Counsel Baez said no problem with the proffer. Baez: **Did not!** Prosecution: **Did too!** (Really boys, if you keep this up, the judge is going to spank both of you!)

Judge: Is the witness being called to testify to general grief? Baez: Yes. Prosecution: She has not interviewed Ms. Anthony, from what I have been told. I have no idea what she is going to say, or be asked. Some of it may be, and some may not be admissible. I have cited many cases that do not allow this kind of testimony. Judge: I hope that there is a well-constructed hypothetical for this witness. I can do it this way, and we'll go in and out like pop tarts tomorrow, dealing with this. How many more witnesses after the grief counselor? Baez: Six. Judge: Prosecution, if you find any cases, e-mail them to me tonight. Make sure you copy the other side with the e-mail. Ms. Finnell's argument on the telephone for the motion will go out to the media and anyone who has ears. In addition, madam court reporter, please e-mail Mr. Grund's short testimony, so I can read the proffer. (Court is in recess for the evening.)

As the media coverage continues to from sea to sea and even overseas, we can make these observations. Much of the coverage has been far more accurate since the trial began. Reporters are working hard to explain the distances involved in this wooded area, and how dense it really is. The media, on most feeds, are bringing uninterrupted coverage, with different courtroom views. Although, some are covering the irrelevant or sensational stories, the sideshows, most are giving their all to bring facts and accurate explanations.

The defense is working hard to introduce psychological testimony on Casey. At this phase of the case, the defense likely intends to try to engender sympathy for her with the jury, and the judge is not likely to allow it. The penalty phase is different, and psychological and psychiatric testimony is almost essential, since some mitigating circumstances involve mental health issues, and even being a model prisoner can be considered as mitigation. Throughout this trial, we have been disappointed with some of the defense's tactics; some we have thought were good. We have pointed out the prosecution's mistakes, which were few in number but when they came, were so major that they were stunning to us. We realize that the investigation was hard because of evidence being tossed into a swamp, but tactical blunders cannot improve the State's case.

We have watched all of Casey's faces and reactions, and we are still left wondering who she really is. More importantly, we have wondered who Caylee would have been, had she been given the chance to grow up. We have tried to give everyone a look at our justice system. It is an enigma involving not just the players in the courtroom, but those outside of it as well. It is not always pretty, or honest, or just. However, in this case it seems to us that Judge Perry has done everything possible to be sure

421

that the proceedings have been fair to the defendant. The prosecution has put on a well-organized, substantial, but circumstantial case. It hinges in large part on complicated scientific evidence. This tells us that even if you attempt to destroy all the evidence, there is no such thing as a perfect murder. The devil is in the details.

"Justice is the concept of moral rightness based on ethics, rationality, law, natural law, religion, fairness, or equity, along with the punishment of the breach of said ethics," to quote Plato. Our symbol, Lady Justice, depicts justice as equipped with three symbols: a sword symbolizing the court's coercive power, a human scale weighing competing claims in each hand, and a blindfold indicating impartiality.

After more than twelve days, the defense is preparing to close its case in the next twenty-four hours. All of us believe at this point that Casey Anthony is likely guilty of first-degree or second-degree murder, but we are split on whether the prosecution has proved beyond a reasonable doubt that Casey killed her daughter. We do not know what the jury will do. When the jury compares the details of the phone records and Google searches, we believe the jurors may return a verdict of First Degree Murder. In the State of Florida, premeditation takes only seconds of thought, not months. We also believe it will be a life sentence, rather than death for the pretty, young, white woman. Justice is not always blind. The jury, we believe, will consider the suffering of this whole family, and mercy, as Finnell told us, can be considered. However, this could be a double-edged sword. Might some jurors find death more merciful than a life sentence for a twenty-five-year-old woman?

June 29th, 2011

The JOA motion will be argued at the close of the prosecution's rebuttal case, or at the close of all evidence, if the defense puts on surrebuttal evidence. Yesterday, we were told that Ann Finnell is arguing some sort of motion by telephone. This will be broadcast, per the judge. She is a highly experienced lawyer, so it will be interesting to hear the basis of the motion and to find out what she will argue. As an interesting note, during every recess, the cameras are focused on the courtroom flagpole with its eagle on top. Just before court resumes, the image rocks back and forth. It is swaying now. Court is about to resume for Finnell's motion.

Judge: A Motion to Reconsider Ms. Anthony's Motion to
Declare Florida Statute 921.1951 Unconstitutional under
Ring v. Arizona, a Death Case is presented. We will see
if counsel shows up. Was Ms. Finnell to appear by phone?
Prosecution: Yes, Your Honor. Judge: Mr. Ashton, do we
know what number she was to dial in on? Finnell: Yes,
Your Honor this is Ann Finnell on the Motion to
Reconsider. I can hear you, thank you. Judge: Okay, Ms.
Finnell, Ms. Anthony is present, and none of your other
co-counsel is present. You scheduled this matter at 8:30
and the time is now 8:32. Mr. Ashton is present. You may
proceed.

Finnell: Thank you Your Honor, I have filed a Motion to
Reconsider Ms. Anthony's Motion to Declare Florida
Statute 921.1951 Unconstitutional under Ring v. Arizona.
I have attached a Memorandum of Law in support of that
motion to reconsider, as well as an appendix to issues of
Paul H. Evans v. Walter A. McNeil out of the United
States District Court for the Southern District, Miami
Division. It is a decision rendered by Federal Court
Judge Jose Martinez on June 20, 2011, in which he granted
habeas relief on this very issue declaring Florida's
death penalty statute unconstitutional. (Habeas is short
for habeas corpus, Latin for produce the body, of the
defendant. Habeas corpus petitions allege unlawful
detention or penalty.) I will rest on the motion, case
law and memorandum unless the court has specific
questions for me, then I will be willing to answer.

Judge: One question, one of the remedies you asked for is
the remedy of a mistrial; is that correct? Finnell: Yes,
Your Honor, that is correct. Judge: Have you consulted
with your client, and does she consent to a mistrial?
Finnell: Your honor, I have not directly consulted with
her, I believe that issue has been discussed with her by
Mr. Baez and/or Mr. Mason, and I believe she does concur
with that. However, if one of those men are present or
Ms. Sims, perhaps they can do that consultation at this
time, just to be on the safe side.

Judge: Unfortunately, they are not here. Ms. Anthony is
at counsel table alone, and you are appearing by phone.
But I will ask them whenever they choose to arrive. Thank
you, that would be fine Your Honor, I feel confident that
Ms. Anthony would agree with this issue as it relates to
the constitutionally of the death penalty. Judge: Ms.
Anthony do you want to answer that question now, or do
you want to wait until Mr. Baez or Mr. Mason or Ms. Sims
arrives?

Casey Anthony: (reaches over and turns on the microphone, then stands and calmly says) "I can answer that now." Judge: Okay. Casey Anthony: "I agree with Ms. Finnell." (She speaks!)

Judge: Thank you, madam. Finnell: Thank you. Judge: Mr. Ashton. Ashton: At the outset, I would point out to the court that according to the Attorney General of the State of Florida, this opinion is not final as of yet. A Motion to Alter Judgment is pending before the District Court of the Southern District of Florida. So at this point, this is not a final order. Further, it is apparent from the Order, starting at page ninety-two that, "This is an as applied finding by the court." The court goes into great length and I will cite the exact language: "Any one single aggravating factor may not have been found beyond a reasonable doubt by a majority of the jury. The court's interpretation of Ring requires, at the very minimum, that the defendant is entitled to a jury's fact-finding on the existence of an aggravating circumstance. Not simply a majority finding of jurors finding the existence of a combination of aggravating factors on which the judge many or may not base a death sentence…"

Judge Perry: "I will rule on the request prior to the receipt of the verdict, if we get this far in this case." The court will reserve the ruling on the defense motion for mistrial and the motion to declare the death penalty unconstitutional. I will rule on this if we get to the verdict. (Meanwhile, the defense lawyers have entered the courtroom.) (The jury enters the jury box.) The defense may call its first witness.

(This to us is a big hint from the Judge to Casey to try to negotiate a plea. We are reasonably sure that Casey understood. Casey was lucid and articulate with well-formed thoughts as she spoke to the judge, agreeing to Finnell's argument for a mistrial. Casey was clearly aware of her surroundings, and was alert enough to turn on the microphone and stand before she spoke to the judge. That was an eye-opening experience. Something the jury will never hear. Since we are against the death penalty, we agree with Finnell on this Motion.)

The Defendant's Fifty-third Witness

Interpretation of Testimony - Cindy Anthony (recalled): I was never made aware of my son going into Casey's room at night. (Sidebar) (Baez slipping things in again) (Sustained) I recall testifying six months ago that Caylee was alive. Part of me believed it. In February of 2009, we had a memorial service. I requested that her

remains be cremated. (Objection) (Sustained) I saw the
video about me telling Casey in jail that her dad had
blown up at the media. This was in response to a
statement that a member of the media asked, Is it true
Caylee died in a drowning accident? At this time, we
believed Caylee to be alive. (Objection)(Sustained) What
I expressed was that this is a new theory or new story
and it was just the media's theory. On July 16th, 2008, I
mentioned the pool ladder being attached to the police.
(Objection) (Sustained) I told the police about the
ladder and the pool. The statement on the jail video, I
said it was the latest story or the theory from the
media. Casey said she was aware that her father had blown
up at the media. I do not know how she heard. She could
have heard it from someone in the jail.

I had made law enforcement aware of the pool ladder.
(Objection) When I related to Casey that George had blown
up at the media, her response was to her dad blowing up.
Her response was to the story, not to the claim that
Caylee drowned. When I came in to see Casey in jail, I
was upset. The media was screaming and saying, what do
you think about you granddaughter drowning in the
swimming pool? This is when she was missing, and we
believed alive.

The Defendant's Fifty-fourth Witness

Interpretation of Testimony - George Anthony (recalled):
On July 24th, 2008, police talked to you about your law
enforcement experience, and you said you found people out
in the woods. (Objection) (The witness is refreshing his
recollection with a statement.) How did you know that
your granddaughter would be found in the woods?
(Objection) (Sustained) Sir, you are clearly taking my
law enforcement background out of context. That question
is when you asked me about my law enforcement background
and experience in decomposition, in a deposition. I told
you I had encountered it in law enforcement, and that we
would find bodies in cars and woods. (Objection)
(Sidebar) I told the police that I had smelled
decomposition in woods, houses, and cars in Ohio, when I
was in law enforcement.

I walked the perimeter of the fenced area on Suburban
Drive. I did that because the police brought a toy to us.
I asked where he had found it. I walked every place. I
walked, walked, and looked in the street. I was over in
the other area because we were looking for a new place
for a Kid Finder tent center. I called the County
Commissioner to see if that area was vacant. I was going
to put up a Kid Finder tent. The first night, in the

early morning, I told law enforcement about the car smell, and asked for an AMBER Alert. I wanted answers to where my granddaughter was. I was hysterical and upset. I did not pull the officer aside. I talked to him in the morning hours, and I told him that Caylee was missing and she was last seen with my daughter. Sir, definitely something happened to Caylee. She's no longer with us, and Casey was the last one that I saw with Caylee. One and one adds up to two, sir, in my mind. And no matter how you're trying to spin it, I'm upset because my granddaughter is missing. I don't know where she's at. I was told that someone had taken my granddaughter, forcibly removed her from my daughter, or my daughter dropped her off at some house.

I'm trying to put all the stories and information together, sir. Was I running on pure emotion and drive and demanding answers? That is my right as a father and a grandfather and as whatever you want to spin it. Was I upset and falling apart at the moment? Absolutely. My family was being torn apart. And for to you say that I was doing something… Baez tries to object, and the witness continues over him, saying …wrong, sir, you're wrong. Baez continues with his objection… the witness commenting on counsel's questions.

Judge Perry steps in, says something that cannot be heard, and tells the witness to just listen. Next question, Mr. Baez.

Baez: Yes, sir. Now, on July 24th, you went in and made this statement to law enforcement that you had smelled that car and you smelled human decomposition. Yes, sir. Baez: And you were sure of it. Witness: On July 24th, 2008, I made a statement to law enforcement and I told them I had smelled decomposition in the car. I am one hundred percent sure of what I smelled. My daughter lives on the edge. Yes, I could have told them that. (Objection) I could have told detectives she lies and she takes things to the end. I am sure I said negative things about my daughter; I was trying to get answers. Then I visited her in jail. I was trying to keep my daughter upbeat and comfortable. I wanted to find Caylee. In twenty-four hours, I said negative things and then on the video I was saying nice things. I was trying to keep her upbeat. I was not undercover. I was a father and grandfather. My daughter wanted out, and I would not put up the house as collateral. I testified under subpoena to the grand jury. (George is emotionally distraught; this is taking a toll on him. Truly, this is blaming the victim's grandfather, brother, or anyone else by Casey for her actions.)

On July 24th, 2008, when I spoke to law enforcement I was one hundred percent sure I smelled decomposition. I gave depositions, including August 5th, if that is what you are talking about, sir. I believed I smelled decomposition, human and like the car, it took my breath away. (Objection) I opened the car and it is out of gas, the attendant said oh, my gosh this really stinks. It did not come to mind that it was my daughter or granddaughter, at that second. Then I can remember the attendant and all I could say, that I remember while getting out of the car, and I did not say it directly, was **don't let this be my daughter or granddaughter!** There was trash with maggots and the attendant disposed it.

Sir, that answer speaks for itself. I could smell it three feet away. I opened the door. It was strong. It was human decomposition in that car, not the garbage in the car. The trash that had maggots was there, the smell was decomposition – human – and neither my daughter nor granddaughter was in that trunk. I do not know if I could have handled that. Ten years as a law officer, and I knew it was decomposition. After I knew that it was not my daughter or granddaughter, my emotions were raw. I was concerned; my emotions were unreal still. Moreover, looking back, going to work, driving the car home, not calling police, I was just an emotional wreck. I went on the media in August 2009, looking for my granddaughter. I did not want to believe that my daughter could take the life of her daughter.

In late January, 2009, I attempted to commit suicide. Did you leave a note expressing guilt? (Objection. Mr. Baez can put the note into evidence. The best evidence is to put the document in.) I was hospitalized. Then a week or so later, I was making media appearances, sure. I was paid by the media, and it was to bring awareness to my missing granddaughter and other missing children. The focus of the media was my daughter. Mine was always to bring focus to my granddaughter or missing children. All these interviews did stop, because you Mr. Baez brought up a claim of child abuse against me. (Sidebar) I was asked the first day of trial about sexual abuse of Casey. I did not abuse Casey. Baez: You would never admit to it, it is a life felony. (Objection) I would never do anything to harm my daughter in that way. Baez: Only in that way? (Objection) (Sustained)

On June 24th, 2008, yes, two gas cans were taken and I reported them stolen. I had asked Casey in the past if she used them. On August 1st, 2008, the gas cans might have had duct tape on one of the cans. The police came

and took it. I had an argument with my daughter on the
twenty-fourth. Myself, my daughter, and God were there.
That was it. Baez: Want to toss the dog in? (Objection)
(Question withdrawn)

I recall giving a deposition. When the police came and
took the cans, there was no duct tape on the can. I saw
the photo in the deposition. I said it was not on the can
that is what I said. These cans were taken two times. I
believe I was shown another photo of this gas can. I see
the tabs where the exhibits and the photos are the same.
Baez: So either the police put the tape on or you are
lying? (Objection) (Sustained) I had the argument with
Casey and she forcibly set the cans out of her trunk down
on the ground. It was an argument; the voices were raised
a bit, and she said "Here are your fucking gas cans." The
tape was not there. Did I put it on it later because
there was no vent cap? I could have, I do not remember.
(Objection to the witness narrative and move to strike.)
Judge: Lawyers and court reporter approach the bench.

When Casey gave me the gas can on June 24th, 2008, it did
not have duct tape on it. On August 1st, 2008, I will say
no. (Objection) (Sustained) I said it did not have duct
tape over the vent, it has it on it, and I did not put it
on. I made a mistake about that, is all. (Objection)
(Sustained) On August 5th, 2009, I still believed that my
granddaughter was killed by someone other than my
daughter.

We sparred in that deposition in August. Yes, I was upset
that I was being asked to give testimony against my
daughter. Do you no longer believe that your
granddaughter had died in the custody of someone other
than you daughter? (Objection) (Sustained) I did not
believe at that time my daughter murdered my
granddaughter, in August, 2009. In December 2008,
Caylee's remains were found. A deep hurt inside, tears,
an emotional loss and breakdown, seeing my wife and son
suffer. I held out the hope until December 2008. (George
is completely breaking down on the stand now.) In January
2009, I went and got a gun. (Objection) (Sidebar) (The
jury is sent out.)

Prosecution: Your Honor, I believe in the note he makes
it clear he was going to use it to make those that he
thought were involved (the young men who were friends of
Casey he incorrectly thought were involved). Prosecutor:
He was going to make them tell who had his granddaughter,
and then kill himself. I am entering the suicide note.
Mr. Baez opened this door. It clearly rebuts that George
Anthony knew anything about his granddaughter's death. I

just discovered the gun was before the attempt at suicide. I will correct with the jury. Baez: I want it stricken and the jury advised. Prosecutor: Okay, that is fine. I will just ask it another way. I intend on bringing it in. Baez: The note is hearsay. Prosecutor: A suicide note can be admissible if it does not contain any admission of guilt. It is admissible because it does not contain anything about the things the defense has questioned him about. If there is a specific issue, he knew about what happened and where she, Caylee, was, it would not be admissible now. However, George says, "she was so close to home, we questioned, you questioned, why did she die? I want this over for Casey. Why could she not come to us, to you, to Lee" and it states that he did not know. Baez: He took blood pressure meds, drank beers, and wrote a note.

Judge: You asked did he attempt to commit suicide. What was the purpose of asking the question? Baez: He did attempt an outcry, or an attempt to kill himself. It could it be that he was guilt-ridden that he had sexually abused his daughter and the law was closing in. Prosecution: Could be among others. Judge: Generally, a witness's state of mind at the time is not an issue. It is rare that it becomes an issue; the defense has made Mr. Anthony's state of mind an issue. All of Mr. Baez's questions have implied that Gorge Anthony had some guilt about matters that Mr. Baez has accused him of in this case. I think the door has been opened, but I want some time to contemplate and read a few cases before I allow the letter. However, it is fair game to cross-examination on the suicide note. Mr. Baez opened the door. (We authors believe that Mr. Baez has opened doors, many ways, many times, and it looks like the judge is going to let the prosecution through this one.) Mr. Baez do you want a proffer?

State's Proffer - George Anthony: In 2008, I obtained a firearm. I wanted to go get answers that I believed at the time were reasonable for finding Caylee, based on what Casey had told me. I had a three day wait to obtain the gun. The Sheriff's Department with the Corrections Department came to my house. Casey was home from jail, and because she was home, they took the gun before I used it. It was still locked and secured in the box. In January 2009, I went to a hotel with an intention of taking my life and I still have those thoughts even as I sit here today. Did you put pen to paper in that hotel leaving a note to your wife and son? Yes, and this is a true and accurate statement of my thoughts, intentions and knowledge. I also sent text messages to my family and my lawyer. I called my sister, my mother and my family to talk, and not tell them that I was saying goodbye. I needed to go be with Caylee because I believe I failed her, and law enforcement stopped me or I would not be here today. In the note are some of the unanswered questions that were in my mind at that time. I wrote it over many hours.

Baez: Objection, beyond the scope, the buying of the firearm has nothing to do with the trial. Prosecution: Counsel questioned the witness about his knowledge from August to January. Judge: The issue of Mr. George Anthony's attempt to commit suicide, the issue that was brought out in the defense direct examination and these questions are a logical progression. The Court will permit this line of questioning. You can mark and have him identify the note and then until it comes in you cannot question him on the note. Return the jury.

George Anthony – State's cross-examination: In August 2008, I purchased a firearm. My purpose was to get answers from people I believed were involved with my granddaughter being missing, friends of my daughters. I was going to use that gun to force them to tell me where my granddaughter was. Law enforcement came to my home and informed me that since Casey was home on bond, a gun could not be there. It was the same day I picked up the gun, and they took it. In January 2009, I traveled to a hotel with plans on taking my life. I do not know why that day. My emotional state even today – I wanted to go be with Caylee. I wanted to call my son, wife, and family, and tell them goodbye without telling them. I was supposed to go to a meeting, and I decided today was the day to go be with Caylee. I wrote the letter to my wife Cindy, and planned to kill myself through pills and alcohol. I included in the letter questions I had about what happened to Caylee. I had to express what I was feeling, and not feeling. I wanted Cindy to know why I was dead when she found me. I could not tell her face-to-face. I would have killed myself if law enforcement had not found me.

George Anthony – Defendant's re-direct: Mr. Ashton questioned me about sparring with you at the deposition. Witness: I recall Mr. Ashton reminding me of my oath, I am sure. The questions had to do with the cans, duct tape, daughter and granddaughter. I would say it was verbal sparring. I classify ours as sparring. When I got the gun, the Department of Corrections explained the rules of house arrest, and we were given a list. I knew I could not have a gun; that Casey would go back to jail, and they almost took her back to jail. My emotional state was to get that gun and go get answers. No, I did not buy the gun before she was home. I do not know how much beer I purchased; I had blood pressure and nerve pills. I do not know what was recovered from my hotel. On December 11th, 2008, law enforcement went through the whole house. It is my stuff. My car, the whole house was searched. I do not know what they took - seventy or more items. When we came home from the Larry King show, our house was upside down. (The judge declares a lunch recess.)

Casey does not appear to care at all about what her family is going through. Her father, mother, brother are battered and distraught, and Casey is smiling and batting her eyes again. The jury is out of course. (Court is back in session.) Casey just came back in after a long lunch, and it appears something was going on in the judge's chambers. She wipes a few tears, we think. It must have been about her fate. Baez is talking with her and he looks unhappy. (The jury returns.)

George Anthony - Defendant's re-direct (cont.): On December 20th, there was a second search warrant. I got conformational with the officers, and I was asked to step outside. I told Sergeant Allen "Take your fucking minions and get out of the house." (Objection) (Sustained) They took other items. The State Attorney's Office issued a subpoena for my fingerprints, maybe in December 2008. How many times have you had an investigative subpoena? (Objection) (Sustained) I did not give my fingerprints to them voluntarily. I saw in late December and early January 2009, the video of Dominic in the woods. In January 2009, when this video first surfaced, did you ask Dominic what are you doing? I did not ask what they were doing.

I was told in December 2008, about the remains being discovered. I never asked him what he was doing there a month before. After all of the investigations and subpoenas, did you feel the walls closing in? Was the pressure getting to you? From July 15th, 2008, I have always cooperated with law enforcement, the FBI, and even you to try to find and bring my granddaughter home. Well sir, the loss of my granddaughter when I knew she was missing and then later found dead – we were all devastated. Then I was facing losing my daughter. I was upset. There have been so many people investigated, and I have opened myself up and cooperated with everyone, but I was upset. I called many people the day I was planning to commit suicide. I might have called you, I do not remember. I did not go on the media twenty-four hours after I left the hospital. I need dates. On January 20, 2009, I tried to take my life. I do not know when I was

on the news after that. Did you stay at the Ritz
Carleton? Yes. Who paid for that? I do not know.

I traveled to California to be on Larry King. The purpose
of the appearance was to publicize the disappearance of
my granddaughter, we learned of her remains by numerous
calls that a child had been found. We arrived from
California to the airport. We had five hours to wonder on
the plane. We were told we could not get off the plane by
police until everyone else was off. We were just falling
apart. I can remember much later that evening, we had
dinner at the Ritz Carlton with Mr. Baez. (So Mr. Baez is
trying to use a dinner he had with the Anthony's to make
George look bad for being at the Ritz.) (Objection by Mr.
Baez) (Sidebar) (Did Baez really think his dinner with
them would not come out?)

George Anthony - State's re-cross: During the time from
July 16th through December 11th, 2008, I cooperated with
law enforcement, Mr. Baez, anyone who could help me find
Caylee. December 20th was the day after I had
confirmation that my granddaughter was dead. I was upset,
and upset with the police. We were taken from the airport
to the Ritz. I stayed at the Ritz and I do not know who
paid. I did not have to do any interviews for it. I do
not who know swept us up from the airport. (Witness is
excused.)

Mr. Anthony made his antagonism to the defense and Baez
clearer than ever this time around. In his emotional,
nearly out of control, much-interrupted testimony, George
Anthony made one pithy comment that continues to ring in
the minds of your authors. "One plus one equals two.
Casey was the last one to be seen with my granddaughter;
I watched her leave with Caylee." That seems to us to be
the highest hurdle that the defense must leap for any
hope at an acquittal of the homicide and child abuse
charges.

The Defendant's Fifty-fifth Witness

Interpretation of Proffer Testimony - Brandon Sparks: I
am on active duty in the Coast Guard, doing drug
interdiction and search and rescue. I go out for three or
four months at a time. Roy Kronk is my biological father.
We have been estranged since I was eight. In 2008, we
reconnected; I reached out to him in 2008. We talked from
June 2008 to February 2009. I live in Maryland now. In
2008, I was in Virginia Beach. It was cell phone calls.
In July to December 2008, he mentioned it before when the
search was going on. He said he knew something about this
case in November 2008. It was before the epiphany on

December 11th, 2008. I asked why he waited so long, and he would avoid the topic. Did he make any other statements about this case? No, sir. (The cell phone records are put it evidence.) He said he found the skull and it was in November, around Thanksgiving. I told my wife and mother. My mother said she held no ill will toward my father, and I do not, either

Brandon Sparks – State's cross-examination: I followed in the footsteps of my mother and father in the Coast Guard. In my statement, I refer to the telephone call that I spoke about in court today. When I instigated contact with my father, I did not tell my mother. I kept it from my mother. I did not remember the call about the skull until December 11th, when it was found, and then it became relevant. I was reminded by my mother and wife of the November conversation about the skull. I did not prepare this statement in October, 2009, I just signed it. My father told me that he had gone to urinate at the woods and found remains in November and *I asked was it the little girl*.

Brandon Sparks – Defendant's re-direct: I saw him on TV on December 19th, 2008. I was questioned by an investigator. I have never been contacted by law enforcement and I do not know Detective Melich. *I did not know about the case until December 11th, 2008*. He always has an imagination, and says far-fetched things, and… (Objection) (Sustained) Did you father tell you he had taken this skull from the scene? He said he located it, then he contacted law enforcement, and there was a media blitz. I had not seen him since I was eight. He told you he was going to be rich. (Objection) (Sustained) (The witness is released.)

The witness's claim is that he knew nothing about the case until December 11th, 2008, yet he testified that when his father told him about finding remains in November, he asked his father if it was the little girl. His father thought he found the remains in August when he called the police and crime line. Roy Kronk wanted to look good to his long-lost son. It is not surprising that he told him in November, but the surprise is that the son would ask about Caylee at a time when he says he knew nothing about the case. The son keeps trying to get out his father's bad past. This is probably why Roy Kronk did not want the media attention. The son sounds a bit like an angry child. There is no fifteen minutes of fame for him here.

The Defendant's Fifty-sixth Witness

Interpretation of Testimony - Roy Kronk (recalled): I
made a second statement on December 11th, 2008. I sat in
my truck where law enforcement ask me to wait, and they
asked me to write a statement. I said the skull fell out
of the bag. I went to the car, and I think I might have
made a recorded statement. It was recorded. I told them
what I saw and did. I wanted to tell them what happened.
I told them I did not touch anything, I used my meter
stick. I told them I put the stick in and lifted the
skull up to see for sure what it was. I guess I did not;
my written statement says that the skull dropped out of
the bag. This is three years ago, refresh my
recollection. I did not state that I called four times. I
said that I called crime line. (Objection) (Sustained,
asked and answered.) The officer that appeared on the
scene, he asked me not to mention it, but he did not tell
me to keep my mouth shut. I gave a statement, I told them
I reported what I saw in August, and that I had called.
(Objection) (Sustained) (Okay, so nobody wanted to look
bad for not wanting to go into the swamp full of
rattlesnakes, in August, in Florida.) On December 11th,
2008, I made two statements, and law enforcement came to
my home about a week later. That is when I first publicly
did the change to my statement, but I had realized it
earlier. A few days afterward, I made the change to the
statement after I calmed down, from being overwhelmed by
what I had seen in the woods. I realized I had made a
mistake. Helicopters were flying over, and I was
overwhelmed after finding the remains of the child. I do
not know how many statements I made all together.

The Defendant's Fifty-seventh Witness

**Interpretation of Testimony - Deputy Edward Turso
(recalled):** I was the first responding male officer to
the scene on December 11th, 2008. Roy Kronk did not tell
me he called crime line.

The Defendant's Fifty-eighth Witness

**Interpretation of Testimony - Detective Yuri Melich
(recalled):** I was the lead investigator in the case. I
responded to the remains scene on December 11th, 2008 and
spoke to Roy Kronk. He had a written statement. I
reviewed it. The statement was brief, so we recorded a
statement from him for that reason. On December 11th,
2008, he did not tell me he called in August. It was
December 17th, when I found out about the early calls and
got the calls. I had obtained another statement to

clarify whether or not the skull had rolled out. We went there for clarification, and he added information. I would need to see the transcript to tell you more. (He reviews the transcript.) Did he tell you…? (Objection, improper extrinsic evidence) (Sidebar) (Sustained)

Yuri Melich (Testimony resumes): On December 17th, 2008, this is the first time I knew more than that he had called previously to crime line. That he had called four times. (The witness is released.)

It is clear to the authors; the man found the remains, and that's all folks. Baez is beating a dead horse.

The Defendant's Fifty-ninth Witness

Interpretation of testimony - Sally Karioth, PhD: (Dorothy Sims is questioning for the defense.) I am old. I have been at Florida State for 40 years and I have a degree in nursing. I was looking for a degree in the theater. I have two master's degrees and a PhD, in nursing, musical theory, foundations of educations, family nursing and then genetics. I am a nurse who works with a doctor. I can do clinical counseling. If patients need medical care, I refer them out. I teach courses in death, religion, clinical, ethnic variations, and holistic medicine. I have been teaching a course in traumatology. We go and interact with first responders, dealing with the stress. I have seen patients for forty years, including terminal patients. I deal with kids that struggle, loss of job, death, and grief. Physicians refer patients when they think it is grief-related.

I do not charge for seeing individuals. Maybe thirty or forty thousand people, individually and in seminars (Objection) (She is just going on and on.) I consult with fifty seniors a year, and I have done hundreds of a mix of people, helping groups and social work groups. When the Chicken Soup for the Surviving Soul Book came out, they asked me to tell one of my stories. I authored chapters that were edited to fit in. I do editing of others' books. I host groups of parents who meet with other parents who have experience a suicide or SIDS loss. Sims: Your Honor, I am tendering the witness as an expert in trauma and grief.

Have you ever published any peer-reviewed articles? Yes, on disposing of dead children's clothes. It was published in South East Research Journal; it is a peer-reviewed journal. Parents Book, it is peer reviewed by Barnes and Noble. Barnes and Noble is a publisher and not a peer reviewer. They have been accepted by the editor of the online magazine. I am an editor of an online trauma journal. Sims: I am looking for peer-reviewed articles, doctor. I just want the name of the journal. Florida Department of Public Health, it is an online journal. The folks at the health department saw it and gave a grant. The experts who review, we do not know. Healing Adjuncts, it is a book. The Nurses Review, it is published quarterly. Sims: You indicated you had testified as an expert on grief approximately 12 times? I testify about the amount of grief a trauma can cause. I testified for the victims. I have been called to testify in the case of a child who was sent to a boot camp and died. Yes, trauma to the victims of those who died. (Accepted as an expert) (State Objects)

Not everyone suffers grief the same way. If I polled the room, everyone does it differently. Like in this case… (Objection) The question is not relevant to this case. (Sidebar)

Sims: Assume a twenty-two-year-old mother of a young child almost three years old, with a loving bond loses that child. Please describe the grief that could be associated with that loss. (Objection)(Sidebar)(The Judge is really bending over on this one.) You authors say, how about assume a mother murders her child, more to the evidence. Mercy is one thing; sympathy or empathy is a not available after what we have heard in this courtroom.

The judge lets her ask again. Again since everyone does it differently. I have seen mothers that cannot get out of bed, they do not wash their clothes. I have seen them coming home to clean the room and give the toys away. They never speak of the child, it is too painful to have memories, and with others, the memories get them through. In younger adults, college age, they exhibit risky behavior. A mother kills a child in a drunk driving accident, yet she continues to drink. We call it survivor guilt. (Objection) (Sustained) Let us add to this the family deals with things by denial. (Objection) (Sidebar) Given that compound hypothetical, we can see that people can deny. Let's add the thirty-one days of Casey's behavior? Well, you have to look at what everyone else did. They go out and do the same thing their friends died of. (I am sure this woman has validity with grief, however this is distasteful in this set of circumstances.)

Sally Karioth, PhD – State's cross-examination: Is being very happy consistent with grief, sad, happy, and mad? Nothing excludes or includes grief. Lack of promiscuity to virginity? Is there anything that is inconsistent with grief? Anything could happen, that could be consistent with grief. I was first contacted by the defense at the end of May or the beginning of June. When you walked in this door, did you know about this case? I did not know at the time of the e-mail. Then I got another note, so then I looked; this is something from several years ago. London did not carry this story. When you walked through the door what facts did you know? I was asked to come and talk on general grief. I worked in the Susan Smith trial. I testified, trying to help people understand why Susan Smith murdered her children. (Objection) (Sidebar) Denial is a coping mechanism, and it is denying the child is around. Someone who loses a father may think their father is in Europe.

State: Let's assume this hypothetical. A twenty-two-year-old mother's child dies, she lives with her parents, tells no one, within a half day goes to her boyfriend, has sex, and rents movies. Over the next thirty-one days, she tells people all kinds of different stories. She tells her family she is in Tampa with the child, but she is in Orlando. Then another fiction for the mother, while everyone else knows she is in Orlando, then another event for child to attend at Disney, and then a wealthy potential boyfriend to stall the mother. She tells the mother she is in Jacksonville, but she is in Orlando, and everyone else knows she is Orlando.

I would agree that this is a young woman in crisis not consistent with denial and grief. It is more consistent with crisis. More like, if I can keep all the balls in the air, maybe it won't be true. State: Let's add one more thing to our hypothetical: the mother deliberately killed the child. (Objection) (Sidebar) Denial is a coping mechanism for guilt. It is documented that many people use denial to cope with guilt and shame. This can be compartmentalized, and they can go on with coping. They can do this with a deliberate horrible act they have committed. They can put it in a box and go on as though nothing happened. Guilt can be from lying and that they can appear to be truthful, and it is denial. In an attempt to stay afloat, they can come up with an almost merry story. Magical thinking is a mother that lost a child, who called and said he had never been out in the dark and rain. We sat on the porch, with umbrellas. She knew the child was dead. The bond between mother and child does not break. (The witness is excused, and the jury is in recess for the evening.)

We believe that in the end, this doctor realized this was not a woman in grief, but in crisis. It is also possible that she was not given information on this case, and her lack of knowledge worked to the State's advantage. The defense will close tomorrow afternoon.

Judge: State, please have some afternoon witnesses ready. A charge conference will be on Friday, and closings on Saturday. If they are not on Saturday, they will be when the jury wants. If they want to work Sunday, we will. Burdick: What about the Fourth of July? Judge: Let me see if the jury wants to work. Burdick: You know they will want to work. Ashton: I hear the fireworks are beautiful from up here. Judge: Then you had all better get ready to work. Court stands in recess. (We like this! This judge is willing to work until they all drop. Our house lawyer had a judge work him until 1 AM, and has often been in trial until well into the evening, so he sympathizes with the lawyers for both sides on this one!)

June 30th, 2011

Last night, the media reported that that a woman has come forth asking to be tested, because she believes she is the biological grandmother of Caylee. According to reports, she states that her son died in a car accident and that he had told her of Casey and her pregnancy with Caylee. We are sure of this; someone will test her and many others in the upcoming months. The story could or could not be true. (Court is in session.)

Judge: Good morning, everyone. You may be seated. I understand you have a couple of matters you want to take up before testimony resumes. Defense: Yes, Your Honor, just a scheduling question from Ms. Finnell. Judge: You may approach the bench. Do we need the court reporter? Defense: No. (Sidebar)

Baez: I was just handed information from the State of Florida on work information for Cindy Anthony, phone logs. There are two hundred and thirty-one pages of a printout that I do not understand. I can only assume it is to rebut Mrs. Anthony's testimony that she did the chloroform searches. It is a discovery violation. I would like to have a continuance and take depositions of people at her work.

Judge: We will be stopping at five, if you want to take depositions from five to midnight. I assume when you put her on the stand, that you knew the answers to the questions you asked her. I assume you were provided with her time cards. Then Mrs. Anthony testified she was not at work, so. We will conduct a **Richardson hearing** at the time of admission of the records. I suggest you get any witness you want to see what they have to say. It is

438

logical if someone tries to testify to A, someone is going to look at B to see if A sails. We will look at whether this is a discovery violation and more. (A Richardson hearing is a hearing held outside the presence of the jury regarding the admissibility of evidence that is not given to the other side on time. The hearing involves whether the violation of the discovery rules is inadvertent or not, whether it could have been given to the other side sooner, whether it could have been known to the side who wants to introduce the evidence, and other factors.) Judge: Who will be the defense's next witness? Defense: Chrystal Holloway. Call the jury.

The Defendant's Sixtieth Witness

Interpretation of Testimony - Krystal Holloway: I am known by River Cruse. My father called me "River" and my mother's maiden name is Cruise. There are no other reasons I use that name. I know George Anthony, and I met him in July or August of 2008, at a tent for his granddaughter. I went there every day. I got to know him better, and I developed an intimate relationship. He came to my home maybe twelve times. Did you loan him money? (Objection) (Sidebar) (Sustained)

I had a conversation with him about his granddaughter. I was on the floor and he was on the couch. He said it was an accident that snowballed out of control. I did not prompt it, he just said it. I said I did not think that he could raise someone that could kill her child and he just said it was an accident that snowballed out of control. My relationship with him ended on the fourth birthday balloon release. I do not know the date, but I had attended. At the memorial for Caylee, I was still in a relationship with George Anthony.

After the relationship ended, I did not tell anyone until I was contacted by police. The police contacted me two years later. They asked how I knew George and if I had an affair. They had a text. They had several text messages. They asked for my phone records and the letters that he had written. (A text message is introduced as an exhibit.) This is a photo of the text. The date is December 16th, no year, and it says "just thinking about you, I need you in my life." The relationship ended on the day of the memorial. He was supposed to come over and he did not. I was not good enough for him to call me (no angry motive here?), and I went crying to my sister. My sister sent a mean message, and I never heard from him again.

There is a guard port at my complex. I told the guard not to let him in. I have been on the media. I was beginning to be harassed. (Objection) (Sustained) Baez: I would like leeway Judge: Sustained. You may approach. (Sidebar)

(Testimony resumes) When the police first asked me about an affair, I denied it. I thought he would get in trouble with the media, and I was in a relationship. I eventually told the police the truth after. That was after I had no choice behind the texts, and I was confronted. Prior to the police finding you and your name released, did you talk to the media? I did not sell my story to a tabloid. I gave an interview. They offered me a chance to tell my story. I felt the media would edit it, and he gave me the chance to tell my story in full. I have a twin and my **sister got compensation for the story**. I wanted to testify here. (Objection) (Sustained) At the time you inserted yourself in their life, they were celebrities. They were on the news and in the media. How much money did you get from the National Enquirer for just talking to them? $4000. Other news organizations who do not pay asked for interviews, correct? I chose the one that paid. The National Enquirer was the one that I could trust. I took that one because of how I was being treated. The National Enquirer was the one and the story was better if you had sex. No, the story is not better if I am having sex and not just a friend. You do not agree that this story is better if you are sleeping with him?

You said George sent you letters. This is a letter sent within a couple of weeks of the text George sent you. I would like this in evidence. (Objection) It is the defense case (Sustained) (Sidebar) Ms. Holloway, in January 2008, you referenced his attempt to leave messages through your daughter, security and husband. Did you ever tell George Anthony you were in a relationship and claiming a husband type relationship with someone else and did George refer to him and his wife in the letter? Yes. And, you were being friends with him and his wife? The text message was sent after the remains were discovered - by the fifth day. I was under oath, and I swore that I was not in a romantic relationship with George. You stated, "no we did not become romantically involved", didn't you? In February, I told the detectives - this was February 17th, 2010. I changed it when my sister went to the media and then after my family goes to the media. I called and changed it to the police. I went to the detective. On February 17th, they found you, and then you go to the media and when does the National Enquirer contact you? How did the National Enquirer or other sources relate to your changing your story? I lied. When and how did this change take place, in that same

440

week? I first discussed giving a story to the media by the end of the week from the first interview with police.

I was talking to him about his daughter and that I did not believe he could raise anyone who could kill anyone. He said, I really believe it was an accident that snowballed out of control. This is from the same statement that you swore to tell the truth. He said, "I really believe," it was an accident, and it went wrong, and she tried to cover it up? Yes, that is what he said. He also said it was an accident that snowballed out of control. He did not tell me he was present when it happened. I just told you he said it was an accident, he did not claim he knew it for sure. He did not say that he knows it or that Casey said it. Did he also tell you on another occasion about an incident involving him attempting to get information about the death of Caylee by throwing his daughter up against the wall? (Objection) (Sustained) (Sidebar)

(The jury will not see what we saw of this woman on TV in interviews. She appears to enjoy herself on television. Did she and George Anthony have an affair? Maybe; who knows, and who cares except Cindy. The letters she received seem to speak from both George and Cindy. She was clearly selling stories and seeking her fifteen minutes of fame. The fact the George was praying his daughter was not a murderer and hoping this nightmare was an accident, we all understand.)

Krystal Holloway - Defendant's direct examination resumes: Baez: The statement that says, He believes; that statement was taken out of context. Before that, it says that he said it was an accident that snowballed out of control. This was a statement he made when he was doing media interviews and looking for his missing granddaughter? Witness: Yes. I never went to anyone; the detectives came to my door. After the relationship was exposed and it came out in the media, I went to the National Enquirer. The media would edit it and say that I have a criminal background, it's not true. Yes, I have had incidents with citations and…(Objection) (Sustained)

Krystal Holloway - State's cross-examination: Read this statement. This is your statement of February 17, 2008. (Objection) (Overruled) He said, I really believe it was an accident and something went wrong. Casey? George gave no verbal response to my asking if it was Casey. (Objection) (Sidebar)

(This is a danger, that is often associated with any type of volunteer groups for any kind of high profile story.

People come out for media attention with many different claims, or send repeated information to the police in an investigation.)

Krystal Holloway - State's cross-examination (resumes):
He did not say that he knew it was an accident, he just said he believed. Correct. He did not say Casey told him. Mrs. Holloway I am confused. In your statement, you said George did not know, he believed. Is that correct? Yes.

(The jury is out for recess, and this fight about the word continues. (The witness steps down.) Judge: Let's clear this up now, and then you can have a break, so talk as long as you want, gentleman. Defense: I have no further questions. The prosecution requests a jury instruction on this witness. Prosecution: The alleged statement by this witness maybe used only as impeachment and for no other purpose as to the cause of death of the child. The judge recites the law to Mr. Baez. Regarding prior inconsistent statements, and quotes Ehrhardt. The statement she gave was to law enforcement. That statement is not proof of how this child died. That is for argument. Baez: Just more blah, blah, blah.

Judge: Mr. Baez, have you read this case? The state got a conviction in a first-degree murder, and it was reversed because the state used an inconsistent statement as substantive evidence. You are not saying this is substantive evidence are you? Baez: No, it is to impeach George Anthony. Prosecution: The evidence is not really to impeach and he is not impeaching. This is put before the jury in hope that they take it for more than it is, and use it in an improper way. Every instruction is to be presented to outline the law. This is argument, and at what point do you stop? (The prosecutor is tossing in a jab.) Judge: An instruction needs to be given. We have two trained lawyers who cannot agree, and how do we expect the jury to understand this testimony? Pursuant to Florida Supreme Court, we will give the following amended instruction: The testimony concerning the statement of George Anthony testified to by this witness, Krystal Holloway. You may not consider this testimony in any way as to the manner of the death of the child or to the guilt or innocence of Casey Anthony. This type of instruction has been upheld in many cases before. They are not lawyers, and even you lawyers cannot agree. I am charged with the responsibility and if we get to that stage, (The judge means an appeal) my paper will be graded. Bring the witness in, if there are no more questions, I will excuse her and give the instruction to the jury.

The lawyers announce that they have no further questions, and the witness is excused. This instruction is given to the jury by the judge: The testimony by the witness Krystal Holloway, you may only consider it as to impeachment. You are not to use her testimony as evidence as to the guilt or innocence of the defendant. (Sidebar)

The Defendant's Sixty-first Witness

Interpretation of testimony - Dominic Casey (recalled): This is a photo of a map attached to an e-mail. I sent it on November 15th, 2008; the map depicts the area and it would not be specific. Luke sent me an e-mail with this map and asked if I could point to where I looked on Suburban Drive. (Objection) (Overruled) It was prepared in 2008, and my mind was fresher then than it is now. I looked on November 15th and 16th. On November 15th, I went to the location and looked around. When I look at the blown up map, they are in the same area; the blown up map is inaccurate. It appears to be a blown up version, but the pin marks would be different. The first pin is allocated off Suburban Drive.

When you marked this map with a pin, it is a best guess, were I went. It was not a search. I use the bend in the road as a guide and the larger one brings it more into perspective of the area. I walked in, took a right turn, and walked maybe a few feet. These pins are not indicative of where I was. It is a general idea of where I would have gone into the woods. I prepared it three years ago. This is the only area where I went to look. The video is a news video of the command center of George. This is a video of the Kid Finder table, duct tape and people. The roll of duct tape with the brand Henkel is on the table. (The witness is excused.)

The Defendant's Sixty-second Witness

Interpretation of Testimony - George Anthony: I saw the video. I saw the duct tape; it could have been mine or someone else's. There were two different Publix stores. There is one on Chickasaw and one on Curry Road. I do not know at which location the video was made. Did anyone else bring Henkel duct tape to the tent? I do not know. I have no idea if that is my roll of duct tape. I do not know if that tape is from the Company in Ohio you asked about. I do not know. Did I have a dog named Mandy in Ohio? Yes. The dog was put down at the vet and buried in the back yard. The dog was deceased and placed in a blanket, probably. I do not know if he was put out in a bag and duct tape. I had a dog Beau, when Casey was four or five. I do not have any idea how we buried him. I took him to the vet; he was sick and dying. We had a cat, and dog, and I do not know how they were put to rest, no. I never had a dog named Misty. When I found out that my granddaughter was wrapped in a blanket and garbage bags with duct tape… (Objection) (Sustained)

George Anthony – State's cross-examination: Have you ever taken a dead pet and thrown him in a swamp? No sir. (Objection) (Overruled) The witness is excused.)

The Defendant's Sixty-third Witness

Interpretation of Testimony – Cindy Anthony (recalled): I had a dog named Manny in Ohio in 1981. Casey was a baby when she passed. She was ill and she was going to be put down, and they told me to bring something. She was my baby before the kids. I took her baby blanket and held her and then they took her from me and she was wrapped in black plastic with packing, not duct tape. Beau was buried in the back yard, taken to the vet and George and Casey took him. The vet secured him. The children and we had a ceremony and buried the dog. Casey was four and Lee was seven. Yes, in plastic and wrapped in tape, and as we did the other pets that died, a towel or whatever and bury them, with a toy in plastic and clear packing tape. We did the same thing with our pets here – we wrapped them and buried them in the back yard.

Cindy Anthony – State's cross-examination: I take it that you did not euthanize your pets with chloroform. (Objection) (Sustained) Did you put duct tape on their faces? No. Casey was a senior in high school. I think Casey was present when the dog was buried. The reason for the tape was make them compact for burial. We designated a spot for the deceased animals, and the children were aware for many years and there was a memorial marker of a dog. Casey was present at some. When she was small, I kept her with neighbors and I buried the animal. When they were older, they knew. The tape was on the top and bottom and we were placing tape to hold it for burial. (The witness is excused.)

The authors see that the defense is now using the "dog defense".

The Defendant's Sixty-fourth Witness

Interpretation of Testimony – Lee Anthony (recalled): I was young when Mandy the dog died. I remember the first time was Beau the dog. I do not remember being present. Cinnamon, I buried her in a black bag and I used duct tape to secure the bag. One that I remember; my grandmother's pet was given to us by the vet, and it was wrapped in a black plastic bag with clear tape on it. The package was cold; she was on ice. Normally, my parents buried our family pets. (The witness is excused.) (A recess is announced.)

We may be ending the defense presentation in this first-degree murder case of a child, by how they buried the family pets. Casey is back in the courtroom for her defense case to close. The question is, will she testify? She is smiling, looks nervous and animated. We do not know from her demeanor. We think she probably should not testify. Will she? Who knows; the defense case is bad, and she appears narcissistic.

(The judge resumes the bench.) Mason: This is a stack of records we received this morning about Cindy Anthony's work. We need a Richardson inquiry. Baez: May we approach without the court reporter? Yes. (Sidebar)

(Back in open court.) Baez: No more live witnesses, and the defendant will not testify. Judge: Ms. Anthony, is it your decision not to testify? Yes, Sir. You understand it is your decision alone. Yes. It is your decision not to testify and you have weighted the pros and cons? Yes. Has anyone used any force or pressure? No. It is your decision freely and voluntarily? Yes. Let's return the jury.

This is a stipulation between State of Florida and the defense that the attached documents are the correct records of Suretape Brands. We are introducing the records regarding the Suretape brand of Henkel duct tape. (Received in evidence) Baez: The defense rests. (The jury is excused for legal argument.)

The State will be presenting its rebuttal case of less than a day, but the defense has raised the question of some discovery in the State's rebuttal, so it needs to be addressed first.

Richardson Hearing

Mason: Yesterday afternoon, counsel advised us that they were expecting documents of the employment and work records of Cindy Anthony for the purpose as to whether she was at work or not. This relates to whether she had made the computer searches of chloroform. They did present us with a few hundred records this morning. Mrs. Cindy Anthony's testimony was not new. She had testified to the same thing in July 2009. They have known since then. She disclosed that she had made the computer searches. They waited until we had called her, and then subpoenaed records for the first time. It is prejudicial to the defense. In fact, counsel crossed-examined, and then goes out to get records and we are prejudiced. We move the court to prohibit that rebuttal testimony.

Prosecution: The documents we intend to present documents regarding Cindy Anthony's user name, CAMATHON. The records are of the login and logout for that user, maintained by Gentiva. It is the employer log. In addition, there is a series of documents that is being presented with deleted e-mails that are Cindy Anthony's, on Monday the 17th and Friday the 21st. Deleted, received, and sent e-mails are what we received from Gentiva. The reason it looks so big is that it is an Excel spreadsheet. This is the work from the desktop login, and an active job enters dates and times. The company removes patient names from their records because of HIPAA, but the terminal affiliation information is not removed. It is correct to say Mrs. Anthony talked about doing chlorophyll searches and did not dispute her work records in July 2009. She talked about records Gentiva would have. She talked about her password and login. The court knows the records were requested on June 24th and we requested a subpoena. They came in pieces the on the 27th, 28th, 29th; they were sent electronically. I informed counsel yesterday and provided it today. The compliance office of records is here from Atlanta to testify. Mrs. Sims started speaking with him over lunch and she states she needs more time.

Mason: Your Honor, you have, on a number of times, said this is not to be a trial by ambush, with all due respect. There are hundreds of depositions. Was there ever an issue of work records? She clearly testified about chlorophyll and they should not be allowed to drop this on us in the eighth week of testimony. This is a material violation; we are prejudiced. My motion to prohibit introducing the documents is fair.

Judge: When did Mrs. Anthony contest the employment records? She said she searched. Prosecution: She said, I may have searched for chloroform. The searches themselves we talked about. Not the work records. They were received yesterday afternoon. I notified the defense that we were expecting records. This is a new issue. I did not anticipate that accuracy of her work records would be disputed. Baez: She may have said she was a salary employee and she never disputed her work history. She looked, and she said she was looking chlorophyll and peroxide. Judge: Was there any awareness that she would come in and say the records were not accurate? The

446

witness testified to the items. She did say she was a salaried employee. The question I ask is, was the defense aware that she would come in dispute the records and say they were meaningless? The prosecution touched on this. Baez: Your Honor, the answer is… a kind of yes.

Judge: What prejudice would the defense suffer? Baez: We are not knowingly presenting false evidence that she did these searches. We did not know it was false. What would prevent her on surrebuttal from taking the Fifth? Judge: We could deal with it at that time. Baez: I think it is too late. It would place the stigmata of false evidence. No witness tells you they are going to lie. Unfortunately, counsel can only rely on witnesses to tell them, and not shade their testimony. This was not intentional; Mrs. Anthony testified to e-mails, passwords and disputed the work records.

Prosecution: There is no discovery violation if it can be cured by counsel, and the man is here to testify as the records custodian. Baez: This is complex. We just got a stack of documents, and the timing is too late. Judge: Before Mrs. Anthony's testimony, did you know she was going to say she was at home and not at work? Baez: Yes. I knew she was going to say that. Judge: Were you aware she was going to testify and dispute the records that she was at work, and the records were meaningless? Baez: Yes. Judge: The work records that have been introduced were computer generated, and the time card history report. Baez: Yes. Judge: Computer generated. Baez: No, there was no question of these records, work records that were submitted into evidence, and we had a stipulation we were going to do.

Prosecution: Unlike in Richardson v. State, this was not a discovery violation; we sought the records immediately and provided them to the defense. The defense raises the issue of prejudice; trial is to be about a search for the truth and the jury is to be provided with accurate records to make a fair verdict. The jury will be given an instruction to weight and that they can credit or discredit all or any part of the testimony of any witness. The defense has said they need a computer expert. They have stipulated to records from this organization, and there is no claim that these records were fabricated, and we all know that any fabrication of records is a problem if it did exist.

Judge: The balance of the day, Mrs. Simms is to talk to him about the records. I will make him miss his doctor's appointment if you need him, but everyone knew this was coming. As an officer of the court, consistent with your admission to the bar, how long will it take, Ms. Sims? Simms: I think an hour or so. The chief custodian had someone else compile the records. Prosecution: She would just say I received an order and I retrieved them. There is only a time difference from Central to Eastern. Judge: Medical issues, can he delay the doctor's appointment? Ashton: Let me step outside and check. Okay, let's return the jury. Just one other issue first, Your Honor.

The judge is inquiring about a few upcoming potential witnesses. Prosecution: Mike Vincent is going to be asked to say he has opened and smelled the air in the can. The odor was still there, just less. These jurors will want to smell the can. I am not asking them to do that, but they will want to. I do not know if Your Honor wants to take this up now. Dr. Furton was placed before this jury to counter that the odor was trash, as the defense has claimed. There have been numerous witnesses that said the smell was decomposition. Everyone was cross-examined about whether this was a trash smell. The defense will continue to present the trash argument.

Judge: The prosecution has had a number of witnesses who testified the smell in the trunk was decomposition. Prosecution: What are we going to do when the jury asks to open the can in the jury room and smell? Judge: Mr. Baez, do you want the jury to open this can? Baez: No.

Ashton: Yes. If the jury asks to smell, are we going to say no? There are many cases on the jury using olfactory sense. The ruling was that the juror's use of the olfactory sense was proper, in a marijuana case.

Judge: The Court called everyone's attention to this early in the trial. The question has been before this court and they condemned the practice of allowing a juror to smell or taste whiskey. The jurors become witnesses. This is a 1948 case, I told you about it in Clearwater. I also told you of other cases. They say you can do it and this was a case to do with alcohol. There are two cases in the State of Florida. The latest case is Lynch. That was a death case. The defense found fault with the judge looking at a gun. The judge was trying to see if his manipulation of the weapon was the same as the experts. Contained in Lynch was a quote from Castillo, the Fourth District Court case. They talked about the jury experimentation. The trial court did not abuse its discretion when a trial judge allowed the juror to replicate what the defense expert had done at trial. A replication of a demonstration that was presented in court may be done. This is the question, whether to allow the can to be opened in the jury room. We are asking the jurors to determine whether the odor is trash or a decomposing body. Three or four jurors said they had smelled decomposition before, during jury selection. How would the defense be able to cross-examine the possible juror that had smelled the odor of decomposition? In my opinion, it would violate the defendant's due process right to confront witnesses, and therefore the request if made by the jury, will be denied. That item will not go back to the jury room. I am well aware of the rule that all evidence must go back. However, I am using my discretion and not allowing that can to go back to the jury room.

The authors think the judges' ruling is right. If the jury opened that can, if one or two jurors can recognize the smell of decomposition, they would unduly influence the remaining jurors with that special knowledge. From musicians to war veterans, we have all heard the words 'we can smell the smell of death.' Casey would have been prejudiced if the jury smelled the air in that can. It would be bad precedent for future cases. It is wrong to have jurors, who cannot be questioned by the lawyers, to possibly base their decision on an odor so strong it never leaves the human mind once smelled. Casey Anthony has enough evidence to face. If she is found guilty, we do not want this case to be overturned for another multi-million dollar, taxpayer-funded trial. Casey Anthony has wasted enough of our money and judicial time with her lies.

PART SIX

THE STATE'S REBUTTAL CASE AND CLOSING ARGUMENTS

Chapter 16

THE STATE'S REBUTTAL CASE AND POST-EVIDENCE MOTIONS

The State's Seventy-first Witness

Interpretation of Testimony - Alina Boroughs (recalled): I am a CSI. These are photos of the clothing that was seized in the search warrant. They were located in the northeast corner of Caylee's room in the Anthony home. (All items are admitted to evidence.) (Additional items are being admitted into evidence at this time. They are the drawings of Dominic Casey, documents of Joe Jordon's report of EquuSearch and maps. George Anthony's suicide letter is admitted into evidence. This item is in evidence and is published.)

The jury is now reading it page by page on the monitor. The judge has advised that it will go back to the jury room for deliberations and they can read it in detail. George's handwriting is clear, upright without much of a slant and compacted at the beginning. It becomes more erratic as the letter goes on.

Judge: At some time tomorrow, we will conclude the presentation of all evidence in this matter; On Saturday, we will have closing arguments. On Saturday night, I will instruct you as to the law. On Sunday, you will begin deliberations. (The jury is excused for the day.)

How a spectator can go to jail, part two. A legal issue has suddenly come forth and is now pending in court about a photo. This has to do with a young man sitting in the courtroom who flipped off one of the attorneys. A camera caught him and the judge sees it. Now he is in a lot of trouble and before the judge. Judge: Your name? I am Mathew Bartlett, and I am 28. Judge: I am going to have a deputy place these photos in the court's evidence as exhibits. Bartlett: It is me in the photo. I am using my middle finger. Judge: What does it mean? Bartlett: It is the F word and I was extending it to Mr. Ashton.

Judge: The court was in session. How far did you go in school? Bartlett: I have gone to twelfth grade and I can read and write. Judge: Do you see this sign? "Any gestures, facial expressions, or outcries are prohibited"? It was posted outside the courtroom. Did you read that sign? Bartlett: Yes, I saw it and read it. Judge: I have instructed the court deputies to tell spectators each day that facial expressions and gestures are not permitted. Did you hear a court deputy say that? Bartlett: When I came in this morning, I was advised that there would not be any gestures or facial expressions, and I understood. Judge: Pursuant to rules of court, can you tell me why you should not be held in contempt of court for gesturing while pointing your middle finger to Jeffery Ashton, who was at the podium in open court? Bartlett: I cannot understand why I did it, and I apologize.

Judge: Was he saying something, or do you think he did something to you? Bartlett: No, I don't know why I did it. Judge: The jury was here; they did not see it, and if they had there could have been severe damage. I will find that you are in contempt of court. Did you have any mitigating evidence or excuse for your behavior prior to the court imposing sentencing? Bartlett: I just apologize. I have never been convicted. Judge: Do you work? Bartlett: I am employed at TJ Fridays. I am a server. Judge: Your actions could have jeopardized all of the work that the attorneys have done and the money spent on this trial by causing a mistrial in this case.

You are guilty of criminal contempt and sentenced to six days in the Orange County jail, a fine of $400.00 plus court cost of $223.00. How long will you need to pay the fine and court costs? Bartlett: I can pay it now. Judge: I will give you ninety days to pay. (To the clerk) Set up a payment schedule in equal installments. (To Bartlett) You can pay it in full within ninety days, or you can pay monthly installments. Would you like to appeal? Bartlett: Yes. (The Judge questions Bartlett about his finances, and finds that he cannot afford an attorney. The Public Defender is appointed for appeal.) Judge: Bailiff, take Mr. Bartlett into custody. (Off to jail. This young man was repeatedly making this gesture in the courtroom gallery. He is lucky; the judge had 179 days to play with. Considering that this young man was the second person to be held in contempt in the gallery, and did not have any obvious mental health problems, unlike the woman in Clearwater, we expected a much stiffer sentence.

Let us return to the trial at hand, that of Casey Anthony. After some matters before the judge, the remainder of the day will be devoted to depositions of the State's newly listed rebuttal witnesses.

Baez: We ask the court to issue a subpoena duces tecum. Judge: I'll grant the request for additional records. If the additional records cannot be obtained until Wednesday, then if, they contain information that is mind-bending, it is what it is. Our translation is, "use it for a motion for new trial, and then argue newly discovered evidence on appeal." (Court is in recess for the day.)

Every death-sentenced defendant's case is automatically appealed to the Supreme Court of Florida, even if the defendant does not want an appeal. Our house lawyer tells us that sort of thing actually does happen sometimes, and some murder defendants even try to prohibit their lawyers from putting on mitigating evidence in penalty phase. The supreme court has come up with a procedure for those defendants - the defense must still put on a penalty phase case against the defendant's wishes, and generally without the defendant's cooperation. The purpose of both the automatic appeal and the requirement of a penalty phase defense for death-seeking defendants are to be a safety net, to insure the integrity of the judicial process, and to minimize the chance of defendants

451

committing suicide by choosing the judiciary as their weapon.

July 1st, 2011

As he entered the courtroom today, Mr. Baez was actually smiling. Our guess is because he feels relief; he has done all he can, pretty much. The defense case is over, and the trial is almost done, one way or the other. Just so you know, a lawyer personally succeeds if he goes home and not jail to for contempt, despite the verdict regarding the defendant. The verdict will tell us if Casey Anthony joins those who go home, or not. Chaney Mason is in a white suit today. Is this his good guy hat? Chaney, it is raining in Florida! Maybe it is his lucky suit. My husband says he did not have a lucky suit, he just has trial suits, in shades like postman blue, dark blue, gray windowpane, and all very conservative. This suit of Chaney's is not conservative. It gives the writers a chuckle. We told you old dog… and old dogs do what they want. We think subconsciously he wants the jury to remember him. We took a poll, and he looks like he should be in an ad for fried chicken! Never underestimate what can be choreographed by a lawyer. Casey is more subdued this morning, she looks and acts like the pressure is building. She looks more in tune with the reality of the situation. The judge is on the bench.

Baez: We are hopefully asking you for a reconsideration to exclude the Gentiva testimony. In reviewing some of the stipulations, there is a login profile and more that goes into the status of the work records of Cindy Anthony. We were going to stipulate. So they knew of the issue. The people from Gentiva were deposed, and my understanding is that Mrs. Simms had requested to speak with two of the State's computer experts. The State stated that they are asking them for new opinions. They said they are not issuing a report, and they were not made available to Ms. Simms; Osborne and the sergeant. We ask that the court hold the State to the same standard as the defense - no opinions if they are not in the report. It appears that Dr. Goldberger and Dr. Warren, the anthropologist, are outside as well. We would like a proffer for new opinions and reports. I think I have lived up to my end.

Prosecution: As it related to the members of the Sheriff Office who were asked to do key word search, Mr. Baez was advised. Mrs. Simms, at 5:15 yesterday, said she wanted to depose them. I told them about what they are testifying to, and that is all, nothing new. They are testifying to what Mrs. Anthony claimed she searched, and that she had remote login. We verified, and there is none. That was brought up yesterday.

Baez: My understanding is that this task would take two days to do. We sure would have liked to have had notice of this testimony, what they did, what hits, it is a whole complexed process. They waited until our case was closed and no such remedy is available. Judge: We are going to submit this case to the jury. How much time do you need? Baez: When reports are written, then I can show it to our experts. In addition, the doctors have new opinions in the rebuttal case.

Prosecution: The doctor provided a report years ago to the defense, and it stated that the brain debris was nothing. This is rebuttal. He is a defense witness. Dr. Warren is going to say that opening a skull is not a standard procedure in the autopsy of skeletal remains. Baez: They are not experts in this, and the rules apply to both. Prosecution: The doctor discussed his opinion on the skull, he has the report and it is not a surprise. This is about the very wash that Mr. Baez just discussed. There is nothing there. This was disclosed and nothing more.

Judge: He is a forensic anthropologist, and he is going to testify. Do you want to take his and other depositions? We will give you the remainder of the morning to take them, but we will be here Saturday and Sunday. Mr. Baez, you have the two alternatives. You are saying that all this is news to you. On the other hand, you will be here to finish this case. Both sides have asked to have the day off to prepare for closing. You can have that time, and we will work tonight, tomorrow, Sunday, Monday and Tuesday. I want to see the report, because you say this is not all there. I do not want to read a report and find it is there. I want a report. Prosecution: He is going to say it is not organic matter; it is not organic matter from decomposition. I just told counsel about the report and it should not take long. Baez: So counsel is admitting it is not in the report. Prosecution: (Voice is raised) No! I am not saying it is not in the report! I want to get to work!

Judge: There are real problems and there are imaginary problems. I will give you the time and this had better not be imaginary problems. I have a jury ready to return to their homes. In addition, you all need to agree on a statement with Dr. Rodriguez. Prosecution: We argued the issue and there is no agreement. Judge: I need some language. Prosecution: Your Honor, two depositions rooms would speed these depositions. Judge: I do not care what you do! (The judge is mad!)

There is an old saying in the defense business. The defense lawyer has not done his job unless the Judge and prosecution are both mad at him. However, there is a line. Mr. Baez, in our opinion, just keeps crossing it.

A lawyer makes many judgment calls based in part on what the client is telling him. We believe Casey knew everything Baez planned to do in court, and fed him information that led him to this plan. Casey is a liar, and her lawyers could just be some of her victims. This is our opinion on the events of the last thirty-five days of the trial.

Well, while we wait, Krystal Holloway, aka River Cruise, is making the media circuit. This woman and/or her twin received money from the National Enquirer after she changed her story from the no affair tale to the affair story. Sex sells. We wonder what Holloway does for a living; no one ever said. The news reports her as unemployed. These writers will rest until the action comes back to Courtroom 23.

They are coming back to court and Baez does not look happy. (The judge is on the bench now.) Baez: We have an objection that the first witness did not download the records himself. Judge: Are they kept in the course of business? That is what establishes them to come in. Bring the jury in now.

The State's Seventy-second Witness

Interpretation of Testimony - John Camperlengo: I am chief counsel and general attorney for Gentiva Healthcare in Atlanta. We are a publicly traded company. I am in charge of all legal affairs and assuring compliance with federal regulations. Gentiva has policies and regulations that records are collected and retained at the branch or our electronic off-site secured facilities. As a company policy, we retain records for a period of time. The patient records are retained for ten years. The electronic records are maintained in Kansas, and the facility has its own security officer. We have many servers that support all of our locations, for permanent storage. They are maintained by the 400 System. These records are HIPPA regulated, and we are under tight control. The records of the actions on terminals at any location are maintained by user identification, and everyone has a unique login. We can retrieve those records based on the identification of each employee. It is a combination of their first and last name. We record that information with the use of a Unity program. It records certain information when someone logs in, and a time stamp is made and recorded.

Cindy Anthony was employed at Gentiva in March 2008; the sheriff contacted me about her records. I requested a subpoena. We were asked for phone records, computer records and more. (He is stipulated to as the custodian of records.) The records of Cindy Anthony include deleted, sent, and recorded e-mails. They were kept in the regular course of our regularly conducted business activities, and the reports were run by our IT department. These are the e-mails for the week of March 17th, 2008. IT Vice President Paul Stein provided these to me. We have done this many times before. We have deleted patient names and identifying information, to fulfill our confidentiality requirements under HIPAA.

(All e-mails are admitted into evidence. He gave a lengthy explanation of the numerous regulations and policies of Gentiva, including their retention of sent, deleted, and received e-mails. He explained how computer activity is recorded at Gentiva's offices. He also explained that each employee had a unique user ID that was not to be shared or used by anyone else. Employees would not be able to do any work on any computers without logging in with their own ID first. A clinical administration management system called Unity would record activity whenever employees would log into a computer, no matter what computer the employee used. The company also could tell if employees were using their own computer or someone else's, and whether it was a desktop or a laptop. The witness confirmed that Cindy Anthony, under the username "CMANTHON," was in fact logged in to her workstation on March 17th, 2008 and on March 21st, 2008.

The witness also denied anyone could ever fix or change Cindy's time card, directly contradicting Cindy's statement that a supervisor could have inaccurately fixed her time card. When asked by the prosecution if there was ever a time that Cindy was allowed to work from home when the records reflected she was actually at work and logged in, he said that would be illegal. These are the login and logout times of Cindy Anthony for the week of March 17th, 2008.)

(The witness is shown a screen in the courtroom.) This is the history log report for Cindy Anthony's password account and her user identification, CMANTHON. If someone is working, it will stay up until the person logs out. The system is the same every day, and it operates twenty-four hours a day. (All remaining records are introduced into evidence.) The system follows what patient's work, or job, that she worked on at any given time. The time and date stamp is applied to each patient file from the user input. There is no outside access to the information on the servers, not even for updates. The servers are updated only by IBM, in person, and are verified by Price Waterhouse audits.

On March 17th, 2008, from 1:30 PM to 3:00 PM EST, the user CMANTHON was entering information. There were at least several changes made to different patient profiles at that time, from that office terminal, by that password of Cindy Anthony on that day. On March 21st, 2008, from 1:27 PM EST at until 4:06 PM EST there was also activity at her desk terminal at the office. Specifically, between 2:00 PM and 3:00 PM EST, she was entering information at her terminal in the office.

John Camperlengo - Defendant's cross-examination: My first contact with this was last Friday, after this trial began. Mrs. Anthony testified, and it was only then I was contacted to impeach her testimony. (The witness is excused.)

The State's Seventy-third Witness

Interpretation of Testimony - Deborah Polisano: In March of 2008, I was a nurse and director in the Winter Park office of Gentiva. I was the Director of Clinical Management, responsible for all staff, both in and out of the office. I supervised twenty employees inside the office. I know Cindy Anthony, and I was her supervisor. I was responsible for oversight, job performance, and evaluation. Cindy had a team of field staff, and was responsible for patient care by that staff. She was responsible for the paperwork; it was an office job. She did not leave many times a day. She was in a cubicle, and had to log in and out and she only had a half hour to hour for lunch. Employees would be allowed to make runs to the drug store or like.

First thing, you log on when you arrive. The computer would log out in fifteen minutes, if the terminal was inactive. Then, the employee would have to log back on. Cindy was a hard working employee. She did not take extended lunches or time off; I know because I would have to do her job when she was gone. I would remember if I had to do her job on any regular basis. Only the person logged on could use that account, because it is a HIPPA compliance issue.

In March 2008, Mrs. Anthony could not have worked from home or a laptop computer. No remote access was allowed by our office. There was no other way for an employee to access our system but to use their terminal at the office. I never fixed anyone's time card or time stamp on anything. The time card is an electronic stamp, (It is submitted into evidence.) On 3/17, she arrived at 8 AM and worked until 6 PM for 10 hours; on 3/21, the time card reflects that she worked from 8 to 5; she worked for 9 hours. I check all cards electronically for accuracy every Friday. Salaried employees work more than forty hours. If the records say she was at work, then she was at work. It would be illegal to do anything else.

Deborah Polisano - Defendant's cross-examination: Employees are allowed to run errands in the middle of the day, if they need to. On July 15th, 2008, she had to go to a tow yard, and left work. I do not recall how long she was gone, maybe an hour and a half or two hours, at most. I have not reviewed the records of July 15th. She came back, there was a lot of commotion, and then she went back to work. We had to force her to go home. She wanted to work. If the circumstances arose where I did her work, she would have to log out, and I would work under my user name and password. (The witness is excused.)

It appears to the authors that Cindy has been changing her testimony in this case to save her daughter. We are not talking about Cindy misspoke or Cindy made a mistake. It looks to us like Cindy is testifying falsely. This is why we think that allowing the Anthony family in the courtroom was wrong. Their presence allows them to figure out what they need to do to save Casey. While we can understand a mother's instinct to protect her child, the mother must be willing to accept the consequences of those instinctive acts. In case you may think Cindy's actions are noble, we would like to remind everyone that this disruption of justice does damage to the entire system, and it does have consequences. For Cindy, the consequences may include felony charges punishable by up to fifteen years in prison. We must understand that lying to derail justice may work, but should you choose to jump in front of the justice train, you must be prepared not just to push your child off the track, but also to be run over by the train. This could be an end result in this case.

The State's Seventy-fourth Witness

Interpretation of Testimony - Bruce Goldberger: I am Professor and Director of Toxicology at the University of Florida College of Medicine. I have a BA degree in Zoology and a Master's and a PhD in Forensic Toxicology. Forensic toxicology is medico-legal toxicology. I work on legal cases. My work involves testing compounds for volatile subjects. I am contacted from all over the state, and I was contacted in this case. I came from Gainesville to Orlando to take samples in this case. Dr. G and I collected samples of the femur, prepared marrow from the femur, and conducted two washes of the skull for residue of brain matter. (Sidebar) I also collected strands of hair, some matted hair, and soil from around the matted hair for examination and testing.

To do the cranial washes in the autopsy room, we sealed the sutures of the skull with wax, and then we added thirty milliliters of saline and shook the skull to dissolve anything inside it. We did that twice. I analyzed the solution that we drained from the skull. Nothing was detected to suggest decomposition product in the skull cavity.

Bruce Goldberger - Defendant's cross-examination: You said you collected something from the femur. (Objection) Baez: This is what he just said. Judge: If you open the door, he gets a chance to go into it. (Sidebar) I collected bone marrow. Then I did the saline wash of the skull. It is a crude technique, but it has been done many times, and it works. Without opening the skull, it is the best thing that I could do. Opening the skull would have disturbed the structure of the cranium [as evidence for the defense to examine.] We do not look for DNA; we are looking for other things from the skull washings. I did not send it for any further testing; I returned them to Dr. G.

The State's Seventy-fifth Witness

Interpretation of Testimony - Michael Warren, PhD (recalled): I am the director of the C.A. Pound Human Identification Laboratory at the University of Florida, and I am an anthropologist. I am a member of the working group that is tasked with best practices in science for all areas. I am not aware of any protocol that requires you to open a skull — it is simply not necessary. You can look inside the skull through the foramen magnum, the large hole where the skull attaches to the spine, see and feel everything. The negative consequences are such that another expert would not be able to see the evidence. It is simply invasive to the remains on a skeleton. A mirror is fine for viewing inside. I have not had to saw any of the skulls currently in my laboratory; and with children, you could break the skull very easily. Yes, that photo is Caylee's skull, and it is fractured. I had examined her skull and it was not fractured before sawing. Nothing recommends sawing the skull, and the Minnesota Protocol, a United Nations protocol, does not recommend it.

Michael Warren, PhD - Defendant's cross-examination: I did the video of Caylee. I am not a medical doctor or a forensic pathologist, and I cannot competently testify to what a forensic pathologist should do in an examination. I am testifying to what a competent anthropologist would do, and in my opinion, this was an anthropological case of remains. My testimony is limited to forensic anthropology. The UN team consists of multiple fields, and the UN protocol is for all sciences doing examination of those remains. I am somewhat familiar with the National Association of Medical Examiner's protocols. Anyone, in any discipline, doing the examination would make a judgment call as to what is necessary, as well as following the best practices of the discipline. I did an examination of the skull. (Objection) (Sustained) (Sidebar) I did not do the cranial washes. This was a skeletal examination, and not an autopsy of a non-decomposed body. I reviewed no reports prior to my examination of the remains. I did not review the autopsy report or the report of Dr. Goldberger. (Objection) (Sustained) No further questions. (The witness is released.)

The State's Seventy-sixth Witness

Interpretation of Testimony - Kevin Stenger (recalled): I am a Computer Forensic Examiner for Orange County. I testified about a portion of the internet history in the deleted files from the HP computer from the Anthony home. The deleted internet history is from March 4th to March 24th. I used many tools and programs to obtain this information. These are the disks with two reports and they are from NetAnalyzer and CacheBack. This report had the entire deleted history and the two days' - 3/17 and 3/21 - histories. Ashton: We admit this into evidence, and the defense wants it conditional pending their review of the disk. The prosecution wants it without condition. (Objection by Baez is overruled) Judge: It is received in evidence. Baez: May we approach? (Sidebar)

I was asked to conduct key word searches for anything related to chlorophyll, chloroform, bamboo, and neck breaking. May we publish to the jury? (The report is shown to the jury.) By using only the first letters, we get all the words that begin with those letters. Using the word chloroform, this was the result. A "chloroform habit" result was obtained. There was a reference to "chlorophyll" of any kind that was returned as a search result. The words "hand sanitizer" do not appear. I searched for sanitizer and it is not in this result. A search for "neck" returned a result of neck in conjunction with other returns. This was not a pop up. This is a Google search for "neck" and "breaking". This was typed into the Google. The user typed "neck breaking". This is not the result of a pop up but a human being entering the words and pressing enter key to search. When I searched for "chlorophyll," there had been no searches for that item in this period. Bamboo returned no searches. There was no access to any Gentiva website in this history. I utilized many different tools to do these searches to confirm the result. On one of the dates, someone searched about how to get rid of fleas.

Kevin Stenger – Defendant's cross-examination: Yahoo.com is a domain for the webpage from Yahoo, which brings up things that are different on that page each day. I was looking at the domain address of what was on this site. For Google, the person must enter the words. Neck breaking, I do not know if it has anything to do with this case, but I do not think so. Therefore, whoever searched for neck breaking then went to a fighting arts site and I cannot say what was on the page. I was not asked to do these searches in 2009. I was contacted after they wanted to impeach the testimony of Cindy Anthony. I did not do a specific search for alcohol. They automatically came up, so I did not have to do the searches for it. (The witness is released.)

The State's Seventy-seventh Witness

Interpretation of Testimony - Sandra Osborne (recalled): I am forensic computer examiner. I was asked to search for key words. I used the Encase software forensics application. I was asked to look on the entire hard drive for chlorophyll, hand sanitizer, and bamboo. These searches run all day and all night. In one place, I found "chlorophyll" in a Microsoft dictionary that comes with the computer software. "Hand sanitizer" does not occur. I found "bamboo furniture", "floors", "jewelry", "rugs", "lights", "panda bears" and "tiki bars". There is no reference to bamboo as a poison substance. There was no remote login under the three specific login names.

When someone deletes something, it goes into unallocated
space, and it does not automatically go in order of the
searches. The file stays in that location. When it is
deleted, the file is stored but the reference to the file
is deleted. The reference to the file is told that the
space is available until some other files overwrite it.
It is hard to tell what has been overwritten, but
otherwise it is there to see. This is why in unallocated
space there are fragments. If it had been overwritten, it
would be obvious due to fragments showing. (Three
stipulations are moved into evidence.) (The witness is
released.)

The State's Seventy-eighth Witness

Interpretation of Testimony - Yuri Melich (recalled): I
am the lead detective of the Casey Anthony case. These
are the home phone records for Hopespring Drive. I
subpoenaed these records. I subpoenaed the cell phone of
George for June and July of 2008, and for Cindy, for June
and July 2008. There were no calls from Cindy to George
during the week of June 16th. I did not know that George
had multiple cell phones.

Yuri Melich - Defendant's cross-examination: Did Krystal
Holloway/River Cruise tell you? (Objection) (Sustained)
(The witness reviews George Anthony's statement.) I did
not recall that George had a work cell phone, and I
therefore did not pull records. Were you ever aware that
all of the family had Boost cell phones? (Objection; this
is a different time frame.) (Sidebar) (The witness is
released.)

The prosecution has no more witnesses to present, and
announces, "The State rests." (Sidebar; we assume this is
to find out if the defense has surrebuttal.) Judge: This
concludes all evidence in the case, and we will reconvene
for closing arguments on Sunday. (The jury is excused.)

The defendant presents a motion for mistrial on the basis
of the video superimposition, and all other motions for
mistrial previously argued. Judge: Denied. The defense
renews its motion to dismiss based on the Ring case
regarding the death penalty. Judge: I reserve ruling,
pending the verdict. The defense renews all previous
motions and objections, and the judge says his rulings
are the same.

Our house lawyer says that there is a reason that the
motions for mistrial and objections are renewed at the
close of all evidence. It is done to preserve the issue
of **cumulative error.** Cumulative error means that the

combined effect of errors that individually would not be enough for reversal has resulted in the defendant being denied a fair trial. These motions are done to preserve appellate issues, not because anyone believes that the trial judge will change his mind on any of his rulings at the eleventh hour.

The Defendant's renewed Motion for Judgment of Acquittal is presented to the court: (This is standard at the end of evidence in every criminal case, and is denied regularly.) Mason: We are not waving anything. I add at the close of all evidence that there is at least as much of a case for drowning, as there is for duct tape or chloroform. The child had the ability to go in and out of the house, and up the pool ladder. There has yet to be any evidence how, where, and with whom Caylee died. You must conclude that the jury must have reasonable doubt. There is no child abuse, no torture, and no premeditated murder. As to the elements as to counts one, two and three, the State has proven only that Casey Anthony lied to the family, that the child was dead, and that she was a loving mother. All of the three hundred and sixty-six documents and exhibits in evidence that are here show a lot of maybes, decomposition, chloroform, duct tape on the hair, and no DNA. What is there excludes the defendant, and shows no evidence that the duct tape was placed on this child's face before death. The whole thing is a bunch of confusion, and you must separate the facts from fiction. The jury should not have to guess; it is your job to take the burden, and I urge you to enter a Judgment of Acquittal.

State: The facts are here for the jury to decide if the evidence is fact or fiction. There is sufficient evidence to go to the jury on every count.

Judge: Judgment of Acquittal is denied. We have a telephone conference at noon tomorrow. Defense: We are going to work out all that, we think. Prosecution: We will discuss it at noon with you, Your Honor. Judge: Do you lawyers remember the judge who was murdered years ago? They never found his body. He went fishing and did not come back. (The judge has tried to say that if there is a plea offer, take it, Casey.) The reality of her situation is showing in Casey's face. We see fear, and her understanding of her complete lack of control over her fate. She looks frantic. (Court is in recess.)

Saturday evening, Pam Plasea, an aunt of Casey Anthony, appeared on the Nancy Grace show by telephone. She stated that she had talked to Cindy's mother, Shirley Plasea. The aunt goes on to say that Cindy loved Caylee very much, much the same as she loved Casey. Cindy was enthralled with Casey when she was born; she was enthralled with the idea of having a daughter. Casey's grandmother had said that on of June 15th, 2008, Father's Day, that Cindy and Caylee came to visit Shirley after going to the nursing home. At that time, Shirley told Cindy she was going to have Casey arrested. Shirley said that money from her husband's, the grandfather's, nursing home account was taken, and Shirley had tracked it to a routing number that Casey had gotten her hands on. Shirley was certain that Casey had stolen her grandfather's money. She felt if she had Casey arrested, it might shock Casey into stopping this behavior. Cindy said she would never speak to her again if Shirley had Casey arrested. Cindy told her she would pay back the money and take care of it. Pam Plasea also said that Shirley told her that Cindy and Casey had a fight at the house that evening and Cindy put Casey against a wall and had her hands around her throat. The grandmother felt guilty, because if she had had Casey arrested, she might have saved Caylee. (We realize that is both untrue and sad; the arrest would not have happened fast enough.) The aunt continued, saying that she did not know if Casey was always like this. They seemed like the perfect family. She goes on to say, I do not believe anything they are saying about George.

We do not know whether to classify this as sideshow, attention-seeking behavior by the aunt, or truth. It may be all three. Because it was not presented as evidence in trial and subjected to the truth-testing inherent in the judicial process, we cannot be certain. What we do know is that the jurors will not be able to consider any of it in their deliberations. The jurors will hear this and many other things… *after their verdict*.

July 3rd, 2011

The judge begins the day by giving his proposed written jury charge to both sides. He tells the lawyers that the document includes the standard jury instruction, plus requested instructions. He says that he went off what the lawyers gave him. He plans to review the final set before they go to the jury. He asks, did you redo these suggestions in writing? You had better get some. I will wait to do the charge conference at noon during the lunch hour. Baez: The charge of False Information to Law Enforcement, the defense argues that these all should be one charge. Judge: This should have been a Motion to Dismiss, when charged. Motion denied.

The judge continues with housekeeping items. As for closing arguments: These photos are in evidence, so the defense can use inferences drawn from the pictures. Therefore, if there is an argument, let me hear it now. Also, there is no evidence of the defense of sex abuse by father or brother. Baez: I submit that a jury can draw from the paternity test by the FBI; she had irregular menstrual cycles and other female problems. Judge: Is there record evidence, consistent with the periods and early female problems? Lee Anthony testified, and no one ever asked if he crept into her room at night. Defense: There is evidence of a hidden pregnancy; there may have been questions that the reason was some kind of abuse. Ms. Anthony's behavior of sexual activity, lying and compartmentalizing could be signs. These are consistent with sex abuse. There is no more evidence of chloroform than sex abuse. Both sides asked the jury to draw inferences. Tony Lazzaro shared secrets and that has to be sex molestation. To pretend that it did not exist because no one witnessed it, or said so, should not preclude the argument.

Judge: "There is absolutely no evidence that the defendant was molested by her father or her brother." Prosecution: We take the position that innuendo is not evidence and there is no evidence to connect this to the case. This is alleged, unproven, and denied by George Anthony. It has nothing to do with this case. Judge: No facts or reasonable evidence exists that either George or Lee molested or attempted to molest Casey Anthony. Next, Dr. Rodriguez, I will give this instruction. Dr. Rodriguez was called as witness for the defense and through no fault of the defense or State, he could not continue. Do not consider his testimony.

Mr. Baez: Is the court precluding me from mentioning the evidence? Judge: You cannot use it to say that sex abuse by the father and brother existed. You can say dysfunction. (The jury is brought in now, and the Dr. Rodriguez instruction is read. The States closing argument begins.)

Chapter 17

THE PROSECUTION'S CLOSING ARGUMENT

Ashton: Good morning and I want to be the first, and I will not be the last, to thank you. All of us appreciate the time you have given. We came in on the low end of time we estimated. Our time is almost done, and then it is your time. (Photos and video of Caylee and Casey are shown.) It is easy to be a parent, sometimes. It is easy

when you are playing and it is easy when the child is a
joy and fun. We all know it is more - it is about
sacrifice, sacrifice of your time, love, and life. When
you have a child, that child becomes your life. This case
is about the clash of that responsibility and the life
Casey wanted. When Caylee was born, Casey was saddled
with responsibility from society and her parents. She
should care for, work hard and support her daughter.

Her response was to lie. She did not work and help
support her daughter. Her solution was to lie; she told
her parents that she went back to the same job at
Universal Studios, they accepted that and they worked
days. There is a pattern and reason why she lied. When
Casey is faced with a problem, her solution is to change
a lie. Casey is very smart. When Casey wants to do
something, she lies. When someone is working and playing,
someone else has to take care of a child. For almost two
years, Casey Anthony pretends to have a job and a nanny.
She had no job. Casey is with Caylee every day and night
because she lies. She solves that with a job of Event
Coordinator with flexible hours so she can see boyfriends
and party, so she can drop Caylee off with her mother.
She can now have Caylee when it is fun and then leave her
with her mom, who believes Casey is at work in the
evening.

Then she meets Ricardo, who accepts her child. How can
she now keep her in the evening? Mom thinks she is
working late and Caylee now can be with a Zanny the nanny
and then really stay at Ricardo's house with Casey. Then
Ricardo decides he is done playing house. Now she has
another problem to solve with a lie. However, the excuse
is not working and Cindy is not allowing Casey to just
drop Caylee at night and go out. The parents are getting
suspicious. Remember the lies about the job at Sport
Authority. George has tried to find out and get beneath
the layer of lies. He is told to stay out of it. Read his
suicide note.

There is another problem now, Caylee is verbal and she is
starting to talk. Caylee is not going to cooperate with
the lies, she cannot. She is a child. Then, at some time,
she is going to say something. Someone is going to say,
"Did you have a good time at Zanny's?", and Caylee is
going to say, "Who?" Casey meets Tony, and he has a free
life, the nightclubs, Fusion, dancing. There is nothing
wrong with young people playing, dancing and having fun.
However, Casey is a mom, and that gives her
responsibilities. That life is what she so wants. In
June, that entire week, Casey got to enjoy being free.
She has a taste of freedom and it is fantastic. So, she

had a choice, a life together with a child or free to be Tony's girlfriend. Why not just give Cindy custody and walk away? Based on the evidence, Cindy would not let her daughter walk away from the responsibility of Caylee. There is no way she would let Casey walk away from being a mother; she wanted Casey to be a good mother. As hard as this is, she has to choose between two things, her child or a party life.

On June 16th, 2008, Casey pretended to leave the house with Caylee. She tells her father, "I have to work late, and we are both spending the night with Zanny." She told the same story to her mother the night before. She was not staying at Tony's with Caylee, because that was not her relationship with Tony. She knew that Caylee would not be staying the night. She knew that that Caylee would be dead. So, on June 16th she spent the night alone with Tony; she knew Cindy would accept that they were staying another night with Zanny. Then there was the third night, and she knew Cindy would not believe that lie anymore. So, she adds an additional lie, the conference and Zanny going with her to the conference with another child for Caylee to play with. Casey is very smart, she adds the element of fun for Caylee, and mom will buy that. Casey is with Tony and Caylee is in all likelihood in the trunk, decomposing. On the 17th, her car is backed into the garage, then again on the next day, and she borrows a shovel. She thinks briefly about burying Caylee in the back like her dogs, but it was too much work, so she throws Caylee in the swamp.

The 19th, she adds a party for Caylee at the theme parks, and tells Cindy she will be home with Caylee on the 21st. On the 21st, it still going on, and she adds people. Defense counsel in questioning stated that these people were imaginary. They are not imaginary; they are in fact just lies. She tells of others, different people, different stories. She lies as it suits the audience and necessity.

By the 22nd, Cindy is told the conference is again running over and Cindy is again placated. On the 23rd, all the evidence shows that Caylee was already in her resting place off Suburban Drive, decomposing. On the 23rd, she comes up with the story of the accident, hospital, and Caylee is with other children having a wonderful time. The excuse is extended a few days longer with updates, then even longer. On the 24th, she has a problem. She came home and ran into her father. Now she needs another excuse, the insurance papers for Zanny in the hospital are the excuse to Cindy. Casey is smart; her mind is nimble and fast. The 25th, she is dropping Zanny off from the hospital; on the 26th, staying over one more night, and Cindy thinks that Caylee is coming home tomorrow. The next day June 27th. New excuse: we are back in town, but we met up with Jeff. Casey has an amazing memory. It is really quite interesting. Cindy is placated. She tells Amy that Caylee is at the beach, and Cindy that she is at the Hard Rock with Caylee and Jeff. He becomes an interesting path of Casey's strategy.

July 3rd, she makes a mistake and she tells Cindy they are at Universal. Cindy goes to Universal and calls Casey. She wants to see her granddaughter. They're not there. Back up story: she is with Jeff, he is wealthy, and we are in Jacksonville. Casey is very bright; her lies are very detailed. But when Casey wants to do what Casey wants to do, she finds a way. Timer 55, in a tape, is related to Caylee. Lee testified and he had to have it researched. She told Lee that it was the date between June 16th and Caylee's birthday. This was the maximum she could stall Cindy. Cindy created a Myspace. "I am in Jacksonville with Jeff and I think I can have a long-term relationship and mom you have to get used to me not being with you." So she is now coming up with a long-term strategy. She is working on extending the Timer 55. Maybe she will marry and go to Europe.

But things do not work. She had extended and Cindy had backed off after that conversation. However, on July 15th, they got the car, and all hell broke loose. On July 15th, the car is discovered, and Cindy is going to find her granddaughter. She finds Casey and says, "You are going to tell me where Caylee is now." Now Casey says she is with Zanny, until finally her brother lays it out, "Let's play this out. I will pretend I am the police." He convinces her that she cannot lie anymore; it will not work. She creates another lie – Caylee was kidnapped. Yes, there is a Zanny, and she kidnapped her thirty-one days ago. Thirty-one of the 55 days were gone. "I have not seen her; I looked." Then the weaves of story are consistent with the story to the police. Initially, they treat her as a victim of a child kidnapping. However, the more they investigated, the more it was falling apart. Even a fiction writer cannot write this one... **She takes them to Universal, walks them in then says, "I do not work here."**

Casey Anthony maintains her lies, and when she realizes this lie had failed, she creates another. In the Melich interview, "I am lying about working here… but everything else is true." She maintains the story with law and her parents. During that period of time, the claims of where she dropped Caylee off had been disproved. She is released from jail for a short time, and then comes up with a kidnapping story; a kidnapping by force. Only when faced with overwhelming evidence comes Casey 3.0, a new version. The problem with that version comes up on December 11th, when the remains are found within a quarter mile of her home. The items found with Caylee are the tape; the tape is on the remains, three piece of Henkel duct tape, the facilitator for Casey 3.0, is tape from her home and it is pretty unusual. That is a problem. That very tape was used unknowingly by her father; the very same tape was used to implore people to look for Caylee. Next, the bag, Caylee's coffin, an identical bag is taken from the Anthony home; this is a make of bags that are sold in sets. This is the square bag, and the cylindrical bag is in evidence from the remains scene.

The shorts that were found, this is photo of Caylee wearing those shorts. This is a photo of the shirt lettering; the last remnants of the shirts and shorts are all that is left. This is a photo of Caylee in the shirt she died in. She was not with a stranger; Caylee was with Casey Anthony. The blanket that was with the remains was a Winnie the Pooh with Piglet blanket. This is the same bedding that was on Caylee's bed… a room minded by the grandparents, all the time she was missing. You see the exact same figure on the bedding and blanket. This blanket was not taken from a stranger's home. It was taken from the same home Casey and Caylee lived in. The claim that it was some stranger is no longer tenable. Just like the claim of Universal Studios, Zanny, and by the time that the body was found, there was no question left. The evidence is that she died by someone in that house. The evidence is the witnesses and testimony.

The judge will instruct you on the definition of reasonable doubt. It is not a forced one, not an imaginary one, or a maybe doubt. Evidence has not established the defense opening statement in this case. George Anthony told you it did not happen, the first witness. You may not speculate or imagine, there is no evidence in this case that supports that allegation. The defense opening was not just to create one villain, they referred to Roy Kronk as someone that was morally bankrupt, and then George Anthony disposed of Caylee's body, somehow. We will admit this tape comes from the home; we agree. But it does not mean that George Anthony placed it on Caylee. Then Roy Kronk came up, took the body home, and put the tape on. Someone put that tape on the child before the child decomposed, and the defense has asked you to leave your common sense at home. Men who love their granddaughters, and how George loved Caylee,

468

take an accident and make it look like a murder? This is the world that the defense invites you to occupy. A man who runs across a skull and reports it three times, takes the skull and mandible that is worth reward money. He takes it home, puts tape on it, and then brings it back. This is the world, the defense invites you to occupy.

Even for the most morally bankrupt and motivated by money, if they are motivated by money, if no one is listening, just walk down the street to the news trucks. He gave up, and then four months later came back. You can tell by looking, you do not need an expert. The body had been there along a time, and the tape decomposed with it. It did not have any cotton in it – left on the tape. The tape did not just get out a few days before. There is absolutely no possibility that George Anthony had anything to do with disposing of his granddaughter. You watched on the video; he was looking for answers. In his suicide note, he wrote that he was going to be with Caylee. There is no way the man who wrote that note knew anything about what has happened to his granddaughter. He has nothing to do with this crime. But Casey – her car – on July 15th, 2008, her car reeked of death. Simon Burke, who had been in towing for 25 years, and a year of waste management, told you. "I have smelled it before; that was a smell of a dead body." He smelled something the first time, and he knew what it was. I know what that is, decomposition. He has no reason to lie. You heard from professional witnesses, Casey's father. It was decomposition, and we know what it smells like. We got help from the one person who has studied the world of decomposition for the last ten years, the odor. Dr. Vass told you when he opened the can, he jumped back three feet and knew. But then he tested it; he removed the carpet and ran tests.

There is no signature of the chemicals, they tell you. However, Dr. Vass, who has researched it more than anyone else, has told you there is a chemical signature. You could put a chemical group together and identify it. It would still not smell like decomposition, it has to be actual decomposition. And it was even on the paper towels. There was a dead body in the back of the car. Others, although not as experienced, agreed with Dr. Vass that it was decomposition, and the smell of the garbage was not sufficient. They tried to talk to around it, and eventually all agreed the myth of the garbage is not sufficient to create the odor on the items; and it was still present two year later. You all have walked past the garage with garbage and when you remove the bag of garbage, the smell goes with it. You have the hair, an artifact that is only found in decomposing bodies. That

469

testimony has never been rebutted. You heard testimony that they tried to recreate this in a living person. "I could not recreate it," he said. He could not replicate decomposition. That hair was from a dead body. It was confirmed to be Caylee's by mitochondrial DNA; it was Caylee's, Casey's, Lee's, Cindy's or the grandmother's hair. Casey, and Cindy and grandmother all have hair that is treated, and Lee's hair is short. This hair is nine inches long. This hair also had the root banding, just like the hair on Caylee's body.

As hard as it is to accept, when Casey was at Blockbuster, walking arm and arm with Tony, Caylee was in her trunk, in early states of decomposition. She backed the car in the garage with the intention of burying her and she actually laid the body down on the ground, then she decided the work was too much, and she tossed her into the swamp. Casey decided the conflict of the life she wanted and her child had to be resolved. She took the life of her child, put her in the trunk and forgot about her until she could not stand the smell, and then tossed her out. The defense will say we cannot prove how she died. There is no good reason to put duct tape over the face of a child. To silence, why do you need three pieces? Three overlapping pieces, why use three? One would silence, three is to make sure she cannot breathe. One over the mouth, another over the nose, and the third to cover any gaps, and then the child dies. There is no other reason to put duct tape over a child, living or dead. That is proof of how Caylee died. There is no other explanation. The Medical Examiner, the anthropologists, told you the tape had to be on before she died, to keep the jaw intact. That tape was placed there for one single purpose. We can only hope the chloroform was used first, so Caylee went peacefully. No matter what, the tape was there to stop her breathing and to kill her. (The jury is given a recess.)

It appears Mr. Ashton sees and we saw the same story from the evidence… a child beginning to talk, the inconvenience on her life, Casey's lies were closing in on her. However, Mr. Ashton put into his closing argument something that has rolled in these writers minds. We do not think either of us would have done it as well as he did; he made the chloroform into a wish for a painless death before the duct tape suffocated her, hoping Caylee was murdered while sleeping. This writers den has also had that wish for Caylee. Bravo, Mr. Ashton. I guess that is why he gets the big bucks. Actually, he is only a public servant, so there are no big bucks. Each side receives a limit of 4 hours for closing arguments. The

470

prosecution used 77.8 minutes in the first part, so they have the balance to use in rebuttal, after the defense.

The judge makes an announcement to the spectators: Once we start the final jury instructions, no one can leave or enter, move or bounce in this courtroom. (The defense is preparing its closing, using four-foot high posters as visual aids. Baez has posters of people with no faces – Casey's imaginary friends.)

Judge: Let's return the jury. Baez: Are we breaking at noon? Judge: Shortly thereafter, or where there is a logical break.

Chapter 18

THE DEFENDANT'S CLOSING ARGUMENT

Baez: May it please the court; my colleagues and I would like to thank you for the time that you have given and we all thank you, individually and collectively. Here we are at the end of the journey, and you probably have more questions than answers. I told you in opening, we would never know how Caylee died. What is proven beyond every reasonable doubt? There was probably a lot you were looking for that you did not get. This is our moment, our opportunity to show you what I think that the evidence did show. The state will have one more chance to talk to you and I will not. That is because they have the burden, and that is why they have the opportunity of the last word. I told you this is not a two-sided affair. While we did put on evidence and witnesses, we could have just as easily not done anything. It was still the State's burden. Mr. Mason is going to come talk more about that. Judge Perry will give you the law and it is important for you to follow it. No one has the right to base his or her decision on emotion.

I am going to tell you what I fear, then outline the State's case. I want to show you what I think it showed. What we say is not evidence. It is a guide. There were many sidebars; sometimes it was not perfect. This is the purpose of closing argument, to show you a guide. We want to tie it together. Mr. Mason will explain the law in the judge's instructions, and how it applies to the State and defense. They will have the last remarks. This is going to be the toughest time for me, when Ms. Burdick is talking last. My biggest fear is that this case deals with deep emotions. Your rules of deliberation must not be decided because you feel sorry for someone, or are angry with anyone. We want you to base your decision on the law. There were times that there were emotions directed at you. This is not what you base your verdict on. Caylee was a beautiful child, her life cut short.

Mr. Ashton started with a video of this beautiful child; this was to set up your emotions. They did not come right out of the gate with evidence. They painted Casey as a party girl and a liar. The State came out with all these witnesses, but everyone said she loved and cared for Caylee. We did not hear one single incident of child abuse. If there is an abused child, someone sees it – broken bones, more. There was nothing other than that this child was loved and cared for. Something changed, and it changed the life of Casey and Caylee Anthony. You have trouble on the evidence, on how she died. I agree with one thing Mr. Ashton said: it was not proven. We can speculate all day long, and the truth must be proven. If you have questions, then it was not proven. You have seen this checkbook prosecution – they used the FBI and established procedures and even new ones to present this style of evidence. You are the first to hear about air, hair banding and dog trainers. This prosecution would reach that level of desperation, and we will not. If you think she is a lying, a no good slut, maybe you will discriminate against her. That is the government's proof in this case, if we can get a jury to hate her, the jury will convict her.

I told you at the beginning, this was an accident that snowballed out of control. You have seen bizarre things were going on in this family before and after Caylee was born. On this bizarre behavior, I ask you not to speculate. I told you the State's evidence about the car would double the length of this trial, and it was all irrelevant. The car tells you how she may have or may not have been transferred. Did George have access? Was there a body in the car? We all know Casey made some mistakes and bad decisions. She should have called the police and reported this. If there are crimes associated with those acts, then so be it. They do not have the right to overcharge her, just because there is a mystery. You heard tons of media and how it focused on this case. I want to start off with the car; I used these boards in my opening. Caylee was last seen on June 16th, according to George Anthony. The indictment reads June 15th. (Objection, the indictment is not evidence, it is a list of charges between the dates. (Sustained, move on.)

On June 20th, Tony went to the shed and got the gas. They poured the gas in with an open car trunk. She could have never gotten assistance if she had a body in the trunk or a smell. Why did he not smell it? Everybody said they could smell it. Marie Kissh, said she did not smell anything. It was during the time she lived with Tony. Yet two years later, this car still smells? The gas cans were reported missing on June 24th. I think the issue is clear who reported the gas cans missing and why that duct tape is on there. Why are there so many lies around this? The odds are like the lottery. The car is towed the 30th, and why did Mr. Anthony wait a week to pick up the car after a notice. He showed up with gas cans; he knew it was out of gas. Birch told me it had been there for three days. Even though Mr. Anthony heard that testimony, how did George Anthony know the car was at the Amscot and out of gas? He showed up with cans. He smelled the smell of death, and he did what every parent would do. He did not call Casey or check on Caylee. He knew she was dead. This evidence does not make sense. If the State of Florida had done more to track him, you would have more answers.

Then July 15th comes around and CSI Bloise testified about human decomposition. Deputy Forgey testified about the dog inspection, everyone else lied, Melich and CSI Vincent. No smell was noticed from the manager of Amscot, or Beasley, who picked up the car and took it to the tow yard. Sergeant Bosey smells it, but the trash seemed plausible. Eberlin, the man who handcuffed her, and Melich, who was advised by George, did nothing. Fletcher does not smell anything and the trunk was open. I know you heard a lot of evidence about the trunk, but once Casey is arrested, Cindy explained why she said that. You still have an abundance of people who did not smell the odor. The State of Florida presents a neighbor; he testified that Casey borrowed a shovel. If you think about the testimony, the police told him to close his eyes and remember the date. Casey returned the shovel, and Casey was not sweaty. She had shovels in the shed and she borrowed one? Buried her as she buried her pets? They are saying let's speculate what happened.

You saw tons of testimony about the trash and garbage. I think what is important is that it was destroyed by drying it. It had fingerprint powder, and they want you to know who cut the cheese. This is not what a police or CSI should be doing. They should be preserving, so you can know. They did the air test from six weeks later. As for the computers, I will point out more later, and talk about the State's so-called premeditation. This evidence will also affect the quality of the case, and so you will have to render a verdict of not guilty. Your Honor, I think this may be an appropriate time for a recess. (The jury is in recess for lunch.)

Baez to the judge: I continue to see Mr. Ashton's facial expressions during the closing arguments. Judge: With the sign, I cannot see; but we do not allow any facial expressions. (The charge conference is completed during the jury's lunch recess). Judge: You have used 38 minutes of your four hours. Let's bring the jury back. (The jury is returned to the jury box.) Please continue.

Baez (to the jury): Good afternoon, we will pick up where we left off - the actual physical evidence, and this fantasy evidence, and the phantom stain. I am looking; we have all seen the photos. This goes back to your emotions. There is no blood. We have heard Bloise and how complete he was. We heard the FBI. They could not find DNA. They have no proof there was a body in this car. They want you to see a figment of your imagination. You might see a stain because your emotions are worked up. Evidence would have been DNA in the car. This car has stains - it is an old car. You heard evidence about this stain, but it is a phantom stain. This investigation reached the level of desperation. Some of these boards have writing, and you must rely on what you have heard, not these boards I have here.

The evidence in this case, as our experts have testified, was the fruit flies and the trash. There is no evidence of decomposition. The flies are from garbage. You heard a doctor say you cannot clean it up with paper towels. They gave you speculation and guesses. They want to anger you and use your emotions. If they talk about maggots, you will get mad. He told you with the maggots if they took DNA from the maggots, they could have tested it. More speculation. There is nothing in the trunk that has anything to do with human decomposition. This is to make up for the lack of evidence. You cannot and should not go there. We had to call the FBI personally. Why is important information being withheld? This is about a high profile case and about winning. (We think this is the pot calling the kettle black from Mr. Media himself.) The science is just not far enough along to know. They conducted a study after we took their depositions, on environmental effects of hair. They were trying to validate their science that is not science. They know it is still ongoing, and they admit they had similar effects. Even the scientists in the lab got it wrong. No one could tell you anything, except that one hair was in the trunk. They went crazy trying to find more hairs that showed something that easily could be from environmental things.

One week it is chloroform, the next week it is duct tape. Chloroform, this has to be a joke. (Objection) (Sustained) Vass testified the chloroform levels were shockingly high, he is an anthropologist, even if Dr.

474

Wise says he is, Dr. Wise is a chemist. They did only qualitative and not quantitative tests. Let's rely on this guy selling a sniffer machine. The witness from the FBI said the levels were low, consistent with cleaning products. Vass or Rickenbach, you can only believe one. These explorers, they push the boundaries of science. Wise was evasive and wanted to say how great his buddy Vass was. Another chemist said it was gasoline, even if the liner was removed. He was hired by the State. Is this a straight-up prosecution and are they giving you a straight-up story? (Objection) (Overruled) Why were these people hidden from you? Is that justice? I suggest that this is lack of straightforwardness; it is a lie. Vass had a financial motive. He has done some research, but others still have too, not just in Greece. They talked of divining rods. These are the speculations that Vass hangs onto. This is the desperation the prosecution has. This is a forensics fantasy. We have the most advanced tools in the world, and they could not find a link, this is all because it is a high profile case. (Objection) (Sustained)

The computer, this shows the sci-spot website one time. He goes to a seminar and gets CacheBack, and they have to rework the software to work. Then they come back with 84 searches. When I saw this, it was a jaw-dropping moment for me. He testified falsely and it was someone else's report. This is fraud… (Objection) (Sustained) (Motion to Strike. Granted.) A human life lies in the balance, and you are being asked to take someone's life. Then there was Myspace. This is outrageous. This is their premeditation. We can hope she used the chloroform first. How can they ask you, how can they come forth with this junk? This is the Myspace posting of Ricardo when he was dating her. March is the month of these searches, first Myspace, and then chloroform.

Then comes Cindy Anthony. In 2009, she claims she made these searches. Then the State spends their entire rebuttal case calling her a liar. I told you she was a liar the first day - so is the entire family. Phantom searches, science, evidence but Casey is a slut and let us make her pay with her life? This is out of control; it snowballed. This case did not have to come out. The truth ends here and the truth started here. All the nonsense should stop. There is an old adage that says, if you find a bug in your food, you do not take out the bug, you send the food back. That's reasonable doubt, if this was your financial statement on this chart. (Objection) (Golden Rule Sustained) (Motion to Strike) If you do not find that it was not proven to you, it is over. Only use what was proven. The law will guide you.

The fantasy continues with the heart sticker. An FBI
agent sees something on the tape. They recover another
piece of tape thirty feet away. This looks nothing like
the stickers at home. This is outrageous! This is the
quality of their case. She was arrested within several
hours, and they went for the evidence later. Let's get
rid of the trash; they are sneaky. (Objection)
(Sustained) In Dr. G.'s autopsy, there are no broken
bones, and no evidence of trauma. The State used
toxicology to try to make this case fit. The cause of
death is unknown – that is where we are. How did the
child die? The police should not be telling anyone not to
report to the media about a body found in a wooded area.
Duct tape appeared to be applied to the lower face. They
cannot establish the cause of death. This had nothing to
do with chloroform in the home. Dr. Schultz wanted to get
you mad by telling you how she was treated after death.
Dr. Warren showed you a Google picture and duct tape.
Caylee could have died any number of ways. Dr. G. jumped
in because it was a high profile case, and so she comes
back in and takes over because of media.

Dr. Spitz did a full autopsy. He found physical evidence.
He found that that the remains were not like Dr. G. and
Kronk said. I believe him over an Anthropologist.
(Objection) (Sustained) He is more qualified. They wanted
to question him on what he had read. He found when you
open a skull that there is discoloration there sometimes.
It does not always happen, and it did not in this case.
Dr. G. botched the autopsy. You may say that this is a
leap. There is no evidence of this, unless you are going
to entertain fantasy. The defense is not required to
present evidence of anything. This is a right. Casey
reacts the way she does and lies because of the
dysfunctional family. This is a photo of her looking
pregnant. Cindy says because Casey was sedentary. Lee is
the only one you can believe. He told Cindy he thought
Casey was pregnant, and they told him to forget about it.

Any witness who tells a lie does not have the right to be
believed. It is like the plate of food. The State told
you to believe Cindy when we want and not when we want.
Casey had issues, and they were there long before Caylee
was born. Casey lived in a world of imaginary friends,
jobs, and boyfriends who are rich. The details the state
told you were shocking. This is something just not right;
this is the world Casey lived in. There is something
wrong with this girl. The police should have handled this
investigation differently. Melich should have dealt with
this investigation differently. All the signs were there.
Casey did not hop on a plane and tell her parents, "You

will never see Caylee." Casey's world had an expiration date, and people were not just going to stop asking about Caylee. These are unhealthy coping skills. Casey had an unhealthy environment; she would lie, go dancing, and go where she felt safe. She went to Tony's. I do not think anyone can justify her actions, but it is not murder. The State says "You understand the why," even though Tony liked Caylee, and it was Monday and there was no party to go to. She now wants her freedom, so she kills and then gets to party every day and night. She had no motive. She treated her well and loved that child. No one said she was a bad mother. Remember when Tony said Caylee was running to the pool and Casey had to stop her. Everyone said she was kind. This is not a person who does murder or aggravated manslaughter.

I told you in the beginning what I expected to prove. Cindy said she took the ladder down that day. The State shows you she is a liar. Cindy is in denial; I understand why she said she took it down. This house had no safety locks, and you can understand how the ladder can be taken down sometimes and not. On June 17th, she went to work and tells people that someone is swimming in my pool. Why would she tell co-workers that? This happened long before the police were called. Caylee told George she liked to swim. Something happened, when both Casey and George were home. Melich was getting calls from Cindy, desperate, and she told him about the swimming pool. He did not ask her about the pool or accident. He did not want to consider that something is wrong with this girl. There is nothing sexy about a drowning. We uncovered a photo of Caylee opening the sliding glass door. She was heavily photographed. There is the proof, short of a video, of what happened. There is a reasonable presumption of innocence. The State cannot rebut this. How did she die? When, where, and why did she die? This is the only thing that makes sense. These people are different, and this girl is different. We have lost our senses here.

The duct tape, George did not give you a clear answer on the duct tape or the gas cans. Almost the whole roll is on the Kid Finder table. George said, "I do not know," and he would not admit it was his duct tape. He cannot lie at all, he cannot tell the truth at all. When I crossed him, I was shut down. This is no longer fantasy evidence, it is cold hard evidence – the duct tape is the only thing linked to this child's death, and his answers all depend on who is asking the questions. (Objection) (Sustained) He played all kinds of games about the gas cans; he lied to Ashton when he was taking his deposition. You remember; we sparred. Why is he lying about the duct tape? He knows he is the only one connected. The only one who had a roll of duct tape, and then he reports it missing. This all connects to George. It only connects to him. The truth is the truth, depending on who is asking the questions, whether it is me or this laughing guy right here (gesturing to Ashton)… (Objection) (Sustained) Judge (to Baez): Approach the bench. (We suspect it is because Baez is arguing to the jury about things that are not in evidence. The judge had warned him in writing before closing arguments started that nothing could be argued if it was not in evidence. This is very unusual, as the lawyers are expected to know the law. The other possibility is that the judge is about to end the contest of overblown egos between Baez and Ashton.) Baez is ordered to the bench mid-sentence.

Court is immediately recessed. The judge removes his robe, storms off the bench, and, with three armed officers, heads down the hallway fast. He returns to the bench a few minutes later. It appears both Ashton and Baez are on the wrong side of the man in the robe. Ashton was laughing with his hand over his mouth at the "no evidence" remarks from Baez to the jury. Baez said something about "the laughing guy" to the jury.

Judge: I viewed the video of Mr. Baez talking and Mr. Ashton's reaction and Mr. Baez's corresponding response. Needless to say the responses on behalf of Ashton and Baez, they have both violated this Court's order. If you both want to look at the video you can, then I am going to do what I am going to do. The video shows it.

Judge: No more sidebars! Burdick: Your Honor, before we decided to see the video of Mr. Ashton and Baez, I would like to know what you are intending on doing? (The lead prosecutor is trying to clean this mess up.) Judge: I am the only one that knows what I intend on doing. I have told both sides about the courtroom decorum policy. I gave everyone a copy. No gestures or facial expression of any kind from counsel, at all times they are prohibited. This action throughout the trial has been going on back and forth. I assumed you were all professionals and I do not have to watch you. Maybe I am misinformed when I think you will follow the law. Ashton: I trust your judgment about what you saw on the video, I do not need to see it. Mason: I want to see it, it has nothing to do with your judgment, Your Honor, it has to do with Ms. Anthony's defense.

(Ashton, Mason and all other lawyers leave the courtroom to look at the video.) Ashton: I appear to smile behind my hand. I was making sure nothing was seen by the jury. Baez: I have no other comments. I would ask that Mr.

Ashton not be held in contempt because of his facial expression. I am sorry for getting caught up and making the argument I made. (We say, if one goes down on contempt the other will go down. Good move, Baez! Baez referred to Ashton as a "laughing guy" and pointed to Ashton who was laughing behind his hand.)

Judge: I will accept that for now. If it happens again, the remedy will be exclusion of that attorney, and there are at least three attorneys on each side. There will be other things that will be not quite pleasant. Because of the delay, I will instruct the jury. I take the responsibility for that, because I should have brought you back on Saturday. However, I took you at your word that it would take a half-hour to complete the charge documents. Return the jury.

(Defendant's closing resumes) As laid out through the course of this trial this duct tape only points to one person. There is something that seems not to add up, and you learned at the end of the trial, how they bury their animals. Why did George never tell police how they bury their pets? There is a chance to save his daughters life. This tape was attached to the hair, near the top of the bag. In a swamp, it can move and it is not reasonable, the constant lies around duct tape. We are not suggesting George killed Caylee. This is nothing but an accident that snowballed out of control. Mr. Anthony has on numerous occasions, has had the opportunity to come up here and to tell the truth about what happened. He did not. He does not have an ounce of paternal instinct in him. He got up here and testified against Casey, and George did not protect her from the jaws of death. Cindy and Lee both tried, but George did not try to save her. He thought it was funny to spar with me at the time. He displayed no affection. Holloway, he told you she had a brain tumor. She was still alive three years later. He went to her apartment night and day to console her. He has a woman at home who needed consoling. The State tried to impeach her until it was public, then she sold her story. He lied. George cares about George, not his wife, daughter, or family. It is about him - his suicide note is not about anyone but him.

The police are closing in. The only reason he got a gun was to get Casey back in jail. He knew the rules. This is not a suicide note. This is a self-serving document. George calling the police for the gas cans is George protecting George. You saw the text message. George was not consoling her for the brain tumor. He denies that this was an accident, and tells her it was. He is still going to the media. If there is one thing you have learned, it is that lies live in this family. Casey was raised to lie. You have something very wrong going on, and it has nothing to do with Casey.

The prosecution did not call the man who found the remains, we had to. (Objection) (Sustained) (Baez goes on to say that Kronk staged the remains scene.) He thanks the jury for their attention, requests that they render verdicts of not guilty

Mason: We are about to put on your shoulders the most awesome responsibility. A dear friend of mine, Milton Hirsch, an author and a judge, reminded me of a parable. On May 19th, 1776, the skies over Hartford, Connecticut went from bright and sunny, to dark and stormy with such speed and force that the people believed that the end of the world was at hand. The Connecticut House of Representatives was in session at the time, and some of its members dropped to their knees in prayer, and others clamored for adjournment. The Speaker of the House restored order with these words: the Day of Judgment is either approaching or it is not. If it is not, there is no cause for adjournment. If it is coming, I wish to be found doing my duty. I wish therefore candles be brought. Today is judgment day as to the Constitution, tomorrow will be judgment day as to the Constitution, and every day will be judgment day as to the Constitution.

Today and every day in which an American stands trial; in which someone is arrested; in which a person's home is searched or property seized; every day in which voices are raised in song; every day in which a newspaper is printed; every day in which a lawyer is asked to defend an unpopular matter or cause, is the judgment day of the Constitution. We can cower before the storm, or we can light candles. Let us light some candles on this eve of the Fourth of July, the anniversary of the freedom of our country, and of our Constitutional government. There are some things that are very important to each of us in this room - our constitutional rights and constitutional freedoms.

There are some special rules incorporated for Casey. After we are done and the prosecution is done, Judge Perry will read some rules and laws to you about this case. There will be questions that will be asked of these laws. You will not have to memorize the law. You will have twelve sets of instructions to discuss. Remember that you all have cumulative and individual strength. There are things that control the light of the candle. Casey Anthony is not required to present evidence or prove anything. Each one of you accepted the responsibility of remembering this. You cannot be caught up in emotional rhetoric. You must remember the defendant is not required to present evidence in this case. The prosecution has the entire burden, and that is what separates our constitutional freedom.

Every element of the offenses must be proven by every reasonable doubt. If they fail to prove any element, then you are required to find the defendant not guilty. Only if it can be said that in conscience and intellect, it has been proven can you vote guilty. You must weigh the evidence, not the sparring between the lawyers. You weigh and decide what evidence is reasonable and what you are skeptical about. The court will give you guidance. Did the witness seem to have an opportunity to see what they are talking about; did they have an accurate memory, were they honest and straightforward? We have seen a lot of that these weeks. Did they have a motive like making money? Did they make a statement that is inconsistent with a previous statement? You have the right to believe or disbelieve any or all, or none, or part of the evidence. You weigh the credibility of every witness.

Expert witnesses, the court will instruct to you weigh the evidence and treat them the same as every other witness – believe all or any part of their testimony. You do not have to believe them, just because Judge Perry ruled them an expert. I want to talk about the elephant in the room, my client took the advice of counsel and did not testify. I have not tried as many cases as I have without knowing what you are thinking. However, she exercised her right and you cannot view this as an admission of guilt. That is a promise you made. Lighting candles for our constitutional rights and freedoms. Counts four, five, six and seven allege that Casey Anthony made false statement to Melich. You must consider the total circumstances, whether she had been threaten or promised. A recording was made where she was questioned in a six-by-eight room and them yelling at her, berating her. She was put in a cage and handcuffed. Consider if she was threatened, in that small room, or if she was freely and voluntarily able to make the statements.

First-degree murder requires the government to prove certain things. We all know Caylee is dead. The death was caused by Casey's acts. What acts? Premeditation and the alternative felony murder, we are trying to make them clear. The main thing is what act? What is the premeditation? Felony murder is that Caylee is dead as a consequence of aggravated child abuse. We have been here. Where is the event of aggravated child abuse? All of the witnesses said Caylee was well fed, bright, and there was no abuse present. Death occurred as she was attempting to commit child abuse. You will get an instruction on what is meant by aggravated child abuse, and it includes willfully. I may not have been able to hear everything; the computers send me the words since I cannot always hear. I heard or read nothing about abuse.

The evidence or the lack of the evidence can be a reasonable doubt. I made a list; you can agree or discard it. There is lack of evidence, no fingerprints on bags. The gas can with the duct tape, the toxicology test with no drugs, there is no DNA – the only DNA excluded Casey and the child. There is no evidence of decomposition at the recovery scene. The entomologists said she must have decomposed somewhere else. The only bugs found were in the trash, not the trunk.

The issue of chloroform was brought up. what a media baby this was. Dr. Michael Sigman was the one who extracted two Tedlar bags of air from the trunk at the same time, in the same time, at the same place. He took one to his lab, and sent one to Dr. Vass. Sr. Sigman's lab said major compounds of gasoline and a small component of chloroform, which he also said was everywhere. Dr. Vass's lab said shockingly high levels, we don't know how much, but it was shockingly high. Search warrants at the house three times; they searched, and they found no chloroform, no papers related to it, and no bottles or ingredients – nothing. Where was the chloroform, used to knock her out and kill her, or was it a natural product of decomposition, as they also alleged? It couldn't be both, but is sounded sexy for the media. The heart-shaped sticker deal from the FBI analyst. She said she saw part of a heart shape on the corner of a piece of tape, if I recall, but when she went to take a picture of it, poof – it was gone.

It is unusual in a murder case, not any admission of anything by the defendant. Why would she kill Caylee when she had a babysitter, her mother, and the boyfriend liked her? I do not know what the odor was or was not in the car. The tow driver or George never called the police; they just tossed out the trash. The tape as a murder weapon, maybe, might me, in all likelihood it was the murder weapon. That's what the State would have you believe. Kronk moved it. The burden of proof chart is of all the possible things along the way to reasonable doubt. The State must prove this to you. Light a candle for our constitutional rights. Do your constitutional duty and find Casey Marie Anthony not guilty because they have not proved her guilt. Thank you. (Mason returns to the defense table.)

It is a good job, from both Mason, who performed honorably, and Baez, who was not so great, but he did his job. We think the beauty of Mason's skills was undercut by Baez using the first three and a half of the four hours allotted. Baez says Roy Kronk hid her remains. We think this is where he lost this shadow jury; it was too far of a reach, Mr. Baez. He wants the jury to discount little Caylee's very remains as having no value to tell what happened to her. He says the entire crime scene is staged. There is something not right here. In our opinion, what is not right is Mr. Baez's story. He wants us to forget what evidence Casey could not destroy. Cheney Mason also brought Mr. Kronk up and again lost us. That was the area where his argument faltered, and lost us. Perhaps he felt obligated to echo Baez's argument and make some sense of what Baez said about Kronk.

We think lead counsel should have used the talent he has more effectively. Mason was much more effective in closing than Baez. Maybe Baez used Mason more behind the scenes. That is often the case with old dogs. Mason has been to a few legal rodeos in his life. His argument was smooth and would be persuasive, except that we are not swayed by closing arguments. When done well, they can be beautiful, but a lawyer uses only some of the evidence or the lack of evidence. We like facts and all of the evidence. We think media-seeking Baez wanted to be the star. Fame, we think, affected his decisions. Mason's style and tone were still good and his presentation strong and clear. However, it does not change the evidence. Casey Anthony has had a fair trial, and the assistance of lawyers with a lot of legal experience. The defense called this case a checkbook prosecution; well thanks to the taxpayers, the defense got about anything they wanted in Casey's defense. Despite what we think of Media Hound Baez, the judge made sure Casey Anthony received a fair trial. It is a lawyer's dream to cross the lines of propriety the way the judge allowed Baez to do. The judge did not want a mistrial or reversal on appeal, although we truly believe that Judge Perry did a good job on this media nightmare case. We think the judge should have started fining Baez personally, outside the presence of the jury, for those questions not asked in good faith. They were solely designed to taint the jury. That is why there has to be a good faith basis for questions in a court of law. Fining him might have stopped Baez.

(Court resumes.) Judge: I am making an executive decision, I can see some of you jurors are tired, and I want you rested. Court is adjourned for the night. (Here is the surprise; we saw no objection from the defense! This is an advantage for the prosecution. They will be rested. They will have time to pick the defense closing argument apart. They will have the last three hours tomorrow with the fresh jury and then the judge will instruct, followed by deliberations. The other side is the jury will have all night to let Baez's and Mason's arguments settle in their minds.)

Judge: We need to complete the charge conference. Page 4 - Murder - The defense has an objection because of the deviation from standard jury instructions. State has no objection. Page 5 - Felony of Aggravated Child Abuse. Defense objects. State no objection. Page 7 - Aggravated Manslaughter of a Child. Change in title to match indictment. Defense objects. State no objection. We will complete and review the rest of the instructions. I draw your attention to two new cases from June 30th, Ballard v. State, a duct tape case with no body, and Scott v. State, a proportionality case. (Court stands in recess.)

Chapter 19

THE PROSECUTION'S CLOSING ARGUMENT - REBUTTAL

July 4th, 2011

Morning has broken, on this the final day of the trial, July 4th, 2011, Independence Day. The jury will be charged after the last three hours of the prosecution's closing argument and deliberations will begin. We looked at the two cases the judge cited to the lawyers at the end of court yesterday. In both cases, the Florida Supreme Court upheld the conviction; however, the death sentences were overturned by the court to life sentences. One thing we would like you to take away from this book, *the law is ever changing*. Casey is in the courtroom. She is unremarkable, except for playing with her hair and looking stressed. (The judge just resumed the bench.)

Judge: Have you received the copy of the final instructions? Baez: We object to the prosecution being allowed to split their rebuttal argument, especially since Mr. Ashton already covered a lot. Judge: If they exceed rebuttal, make a simple objection, and a ruling will happen. It is solely rebuttal. Return the jury.

Prosecution Rebuttal Closing Argument

Ashton: Good morning and happy Fourth of July. Ms. Burdick and I will both be talking to you. The defense presented an aggressive argument as to the science. The science is complicated and with a dispute, you may find one expert or issue is more credible than another. Isolate it by matter. Medical Examiner and pathologists, you heard from Dr. G, the Chief Medical Examiner, Mr. Oien, Dr. Schultz. Forensic Anthropologists: Dr. Warren and Dr. Spitz. All of them agree that there is nothing that tells us anything; there are no fractures. Nothing about how Caylee died. They all also agree that the way the human body decomposes, the skull and the mandible should not be together. When Caylee was found, they were in the same position that they would have been if she were alive. Four out of five told you the tape kept them together. The only other time they had seen this with both still together was in Kosovo with duct tape victims of murder and genocides. One told you that someone had come along and picked up the remains, took them away, duct-taped them, and then returned them to the site. You decide what is reasonable. When I pointed out that the duct tape had deteriorated, and someone would have had to put hair across, he accused the Medical Examiner. When I showed him pictures at the site that looked the same way, he blamed the Sheriff. This is incredible.

The other area there was the difference in opinion was on sawing Caylee's skull. They told you Dr. G. violated protocol. Yet, there is no such protocol. In fact, opening it can and did crack the skull. We brought in doctors who washed the skull and he told you that there was no remains of decomposition inside. Dr. Spitz acknowledged that a forensic anthropologist must know about the circumstances surrounding the death. He told us he went to the house and they have a pool, and something about a nanny. He had no idea of the thorough and complete investigation and medical examination that had taken place.

Let's talk about entomology. You heard you about the car and scene. You have to decide who is more believable, someone with three or twenty-five years-experience. They do agree that in the body's original few days of decomposition, the early flies could not get to her. She was dumped in June to July of 2008. The only place they disagree is with the trunk being a source of early decomposition. Twenty-five years says yes, three years' experience, says no. The important thing is what they agree upon. From June or July, the body was in the woods. Chloroform, Mr. Baez had a big poster of this. You must understand what they were examining and what their perspective was. Dr. Vass and Wise are used to looking at air samples and all different areas. Wise felt the amount in the trunk was high for a car. They told you the sample in the can was in the low parts per million. They told you if they gave you a number it would not mean anything, it would be less than what was there in the beginning. Rickenbach tested the can and the spare tire cover in cardboard. He found it even in the unsealed box of the car tire sample. He found even more in the sealed can. The rough estimate puts it in the low parts per million. He is used to looking at it as liquid, but he found it coming from the carpet, and he had never seen it before. Actual detectable amounts, there would have been far more, it was aired on July 15th, before that, it would have been far greater. There has been no evidence to explain why from the defense. He tested the trunk four days after the carpet was removed, he found detectable amounts of chloroform and it should not have been there. No chlorine, no bleach stains, no other components of cleaning products. All that was found in that trunk was chloroform and decomposition.

The odor of decomposition, the defense attacks Dr. Vass because that he had created a device for scenting decomposition. If the invention is sold to the private sector and not just to governments for their use, they will all share something. Dr. Vass is an anthropologist, a science geek. Counsel sneered at him because he wondered if a divining rod could work. He is a science geek that loves to solve questions. When have you had an expert tell you, "Here is the cool part?" They agree it is decomposition. Dr. Vass told you when you combine the science with thirty years of studying decomposition, that what was in was the air in the can. "I can explain nothing but decomposition in that trunk from the odor I smelled and science." The defense told you the deputy sheriffs removed something from that garbage and it is untrue. The myth of the garbage has been disproven. That smell was from Caylee.

DNA, the defense tested DNA but it is not in evidence. She told you she did not expect to find it on the tape that had been in the wood and swamp for six months. There was one witness who provided us with a report, two days before he testified. Yet, he said, maybe he might have been able to find something, but probably not. The defense called ten non-evidence witnesses. They knew nothing, and they told us nothing. Hair, there is an artifact that has only been found in dead human bodies. They have tried to recreate it and cannot. That evidence was not rebutted. To say there is no evidence that connects Casey to this case is ridiculous.

The reasonable doubt argument by counsel; let's look. The duct tape; counsel went to great lengths to connect it to the Anthony home, and we agree it came from there. Their argument is that George found a drowned Caylee and disposed of the accident and put duct tape on the face of a dead child. People do not make accidents look like murder. It is obscene. (Objection) (Motion to Strike) (Overruled) You have heard nothing to make this less absurd. Let's say George… (Objection) (Overruled)

Let us suppose that George Anthony had placed her remains in the woods, placed duct tape over her mouth. Then he calls law enforcement a week later, and he creates this issue by reporting the gas cans missing. They take the cans and they do not photograph anything. However, they want you to believe that he is doing this to implicate his daughter. Yet, he does not tell the police the first day about the cans. So, they give them the gas cans back. George takes the can back and sticks it in the garage for four months, just lets it sit there. Then in December, the police find it and take it. This criminal George, he takes the very same duct tape to make posters for his missing granddaughter. This is absurd. The reason it does not make sense is because it is not true. He had no idea that the duct tape had anything to do with the death of his granddaughter.

As for this pool theory, they say there is no dispute. George told you he was not there! Mrs. Anthony told you it did not happen! They tell you to follow the duct tape and then tell you Roy Kronk did it and used this same unusual duct tape. Counsel has argued that the crime scene was staged. The only thing that staged this scene is Mother Nature herself. There are leaves, vines, and only Mother Nature staged it. This skull has been unmoved except by animals for six months.

The defense told you Kronk took it home with him. We showed you how the body was disarticulated, because things would decompose separately and because of animal activity. We did not tell you that to upset you. We told you that to so you knew these bones were scarred by Mother Nature and animals. This skull has not been moved for months. It is surrounded with hair and the hair fell straight down when the body decomposed. The duct tape is partially covered by leaf litter and the duct tape goes completely around the skull. The duct tapes wraps around the mandible! It is there, not put there by water, but it is there, because that is where Casey Anthony put it. There are strings from the tape that go over it, and it is not an accident, or the water did it. It is because the tape was placed over her mouth and nose before she decomposed. The scene was not staged, the forces of water, animals, and decomposition moving the tape conclusively rebuts staging, by the evidence. This crime scene was not staged or moved, and this duct tape has been on her face since the day she died.

We did not put Roy Kronk on. He just happened on the skull; it does not mean anything. Roy likes to spin a yarn. The skull he found in August, then reported it three times, then he starts communicating with his son and wanted to look like a hero. So he does go back, and he tells his big story. He found the skull - no question, but he is not a morally bankrupt individual who would take a little skull home and play with it. Mr. Mason told you about first-degree murder. It can be committed two ways. We believe she chloroformed Caylee so she would not suffer, put the duct tape on her mouth and disposed of her body. The State must convince you of premeditated murder or of felony murder. (Objection) (Overruled) You must all agree that what happened is first-degree and you do not need to agree on whether it is premeditated or felony murder. Caylee is dead, a criminal act of Casey and premeditation after deciding to kill Caylee. Felony murder has three elements Caylee died, the death occurred while in the commission of aggravated or attempted child abuse, knowing or willing committing child abuse. Child abuse is intentional infliction of physical or mental abuse that could reasonably be expected to cause her death.

Some may say Casey put the duct tape on her to keep her quiet and she died. If you think that - that is felony murder - then this is first-degree murder. Or you may think that she used chloroform in the trunk so she could have a good time with Tony and Caylee dies, that is also first-degree murder. This is premeditated, but any way you slice it, Casey is guilty of murder in the first degree. You have seen hours with George and Cindy with Casey, and just Casey. These videos give you an unguarded window into George's mind with worry about Caylee and how he is perplexed about why his daughter will not tell him something. He expresses his love and disappointment that he was not a better father. Casey tells him how great he is as a father and grandfather. George is not this Machiavellian monster the defense tells you. The defense asked, "Did you try to commit suicide; did you leave a note of guilt?" They wanted you to think it was something else, but you have received the letter, this man was in pain and he wanted to be with his granddaughter. The effects of the pills and alcohol as he wrote this letter are clear. This is the cry of a man that does not understand the world any more. He does not know what happened to his granddaughter, and why won't Casey tell. I should have done more, she was so close to home, and who put her there? Why could she not come to us? You know for a year or so, I brought stuff up, and I was told not to be negative. This is before Caylee went missing.

I want to thank you all and wish you well in the decision you are about to make. (Aston takes a seat at the prosecution's table.)

Well, it seems Ms. Burdick is a very smart lady. She had given Ashton almost all of the closing, and he was precise and clean, he laid it all out for the jurors. It was all about what has really been said and done, and why this is in a court of law. He gave them choices of how Casey killed Caylee and they are choices we can see. You see, it appears Mrs. Burdick knows that a person is only as smart as the ones around her. That is something Mr. Baez did not seem to get throughout this trial, or he would have used Mason more. (The jury is taken out for a recess, while legal arguments occur.)

Baez: The issue dealing with the computer searches. The number of times that chloroform and the Myspace did not show up on the second report and it is our contention on that false testimony was used. Burdick: Mr. Baez has already made his closing argument.

Judge: I do not know if it is true or false. If it is false, you need to file a motion and I will review it. We will cross that bridge when we get to it. I cannot change arguments. (The jury returns to the courtroom.)

Burdick: Good morning. When Judge Perry took that break for fifteen minutes, I felt like I was called on the field after the other player has taken it to the goal line. The advantage is that no one gets to say anything after me but the judge. You have been listening to what lawyers think, and I realize that you are ready to begin your job. On May 9th, we packed up and spent two weeks in Clearwater. You have made a greater sacrifice for many weeks. I do ask that you indulge me for a few minutes. I am not dragging out a lot of posters or evidence. When I came up in front of you in May, I told you what evidence we would show. I did not make promises that the State would not keep. The evidence and witnesses have proved every element of the prosecution's case. Mr. Baez said his biggest fear was that you would make your decision on emotion. I would not ask you to make a decision based on emotion. I will ask that you make your decision only on the evidence and the testimony of the witnesses. Want to know what my biggest fear is? My biggest fear is that common sense will be lost in the rhetoric, and that you will not look at the evidence as a whole. You must look at the evidence. My fear is that you will not look at the big picture; we spent two weeks looking for people who could see the forest for the trees.

In closing, Mr. Baez used words like liar and fantasy. The truth is the cornerstone of justice, and it is lying that perverts justice. In a case where we had the most documented liar in the court, the defendant, she is accusing everyone else of lying and perjury. Accusing others of lying is classic Casey Anthony. When she wants to divert attention from herself, she accuses others. Ms. Anthony had spent years lying, she spent 31 days lying, and Mr. Baez says that means nothing! A lie told convincingly is still a lie. The defendant, through counsel, has accused everyone, Melich, Vass, Bloise, and many others of being liars. The Orange County Sheriff's Office was painted as desperate, and if there was anything the Orange County Sheriff was, it was desperate to find a little girl, whether she was alive or dead. The FBI, police, citizens, no one had any motive other than to find Caylee. Caylee's grandparents and uncle were searching.

False allegations, a false absurd diversion, cost resources and draws attention away from the perpetrator; it buys them more time. One of things that Casey said when she was picked up at Tony's, was she just wanted another day. She created the kidnapping to divert and buy time. (They put up pictures) They said, there was no smell, because they took no action. That first night, the police did not believe she was dead. The defendant was telling them that she was alive, asking for help in finding her.

So much was made of this episode of Casey being handcuffed for ten minutes. They uncuffed her because they were there to help, to find Caylee. They were there to help. You have three detectives who want to help and are willing to spend resources to find Caylee, but Casey is lying, like she had done with her parents, brothers and friends, for thirty-one days. The defense says the lies are really meaningless. Counsel suggests the State was trying to prove she was a slut. Nothing could be further from the truth. The Orange County Sheriff was trying to backtrack where Casey had been and find Caylee. They were using the records of cell phones to find Zanny, to find Caylee. As they backtracked, it became more apparent that the defendant was lying about everything. The only true statement on her five-page report is that Caylee was born August 9th, 2005, and every, every other statement is a lie. It has been said everyone grieves differently; that may be true and the response to grief may vary. But the response to guilt is constant; they

490

lie, avoid, run, mislead family, and appease. They divert attention and they act like nothing is wrong. That is how you know about the thirty-one days, and this is in no way the grief of someone who has lost a child by accident. The defense said she could have run, but this was a time of desperation. She had no option to go anywhere but away from the family. Those people would ask all the questions. Friends are really easy to appease. She was running from her family, who would want more than a reference to Caylee.

The only question is who killed Caylee? We no longer ask where Caylee is. It is no longer, what happened. For the longest time Caylee was alive, until the remains were found. As the facts and circumstances changed over the time, the defendant's lies changed, they got bigger and better. There must be something wrong with Casey; she has imaginary friends. These were not imaginary friends. They were lies. A lie designed for a specific purpose to get Casey out of a jam. So she lies, Caylee is alive and I have nothing to do with it. The lie must change into a new theory; it is some kind of accident. You know from the evidence that Caylee's death was no accident. The sheriff proposed an accident, and Casey denied it.

(Audio played) Detective Melich - I have sat down with mothers that rolled over on their children, children who died in pools, and boyfriends who killed the child. I have also dealt with people who have done horrible acts and then when they finally come forward, people pass on them, they have lied for the last time to them...

You were told that they did not want to consider this an accident. Casey was asked; no, she says, Caylee is alive. The defendant's mother suggested it in the video at jail. (Audio played) Cindy - Someone just said Caylee was dead she drowned in the pool. That is the newest story out there. Casey: Surprise, surprise.

So when Caylee is found dead, surprise, surprise, at her new lie. No one makes an accident look like murder. Her actions are inconsistent. When there is a child injured or dead in an accident, one hundred percent of the time someone calls 911 and they agonize. Especially if you want to accept that she was a great mother. Every baby loves its mother. Their love is unconditional. That she provides food, shelter, and clothes -- that makes her a mother, not a good mother. And they were provided by her grandparents anyway. Look at her room, her back yard. What parent acts with complete indifference? You heard their grief expert tell of the woman who wanted to go to the gravesite because her child who died, had never been in the rain and dark!

If this were an accident, Caylee would have been found in the pool, and not in a swamp. George told you if there had been an accident, he would have called 911 and tried to save her, and no one would be here. George wanted to go with Caylee in death. The person who disposed of Caylee, the way the remains were disposed of, showed they really thought nothing about her. The Anthony's worshipped her and put a stone base under the playhouse so she would not get wet or get an insect on her. On the jail videos, you heard Mr. Anthony trying to get Casey to talk to the FBI or sheriff. If he were covering up, why would he want her to talk to the cops? The disposal of the remains speaks volumes – how Casey felt about Caylee.

(Jail video is played in part) (A jail call from Casey to the Anthony home is played in part.) We have enclosed the only one excerpt, since the rest was provided earlier. This is during the first 24 hours in jail and while everyone else is trying to find Caylee.

Casey: *They just want Caylee back. That is all they are worried about right now is getting Caylee back.* (And then her afterthought) And you know what, that is all I care about right now.

When you use your common sense, there is nothing that cannot be explained in two words – pathological liar. Her focus is and has been with Tony Lazzaro. You have learned during the course of this trial that Casey Anthony is the only person that had access to every piece of evidence, the duct tape, the laundry bag, the blanket, the shorts, and the car. There is no evidence that anyone but Casey Anthony has been driving around in the car. That trash was placed as a decoy and the car was backed in next to the dumpster as a decoy. George did not have access to that car. They did not know where she was or where the car was. The shirt "big trouble comes in small packages," indeed. Cindy told you she was not familiar with that shirt, it was kept in the car packed in the bag. We saw it twice, at Ricardo's, and at the remains site. They want you to believe it was George in a cover-up of an accident. No one else tried to cover up then lie and lie.

Let's throw Cindy in the mix, for leaving the ladder up. Let's twist the knife in her a little more. Then twist the knife in George for a cover-up. Where is Caylee? She is dead in the woods. At the end of the case, ask yourself whose life was better without Caylee. Was it Cindy? (911 call by Cindy) "My daughter was missing for a month, but I cannot find my granddaughter and we found the car and it smells like a dead body." Was George's life better, we told you what happened to George over losing his loving granddaughter. Whose life was better is the only question you have to answer as to who left Caylee on the side of the road dead. (Photos of Casey's Bella Vita Tattoo and Casey Anthony at the Fusion Nightclub hot body contest are shown as Ms. Drane Burdick returns to counsel table.)

The closings were very good for the prosecution. However, we would have shown the gruesome photos to the jury at the end. This case is about Caylee being dead and tossed into the swamp. No one would have stopped us from reminding the jury that this is not playing to the emotions. It is the facts. Despite the disposal and the ravages of time, the evidence is here for the jury. This readers, is no accident, and hopefully the Day of Judgment is here for Casey Anthony. It is Day 35, the day the case goes to the jury. Casey looks resigned.

Chapter 20

THE JURY INSTRUCTIONS

The judge begins by telling the spectators that once he begins reading the jury instructions, that no one will be permitted to enter or leave the courtroom, so if anyone does not wish to remain, they should exit the courtroom now.

Charging: Judge: Members of the jury I would like to thank you. Please play close attention and you will get copies to take into the jury room. (We are presenting a copy of the written jury instructions; the judge did not read all of the captions after the style of the case.)

IN THE CIRCUIT COURT OF THE
NINTH JUDICIAL CIRCUIT, IN AND
FOR ORANGE COUNTY, FLORIDA

CASE NO.: 2008-CF-15606-A-O

STATE OF FLORIDA, Plaintiff,
v.
CASEY MARIE ANTHONY, Defendant

JURY INSTRUCTIONS:

INTRODUCTION TO FINAL INSTRUCTIONS

Members of the jury, I thank you for your attention during this trial. Please pay attention to the instructions I am about to give you.

INTRODUCTION TO HOMICIDE
In this case, Casey Marie Anthony is accused of Murder in the First Degree, Aggravated Child Abuse, Aggravated Manslaughter of a Child, and four counts of Providing False Information to a Law Enforcement Officer.

Murder in the First Degree includes the lesser crimes of Murder in the Second Degree, Manslaughter and Third Degree Felony Murder, all of which are unlawful. A killing that is excusable or was committed by the use of justifiable deadly force is lawful.

If you find Caylee Marie Anthony was killed by Casey Marie Anthony, you will then consider the circumstances surrounding the killing in deciding if the killing was Murder in the First Degree or was Murder in the Second Degree or was Manslaughter or was Third Degree Felony Murder, or whether the killing was excusable or resulted from justifiable use of deadly force.

JUSTIFIABLE HOMICIDE

§ 782.02, Fla. Stat.

The killing of a human being is justifiable homicide and lawful if necessarily done while resisting an attempt to murder or commit a felony upon the defendant, or to commit a felony in any dwelling house in which the defendant was at the time of the killing.

EXCUSABLE HOMICIDE

§ 782.03, Fla. Stat.

1. The killing of a human being is excusable, and therefore lawful, under any one of the following three circumstances: When the killing is committed by accident and misfortune in doing any lawful act by lawful means with usual ordinary caution and without any unlawful intent, or
2. When the killing occurs by accident and misfortune in the heat of passion, upon any sudden and sufficient provocation, or
3. When the killing is committed by accident and misfortune resulting from a sudden combat, if a dangerous weapon is not used and the killing is not done in a cruel or unusual manner.

I now instruct you on the circumstances that must be
proved before Casey Marie Anthony may be found guilty of
Murder in the First Degree, Aggravated Child Abuse,
Aggravated Manslaughter of a Child, and four counts of
Providing False Information to a Law Enforcement Officer
or any lesser included crime.

MURDER - FIRST DEGREE

§ 782.04(1)(a), Fla. Stat.

There are two ways in which a person may be convicted of
first degree murder. One is known as premeditated murder
and the other is known as felony murder. In order to find
the defendant guilty of murder in the first degree, the
State must convince you beyond a reasonable doubt of the
defendant's guilt of either premeditated murder or felony
murder. While you must all agree that the State has
proven first degree murder beyond a reasonable doubt, you
need not be unanimous in your opinion as to whether that
finding is based upon premeditated murder or felony
murder as I shall now define those terms.

To prove the crime of First Degree Premeditated Murder,
the State must prove the following three elements beyond
a reasonable doubt:

1. Caylee Marie Anthony is dead.
2. The death was caused by the criminal act of Casey
   Marie Anthony.
3. There was a premeditated killing of Caylee Marie
   Anthony.

An "act" includes a series of related actions arising
from and performed pursuant to a single design or
purpose.

"Killing with premeditation" is killing after consciously
deciding to do so. The decision must be present in the
mind at the time of the killing. The law does not fix the
exact period of time that must pass between the formation
of the premeditated intent to kill and the killing. The
period of time must be long enough to allow reflection by
the defendant. The premeditated intent to kill must be
formed before the killing.

The question of premeditation is a question of fact to be
determined by you from the evidence. It will be
sufficient proof of premeditation if the circumstances of
the killing and the conduct of the accused convince you
beyond a reasonable doubt of the existence of
premeditation at the time of the killing.

495

FELONY MURDER - FIRST DEGREE

§ 782.04(1)(a), Fla. Stat.

To prove the crime of First Degree Felony Murder, the State must prove the following three elements beyond a reasonable doubt:

1. Caylee Marie Anthony is dead.
2. The death occurred as a consequence of and while Casey Marie Anthony was engaged in the commission of Aggravated Child Abuse, or the death occurred as a consequence of and while Casey Marie Anthony was attempting to commit Aggravated Child Abuse.
3. Casey Marie Anthony was the person who actually killed Caylee Marie Anthony.

In order to convict of First Degree Felony Murder, it is not necessary for the State to prove that the defendant had a premeditated design or intent to kill.

AGGRAVATED CHILD ABUSE

§ 827.03(2), Fla. Stat.

To prove the crime of Aggravated Child Abuse, the State must prove the following two elements beyond a reasonable doubt:

1. Casey Marie Anthony knowingly or willfully committed child abuse upon Caylee Marie Anthony and in so doing caused great bodily harm, permanent disability, or permanent disfigurement.
2. Caylee Marie Anthony was under the age of eighteen years.

"Willfully" means intentionally, knowingly and purposely.

"Child abuse" means the intentional infliction of physical or mental injury upon a child or an intentional act that could reasonably be expected to result in physical or mental injury to a child or active encouragement of any person to commit an act that results or could reasonably be expected to result in physical or mental injury to a child.

AGGRAVATED MANSLAUGHTER OF A CHILD

§ 782.07, Fla. Stat.

To prove the crime of Aggravated Manslaughter of a Child, the State must prove the following two elements beyond a reasonable doubt:

1. Caylee Marie Anthony is dead.
2. Casey Marie Anthony's act(s) caused the death of Caylee Marie Anthony, or the death of Caylee Marie Anthony was caused by the culpable negligence of Casey Marie Anthony.

I will now define "culpable negligence" for you. Each of us has a duty to act reasonably toward others. If there is a violation of that duty, without any conscious intention to harm, that violation is negligence. But culpable negligence is more than a failure to use ordinary care toward others. In order for negligence to be culpable, it must be gross and flagrant. Culpable negligence is a course of conduct showing reckless disregard of human life, or of the safety of persons exposed to its dangerous effects, or such an entire want of care as to raise a presumption of a conscious indifference to consequences, or which shows wantonness or recklessness, or a grossly careless disregard of the safety and welfare of the public, or such an indifference to the rights of others as is equivalent to an intentional violation of such rights. The negligent act or omission must have been committed with an utter disregard for the safety of others. Culpable negligence is consciously doing an act or following a course of conduct that the defendant must have known, or reasonably should have known, was likely to cause death or great bodily injury.

If you find the defendant guilty of Aggravated Manslaughter of a Child, you must then determine whether the State has further proved beyond a reasonable doubt that Caylee Marie Anthony was a child whose death was caused by the neglect of Casey Marie Anthony, a caregiver. "Child" means any person under the age of 18 years.

"Caregiver" means a parent, adult household member, or other person responsible for a child's welfare.

"Neglect of a child" means:

1. A caregiver's failure or omission to provide a child with the care, supervision, and services necessary to maintain a child's physical and mental health, including, but not limited to, food, nutrition, clothing, shelter, supervision, medicine, and medical services that a prudent

person would consider essential for the well-being of the child. Repeated conduct or a single incident or omission by a caregiver that results in, or could reasonably be expected to result in, a substantial risk of death of a child may be considered in determining neglect.

FALSE INFORMATION TO LAW ENFORCEMENT

§ 837.055, Fla. Stat.

To prove the crime of False Information to Law Enforcement, the State must prove the following five elements beyond a reasonable doubt:

1. Yuri Melich was conducting a missing person investigation.
2. Yuri Melich was a law enforcement officer.
3. Casey Marie Anthony knew that Yuri Melich was a law enforcement officer.
4. Casey Marie Anthony knowingly and willfully gave false information to Yuri Melich.
5. Casey Marie Anthony intended to mislead Yuri Melich or impede the investigation.

"Willfully" means intentionally, knowingly and purposely.

WHEN THERE ARE LESSER INCLUDED CRIMES

In considering the evidence, you should consider the possibility that although the evidence may not convince you that the defendant committed the main crimes of which she is accused, there may be evidence that she committed other acts that would constitute a lesser included crime.

Therefore, if you decide that the main accusation has not been proved beyond a reasonable doubt, you will next need to decide if the defendant is guilty of any lesser included crime. The lesser crimes indicated in the definition of First Degree Murder are: Second Degree Murder, Manslaughter or Third Degree Felony Murder. The lesser crime indicated in the definition of Aggravated Child Abuse is Child Abuse.

MURDER - SECOND DEGREE

§ 782.04(2), Fla. Stat.

To prove the crime of Second Degree Murder, the State must prove the following three elements beyond a reasonable doubt:

1. Caylee Marie Anthony is dead.

2. The death was caused by the criminal act of Casey Marie Anthony.
3. There was an unlawful killing of Caylee Marie Anthony by an act imminently dangerous to another and demonstrating a depraved mind without regard for human life.

An "act" includes a series of related actions arising from and performed pursuant to a single design or purpose.

An act is "imminently dangerous to another and demonstrating a depraved mind" if it is an act or series of acts that:

1. A person of ordinary judgment would know is reasonably certain to kill or do serious bodily injury to another.
2. was done from ill will, hatred, spite or an evil intent.
3. is of such a nature that the act itself indicates an indifference to human life.

In order to convict of Second Degree Murder, it is not necessary for the State to prove the defendant had intent to cause death.

MANSLAUGHTER

§ 782.07, Fla. Stat.

To prove the crime of Manslaughter, the State must prove the following two elements beyond a reasonable doubt:

1. Caylee Marie Anthony is dead.
2. (a) Casey Marie Anthony's act(s) caused the death of Caylee Marie Anthony, or

(b) The death of Caylee Marie Anthony was caused by the culpable negligence of Casey Marie Anthony.

However, the defendant cannot be guilty of manslaughter if the killing was either justifiable or excusable homicide:

The killing of a human being is justifiable homicide and lawful if necessarily done while resisting an attempt to murder or commit a felony upon the defendant, or to commit a felony in any dwelling house in which the defendant was at the time of the killing. § 782.02, Fla. Stat.

The killing of a human being is excusable, and therefore lawful, under any one of the following three circumstances:

1. When the killing is committed by accident and misfortune in doing any lawful act by lawful means with usual ordinary caution and without any unlawful intent.
2. When the killing occurs by accident and misfortune in the heat of passion, upon any sudden and sufficient provocation.
3. When the killing is committed by accident and misfortune resulting from a sudden combat, if a dangerous weapon is not used and the killing is not done in a cruel or unusual manner. In order to convict of manslaughter by act, it is not necessary for the State to prove that the defendant had an intent to cause death, only an intent to commit an act that was not justified or excusable and which caused death.

I will now define "culpable negligence" for you. Each of us has a duty to act reasonably toward others. If there is a violation of that duty, without any conscious intention to harm, that violation is negligence. But culpable negligence is more than a failure to use ordinary care toward others. In order for negligence to be culpable, it must be gross and flagrant. Culpable negligence is a course of conduct showing reckless disregard of human life, or of the safety of persons exposed to its dangerous effects, or such an entire want of care as to raise a presumption of a conscious indifference to consequences, or which shows wantonness or recklessness, or a grossly careless disregard of the safety and welfare of the public, or such an indifference to the rights of others as is equivalent to an intentional violation of such rights.

The negligent act or omission must have been committed with an utter disregard for the safety of others. Culpable negligence is consciously doing an act or following a course of conduct that the defendant must have known, or reasonably should have known, was likely to cause death or great bodily injury.

FELONY MURDER - THIRD DEGREE

§ 782.04(4), Fla. Stat.

To prove the crime of Third Degree Felony Murder, the State must prove the following three elements beyond a reasonable doubt:

1. Caylee Marie Anthony is dead.
2. The death occurred as a consequence of and while Casey Marie Anthony was engaged in the commission of Child Abuse, or the death occurred as a consequence of and while Casey Marie Anthony was attempting to commit Child Abuse.
3. Casey Marie Anthony was the person who actually killed Caylee Marie Anthony.

It is not necessary for the State to prove the killing was perpetrated with a design to effect death.

Child Abuse means the intentional infliction of physical or mental injury upon a child; or an intentional act that could reasonably be expected to result in physical or mental injury to a child, when that person knowingly or willfully abused a child without causing great bodily harm, permanent disability, or permanent disfigurement to the child.

"Willfully" means intentionally, knowingly and purposely.

ATTEMPT TO COMMIT CRIME

§ 777.04(1), Fla. Stat.

In order to prove that the defendant attempted to commit the crime of Child Abuse, the State must prove the following beyond a reasonable doubt:

1. Casey Marie Anthony did some act toward committing the crime of Child Abuse that went beyond just thinking or talking about it.
2. She would have committed the crime except that someone prevented her from committing the crime of Child Abuse or she failed.

It is not an attempt to commit Child Abuse if the defendant abandoned her attempt to commit the offense or otherwise prevented its commission, under circumstances indicating a complete and voluntary renunciation of her criminal purpose.

CHILD ABUSE

§ 827.03(1), Fla. Stat.

To prove the crime of Child Abuse, the State must prove the following two elements beyond a reasonable doubt:

1. Casey Marie Anthony

A. intentionally inflicted physical or mental injury upon Caylee Marie Anthony

Or

B. committed an intentional act that could reasonably be expected to result in physical or mental injury to Caylee Marie Anthony

2. The victim was under the age of eighteen years.

PLEA OF NOT GUILTY; REASONABLE DOUBT; AND BURDEN OF PROOF

The defendant has entered a plea of not guilty. This means you must presume or believe the defendant is innocent. The presumption stays with the defendant as to each material allegation in the indictment through each stage of the trial unless it has been overcome by the evidence to the exclusion of and beyond a reasonable doubt.

To overcome the defendant's presumption of innocence, the State has the burden of proving the crime with which the defendant is charged was committed and the defendant is the person who committed the crime.

The defendant is not required to present evidence or prove anything.

Whenever the words "reasonable doubt" are used you must consider the following:

A reasonable doubt is not a mere possible doubt, a speculative, imaginary or forced doubt.

Such a doubt must not influence you to return a verdict of not guilty if you have an abiding conviction of guilt. On the other hand, if, after carefully considering, comparing and weighing all the evidence, there is not an abiding conviction of guilt, or, if, having a conviction, it is one which is not stable but one which wavers and vacillates, then the charge is not proved beyond every reasonable doubt and you must find the defendant not guilty because the doubt is reasonable.

It is to the evidence introduced in this trial, and to it alone, that you are to look for that proof.

A reasonable doubt as to the guilt of the defendant may arise from the evidence, conflict in the evidence or the lack of evidence.

If you have a reasonable doubt, you should find the defendant not guilty. If you have no reasonable doubt, you should find the defendant guilty.

WEIGHING THE EVIDENCE

It is up to you to decide what evidence is reliable. You should use your common sense in deciding which, is the best evidence, and which evidence should not be relied upon in considering your verdict. You may find some of the evidence not reliable, or less reliable than other evidence.

You should consider how the witnesses acted, as well as what they said. Some things you should consider are:

1. Did the witness seem to have an opportunity to see and know the things about which the witness testified?
2. Did the witness seem to have an accurate memory?
3. Was the witness honest and straightforward in answering the attorneys' questions?
4. Did the witness have some interest in how the case should be decided?
5. Does the witness' testimony agree with the other testimony and other evidence in the case?
6. Has the witness been offered or received any money, preferred treatment or other benefit in order to get the witness to testify?
7. Had any pressure or threat been used against the witness that affected the truth of the witness' testimony?
8. Did the witness at some other time make a statement that is inconsistent with the testimony he or she gave in court?

You may rely upon your own conclusion about the witness. A juror may believe or disbelieve all or any part of the evidence or the testimony of any witness.

WEIGHING THE EVIDENCE CONCERNING CANINE SEARCHES

It is up to you to decide what evidence is reliable. You should use your common sense in deciding which, is the best evidence, and which evidence should not be relied upon in considering your verdict. You may find some of the evidence not reliable, or less reliable than other evidence.

Some things you should consider in evaluating canine searches are:

1. The canine's training and certification records, including an explanation of the meaning of the particular training and certification.
2. The field performance records including any unverified alerts.
3. The experience and training of the officer handling the canine, as well as any other objective evidence known to the officer about the canine's reliability.

You may rely upon your own conclusions about this type of evidence. A juror may believe or disbelieve all or any part of the evidence or the testimony.

EXPERT WITNESSES

Expert witnesses are like other witnesses, with one exception – the law permits an expert witness to give his or her opinion.

However, an expert's opinion is only reliable when given on a subject about which you believe him or her to be an expert.

Like other witnesses, you may believe or disbelieve all or any part of an expert's testimony.

DEFENDANT NOT TESTIFYING

The constitution requires the State to prove its accusations against the defendant. It is not necessary for the defendant to disprove anything. Nor is the defendant required to prove her innocence. It is up to the State to prove the defendant's guilt by evidence.

The defendant exercised a fundamental right by choosing not to be a witness in this case. You must not view this as an admission of guilt or be influenced in any way by her decision. No juror should ever be concerned that the defendant did or did not take the witness stand to give testimony in the case.

DEFENDANT'S STATEMENTS
A statement claimed to have been made by the defendant outside of court has been placed before you. Such a statement should always be considered with caution and be weighed with great care to make certain it was freely and voluntarily made.

Therefore, you must determine from the evidence that the defendant's alleged statement was knowingly, voluntarily and freely made.

In making this determination, you should consider the total circumstances, including but not limited to:

1. Whether, when the defendant made the statement, she had been threatened in order to get her to make it, and
2. Whether anyone had promised her anything in order to get her to make it.

If you conclude the defendant's out of court statement was not freely and voluntarily made, you should disregard it.

RULES FOR DELIBERATION

These are some general rules that apply to your discussion. You must follow these rules in order to return a lawful verdict:

1. You must follow the law as it is set out in these instructions. If you fail to follow the law, your verdict will be a miscarriage of justice. There is no reason for failing to follow the law in this case. All of us are depending upon you to make a wise and legal decision in this matter.
2. This case must be decided only upon the evidence that you have heard from the testimony of the witnesses and have seen in the form of the exhibits in evidence and these instructions.
3. This case must not be decided for or against anyone because you feel sorry for anyone, or are angry at anyone.
4. Remember, the lawyers are not on trial. Your feelings about them should not influence your decision in this case.
5. Your duty is to determine if the defendant has been proven guilty or not, in accord with the law.
6. Whatever verdict you render must be unanimous, that is, each juror must agree to the same verdict.
7. It is entirely proper for a lawyer to talk to a witness about what testimony the witness would give if called to the courtroom. The witness should not be discredited by talking to a lawyer about his or her testimony.
8. Your verdict should not be influenced by feelings of prejudice, bias or sympathy.

Your verdict must be based on the evidence, and on the law contained in these instructions.

CAUTIONARY INSTRUCTION

Deciding a verdict is exclusively your job. I cannot participate in that decision in any way.

Please disregard anything I may have said or done that made you think I preferred one verdict over another.

VERDICT

You may find the defendant guilty as charged in the indictment or guilty of such lesser included crime as the evidence may justify or not guilty.

If you return a verdict of guilty, it should be for the highest offense which has been proven beyond a reasonable doubt. If you find that no offense has been proven beyond a reasonable doubt, then, of course, your verdict must be not guilty.

Only one verdict may be returned as to each crime charged. This verdict must be unanimous, that is, all of you must agree to the same verdict. The verdict must be in writing and for your convenience the necessary forms of verdict have been prepared for you. They are as follows:

[The judge reads the verdict forms to the jury; the verdict forms are provided to the jury with copies of the written instructions.]

SINGLE DEFENDANT, MULTIPLE COUNTS

A separate crime is charged in each count of the indictment and while they have been tried together each crime and the evidence applicable to it must be considered separately and a separate verdict returned as to each. A finding of guilty or not guilty as to one crime must not affect your verdict as to the other crimes charged.

SUBMITTING CASE TO JURY

In just a few moments you will be taken to the jury room by the court deputy. The first thing you should do is elect a foreperson. The foreperson presides over your deliberations like a chairperson of a meeting. It is the foreperson's job to sign and date the verdict form when all of you have agreed on a verdict in this case. The foreperson will bring the verdict back to the courtroom when you return.

Your verdict finding the defendant either guilty or not guilty must be unanimous. The verdict must be the verdict of each juror, as well as of the jury as a whole.

During deliberations, jurors must communicate about the case only with one another and only when all jurors are present in the jury room. You are not to communicate with any person outside the jury about this case. Until you have reached a verdict, you must not talk about this case in person or through the telephone, writing, or electronic communication, such as a blog, twitter, e-mail, text message, or any other means. Do not contact anyone to assist you during deliberations. These communications rules apply until I discharge you at the end of the case. If you become aware of any violation of these instructions or any other instruction I have given in this case, you must tell me by giving a note to the court deputy.

In closing, let me remind you that it is important that you follow the law spelled out in these instructions in deciding your verdict. There are no other laws that apply to this case. Even if you do not like the laws that must be applied, you must use them. For two centuries we have agreed to a constitution and to live by the law. No juror has the right to violate rules we all share. Thank you.

PART SEVEN

THE VERDICT, AFTERMATH, AND POSTSCRIPT

Chapter 21

THE WAIT AND THE VERDICT

Everyone waits. It has been said that by the end of Burdick's closing argument, Casey Anthony and her attorney Simms were both in tears. We did not see this. The jury of twelve men and women began its deliberations in this murder case on the Fourth of July, 2011. They will end deliberations each day at 6 PM. A standard deliberations day will be from 8:30 to 6 PM, until they reach a verdict or become so deadlocked that a mistrial is declared. We expect the jury to be out a week or more to review this evidence, regardless of the verdict. On day one, deliberations last six hours; there is no verdict, and the jury is sequestered for the night.

July 5th, 2011

There are no smiles or eye batting as Casey Anthony enters the room. She is stoic and clearly stressed. The lawyers told you this is a smart woman. It appears she is smart enough to understand the gravity of the juror's deliberations, weighing the evidence on her life. Was there enough evidence or will the jury find Casey not guilty? We believe the four false statement charges are a given. She will be found guilty of those. Six months in the Florida swamp assured we will never know what killed Caylee. We know who she was with the last day she was ever seen; she was with her mother, Casey Anthony. Whatever the jury decides, we will accept it. This is our justice system. However, after watching this entire case, we believe Casey had malice that day. We do not believe Caylee drowned accidentally, and everyone turned an accident into a murder instead of calling 911 in hope of reviving the child. However, we also realize the evidence remaining after Caylee's "proper burial," and Casey's apparent lies and deflecting tactics in court, could affect the jury.

Judge: We will bring the jury in and I will make an inquiry, then they will be discharge to continue their deliberations. Bring the jury in. Good morning ladies and gentlemen of the jury. Did you heed all my admonitions? You make be excused to continue your deliberations. We are in recess, subject to the call of the jury.

Day two's deliberations last another four hours and thirty-three minutes. The verdict is in, and will be read in fifteen minutes. We wait, shocked by the short deliberation on a case with so much technical evidence. The prosecutors look content, and Ashton looks nearly jubilant. Casey Anthony is crying, worried, shocked, chewing her nails, and looks like she is about ready to lose it. She has spoken to her lawyer Simms a couple of times. George and Cindy are in the courtroom. George has been crying and wiping his nose. His hands now folded in a prayer pyramid before his face, and then he rubs his hands together. Cindy is stretching her neck. The Anthony's look worried as they talk a little. Casey appears to push herself up with the support of the table, as the judge takes the bench.

Judge: The defense and prosecution are ready. There will be no remarks of approval or disapproval, return the jury. Have you reached a verdict? All jurors: Yes. Judge: Hand the verdicts to the court deputy, please. The judge reviews, tries to remain stoic but looks slightly alarmed for a split second, and passes the verdicts to the clerk to read.

First Degree Murder: **Not Guilty**
Aggravated Child Abuse: **Not Guilty**
Aggravated Manslaughter of a Child: **Not Guilty**
Four Counts of Providing False Statements to Law Enforcement Officers: **Guilty of each Count**

Judge: I express my sincere thank you for your service. We came in, met with you and took you away from you families. We thank you. Sentencing will be set for Thursday. Ms. Anthony needs to be fingerprinted before the court. Court dismissed.

Chapter 22

AFTERMATH AND POSTSCRIPT

The maximum sentence is four one-year sentences with credit for time served, less any time used up on the financial charges of which she has already been convicted. We assume the judge will sentence her to consecutive (one after another) sentences. We are not pleased with the verdict. However, we accept it, and hope Casey Anthony will go forth in the world, to do no more harm.

Defense press conference a few minutes after the verdict:

Sims says, we are thankful for the verdict. Mason is angry that they have lawyers who know nothing about the case talking on TV. Now you have learned your lesson, he says.

Baez: While we are happy for Casey, there are no winners in this case. Caylee has passed on far too soon. My focus has been to make sure there was justice for Casey and Caylee. Casey did not murder Caylee, and they did not pervert her memory with a wrongful conviction. I would like to thank the man who took me under his wings… (Baez looks to Mr. Mason.) We hope for changes in the justice system and we should all take this in and learn that you cannot convict someone until their day in court. Today and yesterday, there was a breath of light. We want to acknowledge the prosecutors, Linda Drain Burdick is a fine prosecutor, Frank George made them cohesive, Jeff Ashton is a fierce opponent, and they served the State of Florida well. We are very happy for Casey, and we want her to be able to grieve and grow, and get her life back together somehow. This is why we believe the death penalty does not work. (The press conference ends; no questions are entertained.)

It is a sad shock to us to see Baez refer to Mason as his mentor. Maybe Baez has learned from his client how to deflect blame from himself. In our opinion, we have found Mr. Baez's actions in trial an appalling display of questionable legal and ethical behavior. If Mason did take Baez under his wing, we hate to think how badly Baez would have behaved without guidance, assuming that Mason did not goad Baez into some of his antics. During the course of the trial, Judge Perry told both Baez and Ashton that they were facing some sort of sanction at the conclusion of the trial. We do not know if that will occur. We also do not know if the judge will file a complaint with the Florida Bar and what action, if any, the Bar might take. This is one part of the case we will continue to follow. We want to know if the Florida Bar, the regulatory body for lawyers' qualifications, behavior, and ethics takes any action.

Baez and other defense lawyers celebrate with cocktails, near the very courthouse where no one was held responsible in the death and disposal of Caylee. During the cocktail party, Cheney Mason lowers the public's perception of his profession another notch by saluting photographers with his middle finger. We expected better from the old dog.

Maybe Caylee just jumped into the swamp after wrapping herself with duct tape and bags. We agree with Dr. G; one hundred percent of the time in accidents, people call for help, even when there is no hope their loved one can be revived. Nobody puts duct tape over the mouth of a drowning victim and throws them into the swamp. *This is common sense.*

The State Attorney Larson Lamar: In October 2008, after the grand jury indicted, I told you I would not talk until this case was over. This case had been exploited for fifteen minutes of fame. This media has caused us to seek a jury outside out our own area. So much of the expense could have been avoided if counsel did not seek notoriety. Linda Burdick, Jeff Ashton, and Frank George did this skillfully and without histrionics. The lead agency has been the Orange County Sheriff's Office. Its deputies and employees did an excellent investigation.

Sheriff Jerry Demings: We have just celebrated the Fourth of July. Men and women have died to protect this freedom. For three long years, the citizens of Orange County have sought justice for Caylee Anthony since her remains were

510

found on December 11th, 2008. We thank all for their efforts in the investigation, and the prosecution of this murder case. We ask that all respect the jury's decision. There have been many high profile cases which have resulted in civil disobedience. Please respect the verdict. Patrols will be increased to assure peace.

State Attorney Lamar: This was a dry bones case and the delay in recovering the remains made this a very difficult case to prosecute. We are disappointed in the verdict. I never criticize a jury, and tomorrow we go back to seek justice in the many cases of murdered children our attorneys must prosecute. This is not unusual. (The press conference ends; a representative says that no questions will be entertained.)

Crowds of what appears to be hundreds of people, who gathered for the verdict, appear to stir in stun and shock. One of the authors stood in Washington, D.C. to see such a scene when the OJ Simpson verdict was read. The other author had a dream that this case would result in an acquittal, despite her belief that Casey did something to end Caylee's life. There is a difference between a verdict of Not Guilty and innocence. A not guilty verdict can mean that the jury found that the defendant was truly innocent, but more often, it means that the jury found that the prosecution did not prove guilt beyond a reasonable doubt. A legal dictionary defines "not guilty" as declared not guilty of a specific offense or crime; legally blameless. It defines "innocent" as uncorrupted by evil, malice, or wrongdoing; sinless. Casey is now the former relating to the felony charges regarding her daughter, but we do not believe that she is the latter.

July 7th, 2011

Today is the sentencing hearing of Casey Anthony for the four false statements to officers during the investigation of missing Caylee. Court will begin shortly. We want to give you a final update before the sentencing. Some jurors have come forth saying they were sick to their stomachs, but they did not have the evidence to convict. Maybe it was there, maybe not. It was their decision to make. However, we think ten hours was too short to evaluate all of the evidence in this case. Even after watching every movement of this trial, we believe it could have taken a long time to evaluate the evidence present in the jury room.

The news has reported the following events. The State of Florida is seeking to recover from Casey Anthony special costs of the investigation. This is a slippery slope, and interesting legally. EquuSearch is believed to be suing Casey Anthony. The law firm of Morgan and Morgan long ago filed suit on behalf of the woman who was accused of being "Zanny." That suit is now ramping up; it has been delayed by the pending criminal charges until now. Prosecutor Jeffrey Ashton has retired after this case, and spoke on Dr. Drew last night. He said he was glad that the pictures were not released, but if you saw the skull and tape, you know it was put there to stay. Cindy and George are believed to be moving away, but they are in the court this morning. We are sure Casey Anthony will live just fine as a Hollywood golden goose. We hope they toss in a good psychiatrist for Casey, however, even if they had twenty years, we doubt they could figure out the mind of Casey Anthony.

One alternate juror says, No one can say how Caylee died. The prosecution did not meet their burden of proof. Why all the lies? Casey needs to get help. I am sure they looked at all the evidence and law, but I was not in the room.

People have been in line since yesterday waiting for tickets to be present in the courtroom for the sentencing hearing. Crowds are outside the court, the Anthony home on Hopespring Drive, and Suburban Drive. They are protesting. We hope they will stop bothering this family now, the bell has been rung, whether for justice or not.

The judge is on the bench for sentencing, and Casey is in court with her hair down for the first time. She is talking with Mason and Sims. Baez just joined them. Casey looks rested, her makeup is on, and she is prepped for Hollywood. The sheriff's office has said they will not say how she will leave the court, if given time served. The judge enters the courtroom for the last time in this case. Maybe.

Judge: Madam Clerk, call the case. Are the defense and prosecution ready? Defense, you asked me reserve on the mistrial motion. Mason (chuckling): Forget it, Your Honor. Judge: Mr. Baez: Is there any reason why we should not proceed? Mr. Mason: No, Your Honor, on the issue of sentence. Prosecution: We filed a motion for costs of the investigation. The jurisdiction of the court, if the defense appeals the False Statements verdicts, could be lost. We ask that you to bifurcate the sentencing hearing and motion for investigation costs, and retain jurisdiction over the costs motion. They can be handled separately, and the costs are not punitive.

Mason: I do not object to the bifurcation, but we have no invoices; we will review them at the time we receive them. Judge: The Court retains jurisdiction over the issue of the investigation costs. Any mitigation, Mr. Mason? Mason: No, but Ms. Fryer (case law lady) has a legal argument. Fryer: Prior to sentencing, the four counts are a violation of double jeopardy, as they are one continuous act and must be reduced to one charge for sentencing. This is a single criminal act. Judge: Let me stop you, I do not have what you provided to the court. Ms. Fryer: I'm sorry Your Honor; I gave the memo to the clerk. (The judge gets the motion from the clerk and reviews it.) Fryer: This test requires the court to see if there are distinct criminal acts or one continuous act. It is double jeopardy. (Case law is cited.) There was no time for the defendant to pause and reflect during the statement made to Detective Melich. We request the court only sentence her only as to one charge.

Judge: Let's look at Count Four; it alleges that on July 16, 2008, there was a knowing false statement of working at Universal Studios. Judge: Did the police have to take any resulting action due to the statement? Count Five, she identified a person as Zanny, and that she left her child with a babysitter. Did it require the detective to investigate? Fryer: On these charges as a matter of law, we look at the acts of Ms. Anthony as one statement at one time. Judge: Count Six, she made a false statement as too the people Jeffery Hopkins and Juliette. Count Seven, she reported a phone call from Caylee Anthony on that very day of the statement. Let me read these cases right quick before I hear from the State of Florida.

(This is the case law lady, now known as Attorney Fryer and she is good a legal geek. However, Judge Perry is geekier, and he is wearing the robe.)

Judge: One last question Mrs. Fryer. Are you saying that Ms. Anthony did not have time to form a separate act? Fryer: There must be a separation of time and place. State: I was only provided with this motion this morning, however if we look at these cases, the cases require statements to be made as a single act, for jeopardy to attach. These counts are not a single act, this is core conduct and there are several, not just the four charged, and are in three separate statements, at 1 AM, 4 AM and 1 PM. And they are material lies as she said herself, to send them on a wild goose chase. They do not violate double jeopardy. (The Judge is using Westlaw, a computer legal research tool, at his terminal on the bench to research and review cases.)

Judge: Does your client wish to say anything prior to sentencing? (Mason says she does not.) The Court makes the following ruling on the four counts. Count Four dealt with the following conduct: it is alleged that the defendant was working at Universal Studios, diverting a missing person investigation and law enforcement resources were spent to find she did not work there. Count Five: she informed authorities that she had left the child at Sawgrass Apartments with a babysitter during a missing person investigation, and they had to follow many leads. Count Six: she stated that she informed two employees of Universal Studios of the missing child. Count Seven: she received a call and spoke to Caylee and cost many resources. They are four separate and distinct lies. A lot of time and manpower was spent looking for Caylee. The search for her went on from July through December, over several months, trying to find Caylee Anthony. They are four distinct charges and separate lies.

Just as the jury spoke on Counts One, Two and Three, they spoke on Four, Five, Six and Seven. There is no legal basis not to impose sentence. I will sentence you to one year in the Orange County jail, all counts to run consecutively, (one after another), with credit for time served. Mr. Baez and Mr. Mason, we are going to spend time figuring the time served, and it will take some time because of the previous sentences she has been given in the theft case. I expect that she will be released in early August or late July, the jail has to apply good time and jail time.

I will reserve jurisdiction for sixty days to determine the costs of investigation. Prosecution: Thirty days to prepare the entire cost document should be fine. Mason, I need invoices. Prosecution: I believe that will give Mr. Mason time to review the affidavits of the Sherriff. Mason: We waive Casey Anthony's appearance in court for that hearing. Mr. Baez: Do you wish to appeal? You can file a notice of appeal. Baez: We reserve the right. Judge: You have 30 days to appeal. Does she have the financial wherewithal for an attorney? Baez: No. (Not yet…) It will be your responsibility, Mr. Baez before relieved from this case, to file any and all documents for appeal.

Within hours, Casey Anthony's release date is scheduled for July 13th, 2011, then updated to July 17th, 2011; next week. We believe they are trying to make the release date confusing in order to get Casey out of the jail quietly. The media reports that Baez has signed with a talent agency as a package deal, however he denied that Casey has signed any deal.

The same day as the sentencing, attorneys for the media are having an emergency hearing before Judge Perry, to get the judge to release the jurors' names. The argument is that the jurors are open to public scrutiny just like lawyers, defendants, and the judge. It is the norm in high profile cases. The media is arguing, how can we know it was a fair and impartial jury, free from tampering, without being able to contact the jurors?

Judge: Is there any cooling off period? Lawyer: I believe it is something like a week or so. The Supreme Court has stated that in criminal cases the jurors cannot remain anonymous. A few have already chosen to speak about this case. Judge: There are people who want to do them harm, cut them open and pour salt in the wounds, feed their legs to piranhas. In the future, do we need to start telling jurors, "Your name will be disclosed," at the beginning of jury selection? Getting an address will only take seconds. People can go to the door, and they have the juror in their hands. Do we need to provide protection, and for how long? I am trying to figure out in striking this balance between the jurors' right to privacy and the right to transparency. I am concerned for the threats. I am concerned that the journalism field has become unregulated as to its professionalism. I am considering a cooling off period, and then releasing the names. I will withhold ruling for now.

The news reports the following day are that Casey Anthony has refused a jail visit from Cindy Anthony. The media also says that Jose Baez was dropped from the talent agency he is believed to have signed with. These are just a few media stories, to end where we began: in the media's eye. The lawyers in the media say this case was not proved by the prosecution, and whatever the defense did was irrelevant. We do not think this is true; the defense had plenty to do with this verdict. We find most interesting that lawyers are not allowed to put a witness on the stand they know will make false statements – it is a crime.

Judge Perry repeatedly asked Jose Baez if Baez had put Mrs. Anthony on the stand, knowing that she would testify that she was at home when her records show that she was at work. Although the authors clearly believed this was, at a minimum, a case of aggravated child abuse murder or manslaughter, the Anthony family's lawyer was not surprised at the verdict. We have created this interpretation from our viewing, notes, and opinions during the very moments of witness testimony, introduction of evidence, and statements of the lawyers, the judge, and the defendant. We reported the sideshows as they occurred. We hope this will allow you a keyhole look at the trial, every day Courtroom 23 was open. This is our justice system, for good or bad. Now you can render your own shadow juror verdict….

We will never know the truth of how Caylee died. The discarding of her body into a snake-infested Florida swamp like trash served its purpose. Many answers will always remain unknown. What we do know, is that Caylee will never have the opportunity to grow up, laugh, learn, or finish her time on this earth, because Caylee can't dance. The Anthony family was faced with the Hobson's choice, try to keep Casey off death row, or seek justice for Caylee. The changing stories at the end of the trial, the denial of the obvious, told us what we believe was their choice. We do not believe any other family member was involved in the death or disposal of Caylee. Yet, it is very possible their testimony prevented justice for Caylee.

It is our opinion, after looking at the entire trial – the evidence, witnesses, and testimony of experts – that we will never know why Caylee's life was taken. Was it black malice; revenge on Casey's own mother for confronting her the night before for the theft from the grandparents? Was it trying to assure Caylee would not noisily wake from the chloroform with tape? Was it because Casey wanted her freedom to go to New York with Tony and live the Bella Vita? Our opinions varied over time, from cold-blooded murder, to an accident while sedating Caylee, to Casey simply becoming as angry as we saw the real Casey Anthony on the jail video.

We believe for a few reasons that Caylee did not drown. The high chloroform levels were there in that car. Maybe crude chloroform was created from alcohol, chlorine bleach, and nail polish remover or hydrogen peroxide. They are all items in any home. We trust Oak Ridge National Laboratories and its analysis. Second, the gate to the house was unlocked from inside the back yard. We suspect that after Caylee was dead and already in the trunk of the car in the garage, Casey Anthony went out the sliding glass doors to enter the back yard. She closed and locked the doors while calling her mother franticly to make sure her mother had not left work for home. Casey knew her father was at work until late. Perhaps she put the ladder up in the climbing position on the pool. The duct tape and bags were all in the garage for her use. She took the time to wrap the body in the trunk. She left in a hurry, because she was unable to verify where her mother was by phone. She went through the gate, the one that can only be unlocked from inside the yard, to get back to the car in the garage. No one trying to hide a body would carry the body through the gate for all neighbors to see.

She could not go to the house with Caylee's body on June 17th; her father was home. The following day, when her father was back at work, Casey returned and backed into the garage again, borrowed a shovel to bury Caylee near the dollhouse, laid the decomposing body on the grass by the dollhouse, and then decided her dad might find it. She returned the body to the trunk and the shovel to the neighbor. However, she was still faced with the same dilemma; detective dad might notice something had changed in the back yard, if Casey buried Caylee in the yard. She kept the body in the trunk; she disposed of Caylee when she was smelling decomposition. Late at night, she tossed Caylee into the swamp near her home. After that, every time the car and trunk were aired, the smell went away for a while; only to return each time it was closed up again. That is when she dumped the car.

We believe the idea of drowning came from the police questioning of her at the home and at Universal Studios, and because of media speculation and hype. We believe Cindy was sold on the drowning story by Casey at some point. Casey may have convinced her mother that Cindy was so mad at Casey about the grandfather's money that she forgot to take the ladder down. This fight is something the jury never heard, but the aunt has come forth on the media to tell of the fight Casey and Cindy had the night before Caylee died. If the aunt's story is correct, Cindy had learned of the most recent theft only hours before Casey came home in the evening of June 15th, 2008, and Cindy was very angry.

The jury foreman has now stated that the jury was suspicious of George Anthony. One author believes the only thing snowed in this trial was the jury – by Casey Anthony's defense. Again, Casey Anthony has successfully deflected the blame onto someone else, and that the jury did not understand the scientific evidence. A juror would need to sort details, such as when air samples were tested from a car trunk had the carpet has already been removed, unbeknown to the person taking the samples and when a laboratory like Oak Ridge did through tests on the air/carpet samples. This is just one area that would need to be reviewed. We feel this evaluation of the difference kinds of evidence in this case would take many days. This is what circumstantial evidence is, putting the pieces together, it takes time. This has been a rare opportunity to see what the jurors saw. The jurors like the judges, lawyers and defendant are subject to review by the people. Now this said, the bell has been rung and Casey Anthony will be free. Anyone who brings harm to Casey Anthony for vengeance must be laid down with justice's most heavy sword, for their acts. This is our system, change it or live with it.

The other author does not think that the prosecution made a coherent argument for first-degree murder. The evidence was circumstantial, and the evidence presented did not prove beyond a reasonable doubt that Casey killed her daughter under either theory of first-degree murder. The author also believes that the defense did a poor job, and promised things in opening statement that it did not deliver. The author does not think that Casey was proven guilty of either first-degree or second-degree murder, and thinks she might have been convicted of manslaughter, based on culpable negligence. Much as it pains the author to admit, she does not believe that the circumstantial evidence proved beyond a reasonable doubt that Casey Anthony was guilty of more than that. Although the State did not prove more beyond a reasonable doubt, the author is convinced that Casey's thirty-one day delay in reporting her child missing was proof of culpable negligence that caused or contributed to Caylee's death. The author, had she been a juror, would have voted for a verdict of guilty of manslaughter, and then locked herself away for a week and cried, because she wholeheartedly believes that Casey killed her child somehow. There simply was not the proof to convict her of the more serious charges. The law does not always provide justice.

Both authors believe that the Anthony family lied and again saved Casey Anthony from responsibility. The family criminal attorney believes if she had been convicted on the evidence presented at trial, it would not have been overturned on appeal, short of procedural issues. The one thing we can be sure of is that varying opinions on guilt or not, on good science or paid professional expert witnesses, will continue.

We believe George knew less than Cindy to the very end of the trial. He may be dislikeable, deny an affair he probably had, or dance questions about a roll of duct tape he innocently had to put up posters, because he has been accused of everything by the defense from sex abuse to disposal of his granddaughter. But he did not turn an accident into a murder and toss his grandchild in the swamp. The author's opinions are different from first-degree murder for Claudette to a reluctant manslaughter for Matrix. The defense lawyer in the family thinks she did it, but that the circumstantial evidence was insufficient to prove a homicide. We all agree that the State could not show us the moment of murder. Now you can see how different the opinions are among like people. Notice that none of us believe the child drowned or that an accident was turned into a murder. We disagree on what proof the law requires for legal responsibility, not whether we feel Casey is morally responsible. All of us believe that Casey somehow killed her child; we simply disagree on whether it was proved to the standard required by law.

Harry Krop, PhD, the forensic psychologist who was retained to do an evaluation on Casey Anthony for the defense penalty phase in case of conviction, made his observations known after her acquittal on murder charges, with Casey Anthony's consent. He does not believe, based on all his interactions with Casey Anthony, as well as psychological testing, that she has any diagnosable mental illness. He also said that Casey was always competent to proceed from the initial stages of his involvement in 2010 all the way to the end of the trial. He referred to both psychological and psychiatric disorders, meaning both DSM Axis I and Axis II diagnoses. Axis I diagnoses are clinical disorders and learning disorders more like depression and anxiety disorders, and psychotic disorders; and Axis II diagnoses are more like chronic behavioral disturbances, lying and interpersonal chaos. Casey Anthony is not a depressed, anxious person, nor does she have any chronic behavioral disorder or borderline traits or sociopathic traits. Casey Anthony is of average intelligence, but extremely immature. Now after three years in jail she has had time to reflect on the situation, and is unable to understand why she behaved the way she did. Casey Anthony does in fact come from a dysfunctional family, but the psychologist believes the way Casey Anthony acted after the death of her daughter was "out of character." He also said that she was not a negligent or abusive parent. He said he did not think anybody has ever suggested that. He feels it would have been out of character for her in comparison to her prior history or lack of history of violence. He ended with, "So if there was a homicide, it would have been out of character for her." The writers leave it for you and time to judge.

These writers have shared time in the den laughing, debating, knocking heads together, (we are all strong-minded) and sharing the pain we feel for the loss of a little girl, who died much too soon. We have loved every movement of the time we have spent writing this story, as mother and daughter. Hence, the Latin, Matrix Filia, is the pseudonym of the daughter. It is the name under which she has chosen to write this and future books. We will always remember the time we spent together on this story as grown women. Never will we forget Caylee, but we cannot forget Casey soon enough. May Casey Anthony go forth and do no more harm.

Casey Anthony has been found not guilty of the murder of Caylee Anthony, age two, and guilty of providing False Statements to Law Enforcement during the investigation of the 31 days she failed to report the child missing. It is important to keep in mind the number of children who are in danger of death at the hands of a parent every day in America, despite the verdict in this case. This mother and daughter team of writers choose to live with Caylee in our hearts. *Yet, forever we believe, evil lurks.*

POSTSCRIPT

BY LICENSED PSYCHOTHERAPIST LAURA SCHULTZ

When seemingly average mothers such as the infamous Susan Smith kill their children with an apparent calm and even detached demeanor and deflecting the blame to a non-existent stranger, we are collectively shocked and dismayed. Even after scores of these murders have been committed, many people remain in a state of generalized denial that a woman could actually commit such a callous crime toward a person she has nurtured and protected. The truth is, according to FBI statistics, three to five children a day are killed by a parent in the U.S. Further, homicide remains one of the leading causes of death in children under four.

Still, we hold steadfast in the belief that mothers are incapable of killing their children. Even the most veteran of law enforcement officers and experienced judges may have a difficult time believing that a woman could be capable of such heinous crimes. A common response is that a mother who murders her child must be "insane." However, often quite the opposite is true. When a child is killed by his/her mother, there are signs that the child is viewed as a mere nuisance or an "object" that requires too much energy or time and gets in the way of the mother's own desires.

The first and foremost reason that women killers can
continue to escape notice for long periods of time,
according to some leading experts, is that to the human
eye it is very difficult to ascertain whether a woman is
an actual killer. The frightening truth is that many
female killers have a quiet veneer of normality. For the
most part, they appear to be ordinary women living the
roles of loving spouse, nurturing mother to their
children, and trusted caregivers. For this reason, as
well as a still somewhat unchanged societal viewpoint
towards women as the more nurturing, physically weaker of
the sexes, such killers are thought to be incapable of
such horrendous brutality. Consequently, women are less
often suspected to be the culprit in the death of their
children and even when convicted, often receive lighter
sentences than their male counterparts.

The female predator plays on the weaknesses of others to
her advantage. By using an uncanny ability to manipulate
people's disbelief regarding their potential to commit
murder, these deadly women can continue to live their
lives without arousing suspicion. As part of their highly
seductive and superficially charming nature, they are
more than able and willing to pull off a skillful ruse.
They often dress or act in ways to enhance their physical
appearance to seem helpless or innocent beyond reproach,
particularly during a court appearance or in the first
few meetings with a newly intended target of her charm.
The targets who she is trying to convince of her
innocence may include lawyers, prosecutors and
especially, members of her own family.

In order to make an accurate diagnosis of an individual,
a professional clinician should be called in to conduct a
1-1 interview and complete a full psychological
assessment. However, based on the evidence presented in
the State v. Casey Anthony case thus far, including court
records, live video feed from the trial, and the massive
amounts of information available, there are certain
traits of Casey Anthony that are quite visible to a
clinician.

Casey Anthony deflects blame away from herself by her
insistence that someone else is responsible for her
daughter's death. Her claim of "Zanny the Nanny"
abducting and/or killing little Caylee has been proven
false. Reporting the disappearance a month after the
occurrence is suspicious in and of itself and is highly
atypical when a child is missing.

In addition, throughout her taped interviews and
conversations with police, not only did her version of

the facts repeatedly change, but more telling is the fact that she spoke of her child in the past tense even before the body was discovered. This type of behavior gives very specific clues to a clinician. Her casual demeanor and detached statements as well as her party lifestyle while her child was missing are indicative of someone who has a callous and unstable nature i.e. not the normal grief pattern experienced by a mother who has lost her beloved child.

While being interviewed by Detective Melich, Casey Anthony appeared as if she was talking to friends or colleagues, bantering with officers in a collected and calm, even humorous manner. It was quite stunning to hear her state to Detective Melich, "This in no way means that I would ever do anything or let anything happen or harm come to 'that child.' She's the one thing in this world that I love more than anything." Her lack of agitation, excitement, sadness, anger, or any emotion whatsoever while speaking of her (at that point) missing child, Caylee, is quite chilling to observe. Though an exact profile cannot be totally accurate from afar, it appears that Casey Anthony lacks a connection with and empathy for her daughter during the trial. There also appeared to be a total disconnect between what the public viewed in pictures of her and of Caylee playing together at home and her mood swings in the courtroom that varied from laughter to anger.

In short, while Caylee was missing (and perhaps dead at that point) Casey's concerns appeared to be solely about her own welfare and comfort, and her connections with people (even her own parents) seem to be shallow in nature. Her behavior demonstrated a lack of concern about what her child went through, as most parents would during such an ordeal. Casey Anthony has been found not guilty in the death of her daughter. However, the numerous guilty verdicts of making false statements to law enforcement during a missing child investigation, the pattern of behavior, inclusive with videos presented in court, leave us with a myriad of questions.

The death of Caylee Anthony, regardless of the who or how, reminds us that it is important to recognize the number of children who are in danger of death at the hand of a mother every day in America and the world. All of our eyes have been opened to this very real possibility and we as a society must never ignore the silent cry of the children. It is incumbent upon us to look for the signs of unusual behavior in those charged with guarding our most precious resources, our children.

This is the opinion of Laura Schultz, Psychotherapist, based on evidence presented in the case and behavioral clues but is NOT an actual clinical evaluation of Casey Anthony.

Laura Schultz has been a licensed psychotherapist (Licensed Marriage and Family Therapist) in private practice in Los Angeles, California for over 25 years. She has expertise in the field of relationships, sexuality, addiction, and childhood trauma. She is also a freelance writer who has many years of expertise in the true crime arena.

Her treatise called "Hiding in Plain Sight: The Psyche of Serial Killers" is published in Crime Magazine. Her latest essay can be found in Crime Spree Magazine entitled, "Strychnine and Stilettos: The Anatomy of Female Serial Killers". Additionally, she is a book reviewer in the true crime genre for the New York Journal of Books.

We would like to express our deepest appreciation to Laura Schultz, for peering into the mind of women who kill, in an attempt to give our readers a look behind the eyes of mothers who kill their children. *Casey Anthony has been found not guilty of the murder of her daughter Caylee.*

WITNESS LIST

Who were the witnesses in this American tragedy?

Prosecution Witnesses

1.   May 24th - George Anthony, Casey's father

2.   May 25th - Cameron Campania, Former roommate of Tony Lazzaro

3.   May 25th - Nathan Lezniewicz, Former roommate of Tony Lazzaro

4.   May 25th - Roy "Clint" House, Former roommate of Tony Lazzaro

5.   May 25th - Maria Kissh, Ex-girlfriend of Clint House

6.   May 25th - Brian Burner, Next-door neighbor of Anthony family

7.   May 25th - Jamie Realander, Shot girl at Fusion

523

8.   May 25th - Erica Gonzalez, Shot girl at Fusion

9.   May 25th - May 26th - Anthony "Tony" Lazzaro, Casey's ex- boyfriend (June to July 2008)

10.   May 26th - George Anthony (2nd testimony)

11.   May 26th - Ricardo Morales, Casey's ex-boyfriend (February to May 2008)

12.   May 26th - Melissa England, Ex-girlfriend of Troy Brown, met Casey in July 2008

13.   May 26th - Troy Brown, Friend of Ricardo Morales

14.   May 26th - Iassen Donov, Friend of Casey since 2007

15.   May 26th - Dante Salati, Friend of Casey since 2000

16.   May 26th - Christopher Stutz, Friend of Casey since 2005

17.   May 26th - Matthew Crisp, Friend of Casey since 2002

18.   May 27th - Mallory Parker, Lee Anthony's fiancée

19.   May 27th - William Waters, Friend of Amy Huizenga, met Casey on July 4, 2008

20.   May 27th - Catherine Sanchez, Amscot district manager

21.   May 27th - Simon Birch, Johnson's Wrecker towing company manager

22.   May 27th - George Anthony (3rd testimony)

23.   May 27th -May 28th - Anthony "Tony" Lazzaro (2nd testimony)

24.   May 28th -May 31st - Cindy Anthony, Casey's mother

25.   May 31st -June 1st - Amy Huizenga, Friend of Casey since 2008

26.   June 1st - Lee Anthony, Casey's older brother

27.   June 1st - Rendon Fletcher, Orange Co. Sheriff's Office in July 2008

28.   June 1st - Adriana Acevedo, Orange Co. Sheriff's Office
29.   June 1st - Amanda Macklin, Sawgrass Apartments property manager in July 2008
30.   June 1st - Reginald Hosey, Orange Co. Sheriff's Office
31.   June 1st - Yuri Melich, Orange Co. Sheriff's Office
32.   June 2nd - Jeffrey Hopkins, "Acquaintance" of Casey since middle school
33.   June 2nd - Leonard Turtora, Assistant manager at Universal Orlando Resort
34.   June 2nd - Yuri Melich (2nd testimony)
35.   June 3rd - Charity Beasley, Orange Co. Sheriff's Office
36.   June 3rd - Awilda McBryde, Orange Co. Sheriff's Office
37.   June 3rd - Christine Narkiewicz, Orange Co. Sheriff's Office
38.   June 3rd - Gerardo Bloise, Orange Co. Sheriff's Office
39.   June 4th - Karen Korsburg-Lowe, FBI forensics expert
40.   June 4th - Michael Vincent, Orange Co. crime scene investigator
41.   June 6th - Arpad Vass, PhD, Forensic anthropologist at Oak Ridge National Lab
42.   June 7th - Gerardo Bloise (2nd testimony)
43.   June 7th - Arpad Vass, PhD (2nd testimony)
44.   June 7th - Michael Rickenbach, PhD, FBI forensic chemist examiner
45.   June 7th - Jason Forgey Cadaver, dog handler, Orange Co. Sheriff's Office
46.   June 8th - Kristin Brewer, Cadaver dog handler, Osceola Co. Sheriff's Office

47.   June 8th - Sandra Osborne, Computer examiner,
Orange Co. Sheriff's Office

48.   June 8th - Kevin Stenger, Computer crimes
supervisor, Orange Co. Sheriff's Office

49.   June 8th -June 9th - John Dennis Bradley,
Computer expert, CacheBack software developer

50.   June 9th - Lee Anthony (2nd testimony)

51.   June 9th - Edward Turso, Orange Co. Sheriff's
Office

52.   June 9th - Jennifer Welch, Orange Co. crime scene
investigator

53.   June 9th - Stephen Hanson, Chief investigator,
Medical Examiner's Office

54.   June 9th - June 10th - Gary Utz, MD, Deputy Chief
Medical Examiner

55.   June 10th - John Schultz, PhD, UCF anthropology
professor, forensics expert

56.   June 10th - Jan "Dr. G" Garavaglia, MD, Orange-
Osceola Chief Medical Examiner

57.   June 10th - Michael Warren, PhD, UF anthropology
professor

58.   June 10th - Michael Vincent, 2nd testimony

59.   June 10th - Robin Maynard, Former Orange Co.
crime scene investigator

60.   June 11th - Neal Haskell, PhD, Forensic
entomology expert

61.   June 11th - Jennifer Welch, 2nd testimony

62.   June 11th - Ronald Murdock, Forensics supervisor,
Orange Co. Sheriff's Office

63.   June 11th - Gerald Johnston, Land surveyor

64.   June 13th - Stephen Shaw, FBI hair and fiber
examiner

65.   June 13th - Elizabeth Fontaine, FBI latent print
expert

66.   June 14th - Catherine Theisen, PhD, FBI quality assurance specialist, DNA expert

67.   June 14th - Alina Burroughs, Orange Co. crime scene investigator

68.   June 14th - Cindy Anthony (2nd testimony)

69.   June 14th - Jennifer Welch (3rd testimony)

70.   June 14th - Bobby Williams, Tattoo artist

Defense Witnesses

71.   June 16th - Gerardo Bloise (3rd testimony)

72.   June 16th - Heather Seubert, FBI former supervisory DNA examiner

73.   June 16th - Robin Maynard (2nd testimony)

74.   June 16th - Ronald Murdock (2nd testimony)

75.   June 16th - Jennifer Welch (4th testimony)

76.   June 16th - Lorie Gottesman, FBI forensic document examiner

77.   June 16th - Cary Oien, FBI hair and fiber analysis expert

78.   June 17th - Tim Huntington, PhD, Forensic entomologist

79.   June 18th - William Rodriguez, PhD, Forensic anthropologist

80.   June 18th - Werner Spitz, MD, Autopsy expert

81.   June 21st - Jennifer Welch, 5th testimony

82.   June 21st - Jane Bock, PhD, Forensic botanist

83.   June 21st - Richard Eikelenboom, PhD, DNA scientist

84.   June 21st - Yuri Melich (3rd testimony)

85.   June 21st - Marcus Bain Wise, PhD, Analytical chemist, Oak Ridge National Lab

86.   June 22nd - Maureen Bottrell, FBI forensic examiner, geologist

87.   June 22nd - Madeline Montgomery, FBI forensic toxicologist

88.   June 22nd - Michael Sigman, PhD, UCF forensic chemistry expert

89.   June 22nd - Susan Mears, Orange Co. crime scene supervisor

90.   June 22nd - Michael Rickenbach, PhD, (2nd testimony)

91.   June 22nd - Karen Korsburg-Lowe (2nd testimony)

92.   June 23rd - Susan Mears (2nd testimony)

93.   June 23rd - Stephen Shaw (2nd testimony)

94.   June 23rd - Barry Logan, PhD, Forensic toxicologist

95.   June 23rd - Jennifer Welch (6th testimony)

96.   June 23rd - Cindy Anthony (3rd testimony)

97.   June 23rd - Sandra Osborne (2nd testimony)

98.   June 23rd - Kevin Stenger (2nd testimony)

99.   June 24th - Cindy Anthony (4th testimony)

100.   June 24th - Lee Anthony (3rd testimony)

101.   June 24th - Cindy Anthony (5th testimony)

102.   June 24th - Ryan Eberlin, Orange Co. Sheriff's Office

103.   June 24th - Eric Edwards, Orange Co. Sheriff's Office

104.   June 24th - Linda Tinelli, Texas EquuSearch volunteer

105.   June 24th - Yuri Melich (4th testimony)

106.   June 27th - Yuri Melich (5th testimony)

107.   June 27th - Michael Vincent (3rd testimony)

108.   June 27th - Gerardo Bloise (4th testimony)

109.   June 27th - Jason Forgey (2nd testimony)

110.   June 27th - Kenneth Furton, Forensic chemist

111.   June 27th - John Allen, Orange Co. Sheriff's Office

112.   June 27th - James Hoover, Private investigator

113.   June 27th - Dominic Casey, Private investigator

114.   June 28th - Joe Jordan, Texas EquuSearch volunteer

115.   June 28th - George Anthony (4th testimony)

116.   June 28th - Cindy Anthony (6th testimony)

117.   June 28th - Lee Anthony (4th testimony)

118.   June 28th - Yuri Melich (6th testimony)

119.   June 28th - Roy Kronk, Meter reader, found Caylee's remains

120.   June 28th - David Dean, Meter reader

121.   June 28th - Alex Roberts, Roy Kronk's former supervisor

122.   June 28th - Dennis Moonsammy, Orange Co. Jail

123.   June 29th - Cindy Anthony (7th testimony)

124.   June 29th - George Anthony (5th testimony)

125.   June 29th - Brandon Sparks, Roy Kronk's son

126.   June 29th - Roy Kronk (2nd testimony)

127.   June 29th - Edward Turso (2nd testimony)

128.   June 29th - Yuri Melich (7th testimony)

129.   June 29th - Sally Karioth, Grief expert

130.   June 30th - Krystal Holloway, George Anthony's alleged mistress

131.   June 30th - Dominic Casey (2nd testimony)

132.   June 30th - George Anthony (6th testimony)

133.   June 30th - Cindy Anthony (8th testimony)

134.   June 30th - Lee Anthony (5th testimony)

135.   June 30th - Alina Burroughs (2nd testimony)

Prosecution Rebuttal Witnesses

136.   July 1st - John Camperlengo, Gentiva Health Attorney

137.   July 1st - Deborah Polisano, Gentiva Health, former supervisor of Cindy

138.   July 1st - Bruce Goldberger, PhD, University of Florida toxicology

139.   July 1st - Michael Warren, PhD (2nd testimony)

140.   July 1st - Kevin Stenger (3rd testimony)

141.   July 1st - Sandra Osborne (3rd testimony)

142.   July 1st - Yuri Melich (8th testimony)

CELL PHONE ACTIVITY FOR CASEY ANTHONY: JUNE 16th, 2008
(As reported in the media)

According to records, Anthony's cell phone "pinged" 20 different cell towers 754 times in a two-week period. Each time, her cell phone received or sent a text message, or a phone call was made.

Ninety-seven percent of the pings were to either her boyfriend's apartment near Winter Park, her friend's home in Orlando where she sometimes stayed, her parents' home off Chickasaw Trail, or the Fusion nightclub, where she was photographed partying while Caylee was missing.

The other 3 percent of the pings - especially during three days in June - have raised questions.

On Monday, June 16th, Casey Anthony's father, George Anthony, said he saw his daughter and granddaughter leave his house at about 1 PM. If they did leave at that time, the cell records show they did not go far. Casey's cell phone communicated that afternoon through the same three cell towers she could reach from her home.

At 1 PM, Casey Anthony made a 14-minute call to her boyfriend, Tony Lazzaro. At 1:44 PM, she made a 36-minute call to her then-best friend, Amy Huizenga. At 2:52 PM, there was an 11-minute call with ex-fiancé Jesse Grund. All of the calls used cell towers that can be reached from her parents' home.

At 4:11 PM, Casey Anthony began trying to reach her mother, Cindy Anthony, making four attempts in two minutes, according to records. Anthony then traveled north from her parent's home and called Lazzaro for one minute at 4:19 PM. Two minutes later, she talked to Grund for a minute, and tried to call her mother again at 4:25 PM. There was no other communication from Anthony's cell phone until a call was made to Lazzaro's apartment at 5:57 PM, records show.

THANK YOU

We would like to express our sincere thank you to the many media outlets that provided the moment-by-moment video coverage by feed from the courtroom, from start to verdict. For the Casey Anthony trial, the Orlando Sentinel provided the still photography and the video feeds came from In Session. The video from In Session was provided in a live stream to the many other news outlets who broadcast this live.

We would also like to thank the investigators, searchers, police, the Medical Examiner's and FBI employees, who did an excellent job, trying to find Caylee, recovering her remains from a Florida swamp (that must have been hellish to work in), and in analyzing the results.

The scientists from Oak Ridge National Laboratory will always hold a special place in these authors' minds, for stepping up to test what was really in the trunk. Regardless of the outcome of this case, you proved to us three things that never should have been in the trunk, chloroform, decomposition, and Caylee.

Casey Anthony has altered the lives of so many innocent young people by her actions and by involving them in this public murder trial. The authors would like to wish them a life free of any further infliction of evil.

This has been…

The Casey Anthony Murder Trial

Written by Claudette Walker and Matrix Filia

© Abacus Books, Inc., www.abacusbooks.com

3756936R00298

Printed in Great Britain
by Amazon.co.uk, Ltd.,
Marston Gate.